AF541044

Risk Assessment in Chemical Process Industries

Advanced Techniques

RISK ASSESSMENT IN CHEMICAL PROCESS INDUSTRIES

ADVANCED TECHNIQUES

F.I. KHAN
ME, PhD, MIE, MIPHE
Head, Computer-Aided Environmental Management Unit
Centre for Pollution Control & Energy Technology,
Pondicherry University, Kalapet, Pondicherry-605 014

S.A. ABBASI
PhD, DSc, FIPHE, FIE, PE
Senior Professor & Director
Centre for Pollution Control & Energy Technology,
Pondicherry University, Kalapet, Pondicherry-605 014

DISCOVERY PUBLISHING HOUSE
NEW DELHI-110002

First Published-1998

ISBN 81-7141-422-2

Published by:
Discovery Publishing House
4831/24, Ansari Road, Prahlad Street,
Daryaganj, New Delhi-110002 *(INDIA)*
Phone: 3279245
Fax: 91-11-3253475

Printed at:

Tarun Offset Printers

DEDICATED TO

PROFESSOR FRANK P. LEES AND PROFESSOR P.F. NOLAN

Our *Gurus* with whom we have never met but whose writings have taught and inspired us

Preface

The Vishakhapatnam refinery disaster of September 1997 was the worst industrial accident of the 1990s. The Bhopal gas tragedy of 1984 was the **worst-ever** such accident in the history of process industries. India, thus has the dubious distinction of setting two world records in the realm of industrial accidents within a span of 13 years.

Indeed, during the last two decades India has witnessed thousands of industrial accidents involving fires, explosions, toxic releases or combinations of these. The experience of the rest of the developing world is similar - with increasing population, industrialisation, and number of hazardous chemicals/process, the frequency as well as severity of industrial accidents is increasing.

Why is the situation in the Third World countries particularly grim? In these regions it is common to find several industries clustered together, with towns and villages lying in close proximity. Even when an industry sets itself up some distance away from populous areas, the growing neighbourhoods soon reach its periphery. In such settings the impact of industrial accident on human lives as well as property is always severe.

How to deal with this situation?

Attempts to search for answers to this question have given rise to the field of risk assessment in chemical process industries (RACPI). Finding ways and means to prevent accidents, and to cushion the damage if accidents do occur, are integral parts of this new science of RACPI.

The Government of India has acknowledged the hazards of Bhopal-like accidents posed by chemical process industries and has made it mandatory that all industries conduct elaborate risk assessment. Apart from being in the interest of public welfare, risk assessment is also extremely important for the welfare of the concerned industry because accidents can damage the industry's infrastructure causing enormous direct loss in terms of assets and indirect loss in terms of hindrance in production. Sometimes an accident can even totally destroy an industry.

When we began work in the field of risk assessment in 1991, we were fortunate to have the 'shoulder' of Professor Frank P. Less — in the form of his pioneering books on risk assessment — on which to climb and look further. We also found the writings of Prof P.F.Nolan and others to help us along. But very soon we realised that know-how indigenous to India is very little and patchy. R & D institutions and consultancy firms based their risk assessment of industries almost entirely on a few software packages imported from abroad. When we, too, used those packages we became sharply aware of their inadequacy. We also became aware of the dangers in relying on imported packages as they are always 'locked' - we can't really learn from them nor 'touch' them for making any improvements. Consequently we decided to go for R&D in a big way to generate a comprehensive body of methodologies and computer-automated tools for risk assessment. Such a body of expertise, we hoped, would not only add to the Indian thrust towards risk assessment but also contribute, in its small way, towards the global know-how. This book embodies results of our first few faltering steps.

The authors are thankful to Mrs. V Venilla and Ms K. Chellam who were with us when it all began. The effort has been given impetus recently by All India Council of Technical Education through a CAEM (Computer Aided Environmental Management) Unit awarded by them. We also acknowledge numerous industries - notably MRL, MFL, HOCL, IOCL, CutFast Abrasive, Zuari Agro Limited, etc for whom we have done risk assessment, thus getting an opportunity to compare the performance of our packages with the commercial ones.

FAISAL I KHAN
S.A. ABBASI

Contents

PART IV

QUANTITATIVE METHODS OF RISK ASSESSMENT- II :

RAPID RISK ASSESSMENT

PART V

QUANTITATIVE METHODS OF RISK ASSESSMENT- III :

PROBABILISTIC HAZARD ASSESSMENT

PART VI

STUDIES ON CHAIN OF ACCIDENTS (DOMINO EFFECTS)

PART VII

METHODS OF HAZARD IDENTIFICATION, SCREENING AND RANKING

PART VIII

APPLICATION OF RISK ANALYSIS IN PROCESS DESIGN

Part 1

Introduction

This part consists of two chapters, presenting a general introduction to the book and a brief review of risk assessment methodologies.

Of these, Chapter 2 is a pre-print of our paper, Techniques and methodologies for risk analysis in chemical process industries due to appear in Journal of Loss Prevention in Process industries.

1

GENERAL INTRODUCTION AND LEAD-UP TO THE PRESENT WORK

The history of chemical process industries is replete with major accidents. Such accidents have had catastrophic implications, causing massive losses of property, human lives, and environmental quality. The reverberations of the worst such disaster which happened in Bhopal in 1984, are being still felt even though over a decade has passed. Even as Bhopal gas tragedy was catastrophic in its dimensions—leading to a death toll that is by far the worst ever in the history of industrial accidents — it is by no means an isolated instance. Indeed several serious industrial accidents have taken place before and after Bhopal gas tragedy in India as well as abroad. Indeed, in India itself such accidents keep occurring with frightening regularity.

Indeed the biggest industrial accident of the 1990s - the 'HPCL Disaster' (also known as 'The Vishakhapatnam Disaster') has also occurred in India on 14 September 1997 at the HPCL (Hindustan Petroleum Corporation Limited) refinery near the city of Vishakhapatnam, India. It brought into sharp focus the destructive potential of domino effect vis a vis industrial accidents. It was this effect (also variously called 'cascading effect' or 'chain of accidents') which was responsible for a single failure in the HPCL refinery with limited damage potential to escalate into a series of major accidents, eventually claiming over 60 lives, causing damage to property worth over Rs 600 million ($ 20 million), and terrorising a sprawling city of over 2 million inhabitants (The Hindu, 1997; Subramanian, 1997)

The death toll which eventually crossed 60 would have been higher had the fire started half-an-hour later than it did, when the first shift staff would have come in to relieve the night shift. And Sunday being a holiday, the administrative personnel, who number over 200, were saved as they were not on duty (The Hindu,1997; Subramanian, 1997).

The compulsions of increasing population and developmental needs keep putting ever increasing pressure on available land space. Even those industries which were earlier set up in remote areas away from human dwellings now find themselves being enveloped by residential colonies. The risk posed by industrial accidents is thus increasing even in situations where the quantities of the hazardous materials being handled, or the manner in which they were being handled, remains the same as before.

Unlike the normal release of gaseous, liquid, or solid wastes from industrial process — which take place slowly and are controllable — accidental toxic releases, explosions, or fires occur all of a sudden leaving no chance for impacted people to escape, let alone control the accident. In order to prevent or at least reduce the frequency of occurrence of such accidents, major efforts are needed towards raising the safety level, hazard management and emergency preparedness. This realisation and the increased public awareness towards this issue, has prompted techniques development of new process to carry out risk assessment (RA) and safety evaluation of chemical process industries, singly or in combinations (as they exist in chemical complexes). Over the last few years, several methodologies have been developed for qualitative as well as quantitative risk assessment in chemical process industries. These methodologies (reviewed in Chapter 2) have served very useful purpose. Yet there is significant scope of advancement in terms of the following:-

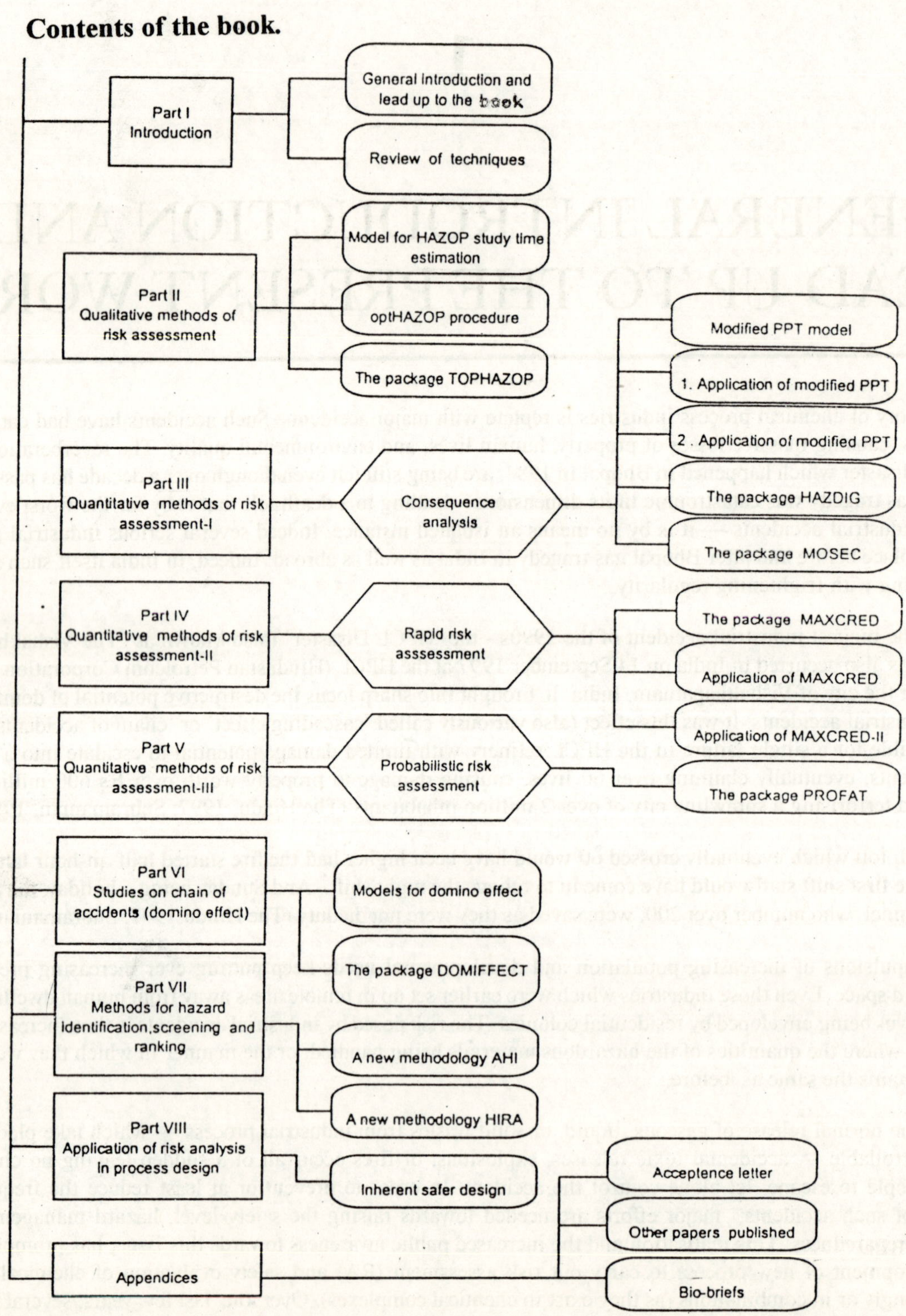

(Figure1. The structure of the book)

Reduction in experts' time and computational costs

Techniques such as hazard and operability problem (HAZOP), failure mode effect analysis (FMEA), checklist, and probabilistic risk assessment (PRA) need huge resource inputs in terms of expert-time and computational costs. Moreover the results obtained by these techniques are largely qualitative in nature.

Increase in the accuracy and precision of the forecasts

a) Quantitative techniques such as consequence analysis, indices, detailed maximum credible accident analysis (MCAA), and quantitative risk assessment (QRA) can be made more accurate and realistic; further the accident scenarios generated by them can be made more precise and sophisticated.

b) Most of the techniques ignore site characteristics; this mar the effectiveness and applicability of the forecasts to some extent.

c) Techniques such as frequency prediction, PRA, and fault tree analysis (FTA) demand highly accurate and precise data of the components; getting such highly reliable data is difficult and even a small inaccuracy in the data may lead to great inaccuracy in the results.

Increasing the gamut of RA study

The existing RA techniques either do not account for, or not very strong in, handling phenomena such as the effects of heavy gas dispersion, effect of surrounding industries on domino/cascade effects, improper safety management, and lack of adequate emergency planning.

Improving the reliability of rapid risk assessment

The existing rapid risk assessment techniques such as indices and MCAA have limitations in terms of identification and assessment of hazards relating to types of operations, states of processes, process conditions and site characteristics.

THE PRESENT WORK

We have made a few humble efforts towards introducing improvements in the various RA techniques and methodologies. We have also developed software packages aimed at user-friendliness, swiftness, larger coverage, and sophistication in risk analysis.

Attempts have been made towards :

- Developing a more reliable indexing technique for hazard identification and ranking in process industries.
- Developing a combination of techniques for qualitative hazard assessment and probabilistic hazard assessment. The techniques have been packaged as TOPHAZOP and PROFAT.
- Developing better tools for quantitative risk assessment based on more precise and accurate forecasting of the nature and impacts of accidents. These efforts have resulted in software MOSEC and HAZDIG. These have also led us to develop a new model based on modification in plume path theory for studying the dispersion of heavy gases and evolving damage control strategies when such gases are released in large quantities.
- Developing methodology for rapid risk assessment. This methodology has been coded in software package MAXCRED.
- Developing a conceptual model for the simulation of chain of accidents (domino/cascading effects) and forecasting their consequences. A software package DOMIFFECT has been developed over this.
- Developing application of risk analysis during design stage to make plants inherently safer.

The applicability of the methodologies and the software packages has been tested with real-life case studies.

CONTENTS OF THE BOOK

The contents of the book are summarised in Figure 1.

We hope that the book which presents a multi-module system of methodologies and software packages would contribute some new knowledge to the subject and would stimulate further work in the area of risk assessment.

REFERENCES

1. The Hindu, (1997). Major fire in Visag refinery, *The Hindu Publications*, **September** 15, 1, Chennai.
2. Subramanian, T S,(1997). Close call. *The Hindu Publications*, **October** 17, 41-43, Chennai.

2

TECHNIQUES AND METHODOLOGIES FOR RISK ANALYSIS IN CHEMICAL PROCESS INDUSTRIES*

This paper presents a state-of-art-review of the available techniques and methodologies for carrying out risk analysis in chemical process industries. It also presents a set of methodologies developed by the authors to conduct risk analysis effectively and optimally.

Key words: Risk assessment, hazard assessment, quantitative risk assessment, industrial hazard assessment, process safety assessment

INTRODUCTION

Chemical process industries often involve reactors, conduits and storage vessels in which hazardous substances are handled at elevated temperatures and/or pressures. Accidents in such units caused either by material failure (such as crack in the storage vessels), operational mistakes (such as raising the pressures temperature/flow-rate beyond critical limits), or external perturbation (such as damage caused by a projectile) can have serious - often catastrophic - consequences. The most gruesome example of such an accident is the Bhopal Gas Tragedy of 1984 which killed or maimed over 20,000 persons but there have been numerous other accidents (Flixborough-1974, Basel-1986, Antwerp-1987, Pasadena-1989, Panipat-1993, Mumbai-1995, and Vishakhapatnam-1997) in which the death toll would have been as high as in Bhopal if the areas where the accidents took place were not less densely populated(Less, 1996; Marshall, 1987).

Along with the rapid growth of industrialisation and population the risk posed by probable accidents also continues to rise. This is particularly so in the third world where population densities are very high and industrial areas which are surrounded by dense clusters of neighbourhoods. Further it is common to find 'industrial areas' or 'industrial complexes' where groups of industries are situated in close proximity to one another. The growth in the number of such industrial areas and in the number of industries contained in each of the areas gives rise to increasing probabilities of 'chain of accidents' or cascading/domino effects wherein an accident in one industry may cause another accident in a neighbouring industry which in turn may trigger another accident and so on. Some of the past experience like Mexico-1984, Antwerp-1987, Pasadena-1989 and recently Vishakhapatnam-1997 are examples of

* Reproduced from *Journal of Loss Prevention in Process Industries,* UK.

such disasters(Hindu, 1997). In order to prevent -or at least reduce the frequency of occurrence of such accidents major efforts are needed towards raising the level safety, hazard management and emergency preparedness. This realisation and the increased public awareness towards this issue, has prompted techniques development of new process to carry out risk assessment and safety evaluation of chemical process industries, singly or in combinations (as they exist in chemical complexes).

The resulting science of risk assessment, which has emerged in recent years with ever - increasing importance being attached to it, deals with the following key aspects of accidents in chemical process industries

a) Development of techniques and tools to forecast accidents.

b) Development of techniques and tools to analyse consequences of likely accidents. Such consequence analysis fulfils two objectives:-

    * it helps in sitting of industries and management of sites so as to minimise the damage if accident does occur;

    * it provides feedback for other exercises in accident forecasting and disaster management;

c) Development of managerial strategies for 'emergency preparedness' and 'damage minimisation'.

RISK ASSESSMENT

The terms hazard and risk are sometimes used interchangeably by the process/environmental engineer or safety personnel. However, hazard relates to the source of harm, while risk is the probability of the harm being experienced(Lees, 1996; Greenberg and Cramer, 1991). In the authors' opinion risk may be defined as a combination of hazard and probability of hazard occurrence, where hazard is defined as the degree of harm to the human beings, property, society or environment. In this context risk analysis can be defined as an exercise, which includes both qualitative and quantitative determination of risk and its multidimensional impacts.

TECHNIQUES AND METHODOLOGIES FOR RISK ASSESSMENT

Several techniques and methodologies have been proposed from 1970 onwards for risk and safety study. A brief review of the important ones is presented here;

Checklist

Checklist represents the simplest method used for hazard identification (Balemans, 1974;

Rose *et al.*, 1978; Hessian and Rubin, 1991; Oyeleye and Kramer, 1988). A checklist is a list of questions about plant organisation, operation, maintenance and other areas of concern to verify that various requirements have been fulfilled and nothing is neglected or overlooked. Checklist is primarily based on the prepares' prior experience, but it can also be based on codes and standards(Hessian and Rubin, 1991; Oyeleye and Kramer, 1988).. The checklist has to be maintained during the life of project and should be updated after each modification, and after every major outage when equipment is replaced or modified substantially.

Although checklist development requires trained and experienced personnel, even relatively untrained personnel can use it effectively. The main limitations of this methodology are:

· it takes long time to develop a checklist but it yields only qualitative results, with no insights into the system. It merely provides the status of each item in terms of 'Yes' or 'No'.

· a checklist can focus only on a single item at a time, so it can't identify hazards as a result of interaction among different units or components (equipment).

· it is only as good as the ability and prior experience of the person preparing it. There is always a significant probability of some critical item being neglected.

· it is unable to identify hazard due to the type of unit operation (reaction, heat transfer, storage etc.), severity of operating conditions (temperature, pressure), and any mis-operation (leak or excess heat generation etc.).

Due to above mentioned drawbacks this technique is not recommended for detailed risk analysis. However, it continues to be used(Eley, 1992; Ozog and Stickles, 1991).

Table 1. Guide words and their physical significance

Guide Word	Meaning	Parameter	Deviation
None	Negation intention	Flow Level	No flow Zero level
Less	Quantitative decrease	Flow Level Temperature Pressure Concentration	Low flow rate Low level Low temperature Low pressure Low concentration
More	Quantitative increase	Flow Level Temperature Pressure Concentration	High flow rate High level High temperature High pressure High concentration
Reverse	Logical opposite	Flow Pressure	Reverse flow rate Reverse pressure
Part of	Qualitative decrease	Concentration Flow Level	Concentration decrease Flow decrease Level decrease
As Well-As	Qualitative á increase	Concentration of impurity impurity substance	Concentration increase impurity
		Level of impurity	Level increase
		Pressure of substance	Pressure increase
		Flow of impurity	Flow increases
Other Than	Complete - substation	Concentration of desired substance	Concentration zero
		Level of desired substance	Level zero
		Flow of desired substance	Flow rate zero

HAZOP

HAZOP is a simple yet structured methodology for hazard identification and assessment(ICI, 1974; Lawley, 1974; CIA, 1977; Knowlton, 1976; ILO, 1988; Kletz, 1983,1985; Freeman, 1991; Sherrod and Early, 1991; Venkatasubramanian and Vaidyanathan, 1994; Medermid *et al.* 1995). It had been developed at Imperial Chemical Industries (ICI) in 1974 and later went through several modifications(ICI, 1974; Kletz, 1985; Andow *et* al., 1980; Knowlton, 1982,1989; McKelvey, 1988; Montague, 1990). The basic principle of a HAZOP study is that normal and standard conditions are safe, and hazards occur only when there is a deviation from normal conditions. It is a procedure that allows its user to make intelligent geniuses in the identification of hazard and operability problems.

In a typical HAZOP study, design and operation documents (PI&D's, PFD, material flow diagrams, and operating manuals) are examined systematically by a group of experts. Abnormal causes and adverse consequences for all possible deviations from normal operation that could arise are identified for each unit of plant. HAZOP is considered by a multi-disciplinary team of experts who have extensive knowledge of design, operation and maintenance of the process plant. To cover all the possible malfunctions in the plant the imagination of the HAZOP team members is guided systematically with a set of guide words for generating the process variable deviations. A list of guide words and their definitions is given in Table 1. The salient features of HAZOP study are:

- it gives an idea of priorities basis for detailed risk analysis,
- it provides first hand information of the potential hazards, their causes, and consequences,
- it indicates some ways to mitigate the hazards,
- it can be performed at the design stage as well as operational stage,
- it provides a basis for subsequent steps in the total risk management program.

A number of applications of HAZOP in Chemical process industries (PI) have been reported in literature; Freeman *et al.* (1992), Sweeney (1993), Pully (1993), Kolodji (1993), Shafagi and Cook (1988) , Mulvihill (1988) , Parmer and Lees (1987) , Piccinini and Levy (1984) , etc.

In its original, and thus far widely used form, HAZOP has some limitations; these limitations are of two kinds. The first kind arises from the assumptions underlying the method and is a limitation (perhaps intended) of scope. The method assumes that the design has been carried out in accordance with the appropriate codes. For example, it is presupposed that the design is appropriate for the requirements of normal operating conditions, as HAZOP only tries to identify deviations from these supposedly ideal situations.

The other kind of limitation is one which is neither intended, nor desirable, but is inherent in the method. For example Hazop is not, inherently well-suited to deal with spatial features associated with plant layout and their resultant effects. Furthermore HAZOP needs large inputs of time and expert manpower.

As the efficiency and accuracy of study is fully dependent on the experience and sincerity of the expert team members, any lacunae in manpower selection or performance can seriously harm the success of any HAZOP.

McKelvey (1989), Montague (1990), Mulvihill (1988), and Khan and Abbasi (1997a) have made suggestions to increase the effectiveness and reliability of HAZOP. According to them the duration of the study can be reduced drastically using automated systems to study the commonly occurring equipment. This may reduce the work load of team members and increase the efficiency and reliability of the study

Inspite of its limitations HAZOP remains the most favoured technique for hazard identification and assessment.

Fault tree analysis (FTA)

Fault tree(FTA) is an analytical tool that uses deductive reasoning to determine the occurrence of an undesired event analysis(Parmer and Lees, 1987; Lapp and Powers, 1976, 1979; Hauptmanns, 1988). FTA, along with component failure data and human reliability data, can enable determination of the frequency of occurrence of an accidental event.

FTA was developed in 1960's by Bell Laboratories during the Polaris missile project. Initially it was applied in the aerospace industry. Later its use was extended to nuclear and chemical industries(Less, 1996; Greenberg and Cramer, 1991; Lapp and Powers, 1979; CCPS, 1989; Rauzy, 1993; Cummings *et* al., 1983; Hauptmanns and Yllera, 1983; Ulerich *et al.*, 1988; Guymer *et al.*, 1987). FTA yields both qualitative as well as quantitative information.

FTA has the following advantages.

1) it directs the analyst to ferret out failures deductively;

2) it points out the aspects of the system which are relevant to an understanding of the mechanism of likely failure;

3) it provides a graphical aid enabling those responsible for system management to visualise the hazard; such persons are otherwise not associated with system design changes;

4) providing avenues for system reliability analysis (qualitative , quantitative);

5) allowing the analyst to concentrate on one particular system failure at a time;

6) providing the analyst with genuine insights into system behaviour.

Yllera (1988) and Lai, *et al.,* (1986) have drawn attention to the difficulties associated with FTA. According to them FTA is a sophisticated form of reliability assessment and requires considerable time and effort by skilled analysts. Although it is the best tool available for a comprehensive analysis, it is not foolproof and, in particular, it itself does not does assure of detection of all failures, especially common cause failures. The accuracy of prediction is limited and depends upon the reliability and failure data of components of the fault tree.

In many real-world applications, it may be difficult to assign exact values to the probabilities of occurrence of the fundamental events. This problem is likely to arise in dynamically changing environments or in systems in which accidents occur so frequently that reasonable failure data are not available. In the absence of genuine probability data, estimates of failure probabilities are customarily supplied by personnel familiar with the operation of the system. Usually they prefer to express their knowledge in general terms and find it extremely difficult to specify the exact numerical values that are required in conventional fault tree analysis.

To cope with this problem associated with the assignment of exact numerical values to failure probabilities, modifications have been suggested by Lai *et al.*, (1986), and Rauzy (1993), and Camarinopoulous (1985) to dilute FTA's dependency on reliability data and cut short the time of analysis using Fuzzy mathematics. Lapp and power (1976,1979),, Lapp (1991) and Bossche (1991) have proposed algorithms for computer aided fault tree design and analysis, which seems to be useful.

Failure mode effect analysis (FMEA)

FMEA is an examination of individual component such as pumps, vessels, valves, etc. to identify the likely failures which could have undesired effects on system operation(Lees, 1996; Greenberg and Cramer, 1991; Khan and Abbasi, 1995; MIL, 1977; Henevely and Kumanoto, 1981; Klaassen and Van Pepper, 1989; O'Mara, 1991). FMEA involves following steps:

1) identification of each failure mode, of the sequence of events associated with it, its causes and effects;

2) classification of each failure mode by relevant characteristics, including deductibility, diagnosability, testability, item replaceability, and compensating and operating provisions.

Typical information required for an FMEA includes :

a) system structure;

b) system intimation, operation, control and maintenance;

c) system environment;

d) system modelling;

e) system software;

f) system boundary;

g) system functional structure;

h) system functional structure representation;

i) block diagrams; and

j) failure significance and compensating provisions.

FMEA is a qualitative inductive method and is easy to apply. FMEA is assisted by the preparation of a list of the expected failure modes in the light of (1) the use of the system, (2) the elements involved, (3) the mode of operation, (4) the operation specification, (5) the time constraints and (6) the environment.

FMEA is an efficient method of analysing elements which can cause failure of the whole, or of a large part, of a system. It works best where the failure logic is essentially a serial one. It is much less suitable where complex logic is required to describe system failure(Lees, 1996; Klaassen and Van Pepper, 1989).

In essence FMEA is an inductive method. FTA serves as complementary deductive method to FMEA and is needed where analysis of complex failure logic is required. FMEA is good for generating the failure data and information at component level(Henevely and Kumanoto, 1981; Klaassen and Van Pepper, 1989). It has been recommended for use as a hazard identification technique mainly to the systems dealing with low/moderately hazardous operations and the ones which cannot support expensive and time taking HAZOP study(AICHE, 1985).

It has been stated that FMEA can be a laborious and inefficient process unless judiciously applied. FMEA is unable to deal with the interaction among different components and needs highly expert team with sufficient experience and time to carry out the study. More seriously, FMEA is restricted up to component level, while actual hazard may start at sub-component level (failure of transmission line, failure of temperature transducer, failure of controller etc.).

What-If analysis

The What if method involves asking a series of questions beginning with what if as a means of identifying hazards(CCPS, 1989; IChemE; Zoller and Esping, 1993). Apart from checklists, What if analysis is possibly the oldest method of hazard identification and is still popular(AIChE, 1985; Buck, 1992; Kavianian *et al.*, 1992). What if analysis is performed with questions such as:

What if the pipe leaks?

What if the flow controller fails?

The questions need not necessarily start with What if; other phrases may also be used.

The method essentially involves a review of the entire design by a team using questions of this type, often using a checklist.

The advantages of this technique are;

I) no specialised technique or computational tool is required,

II) once the questions have been developed they can be used throughout the life of the project with slight modifications,

III) provide a simple tabular summary.

The major disadvantages are :

1) it requires a team of experts to perform the study; it thus has disadvantages (in terms of expert available and costs) similar to HAZOP.

2) the heavy reliance on the experience and intuition of the study team both to develop questions imaginatively and to get the answer implies that any lacunae in this aspect of the study can render the study totally useless (worse still -misleading).

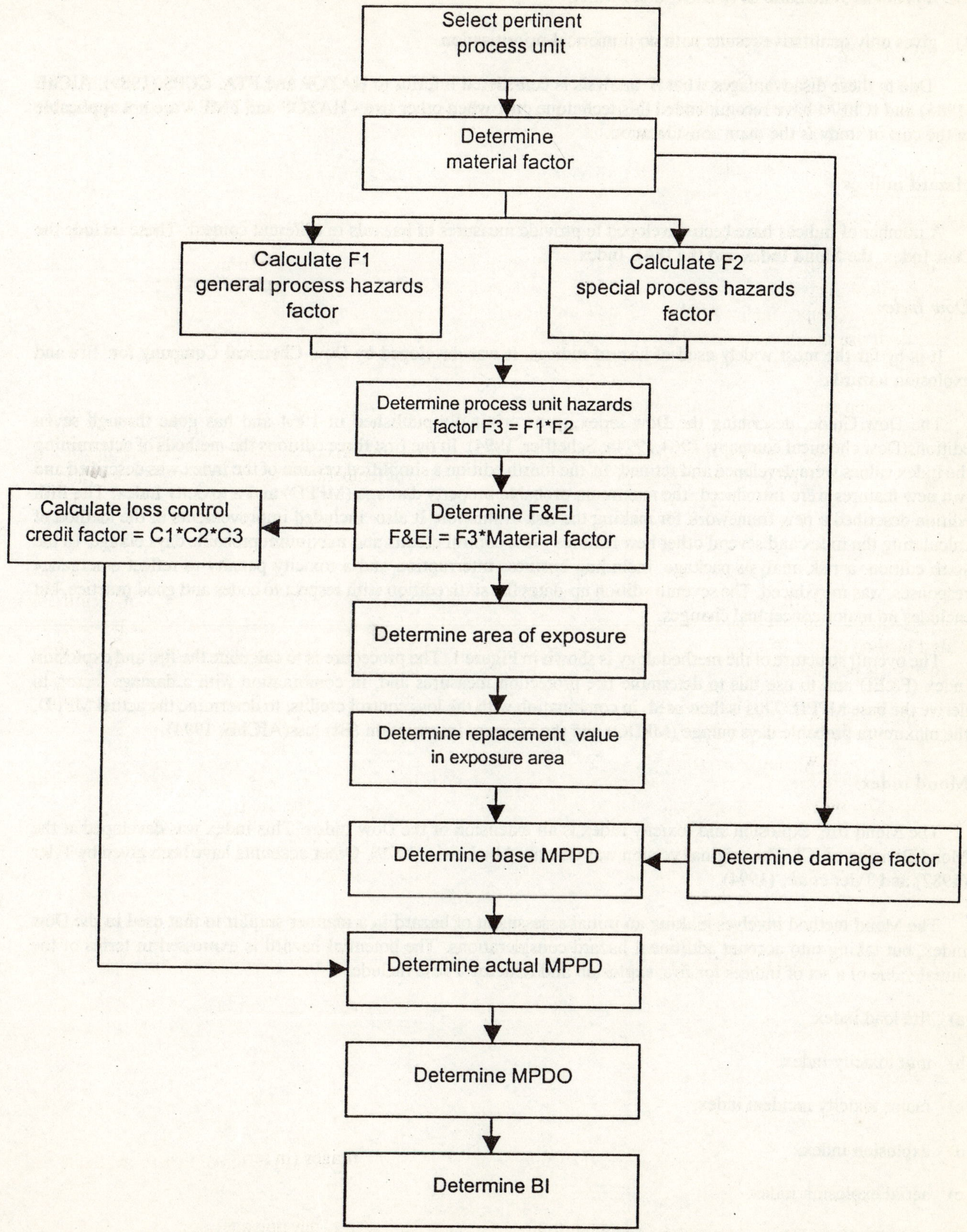

Figure 1. Procedure for calculating the Dow Fire and Explosion Index and other quantities (Lees, 1996)

3) it is not as systematic as HAZOP, and FMEA,

4) gives only qualitative results with no numerical prioritisation.

Due to these disadvantages what if analysis is considered inferior to HAZOP and FTA. CCPS (1989), AIChE (1985) and IChEM have recommended this technique only when other two - HAZOP and FMEA are not applicable or the cost of study is the main consideration.

Hazard indices

A number of indices have been developed to provide measures of hazards in different context. These include the Dow Index, the Mond Index and the IFAL Index.

Dow Index

It is by far the most widely used of hazard indices. It was developed by Dow Chemical Company for fire and explosion hazards.

The Dow Guide, describing the Dow index, was originally published in 1964 and has gone through seven editions(Dow chemical company, 1964,1994a; Scheffler, 1994). In the first three editions the methods of determining the index values were developed and refined. In the fourth edition a simplified version of the index was described and two new features were introduced: the maximum probable property damage (MPPD) and a toxicity index. The fifth edition described a new framework for making the risk evaluation. It also included improvements in the method of calculating the index and several other new features - loss control credits and maximum probable days outage. In the sixth edition, a risk analysis package, including business interruption and a toxicity penalty to reflect emergency responses, was introduced. The seventh edition up-dates the sixth edition with respect to codes and good practice, but includes no major conceptual changes.

The overall structure of the methodology is shown in Figure 1. The procedure is to calculate the fire and explosion index (F&EI) and to use this to determine fire protection measures and, in combination with a damage factor, to derive the base MPPD. This is then used, in combination with the loss control credits, to determine the actual MPPD, the maximum probable days outage (MPDO) and the business interruption (BI) loss(AIChE, 1994).

Mond index

The Mond fire, explosion and toxicity index is an extension of the Dow Index. This index was developed at the Mond Division of ICI. The original version was described by Lewis (1979). Other accounts have been given by Tyler (1982) and Tyler *et al.,* (1994).

The Mond method involves making an initial assessment of hazard in a manner similar to that used in the Dow index, but taking into account additional hazard considerations. The potential hazard is expressed in terms of the initial value of a set of indices for fire, explosion and toxicity. These include:

a) fire load index,

b) unit toxicity index,

c) major toxicity incident index,

d) explosion index,

e) aerial explosion index,

f) overall index, and

g) overall risk rating.

Start

Identification of hazards

. Check-lists

. Matrix diagrams of interaction

Assessment of hazards

. Accident sequence analysis

. Failure effect analysis

Accident consequence analysis

Stop

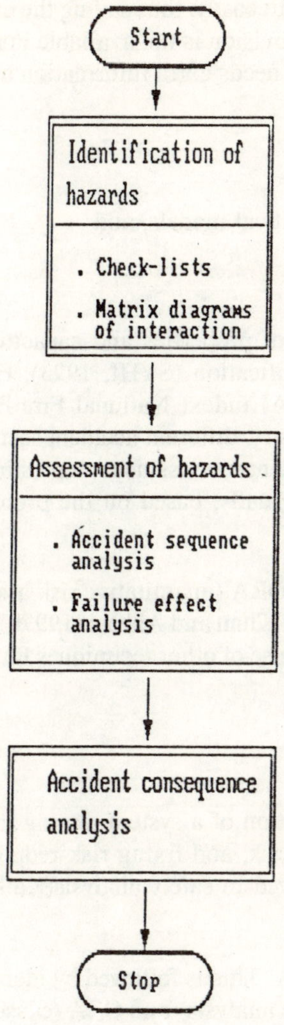

Figure 2. WHO's hazard assessment procedure

IFAL index

The instantaneous fractional annual loss (IFAL) index was developed by the Insurance Technical Bureau (1981), U K, in 1981 primarily for insurance assessment purposes(Singh and Munday, 1979; Whitehouse, 1985). Procedure for the calculation of the index is described in the IFAL Factor workbook (1981) (Insurance Technical Bureau, 1981). It involves considering the plant as set of blocks and examining each major item of process equipment in turn to assess its contribution to the index. The main hazards considered in the index are

a) pool fires,

b) vapour fires,

c) unconfined vapour cloud explosions,

d) confined vapour cloud explosions,

e) internal explosions.

In contrast to the Dow and Mond Indices, the IFAL index is too complex for manual calculation and needs a computer.

PROPOSED SCHEMES OF RISK ASSESSMENT BASED ON COMBINATION OF VARIOUS TECHNIQUES

WHO

World Health Organisation (WHO) and International Labour Office (ILO) have jointly proposed a scheme for conducting hazard assessment(1984). The scheme consist of three-steps procedure (Figure 2). As most of the constituent techniques are quantitative in nature this procedure is not as amenable to quantification as some other procedures described below are.

ISGRA

This scheme, authored by International Study Group on Risk Analysis(ISGRA, 1985) , comprises of three steps 1) hazard identification, 2) consequence analysis, and 3) quantification of risk. The hazard identification step identifies and assesses hazards based on the chemical properties, capacity, and deviation in operating parameters. HAZOP, FMEA, and FTA/ETA have been recommended for this step. The consequence analysis step is to estimate the damage potential using standard mathematical expressions. The last step - quantification of risk is based on the frequency of occurrence of an accident and its damage consequences. The frequency of occurrence is estimated based on the past history of similar accidents.

The use of this scheme, unless he/she is very well-versed with the techniques and tools of risk assessment, may be misled into by passing causes of hazards and frequency of their occurrence. These being crucial inputs for any risk assessment study, may lead to wrong conclusions.

Maximum Credible Accident Analysis (MCAA)

MCAA is an approach to forecast the damage likely to be caused if an accident takes place in a chemical plant(AIChE, 1985; API, 1992; Mallikarjunan *et al.,* 1988; Khan and Abbasi, 1997b). MCAA comprises of the following main steps:

i) study of the plant to identify hazardous materials, the non/less-hazardous unit easily, thus saving the efforts and duration going to wasted in studying non/less hazardous units. While this provision is not available in QRA and to estimate the same parameters using Dow's index and/or Mond's index it needs extra information and calculations.

ii) development of credible accident scenarios,

iii) assessment of damages likely to be caused in each scenario using mathematical models, and

iv) delineation of the maximum credible accident scenario.

The first step identifies the hazards in any process industry on the basis of properties and capacities of the chemicals and by employing different indices such as System of Hazard Identification (SYHI, 1993), Extremely Hazardous Substance (EHS 1987), and National Fire Protection Agency (NFPA) index(National Fire Protection Association, 1991). On the basis of the storage or handling situations in the industry, different accident scenarios are generated, representing plausible accidental events. The next step - the consequence assessment step estimates the consequences of each accident scenario in terms of likely extent of damage. Finally, based on the probability of occurrence and damage potential, the worst disaster scenario is identified.

MCAA has been extensively used in risk assessment and forms the basis of QRA (quantitative risk assessment) schemes proposed and applied by Arendt (1990a,1990b), Van Sciever (1990), and Khan and Abbasi (1997b). It forms one of the key steps in any elaborate risk assessment exercise but necessitates the use of other techniques for identifying causes of hazards and estimating frequency of likely accidents.

Safety analysis

Safety analysis is defined as a systematic examination of structure and function of a system aiming to identify accident contributors, modelling sequence of potential accidents, estimation of risk, and fixing risk-reducing measures. Safety analysis can be extended to risk analysis. The various steps involved in safety analysis(Kafka, 1984; Suokas, 1988) are presented in Figure 3.

The procedure starts with identification of hazards using HAZOP and FMEA. This is followed by identification of different accidents and their causes. FTA (fault tree analysis), ETA (event tree analysis) and CCA (cause - consequence analysis) have been recommended for this step. This logical model is later analysed for further results (frequency and loss in terms of economic and fatal). The procedure can be extended to the use in risk analysis by incorporating the consequence analysis step.

Quantitative risk analysis

Quantitative Risk Analysis (QRA) has been in existence for many years. Before its use in the chemical process industries (PI), it was used extensively in the nuclear industry. Unfortunately, the application of QRA in the PI is much more difficult than in the nuclear industry. This is because of the greater diversity of processes, hazardous materials, equipment types and control schemes in the PI. This diversity requires continuous addition of new capabilities in QRA(CCPS, 1989; Arendt, 1990b;1990b; Van Sciver, 1990; ICI, 1982; CMA, 1985; CCPS, 1994) . A typical QRA comprises of four steps (Figure 3).

1) hazard identification,

2) frequency estimation,

3) consequence analysis and

4) measure of risk.

The first step seeks answer to the question: what can go wrong? This is the most important step because hazards that are not identified will not be quantified, leading to an underestimated risk(Van Sciver, 1990). The techniques used for hazard identification include HAZOP studies, FMEA, 'What If' Analysis, and Checklists . After the hazards are identified, the scope of a QRA is defined.

The second step involves another key question how likely is occurrence of each accident?. Answering this question involves quantification of the probability of each accident scenario. FTA may be used for third purpose.

The third step of consequence analysis aims to quantify the negative impacts of the likely events. The consequences are normally measured in terms of the number of fatalities, although they could also be measured in terms of number of injuries or value of the property lost. The analysis of consequences in the PI is very complex due to the great variety of materials, chemical reactions, and technologies involved. Consequence analysis is the aspect of QRA that is growing most rapidly.

The last step of a QRA is to calculate the actual risk. This is done by estimating the areas that are at risk, and the extent of that risk.

Inspite of being lengthy (needs large time for implementation), high cost of implementation (due to the need of highly expert professionals of various discipline for longer duration), and needs sophisticated tools and data, it is the most favoured and presently most frequently used scheme for the risk analysis of chemical process industries(Lees,1996; Greenberg and Cramer, 1991; Khan and Abbasi, 1997b,c,d).

Improvements in terms of reducing the duration of the implementation of various steps by screening the non-hazardous units, cutting short the time of each step (use of already developed information base) would bring down the cost of study drastically and thus make the study optimal in all respect (cost, duration and reliability of results).

Probabilistic safety analysis

In subsequent years Guymer *et al.* (1987), Popazoglou *et al.* (1992), and Kafka (1991,1993), have proposed a combination of different techniques for probabilistic safety analysis (PSA) in chemical process industries. PSA provides, a framework for a systematic analysis of hazards and quantification of the corresponding risks. It also provides, a basis for supporting safety-related decision-making. The

HAZARD IDENTIFICATION
. Identification of plant operating stage
. Initiating event selection
. Function system relationship
. Screening of initiating event

ACCIDENT SEQUENCE MODELLING
. Event sequence modelling
. System modelling
. Human performance analysis

DATA ACQUISITION AND PARAMETER ESTIMATION
. Initiating events
. Component failure data
. Human error probability

ACCIDENT SEQUENCE QUANTIFICATION
. Determination of accident sequence
. Boolean reduction

HAZARDOUS SUBSTANCE RELEASE CATEGORIC ASSESSMENT
. Outflow model
. Evaporation model
. Weather conditions
. Relation of plant damage state & release category

CONSEQUENCE ASSESSMENT
. Dispersion models
. Assessment of doses
. Dose response models

INTEGRATION OF RESULT

Figure 3. Steps of probabilistic safety analysis in chemical industries.

methodology and the procedures followed for the PSA of a typical chemical installation involved in handling a hazardous substance can be outlined in the following seven major steps(Popazoglou *et al.*, 1992) (Figure 4).

1. **Hazard identification**

The main potential sources of hazardous substance releases are identified and the initiating events that can cause such releases are determined.

2. **Accident sequence modelling**

A logical model for the installation is developed. The model includes each and every initiator of potential accidents and the response of the installation to these initiators.

3. **Data acquisition and parameter estimation**

Parameters which must be estimated include the frequencies of the initiating events, component unavailability and probabilities of human actions.

4. **Accident sequence quantification**

This step quantifies the accident sequences, that calculates their frequency of occurrence. In particular, the plant model built in the second step is quantified using the parameter values estimated in the third step.

5. **Hazardous substance release categories assessment**

Release categories of the hazardous substance are defined in order to streamline the calculation of the consequences of the accidents and the associated frequencies.

6. **Consequence assessment**

Undesirable consequences and associated probabilities are calculated for each release category. If the hazardous substance is toxic, immediate health effects can be estimated by calculation of the atmospheric dispersion of the released substance, the assessment of the dose an individual would receive at each point around the site, and by establishing a dose/response model.

7. **Integration of results**

Integrating the models and the associated results, developed in steps 4,5 and 6, results in the establishment of the range of possible consequences and the associated uncertainties.

Beckjord *et al* (1990) have reported a few applications of PSA in chemical process industries. For the same level of accuracy PSA takes about 50% more time than QRA. Moreover, the application of PSA is limited to the operational stage as because many of its steps (data acquisition and parameter estimation, and accident sequence quantification) need precise operational data, which are available only during operation.

THE PRESENT WORK

It emerges from the foregoing review that several of the existing methodologies are useful in conducting one or other aspect of risk analysis. For example; HAZOP is a powerful technique for identifying and assessing hazards qualitatively, while MCAA is widely applicable in consequence analysis. All conventional risk analysis procedures require a combination of these methodologies. As some of them - such as HAZOP- are cumbersome and costly, and some other - such as FMEA,FTA - require extensive reliability data which might not be easy to obtain, the conventional RA procedures become tedious, costly, and prone to serious errors (when precise basic data is required but is not available).

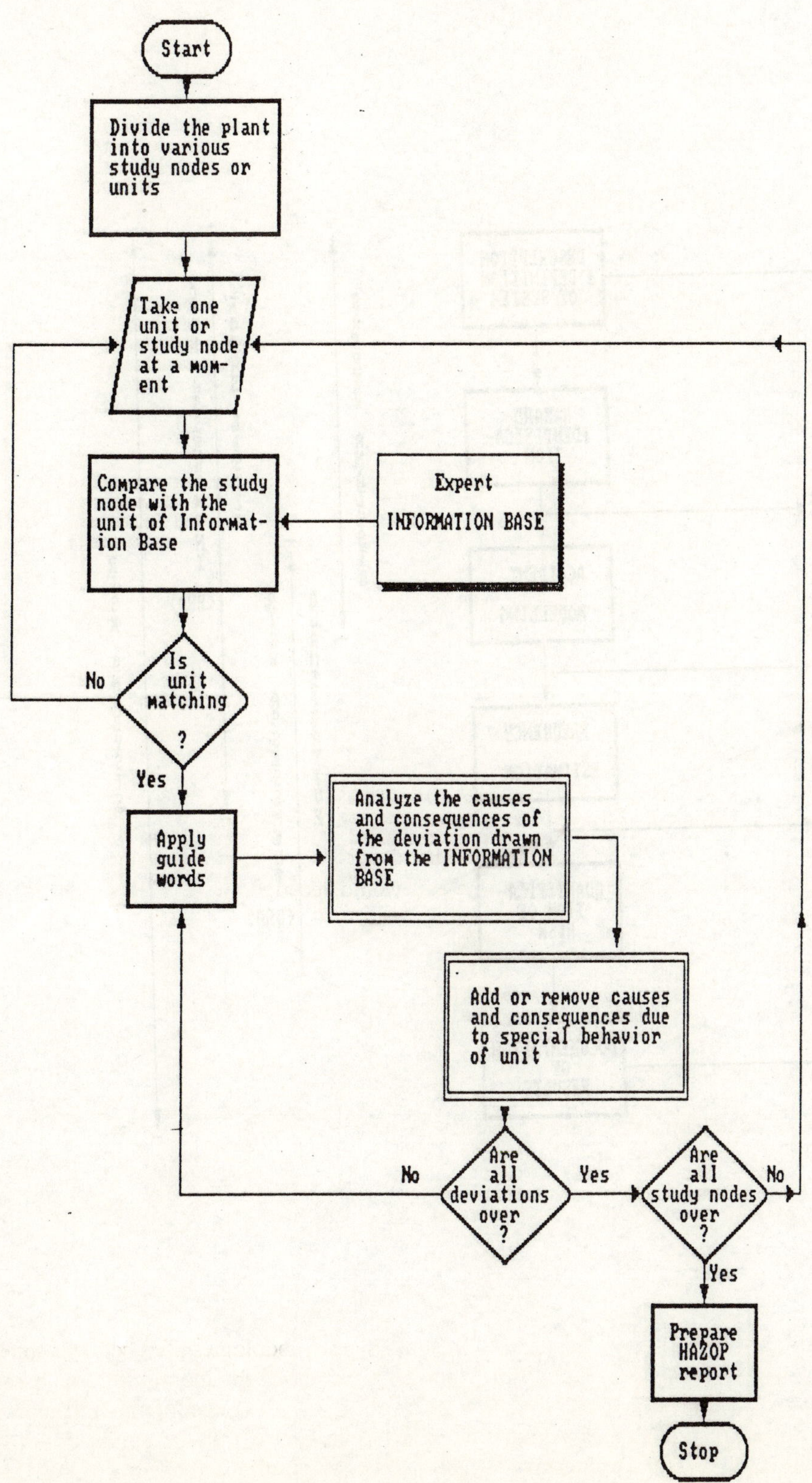

Figure 4. optHAZOP study procedure

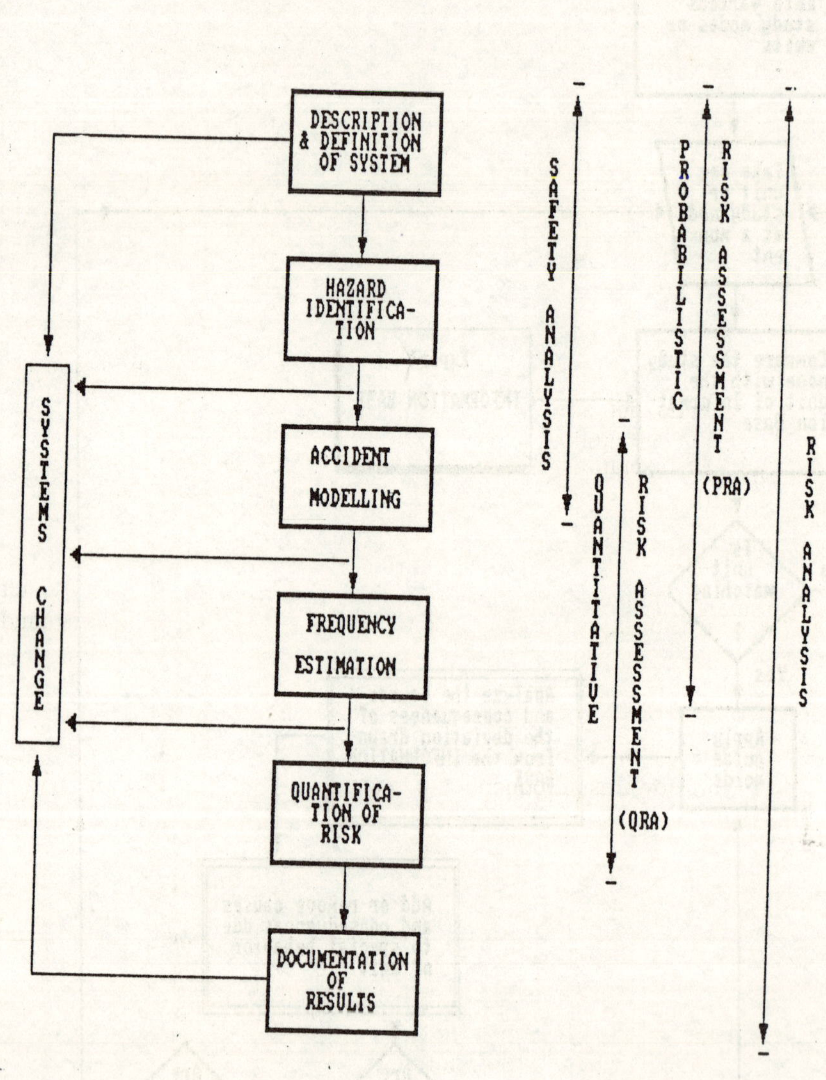

Figure 5. Simplified block diagram showing main steps of different risk and safety assessment procedures

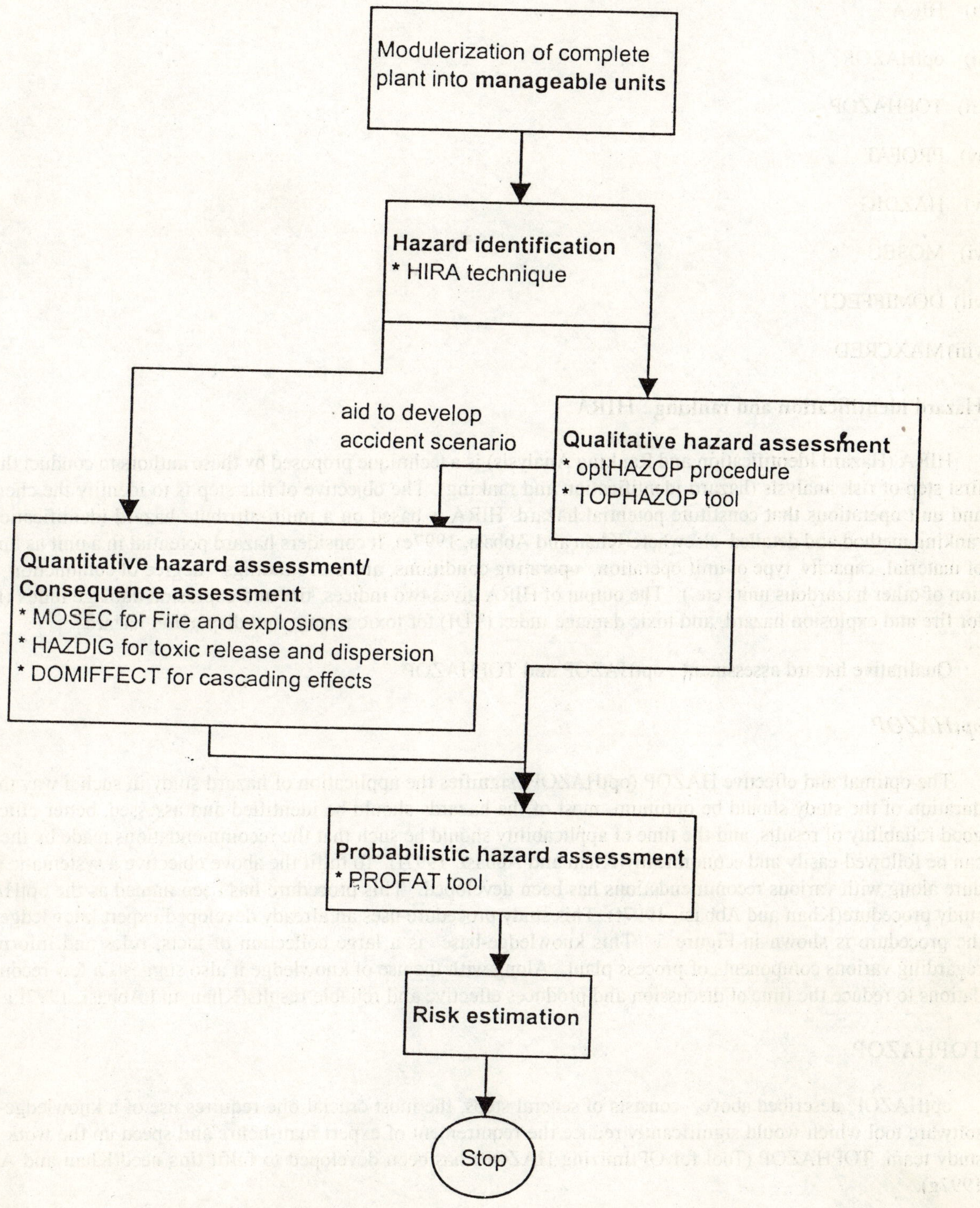

Figure 6. Simplified block diagram showing various steps with techniques and/or tool to conduct optimal risk analysis

We have tried to improve the situation modifying some of the conventional methodologies and strengthening some others in terms of enhancing their analytical and computational capabilities. These efforts have led to the following:

i) HIRA

ii) optHAZOP

iii) TOPHAZOP

iv) PROFAT

v) HAZDIG

vi) MOSEC

vii) DOMIFFECT

viii) MAXCRED

Hazard identification and ranking : HIRA

HIRA (Hazard Identification and Ranking Analysis) is a technique proposed by these authors to conduct the very first step of risk analysis (hazard identification and ranking). The objective of this step is to identify the chemicals and unit operations that constitute potential hazard. HIRA is based on a multi-attribute hazard identification and ranking method and detailed elsewhere(Khan and Abbasi, 1997e). It considers hazard potential in a unit as function of material, capacity, type of unit operation, operating conditions, and surroundings (degree of conjunction, location of other hazardous units etc.). The output of HIRA gives two indices, fire and explosion damage index (FEDI) for fire and explosion hazard, and toxic damage index (TDI) for toxic release and dispersion hazard.

Qualitative hazard assessment : optHAZOP and TOPHAZOP

optHAZOP

The optimal and effective HAZOP (optHAZOP) signifies the application of hazard study in such a way that the duration of the study should be optimum, most of the hazards should be identified and assessed, better efficiency, good reliability of results, and the time of applicability should be such that the recommendations made by the study can be followed easily and economically(Khan and Abbasi, 1997f). To fulfil the above objective a systematic procedure along with various recommendations has been developed. This procedure has been named as the optHAZOP study procedure(Khan and Abbasi, 1997f). This study procedure uses an already developed expert knowledge-base; the procedure is shown in Figure 5. This knowledge-base is a large collection of facts, rules and information regarding various components of process plant. Along with the use of knowledge it also suggests a few recommendations to reduce the time of discussion and produces effective and reliable results(Khan and Abbasi, 1997f,g).

TOPHAZOP

optHAZOP, described above, consists of several steps, the most crucial one requires use of a knowledge-based software tool which would significantly reduce the requirement of expert man-hours and speed up the work of the study team. TOPHAZOP (Tool for OPtimizing HAZOP) has been developed to fulfil this need(Khan and Abbasi, 1997g).

TOPHAZOP is a knowledge-based user-friendly software for conducting HAZOP study in a comprehensive, effective, and efficient manner within a short span of time. TOPHAZOP overcomes several major limitations (time, effort, repetitious work, etc.) of the existing HAZOP procedure. The software has an in-built knowledge-base which is extensive and dynamic. It incorporates process units, and works out numerous modes of failure for certain input operational conditions. It drastically minimises the need of expert time. The knowledge-base has been developed in two segments: process general knowledge, and process specific knowledge. The process specific knowledge segment handles information specific to a particular process unit in a particular operation, whereas the process general knowledge segment handles general information about process unit. At present the knowledge-base incorporates information pertaining to 15 different process units including their characteristics and modes of failures. The availability of on-line help and graphical user-interface enhances its user-friendliness so that even an inexperienced professional can utilise the software with relative ease.

Probabilistic hazard assessment : PROFAT

Fault tree analysis involves identification of causes of an accident, frequency of occurrence of an accident, and contribution of each cause to the accident. It is a useful methodology but is besieged with the same types of limitations which we find with other methodologies such as: need of large volumes of precise data, and requirement of large expert time. We have made attempts to overcome these limitations by incorporating a combination of analytical method(Hauptmanns, 1988), and Monte-Carlo simulation technique(Rauzy,1993; Hauptmanns, 1983) with fuzzy set theory(Tanaka *et* al., 1983; Khan and Abbasi, 1995). A software PROFAT (Probabilistic Fault Tree Analysis) has been developed on the basis of this recipe.

Consequence Analysis : MOSEC HAZDIG and DOMIFFECT

Consequence analysis involves assessment of likely consequences if an accident scenario does materialise. The consequences are quantified in terms of damage radii (the radius of the area in which the damage would readily occur), damage to property (shattering of window panes, caving of buildings) and toxic effects (chronic/acute toxicity, mortality). The assessment of consequence involves a wide variety of mathematical models. For example source models are used to predict the rate of release of hazardous material, the degree of flashing, and the rate of evaporation. Models for explosions and fires are used to predict the characteristics of explosions and fires. The impact intensity models are used to predict the damage zones due to fires, explosion and toxic load. Lastly toxic gas models are used to predict human response to different levels of exposures to toxic chemicals.

MOSEC

A software MOSEC (MOdeling and Simulation of fire and Explosion in Chemical process industries) has been developed specifically to estimate the impacts of accidents involving explosion and/or fire(Khan and Abbasi, 1997h). MOSEC comprises of state-of-the-art models to deal with : i) pool fire, ii) flash fire, iii) fire ball, iv) jet fire, v) boiling liquid expanding vapour explosion (BLEVE), vi) confined vapour cloud explosion (CVCE), vii) unconfined vapour cloud explosion (UVCE), and viii) vented explosion. The software has been developed in object-oriented programming environment using C++ as a coding tool. It has been made user-friendly by incorporating such features as graphics, on-line help, ready-to-use output format, etc.

HAZDIG

HAZDIG(Hazardous dispersion of gases) is a computer software specifically developed to estimate the consequences (damage potentials and risks) due to release of toxic chemicals, accidentally or voluntarily (Khan and Abbasi, 1997i). The modular structure of HAZDIG (developed in object oriented environment) enables swift processing of data and computation of result. It is also easy to maintain and up-grade. HAZDIG incorporate latest models for estimating atmospheric stability(Van Ulden and Hostlag, 1985) and dispersion(Pasquill and Smith, 1983; Wrbink, 1993; Erbink, 1995; and Khan and Abbasi,1997j,k). The data needed to run the models is easy to obtain and feed e.g. properties of chemicals, operating conditions, ambient temperature, and a few commonly available meteorological parameters. A database containing various proportionality constants and complex empirical data has been built into the system. It is capable of handling various types of release and dispersion scenarios: two phase release followed by dispersion, momentum release followed by dispersion, dispersion of heavier-than-air gases, etc. The Graphics option enables the user to draw any industrial site/layout using freehand drawing or using any already defined drawing tool. The contour drawing option has the facility for drawing various damage/risk contours over the accident site.

Table 2. Parameters used in the effectiveness study of various i risk assessment schemes

Parameters	Detail description
A	Quantitative results
B	inexpensive to execute (in terms of expert time/computational time/data requirement)
C	Sequence of steps optimal
D	In some steps numerous techniques have been clustered without giving criteria of which to choose in which situation, this may lead persons not very well-versed to either waste time or bypass some crucial aspects
E	Precision
F	Applicability at various stage of project
G	Covers most of the aspect of risk study
H –	Cumulative performance index

DOMIFFECT

Most of the risk analysis methodologies deal with accidents in a single industry, more so in one of the units of an industry. But it is always possible that a major accident in one unit -say an explosion or a fire - can cause a secondary accident in a nearby unit which in turn may trigger a tertiary accident(Khan and Abbasi, 1997l; Pasman *et* al., 1992). The probability of such domino or 'cascading' effects occurrence is increasing day by day with more new industries coming up in already congested industrial areas(Khan and Abbasi, 1997l).

We have developed a computer automated methodology DOMIFFECT (DOMIno efFECT) which enables one to know a) whether domino effects are likely to occur in a given setting, b) if they do what would be the likely accident scenarios, and c) what would be the likely impacts of the different scenarios(Khan and Abbasi, 1997m). Finally, the tool guides us towards strategies needed to prevent domino effects(Khan and Abbasi, 1997m). DOMIFFECT is menu driven and interactive, capable of the following:

- estimation of all possible hazards from toxic release to explosion;
- handling of interaction among different accidental events (generation of domino or cascading accident scenarios);
- estimation of domino effect probability;
- estimation of domino effect consequences.

Rapid risk analysis : MAXCRED

A total risk assessment exercise covering all steps exhaustively from beginning to end is expensive in terms of time as well as monetary and personnel inputs(Greenberg and Cramer, 1991; Khan and Abbasi, 1995; CCPS, 1989; AIChE, 1985; WHO, 1984; Suokas, 1988; Popazoglou, 1992; Pasman *et* al., 1992). It often becomes necessary to conduct rapid risk assessment (RRA) to draw the same conclusions that a full fledged risk assessment would lead to, albeit with lesser (yet practicable) accuracy and precision(Khan and Abbasi, 1996,1997h).

We have proposed a software package, and the system of methodologies on which the package is based, for conducting RRA in chemical process industries. The package is named MAXCRED (MAXimum CREDible rapid risk assessment)(Khan and Abbasi, 1997h). The package, coded in C++, has the following attributes:

i) it incorporates larger number of models to handle larger variety of situations useful in RRA;

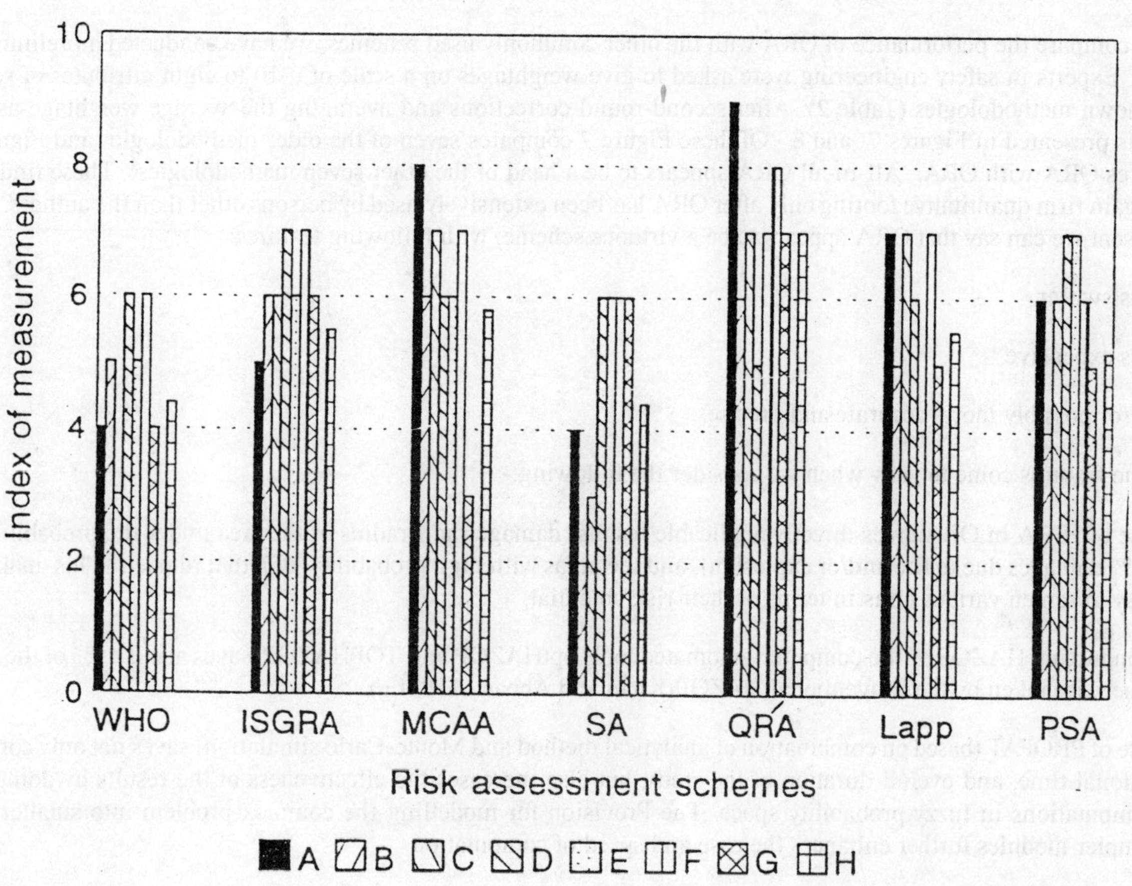

Figure 7. Comparison of parameters for various scheme of risk assessment (legends A, B....H is defined in Table 2)

ii) it includes more precise, accurate, and recent models than handled by existing commercial packages;

iii) greater user-friendliness;

iv) ability to forecast whether second or higher order accidents may occur.

Optimal Risk Analysis (ORA)

We have combined the first seven of the methodologies described above into a framework, named ORA (Optimal Risk Analysis). ORA involves four steps : i) hazard identification and screening, ii) hazard assessment (both qualitative and probabilistic), iii) quantification of hazards or consequence analysis, and iv) risk estimation. These steps of ORA and corresponding methodology to be used in each step are presented in terms of ORA algorithm (Figure 6).

To compare the performance of ORA with the other commonly used schemes we have conducted a preliminary Delphi. Experts in safety engineering were asked to give weightages on a scale of 0-10 to eight attributes of seven well-known methodologies (Table 2). After second-round corrections and averaging the average weightage as obtained is presented in Figures 7 and 8. Of these Figure 7 compares seven of the older methodologies and Figure 8 compares QRA with ORA. All-in-all ORA appears to be a head of the other seven methodologies. These findings would gain firm quantitative footing only after ORA has been extensively used by persons other than the authors. For the present we can say that ORA appears to be a virtuous scheme, with following features:

a) it is swifter,

b) less expensive,

c) as (or possibly more) accurate and precise.

The features come to view when we consider the following:-

1) Use of HIRA in ORA gives directly applicable results: damage radii(radius of the area under the probability of 50% damages due to fire and/or explosion), and the areas with high probability of lethal impacts. This makes it easy to screen various units in terms of their risk potential.

2) Conducting HAZOP by the computer-automated tools optHAZOP and TOPHAZOP saves about 45% of the time otherwise taken by the conventional HAZOP(Khan and Abbasi, 1997f,g).

3) Use of PROFAT (based on combination of analytical method and Monte-Carlo simulation) saves not only computational time, and overall duration of the study, but also increases the effectiveness of the results by doing the computations in fuzzy probability space. The Provision for modelling the complex problem into smaller and simpler modules further enhances the ease and speed of computation.

4) Use of HAZDIG, MOSEC and DOMIFFECT (based on the state-of-the-art models) enables easy, fast, and reliable consequence assessment.

DOMIFFECT enables study of the possibility and likely impacts of domino effects; without such a study no risk assessment exercise can be considered complete or 'safe'.

REFERENCES

1. AIChE, (1985). Guidelines for hazard evaluation procedures, *prepared by Battle Columbus division* : *AIChE,* New York.

2. AIChE, (1994). Dow's Fire and Explosion Index classification guide, AIChE *Technical manual LC 80-29237* :*AIChE,* New York.

3. Andow, P K, Lees, F P, and Murphy, C P, (1980). The propagation of faults in process plants; a state of the art reviews. *Int.Chem.Eng.Sym.Ser*, **58**, 225.

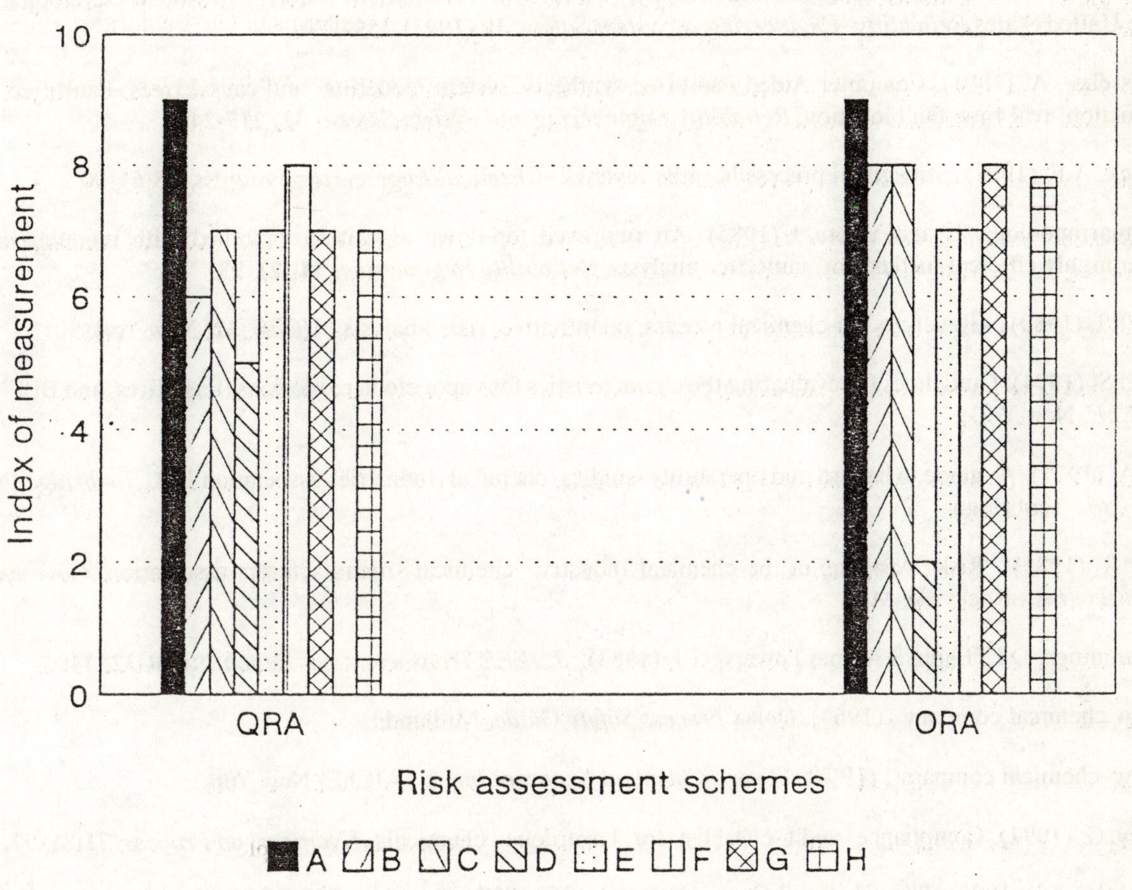

Figure 8. Comparison of effectiveness of ORA over QRA (legends A, B,... H are explained in Table 2).

4. API, (1992). Management of Process Hazards, *Recommended Practice 750*, American Petroleum Institute, Washington D C.

5. Arendt, J S, (1990a). Using quantitative risk assessment in the CPI, *Reliability Engineering and system safety*, **29**, 133-149.

6. Arendt, J S, (1990b). Management of quantitative risk assessment in chemical process industries. *Plant/ Operation Progress,* **4**,262-268.

7. Balemans, A W M, (1974). Check-list. *Loss Prevention and Safety Promotion*,**1**, 7-15.

8. Beckjord, E S, Cunningham, M A and Murphy, J A, (1990). Probabilistic Safety Assessment Development in the United States,*Reliability Engineering & System Safety,* **39** (1993) 159-170.

9. Bossche, A, (1991). Computer Aided Fault tree synthesis; system modeling and causal trees; Fault tree construction; real time fault location, *Reliability Engineering and System Safety,* **32,** 217-241.

10. Buck, A F, (1992). Strengthen process hazards reviews. *Chemical Engineering Progress,* **88**(6), 90.

11. Camarinpoulous, L and Yllera, J, (1985). An improved top-down algorithm combined with modularization as a highly efficient method for fault tree analysis, *Reliability Engineering,* **11** (2), 93.

12. CCPS, (1989). Guidelines for chemical process quantitative risk analysis, *AIChE*, **32**, New York.

13. CCPS, (1994). Guidelines for evaluating the characteristics for vapor cloud explosions, flash fires, and BLEVEs, *AIChE*, New York.

14. CIA, (1977). A guide to hazard and operability studies chemical industries association Ltd., *Tonbridge Printers Ltd.,* Tonbridge.

15. CMA, (1985). Risk Analysis in the chemical industry, chemical manufacturers association, *Government Institute Inc.,* Rockville, MD.

16. Cummings, D L, Lapp, S A, and Powers, G J, (1983). *J. IEEE Transaction on Reliability,* **R-32**, 140.

17. Dow chemical company , (1964). *Dow's Process Safety Guide,* Midland.

18. Dow chemical company , (1994a). *Dow's Chemical Exposure Index* , AIChE, New York.

19. Eley, C, (1992). Compliance audit checklist for hazardous chemicals, *Hydrocarbon Process,* **71**(8), 97.

20. Erbink, J J, (1993). The advanced Gaussian model STACKS, Procd. of ERCOFTAC, *Work shop on Inter comparison of Advanced Practical Short range Atmospheric Dispersion Modeling*, Manno, Switzerland.

21. Erbink, J J, (1995). Turbulent diffusion model from tall stacks, *Ph.D. thesis submitted to VRIJ University*, The Netherlands.

22. Extremely hazardous substances, (1987). *Environment Protection Act -40CFR part 355*, Washington DC.

23. Freeman, R A, (1991). Documentation of Hazards and operability studies, *Plant/Operation Progress,* **10**(3), 155, July.

24. Freeman, R A, Lee, R, and MeMamara, T, (1992). Plan HAZOP studies with an expert system, *Chemical Engineering Progress,* August.

25. Greenberg, H R, and Cramer, J J, (1991). Risk assessment and risk management for chemical process industries, *Van Nostrand Reinhold*, New York.

26. Guymer, P, Kaiser, G D, and Mckelvey, T C, (1987). Probabilistic risk assessment in the CPI, *Chemical*

Engineering Progress, January, 37-45.

27. Hauptmanns, U, (1988).Fault tree analysis for process industries : engineering risk and hazard assessment, (Ed: *Kandel and Avani), CRC Press Inc.,* Florida,.

28. Hauptmanns, U and Yllera, J, (1983). Fault-tree evaluation by Monte- Carlo simulation, *Chemical Engineer*, **90**.

29. Henevely, E J and Kumanoto, M, (1981). Reliability engineering and risk assessment, *Englwood Cliffs*, New Jercy.

30. Hessian, R T, and Rubin, J N, (1991). Check list reviews, Risk assessment and risk management for the PI, *(ED: Greenberg and Creamer), Van Nostrand Reiǹholdm,* New York.

31. Hindu, (1997). Major fire in Vizag refinery, *The Hindu publication*, September 15, **1**.

32. IChemE , Risk analysis in the process industries, *EFCE publication series No 45,* IChemE, Rugby.

33. ICI , (1974). Hazard and operability studies, *Imperial Chemical Industries*, Process Safety Report 2, London.

34. Quantified Risk analysis in the process industries, *The Chemical Engineer,* **385,** 355-367.

35. ILO**,** (1988). Major hazard control : a practical manual, *I L O Office*, Geneva.

36. Insurance Technical Bureau **,** (1981)**.** *IFAL Factor Workbook* , London.

37. ISGRA, (1985). Risk analysis in the process industries- an ISGRA update, *Plant/Operation progress,* **4**(2), April, 63-67.

38. Kafka, F L, (1984). The European chemical industry's view of major hazards legislation. *The 1984 European Major Hazards Conference*, London.

39. Kafka, P, (1991). Probabilistic Safety assessment: Quantitative process to balance design, manufacturing and operation for safety of plant structures and systems. Principal Division Lecture, *Transactions SMiRT 11*, A Tokyo.

40. Kafka, P, (1993). Important issues using PSA technology for design of new system and plants, *GRS mbH 85748 Garchirg,* Germany.

41. Kavianian, H R, J K and Brown, G V, (1992). Application of Hazard Evaluation Techniques to the Design of Potentially Hazardous Industrial Chemical Processes. Report. Div. of Training and Manpower Dev., *Nat. Inst. Occup. Safety and Health*, Cincinnati, Ohio.

42. Khan, F I and Abbasi, S A, (1995). Risk analysis: a systematic method of hazard assessment and control, *J of Industrial Pollution Control,* **11**(2), 89-98.

43. Khan, F I, and Abbasi, S A, (1995). Analytical Simulation : a procedure to conduct FTA in chemical process industries, *CPCE/RA 012/95*: Pondicherry University, Pondicherry.

44. Khan, F I, and Abbasi, S A, (1996). Simulation of accidents in a chemical process industry using software MAXCRED, *Indian J of Chemical Technology,* **3,** 338-344.

45. Khan, F I, and Abbasi, S A, (1997a). Mathematical model for HAZOP study time estimation, *J of Loss Preven tion Process Industries*, **10**(4), 249.

46. Khan, F I, and Abbasi, S A, (1997b). Risk analysis of epichlohydrin manufacturing industry using new computer automated tool MAXCRED, *J Loss Prevention Process Industries,* **10**(2), 91-100.

47. Khan, F I, and Abbasi, S A, (1997c). Risk analysis of a cloralkali industry situated in densely populated area,

Process Safety Progress, **16**(3), 172-185.

48. Khan, F I, and Abbasi, S A, (1997d). Rapid quantitative risk assessment of a petrochemical industry using a new software package MAXCRED, *J of Cleaner Production* (in press).

49. Khan, F I, and Abbasi, S A, (1997e). Hazard identification and Ranking : a multi-attribute technique for hazard identification, *Research report CPCE/RA 22/97* Pondicherry University, Pondicherry.

50. Khan, F I, and Abbasi, S A, (1997f). optHAZOP an optimal and effective procedure to conduct HAZOP study, *J of Loss Prevention in Process Industry*, **10**(3), 191-204.

51. Khan, F I and Abbasi, S A, (1997g). TOPHAZOP: a knowledge based software tool for conducting HAZOP in a rapid, efficient yet inexpensive manner, *J Loss Prevention Process Industries*, (in press).

52. Khan, F I, and Abbasi, S A, (1997h). MOSEC : MOdeling and Simulation of fire and Explosion in Chemical process industries, *Research report CPCE/RA 21/97*, Pondicherry University, Pondicherry.

53. Khan, F I, and Abbasi, S A, (1997i). HAZDIG : Hazardous dispersion of gases, *J of Loss Prevention Process Industries* (communicated).

54. Khan, F I, and Abbasi, S A, (1997j). Application of the recently modified plume path theory on the dispersion of some heavy gases, *Sym. of Air Quality Management at an Urban, Regional, and Global Scale*, 23-26 September, Istanbul.

55. Khan, F I, and Abbasi, S A, (1997k). Modeling and simulation of heavy gases released by petrochemical industries, *2nd International Speciality Conference on Environment Progress in the Petroleum & Petrochemical Industries*, November 17-19, Bahrain.

56. Khan, F I, and Abbasi, S A, (1997l). Models for domino effect analysis in chemical process industries, *Process Safety Progress*, (in press).

57. Khan, F I, and Abbasi, S A, (1997m). DOMIFFECT: a user-friendly software for domino effect analysis, *Environmental Modeling & Software*, (Communicated).

58. Khan, F I, and Abbasi, S A, (1997n). MAXCRED: a new software package rapid risk assessment, *Environmental Modeling and Software*, (in press).

59. Klaassen, K B, and Van Pepper, J C L, (1989). System reliability concept and applications, *Chapman and Hall Inc.*, New York.

60. Kletz, T A, (1983). HAZOP and HAZAN Notes on the identification and assessment of hazards, *The Institution of Chemical Engineers*, Rugby.

61. Kletz, T A, (1985). Eliminating potential process hazard, *Chemical Engineer,* **48**.

62. Knowlton, R E, (1976). Hazard and operability studies and their initial application in R&D, *R&D Management*, 7, 1-8.

63. Knowlton, R E, (1982). An introduction to hazard and operability studies, *Chematics International Ltd,* Vancouver, Canada.

64. Knowlton, R E, (1989). Hazard and operability studies: The guide word approach, *Chematics International Co.,* Vancouver.

65. Kolodji, B P, (1993). Hazard resolutions in sulfur plants form design through start up, *Process Safety Progress,* **12**(2), 127-731.

66. Lai, F S, Shenoi, S, and Fan, L T, (1986). Fuzzy fault tree analysis theory and applications, *(Engineering risk*

and hazard assessment, Ed:Kandel and Avni), CRC press, Florida.

67. Lapp, S A, (1991). A risk evaluation system, *ChemTech.,* 700-704.

68. Lapp, S A, Powers, G J, (1976). *Chemical Engineering Progress,* **72**(4), 89.

69. Lapp, S A, Powers, G J, (1979). *J IEEE Transaction on Reliability,* **R-28,** 12.

70. Lawley, H G,(1974). Operability studies and hazard analysis, *Chemical Engineering Progress,* **70** (4), 45-54.

71. Lees, F P, (1996). Loss prevention in process industries, *Butterworths,* **1-3**, London.

72. Lewis, D J , (1979). The mond fire, explosion and toxicity index - a development of the Dow Index. *AIChE on Loss prevention* (New York).

73. Mallikarjunan, M M, Raghvan, K V and Pietersen, C M, (1988). An approach to Maximum Credible Accident Analysis of cluster of industries, *Proceeding of Envirotech International Conference* , September 21-24, Bombay.

74. Marshall, V C, (1987). Major chemical hazards, *John Wiley & Sons,* New York.

75. McKelvey, C T, (1988). How to improve the effectiveness of hazard and operability analysis, *IEEE Transactions on Reliability,* **37**(2), 167-170.

76. Medermid, J A, Micholson, M, Pumfrey, D J, and Fenelon, P,(1995). Experience with the application of HAZOP to computer based systems, *Dept. of Computer Science,* University of York, Helington.

77. MIL, (1977). Procedure for performing a failure mode effect analysis, *Dept. of Navy,* Report MIL-STD-1629A Washington DC.

78. Montague, D F, (1990). Process Risk Evaluation - what method to use ?, *Reliability Engineering & System Safety,* **29**(1), 27-33.

79. Mulvihill, R J, (1988). Design safety enhancement through the use of hazard and risk analysis, *IEEE Transactions on Reliability.,* **37**(2), 149-153.

80. National Fire Protection Association, (1991). Hazardous chemical data, *NFPA code-325M,* New Jercy.

81. O'Mara, R, (1991). Calculation of human reliability, *Risk assessment and risk management for the CPI, (ED: Greenberg and Creamer) : Van Nostrand,* New York.

82. Oyeleye, O O, and Kramer, M A, (1988). Qualitative simulation of chemical process system : steady state analysis, *AIChE Journal,* **34**(9), 1441.

83. Ozog, H, and Stickles, R P, (1991). Process hazard management documents, practice compared, *Oil and Gas Journal,* January, 81-90.

84. Parmer, J C, and Lees, F P, (1987). The propagation of faults in Process plants : Hazard identification, *Reliability Engg.,* **7**, 277 & 303.

85. Pasman, H J, Duxbury, H A, and Bjordal, E M, (1992). Major hazards in the process industries. Achievements and challenges in loss prevention, *Journal of hazardous materials,* **30**, 1-38.

86. Pasquill, F, and Smith, F B, (1983). Atmospheric diffusion, (third edition), *John whiley,* New York.

87. Piccinini, M, and Levy, G, (1984). Ethylene oxide reaction; safety according to operability analysis; *Canadian J. of Chemical Engineering,* **62,** 547.

88. Popazoglou, I A, Nivoliantiou, A O, and Christou, M, (1992). Probabilistic safety analysis in chemical installation, *J Loss Prevention Process Industries,* **5**(3), 181-191 .

89. Pully, A S, (1993). Utilization and results of Hazard and operability studies in a petroleum refinery, *Process Safety Progress*, **12**(2), 106-110.

90. Rauzy, A, (1993). New algorithms for fault tree analysis, *Reliability Engg. and System Safety*, **40**, 203-211.

91. Rose, J C, Wells, G L, and Yeats, B H, (1978). A guide to project procedure, *Institution of Chemical Engineers*, London.

92. Scheffler, N E, (1994). Improved fire and explosion index hazard classification, *Process Safety Progress*, **13**(4), 214-218.

93. Shafagi, A and Cook, B F, (1988). Application of a hazard and operability study to hazard evaluation of an absorption heat pump,*IEEE Transactions on Reliability,* **37**(2), 161-165.

94. Sherrod, R M, and Early, W F, (1991). Hazard and operability studies, (Risk assessment and management in PI, *(Ed: Greenberg and Creamer)* ,*Van Nostrand Reinhold,* New York.

95. Singh, J, and Munday, G , (1979). IFAL: a model for the evaluation of chemical process losses. *Design 79 : Instn Chem. Engrs,* London.

96. Suokas, J, (1988). The role of safety analysis in accident prevention, *Accident Analysis & Prevention*, **20**(1), 67-85.

97. Sweeny, J C, (1993). ARCO Chemical's HAZOP experience, *Process Safety Progress*, **12**(2), 83-90.

98. SYHI, (1993). Chemical ranking for potential health and environmental impacts, *Environment Protection Act CR-816735*, Washington, D C.

99. Tanaka, H, Fan, L T, Lai, F S, and Toguchi, K, (1983). Fault tree analysis by Fuzzy probability, *IEEE Transactions on Reliability*, **R-32/51**, 453-456.

100. Tyler, B J, (1982). Using the Mond index to measure inherent hazards, *Plant/Operation Progress*, **4**, 172.

101. Tyler, B J, Thomas, A R, Doran, P, and Grieg, T R, (1994). A toxicity hazard index, Hazards, **XIII**, 351.

102. Ulerich, N, (1988). 'On-Line Hazard Aversion and Fault-Diagnosis in Chemical Processes: The Digraph+Fault-tree Method', *IEEE Transaction on Reliability,* **37**(2), 171.

103. Van Ulden, A P and Hostlag, A A, (1985). Estimation of atmospheric boundary layer parameters for diffusion application, *Journal of Climate and Applied Meteorology*, **24**, 1196.

104. Van Sciver, G R, (1990). Quantitative risk analysis in the chemical process industries, *Reliability Engg & System Safety*,**29**, 55-68.

105. Venkatasubramanian, V, and Vaidyanathan, R, (1994). A knowledge based frame work for automating HAZOP analysis, *AIChE Journal,* **40**(3).

106. Whitehouse, H B, (1985). IFAL - a new risk analysis tool. The assessment and control of Major hazards : *Instn Chem. Engrs*, Rugby, 309.

107. WHO, (1984). Major Hazard Control : A practical manual, *International Labor Office*, Geneva.

108. Yllera, J, (1988). Modularization methods for evaluating fault tree of complex technical system, *(Engineering risk and hazard assessment, Ed:Kandel and Avni), CRC Press Inc, Florida.*

109. Zoller, L and Esping, J P , (1993). Use 'What if method for process hazard analysis. *Hydrocarbon Processing*, **72**(1), 132.

Part II

Qualitative Methods of Risk Assessment

Hazop (Hazard and Operability study) forms a part of most risk assessment exercises. It involves a detailed study of the entire process line from start to finish with the help of 'piping and instrument diagrams' (PIDs) covering each and every vessel, conduit, valve, and other control equipment employed in the process line. In HAZOP these PIDs are studied in relation to the operation of the process, the causes that may lead to variations in the plant operation due to human errors, process or material failures, and the likely consequences. HAZOP thus takes into consideration the conditions such as temperature, pressure, creep, fatigue, etc., under which the piping and instruments, and the possible aberrations that may occur due to human errors, loss of process control, or material failures.

Inspite of its popularity, HAZOP suffers from being a very tedious, lengthy, and costly exercise. When used in its conventional form HAZOP is also prone to human errors which can eventually prove very harmful.

In Part II we present three studies which have aimed at:

a) Improving the planning of conventional HAZOP to reduce its costs and margins of error;

b) modifying the conventional HAZOP procedure to make it more quick and exhaustive yet less expensive;

c) developing a computer-automated tool to facilitate the above.

Two of these studies have been published, in Journal of Loss Prevention in Process Industries, and one is in press with the same journal. The three papers are reproduced as Chapters 3-5.

3

MATHEMATICAL MODEL FOR HAZOP STUDY TIME ESTIMATION*

To conduct effective and efficient HAZOP (Hazard and Operability) study it is essential that the study should be planned and managed well. The planning and management can be done effectively only when the various steps of the study, scope of each step, and duration of each step are well defined. Significant work has been done over the identification of various applications of HAZOP, but not much work has been done over HAZOP study duration estimation, which is a key parameter for proper planning and management of HAZOP study. Freeman et al. (1992) has proposed a model for HAZOP study time (duration) estimation, however, still it needs modification in terms of easy application and more reliable estimation.

The present work is an effort in the same direction, a mathematical model being proposed to forecast (estimate) the HAZOP study duration for varying capacity and complexity of the problem. The accuracy of the results have been checked with some of the past case studies carried out by various agencies. It has been observed that the authors' model predicts result with accuracy of about 90-95%, while Freeman's model is restricted to 85-90%. Moreover, the proposed model is simple, easy to implement, and can be automated to software.

INTRODUCTION

HAZOP (Hazard and Operability Study) is one of the commonest tools to accomplish hazard assessment, qualitatively. It involves a detailed study of each and every part of the entire process line from start to finish with the help of 'piping and instrument diagrams' (PIDs) covering each and every vessel, conduit, valve, and other control equipment employed in the process line. In HAZOP these PIDs are studied in relation to the operation of the process, the causes that may lead to variations in the plant operation due to human, process, or material failures, and the likely consequences. HAZOP thus takes into consideration the conditions such as temperature, pressure, creep, fatigue, etc. under which the physical parts (piping and instruments) are used, the aspects of human interaction with the piping and instruments, and the possible aberrations that may occur due to human errors, loss of process control, or material failures.

HAZOP technique was developed in the early 1970s at Imperial Chemical Industries (ICI), in the U.K. The basic principle of HAZOP study is that hazards arise in a plant due to deviations from normal behavior. In HAZOP study, process piping and instrument diagrams (PIDs) are examined systematically by a group of experts (HAZOP team), and the abnormal causes and adverse consequences for all possible deviations from normal operation that could arise are found for every section of the plant. Thus, the potential problems in the process plant are identified. The HAZOP team is a multi-disciplinary team of experts who have extensive knowledge on design, operation, and maintenance of the process plants. The HAZOP team members try to imagine ways in which hazards and operating problems might

* Reproduced from Journal of Loss Prevention in Process Industries, UK, 10 (4), 249-257, 1997.

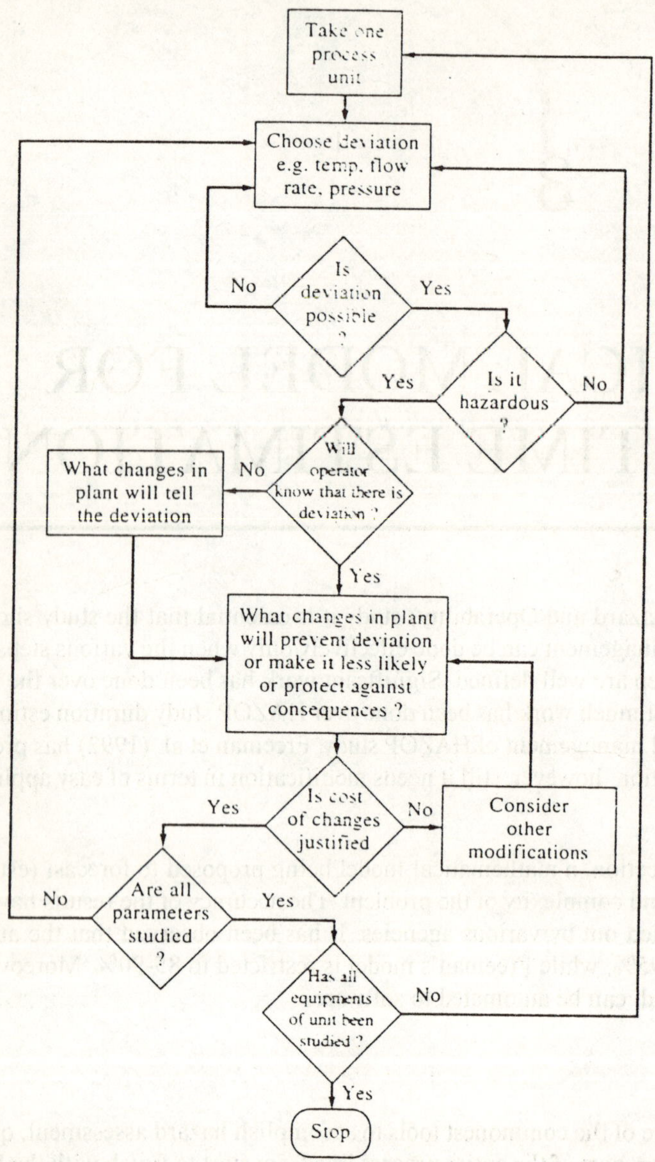

Figure 1. Procedure of HAZOP study

arise in a process plant. To cover all the possible malfunctions in the plant the imagination of the HAZOP study team members is guided in a systematic way using a set of 'guide words' for generating the process variable deviations to be considered in the HAZOP study.

The set of guide words that are often used are NONE, MORE Of, LESS OF, PART OF, and MORE THAN. When these guide words are applied to the process variables in each line or unit of the plant, we get the corresponding process variable deviation to be considered in the HAZOP study. A list of guide words with their meaning and the parameters where they can be applied is presented in Table 1.

The guide words and process variables should be combined in such a way that they lead to meaningful process variable deviations. Hence, all the guide words cannot be applied to all process variables. For example, when the process variable under consideration is temperature, only the guide words MORE OF and LESS OF lead to meaningful process variable deviations. The sequence of typical HAZOP study is shown in Figure 1.

It has been well understood that HAZOP is a comprehensive and time taking technique (Roach and Lees -1984, Greenberg and Crammer-1991, WHO-1984, Kletz-1983, Ozog and Bendixen-1987, Khan & Abbasi-1995). Moreover, the performance of study is dependent on many factors such as; duration of study, proper planning and management of study schedule, team content, number of team members, experience of team leader and participation of team members. Considerable work has been done on the application of HAZOP study in different stage of projects (conceptual design, start up, shut down, etc.) and for different industries (chloralkali, chemical, petrochemical, fertilizer, etc.). Some of the important references concerning application of HAZOP study to various industrial applications are; Lawley (1974), Ozog (1985), Shafaghi & Cook (1988), Knowlton (1989), Montague, (1990), Pully (1993), Kolodji (1993), Sweeny (1993) and Tait (1995). However, a little attention has been paid on the effectiveness, efficiency and performance of HAZOP study. For effective HAZOP study Mckelvey (1988) has suggested some key parameters (factors) such as, skill and experience of team leader, proper planning, and availability of information which should be given proper attention. Mulvihill (1988) has presented an efficient and effective HAZOP application in studying offshore platform using past experiences of similar case studies and guidelines proposed by Mckelvcy (1988). Khan and Abbasi (1996) have proposed an optimum HAZOP study procedure which uses expert system and proper management of some of the key steps. This procedure is optimal in terms of duration of study, effectiveness and reliability of the results.

The proper planning and management of HAZOP study is one of the crucial factor for better effectiveness and good reliability of the results. The HAZOP study can be planned and managed properly only when duration of each activity and for complete study is known. In practical situations duration of HAZOP study is assigned by the authority or administration and in most of the cases it has been observed that the assigned time is either too short or it is too lengthy. A short time gives a crash scheduling of the study which of course affects the efficiency and reliability of the results adversely. Moreover, it leads to the possibility that important aspect of study may be ignored or not given proper attention due to shortage of time. Besides shortage of time, the excess time also has its own disadvantages, more time decreases the momentum of study, loss of interest and more financial expenditure. Hence, the duration of study directly affects the efficiency and reliability of the HAZOP study.

Table 1. The list of guide words and their meaning

Guide words	Meaning	Applicable to following parameters
No/None	Complete negation to design intention	flow rate, level, capacity
More	Quantitative increase temperature, level	flow rate, pressure,
Less	Quantitative decrease	flow rate, capacity, pressure, temperature, level
Part Of	Only part of intention is fulfilled	concentration, signal
As Well As	In addition to design intention , some thing else occurs	concentration, signal
Reverse	Logical opposition of design intention occurs	Signal, flow.
Other Than	Complete Substitution	Concentration, signal

The above discussion gives calls for some technique to predict the time needed to carry out a particular HAZOP study. CIA-1990, AIChE (1992) Freeman et al. (1992) have suggested models for HAZOP study time estimation. The HAZOP time estimation model proposed by AIChE and CIA are based on the qualitative assessment of experts experience and the objective of study. It gives a rough idea with accuracy of 60 to 70%. The method proposed by Freeman et al. (1992) is a structured one and incorporates many steps. However, the empirical equations used in the model to estimate different operational times are not well defined (justified). The accuracy of the HAZOP duration estimated by Freeman's model bounces in accuracy band of 75-85% (for typical chemical industries), which in authors' opinion can be further improved. This gives an opportunity to work for better method of HAZOP time estimation gives more accurate and reliable results. Authors have worked on similar lines as of Freeman et al. and proposed a better and simple model for HAZOP time estimation. The model incorporates some additional features (not defined in Freeman's model) and gives higher accuracy (around 85 to 95%). In order to serve swift understanding a comparison of proposed model with Freeman's model is presented in Table 2. The detailed description of the model is presented in subsequent sections.

HAZOP STUDY PROCEDURE AND TIME ESTIMATION MODEL

HAZOP study is carried out by a team of expert personnel of different disciplines. Generally, a team of six members consisting of team leader, process engineer, operation representative, safety representative, control system engineer, and maintenance engineer is recommended for the study. Growing concern towards the environment protection made it mandatory to analyze the problem in an industry keeping environment (with in plant and surrounding) and society in account. Authors feel that a team of seven members is optimum (Khan & Abbasi-1996) in order to cover all aspects of study and the seventh member should be an environmental engineer. This is to identify and asses the adverse impact of any mishappening / operating problem to the environment and surrounding, particularly in case of chemical process industries dealing with hazardous chemicals. Among the team of seven members, team leader plays a crucial role, (efficiency, accuracy and duration of the study are direct function of team leader's skill). The other parameters which affect the study are, duration of study, availability of information, complexity of problem, objective of study, the extent of the in-depth analysis, and participation of team members (Mckelvey-1988, Khan & Abbasi-1996).

The HAZOP study procedure (Figure 1) consists of four main activities (steps);

a) selection of study team and procurement of relevant information,

b) brainstorming discussion,

c) preparation of uncleared points, and

d) report writing.

The steps 'b' and 'c' are the most crucial and control over the total study duration, effectiveness and reliability of the results. The report writing step is again a dependent activity on the second and third step (step b and c).

Table 2. The comparison of the proposed model with the recent work (Freeman et al. -1992)

Freeman's model	Proposed model
This model takes into account only three parameters namely- number of PIDs, complexity of PIDs and skill level of team leader	This model takes into account four different parameters namely- preparation time, study or meeting time, delay, and repor Writing. The preparation and study time is again a function of three parameters: number of PIDs, complexity of PIDs and the skill of team leader
This model takes into account only team leader preparation time	This model takes account team leader as well as team members preparation time.
This model does not take account of any cushion to cover uncertainty or delay	This model takes care uncertainty and delay (two or delay factors) into consideration.
This model converts each duration (due to different- parameters) in weeks and then adds to get the total	This model first estimate total duration in hours and then converts it into number of weeks through analytical equation.
Most of the equations used in the model are empirical (single variable) in nature	This model uses multivariable empirical equations instead of single variable equations. These equations are derived from detailed study of past case studies and with the help of references (cited accordingly)

MODEL

The total duration of HAZOP study has been modeled as a combination of four different time steps. A brief description about each step and method to estimate the duration is presented below. (These four steps are further function of many variables and sub-time steps).

i) preparation time,

ii) study or meeting time,

iii) delay, and

iv) report writing.

Preparation time

Prior to start the discussion on the process system, there are many things that the team leader and team mates have to do. Firstly, the team leader should plan and decide the schedule, duration of review meetings, and arrange the essential documents such as; PIDs (Process instrumentation diagrams), PFDs (Process flow diagrams), plot plans, operating procedure, etc. Subsequently, the team leader has to decide the beginning point (scope of the study) and boundaries of study.

During the brainstorming discussions, the team leader should take care that the discussion should be on the objectives and should not go beyond the boundaries of study. Every discussion should be followed by a home work on the points (problems) identified and not well understood/discussed in the meeting. These points should be put up in next discussion session before starting the new discussion. In other words, this time step takes account steps 'a' (procurement of relevant information) and 'c' (preparation of uncleared points) of the HAZOP study procedure.

More number of PIDs means more information collection, and identification of more unclear points, which needs high preparation time. Hence, the preparation time is defined as a direct function of number of PIDs and the degree of complexity of PIDs, and can be represented as;

$$Tprep = 1.5 \{ X_1 + 2X_2 + 3X_3 + 4X_4 \} \quad \ldots 1$$

Where, X_1, X_2, X_3, X_4 are number of PIDs of different class of complexity. The classification of the complexity of PIDs is presented in Table 3.

Table 3. Classification of PIDs complexity

Serial Number	PIDs Groups	Number of Equipments	Number of Pipe lines	Coefficient C	Power factor,P
1	Simple	1 to 4	1 to 7	1	1
2	Standard	4 to 6	7 to 15	2	1
3	Complex	6 to 8	15 to 25	1	2
4	Very Complex	> 8	> 25	8	2

Study or meeting time

Study or meeting time is the duration of brainstorming discussion, which is the most important and main activity of HAZOP study. Hence, it is the main contributor to the total HAZOP study duration. This time step (duration of meeting time) depends upon three important parameters namely:

a) effectiveness or skill of the team leader;

b) number of PIDs to be studied; and

c) complexity of PIDs.

The total duration of meeting (study) is a non linear function of these three parameters. A brief discussion on the mode of quantification of each parameter is presented below.

Effectiveness or skill of team leader

The effectiveness (skill) of team leader is a main factor for the success of HAZOP study and major factor which affects the meeting duration. The skilled leader can reduce the lengthy and irrelevant discussions and keep the team mates on the main discussion. Moreover, a skilled leader can check the participation of each member and hence can enhance the effectiveness of study. Thus, a skilled leader can reduce the working load, or in other words duration of study and increase the effectiveness of study.

To quantify the skill of a team leader, skill factor 'L_{eff}' has been defined based on the experience of team leader to handle HAZOP study. The duration of meeting is directly proportional to factor L_{eff}, where, factor L_{eff} decreases with increase of the experience of team leader in handling HAZOP study. The skill factor L_{eff} has been classified mainly in four groups:

Novice-	Never led any team for HAZOP study	L_{eff}=2.0
Moderately - experienced-	Led one or two major HAZOP study team	L_{eff}=1.5
Experienced-	Led more than three major	L_{eff}=1.0

HAZOP-	study team	
Highly -	Led more than five major	L_{eff}=0.75
experienced-	HAZOP study team	

The quantification of L_{eff} has been done as per the recommendation of HAZOP experts of different organizations and with the help of references - namely; Roach and Less (1984), Mckelvey (1988), Oyeleye and Kramer (1988), Freeman (1991), and Freeman et al. (1992).

Number of PIDs or PFDs

The number of PIDs and/or PFDs to be studied during HAZOP study is the second most important factor contributing to the duration of meetings. The duration of meeting is directly proportional to the number of PIDs or PFDs to be studied.

Complexity of PIDs

The complexity of PIDs is another factor contributing to the duration of meeting. The complexity has been classified on the basis of number of study node, number of equipment and number of piping systems in each PID (Table 3). To quantify the effect of complexity of PIDs on the duration of meeting, it has been categorized in four main groups as simple, standard, complex and very complex. The effect of complexity is estimated through the coefficient, C_i and power factor, P_i. These parameters C_i, and P_i can be estimated through the Table 3. The quantification of empirical parameters C_i and P_i have been done according to the guideline suggested by Roach and Less (1984), Knowlton (1991), and authors' experience.

Finally the combination of different parameters for HAZOP meeting time estimation is represented as;

$$T_s = L_{eff}*f(\ C_i*X_i^{Pi}) \quad \ldots\ 2$$

Where,

L_{eff} - skill factor of team leader

C_i - represents the coefficient for different degree of complexity.

P_i - represents the effect of degree of complexity on number of PIDs (power factor).

X_i - represents the number of PIDs of each complexity.

Finally the expanded form of the meeting time function (total duration of brainstorming discussion) can be represented as;

$$Ts = K*L_{eff}*(C_1*X_1 + C_2*X_2 + C_3*X_3^2 + C_4*X_4^2) \quad \ldots\ 3$$

Where,

K is a proportionality constant and equals to one for chemical process industries and higher than one (1.5) for petrochemical industries.

Report writing duration

A written report of the HAZOP study is the out put of the team work. There has been standard format for the HAZOP report presentation (Greenberg & Crammer - 1991, Ozog and Bendixen-1987)The report should be clear, concise so that one should understand what had been highlighted in the meeting and what are the outcomes of the study. . The report should also consist of recommendations to eliminate or to control the problems identified by the study team. The follow up of the recommendations is totally based on the report and feasibility analysis.

The time taken in writing a rough draft of report has been approximated as 45 % of the preparation time. Freeman et al (1992) has suggested draft report time as 50% of the team leader's preparation time. However, the author feels that report writing is an activity which depends upon the feed back of all team members and is strongly dependent on how well the team is involved in the study. Hence it should be a function of total preparation time. This duration is only for the first draft of report preparation.

$$T_{report} = 0.45 * T_{prep} \quad \ldots 4$$

Delay time

Since the participants of HAZOP study have other duties and responsibilities at the plant site or at other places, the actual elapsed time would be greater than the estimated time. Moreover, as every team member has his own responding time to understand the problem and to propose the recommendations, there should be some provision to estimate the excess time to take care of the elapsed time in unforeseen activities and individuals responding time. This excess time has been defined as delay. This delay time includes the time lapsed due to non availability of members, documents or any other essential items, and individuals responding time. The delay time can be categorized in two main groups.

a) delay in schedule of preparation and discussion,

b) final report writing

The first delay 'a' signifies and quantifies the duration due to lack of any activity, information and responding time of individuals. This delay is estimated as 15 % of the preparation time.

$$T_{delay\ 1} = 0.15 * T_{prep} \quad \ldots 5$$

The second delay 'b' is estimated to take into account the preparation of final report from rough draft. This is estimated as 25 % of the draft report preparation time.

$$T_{delay\ 2} = 0.25 * T_{report} \quad \ldots 6$$

The total delay is the sum of these two delays,

$$T_{delay} = T_{delay\ 1} + T_{delay\ 2} \quad \ldots 7$$

Finally, the total HAZOP study time in hours is the sum of all available time (meeting, preparation, draft report and delay) and can be written as;

$$T_{HAZOP} = T_s + T_{prep} + T_{report} + T_{delay} \quad \ldots 8$$

The man-hours requirement for the HAZOP study can be estimated as;

$$T_{man\ hours} = T_{HAZOP} * \text{number of team mates} \quad \ldots 9$$

The total duration of comprehensive HAZOP study in terms of weeks can be estimated as;

$$T_{weeks} = \{1+1/W_{o/o}\} * T_{HAZOP}/T_w \quad \ldots 10$$

Where, $W_{o/o}$ specifies frequency of rest (1,2,3)

T_w hours per week assigned for study (number of hours per day * number of days per week).

Testing of proposed model

The above proposed model for time estimation of HAZOP study has been tested for three different case studies. The results obtained by this model have been compared with actual duration and the model proposed by Freeman *et al* (1992).

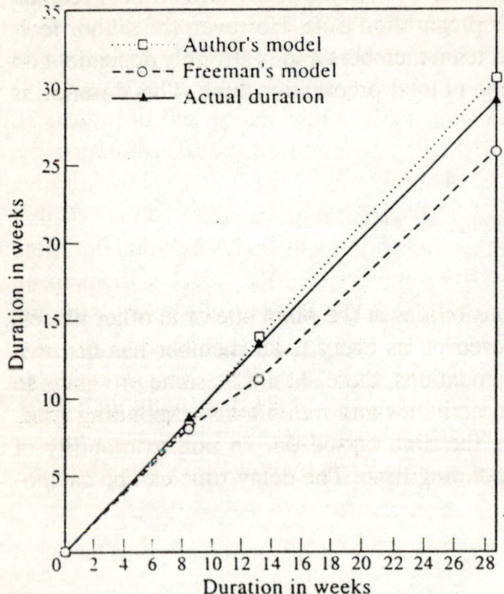

Figure 2. Comparison of the authors' and Freeman's models predictions with actual duration of HAZOP study

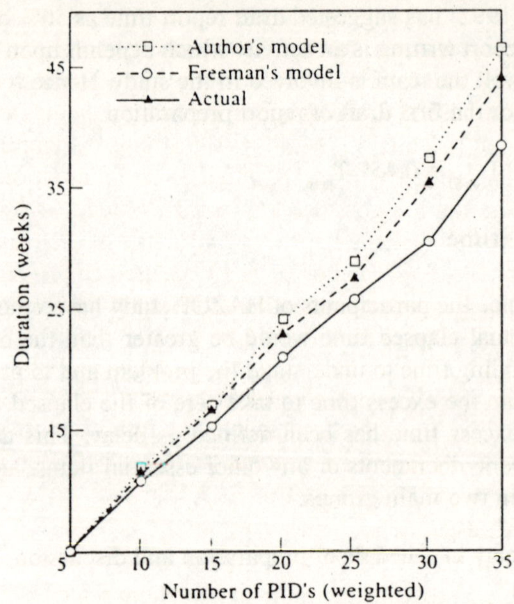

Figure 3. Comparison of different models predictions for various complexities of the problem

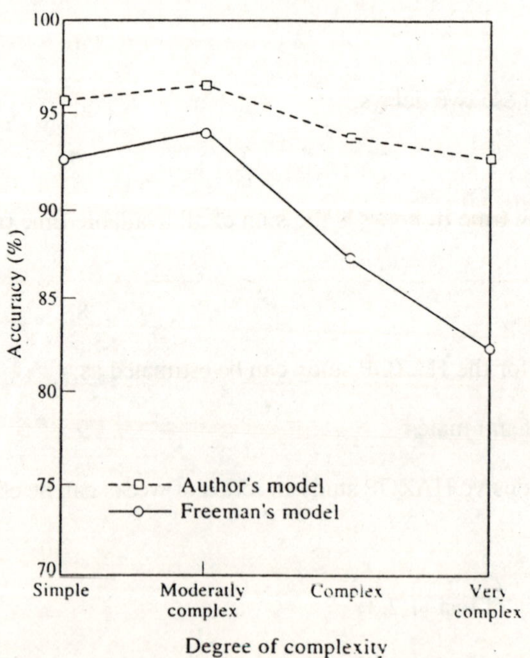

Figure 4. Variation in the accuracy of the authors' and Freeman's models predictions with the complexity of the problem

Case Study 1

Table 4 lists the result of moderately complex (standard problem) HAZOP study (duration of various HAZOP study step and total duration of study). The problem consists of a total of 8 PIDs, two of each degree of complexity. The table also lists the result of Freeman's model, and actual duration of the study conducted by cell of industrial safety and risk analysis (CISRA-1993). It is evident from the table that HAZOP study duration (hours) estimated by Freemen's model is more than that of actual duration (in hours) as well as authors' model prediction. However, the total duration in weeks due to Freeman's model is lower than actual duration as well as authors' model. It is because Freeman has used the step-wise conversion of each duration to week and then finally did addition to get total duration of study in weeks. Moreover, they have used empirical relation to calculate the number of weeks, where as the present model suggests that first estimate the total number of hours and then convert into the number of weeks, using an analytical equation.

In summary the results of first case study suggests that the actual duration (in weeks) of study is more than what has been predicted by any model. The result of authors' model is close to the real durations than Freeman's model prediction. An accuracy of about 97 % has been observed by authors' model while 92 % by Freeman's model.

Case Study 2

Table 5 presents the result of a medium scale HAZOP study, consisting of 10 PIDs, with more number of complex PIDs The results show that for complex problem (medium scale) Freeman's model gives a lower value (duration in weeks) than the actual value whereas the authors' model report a slightly higher value. In this case study the uncertainty by Freeman's model is more than authors'. Moreover authors' model gives a positive error (value higher than actual one), while Freeman's model gives a negative error (values lower than actual). As far as planning of HAZOP study is concerned a positive error is more tolerable because a little over estimate won't have much effect and can be treated as cushion to deal unwanted situations while a negative error would lead to shortage of time and may lead to chances of missing of some important hazards. In this particular case study an accuracy of more than 95% has been observed.

Case Study 3

Table 6 presents the result of a case study classified as major HAZOP study. The study consists of a total of 25 PIDs of different complexity level. It is clear from the results that the actual number of hours of study is maximum for author's model and minimum for Freeman's model. Moreover, the total duration of the study in weeks for Freeman is far lower than actual duration while authors' prediction is closer to actual duration.

Table 4. Results of case study 1.

Parameter	Values		
	Freeman model	Actual duration	Proposed model
INPUTS			
Number of simple PIDs	2	2	2
Number of standard PIDs	2	2	2
Number of complex PIDs	2	2	2
Number of very Complex PIDs	2	2	2
HAZOP team leader still	experienced	experienced	experienced
Meeting per week	15	15	15
OUTPUTS			
Hazop meeting time(hrs)	72.0		42.0
Preparation time (hrs)	54.0		30.0
Draft Report	27.0		13.5
Delay	--		7.9
Total time in hours	--	95	93.4
Total man hours	639.0	665.0	653.0
Total elapsed time (weeks)	8.1	8.5	8.3

Table 5. Results of case Study 2

Parameter	Values		
	Freeman model	Actual duration	Proposed model
INPUTS			
Number of simple PIDs	2	2	2
Number of standard PIDs	2	2	2
Number of complex PIDs	3	2	2
Number of very Complex PIDs	3	2	2
HAZOP team leader still	experienced	experienced	experienced
Meeting per week	15	15	15
OUTPUTS			
Hazop meeting time(hrs)	99.0		87.0
Preparation time (hrs)	60.0		39.0
Draft Report	30.0		17.5
Delay	--		10.2
Total time in hours	--	150	153.7
Total man hours	876.0	1050.0	1075.0
Total elapsed time (weeks)	11.1	13.3	13.6

Table 6. Results of case study 3.

Parameter	Values		
	Freeman model	Actual duration	Proposed model
INPUTS			
Number of simple PIDs	7	2	2
Number of standard PIDs	7	2	2
Number of complex PIDs	7	2	2
Number of very Complex PIDs	4	2	2
HAZOP team leader still	experienced	experienced	experienced
Meeting per week	15	15	15
OUTPUTS			
Hazop meeting time(hrs)	186.7		198.0
Preparation time (hrs)	105.0		87.0
Draft Report	52.5		39.2
Delay	--		22.9
Total number of hours	--	325	347.1
Total man hours	2414.0	2275.0	2356.0
Total elapsed time (weeks)	25.5	28.5	30.7

DISCUSSION

The result of Freeman's and authors' model along with actual duration (studies conducted by various agencies, NEERI-1992,1993, CPCE-1995, etc.) have been plotted in Figure 2. It is evident from the Figure 1 that as complexity increases the estimation due to Freeman's model starts deviating more from actual duration. The result of authors' model also deviates with increase in complexity, however, this deviation is less and is towards over estimation side while the result of Freeman's model deviate towards negative side (under estimation). The reasons for these deviations are, as complexity increases more uncertainty in prediction of preparation time and delay time. As Freeman has used only leader preparation time and no delay estimation it faces more deviation and that also in negative side (under estimation) while in authors' model it goes a little over estimation side.

The result of Freeman's and authors' model have been plotted against different numbers of PIDs with varying degree of complexity in Figure 3. The trend of curve suggests that as number of PIDs increases, the number of weeks needed to complete the study increases more rapidly for authors' model than Freeman's. The trend of authors' model is more closer to the actual results. The number of weeks needed to study the same degree of complexity is more in authors' model while Freeman's model underestimates the results. It can also be visualized from the curves (Figure 3) that as number of PIDs to be studied increases, model proposed by author gives more realistic results in comparison to any other model. Figure 4 shows a plot of accuracy versus various complexity of problem. The figure reveals that the above proposed model is closer to the realistic duration of HAZOP study with an error of 5 to 7%, while for the same studies Freeman's model deviates 7-15% from actual duration.

Finally, it can be concluded that the model suggested here is a good tool for estimation of HAZOP study duration.

REFERENCES

1. AIChE-1992. Guidelines for hazards evaluation procedures (2nd edition), Center for Chemical Process Safety (AIChE), Washington, D.C.
2. CIA-1990. A guide to hazard and operability studies, Chemical Industries Association, London.
3. CISRA-1993. Risk analysis for the Chloralkali plant, Cell for industrial safety and risk analysis, Madras, 105.
4. CPCE-1995. HAZOP study of Linear alkyl Benzene industry situated in a congested industrial complex, report CPCE/RA 17/95, Pondicherry, 120.
5. Freeman, R A, 1991. Documentation of hazards and operability studies, Plant/Operation Progress, 10(3), 155-158.
6. Freeman, R A, Lee, R, and McNamara, T P, 1992. Plan HAZOP studies with an expert system, Chemical Engineering Progress, August.
7. Greenberg, H R, and Crammer, J J, 1991. Risk Assessment and risk management for the chemical process industries, Van Nostrand Reinhold, New York.
8. Khan, F I and Abbasi, S A, 1995. HAZEXPT: A comprehensive Knowledge Base system for HAZOP study, Research report number CPCE/R&D 15/95, Pondicherry University.
9. Khan, F I and Abbasi, S A, 1996. optHAZOP an effective and efficient approach for HAZOP study, J Loss Prevention Process Industries (in press).
10. Kletz, T A, 1983. HAZOP & HAZAN, notes on the identification and assessment of hazards. The Institution of Chemical Engineers, Hazard workshop modules, Rugby.
11. Knowlton, R E, 1989. Hazard and operability studies: The guide word approach, Chematics International Co., Vancouver.
12. Kolodji, B P, 1993. Hazard resolutions in sulfur plants form design through start up, Process safety progress, 12(2), 127-731.
13. Lawley, G, 1974. Operability studies and hazard Analysis, Loss Prev., Chemical Engineering Progress, April.
14. McKelvey, C T, 1988. How to improve the effectiveness of hazard and operability analysis, IEEE Transaction on Reliability, 37(2), 167-170.
15. Montague, D F, 1990. Process risk evaluation - what method to use, Rel. Eng. Syst. Safety, 29(1), 27-53.
16. Mulvihill, R J, 1988. Design - safety enhancement through the use of hazard and risk analysis, IEEE Transaction on Reliability, 37(2), 149.

17. NEERI-1992. Risk assessment of Hindustan Organic Limited, National Environmental Research Institute, Nagpur, 245.

18. NEERI-1995. Rapid risk assessment of a Fertilizer plant, National Environmental Research Institute, Nagpur, 245.

19. Oyeleye, O O, and Kramer, M A, 1988. Qualitative simulation of chemical process system : steady state analysis, AIChE J., 34(9), 1441.

20. Ozog, H., 1985. Hazard identification analysis and control, Chemical Engineering, 161.

21. Ozog, H and Bendixen, L M, 1987. Hazard identification and quantification, Chemical Engineering Progress, April.

22. Pully, A S, 1983. Utilization and results of Hazard and operability studies in a petroleum refinery, Process Safety Progress, 12(2), 106-110.

23. Roach, J R, and Lees, F P, 1984. Some features of and activities in hazard and operability analysis, Can. J. of Chem. Eng., 62, 547.

24. Shafaghi, A and Cook, B F, 1988. Application of a Hazard & Operability study to hazard evaluation of an absorption heat pump", IEEE Transaction on Reliability, 37(2), 161-165.

25. Sweeny, J C, 1993. ARCO Chemical's HAZOP experience, Process Safety Progress, 12(2), 83-90.

26. Tait, J I, 1995. Building an HAZOP studies to reproduce knowledge-based system, IEEE colloquium, Stevenage, England, 2/1-8.

27. WHO-1984. Major hazard control : A practical manual, International Labor Office, Geneva.

Reproduced from *Journal of Loss Prevention in process Industries*, **10**(4), 249-257, 1997

4

OPTHAZOP- AN EFFECTIVE AND OPTIMUM APPROACH FOR HAZOP STUDY[*]

Qualitative hazard assessment is a part of the detailed risk analysis of chemical process industries and hazard and operability (HAZOP) study is the best technique to carry out this step. It is a systematic study conducted by a team of experts of different disciplines to identify and assess hazards using brainstorming discussion of deviation in operational parameters from normal/standard conditions. This study needs high expertise and substantial time commitments. The various steps involved in any typical HAZOP(application of deviation, cause finding and consequence analysis of each and every line and equipment) need a substantial high level of mental performance and alertness for a long span of time, but the repetitious nature of these steps inevitably generates a feeling of drudgery and mental fatigue, even exhaustion. This may not only reduce the effectiveness of HAZOP, but even render it incomplete or erroneous.

This paper is devoted to a discussion about the factors that have direct influence on the efficiency, effectiveness and reliability of such study. It also suggests an optimal approach to HAZOP study procedure (optHAZOP) based on the utilization of an already developed Information base optHAZOP technique reduces the mental execution load of experts by a half, and thus provides more time to study typical hazardous units and conceptualize better control strategies. This technique takes around 45% less time than that of conventional HAZOP study procedure (estimated using CPM networking and time analysis of different steps of study) with better efficiency and effectiveness.

INTRODUCTION

The severe accidents at Bhopal, Mexico city, Samton, Brazil, Panipat, Mumbai and many others have increased the public awareness towards the health, property and environmental risk posed by the chemical installations. This awareness gives a need of systematic analysis of safety, hazard and risk attached with the various units (storage, process, etc.), in a chemical process industry (CPI) or in other words, estimation of risk to the public health, plant and environment due to unsafe operation/mishap in a chemical process plant. Risk analysis (RA) is one of such study, where potential hazards to the plant, to the on-and-off site personnel, and to the environment are identified, assessed and finally various risk factors are computed based on the likelihood of occurrence and the consequences of such hazards. RA is mainly a three step procedure, one is hazard identification, second is hazard assessment and third is consequence analysis.

In last two decades few different procedures (set of various steps with applicable techniques) have been proposed to carryout the detailed risk analysis. Among them, contribution of Knowlton-(1976), Lawley-(1974), Lees-(1980),

* Reproduced from Journal of Loss Prevention in Process Industries, UK, 10 (3), 191-204, 1997.

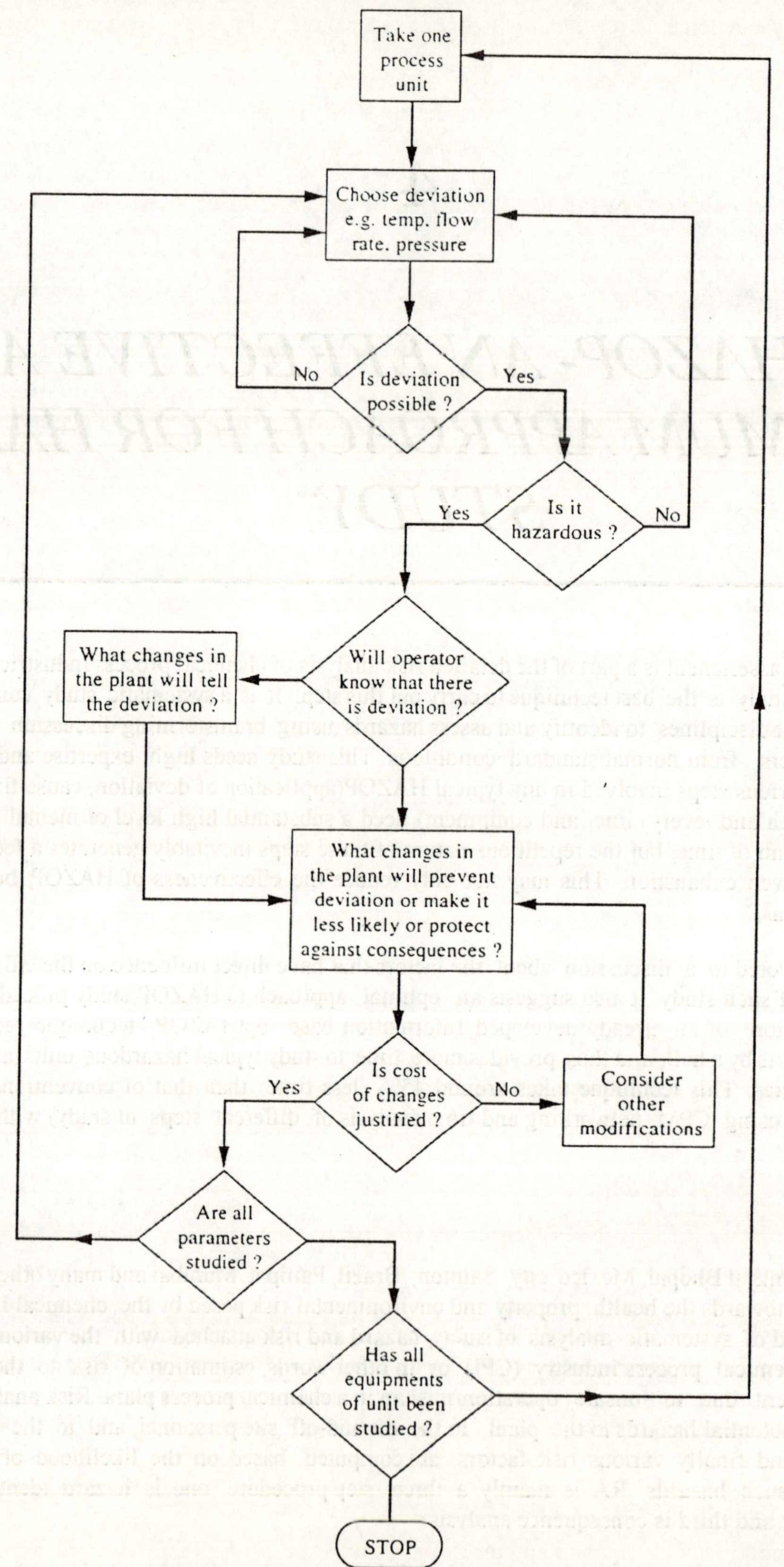

Figure 1. Procedure of conventional HAZOP study

Kletz-(1983) WHO & ILO-(1984), Suokas-(1988), McGrath-(1990), Van Sciever-(1990), Lapp-(1991), Greenberg & Crammer-(1992), Papazoglou et al.-(1992) are highly appreciable.

WHO & ILO (1984) has proposed a three step procedure for hazard assessment. The first and second step (hazard identification and accident modeling) are conducted using HAZOP technique. Suokas (1988) has suggested a three step procedure for safety analysis of chemical installations. For hazard identification step, it suggests HAZOP as a best tool. Van Sciever (1990) has suggested a scheme for quantitative risk analysis in chemical process industries. It is a four step scheme that suggests HAZOP as a tool for hazard identification step. Papazoglou et al.(1992) have suggested a seven step scheme for probabilistic safety analysis in chemical installations. The scheme recommends HAZOP as a tool for hazard identification and accident sequence modeling steps. Similarly, Khan & Abbasi (1995) have suggested a four step scheme for risk analysis in CPI. The scheme recommends HAZOP as a tool for preliminary hazard assessment step. Other than these various other applications of HAZOP technique in hazard identification and assessment have been reported; notably -Ozog-(1985), Quershi-(1988), Mulvihill-(1988), Shafaghi & Cook-(1988), Sweeny-(1993), Pully-(1993). Whatever be the step or purpose; HAZOP has been recognized as an important tool for hazard / risk / operability / safety analysis. By a comprehensive literature survey it has been concluded that HAZOP is the best tool for hazard identification and qualitative hazard assessment.

HAZard and OPerability (HAZOP) study

HAZOP was first introduced by Imperial Chemical Industries (U.K.) in 1966 as a mode of operability problem studies. Later its application in hazard identification and assessment have been explored and subsequently the technique has been modified to deal this aspect comfortably. HAZOP study procedure can be applied to any type of industries (refinery, chemical, petrochemical, metallurgical, pharmaceuticals, etc.) and at any stage of operation.

HAZOP is defined as, a study conducted by a team of experts of different disciplines to identify and assess hazard using brainstorming discussion of deviation in operational parameters from normal / standard conditions. These deviations are generated by using standard guide words. Normally the team consisting of 6 to 8 expert members of different disciplines will sit together to identify and assess the hazards associated with each and every process/plant component by analyzing the behavior of process/plant component under deviation from the normal operation. The procedure of HAZOP study can be divided in three main steps:

i) identification of abnormal behavior of the unit under different abnormal inputs/outputs;

ii) qualitative assessment of the abnormal behavior as it propagates to other units;

iii) basic recommendation to encounter this abnormality.

A detailed HAZOP study should carryout these three steps. These steps are repeated for each and every process/ plant component, which make the scheme a lengthy and time consuming technique. Moreover, due to repetitive nature of the study team members may lose interest and hence the effectiveness of study, which is based on the interaction of these experts, may be reduced (Roach and Lees-1981, McKelvey-1988, Freeman-1991). This will automatically lower the reliability of the results.

His paper has been devoted to present a set of recommendations to increase effectiveness, efficiency and reliability of HAZOP procedure. Considering these recommendations an optimal HAZOP procedure has been suggested. This optimal HAZOP procedure (optHAZOP), has been specifically proposed for qualitative hazard assessment; a step for detailed risk analysis.

Conventional HAZOP study procedure

HAZOP is a method for simulating creativity and a procedure for generating ideas involving brainstorming meeting of multi-disciplinary experts. The brainstorming approach to problem solving is based on two principles, judgment and the interaction among the participants (team members). The team normally consist of 6 to 8 experts, headed by a leader, who is expert in HAZOP study or safety study. The composition of the team depends on the requirement and the objective of the study. For a chemical process industry, process engineer is a basic member and other members should be control and instrumentation engineer, design engineer, member from

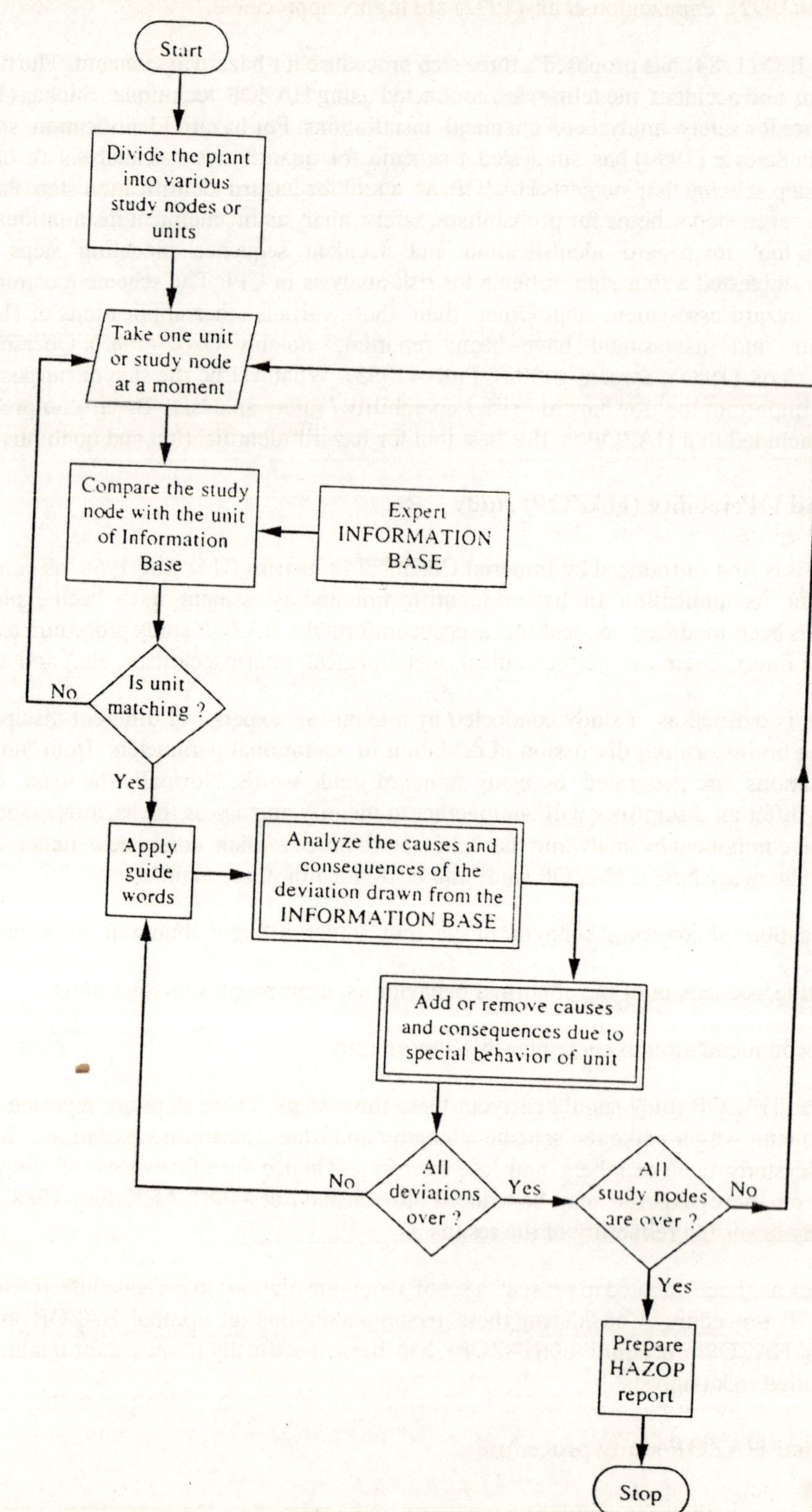

Figure 2 Algorithm for optHAZOP study

operational crew, member from maintenance crew, management representative, and an expert of HAZOP study. The HAZOP study team leader should be a technical person, having exposure of safety and hazard management.

The algorithm of conventional HAZOP study is presented in Figure 1. The procedure of HAZOP study starts with defining the objective, scope, and boundaries of the study. In general, the objective of study will be identifying the deviations from design/operating intention (normal operation) and subsequently the causes and consequences of this deviation. In some cases remedies are also included in study objectives. The main tool of this study is the guide words; an abstract concept of deviation. A set of common guide words with their physical meaning is given in Table 1. These guide words are applied to process variable, to yield the deviation in that particular variable.

guide word + variable = deviation

These deviations, will be analyzed by the brainstorming discussion for hazard and operating problem in process step or equipment. Subsequently, the main causes of these hazard/problem will be anticipated by discussion. In this way all possible deviations are applied to each and every component of the plant/process and the outcome of each deviation is documented for further action. The final results of HAZOP study are presented in a particular format as shown in Table 2.

Factors affecting the effectiveness and efficiency of HAZOP study

By carefully reviewing the failure and success of HAZOP, Roach and Lees-(1981), Kletz-(1985), Oyeleye and Kramer (1988), Mckelvey-(1988), Mulvihill-(1988), Montague-(1990), Freeman-(1991), Pully-(1993), Sweeny-(1993), it has revealed that HAZOP studies have ten key problem areas such as;

i) lack of experience of team members and leader,

ii) inappropriate team selection,

iii) incorrect scope of study,

iv) repetitious work,

v) inadequate/inaccurate information,

vi) management shortcoming,

vii) poor loss prevention practice,

viii) shortage of technical information,

ix) lack of interest,

x) the ultimate limitation (human error, wrong documentation etc.)

Lack of experience of team leader and members seems to be the most pronounced reason for the failure of HAZOP study. Among these; the experience of team leader is most crucial to make HAZOP study successful. However, the team leader and members should have;

a) sense where and when to purse a line of investigation, as experience says another hazard is hiding nearby, if one neglects any component of the plant without proper reason or justification;

b) sense to understand and avoid unproductive discussion;

c) experience in their respective disciplines and should be open minded to accept suggestions or comments made by other experts.

Table 1. Guide words and their physical significance

Guide Word	Meaning	Parameter	Deviation
None	Negation intention	Flow Level	No flow Zero level
Less	Quantitative decrease	Flow Level Temperature Pressure Concentration	Low flow rate Low level Low temperature Low pressure Low concentration
More	Quantitative increase	Flow Level Temperature Pressure Concentration	High flow rate High level High temperature High pressure High concentration
Reverse	Logical opposite	Flow Pressure	Reverse flow rate Reverse pressure
Part of	Qualitative decrease	Concentration Flow Level	Concentration decrease Flow decrease Level decrease
As Well-As	Qualitative increase	Conc. of -impurity Temp. of - substance Level of -impurity Pressure of -substance Flow of - impurity	Concentration increase Temperature increase Level increase Pressure increase Flow increases
Other Than	Complete - substation	Conc. of -desired substance Level of -desired substance Flow of -desired substance	Concentration zero Level zero Flow rate zero

Inappropriate team selection is the second major problem leading to unsuccessful study. The correct choice of technical participants from various areas -research, safety, production, maintenance and management sections require a careful consideration. Personal behavior should also be considered, while selecting personal for HAZOP study team based on technical knowledge, years of experience.

If the scope of study is not well defined, the hazards may be overlooked because they fall outside the objectives of narrowly defined scope. A complete scope of study, therefore, should be defined before starting the study. The scope should include, what units of the plant should be studied, what main type of hazards or operating problems are to be identified, whether the detailed consequences should be studied or not, and whether remedies to these hazards/problems should be suggested.

In conventional HAZOP study, while analyzing the different units for various deviations, the causes and consequences are repeated most of the time. Therefore, repeating the same discussion again and again gives an excess work and boredom the team members, which adversely affects the performance of HAZOP team. It is the main subject that really needs optimization. Some means should be developed which would eliminate or reduce the repetitious work.

The validity of HAZOP is squarely dependent upon the information available for the study. So if the process information is not up-to-date the HAZOP study will be having flaws. Moreover, any unaccounted change in process/equipment or operating conditions without updating the documents may lead to incorrect assumptions about the plant and therefore may lead to over/under estimation or sometimes negligence of hazards.

Figure 3. Network of various activities of conventional HAZOP study procedure.

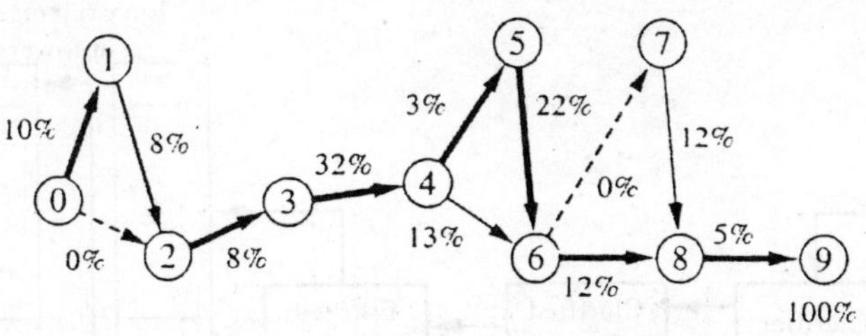

Figure 4. Network of various activities of conventional optHAZOP study procedure.

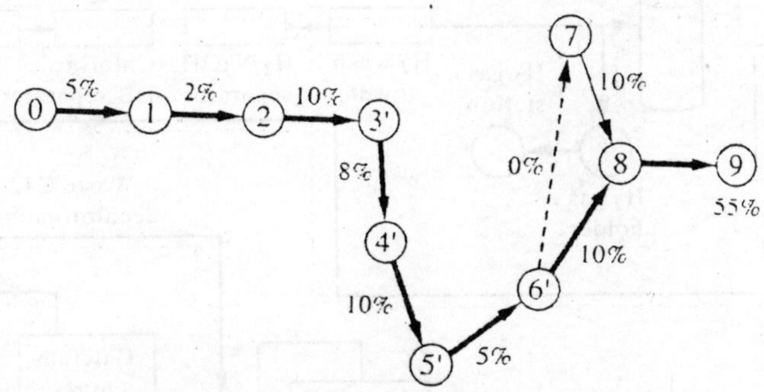

The irregular presence of team members in study session, because of their other duties, produces inconsistent results. Another problem leading to inconsistent results is discontinuity of study sessions, either due to frequent interruption from the authority (management) or due to improper scheduling of the session. So it is management's duty to insure that the HAZOP team members are set free for sufficient time to participate in study sessions. Moreover, time bound pressure on the study team is another management problem. Management should give a good span of time for the study, as it is a process of discovery and creativity and such thing cannot always be completed in short time span.

Abundant equipment or lines not well mentioned in document also leads to errorfic assessment. Moreover, poor practice on loss prevention directly affects the plant performance and can not be assessed unless and until it is well documented. A process reviewer (lacking of standard loss prevention practice) says, *it is an old process and nothing ever gone wrong*, so it is expected that it will work in future also. This type of statements gives a biased feeling about the plant and the hazard not identified yet may be overlooked.

Shortage of technical information is a common problem to most of the chemical processes and it is difficult to overcome. The complexity and the newness of technologies (process) place even greater demands for the need of information and experience. Incomplete kinetic data, lack of thermal stability data and toxicological data are such problems. For example; thermally unstable compound may go for an explosive decomposition by absorbing the energy from dead headed pump, by shock or by solar radiation. This factor (non-availability of technical information) is getting more and more importance as industries are moving from the usage of common to specialized chemicals. The only solution to this problem is that the team should make assumptions from the guidance of past experience and experimental values.

Lack of interest of the team members may lead to total failure of study as the output of study is fully based on the participation of team members. At the initial stage of study; the leader or higher management personnel should

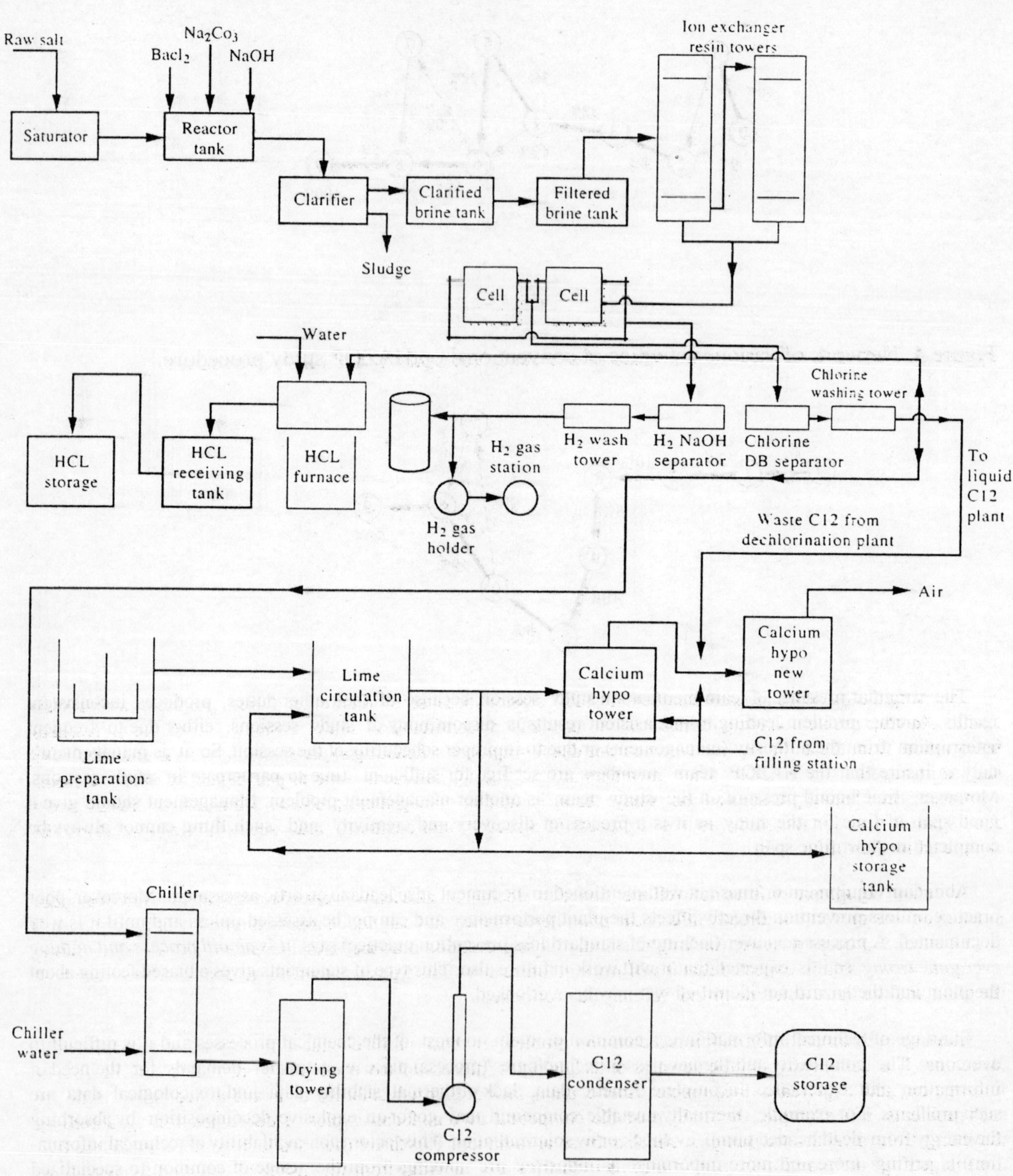

Figure 5. Process flow diagram of chloarakali industry

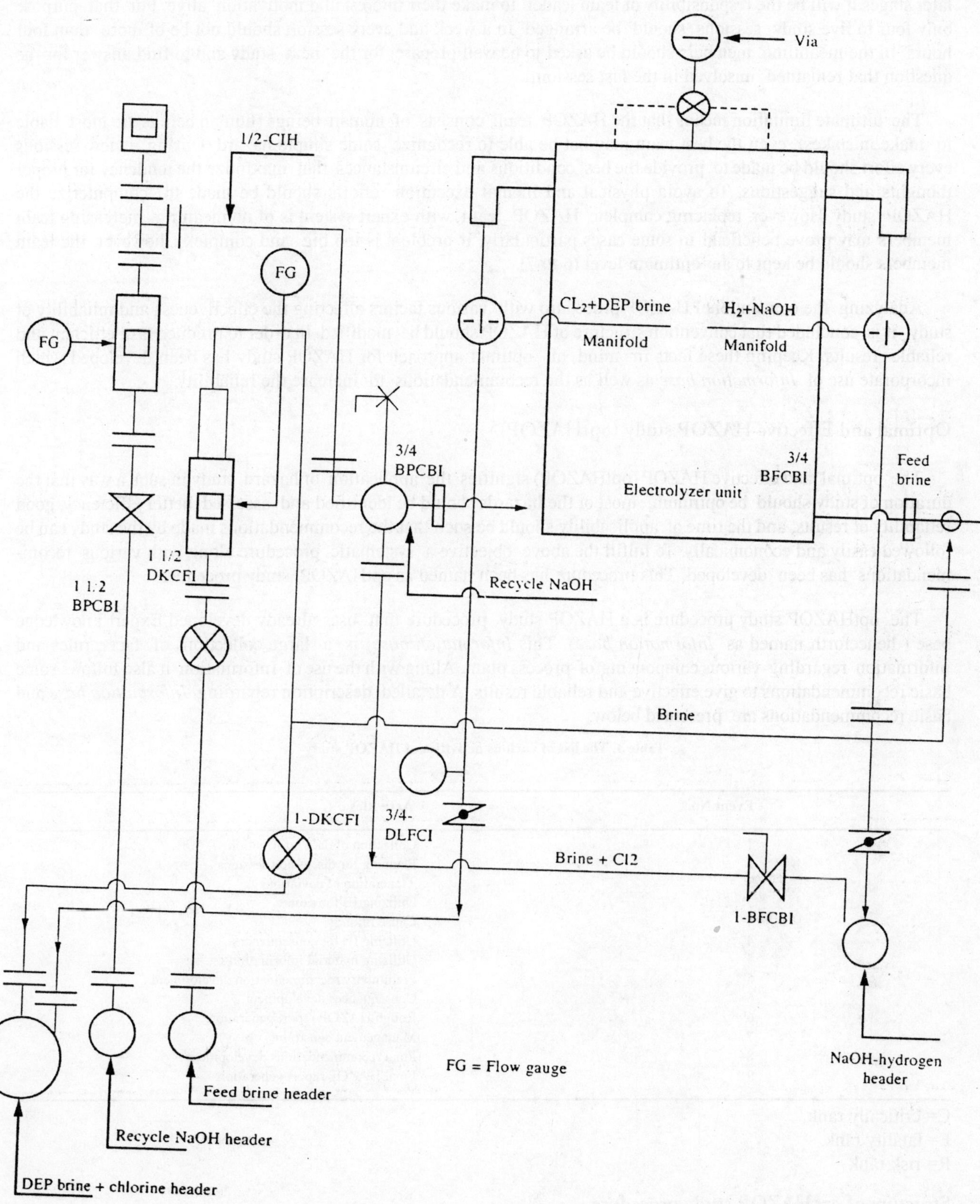

Figure 6. Process instrumentation diagram of electrolyzer.

explain the importance and need of study to all members by citing the past accidents and operational problems. In later stages it will be the responsibility of team leader to make their interest and motivation alive. For that purpose only four to five study sessions should be arranged in a week and every session should not be of more than four hours. In the meantime; members should be asked to be well prepare for the next study and to find answer for the question that remained unsolved in the last session.

The ultimate limitation means that the HAZOP team consists of human beings (human beings are most liable to make mistakes), even the best team may not be able to recognize some simple hazard. During review sessions every effort should be made to provide the best conditions and circumstances that maximize the tendency for proper thoughts and suggestions. To avoid physical and mental execution efforts should be made to computerize the HAZOP study. However, replacing complete HAZOP team with expert system is of no meaning. Increasing team members may prove beneficial in some cases particularly, if problem is too big and complex, however, the team members should be kept to an optimum level (6 to 7).

Analyzing the conventional HAZOP procedure with various factors affecting the effectiveness and reliability of study, it is concluded that convention structure of HAZOP should be modified in order to produce fast, efficient and reliable results. Keeping these facts in mind an optimal approach for HAZOP study has been developed which incorporate use of *Information base* as well as the recommendations to increase the reliability.

Optimal and Effective HAZOP study (optHAZOP)

The optimal and effective HAZOP (optHAZOP) signifies the application of hazard study in such a way that the duration of study should be optimum, most of the hazards should be identified and assessed, better efficiency, good reliability of results, and the time of applicability should be such that the recommendations made by the study can be followed easily and economically. To fulfill the above objective a systematic procedure along with various recommendations has been developed. This procedure has been named as optHAZOP study procedure.

The optHAZOP study procedure is a HAZOP study procedure that uses already developed Expert knowledge base (henceforth named as *Information base*). This *Information base* is a large collection of facts, rules and information regarding various components of process plant. Along with the use of Information it also follows some basic recommendations to give effective and reliable results. A detailed description regarding *Information base* and basic recommendations are presented below;

Table 3. The list of various activities of HAZOP study

Event No.	Activities
1	Collection of data/information
2	Planning for discussion sessions
3	Generation of deviations
3'	Utilizing IB for causes
4	Cause finding
4'	Utilizing IB for consequences
5	Utilizing material information
5'	Preliminary recommendation development
6	Consequences development
6'	Rough HAZOP report generation
7	Management constraint
8	Final recommendations development
9	Final HAZOP report generation

C= critically rank,
F= fatality rank.
R= risk rank

Structure of optHAZOP study procedure

It is true that most of chemical/petrochemical industries have more or less similar type of unit operations/ equipment, the only thing changes from industry to industry are - process, operating conditions, chemicals in use, and capacity of equipment. By analyzing a particular equipment it has been observed that, the type of failure and its causes are not going to change much from plant to plant, however, the consequences may differ from one plant to another depending upon its capacity, chemical in use and operating conditions. A detail analysis of HAZOP study procedure revealed that around 35 to 42 % of total study time is spent on identifying the failure, hazards, and causes of these failures/hazards, and around 25 to 30% time is spent to draw the consequences. Hence, the optimization should be done on identification of hazards, cause finding and consequence assessment work that is repetition of past work and repeats several times in the same study too. Therefore, it is suggested that the *Information base* (an Expert Knowledge base) should be used in order to reduce the repetition load. The Information base is a knowledge base that contains information regarding failure mode, causes and consequences of various equipments. In *Information base* the process unit/equipment (process components) are characterized based on the type of operation they deal and the attributes attached with them (process variables). The systematic procedure to carry out optimum HAZOP study is presented in Figure 2.

In optHAZOP study, more emphasis has been given on the analysis of the information obtained (causes/ consequences) by the Information base and it's suggest recommendations to mitigate such failure/hazard other than spending more time on finding the causes and general consequences. Due to reduction in work load many more new ideas may be suggested which can further improve the quality of study.

Table 4. List of chemicals used in different units

Unit (study node)	Chemicals	Quantity
Brine purification unit	Brine	50 m3/hr
	Barium chloride	5 kg/hr
	Sodium carbonate	5 kg/hr
	Caustic soda	10 m3/hr
Electrolyzer unit	Caustic soda lye	7 m3/hr
	Chlorine	75 m3/hr
	Hydrogen	35 m3/hr
	Brine solution	20 m3/hr
Process unit	Hydrogen	35 m3/hr
	Caustic soda lye	1692 kg
	Chlorine	2657 kg
Chlorine liquication unit	Chlorine	7848 kg
Hydrogen bottling unit	Hydrogen	160 m3/hr
Hydrogen chloride - acid unit	Hydrogen	78 m3/hr
	Hydrogen chloride acid	22 m3/hr
Hypochlorite unit	Calcium hypochlorite	15 ton

Information base

As already described *Information base* is an expert knowledge base consisting of information for process deviations, their causes, and their immediate consequences for various components (process / equipment / pipeline etc.). The information regarding various aspects of process plant is developed based on the past experience, experimental study and the operational study.

Studying the past accidents it has been observed that the causes for failure of an equipment or process component are more or less independent of process type but have some degree of dependency on operating conditions. The consequences are functions of process type, process conditions, and chemicals in use but still general consequences due to failure of a unit can be drawn. The other factors, chemicals, operating conditions, process type only enhance and sometimes reduces the severity. The Information base developed by using practical industrial case studies and suggestions from safety experts and properly maintained by regular updating with new concepts, can serve for longer time, and can be used for other safety related studies too (safety assessment, emergency planning etc.). The inclusion of recommendations in expert system to overcome or reduce the consequences will not be much effective as the recommendation will be based on the type of failure, consequences and economic feasibility. However, a general set of recommendations for various failure scenarios of a particular component can be developed in Information base. These recommendations will serve as a base to find out more economical feasible and reliable recommendations.

Few attempts have been made in last one decade to computerize the knowledge about various process/plant components.

Chae et al. (1994) proposed an expert system that consists of a knowledge base regarding causes and consequences of various deviations in different process equipment. The knowledge is constructed in terms of rule network and uses forward chaining method as a mode of querying the knowledge base. However, systems still need modification in terms of incorporating more process component, refinement in knowledge, efficient retrieval and more reliable results.

Venkatasubramanian and Vaidyanathan (1994) developed a more advanced expert system by considering two types of knowledge -process specific and process general. This knowledge has been developed for 15 different process components. However, this work can be further refined by considering more reliable process specific knowledge, a mechanism to study the propagation of fault in complete system, and more detailed consequences (immediate and ultimate).

An attempt has been made by authors to developed a huge knowledge base consisting of more reliable general and process specific knowledge.

Khan and Abbasi (1995) have developed a knowledge base for twenty different types of process components. The knowledge base is divided in two main sections -process general and process specific. The process general knowledge consists about the information of general causes and immediate consequences of deviations in process components. The process specific knowledge consists of information considering specific operation in process component, specific causes of various deviations, ultimate consequences and propagation of these consequences to other subsequent units. A combination of forward and backward querying method have been used for efficient extraction of knowledge. This knowledge base (information base) has successfully been applied to various HAZOP studies.

Time of applicability

HAZOP study can be carried out at any stage of project from conceptual design to operation and even later at modification stage too. However, HAZOP study carried out after firm design does not have much liberty to follow up the recommendations made by it. In general, recommendations made by this study will either ask to modify the operating procedure or will suggest some additional protective equipment (control systems) to control the assessed hazards. Doing modification in already designed / fabricated process or plant may not be economically feasible solution. Moreover, putting more and more protective equipments is also not going to be economical feasible solution. Hence one should work out the stage where the recommendations are easily followed by simply altering the design / chemical / process / operation hazards and can be avoided instead of implementing more controlling measures. In authors' opinion the best stage of HAZOP application is after conceptual design but before the stage has proceeded too far to incorporate any modification (before making any firm decision regarding fabrication or installation). In other words, the best time of HAZOP study is just after the basic design. It can be understood, similar to *a lesson to 6 to 8 year old child, what ever be the lesson one will suggest, he/she will learn without much difficulty*. The modification suggested at this stage will be cost effective as; at this stage various options to incorporate modifications can be done due to the fact that the process/plant is still on paper only.

Some experts may feel that during the basic design stage, sufficient information may not be available, so, applicability of HAZOP will not be much effective. However, authors feel that the basic design is a final step of plant/process development (starting of fabrication) and it can be executed only when all relevant information regarding the chemicals, process equipment and operating conditions has made available. Moreover, The information necessary for HAZOP study such as PFDs, and PIDs, material data sheet and operating procedure are developed far before finalizing the basic design, thus authors feel and suggest the best time of HAZOP study is just after the basic design.

Information required

As HAZOP study is based on the brainstorming discussion of the available information regarding process, material and equipment used in the process, it is advised that before starting HAZOP study all the relevant information needed for the study should be collected. The total information needed for HAZOP study can be characterized in three main groups namely - chemicals, process equipment, and off-and-on-site information (Freeman et al.-1992, Khan & Abbasi-1994).

a) The information needed for chemicals are;

toxicity data

flammability data

physical state and transportation properties

chemical reactivity data

b) The process and equipment details are;

process flow diagram

piping and instrumentation diagram

plot plant

material of construction of major equipment/pipeline

physical properties of material of construction

c) Information to analyze the consequences are;

. population density on-and-off-site,

. degree of conjunction at plant site

. weather conditions

The information under the groups of chemicals 'a' is available with the *Information base*. However if the process is using any specific chemicals their data should be made available before the study.

If detailed information is available then the HAZOP study can be completed within 4 to 6 sessions and the result of this study will be far superior and realistic than that obtained by conventional HAZOP study. A quantitative assessment of expert opinion regarding collection of information reveals that if relevant information has been collected before HAZOP study, it may save more than 15% of time of total HAZOP study.

The role of team leader

The team leader has critical responsibility in HAZOP study, he should arrange all documents, essential information and decide about discussion sessions according to the convenience of members. The discussion sessions should be conducted in relaxed atmosphere such that every one should feel free to contribute in the study. The leader should take care that every one should involve in discussion and should present his ideas and views. During the discussion, the leader should also take care that no one should dominate the discussion and discussion should not digress from main track. A very important point to be remembered during the discussions is *more emphasis should be given to the problem (hazard) identification and assessment* rather than problem solving (hazard management).

Duration of HAZOP meeting

A HAZOP session should be limited to 3-4 hours. McKelvey-(1988), Freeman et al. (1992) suggested that a session less than three hours would not be effective, and a session of more than four hours, will becomes excessive for the members. Moreover, the number of sessions per week should be restricted to three to four only.

Table 5. HAZOP study report for electrolyzer unit

Plant : Eletrolysis			Draw. number:1FI2425	
Unit: Reactor/Electrolyzer			Date : 5-6-1996	
Guide word	Deviation	Causes	Consequences	Any specific remark
No	no flow of reactants	valve stuck pipe rupture pump fail no reactant available	no big consequence	
	no reaction	no flow of reaction	chances ofleak of reactant	Additional Causes power fail electrode fails
		no catalyst vent/relief system open operating conditions not satisfactory reactor leak		
Less				
	Low flow rate of brine	Leak in pipe Valve not working properly Not enough material	excess heat generation effect to next unit product unit conc get product unit conc get chances of side reaction	no chance of side reaction
	Low flow rate of caustic	Pump not working properly		
		....Same as above	...Same as above	Additional Causes no chance of side reaction voltage increase
	Low temperature	vent valve is open temp. of reactants are low	quality decreases chances of side reaction	Additional Causes low current density
		insulation fail	effect to next unit	Additional Consequences chances of release of toxic gases
		excess cooling some endothermic reaction low reaction flow rate leak in reaction temp. control fail		
	Low pressure	low reactant pressure pressure control fail leak in reactor	chance of side reaction product quality decrease adverse effect to next unit	Additional Consequences membrane damage
	Low reaction	vent valve open impure reactant operating condition not proper reactor leak low catalysis high flow cooling heating ratio changes	excess heat generated product impure side reaction changes of reactant reactant release low efficiency of reaction	Additional causerate excess voltage consumption
More				
	High flow rate	over speed of pump control valve not working properly side reaction	rate of reaction decrease chances of reactant release	
	High temperature	cooling system fail high reactant temp mechanical heating	no reaction side reaction chances of toxic	Additional Cause high current density rupture of membrane

{Cont.}			release
		insulation loss explosion	chances of fire &
	High pressure	pressure control fail	chances of explosion chances of toxic release
		side reaction reactant at high pressure excess heating relief/ vent valve stuck	chances of fire
As well as	Some impurity with rectant	leak in pump/line/valve purging or recycle no proper	Chances of side reaction and associated hazard
	Some side reaction	improper operating condition	Chances of explosion
		leak in reactor pressure control fails	chances of fire chances of toxic release

Follow-up (recommendation) Session

By reduction in identification load more emphasis can be given to follow-up session. Here, the consequences developed in previous steps should be evaluated and based on the experts' team recommendations control strategies should be developed. In normal HAZOP study two to three sessions are devoted to follow-up (recommendation) sessions. For the same limited time, optHAZOP approach gives more time to follow-up session that can suggest better results. The follow-up session should more concentrate on controlling / eliminating hazards rather than identifying hazards and finding the causes (this work has already completed in earlier discussions). This way the efficiency of HAZOP study can be increased around 50 to 75% using optHAZOP procedure.

Table 6. Duration of study for various units of Chloralkali industry

Units	Time (hours) Conventional Hazop	OptHazop
Brine purification unit	3	3
Electrolyzer unit	6	3
Process unit	15	6
Chlorine liqufication unit	9	5
Hydrogen bottling unit	9	5
Hydro chloride acid unit	12	5
Hypo chlorite unit	6	3
Total study time (hours)	60	30

TIME SERIES EVALUATION

To prove the optimization in HAZOP study duration, a time series evaluation of each step in conventional and optimal HAZOP technique has been carried out using CPM networking technique (Reed and Sherwood-1982). The various events of HAZOP network have been listed in Table 3. After developing the network the critical path and critical time have been evaluated using processing time of each activity. Using this critical path and critical time values a percentage contribution of each activity has been derived. It is clear by the Figure 3 (for conventional HAZOP study) that activity 1-5, 3-4, 5-6 are most important and use to take good quantum of time. In the same way the network for optimal HAZOP study (Figure 4) has been drawn and evaluated. It is observed that optHAZOP study procedure takes 45% less time than HAZOP study time. The figure also reveals that most of the steps of optHAZOP procedure contribute equally to the total study.

To show the application of the technique a case study has been solved and presented below.

CASE STUDY

A HAZOP study has been carried out for a chloralkali industry. A complete Process Flow Diagram of industry has been shown in Figure 5.

After collecting all relevant information (PFD, P&ID, material properties, equipment data sheet, plot plan, control strategies) and identifying the different chemicals used in the process, the whole industry has been divided into seven different units (study nodes). Where, a unit is defined as a part of plant or process having independent unit operation and linked with other units to complete the process. A unit can further be divided into sub-units in a way to analyze the unit thoroughly. The list of chemicals used in the different units with the quantity in use is shown in Table 4.

The classified units have been matched with appropriate units of information base. If the matching is not of order then a unit will be further classified into sub-units and sub-units will be matched with the pre-defined (Information base) units. When the matching is of order than the different deviations will be applied to the unit. The causes and consequences for this deviation have been analyzed according to the physical significance of causes and consequences to practical situation.

Due to limitation of space an optimal HAZOP study for electrolyzer unit of chloralkali plant has been discussed here. The detail process instrumentation diagram for electrolyzer unit is shown in Figure 6. The unit is compared with the standard reaction unit and deviation like More, Less, None, As Well As, etc. are applied to it. The causes and consequences of this deviation obtained from *Information base* are analyzed. It is observed that only 15% alteration has been done to the original output of *Information base* to make the results significant to this particular case study. It is due to typical reaction process (electro-chemical reaction) which yield some additional causes and consequences. The HAZOP study result for a conventional reaction unit along with the added information for electrolyzer is presented in Table 5. In the same way the other units such as; brine purification, process unit, HCl unit, hypochlorite unit, has been analyzed. To show the importance and significance of optimization of HAZOP study chloralkali industry has been analyzed using time series network as described earlier (Table 6). It has been observed that for complete study of the plant by conventional HAZOP technique takes more than 12 sessions or 60 hours, while using the optimum approach the total time of study takes only 6 sessions or 30 hours (Table 6). Thus finally, it can be concluded that the optimized HAZOP study (optHAZOP) is a less-time consuming, efficient, and hence more effective technique for qualitative hazard assessment.

REFERENCES

1. Chae, Hee Yeop, Yoon, Y H, and Yoon E Sup, 1994. Safety Analysis using an Expert System in Chemical Process, *Korean Journal of Chemical Engineering*, **11**(3), 153-161.

2. Freeman, R A, 1991. Documentation of hazards and operability studies, *Plant/Operation Progress*, **10**(3), 155-158.

3. Freeman, R A, Lee, R, and Mc Namara, T P, 1992. Plan HAZOP studies with an expert system, *Chemical Engineering Progress*, August.

4. Greenberg, H R, and Crammer, JJ, 1992. Risk Assessment and risk management for the chemical process industries, *Van Nostrand Reinhold*, New York.

5. Khan, F I, and Abbasi, S A, 1994. Guidelines to carryout optHAZOP study using Information Base, *Research report number* **CPCE/R&D 06/94**, 45.

6. Khan, F I and Abbasi, S A, 1995. Risk Analysis: A systematic method for hazard identification and assessment, *Int. J. of Industrial Pollution Control*, **9** (2).

7. Khan, F I and Abbasi, S A, 1995. HAZEXPT: A comprehensive Knowledge Base system for HAZOP study, *Research report number* **CPCE/R&D 15/95**, Pondicherry University.

8. Kletz, T A, 1983. HAZOP & HAZAN, notes on the identification and assessment of hazards. *The Institution of Chemical Engineers*, Hazard workshop modules, Rugby.

9. Kletz, T A, 1985. Eliminating potential process hazard, *Chemical Engineer*, **48**.

10. Knowlton, R.E, 1976. Hazard and operability studies and their initial application in R&D, *R&D management*, 7, 1-8.

11. Knowlton, R.E, 1989. Hazard and operability studies: The guide word approach, *Chematics International Co.*, Vancouver.

12. Lapp, S A, 1991. A risk evaluation system, *ChemTech.*, 700-704.

13. Lawley, G, 1974. Operability studies and hazard Analysis, Loss Prev., *Chemical Engineering Progress*, April.

14. Lees, F P, 1980. Loss prevention in process industries, *Butterworths*.

15. McGrath, P F, 1990. Using Qualitative methods to manage risks, *Rel. Eng.*, **29**(1), 15-22.

16. McKelvey, C T, 1988. How to improve the effectiveness of hazard and operability analysis, *IEEE Transaction on Reliability*, **37**(2), 167-170.

17. Montague, D F, 1990. Process risk evaluation - what method to use, *Rel. Eng.* Syst. Safety, **29**(1), 27-53.

18. Mulvihill, R J, 1988. Design - safety enhancement through the use of hazard and risk analysis, *IEEE Transaction on Reliability*, **37**(2), 149.

19. Oyeleye, O O, and Kramer, M A, 1988. Qualitative simulation of chemical process system : steady state analysis, *AIChE J.*, **34**(9), 1441.

20. Ozog, H., 1985. Hazard identification analysis and control, *Chemical Engineering*, 161.

21. Papazoglou, I A, Nivoliantiou, A O, and Christou, M, 1992. Probabilistic safety analysis in chemical installation, *J. Loss Prev. Process Ind.*, **5**(3), 181-191.

22. Pully, A S, 1983. Utilization and results of Hazard and operability studies in a petroleum refinery, *Process Safety Progress*, **12**(2), 106-110.

23. Quershi, A R, 1988. The role of HAZOP in risk analysis of major hazard plant, *J.Loss Prev. Process Indt.*, **1**(2), 104-110.

24. Reed, S R and Sherwood, F P, 1982. Project engineering management, *PHI*, New york.

25. Roach, J R, and Lees, F P, 1984. Some features of and activities in hazard and operability analysis, *Can. J. of Chem. Eng.*, **62**, 547.

26. Shafaghi, A and Cook, B F, 1988. Application of a Hazard & Operability study to hazard evaluation of an absorption heat pump", *IEEE Transaction on Reliability*, **37**(2), 161-165.

27. Suokas, J, 1988. The role of safety analysis in accident prevention, *Accident Analysis & Prev.*, *20*(1), 67-85.

28. Sweeny, Joseph C, 1993. ARCO Chemical's HAZOP experience, *Process Safety Progress*, **12**(2), 83-90.

29. Van Sciever, G R, 1990. Quantitative risk analysis in the chemical process industry, *Reliability Engineering and System Safety*, **29**, 56-68.

30. Venkatasubramanian, V, and Vaidyanathan, R, 1994. A knowledge-based frame work for automating HAZOP analysis, *AIChE Journal*, **40**(3).

31. WHO & ILO, 1984. Major hazard control : A practical manual, International Labor Office, Geneva.

Reproduced from *Journal of Loss Prevention in Process Industries*, U.K.

5

TOPHAZOP: A Knowledge Based Software Tool for Conducting Hazop in a Rapid, Efficient Yet Inexpensive Manner**

Hazard and operability (HAZOP) studies constitute an essential step in the risk analysis of any chemical process industry and involve systematic identification of every conceivable abnormal process deviation, its causes, and abnormal consequences. These authors have recently proposed optHAZOP as an alternative procedure for conducting HAZOP study in a shorter span of time than taken by conventional HAZOP procedure, with greater accuracy and effectiveness (Khan and Abbasi -1997). optHAZOP consists of several steps, the most crucial one requires use of a knowledge-based software tool which would significantly reduce the requirement of expert man-hours and speed up the work of the study team. TOPHAZOP (Tool for OPtimizing HAZOP) has been developed to fulfil this need.

The TOPHAZOP knowledge-base consists of two main branches : process specific and general. The TOPHAZOP framework allows these two branches to interact during the analysis to address the process-specific aspects of HAZOP analysis while maintaining the generality of the system. The system is open-ended and modular in structure to make easy implementation and/or expansion of knowledge. The important features of TOPHAZOP and its performance on an industrial case study are described.

Introduction

Chemical industries which often handle hazardous chemicals and operate reactors/storage vessels under extreme conditions of temperature and pressure are susceptible to accidents. These accidents may be triggered by human, process, or material failures. The increasing density of industries alongside increasing density of human population has not only increased the frequency of accidents but also the extent of damage caused by such accidents. The most gruesome example is the Bhopal gas tragedy which claimed over 20,000 lives.

The science of risk analysis has emerged to a) forecast the likelihood of accidents, b) assess the consequences of the likely accidents, c) work out strategies to prevent the accidents, and d) to cushion the adverse impacts if an accident does occur. Risk analysis essentially involves three steps:

1. Hazard identification

2. Hazard quantification and consequence analysis

* Reproduced from Journal of Loss Prevention in Process Industries, UK, 10 (6), 151-162, 1997.

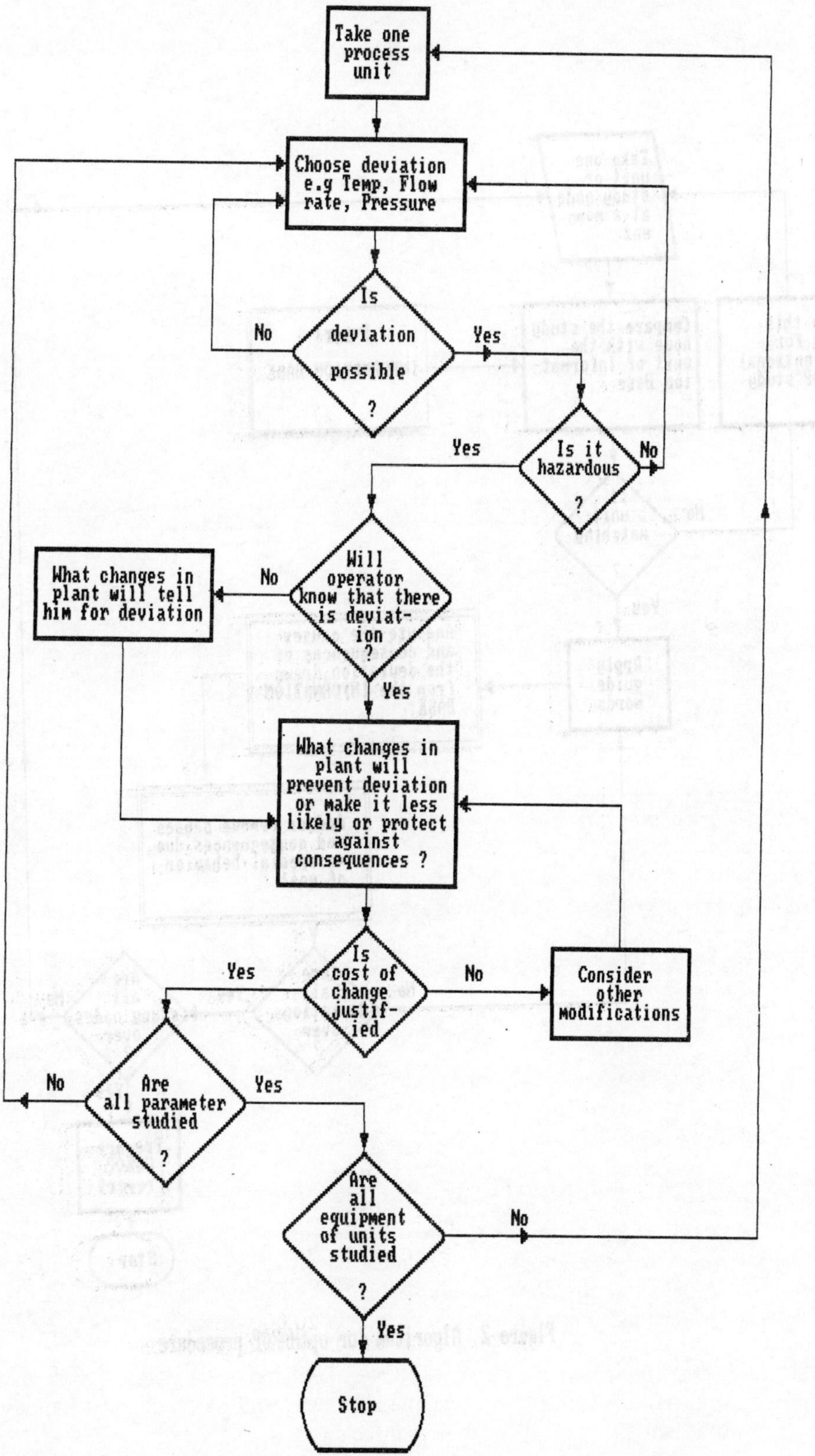

Figure 1. HAZOP study procedure

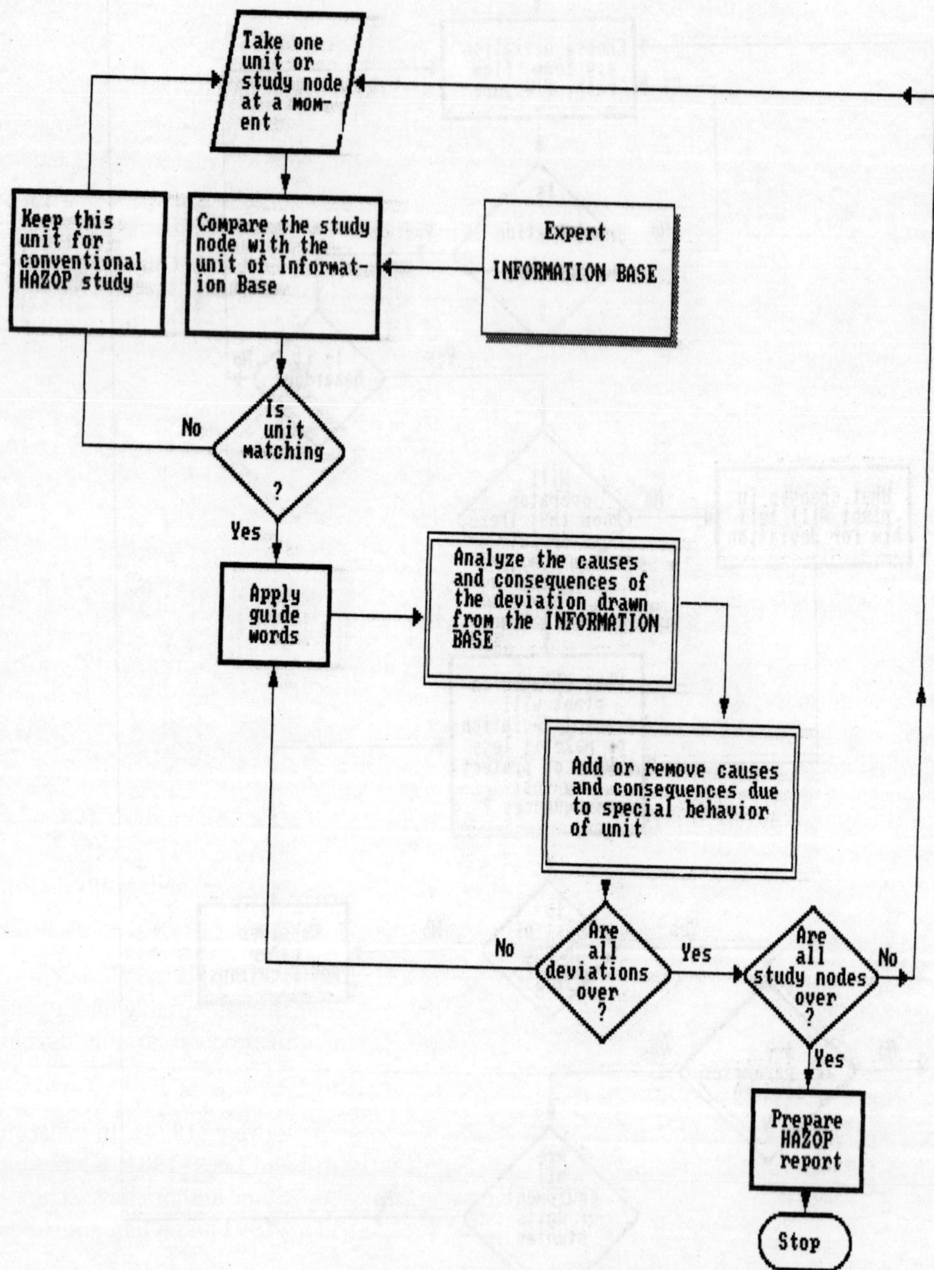

Figure 2. Algorithm for optHAZOP procedure

3. Development of hazard minimization strategies

The first two steps come under the broader classification of 'hazard assessment', the first step covers its qualitative aspect and the second its quantitative dimension.

Different agencies and individuals have proposed different variants of this three-pronged process (CCPS - 1985; Guymer et al-1987; Greenberg and Crammer - 1992) but they all essentially involve the three steps mentioned above.

HAZOP (Hazard and Operability Studies) is one of the commonest tools to accomplish hazard assessment, qualitatively and quantitatively. Thus HAZOP is one of the essential tools for all the three steps mentioned above. It involves a detailed study of each and every part of the entire process line from start to finish with the help of 'piping and instrument diagrams' (PIDs) covering each and every vessel, conduit, valve, and other control equipment employed in the process line. In HAZOP these PIDs are studied in relation to the operation of the process, the causes that may lead to variations in the plant operation due to human, process, or material failures, and the likely consequences. HAZOP thus takes into consideration the conditions such as temperature, pressure, creep, fatigue, etc. under which the physical parts (piping and instruments) are used, the aspects of human interaction with the piping and instruments, and the possible aberrations that may occur due to human errors, loss of process control, or material failures.

The concept of HAZOP was developed in the early 1970s at the Imperial Chemical Industries (ICI) based in UK. In subsequent years refinements have been introduced in the HAZOP procedure but it essentially remains very similar in form and content to the original ICI system (Lawley - 1974; Lees -1980; Mckelvey - 1988; Mulvihill - 1988). Even other schemes of risk analysis proposed from time to time such as *Qualitative Risk Analysis* (Arendt-1990; Van Sciver-1990), Probabilistic Risk Analysis (Papazoglou et al-1992), *Safety Analysis* (suokas-1988), and *Comprehensive Risk Analysis* (Khan & Abbasi -1995, 1996) have all included HAZOP as an integral part of the overall risk assessment process. All this points towards the prominent position of HAZOP in risk assessment.

During HAZOP studies, the process piping and instrument diagrams (PIDs) are examined systematically by a group of experts, and the abnormal causes and adverse consequences for all possible deviations from normal operation that could arise are searched out. The imagination of HAZOP study team is helped along by 'guide words' to cover all possible malfunctions in the plant in a systematic way.

The set of guide words that are often used are NONE, MORE OF, LESS OF, PART OF and MORE THAN. When these guide words are applied to the process variables in each line or unit of the plant, we get the corresponding process variable deviation to be considered in the HAZOP analysis. A list of process variables and their associated deviations are given in Table 1.

All the guide words cannot be applied to all process variables because the two should be combined in such a way that they lead to meaningful process variable deviations. For example, when the process variable under consideration is pressure, only the guide words MORE OF and LESS OF lead to meaningful process variable deviations. The sequence of a typical HAZOP analysis is shown in Figure 1.

The application of HAZOP in hazard identification was first presented by Lawley (1974). In subsequent years various other studies on the application of HAZOP have been reported (Roach and Lees -1981; Kletz -1983, 1985; Shafaghi and Cook -1988; Quershi-1988; Montague -1990; and Sweeny -1993). Some authors have suggested modifications in HAZOP to improve its effectiveness (Mulvihill -1988; Freeman et al -1992 and Khan and Abbasi -1997) in terms of speed and reliability.

Even as HAZOP is important and essential - as explained in the preceding section - it also happens to be the most costly and time consuming of all the steps needed in risk assessment. This is due to the following reasons:

a) In order to conduct HAZOP successfully by the existing methods it is essential to put together a fairly large team of experts (six or more) who have to systematically and critically examine the piping and instrument diagrams (PIDs) in relation to the process conditions and human factors. The team has to work out the various permutations and combinations of possible deviations that can occur during the operation of the plant and the adverse consequence of all such deviations. The end objective is to identify the potential problems or the 'soft spots'.

b) In order to do justice to the study as mentioned above the HAZOP team must be fairly multi-disciplinary and

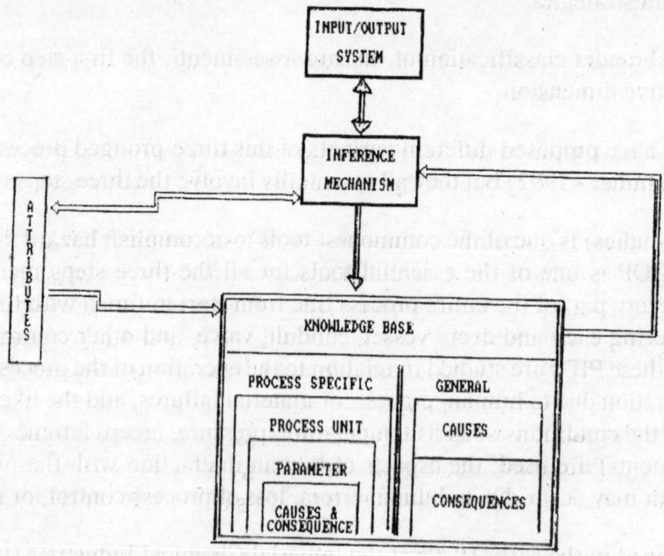

Figure 3. The Architecture of the HAZEXP.

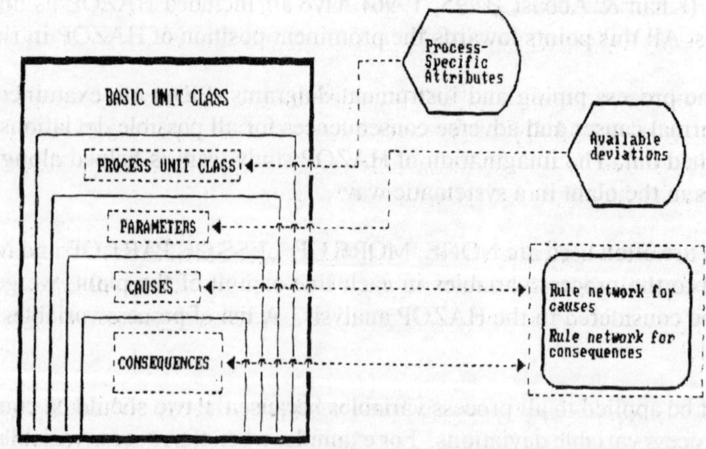

Figure 4. Architecture of knowledge-base

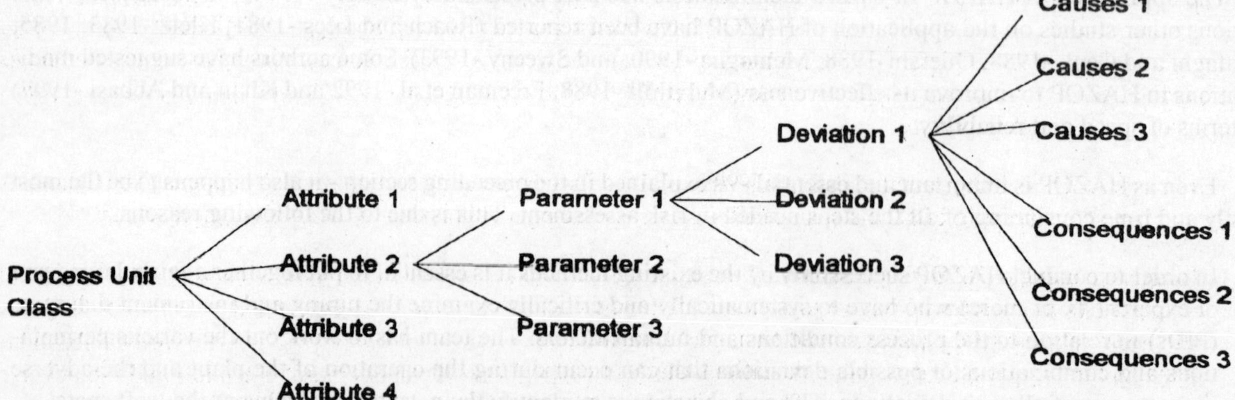

Figure 5. Typical menu of TOPHAZOP

must be composed of experts who have extensive knowledge of the design, operation, and maintenance aspects of the process plant. The experts must also be senior enough to be able to foresee all possible ways in which hazards and operational problems might arise in a process plant.

HAZOP thus becomes costly due to its requirement of highly paid manpower for fairly large number of man-days. As HAZOP is a prelude to other major steps in risk assessment and damage prevention it is unsafe to compromise on thoroughness ; in other words it would be dangerous to cut costs at the expense of exhaustiveness of the study. Hence HAZOP continues to be used in-spite of its costly and cumbersome form.

Other limitations of HAZOP are;

a) Non-availability of experts : even when a company is willing to foot the bill it might be difficult to get personnel of desired level of sophistication and experience.

b) Work of repetitious nature : a large number of likely deviations from normal are of routine nature yet the HAZOP team has to consider and study each one to them. This makes the team's task rather tedious. At the same time the team can't overlook or bypass any of the large number of routine causes as each one of them has the potentiality to cause an accident.

Table 1: Parameters and applicable guide words

Process variables	Guide words
Pressure	More, Less, None
Temperature	More, Less
Flow rate	More, Less, None, Reverse
Capacity	More, Less, None
Level	More, Less, None
Concentration	More, Less, Part of, Other than
Signals	No, Other than

REVIEW OF PAST WORK

Even though experts have felt the need for automating HAZOP in the past (Parmar and Lees 1987a, 1987b; Freeman et al 1992), there has been only limited work and even less success in this area. We have conducted a very thorough literature search in the following manner: a) manual search through Current Contents b) search through CD-ROM Current Contents c) INSPEC d) COMPENDEX. These multiple searches were made just to ensure that no relevant report is left out. The search reveals that as one of the first attempts, Parmar and Lees (1987a,87b) have developed a rule-based system approach utilizing qualitative reasoning and have described its application for the hazard identification of a water separator system. Other attempts in this area have been by Karvonen et al (1990) and Chae et al (1994). Karvonen et al. (1990) have developed a frame-and-knowledge-based system to study the fault propagation in the process plant. The limitations of their system are:

i) large volume of data regarding process and equipment is to be keyed-in each time for analyzing a single deviation;

ii) the applicability of the system is restricted to pre-design stage;

iii) the system places greater emphasis on the identification of causes of deviations rather than the effect (consequences) of these deviations;

iv) the acquisition of knowledge is limited, as it identifies only four types of equipment - storage vessel, pipe lines, operational unit, and control systems. It neglects typical process operations such as mass transfer, heat transfer, reaction, etc.;

v) the system uses fault-tree analysis technique to identify the deviation and causes, which decreases the speed of knowledge extraction;

vi) there is no direct avenue to study fault propagation (deviation propagation) from one unit to other;

vii) the knowledge-base has been constructed in terms of rule networks; for every cause of deviation and its consequences all rules have to be checked which further slows down the knowledge extraction process.

The work of Chae et al (1994) has some limitations common with the system of Karvonen et al (1990) - serialized as i-iii above. In addition it has the following drawbacks:

i) it specifies only three general category of equipment vessels, transportation, and adjunct equipment. It does not take account of process operations in these equipment, which is a key factor in deciding causes and consequences.

ii) the knowledge-base incorporates only limited deviations, their causes and consequences, for each equipment type;

iii) it does not take into account the fault propagation from one unit to other;

iv) it does not take cognizance of process operation and process conditions in development of (creation of) knowledge-base;

v) a total of only six different equipment in three different type of equipment category are considered and several other relevant ones are left out.

Recently a knowledge-based expert system has been reported by Venkatasubramanian and Vaidhyanathan (1994). This system is relatively more elaborate; indeed it is the best reported thus far, but it still has several short-comings which we wish to overcome as detailed in Table 2. Since 1994 no other report on automating HAZOP (elaborate knowledge-based expert system) has appeared though the above mentioned work of Venkatasubramanian and Vaidhyanathan (1994) has been cited in several recent publications on computer aided HAZOP (Coyle, 1995; King et al, 1995; Tait, 1995, Stevens and Humphreys-1996, and McDermid et al-1996, Leone-1996, Shimada et al.-1996).

OPTHAZOP PROCEDURE AND THE TOPHAZOP SOFTWARE

These authors have recently proposed optHAZOP as an alternative procedure for conducting HAZOP study in a shorter span of time than taken by conventional HAZOP procedure, with greater accuracy and effectiveness (Khan and Abbasi -1997). The algorithm of optHAZOP is presented in Figure 2. In this procedure, a knowledge-based software tool is needed to identify general and specific causes and consequences of all probable deviations in the functioning of a process unit. It is the use of this type of knowledge-based software that is envisaged to play a major role in optHAZOP towards a) cutting short the total study time by more than 45%, b) significantly reducing the requirement of expert manpower, thus drastically reducing the HAZOP costs as well as margins of error (Khan and Abbasi -1997). We have since developed TOPHAZOP (Tool for OPtimizing HAZOP) to serve as the requisites tool, the details of which are presented in this paper.

Structure of TOPHAZOP

TOPHAZOP consists of the following main modules:

a) knowledge-base,

b) inference engine, and

c) user interface.

The object-oriented architecture (OOA) of TOPHAZOP is presented in Figure 3.

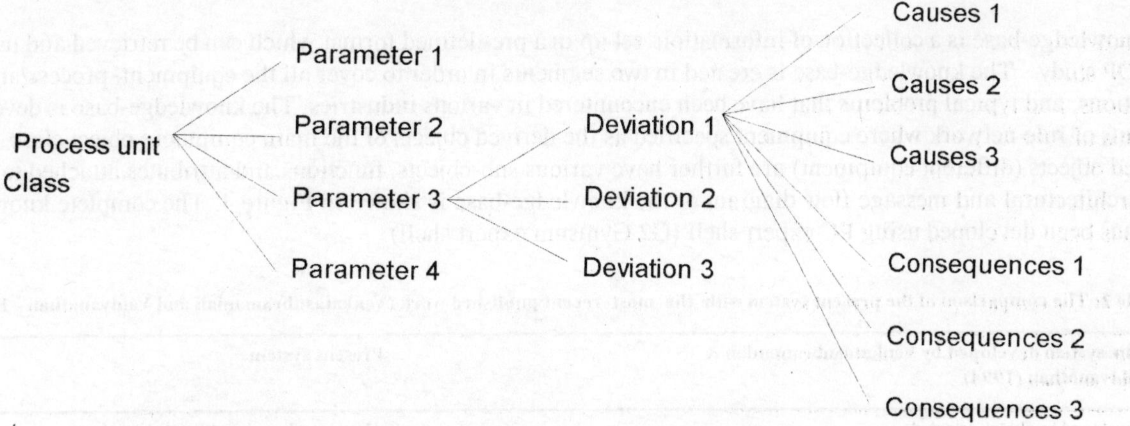

Figure 6. Rule network for general causes and consequences

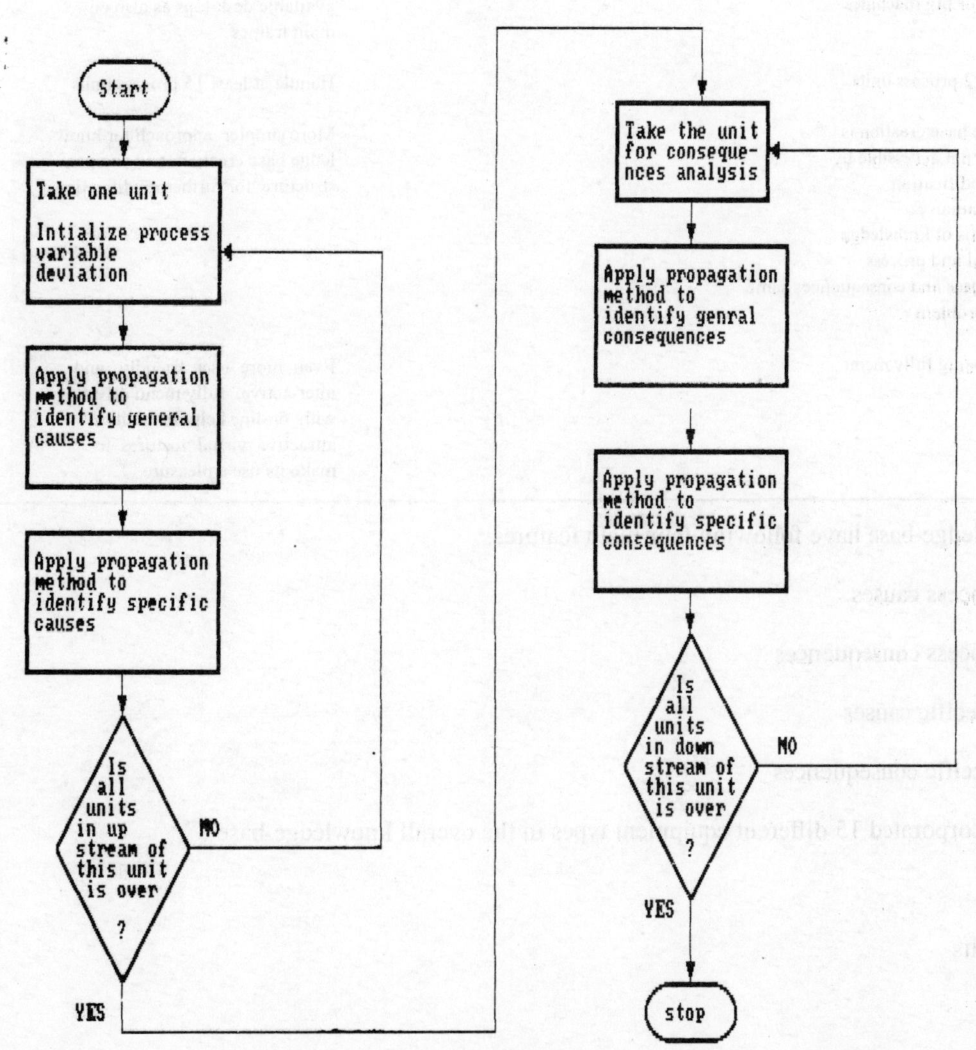

Figure 7. The inference engine for knowledge-base

Knowledge Base

Knowledge-base is a collection of information set up in a pre-defined format which can be retrieved and used for HAZOP study. The knowledge-base is created in two segments in order to cover all the equipment, process/ambient conditions, and typical problems that have been encountered in various industries. The knowledge-base is developed in terms of rule network where equipment specified as the derived objects of the main equipment object class. These derived objects (different equipment) are further have various sub-objects, functions and attributes attached to them. The architectural and message flow diagram of the knowledge-base is shown in Figure 4. The complete knowledge base has been developed using PC expert shell (G2 Gymsum expert shell).

Table 2: The comparison of the present system with the most recent published work (Venkatasubramanian and Vaidyanathan - 1994)

The system developed by Venkatasubramanian & Vaidyanathan (1994)	Present system
Developed in object-oriented architecture with G2 expert shell system	Developed under object oriented environment using C++ language
Needs large memory which restricts running of the system on main frame or big machines	Envisaged to be PC compatible so that it can be run on commonly available desk tops as also on main frames
Handles upto 12 process units	Handle at least 15 process units
The knowledge base creation is complex and is not accessible by user for any modification Venkatasubramanian &	More simpler approach for knowledge base creation and an open structure for further modification
Versatile in terms of knowledge (process general and process specific) on causes and consequences of operability problem	same
User friendly, being fully menu driven	Even more user friendly and inter-active; fully menu driven with on-line help. In addition attractive visual features to make its use a pleasure

The knowledge-base have following four main features:

a) general process causes

b) general process consequences

c) process specific causes

d) process specific consequences

We have incorporated 15 different equipment types in the overall knowledge-base :

1. Pipelines
2. Storage units
3. Reactors
4. Mass transfer units
5. Heat transfer units

6. Mass and heat transfer combined units
7. Transportation units
8. Indirect heating units (furnaces)
9. Direct heating units (boilers, evaporators, etc.)
10. Compressors/blowers
11. Pumps
12. Control systems
13. Settling tanks
14. Valves
15. Sensoring and measuring devices

We have implemented the knowledge base in terms of frame structure and rule networks. The equipment are defined in terms of frame structure while causes and consequences are defined in rule networks. The design architecture and hierarchy of knowledge base is shown in Figure 4.

Process-specific knowledge

The process specific knowledge varies from plant to plant and is related to the type of unit operations, chemical in use and operating conditions.

The process specific knowledge has been classified in two main groups: objects (process unit) and its attributes, causes and consequences. The objects are developed in frame structure with attributes while causes and consequence are developed in rule networks attached to the frame. The causes and consequences for a particular object are invoked by forward chaining technique, while verification (justification) of results is done by backward chaining. The rule sequence for specific causes and consequences is shown in Figure 5. The attributes attached to process-specific knowledge-base are:

1. Equipment (process units)
2. Types of operation
3. Operating conditions
4. Atmospheric conditions
5. Chemical properties
6. Masses of chemicals
7. Interaction among different units

General Knowledge

General knowledge is the information which is independent to process/unit operation. This knowledge has been developed in the same way as for process specific knowledge, except that there are no attributes attached to the objects. The general knowledge is classified in generic causes and generic consequences. These information are created in rule network similar to process specific information. The parameters associated with general process knowledge are: 1) equipment and their capacities, 2) physical state of the chemicals, 3) attributes such as flammability / non-flammability / toxicity 4) reactivity / corrosiveness 5) physical properties of chemicals such as vapor pressure. The simplified rule network for general knowledge is presented in Figure 6.

Inference engine

The inference engine is a type of controller which acts as a manager of the knowledge base, according to the user intention and requirements of the problem under study. The user interface enable the user to easily and swiftly interact with various modules of the software. It also provide on-line help for each option. The flow and control information in the HAZOP inference engine of the knowledge-based system TOPHAZOP is presented in Figure 7 and a brief description is given below.

1. The exercise of mapping starts with the identification of process variable deviations.
2. The deviation is applied to that particular process unit and to all up-stream units to find the general and specific causes.
3. Later the same deviation is applied to all down-stream units to find general and specific consequences.
4. The propagation of deviation (fault) to various up-stream units is done by 'find cause' method which is a function of the basic process unit class.
5. Similarly the propagation of the fault to analyze the consequences is done by 'find consequence' method which is again a function of basic process unit class. These function uses forward chaining for retrieving the information while backward chaining technique to verify the retrieved information.

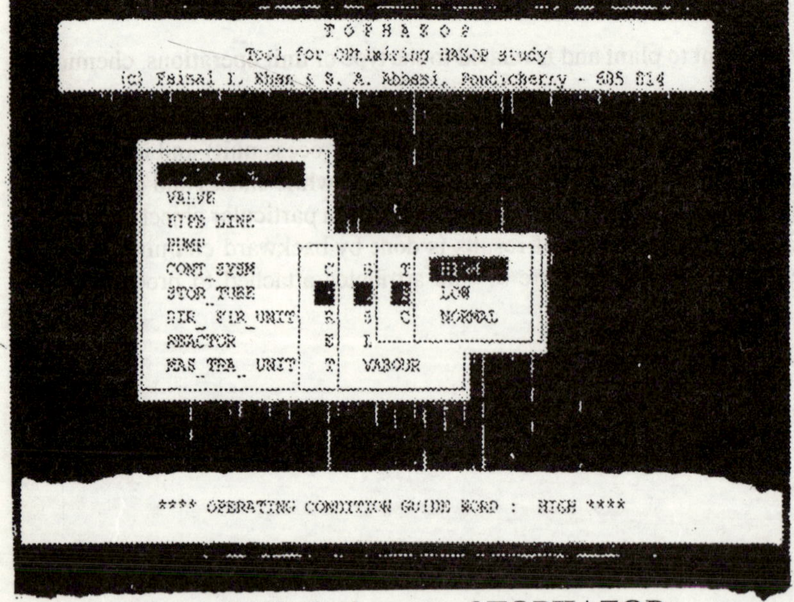

Figure 8. Typical menu of TOPHAZOP.

User interface

This option provides a mode of external interface between the knowledge and the user. This option enables the user to choose a particular equipment from the set of equipment and associated parameters and interact with knowledge-base to carry out the HAZOP study. This option also provides a means of modification or upgradation of knowledge-base according to the need and experience of the expert user (Figure 8).

The user interface has two options: analysis and modification. Choosing one of these options will link the user to the appropriate module of knowledge and on keying in the necessary information the results of the HAZOP study will be obtained. The user has the liberty to check, and modify the knowledge-base or add new information to it. The out put of TOPHAZOP is in the form of normal HAZOP reports and can be directly used in the presentation of the HAZOP study. The user interface also has file processing and other user-friendly options such as on line help and examples.

The application of the TOPHAZOP is illustrated by a real-life case study discussed below.

CASE STUDY

TOPHAZOP has been applied to the HAZOP study of a LPG (liquefied petroleum gas) plant. The plant includes LPG storage units, LPG transportation system and a fractionating column (Table 3). The full plant has been considered in three different study nodes: storage, transportation (containing pipes, valves and heat exchangers) and fractionating column. For the sake of brevity we shall discuss here results of only one of the units of each study node with reference to the general and specific information on the causes and consequences.

Table 3: List of equipment along with associated parameter available in TOPHAZOP

Equipment	Parameters
Reactor	pressure, volume,temperature, concentration, flow rate
Heat exchanger	flow rate, temperature, pressure
Distillation column	concentration, flow rate, temperature pressure
Mass transfer unit	concentration, flow rate, temperature
Evaporator/Condenser	temperature, concentration, pressure flow rate
Pump	flow rate, pressure
Pipe line	temperature, pressure, flow rate
Valve	flow rate, pressure
Storage unit	level, temperature, pressure
Transportation vessel	temperature, pressure, capacity
Control valve	temperature, pressure, flow rate
Control system	signal, temperature pressure, flow rate
Direct combustion unit	temperature, Pressure, flow rate/capacity
Non processing unit (settling tank, agitation tank)	temperature, pressure, level
Sensing and Measuring devices	signal, transmission

Table 4: Output of TOPHAZOP for a deviation - decrease in pressure at outlet stream

TOPHAZOP (c)F.I. Khan & S.A. Abbasi, Pondicherry Result of HAZOP study of a PUMP Plant : LPG Unit: Transportation

Deviation	**Causes**	**Consequences**
	General Analysis	
Low pressure atoutlet	• leak in pump/line • seal fail • lubricant loss • pump running under speed • suction line plugged • relief valve open	• over heating of pump • adverse effect to next unit
	Specific Analysis	
Low pressure atoutlet	• storage tank leak • cavitation occur • line L1 leak • Valve VL1 closed • Pump running under speed	• low pressure and flow rate in fract-ionating column • excessive high temp erature in column • good chances of column failure

Operational data (attributes)
Inlet to unit : Line L1, Valve VL1, Storage S1,
Outlet of unit: Line L2, Fractionating column DS1
Chemical : Highly flammable, low autoigniation temperature
Pressure : High
Temperature : Normal
Flow rate : High
Phase : Liquefied gas

Pump

The function of the pump is to increase the flow and pressure of LPG and send it to the fractionating column. The guide words applicable here are low, more, and no. The TOPHAZOP output if there is a deviation (fall) in the pressure at the outlet is shown in Table 4. Besides maintaining the flow, the pump also serves the specific purpose of maintaining the design pressure of the flow. Further the step involves a highly volatile and flammable chemical. This makes it imperative to study the specific causes and consequences of all such deviations. The study concludes that among various causes the one that may lead to the worst consequence (failure of the column) is rise of temperature of the chemical.

Table 5: Output of TOPHAZOP for a deviation -increase in pressure - in storage vessel

TOPHAZOP (c)F.I. Khan & S.A. Abbasi, Pondicherry Result of HAZOP study of a storage vessel
Plant : LPG Unit: Storage unit

Deviation	Causes	Consequences
	General Analysis	
High pressure in vessel	• overfilling the tank • relief valve fail • external heating • out to tank closed • phase change • leak in line or vessel	• high pressure in vessel • chances of failure of tank accidentally
	Specific Analysis	
Low pressure in vessel	• phase change of LPG • leak in vessel • external heating • cooling system fail • relief valve to flare- • got stuck • valve VL1 closed	• high pressure in the vessel • high chances of boiling liquid expanding vapor explosion (BLEVE)

Operational data (attributes)
Inlet to unit : External loading, addition.
Outlet of unit: Relief valve to flare, Valve VL1, Line L1
Chemical : Highly flammable, low autoigniation temperature
Pressure : Very high
Temperature : Low
Flow rate : High
Phase : Liquefied gas

Storage Unit

The storage unit is a vessel capable of withstanding high internal pressure for, storing liquid LPG. As illustrated in the preceding example of the pump, the general as well as a specific causes and consequences have been searched for all possible deviations for this unit. The result for the deviation involving rise in pressure in the vessel is presented in Table 5. It reveals that this unit is susceptible to boiling liquid expanding vapor explosion (BLEVE), which could be a disastrous event. Among the various causes that may lead to this accident, failure of flair, and choking of valve are the most serious ones.

Fractionating Column

The fractionating column is a process unit that performs a specific operation in each plant. This unit is matched with mass and heat transfer unit of TOPHAZOP. The cause-consequence analysis in general as well as specific terms has been performed for this unit. The results pertaining to a deviation - lowering of concentration - in the feed stream, are given in Table 6. It is evident that the main causes leading to the deviation are changes in feed conditions and/or failure of the reboiler. The ultimate consequence of this deviation is explosion (BLEVE). It is because the chemical is highly flammable and is processed under hazardous working conditions (high temperature and pressure).

This entire case study has been performed by a single person who took only three hours to formulate the problem as well as to run TOPHAZOP, and one and half hours to interpret the results. Using conventional HAZOP study procedure the same study took 2.5 weeks. Moreover, the results obtained by TOPHAZOP are comparable with a study of a team of experts using conventional HAZOP study procedure (Khan and Abbasi-1997).

Table 6: Output of TOPHAZOP for a deviation - decrease in concentration - at the feed stream of the fractionating column TOPHAZOP (c)F.I. Khan & S.A. Abbasi, Pondicherry Result of HAZOP study of fractionating column

Plant : LPG Unit: Distillation

Deviation	Causes	Consequences
	• General Analysis	
Low concentration in feed stream	• impure raw material • leak in line • phase change • excess ingredient • working conditions • chances of equipment • failure	• performance of equi- • pment get effected • impure product • chances of severe -
	Specific Analysis	
Low concentration in feed stream	• impure feed • excess N_2 in storage	• high temperature in • fractionating column • low product quality • high pressure • high chances of- explosion
Operational data (attributes)		

Inlet to unit : Line L1, Valve VL1, Storage S1, Pump PP1 and PP2
Outlet of unit: to final product, to reboiler, to condenser
Intermediate : Heat to the column
Chemical : Highly flammable, low autoigniation temperature
Pressure : High
Temperature : High
Flow rate : High
Phase : Liquefied gas

CONCLUSION

TOPHAZOP is a knowledge-based user-friendly software for conducting HAZOP study in a comprehensive, effective, and efficient manner within a short span of time. TOPHAZOP overcomes several major limitations (time, effort, repetitious work, etc) of the existing HAZOP procedure. The software has an in-built knowledge-base which is extensive and dynamic. It incorporates process units, and works out numerous modes of failure for certain input operational conditions. It drastically minimizes the need of expert time. The knowledge-base has been developed in two segments: process general knowledge, and process specific knowledge. The process specific knowledge segment handles information specific to a particular process unit in a particular operation, whereas the process general knowledge segments handles general information about process unit. At present the knowledge-base incorporates information pertaining to 15 different process units including their characteristics and modes of failures. The availability of on-line help and graphical user-interface enhances its user-friendliness so that even an inexperienced professional can utilize the software with relative ease.

In order to test the effectiveness of the software, a real-life industrial case study has been performed using TOPHAZOP. It reveals that by using TOPHAZOP the time taken in conducting HAZOP can be drastically reduced in comparison to the conventional HAZOP. In the present case the use of TOPHAZOP enabled the HAZOP to be completed within four and half hours while same study by conventional procedure took two and half weeks. The expert manpower requirement were also drastically lesser: TOPHAZOP could be completed by just one engineer whereas conventional HAZOP required six experts.

Further advancements are possible in the TOPHAZOP system in terms of incorporating : more complex process units, more efficient search methods, ability to handle more complex process situations such as reverse flow, recycle loop, purging, etc; and user-interactive flow charting option. Further work along these lines is in progress.

REFERENCES

1. Arendt,J.S., 1990.Management of quantitative risk assessment in chemical process industries. *Plant/Operation Progress*, **9**(4), 262-268.

2. Center for Chemical Process Safety (CCPS), 1985.Guidelines for Hazard Evaluation Procedures,*AIChE*, New York.

3. Chae, H., Yoon, E.P., and Yoon, E. S., 1994. Safety analysis using an expert system in chemical processes, *Korean Journal of Chemical Engineering*, **11**(3),153-161.

4. Coyle, W., 1995. HAZOP studies, *Non Destructive Testing and Evaluation*, 11(1),28-29.

5. Freeman, R. A., Lee, R., and McYamana, T. P., 1992. Plan HAZOP studies with an expert system, *Chemical Engineering. Progress*, **88**(8), 28-32.

6. Greenberg, H.R., and Crammer, J.J., 1992. Risk assessment and risk management for the chemical process industry,*Van Nostrand Rednhold*, New York.

7. Guymer, P., Kaiser, G.D., Mckelvey, T.C., 1987. Probabilistic risk assessment in the CPI, *Chemical Engineering Progress*, January, 37-45.

8. Karvonen, I., Heino, P., and Suokas, J., 1990.Knowledge Based Approach to Support HAZOP studies, *Research Report*, Technical Research Center of Finland.

9. Khan, F.I., and Abbasi, S. A., 1995. Risk analysis : a scheme for hazard assessment and control, *J. of Industrial Pollution Control*, **11**(2), 89-97.

10. Khan, F. I. and Abbasi, S. A., 1996. Accident simulation in chemical process industry using MAXCRED, *Indian Journal of Chemical Technology*, **3**, 338-344.

11. Khan, F. I. and Abbasi, S. A., 1997. optHAZOP. An effective and efficient technique for hazard identification and assessment. *J Loss Prevention in Process Industries* (in press).

12. King, S. D. J., Killick, R.C., Bonner, M., and Gilbert, T. J., 1995. HAZOP implementation an major North sea project, *Proceeding of the Europe Petroleum Conference*, U.K.

13. Kletz, T A, 1983. HAZOP & HAZAN, notes on the identification and assessment of hazards. *The Institution of Chemical Engineers*, Hazard workshop modules, Rugby.

14. Kletz, T A, 1985. Eliminating potential process hazard, *Chemical Engineer*, 48.

15. Lawley, G, 1974. Operability Studies and hazard Analysis, *Chemical Engineering Progress* (*loss prevention*), **70**(4),45-55.

16. Lees, F.P., 1980. Loss prevention in process industries, *Butterworths Ltd.*, **1**, London.

17. Leone, H, 1996. A knowledge-based system for HAZOP studies. The knowledge representation structure, *Computer and Chemical Engineering*, **20**(A), S369-S374.

18. McDermid, J.A., Nicholsen, M., Pumfrey, D.J., and Fenelon, P., 1996. Experience with the application of HAZOP to computer based systems, *Dept. of Computer Science*, University of York, Heslington.

19. McKelvey, C. 1988. How to improve the effectiveness of hazard and operability analysis,*IEEE Transactions on Reliability*, **37**(2), 167-170.

20. Montague, D F, 1990. Process risk evaluation - what method to use, *Reliability Engineering System Safety*, **29**(1), 27-53.

21. Mulvihill, R J, 1988. Design - safety enhancement through the use of hazard and risk analysis, *IEEE Transaction on Reliability*, **37**(2), 149.

22. Papazoglou, I. A., Nivolianitou, A. O., Olga, A. and Christou, M., 1992. Probabilistic safety analysis in chemical installation", *J. Loss Prevention Process Industries*, **5**(3), 181-191.

23. Parmar, J.C., and Less, F.P., 1987a. The Propagation of Faults in Process Plants : Hazard Identification, *Reliability Engineering*, **17**, 277-302.

24. Parmar, J.C., and Less, F.P., 1987b. The Propagation of Faults in Process Plants: Hazard Identification for a Water Separator System, *Reliability Engineering*, **17**, 303-309.

25. Quershi, A R, 1988. The role of HAZOP in risk analysis of major hazard plant, *J. Loss Prevention Process Industries*, **1**(2), 104-110.

26. Roach, J R, and Lees, F P, 1984. Some features of and activities in hazard and operability analysis, *Can. J. of Chem. Eng.*, **62**, 547.

27. Shafaghi, A and Cook, B F, 1988. Application of a Hazard & Operability study to hazard evaluation of an absorption heat pump", *IEEE Transaction on Reliability*, **37**(2), 161-165.

28. Shimada, Y, Suzuki, K, and Sayama, H, 1996. Computer-aided operability study, *Computer and Chemical Engineering*, **20**(6-7), 905-913.

29. Stevens, G.C., and Humphreys, A.M., 1996. Calibrating HAZOP studies, *Arthur D. Little Limited*, Cambridge.

30. Suokas, J, 1988. Evaluation of the quality of safety and risk analysis in chemical industries, *Risk Analysis*, **8**(4), 581-591.

31. Sweeny, J.C., 1993. ARCO Chemical's HAZOP experience, *Process Safety Progress*, **12**(2), 83-90.

32. Tait, J. I., 1995. Building an HAZOP studies to reproduce knowledge-based systems. *IEEE colloquium*, Stevenage, England, 2/1-2/8.

33. Van Sciver, G.R., 1990. Quantitative risk analysis in the chemical process industries, *Reliability Engg & System Safety*, **29**, 55-68.

34. Venkatasubramanian, V., and Vaidhyanathan, R., 1994. A knowledge-based framework for automating HAZOP analysis, *AIChE Journal*, **40**(3), 496-550.

¨ Reproduced from *Journal of Loss Prevention in Process Industries*, UK

Part III

Qualitative Methods of Risk Assessment-I : Consequence analysis

This part is devoted to the quantitative methods we have developed for analyzing some of the consequences if an accident takes place in a chemical process industry. Chapters 6-8 describe a model for heavy gas dispersion, and its applications. The model helps in forecasting the pattern of dispersion and consequently the area-of-impact, when heavy gases are released voluntarily or involuntarily. We have also presented a methodology for controlling dispersion so as to reduce its adverse impacts (Chapter 7-8).

Chapters 9 and 10 presents systems developed by us in simulating and forecasting consequences of release of toxic gases, fires, and explosions.

All of these studies have either been published or in press. We have reproduced full texts of the published/accepted papers in the forms of Chapter 6-10.

6

MODELLING AND SIMULATION OF HEAVY GAS DISPERSION ON THE BASIS OF MODIFICATIONS IN PLUME PATH THEORY

An analytical model for heavy gas dispersion based on the modifications in plume path theory has been developed. The model takes into account the variations in temperature, density, and specific heat during the movement of heavy gas plume.

The model has been tested for three hazardous gases - chlorine, natural gas and liquefied petroleum gas. The results have been compared with the recently generated experimental data as also with the outputs of other models. A good agreement is observed qualitatively as well as quantitatively.

A study has also been carred out to simulate the effect of the wind speed, density of the gas, and venting speed on dispersion. Based on the simulation study a set of empirical equations have been developed. The equations are validated by theoretical as well as experimental studies.

INTRODUCTION

Modelling of the dispersion of the 'dense' gases - gases with density higher than air - has been assuming ever greater importance as many of the hazardous gases (chlorine, hydrogen fluoride, liquefied petroleum gas) are denser than air. Numerous air pollution models, which were developed for lighter-than-air or light-as-air gases, have not been successful with dense gases; accentuating the need for mathematical models appropriate for dense gas dispersion. In recent years, a few mathematical models have been proposed for the study of heavy gas dispersion - notably by Ooms *et al.* (1974), Ooms and Duijm (1983), Colenbrander (1980), Eidsvik (1980), Ermak and Chan (1985), Van Ulden (1983, 1987), Langlo and Schatzmann (1991) and Deaves (1983, 1992).

One of the first attempts to model the heavy gas dispersion was made by Ooms *et al..* (1974). They proposed an analytical model based on using the conventional transport phenomena and the plume path theory (Ooms, 1972). Later Colenbrander (1980) proposed slab (continuous release box) model which assumes normal distribution of concentration within the slab. Around the same time Eidsvik (1980) proposed a refined box model with equations modified to estimate vertical entrainment of air. Van Ulden (1983), Van Ulden and Holtslag (1985), and Van Ulden (1987) used K-theory with atmospheric scaling parameters to model heavy gas dispersion. Ermak and Chan (1985) proposed a model based on the turbulence dissipation and boundary layer parameters. In subsequent years, Langlo and Schatzmann (1991) modelled the heavy gas dispersion using Langrangian approach based on similarity theory.

* Reproduced from Atmospheric Environment, USA

Deaves (1992) modelled the atmospheric turbulence and analysed the way it affects dense gas dispersion. He also used K-theory and employed more extensive meteorological data than the other models did :wind profile, turbulence and boundary layer profiles.

Surprisingly in the present age of computer-based application software, very few such models have been proposed. They include finite difference models which use K-theory : MARIAH (Taft *et al.* 1983),SMART (Tran and Liu , 1981), SIGMET (England *et al.* 1978; Havens, 1982) and MERCUR-GL (Riou, 1986), or box model such as HEGADAS (Colenbrander, 1980; Puttock , 1986). Of these the last named is the most often cited one. The output of these models are well tested with experimental values and are found to be in fairly good agreement.

Although the above mentioned models have been reasonably successful in some cases, they are limited in scope and have found applicability in only certain specific conditions only. In this paper we present a model based on plume path theory (PPT) which, we hope, may enrich the existing repertoire of the heavy gas dispersion models presently available.

Plume path theory (PPT) was proposed by Ooms (1972) and has been used mainly to calculate the plume path of the lighter-than-air and light-as-air gases escaping from the stacks into the atmosphere at atmospheric temperature and pressure. Later this theory was extended to 'heavy' gases (of density higher than air; Ooms *et al.* 1974) with a number of assumptions. Numerous applications of the PPT have been reported for example, Rottman *et al.* (1985) and McQuaid (1986) have used the theory for analysing toxic gas dispersion; Niewstadt (1982,1992), Blewitt *et al.* (1987) and Weil (1988) have used the same for vapour cloud modelling; and Ooms and Duijm (1983) have used the theory to estimate the dispersion of heavy gases coming out of the stacks with high momentum. The theory has also been the basis of the commercial packages PLUME and HFPLUME. In spite of the obvious potential of Ooms' theory, it has not enjoyed wider applicability because the main assumptions have not yet been overcome. The authors of this paper have recently modified Ooms's theory to significantly enhance its range, accuracy, and precision. Most importantly we have enabled application of the theory to 'heavy gases' which is a much less explored domain of air quality modelling than the dispersion of the lighter-than-air or light-as-air gases.

PPT (Ooms, 1972; Ooms *et al.* 1974; Ooms and Duijm, 1983) is a simple approach based on the fundamental principles of fluid dynamics such as Fick's law of diffusion, turbulent kinetic energy and fluid flow. It is based on the assumption that the density and the specific heat of a gas do not differ significantly from that of air. In dispersion calculations, it neglects density spread as well as buoyancy effect. However, these assumptions do not hold true for heavy gas dispersion. In the present paper we have modified PPT in an attempt to make it suitable to model heavy gas dispersion. Some empirical correlations have also been developed to show the dependency of plume variables (concentration, density, plume width, plume velocity) on atmospheric operating variables such as wind velocity, venting velocity and density difference. The applicability of the model developed by us has been demonstrated.

MATHEMATICAL REPRESENTATION

In its original form (Ooms, 1972) plume path theory takes into account only plume dimensions namely velocity and concentration Later it was modified to take into account density and specific heat variations(Ooms and Mahiue,1974). Ooms *et al.* (1974) demonstrated its application to the modelling of venting gases heavier than air at high temperature. However, the modified PPT was based on a number of assumptions (Table 1). The present work is an attempt to make the existing theory more reliable by redefining the assumptions (Table 1) and developing empirical relations to estimate the effect of release and atmospheric parameters on dispersion.

Profiles

Let s, r, and ϕ be the plume cc-ordinates at the plume axis as shown in Figure 1. These co-ordinates are related to the horizontal and vertical axis as :

$$dx/ds = \cos\phi \qquad (1)$$

$$dz/ds = \sin\phi$$

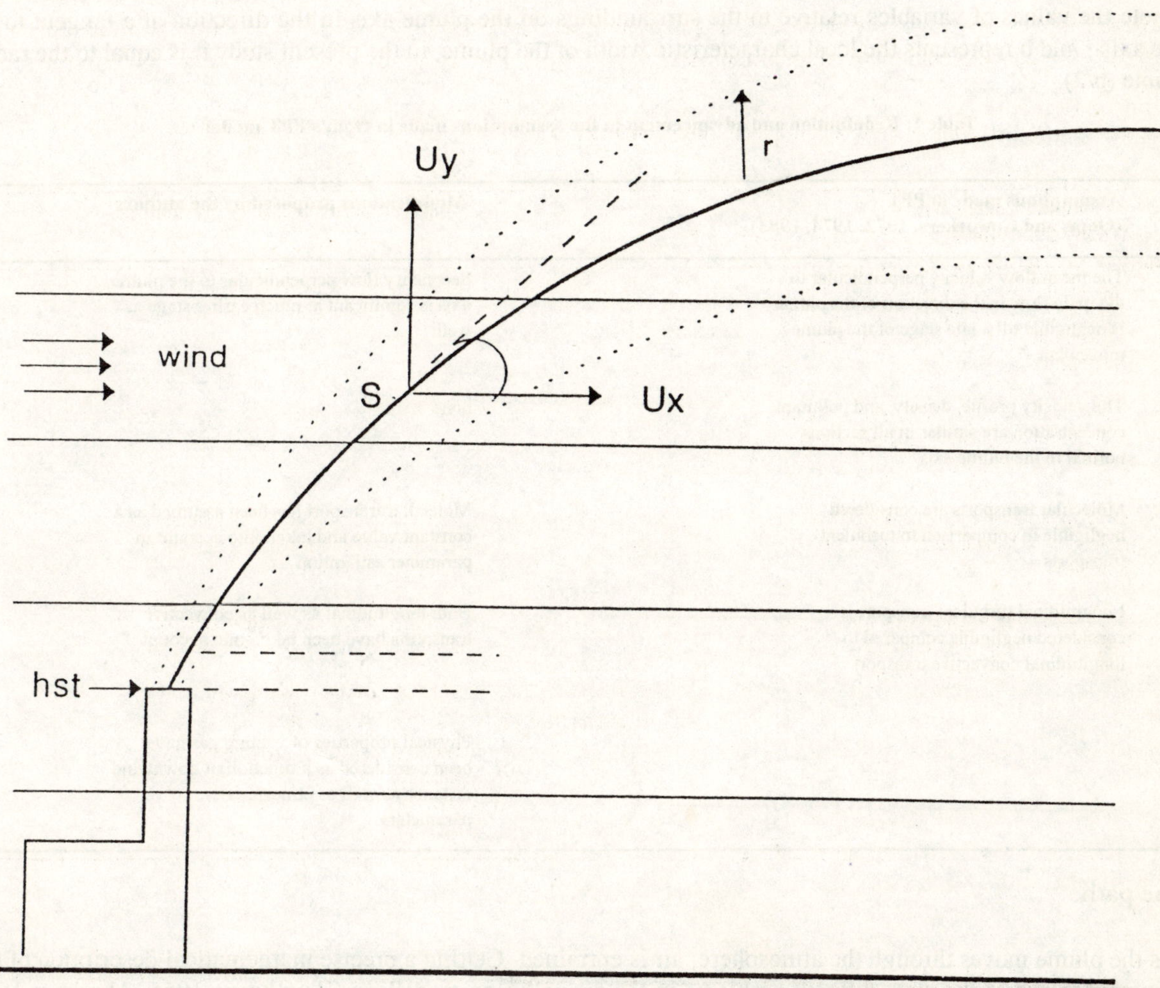

Figure 1. The plume coordinates as used in the present study.

In the earlier form of PPT (Ooms and co-workers,1972; 1974; 1983) only three parameters (u,p,c) have been considered as significant. In the present work temperature also has been taken as one of the dominant parameters. Incorporating the aspects of plume density, temperature and specific heat, the plume characteristics can be written as:

$$u(s,r,\varphi) = u_a\cos\varphi + u^{*}\exp(-r^2/b_s^2) \quad (2)$$

$$\rho(s,r,\varphi) = \rho_a + \rho^{*}\exp(-r^2/\lambda^2 b_s^2) \quad (3)$$

$$c(s,r,\varphi) = c^{*} * \exp(-r^2/\lambda^{2}*b_s^2) \quad (4)$$

$$T(s,r,\varphi) = T_a + \exp(-r^2/Pr^{2}*b_s^2) \quad (5)$$

Where $u(s,r,\phi)$, $\rho(s,r,\phi)$, $c(s,r,\phi$ represent the values of the variables at an arbitrary point in the plume; u^*, r^*, c^*, denote the values of variables relative to the surroundings on the plume axis in the direction at a tangent to the plume axis.; and b represents the local characteristic width of the plume, in the present study it is equal to the radius of plume (b/2).

Table 1: Redefinition and advancement in the assumptions made in Oom's PPT model

	Assumptions made in PPT (Ooms and Coworkers, 1972, 1974, 1983)	Modifications proposed by the authors
1.	The mean flow velocity perpendicular to the main flow in the direction of the plume is negligible till a late stage of the plume movement	Secondary flow perpendicular to the plume axis is significant at much earlier stage as well.
2.	The velocity profile, density, and pollutant concentration are similar in all sections normal to the plume axis	none
3.	Molecular transports are considered negligible in comparison to turbulent transports	Molecular transport has been assumed as a constant value and taken into account in parameter estiamtion
4.	Longitudinal turbulent transport is considered negligible compared to longitudinal convective transport	Both longitudinal as well as convective transports have been taken into account
		Physical properties of venting gas have been considered as a function of downwind distance as well as atmospheric parameters.

Plume path

As the plume moves through the atmosphere, air is entrained. Getting a precise mathematical description of this entrainment is one of the most difficult problems in the air pollution modelling (Hawthrone-1955, Abraham-1970, Briggs-1984, McQuaid-1986). Here we have tried to represent the entrainment in terms of mass flow equations keeping the following facts in mind :

a) in the vicinity of vent or release point venting velocity is higher than wind velocity,

b) at a sufficiently long distance downwind, the velocity of the plume may equal the wind velocity,

c) atmospheric turbulence is one of the most effective factors causing entrainment.

These three facts have been taken into account independently by Abrahám (1970), and recently by Briggs (1984), Fay and Zemba (1985) who proposed different flow equations for each type of entrainment. The final mass flow equation will be a combination of these three entrainment modes with modified profiles of plume characteristic

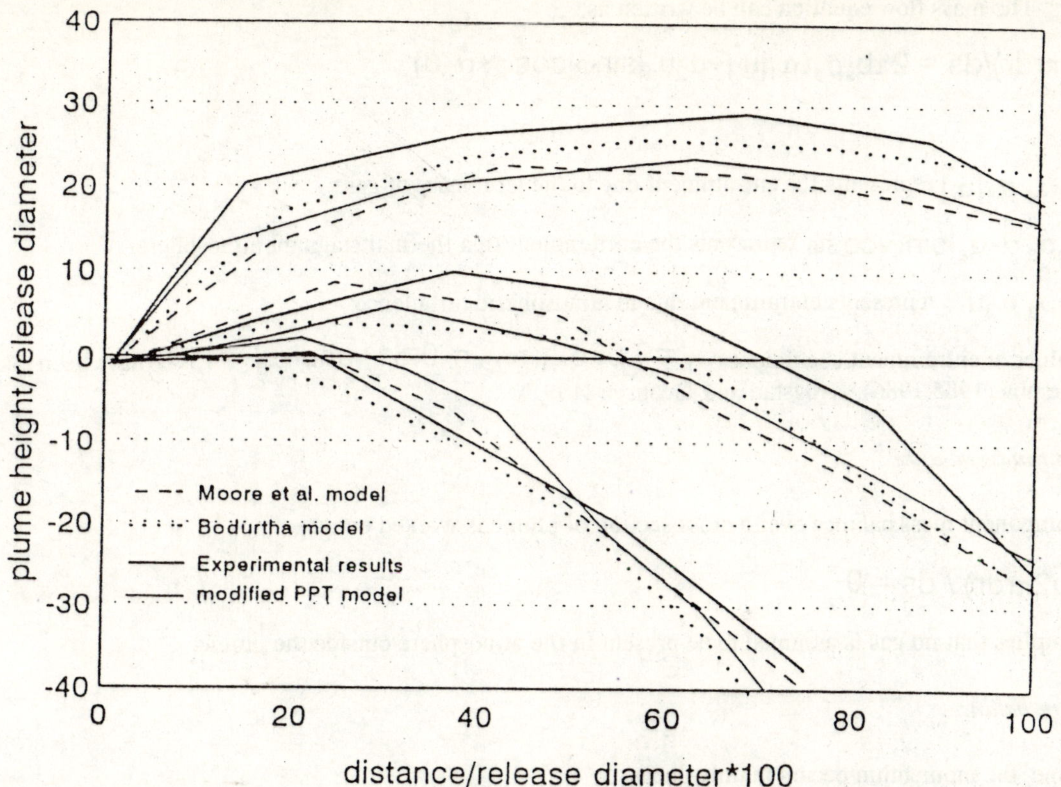

Figure 2. Comparison of plume path estimated by PPT with other models and experimental results

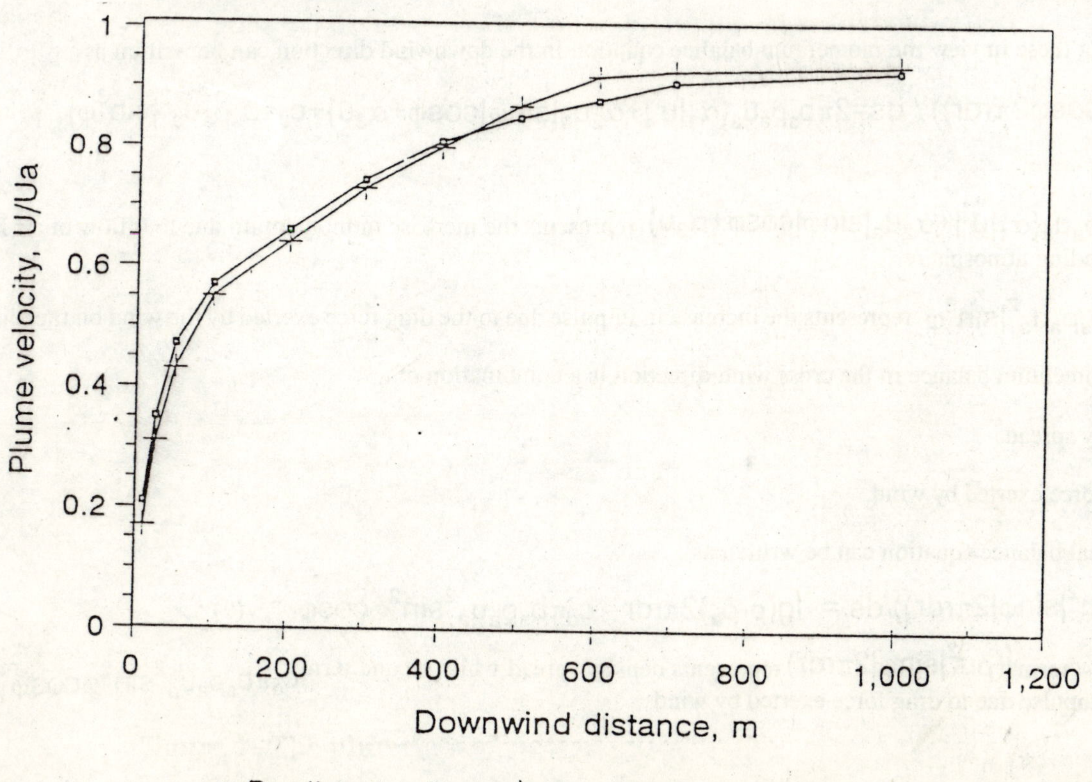

Figure 3. Comparison of observed values of plume velocity with experimental values

parameters. The mass flow equation can be written as;

$$d(\int \rho u 2\pi r dr)/ds = 2\pi b_s \rho_a \{\alpha_1 |u^*| + \alpha_2 u_a |\sin\varphi| \cos\varphi + \alpha_3 u\} \quad (6)$$

where,

$2\pi b_s \rho_a \alpha_1 |u^*|$ represents the entrainment due to the jet release of gas.

$2\pi b_s \rho_a \alpha_2 u_a |\sin\varphi| \cos\varphi$ represents the entrainment in a thermal stagnant atmosphere.

$2\pi b_s \rho_a \alpha_3 u$ represents entrainment due to atmospheric turbulence.

The values of entrainment coefficient $\alpha_1 = 0.0762$, $\alpha_2 = 0.61$, and $\alpha_3 = 1.0$ have been taken from Fay and Zemba (1985,1986), Krogstad and Jacobsen (1991).

Component mass balance

The component mass balance over a cross section of plume is worked out as :

$$d(\int c u 2\pi r dr) / ds = 0 \quad (7)$$

This implies that no gas is assumed to be present in the atmosphere outside the plume.

Momentum balance

In plume, the momentum occurs mainly due to

a) entrainment of air,

b) force exerted by wind.

Keeping these in view the momentum balance equation in the downwind direction can be written as :

$$d(\int(\rho u^2 \cos\varphi 2\pi r dr)) / ds = 2\pi b_s \rho_a u_a \{\alpha_1 |u^*| + \alpha_2 u_a |\sin\varphi| \cos\varphi + \alpha_3 u\} + c_d \pi b_s \rho_a u_a^2 |\sin^3\varphi| \quad (8)$$

Where,

$2\pi b_s \rho_a u_a \{\alpha_1 |u^*| + \alpha_2 u_a |\sin\varphi| \cos\varphi + \alpha_3 u\}$ represents the increase in momentum due to inflow of air from the surrounding atmosphere.

$c_d \pi b_s \rho_a u_a^2 |\sin^3\varphi$ represents the increase in impulse due to the drag force exerted by the wind on the plume.

The momentum balance in the cross wind direction is a combination of

- density spread,
- drag force exerted by wind.

The final balance equation can be written as :

$$d(\int(\rho u^2 |\sin\varphi| 2\pi r dr))/ds = \int g(\rho - \rho_a) 2\pi r dr - c_d \pi b_s \rho_a u_a^2 \sin^2\varphi \cos\varphi \quad (9)$$

The first term $\int(\rho u^2 |\sin\varphi| 2\pi r dr)$ represents density spread while second term $c_d \pi b_s \rho_a u_a^2 \sin^2\varphi \cos\varphi$ represents the impulse due to drag force exerted by wind.

Energy balance

The energy balance for the plume implies that the amount of heat emitted by the gas per unit time is conserved

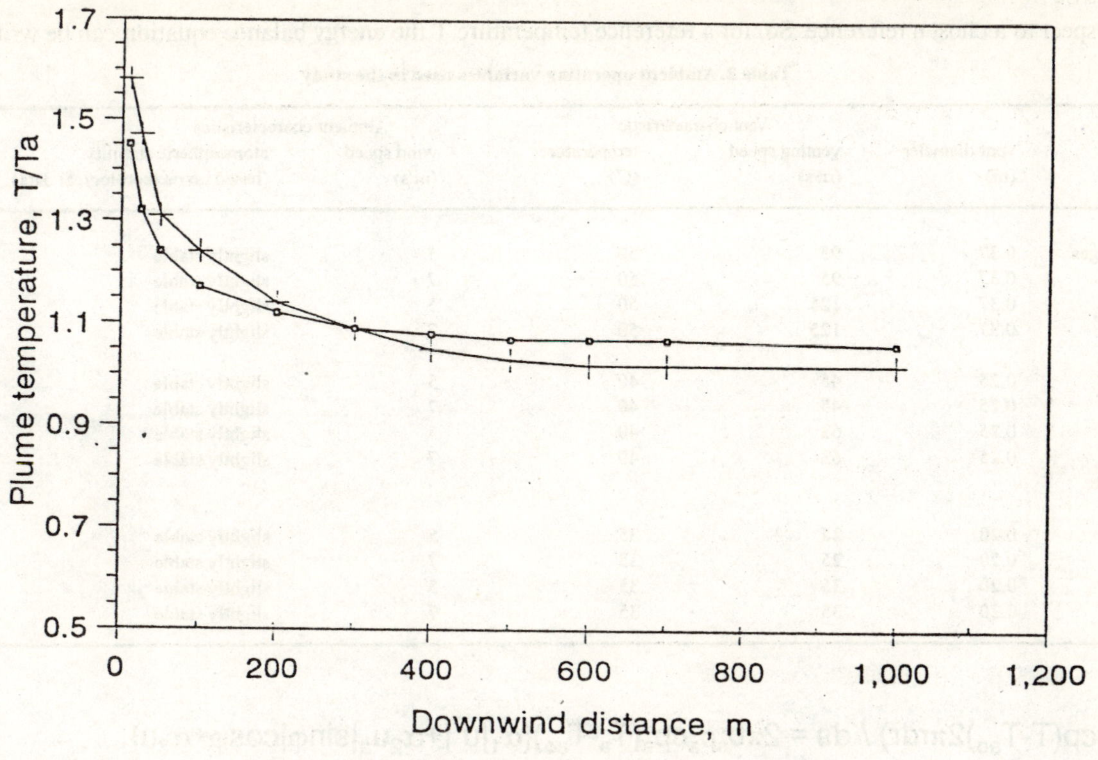

Figure 4. Comparison of observed values of plume temperature with experimental values.

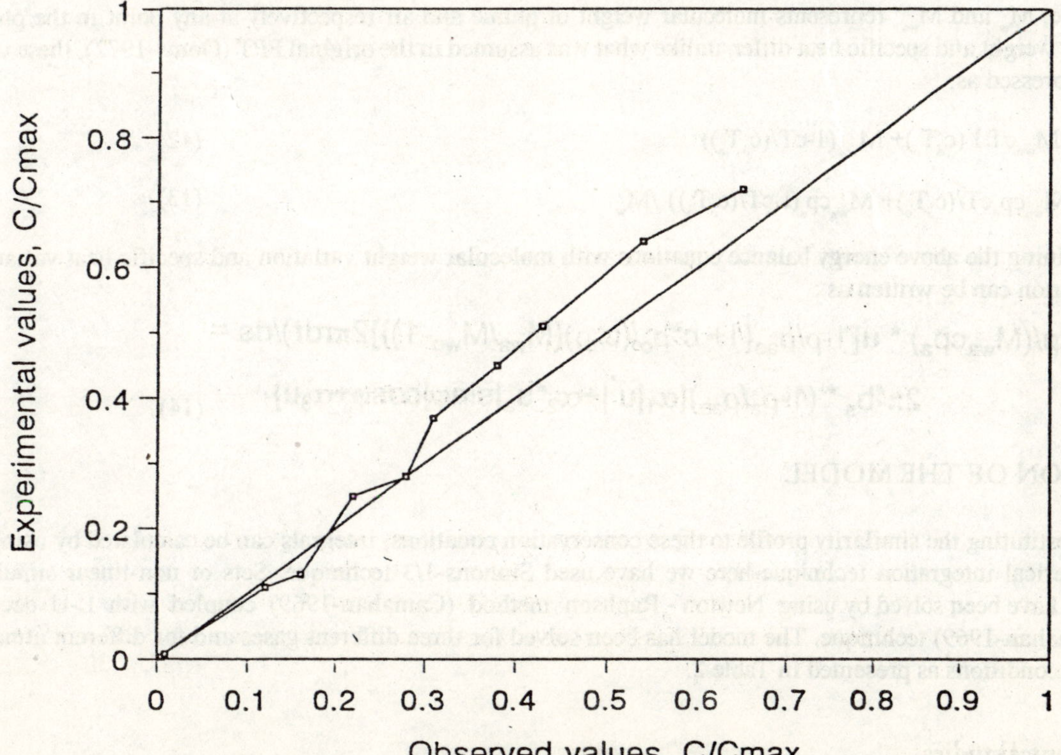

Figure 5. Comparison of concentration of gas in the plume with experimental values (venting of ammonia)

with respect to a chosen reference. So, for a reference temperature T the energy balance equation can be written as:

Table 2. Ambient operating variables used in the study

Gas	Vent characteristic			Ambient characteristics	
	vent diameter (m)	venting speed (m/s)	temperature (C)	wind speed (m/s)	atomospheric stability (based on meteorological data)
Natural gas	0.37	95	50	5	slightly stable
	0.37	95	50	7	slightly stable
	0.37	125	50	5	slightly stable
	0.37	125	50	7	slightly stable
LPG	0.25	45	40	5	slightly stable
	0.25	45	40	7	slightly stable
	0.25	63	40	5	slightly stable
	0.25	63	40	7	slightly stable
Chlonrine					
	0.20	25	35	5	slightly stable
	0.20	25	35	7	slightly stable
	0.20	35	35	5	slightly stable
	0.20	35	35	7	slightly stable

$$d(\int \rho u cp(T-T_{ao})2\pi r dr) / ds = 2\pi b_s \rho_a cp_a(T_a-T_{ao})\{\alpha_1|u^*|+\alpha_2 u_a|\sin\varphi|\cos\varphi+\alpha_3 u\} \quad (10)$$

If it is assumed that air and vent gas obey ideal gas law, then the temperatures (plume and air temperature) can be expressed as

$$T = M_w P/(R\rho) \text{ and } T_a = M_{wa} PI(R\rho_a) \quad (11)$$

Where, M_w and M_{wa} represents molecular weight of plume and air respectively at any point in the plume. As molecular weight and specific heat differ, unlike what was assumed in the original PPT (Ooms-1972), these variables can be expressed as:

$$M_w = M_{wo} cT\, I\, (c_o T_o) + M_{wa}(1-cT/(c_o T_o)) \quad (12)$$

$$cp = \{M_{wo} cp_o cT/(c_o T_o) + M_{wa} cp_a(l-cT/(c_o T_o))\} / M_w \quad (13)$$

Combining the above energy balance equations with molecular weight variation and specific heat variation, the final equation can be written as :

$$d(\int M_w cp/(M_{wa} cp_a) * u[1-\rho/\rho_{ao}\{1+ c^*\rho_o/(c_o\rho)(M_{wa}/M_{wo}-1)\}]2\pi r dr)/ds =$$

$$2\pi^* b_s^* (1-\rho_a/\rho_{ao})\{\alpha_1|u^*|+\alpha_2^* u_a|\sin\varphi|\cos\varphi+\alpha_3 u\} \quad (14)$$

SOLUTION OF THE MODEL

By substituting the similarity profile to these conservation equations, integrals can be calculated by using a suitable numerical integration technique-here we have used Siphons-1/3 technique. Sets of non-linear simultaneous equations have been solved by using Newton - Raphson method (Camahan-1969) coupled with L-U decomposition (Camahan-1969) technique. The model has been solved for three different gases and for different atmospheric operating conditions as presented in Table 2.

Experimental studies

An extensive study to measure the quality of stack emissions and the behaviour of the plume formed when ammonia is released from a pressurised storage vessel was conducted at Manali (near Madras, southern peninsula of India). The initial and boundary conditions of the release are given in Table 3. The study area has flat terrain and is made up of rural habitat. The study included meteorological parameters (vertical temperature profile, vertical as well as horizontal wind velocity profile), air quality (concentration profiles), and behaviour of the plumes (of heavier-than-air as well as heavy-as-air gases) under different sets of conditions influencing dispersion for a continuous as well as an instantaneous release. The following characteristics of the plume were studied measuring various parameters such as; temperature variation within the plume, concentration profiles in the cross wind and downwind directions, plume width, plume height, and the effect of the meteorological parameters on the plume behaviour. A gist of the experimental results obtained in the present study is presented in Table 4.

Table 3. The initial and boundary conditions for release of ammonia from pressurized vessel through vent valve

Parameters	Values
Storage capacity	200 tons
Storage temperature	45 °C
Storage pressure	1625 kPa
Height of the vessel	10.5 m
Height of vent pipe	25 m
Vent diameter	0.2 m
Ambient temperature	27 °c
Ambient pressure	107.3 kPa
Wind speed (at 10 m)	5.5 m/s
Wind direction	North-West
Terrain of the area	Flat rural area with a roughness height of 1.2 m

RESULTS and DISCUSSION

The comparison of the plume path (height of plume rise) obtained by our model with the results reported by Bodurtha (1961) Moore *et al.* (1988) and our own recent experimental studies are presented in Figure 2. Good, qualitative as well as quantitative, agreements have been observed.

The temperature and the plume velocity variations have also been compared with that of the experimental data (Table 4), and a fairly good agreement has been observed (Figures 3 and 4). When the concentration profile obtained by the present model (for release of ammonia) is compared with our experimental results (Figure 5) the predicted results are seen to lie within the confidence interval of 40-50%, a match acceptable for air pollution models.

The simulation study reveals that the plume width and the plume velocity both increase in the downwind direction, while density of the plume, temperature of the gas (above atmospheric temperature) and gas concentration all decrease downwind. We see that the trend diminishes as the distance of travel of the plume increases. This has been observed for all the three gases studied (natural gas, LPG, chlorine). The observations on the individual gases are summarised below.

Natural gas

Figure 6 shows the behaviour of plume variables (dimensionless form) in downwind direction due to the change (step increase) in wind and venting speeds. An increase in the wind speed causes an increase in the plume velocity and the plume width. A similar trend is also observed for an increase in the venting speed. However, the trend is more marked in the case of increase in the venting velocity compared to the increase in wind speed. Perhaps high venting speed creates high turbulence and wake formations in the atmosphere which consequently lead to the rapid entrainment of air and swift dispersion too. Wind speed effects the downwind transportation of the plume more strongly than it does the entrainment of air and its dispersion. As the density of the gas (vapour density =1.34) is not much higher than air a fast response due to a change in the controlling parameters viz, wind velocity and venting velocity, has been observed. For example, a venting velocity of 125 m/s (mass release rate 10 kg/s for 5 min) covers a smaller area under flammability limits compared to a venting velocity of 95 m/s (mass release rate 5 kg/s for 10 min) under high wind (15 m/s). This reveals that a high release (venting) velocity of this gas for shorter periods is safer than a slow release under unstable conditions for longer duration.

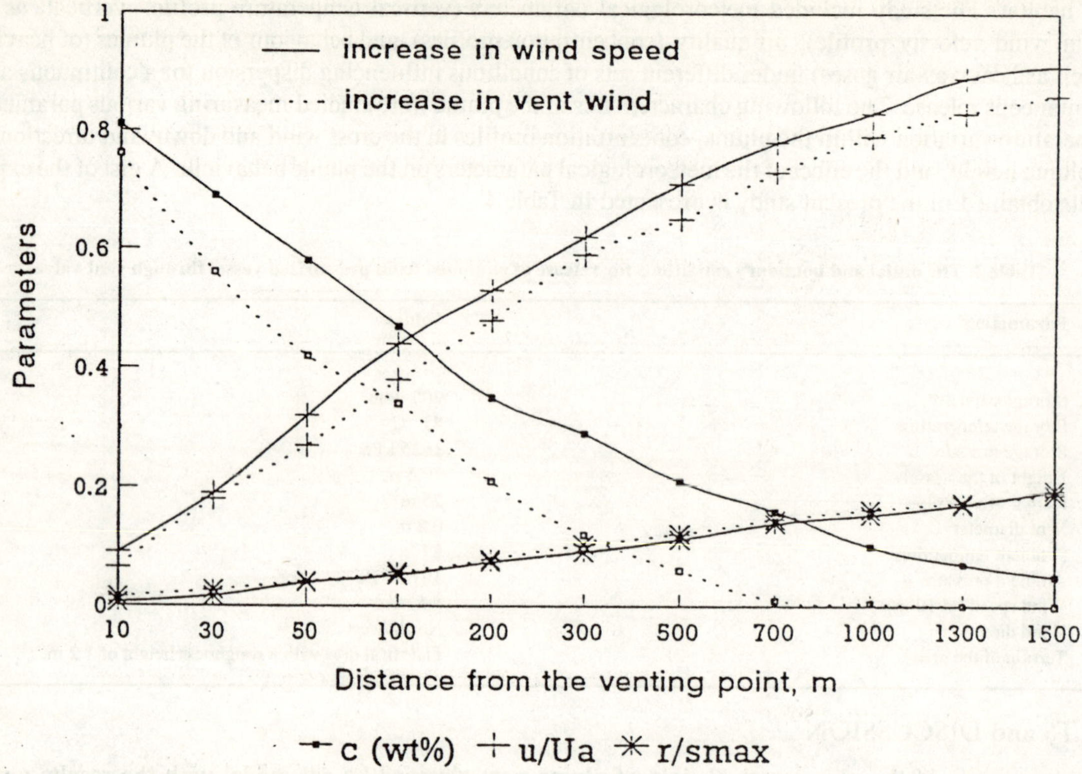

Figure 6. Impact of a 40% change in wind speed (from 5 m/s to 7 m/s) as compared to the impact of 40% change in venting speed (from 95 m/s to 125 m/s) on three plume variables (Natural gas)

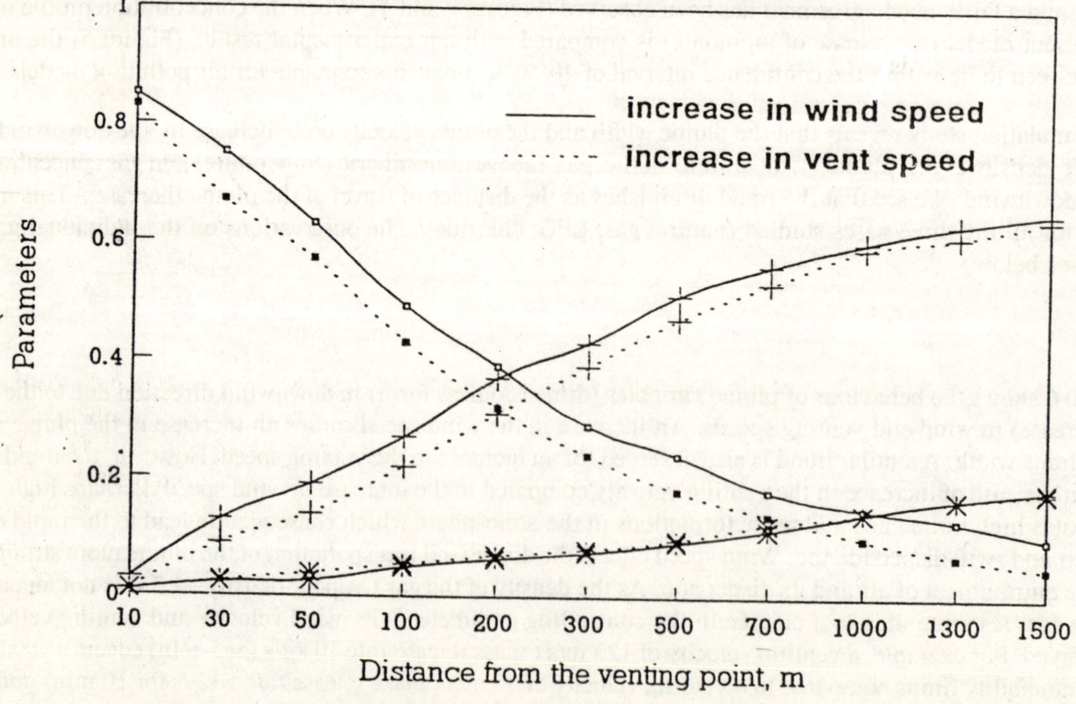

Figure 7. Impact of a 40% change in wind speed (from 5 m/s to 7 m/s) as compared to the impact of 40% change in venting speed (from 45 m/s to 63 m/s) on three plume variables (LPG)

Table 4. Experimental results obtained in the present study

Down wind distance meters	Plume velocity meters	Ground level concentration (wt%)	Plume with meters	Plume temperature °C
10	0.85	0.001	0.027	42.66
50	1.55	0.002	0.065	39.69
100	2.15	0.038	0.097	35.40
200	2.75	0.045	0.137	33.48
300	3.25	0.087	0.174	30.78
400	3.65	0.098	0.202	29.43
500	4.00	0.129	0.245	28.35
600	4.35	0.157	0.312	27.81
700	4.50	0.175	0.357	27.54
1000	4.75	0.224	0.415	27.46
1300	4.85	0.254	0.447	27.41
1750	4.90	0.354	0.521	27.39

Liquefied petroleum gas (LPG)

The pattern of dispersion of LPG is by and large similar to the pattern of dispersion of natural gas discussed above. However a low venting speed (45 m/s) and a higher density causes slower dispersion. It is evident from Figure 7 that at any distance along the downwind direction, plume velocity and the concentration of gas in the plume are higher while plume width is less due to an increase in the wind speed when compared with the increase in venting speed. Thus high venting speed has stronger influence on the entrainment of air and the plume width leading to faster dispersion. But high wind speed also transports the plume to a larger distance with higher velocity.

Chlorine

Of the three hazardous gases discussed in this work, chlorine has by far the slowest rate of dispersion. Otherwise the trend observed with chlorine is broadly similar to the trends seen with the other two gases. As is evident from Figure 8 the dispersion increases with an increase in the wind speed and is faster with the higher venting speeds. For any given distance, the concentration of chlorine is higher and the plume velocity is lower compared to the other two gases. As chlorine gas is the most toxic of the three gases studied and is also the most sluggish to disperse, lethal concentration of this gas can easily build up over large areas and persist for long durations over larger areas.

Parametric effect

To generalise the effect of wind speed, density and venting speed on the plume path, we have developed some empirical equations. These equations directly predict the behaviour of plume variables (gas concentration in plume, plume density, local plume width, plume velocity) with other operating variables viz : density of gas, venting speed, etc.

For this purpose a dimensionless number Q_f has been defined as: (15)

$$Q_f = u_a/u_v*(p_a/p)$$

$$p^{\cdot} = A*\ln(s) + B$$

$$A = -0.00395848*\log(Q_f) - 0.01925951$$

$$B = -0.16083*\log(Q_f) + 0.091579$$

$$u^{\cdot} = A*\ln(s) + B$$

$$A = 0.159874 + 0.960923 * O_f - 1.24869*Q_f^2 + 0.3728' Q_f3$$

$$B = -0.47832 + 0.0418951 *Q_f + 0.\sim 53298 * Q_f^2$$

$C^{*} = A*\ln(s) + B$

$A = -0.0161965 + 0.00543481 * Q_f 0.00128631 * Q_f^2$ (16)

$B = 0.183894 * \exp(-0.382484 * Q_f)$

$b_s = A*\ln(s) + B$

$A = 0.0157719 + 0.104969 * Q_f - 0.0347085 * Q_f^2$

$B = 0.953469 * Q_f^{2\ 0.22422}$

$T = A*\ln(s) + B$

$A = 3.67477 + 7.61097 * Q_f - 2.42655 * Q_f^2$

$B = -8.5476 - 58.7278 * Q_f + 26.7875 Q_f^2$

The equations have been validated with experimental values. A plot representing different plume variables at Y axis with dimensionless number Q_f is shown in Figure 9. It can be seen that with an increase in Q_f variables like plume width and plume velocity (shown on Y axis) increase while gas concentration and density difference both decrease.

CONCLUSION

The plume path theory as modified by us gives satisfactory results for the dispersion of heavy gases. It also enables simulation of plume profiles along the cross section of plume as well as in the downwind directions. The empirical equations developed by us on the basis of the present model, we hope, would prove to be helpful in air-pollution studies, as they can predict responses to the different ambient operating conditions over the plume variables (concentration, density, local width, temp etc.) with relative ease and fair accuracy.

LIST OF SYMBOLS

b_s = Local characteristics width, m

c = Concentration of gas at any point inside the plume, kg/m^3

c^{*} = Concentration of gas on the plume axis, kg/m^3

c_o = Concentration at out let, kg/m^3

cp_o = Specific heat at outlet, J/kg/K

cp = Specific heat of the gas at any arbitrary point, J/kg/K

cp_a = Specific heat of air, J/kg/K

cd = Drag coefficient

g = Acceleration due to gravity, m/s^2

r = Radial distance to plume axis in a normal section of plume, m

s = Distance along the plume axis from the release point to a certain point, m

M_{wo} = Molecular weight of plume at the exit of the gas (gas and air)

p = Absolute Pressure, kPa

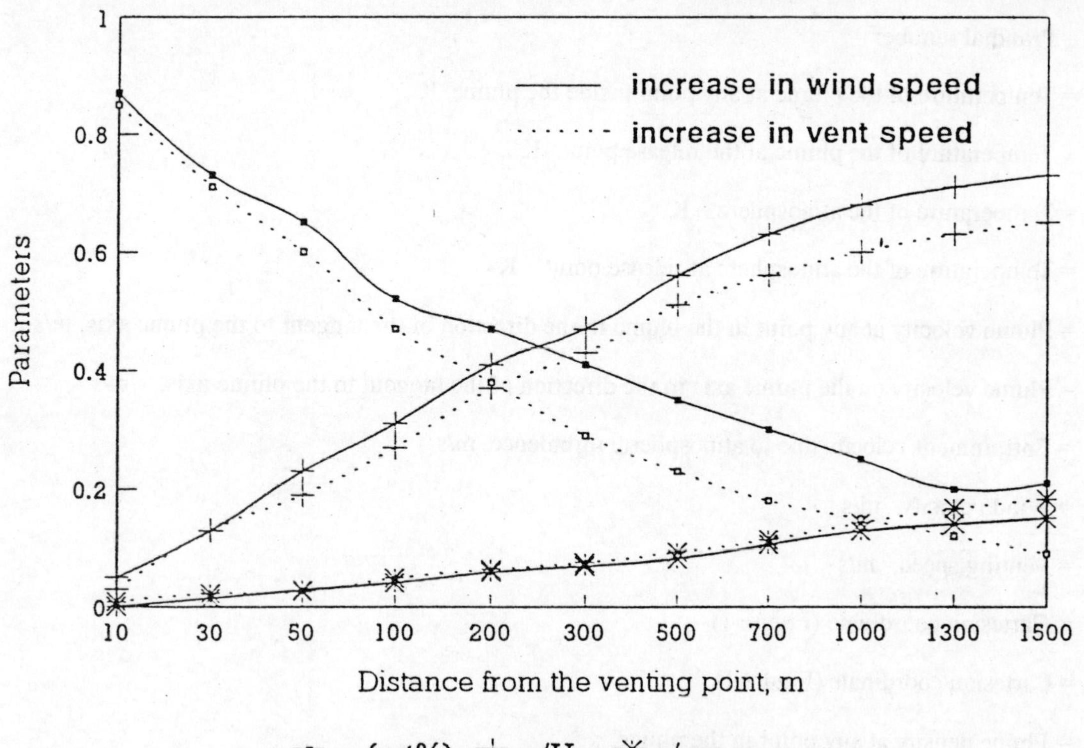

Figure 8. Impact of a 40% change in wind speed (from 5 m/s to 7 m/s) as compared to the impact of 40% change in venting speed (from 25 m/s to 35 m/s) on three plume variables (Chlorine gas)

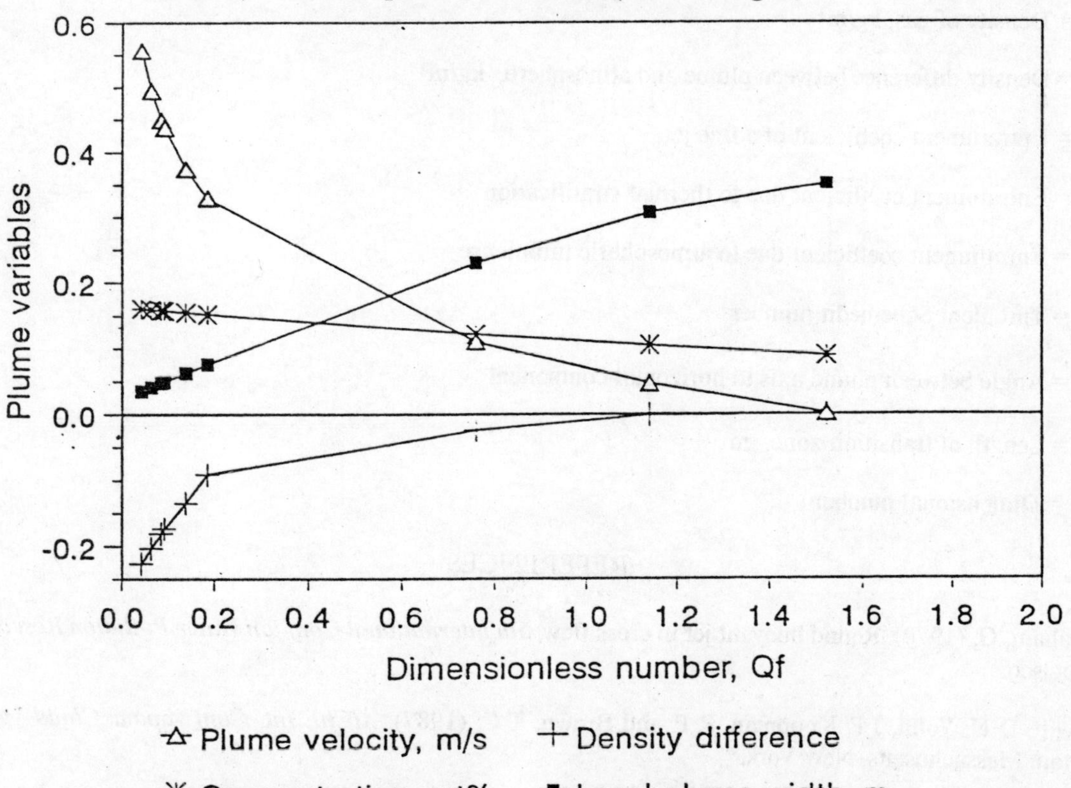

Figure 9. Relationship of the dimensionless number Qf (c.f. equation 16) with different plume characteristics.

Pr = Prandtal number

T = Temperature of the plume at any point inside the plume, K

T_o = Temperature of the plume at the release point, K

T_a = Temperature of the atmosphere, K

T_{ao} = Temperature of the atmosphere at release point, K

u = Plume velocity at any point in the plume in the direction of the tangent to the plume axis, m/s

u^* = Plume velocity on the plume axis in the direction of the tangent to the plume axis, m/s

u' = Entrainment velocity due to atmospheric turbulence, m/s

u_a = Wind velocity, m/s

u_v = Venting speed, m/s

X = Cartesian coordinate (Figure 1)

z = Cartesian coordinate (Figure 1)

p = Plume density at any point in the plume,

p_a = Density of air, kg/ m3

p_{ao} = Density of air at release point, kg /m^3

P_g = Density of gas, kg/m^3

p^* = Density difference between plume and atmosphere, kg/m^3

a_1 = Entrainment coefficient of a free jet

a_2 = Entrainment coefficient due to thermal stratification

a_3 = Entrainment coefficient due to atmospheric turbulence

λ = Turbulent Schemedit number

ϕ = Angle between plume axis to horizontal component

δ = Length of transition zone, m

Q_f = Dimensional number

REFERENCES

1. Abraham, G, (1970). Round buoyant jet in cross flow, *5th international Conf. on Water Pollution Research*, San Francisco.

2. Blewitt, D N, Yohn, J F, Koopman, R P, and Brown, T C, (1987). *AIChE Int. Conf Vapour Cloud Modelling*, Boston, Massachusetts, New York.

3. Bodurtha, F T, (1961). The behaviour of dense stack gases, *J. Air Pollution Contr. Asso*, Il, 431.

4. Briggs, G A, (1984). Plume rise and buoyancy effects, *In: Atmospheric science and power production (ed: RD*

Andersen) DOE/TIC 27601, Spring Field.

5. Carnahan, B, (1969). Applied numerical methods, *John Willy & Sons*, New York.

6. Colenbrander, G, (1980). A mathematical model for the transient behaviour of dense vapour clouds, *3rd Int Sym. on Loss Prevention and Promotion in the Process Industries*, Bassel.

7. Deaves, D M, (1983). Application of advanced turbulence models in determine the structure and dispersion of heavy gas cloud, *IUTAM symposium*, Delft.

8. Deaves, D M, (1992). Dense gas dispersion modelling, *J of Loss Prev. Process Ind*, 5(4), 219-227.

9. Eidsvik, K J, (1980). A model for heavy gas dispersion in the atmosphere. *Atmos. Environ.*, 14, 769-777.

10. England, WC, Teuscher, LH, Hauser, L E, and Freeman. B, (1978). Atmospheric dispersion of liquefied natural gas vapour clouds using SIGMET, a three- dimensional time-dependent hydrodynamics computer model, *Lecture notes heat transfer and fluid mechanics institute*, Washington state University.

11. Ermak, D L, and Chan, S T, (1985). A study of heavy gas effects on the dispersion of dense gases, 15 Inter. *Technical Meeting on Air Pollution Modelling and its Application*, St. louis, USA.

12. Fay, J A, and Zemba, S G, (1985). Dispersion of initially compact dense *gas Environ.*, 19(8), 1257.

13. Fay, J A, and Zemba, S G, (1986). Integral model of dense gas plume dispersion, *Atmos. Environ.*, 20(7), 1347.

14. Havens, J R, (1982). A description and computational assessment of SIGMET LNG vapour dispersion model, *J. Hazardous Materials*, 8, 181-210.

15. Hawthorne, WR, (1955). The growth of secondary circulation in friction flow. *Proc Camb. Phil. Sec.*, 51, 737.

16. Krogstad, P A, and Jacobsen, O, (1991). Dispersion of heavy gas, (Air pollution control), *Elsevier science publication*, 632.

17. Langlo, G K, and Schatzmann, M, (1991). Wind tunnel modelling of heavy gas dispersion., *Atmos. Environ..*, 25A, 1189.

18. McQuaid, J, (1986). Refinement of Estimates of conseequence of toxic vapour release, *Proc. IChmE Sym.*, Manchester.

19. Moore, G E, Milich, L B, and Liu, M K, (1988). Study of Plume behaviour using lidar and SF tracer at a flat and heavy site, *Atmos. Environ.*, 22, 1673.

20. Niewstadt, F T M, and Vand Dop, H, (1982). Atmospheric turbulence and air pollution modelling, *Reidel publishing company*, Boston, USA.

21. Niewstadt, F T M, (1992). A large -eddy simulation of a line source in a convective atmospheric boundary layer -II. Dynamics of a buoyant line source., *Atmos. Environ.*, 26 A, 499.

22. Ooms, G, (1972). A new method for the calculation of the plume path of gases emitted by a stack, *Atmos. Environ.*, 6, 899.

23. Ooms, G, Mahiue, A P, (1974). The plume path of vent gases, Loss prevention & safety promotion in process industries, *Elsevier science publication*, New York.

24. Ooms, G, Mahiue, A p, and Zelis, F, (1974). The plume path theory of vent gases heavier than air, *Proceeding of the first International Loss Prevention Symposium*, Hague/Delft, The Netherlands.

25. Ooms, G, and Duijm, N J, (1983). Dispersion of a stack plume heavier than air. *IUTAM Sym on Atmospheric Dispersion of Heavy Gases and Small Particles, Delft*, , The Netherlands,.

26. Puttock, J S, (1986). Comparison of Thorney Island data with prediction of HEGABOX/HEGADAS, *2nd symposium on heavy gas dispersion trials at Thorney Island,* Sheffield.

27. Riou, Y, (1986). Comparison between MERCURE -GL code calculations, wind tunnel measurements and Thorney Island field trials, *2nd symposium on heavy gas dispersion trials at Thorney Is/and, Sheffield.*

28. Rottman, J W,. Simpson, J E, Hunt, J C R, and Bitter, R E. (1985). *J Hazardous Material*, 1, 325.

29. Taft, J R, Ryne, M S, and Weston, D A, (1983). MARIAH a dispersion model for evaluating realistic heavy gas spills scenarios, *Proc AGA Transmission Conf,* seattle.

30. Tran, K T, and Liu, C Y, (1981). Development of a predictive dispersion modelling system for real-time emergency application, *5th symposium on turbulence diffusion and air pollution,* American met. Soc., Atlanta.

31. Van Ulden, A P, (1983). A new bulk model for dense gas dispersion two dimensional: two dimensional spread in still air, *IUTAM Sym on Atmospheric Dispersion of Heavy Gases and Small particles,* Delft.

32. Van Ulden, A P, and Holtslag, A A M, (1985). Estimation of atmosphere boundary layer parameters for diffusion application, *J. CI. App. Metrol.*, 25, 1609.

33. Van Ulden, A P, (1987). The spreading and mixing of a dense cloud in still air, *KNMI Afdeling Fysishe meterologie, Personal memorandum*, FM-87-11.

34. Weil, J C, (1988). Plume rise, (eds. A Venkatram, J C Wyngaard), *Amer. Metr. Soci., Boston,* USA.

7

Second Specialty Conference on Environmental Progress in the Petroleum & Petrochemical Industries
Saudi Arabian Section - Air & Waste Management Association
and Bahrain Society of Engineers
November 17-19, 1997, Manama, Bahrain

*MODELING AND SIMULATION OF 'HEAVY' GASES RELEASED BY PETROCHEMICAL INDUSTRIES**

FAISAL I. KHAN AND S.A. ABBASI
Risk Assessment Division
Centre for Pollution Control & Energy Technology
Pondicherry University, Pondicherry -605 014, India

ABSTRACT

Dispersion of several common 'heavy' gases (ethylene, propylene, isobutylene, natural gas, chlorine, and ammonia) has been modeled on the basis of empirical equations recently developed by us (Khan and Abbasi, 1997a;1997b) and has been validated by theoretical as well as experimental studies.

Studies have also been carried out to simulate the effect of venting speed (manipulated by injecting hot air with the released gas) on the plume dispersion. The study reveals that the effect of venting speed on dispersion is very pronounced and can be used to reduce the risk posed by the accidental luxury release of toxic/flammable gases. For example an increase of 20% in venting speed of chlorine (54.1 m/s) can reduce the distance up to which toxic concentration would occur by about 1100 meters.

INTRODUCTION

Petrochemical industries which often handle hazardous chemicals and operate reactors/storage vessels under extreme conditions of temperature and pressure are susceptible to accidents. The history of petrochemical industries is replete with several such accidents which have had catastrophic consequences (Lees, 1996). The hazardous (toxic and/or flammable) chemicals normally handled by petrochemical industries are in the form of liquids and gases (lighter-than/light-as-air, and heavier-than-air). To study the accidental release and dispersion of such chemicals one needs models that can handle various types of release scenarios. Modified plume path theory is one such model (Ooms and Duijm ,1983; Khan and Abbasi, 1997 a;1997b).

* Reproduced from Proceeding of Second Specialty Conference on Environmental Progress in the Petroleum & Petrochemical Industries, November 17-19, Bahrain,

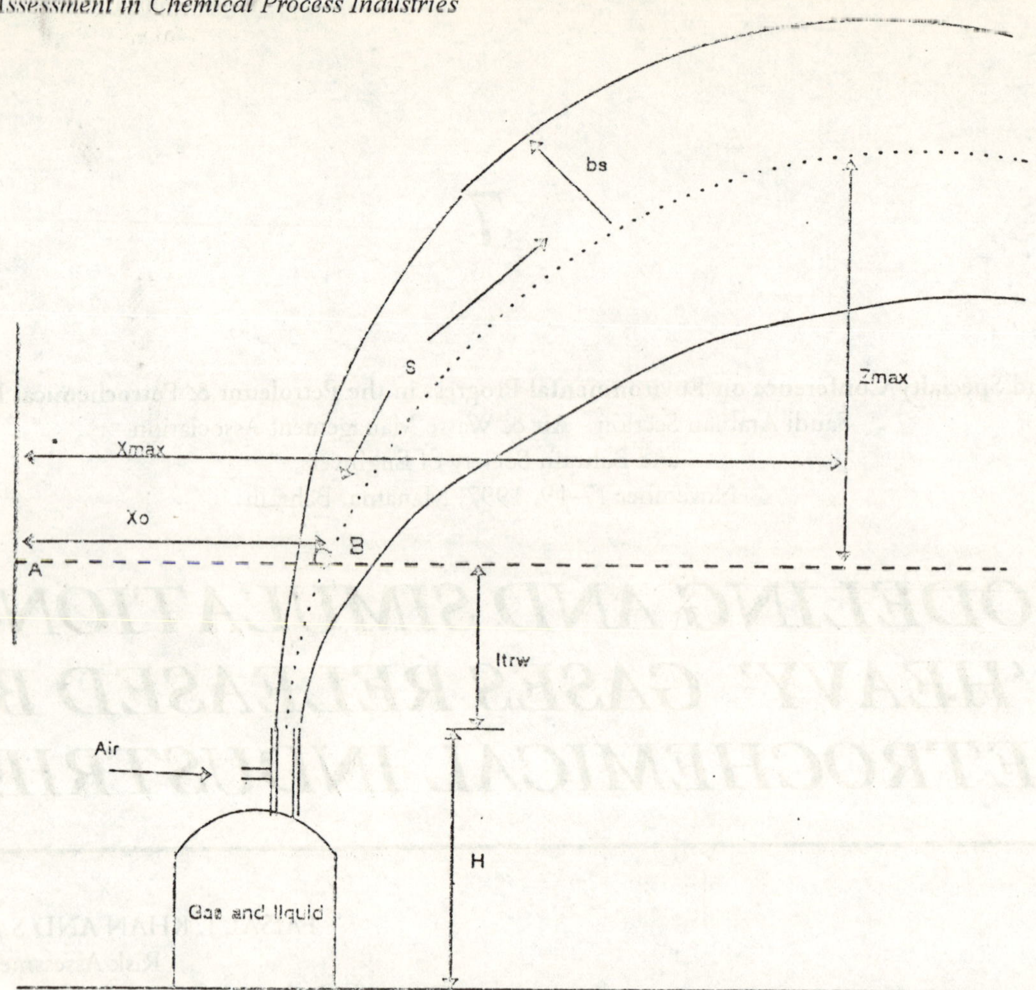

Figure 1. Illustrative figure showing coordinates of the plume as influnced by hot air injection.

Originally, plume path theory (PPT) was proposed by Ooms (1972) and has been used mainly to calculate the plume path of lighter-than-air and light-as-air gases escaping from stacks into the atmosphere at standard atmospheric temperature and pressure. Later this theory was extended to 'heavy' gases (of density higher than air; Ooms and Mahiue, 1974; Ooms *et al.* 1974) with a number of assumptions.

Recently we have modified the plume path theory to improve its versatility (Khan and Abbasi, 1997a). The resultant model, which has been validated with the data generated by the authors and others, overcomes several limitations which had thus far restricted the applicability of PPT. The features of the original PPT and the modifications done by us are summarized in Table 1. They have been detailed elsewhere (Khan and Abbasi,1997a;1997b).

We have subsequently developed and validated several empirical models to study the effect of various parameters on the dynamics of gaseous dispersion (Khan and Abbasi, 1997b).

In this paper the authors present the applications of the aforesaid models in controlling dispersion of flammable and/or toxic gases coming out of petrochemical industries, by injecting hot air into the gaseous plume at the latter's point of exit. The models aim to handle involuntary accidental release as well as voluntary strategic release (to avert accidents).

A brief description of the methodology is presented below.

OBJECTIVES

1. To study the dispersion after accidental or voluntary release, of hazardous gases common in most of the petrochemical industries. For this purpose we have taken a real-life case study of the storage unit of Paplani Petrochemical Limited, situated at Paplani, Gujrat, India. The release of the gases have been assumed to occur through the vent valve/pressure relief valve of the unit around 5 to 7 meter (including height of vessel and vent) above ground level, for six different chemicals stored in different vessels. The initial set of atmospheric and operating conditions used in the present study is given in Table 2.

2. To study the effect of increase in venting speed (by injecting hot inert air) over the dispersion process (distance up to which flammable/lethal concentration would occur).

METHODOLOGY

To generalise the effect of wind speed, density, and venting speed on the plume path, we have developed empirical equations. These equations predict the behavior of the plume variables (gas concentration in plume, plume density, local plume width, plume velocity) as a function of such variables as density of gas, venting speed, etc.

For this purpose a dimensionless number Q_f has been defined as:

$$Q_f = w/u_v*(\rho_a/\rho_{eff}) \quad (1)$$

$$p^* = A*\ln(s) + B$$

ü

$$A = -0.00395848*\log(Q_f) - 0.01925951$$

$$B = -0.16083 *\log(Q_f) + 0.091579$$

$$u^* = A*\ln(s) + B$$

$$A = 0.159874 + 0.960923 * Q_f - 1.24869*Q_f^2 + 0.3728 * Q_f^3$$

$$B = -0.47832 + 0.0418951 *Q_f + 0.153298 * Q_f^2$$

$$c^* = A*\ln(s) + B$$

$$A = -0.0161965 + 0.00543481 * Q_f - 0.00128631 * Q_f^2 \quad (2)$$

$$B = 0.183894 * \exp(-0.382484 * Q_f)$$

$$b_s = A*\ln(s) + B$$

$$A = 0.0157719 + 0.104969 * Q_f - 0.0347085 * Q_f^2$$

$$B = 0.953469 * Q_f^{0.22422}$$

$$T = A * \ln(s) + B$$

$$A = 3.67477 + 7.61097 * Q_f - 2.42655 * Q_f^2$$

$$B = -8.5476 - 58.7278 * Q_f + 26.7875Q_f^2$$

Table1. Redefinition and advancement in the assumption made in Oom's PPT model

Assumptions made in PPT (Ooms and cowrokers,1972 1974)	Modifications proposed by the authors
The mean flow velocity perpendicular to the main flow in the direction of the plume is negligible till a late stage of the plume movement	Secondary flow perpendicular to the plume axis is significant at much earlier stage as well
The velocity profile, density, and pollutant concentration are similar in all sections normal to the plume axis	none
Molecular transports is considered negligible in comparison with turbulent transports	Molecular transport has been treated as significant and taken into account in parameter estimation
Longitudinal turbulent transport is considered negligible compared with longitudinal convective transport	Both longitudinal as well as convective transports have been taken into account
------	Physical properties of venting gas have been considered as a function of downwind distance as well as atmospheric parameters

Effective plume height

The effective plume height is the height reached by the plume from the point of its exit from a stack/vent valve. The calculation of effective plume height assumes (as shown in Figure 1) that there is a virtual source of the plume at point A which is at a distance x_o upwind from the transition point B. This assumption allows for the mixing effect of the jet. The distance x_o is that which would be necessary to achieve the same concentration at the transition point if the mixing were done by the wind (Lees,1996). Then the rise of the plume is given as:

$$Z = 2K_7/w*(x^{1/2}- x_o^{1/2}) \qquad (3)$$

Subsequently maximum rise of the plume is estimated as:

$$Z_{max} = 2*K_7/w*(x_{max}^{1/2}- x_o^{1/2}) \qquad (4)$$

Where, $x_{max} = K_8*w + x_o$ and $K_8 = 200.0$; (Cude,1974), and (5)

$$K_7 = (g*Q/(2*\pi*Dc*\tan\phi*)*ABS((\rho_a-\rho_{eff})/\rho_a)) \text{ (Cude,1974)} \qquad (6)$$

The half angle of a plume (ϕ) from a stack is generally 5° or 6° so that $\tan\phi = 1$. The drag coefficient Dc, as estimated by Cude (1974), is 0.4.

Since length of the jet is inversely proportional to the root of momentum flux, the transition heights of the jet in still air conditions, *ltr* and in windy conditions, *ltrw* are related as:

$$ltrw = ltr/1.2 \qquad (7)$$

Finally the maximum effective rise of the plume is estimated using the following equation,

$$hpl = H + ltrw + Z_{max} \qquad (8)$$

Briggs (1984) and Hanna *et al* (1982) have further modified the equations of maximum and effective rise of the plume taking the temperature of venting gas into consideration. They have proposed equations:

$$Z_{max} = 4(m_o/sta)^{1/4} \qquad (9)$$

$$Z_{eff} = 2.44(m_o/sta)^{1/4} \qquad (10)$$

Where, stability is defined as, $sta = g/T(dT/dy+R)$, (12)

The outcome of all these equations with the modification of Briggs (1984) and Hanna *et al.* (1982) have been validated with experimental data for a range of distance 5 to 3,000 meter (Khan and Abbasi,1997a;

1997b). The results match well in the distance range 15 to 2,500 meter for the gases having effective density of plume higher than air at exit point.

Table 2. The study setting

Parameters	Values
Wind velocity	3.5 m/s
Climatic conditions	Cloudy evening
Atmospheric boundary layer	45 m
Friction velocity	0.435 m/s
Atmospheric temperature	22 oC
Atmospheric pressure	1.01 atm
Terrain of the area	Urban
Height of the source	5-7 m
Atmospheric stability	Slightly stable
Normal venting speed	45.15 m/s

SIMULATIONS: FLAMMABLE GASES

Ethylene

Ethylene is a highly flammable gas which is stored under high pressure (above saturation pressure). Building of further pressure in the storage unit may cause release of gas through vent valve forming a jet which may subsequently take the shape of a plume (Table 3). The profile of various plume parameters (plume width, plume velocity, and gas concentration, in the plume) as estimated by the model are plotted in Figure 2. It reveals that the value of the parameters change sharply in the initial downwind travel of the plume: the velocity increases, the concentration of the gas in the plume decreases and the plume width increases. Subsequently extent of change decreases. This happens because at the initial stage of travel of the plume, turbulence (eddies) are generated which causes rapid entrainment of air in the plume. Subsequently a layer is developed around the edges of the plume which suppresses further entrainment of air and hence slows down the rate of dilution. Eventhough at the initial stage the effective density of the plume is higher-than-air, it disperses swiftly. It is due to highly energized release (with a venting velocity of 45.10 m/s) which imparts momentum to air and causes fast entrainment of air. The lower flammable concentration (LFC) for ethylene has been observed at around ~385 m from the release point. The plume width at this distance is ~1.28 m. The flammable concentration occurs high above the ground level (around 10.45 meters).

Propylene

Propylene is another flammable gas mostly stored in large quantities under pressure. A continuous release of gas through vent valve/pressure relief valve about 7 m above the ground forms a plume. The behavior of plume variables reveals that the dispersion of propylene is sluggish compared to ethylene (Table 3). It is because the effective density of the propylene plume is higher than ethylene. The flammable zone has been observed over an area of 415 m radius from the release point. The release and dispersion of propylene poses considerable hazards as the flammable zone envelops a large area that is also close to the ground level (~7.45 meters).

Isobutylene

Isobutylene is a flammable gas stored in lesser quantities compared to ethylene and propylene. Release of vapors (gas with aerosol) through vent valve would form a plume of density higher than air, which would subsequently get diluted by entrainment of air. The behavior of dispersion parameters (Table 3) reveals a very slow dilution rate and hence building of flammable concentration over a large area. It is because:

i) a comparatively low venting speed would favor gravity-dominant dispersion due to the high density of the plume.

ii) relatively high density would favor formation of suppression layer around the plume edges which would inhibit entrainment of air and hence dilution.

Natural gas

Natural gas is a mixture of light flammable gases (such as methane and ethane) which is stored at saturation pressure. Release of natural gas through a narrow opening would form a plume (~12 meters above the ground level). The results of the model output for this gas show a relatively fast dispersion compared to propylene and isobutylene. The lower limit of flammable concentration would be observed at a distance ~90 m from point of release (at around 12.45 m above the ground level). It is because the effective density of this plume is low and the venting velocity is sufficiently high, allowing rapid entrainment of air, consequently swift dilution.

Table 3. Model output concerning dispersion of the gases

Chemicals	Parameter		Distance along down wind direction, meters				
			20	50	100	300	500
Flammable gases							
Ethylene	maximum plume rise	= 12.06 m					
	plume concentration*10 -2@ kg/m3		6.13	4.61	4.03	3.25	2.75
	plume width, m		0.870	1.051	1.171	1.263	1.343
Propylene	maximum plume rise	= 11.67 m					
	plume concentration 10 -2@ kg/m3		7.41	6.07	5.25	4.55	3.97
	plume width, m		0.600	0.831	1.022	1.173	1.295
Isobutylene	maximum plume rise	= 10.36 m					
	plume concentration 10 -2@ kg/m3		7.66	6.643	5.57	5.09	4.57
	plume width, m		0.554	0.684	0.794	0.904	0.976
Natural gas	maximum plume rise	= 12.58 m					
	plume concentration 10 -2@ kg/m3		6.79	5.07	3.56	1.75	0.83
	plume width, m		0.985	1.314	1.546	1.697	1.735
Toxic gases							
Chlorine	maximum plume rise	= 9.56 m					
	plume concentration 10 -6# kg/m3		5.09	4.12	3.32	2.96	2.54
	plume width, m		0.512	0.644	0.714	0.864	0.944
Ammonia	maximum plume rise	= 10.76 m					
	plume concentration 10 -6# kg/m3		4.15	2.19	1.23	0.54	0.03
	plume width, m		0.752	1.071	1.342	1.551	1.730

@ Concentration estimated at the plume axis
# Concentration estimated at the edge of the plume

SIMULATIONS: TOXIC GASES

Chlorine

Of the two toxic heavier-than-air gases studied here, chlorine (Cl_2) has the slowest rate of dispersion. Otherwise the trend observed with chlorine is similar to the trends seen with the other five gases. For any given distance, the rate of change in concentration and plume velocity as well as plume width are lower compared to the other toxic gas ammonia (Table 3). A!s chlorine is the most toxic of the gases studied here and is also the most sluggish to disperse, lethal concentrations of this gas would easily build-up over large areas and persist for long durations.

Ammonia

Ammonia is stored and processed in liquid state under refrigerated or pressurized conditions. When released, it forms an aerosol of ammonia liquid carried away as droplets along with ammonia vapor. As such ammonia gas has density (0.778 kg/m^3) lower-than-air but due to aerosol formation the effective density of the plume (released vapors with aerosol) becomes higher than air. Hence the dispersion of ammonia is generally treated as if it were a heavy gas.

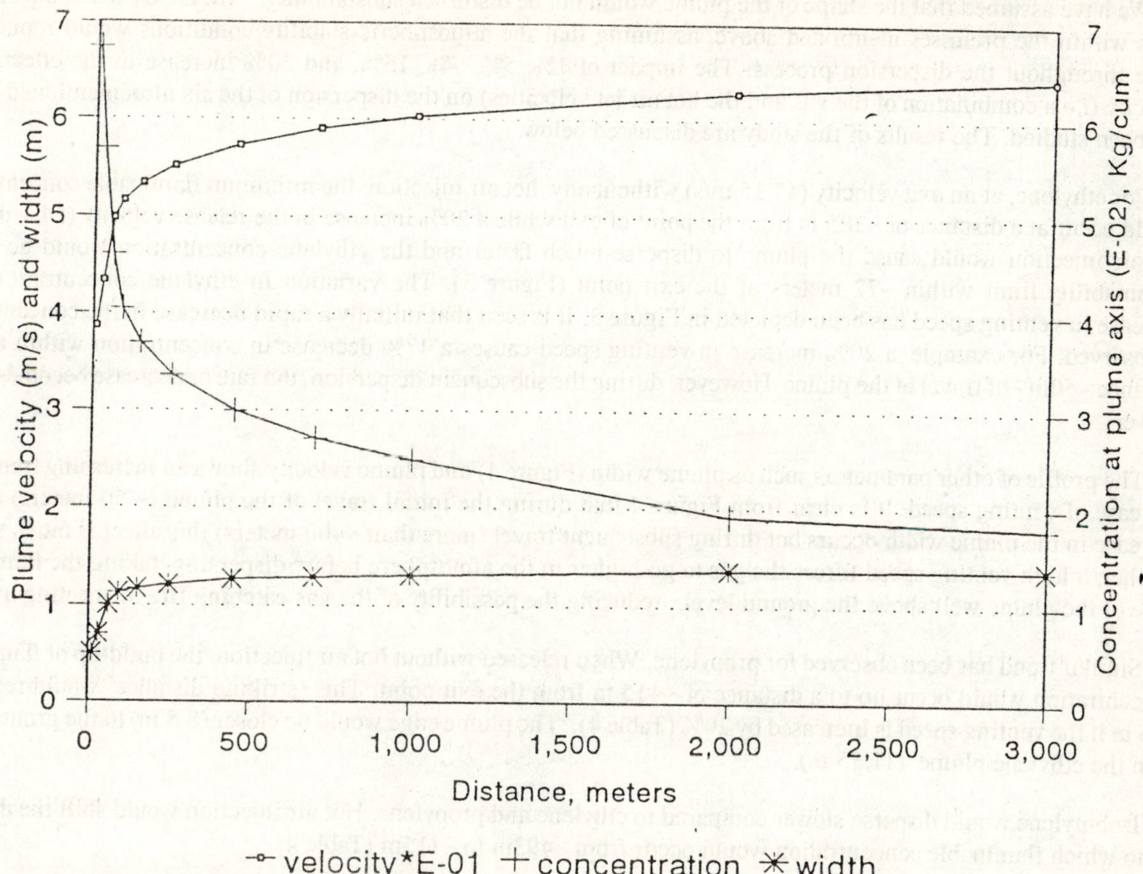

Figure 2. Comparison of plume path estimated by PPT with other models and experimental results.

The model output shows that ammonia disperses in a manner similar to chlorine but the trend is much more steep. The variations in plume width and plume velocity with distance are higher compared to Cl_2. It is because droplets of ammonia liquid settle faster due to gravity leading to the formation of gradient for mixing, subsequently facilitating dilution. At the initial stage of release the effective density of the plume is 3 times higher than air but by the time it travels 375 meters, the density drops to 21% of the initial value. The lethal concentration of the gas at the plume edge extends up to ~645 m downwind at about 9.31 m above the ground.

IMPACT OF HOT AIR INJECTION : FLAMMABLE GASES

In order to contain the damage, if these hazardous gases get released (accidentally, or voluntarily to control bigger accidents such as explosions), we have studied the option of increasing the release velocity by injecting hot air as a possible means of diluting the gases and facilitate their dispersion. Such an act has the following consequences:

a) hot inert air makes the released gas move higher and faster from the exit point; the effective release velocity is a combination of the velocities of hot inert air and the hazardous gas;

b) turbulence is generated which effects the density of the plume as well as its momentum distribution;

c) the high temperature of the air jet further disturbs the momentum balance by energizing the gas; however the air temperature should not be so high that it sparks a fire;

d) thorough mixing takes place at the maximum height of jet and along the downwind direction.

We have assumed that the shape of the plume would not be disturbed substantially. We have carried out simulations within the premises mentioned above, assuming that the atmospheric stability conditions would remain the same throughout the dispersion process. The impact of 1%, 5%, 7%, 15%, and 20% increase in the effective jet velocity (*i,e* a combination of the gas and the hot air jet velocities) on the dispersion of the six aforementioned gases, has been studied. The results of the study are discussed below.

For ethylene, at an exit velocity (45.15 m/s) without any hot air injection, the minimum flammable concentration would occur at a distance of ~385 m from the point of exit while a 20% increase in the release velocity (54.1 m/s) by hot air injection would cause the plume to disperse much faster and the ethylene concentration would go below flammability limit within ~77 meters of the exit point (Figure 3). The variation in ethylene concentration with increase in venting speed has been depicted in Figure 3. It is seen that initially a rapid decrease in the concentration is observed. For example, a 20% increase in venting speed causes a 47% decrease in concentration within a short distance - 50m - of travel of the plume. However, during the subsequent dispersion, the rate of decrease becomes much slower.

The profile of other parameters such as plume width (Figure 4) and plume velocity shows an increasing trend with increase of venting speed. It is clear from Figure 4 that during the initial travel of the plume (~ 50 meters) a large increase in the plume width occurs but during subsequent travel (more than ~400 meters) this effect is much slower. Further, a high venting speed forces the gas to go higher in the atmosphere before dispersing, taking the flammable zone of the plume well above the ground level, reducing the possibility of the gas catching fire by meeting a spark.

Similar trend has been observed for propylene. When released without hot air injection, the build-up of flammable concentration would occur up to a distance of ~415 m from the exit point. This 'striking distance' would reduce to ~96 m if the venting speed is increased by 20% (Table 4). The plume edge would be closer (8.5 m) to the ground level than the ethylene plume (11.35 m).

Isobutylene would disperse slower compared to ethylene and propylene. Hot air injection would shift the distance up to which flammable concentration would occur from ~493m to ~115m (Table 4).

The results for natural gas reveal that at the initial exit velocity (45.1 m/s), the flammable concentration occurs up to observed at ~90 m (about 12.45 m above the ground). It is because the effective density of natural gas is lower than all other flammable gases studied here. An increase of 20% in venting speed (54.1 m/s) would make the gas shoot up high enough in the atmosphere to drastically reduce the probability of it catching fire.

Table 4. Impact of change in venting speed on `striking distance' and plume width

Chemicals	Parameter	Percent increase in venting speed				
		1%	5%	7%	15%	20%
Flammable gases						
Ethylene	distance of occurrence of flammable concentration,m	332	260	200	125	77
	plume width@, m	1.01	1.29	1.41	1.85	2.03
Propylene	distance of occurrence of flammable concentration,m	375	295	221	154	96
	plume width, m	0.95	1.21	1.33	1.77	1.93
Is Isobutylen	distance of occurrence of flammable concentration,m	421	326	279	177	115
	plume width, m	0.71	1.13	1.25	1.63	1.85
Natural gas	distance of occurrence of flammable concentration,m	45	19	4	-	-
	plume width, m	1.35	1.67	1.89	-	-
Toxic gases						
Chlorine	distance of occurrence of toxic concentration, m	1345	1060	815	634	380
	plume width, m	1.11	1.37	1.46	1.71	1.91
Ammonia	distance of occurrence of toxic concentration, m	545	378	235	107	65
	plume width, m	1.39	1.63	1.79	2.03	2.27

@ plume width where flammable/toxic concentration ceases

IMPACT OF HOT AIR INJECTION : TOXIC GASES

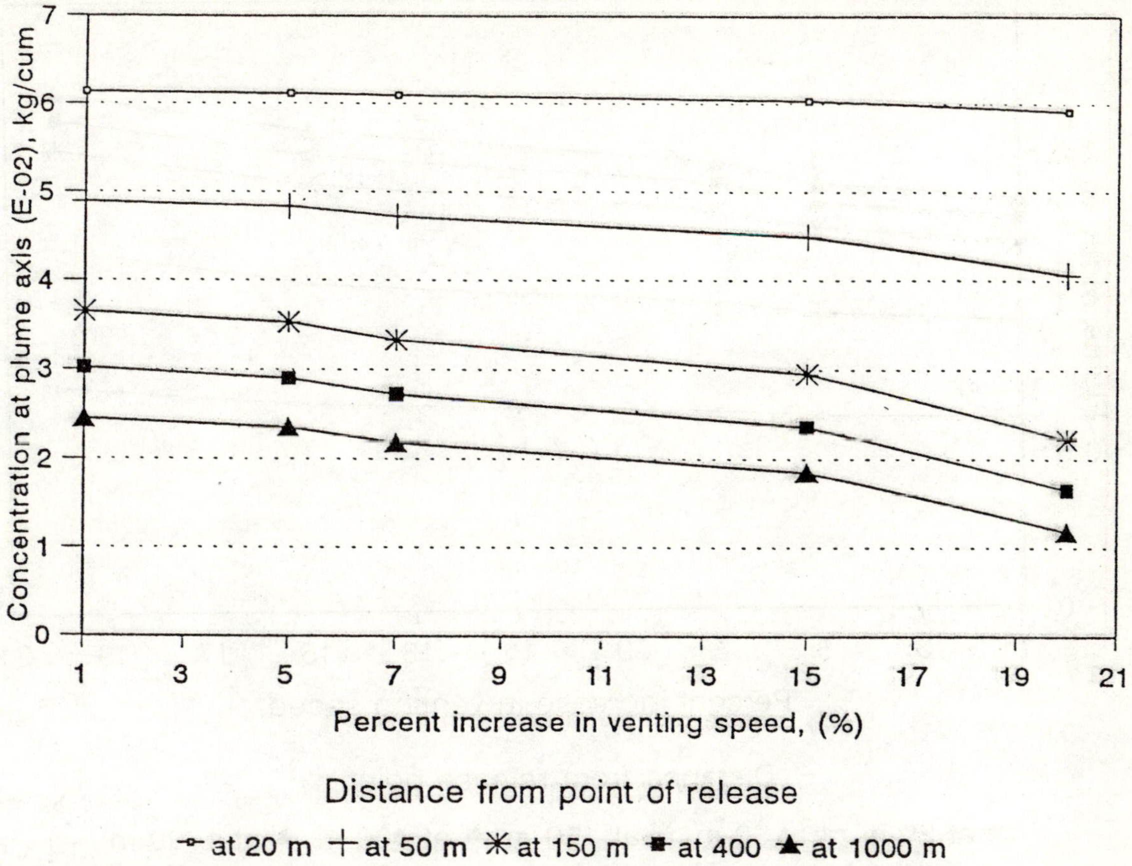

Figure 3. Illustrative figure showing change in concentration at plume axis with increase in venting speed (for ethylene)

The study of the chlorine plume reveals that at a venting speed of 45.1 m/s (without hot air injection) the lethal concentration load (based on immediate fatal concentration for 30 minutes exposure; Contini *et al.* 1991; Lees, 1996) would be observed up to a distance ~1450 m from the point of release in downwind direction. This 'striking distance' would shrink to ~380 m when the venting speed is increased by 20%. Moreover, the plume edge in the later case would be ~ 8.12 m above from the ground level. This would further reduces the probability of the gas coming in direct contact of living organisms.

Ammonia would disperse faster than chlorine. The lethal concentration (based on immediate fatal concentration for 30 minutes exposure) if ammonia is released at 45.1 m/s would spread across ~645 m downwind, this distance would reduce to ~67 m for 20% increase in the gas exit speed. The plume edge would be farther away from the ground level compared to chlorine. The possible reasons are:

a) a comparatively lower effective density of ammonia,

b) greater impact of hot air injection on the effective density of the plume and momentum distribution.

CONCLUSION

We have presented empirical equations developed by us on the basis of Modified Plume Path Theory (MPPT) reported earlier by us. The MPPT, which was duly validated by us, enables one to study the dispersion of heavier-than-air, lighter-than-air, and light-as-air gases. It is especially useful in assessing the risks posed by accidental release of hazardous gases.

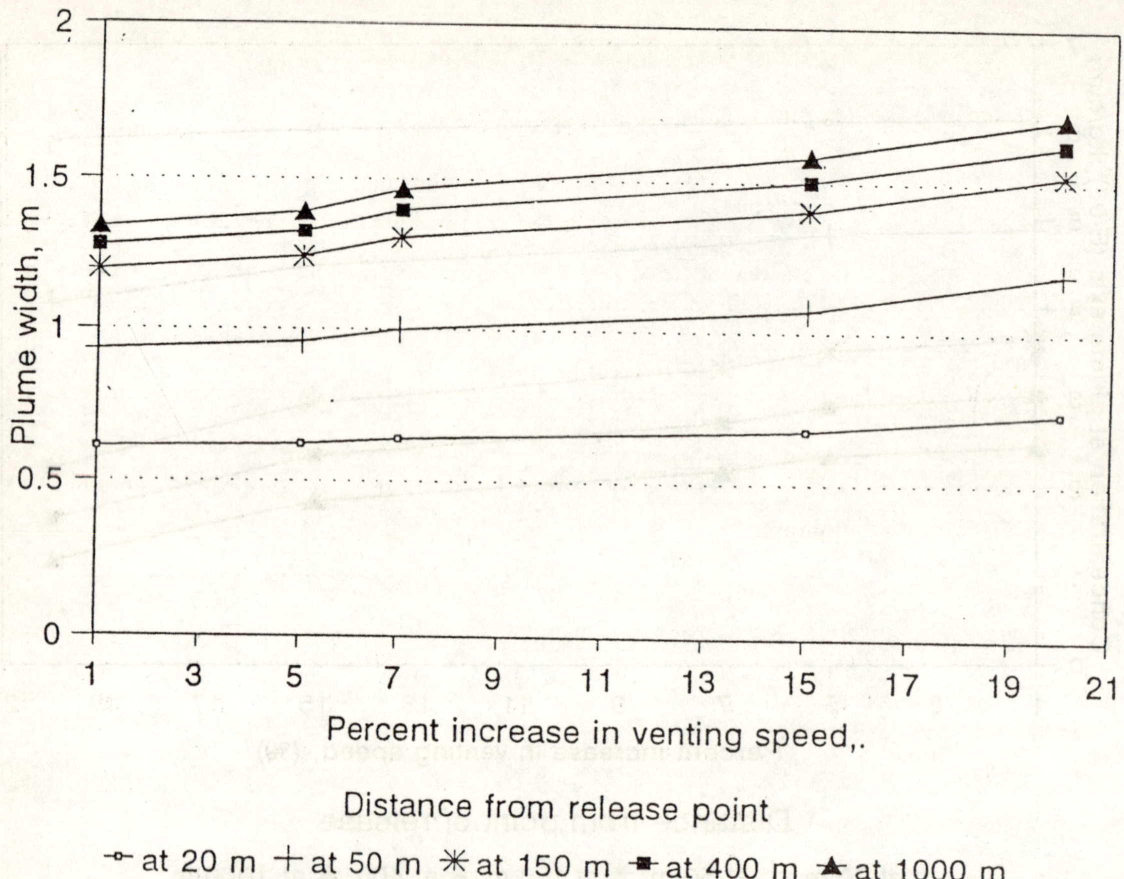

Figure 4. Illustrative figure showing variation of plume width and plume velocity with distance of travel (for ethylene).

The empirical equations described in this paper have been applied to possible accidental release of six hazardous gases from their storage vessels. It is seen that isobutylene release is the most hazardous as it would result in the formation of a flammable cloud covering a large distance downwind.

The effects of decreasing the concentration and increasing the exiting velocity of the gases by injecting hot inert air at the point of exit were simulated. The studies reveal that a) the plumes of hazardous gases can be raised higher (thereby reducing the probability of they catching fire); b) the rate of dilution of the hazardous gases in the plume can be made faster; and c) the 'distance of impact' (in other words 'striking distance') can be significantly reduced, by hot air injection. For example, an increase of 20% in venting speed of isobutylene by hot air injection raises the plume edge to an additional above ground and reduces its 'striking distance' by ~370 m. Similarly an increase in the venting speed of chlorine by 20% increases the plume height by 0.95m and reduces the range of lethal toxic concentration build-up by ~1100 m.

ACKNOWLEDGMENT

Authors are thankful to All India Council of Technical Education (AICTE) for sponsoring "Unit for Computer Aided Environmental Management (CAEM)" which made possible this study.

LIST OF SYMBOLS

b_s = local characteristics width, m

c^* = concentration of gas on the plume axis, kg/m^3

s = distance along the plume axis from the release point to a certain point, m

T = temperature of the plume at any point inside the plume, K

u^* = plume velocity on the plume axis in the direction of the tangent to the plume axis, m/s

u_v = venting speed, m/s

ρ_a = density of air, kg/m^3

ρ_{eff} = effective density of plume/jet, kg/m^3

Q_f = dimensional number

Z = vertical distance above transition point, m

Z_{max} = maximum rise of plume, m

Z_{eff} = effective rise of plume, m

x_{max} = lateral distance where maximum rise of plume occur, m

x = lateral distance along down wind direction, m

x_o = lateral distance from virtual source to transition point, m

w = wind velocity, m/s

Q = volumetric flow rate of gas, m^3/s

g = gravitational acceleration , m/s^2

Dc = drag coefficient

ltr = transition height in still air, m

ltrw = transition height in windy conditions, m

hpl = total effective height reached by the plume, m

H = height of the vent, m

m_o = momentum flux at exit point

R = dry adiabatic laps rate, °C/m

y = vertical distance, m

ϕ = half angle of the plume from the stack

REFRENCES

1. Briggs, G A, *Plume rise by buoyancy effects*, Atmospheric science and power production, **1984** , p.327.

2. Contini, S, Amendola, A, and Ziomas, I, *Benchmark exercise on major hazard analysis, Commission of the European Communities*, Joint Research Centre, ISPRA, Itlay, **1991**, p2.

3. Cude, A L,. Dispersion of gases related to atmosphere from relief valves, Chemical Engineer, **1974**, 290, p 629.

4. Hanna, S R, Briggs, G A, and Hosker, R P,. Handbook on atmospheric diffusion, *Report DOE-TIC 11223 Atmos. turbulence and diffusion lab*, Dept. of Energy, Washington, D.C., **1982.**

5. Khan, F I, and Abbasi, S A, Modelling of dispersion of heavy gas based on modification in Plume Path Theory, Atmos Environ (in press), **1997a**.

6. Khan, F I, and Abbasi, S A, "Application of the recently modified PPT on the dispersion of some heavy gases", *10th regional IUAPPA conference*, Gumu, Ssuyu, Istanbul, Turkey, 23-26 September, **1997b**

7. Lees, F P, *Loss prevention in process industries*, Butterworths, London, **1996**.

8. Ooms, G, A new method for the calculations of the plume path of gases emitted by stack, Atmos Environ, **1972**, 6 , p 899.

9. Ooms, G, and Mahiue, A P, The plume path of vent gases, *Loss prevention and safety promotion in process industries*, Elsevier, New York, **1974**.

10. Ooms, G, Mahiue, A P, and Zelis, F. The plume path theory of vent gases heavier than air, *Proceeding of the first International loss prevention symposium*, Delft, The Netherlands, 2-3 May, **1974**.

11. Ooms, G an Duijm, N J, Dispersion of stack plume heavier than air, *Atmospheric dispersion of heavy gases and small particluates symposium*, Delft, The Netherlands, 1983

¨ Reproduced from Proceeding of *Second Specialty Conference on Environmental Progress* in the Petroleum & Petrochemical Industries

8

APPLICATIONS OF THE RECENTLY MODIFIED PLUME PATH *THEORY ON THE DISPERSION OF SOME HEAVY GASES*[**]

Dispersion of several common 'heavy' gases (sulphur dioxide, ammonia, hydrogen sulphide, and chlorine) has been modelled on the basis of modifications in plume path theory recently done by us (Khan and Abbasi, 1997). The model takes into account, among other things, the variations in temperature, density, and specific heat during the movement of the heavy gas plume. Studies have also been carried out to simulate the effects of wind speed, density of gas, and venting speed on the plume dispersion. Based on the simulations a set of empirical equations have been developed. The equations have been validated by theoretical as well as experimental studies.

Release rate is found to be one of the most important parameter which dictate plume behaviour and geometry.

Key words : gaseous dispersion, heavy gases, plume path theory, industrial hazards

INTRODUCTION

Plume path theory (PPT) was proposed by Ooms (1972) and has been used mainly to calculate the plume path of lighter-than-air and light-as-air gases escaping from stacks into the atmosphere at atmospheric temperature and pressure. Later this theory was extended to 'heavy' gases (of density higher than air; Ooms *et al.* 1974) with a number of assumptions. .

Numerous applications of the PPT have been reported, for example, Rottman *et al.*. (1985) and McQuaid (1986) have used the theory for analysing toxic gas dispersion; Niewstadt (1992), Blewitt *et al.* (1987) and Weil (1988) have used the same for vapour cloud modelling; and Ooms and Duijm (1983) have used it to estimate the dispersion of heavy gases coming out at high momentum from stacks. The theory has also been the basis of commercial packages PLUME and HFPLUME. But in-spite of the obvious potential of Ooms' theory, it has not enjoyed wider applicability because the main assumptions which had limited its applicability, have not yet been overcome. Recently these authors have modified Ooms's theory to significantly enhance its range, accuracy, and precision (Table 1). Most significantly we have enabled application of the theory to 'heavy gases' which is a much less explored domain of air quality modelling than dispersion of lighter-than-air or light-as-air gases. Based on simulations done with the help of model

* Reproduced from *Proceeding of Symposium on Air Quality Management at Urban, Regional, and Global scales, September 23-26, 1997, Turkey.*

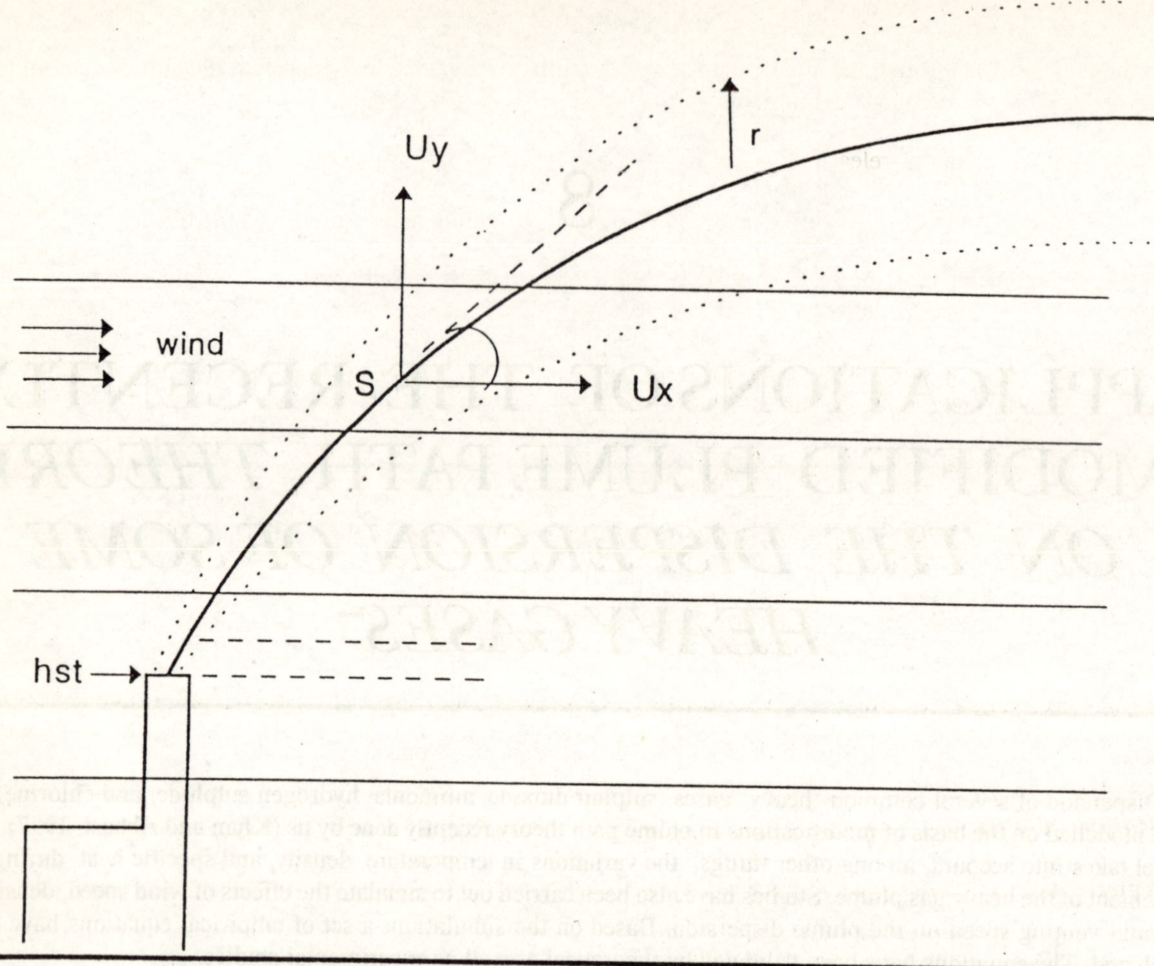

Figure 1. The plum coordinates as used in the present study.

developed by us, we have evolved a few empirical relations to study the effect of atmospheric operating variables (wind velocity, venting speed, venting temperature, atmospheric temperature, etc.) over dispersion. These equations enable air pollution dispersion studies with less computational costs and greater accuracy.

MODIFIED PPT MATHEMATICAL MODEL

In the earlier form of PPT (Ooms and co-workers, 1972; 1974; 1983) only three parameters (u,r,c) have been considered as significant. In the present work temperature also has been taken as one of the dominant parameters. Incorporating the aspects of plume density and temperature, and specific heat, the plume characteristics can be written as:

$$u(s,r,\varphi) = u_a\cos\varphi + u^* \exp(-r^2/b_s^{\,2}) \quad (1)$$

$$\rho(s,r,\varphi) = \rho_a + \rho^* \exp(-r^2/\lambda^2 b_s^{\,2}) \quad (2)$$

$$c(s,r,\varphi) = c^* * \exp(-r^2/\lambda^2 * b_s^{\,2}) \quad (3)$$

$$T(s,r,\varphi) = T_a + \exp(-r^2/Pr^2 * b_s^{\,2}) \quad (4)$$

Where $u(s,r,\varphi)$, $\rho(s,r,\varphi)$, $c(s,r,\varphi)$ represent the values of the variables at an arbitrary point in the plume; u^*, r^*, c^* denote the values of variables relative to the surroundings on the plume axis in the direction at a tangent to the plume axis (Figure 1).

Plume path

As the plume flows through the atmosphere, air is entrained. We have tried to represent the entrainment in terms of mass flow equations keeping the following facts in mind :

a) in the vicinity of vent or release point venting velocity is higher than wind velocity,

b) at a sufficiently long distance downwind, the velocity of the plume may equal the wind velocity,

c) atmospheric turbulence is one of the most effective factors causing entrainment.

Mass flow equation

$$d(\int \rho u 2\pi r dr)/ds = 2\pi b_s \rho_a \{\alpha_1 |u^*| + \alpha_2 u_a |\sin\varphi| \cos\varphi + \alpha_3 u\} \quad (5)$$

The values of entrainment coefficient $\alpha_1 = 0.0762$, $\alpha_2 = 0.61$, and $\alpha_3 = 1.0$ have been taken from Krogstad and Jacobsen (1991).

Component Mass Balance :

The component mass balance over a cross section of plume is worked out as :

$$d(\int c u 2\pi r dr) / ds = 0 \quad (6)$$

This implies that no gas is assumed to be present in the atmosphere outside the plume.

Momentum Balance :

In plume, the momentum occurs mainly due to

a) entrainment of air,

b) force exerted by wind.

Keeping these in view the momentum balance in downwind direction can be written as :

$$d(\int(\rho u^2 \cos\varphi 2\pi r dr))/ds = 2\pi b_s \rho_a u_a \{\alpha_1 |u^*| + \alpha_2 u_a |\sin\varphi| \cos\varphi + \alpha_3 u\} + C_d \pi b_s \rho_a u_a^2 |\sin^3\varphi| \quad (7)$$

The momentum balance in the cross wind direction is a combination of

- density spread,
- drag force exerted by wind.

The final balance equation can be written as :

$$d(\int(\rho u^2 |\sin\varphi| 2\pi r dr))/ds = \int g(\rho - \rho_a) 2\pi r dr - C_d \pi b_s \rho_a u_a^2 \sin^2\varphi \cos\varphi \quad (8)$$

Energy Balance :

The energy balance for the plume implies that the amount of heat emitted by the gas per unit time is conserved with respect to a chosen reference. So, for a reference temperature T_{ao}, the energy balance equations can be written as:

$$d(\int \rho u c_p (T - T_{ao}) 2\pi r dr) / ds = 2\pi b_s \rho_a c p_a (T_a - T_{ao}) \{\alpha_1 |u^*| + \alpha_2 u_a |\sin\varphi| \cos\varphi + \alpha_3 u\} \quad (9)$$

If it is assumed that air and vent gas obey the ideal gas law, than the temperatures (plume and air temperature) can

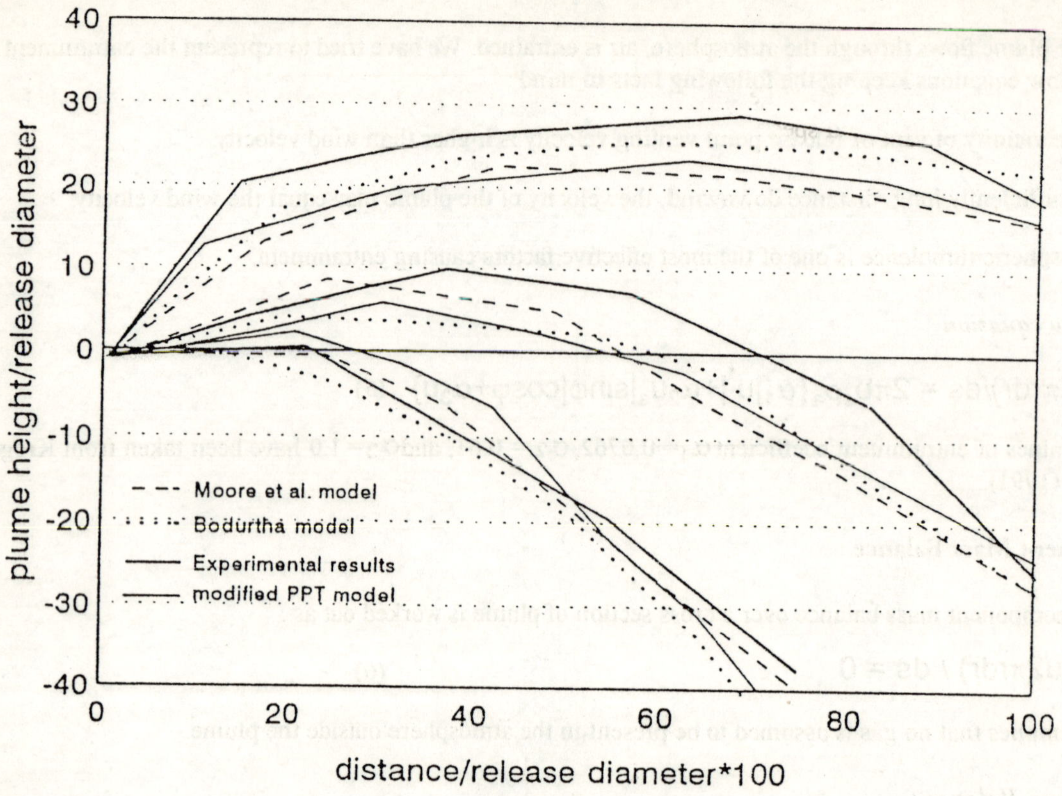

Figure 2. Comparison of plume path estimated by PPT with other models and experimental results.

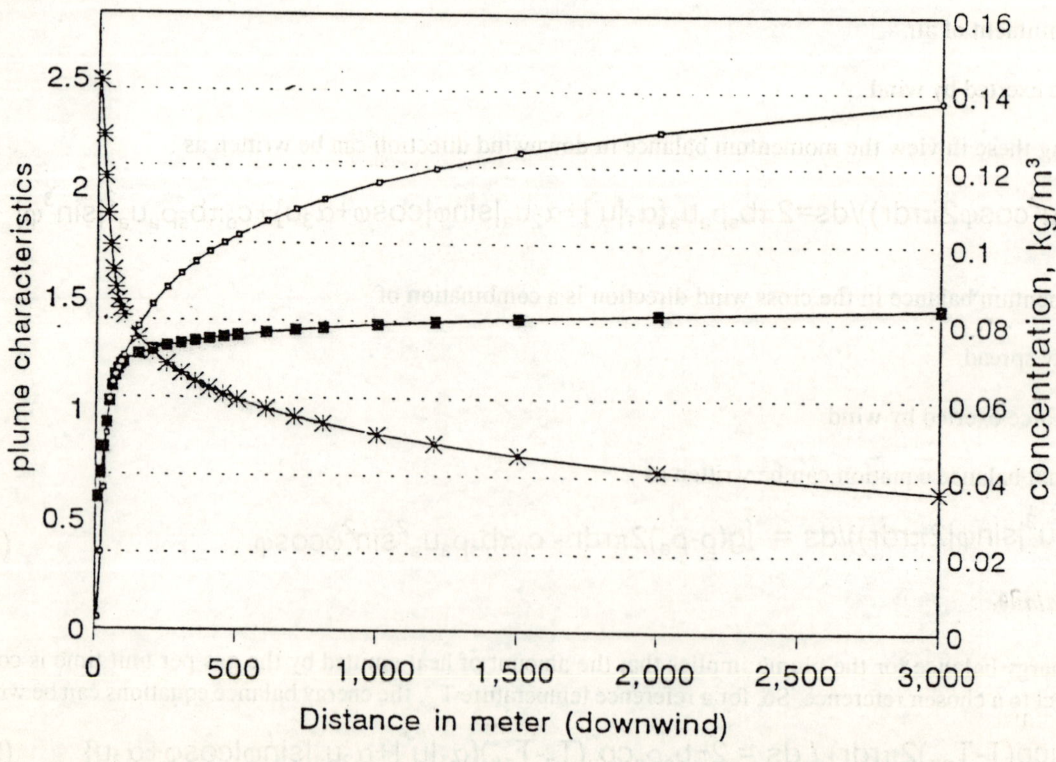

Figure 3. Variation of the plume parameters along downwind distance for sulfur dioxide

be expressed as

$$T = M_w P/(R\rho) \text{ and } T_a = M_{wa} P/(R\rho_a) \tag{10}$$

Where, M_w and M_{wa} represent molecular weights of plume (air and gas) and air respectively at any point in the plume. As molecular weight and specific heat differ, unlike what was assumed in the original PPT (Ooms, 1972), these variables can be expressed as:

$$M_w = M_{wo} cT / (c_o T_o) + M_{wa}(1\text{-}cT/(c_o T_o)) \tag{11}$$

$$cp = \{M_{wo} cp_o cT/(c_o T_o) + M_{wa} cp_a (1\text{-}cT/(c_o T_o))\} / M_w \tag{12}$$

Combining the above energy balance equations with molecular weight variation and specific heat variation, the final equation can be written as :

$$d(\int M_w cp/(M_{wa} cp_a) * u[1\text{-}\rho/\rho_{ao}\{1+ c^*\rho_o/(c_o\rho)(M_{wa}/M_{wo}\text{-}1)\}]2\pi r dr)/ds =$$

$$2\pi^* b_s * (1\text{-}\rho_a/\rho_{ao})\{\alpha_1|u^*|+\alpha_2^* u_a|\sin\varphi|\cos\varphi+\alpha_3 u\} \tag{13}$$

SOLUTION OF THE MODEL and VALIDATION

By substituting the similarity profile to these conservation equations, integrals can be calculated by a suitable numerical integration technique-here we have used Siphons-1/3 technique. Sets of non-linear simultaneous equations have been solved by using Newton-Raphson method coupled with L-U decomposition technique. The model has been solved for and different atmospheric operating conditions are presented in Table 2. The results of the models have been validated against experimental data (Khan and Abbasi, 1997). The comparison of the plume path (height of plume rise) obtained by our model with the results reported by Bodurtha (1961) and Moore *et al.* (1988) and the experimental results (Khan and Abbasi, 1997) are presented in Figure 2. Good qualitative as well as quantitative agreements have been observed.

Parametric effect

To generalise the effect of wind speed, density and venting speed on the plume path, we have developed some empirical equations. These equations directly predict the behaviour of plume variables (gas concentration in plume, plume density, local plume width, plume velocity) with other operating variables viz : density of gas, venting speed, etc.

For this purpose a dimensionless number Q_f has been defined as:

$$Q_f = u_a/u_v^*(\rho_a/\rho) \tag{14}$$

$\rho^* = A^*\ln(s) + B$

$A = -0.00395848^*\log(Q_f) - 0.01925951$

$B = -0.16083 ^*\log(Q_f) + 0.091579$

$u^* = A^*\ln(s) + B$

$A = 0.159874 + 0.960923 * Q_f - 1.24869^*Q_f^2 + 0.3728 * Q_f^3$

$B = -0.47832 + 0.0418951 ^*Q_f + 0.153298 * Q_f^2$

$c^* = A^*\ln(s) + B$

$A = -0.0161965 + 0.00543481 * Q_f - 0.00128631 * Q_f^2$ (15)

$B = 0.183894 * \exp(-0.382484 * Q_f)$

$b_s = A*\ln(s) + B$

$A = 0.0157719 + 0.104969 * Q_f - 0.0347085 * Q_f^2$

$B = 0.953469 * Q_f^{0.22422}$

$T = A * \ln(s) + B$

$A = 3.67477 + 7.61097 * Q_f - 2.42655 * Q_f^2$

$B = -8.5476 - 58.7278 * Q_f + 26.7875Q_f^2$

The outcome of equations have been validated with experimental data for a range of distance (20 to 5,000 meters). The results match well in the distance range 50 to 3,500 meter.

Table 1. Redefinition and advancement in the assumption made in Oom's PPT model

Assumptions made in PPT (Ooms and cowrokers,1972; 1974)	*Modifications proposed by the authors*
The mean flow velocity perpendicular to the main flow in the direction of the plume is negligible till a late stage of the plume movement	Secondary flow perpendicular to the plume axis is significant at much earlier stage as well
The velocity profile, density, and pollutant concentration are similar in all sections normal to the plume axis	none
Molecular transports is considered negligible in comparison with turbulent transports	Molecular transport has been treated as significant and taken into account in parameter estimation
Longitudinal turbulent transport is considered negligible compared with longitudinal convective transport	Both longitudinal as well as convective transports have been taken into account
———	Physical properties of venting gas have been considered as a function of downwind distance as well as atmospheric parameters

RESULT AND DISCUSSION

The simulation study reveals that the plume width and the plume velocity increase in the downwind direction, while density of the plume, temperature of gas (above atmospheric temperature) and gas concentration decrease downwind. We see that the trend diminishes as the length of travel of the plume increases. This has been observed for all the four gases studied (ammonia, hydrogen sulphide, sulphur dioxide, chlorine). The observations on the individual gases are summarised below.

Sulphur dioxide

Industries commonly store sulphur dioxide (SO_2) in large quantities in pressurised vessels. Possible release of SO_2 through pressure relief valve or accidental opening threatens the plant personnel as well as the surrounding population. In several industries sulphur dioxide is continuously or semi-continuously purged to atmosphere. A continuous pressurised release of SO_2 has been studied here. As the density of SO_2 is much higher (2.92 kg/m^3) than air, its plume resists entrainment of air (dilution) and travels longer distance downwind than a plume of a lighter gases would. However, due to the fast release rate (45 m/s) and consequent turbulence an initial mixing occurs (to a distance up to 600 m) but further mixing is limited and only a change of 20 % concentration occurs over the next 1500 m (Figure 3). It is also evident form Figure 3 that not only concentration but plume width also first increases very rapidly during the initial phase of dispersion but later the rate of increase slows down drastically. The plume velocity in the initial stage rises sharply upto a distance of 750 m due to the fast movement of air which dictates the flow of the plume. Subsequently the trend diminishes as the plume velocity approaches the wind velocity. For a release rate 45 m/s under the atmospheric conditions given in Table 2 the lethal concentration (threshold lethal value-

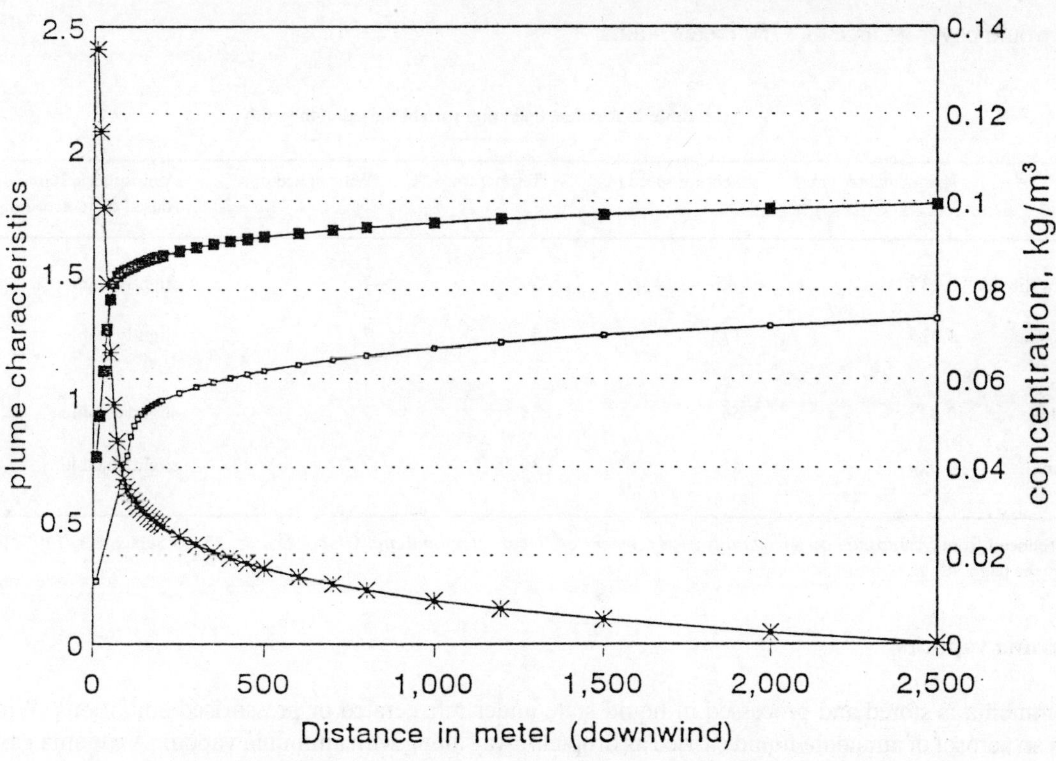

Figure 4. Variation of the plume parameters along downwind distance for ammonia.

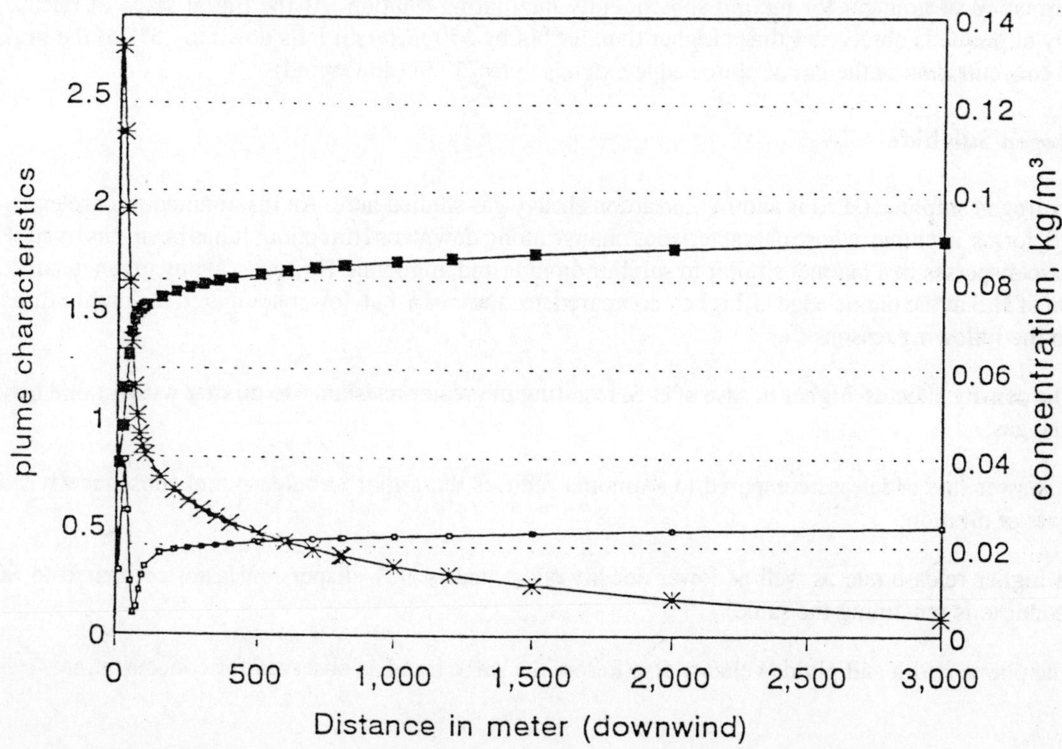

Figure 5. Variation of the plume parameters along downwind distance for hydrogen sulfide

TLV) would cover an area of 1750 meter radius.

Table 2. Ambient operating variables used in the study

Gas	*Vent diameter* m	Venting speed m/s	Temperature °C	Wind speed m/s	Atmospheric stability (based on meteorological data)
Sulphur dioxide	0.037	45	50	7	slightly stable
Ammonia	0.025	125	5	7	slightly stable
Hydrogen sulphide	0.025	65	25	7	slightly stable
Chlorine	0.020	45	35	7	slightly stable

" Reproduced from *Symposium on Air Quality Management at Urban, Regional and Global Scales*, 23-26 September, 1997, Istanbul, Turkey, (kindly see page A3)

Ammonia vapours

Ammonia is stored and processed in liquid state under refrigerated or pressurised conditions. When released it forms an aerosol of ammonia liquid carried as droplets away along with ammonia vapour. Ammonia gas has a density (0.778 kg/m^3) lower than air but due to aerosol formation the effective density of the gas (with aerosol) becomes higher than air. Hence the dispersion of ammonia is generally treated as dispersion of a heavy gas and we have employed the same equations we had used in the sulphur dioxide study. It is seen (Figure 4) that ammonia disperses in a manner similar to SO_2 but the trend is much more steep. The variations in plume width and plume velocity with distance are higher compared to SO_2 . It is because droplets of ammonia liquid settle faster due to gravity leading to the formation of gradient for mixing subsequently facilitating dilution. At the initial stage of release the effective density of plume is observed 4 times higher than air but by 650 meters it falls down to 25% of the initial value. The lethal concentration of the gas at plume edge extends upto 750 m (downwind).

Hydrogen Sulphide

Hydrogen sulphide (H_2S) is another hazardous heavy gas studied here. An instantaneous jet release (1.54 Kg/m^3) of H_2S forms a plume whose characteristics change along downwind direction. It has been observed (Figure 5) that H_2S also disperses in a manner similar to sulphur dioxide and ammonia. However, at any given distance the concentration of H_2S at the plume edge is higher compared to ammonia but lower compared to sulphur dioxide. It may be due to the following reasons :

i) the density effect is higher in case of H_2S, resulting in greater resistance to mixing with air and hence dilution of the gas;

ii) a slower rate of release compared to ammonia reduces the initial turbulence and subsequently slows down the rate of dilution;

iii) a higher release rate as well as lower density effect makes H_2S dispersion faster compared to SO_2 (all other conditions remaining the same).

The plume width and plume velocity also follow the same trend as observed for concentration.

Chlorine

Of the four hazardous gases discussed in this work, chlorine (Cl_2) has the slowest rate of dispersion. Otherwise the trend observed with chlorine is similar to the trends seen with the other three gases. For any given distance, the

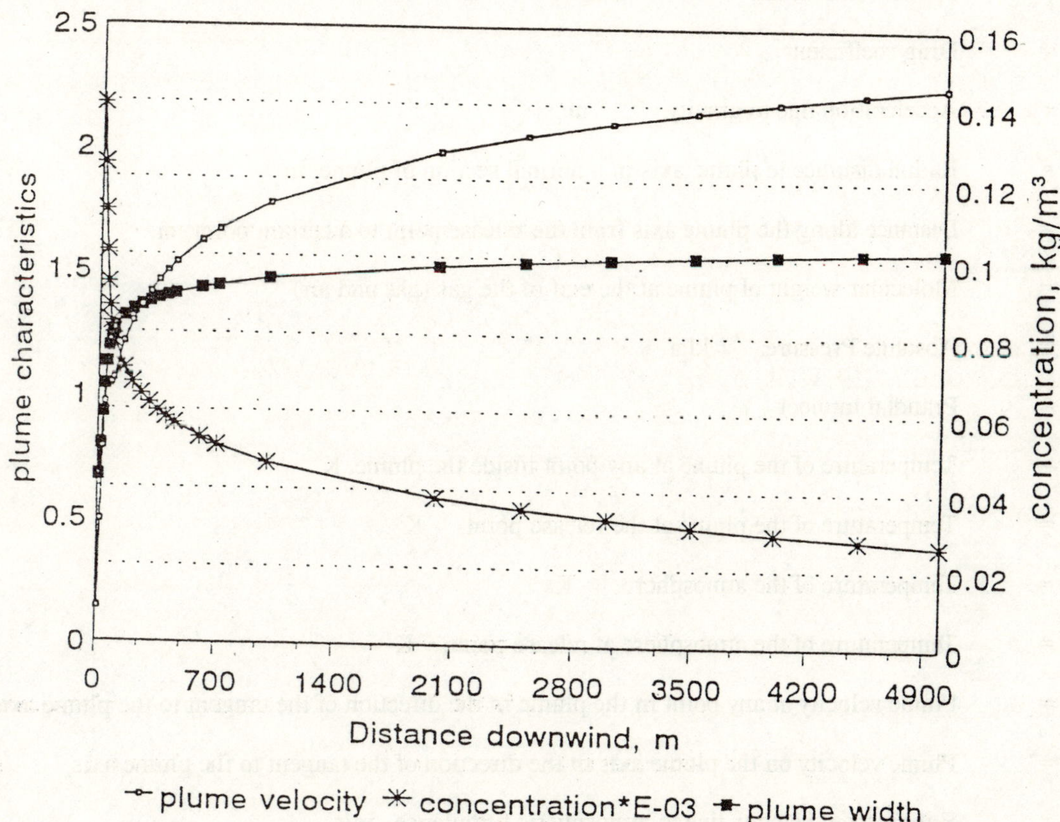

Figure 6. Variation of the plume parameters along downwind distance for Chlorine.

concentrations of chlorine is higher and plume velocity as well as plume width are lower compared to the other three gases (Figure 6). As chlorine gas is the most toxic of the four gases studied and is also the most sluggish to disperse, lethal concentrations of this gas can easily build up over large areas and persist for longer durations.

CONCLUSIONS

The modified plume path theory is a simple but adequately reliable mathematical model to study dispersion of heavy gases. Further the empirical equations developed by us on the basis of the model and validated with experimental data make the study even more versatile and simple. Studies on four hazardous gases (sulphur dioxide, hydrogen sulphide, ammonia, chlorine)reveal that Cl_2 is most sluggish to disperse and generates a lethal load over the widest area. Ammonia is to disperse swiftest.

LIST OF SYMBOLS

b_s	=	Local characteristics width,	m
c	=	Concentration of gas at any point inside the plume,	kg/m³
c^*	=	Concentration of gas on the plume axis,	kg/m³
c_o	=	Concentration at out let,	kg/m³
cp_o	=	Specific heat at outlet,	J/kg/K

cp = Specific heat of the gas at any arbitrary point, J/kg/K

cp_a = Specific heat of air, J/kg/K

cd = Drag coefficient

g = Acceleration due to gravity, m/s^2

r = Radial distance to plume axis in a normal section of plume, m

s = Distance along the plume axis from the release point to a certain point, m

M_{wo} = Molecular weight of plume at the exit of the gas (gas and air)

P = Absolute Pressure, kPa

Pr = Prandtal number

T = Temperature of the plume at any point inside the plume, K

T_o = Temperature of the plume at the release point, K

T_a = Temperature of the atmosphere, K

T_{ao} = Temperature of the atmosphere at release point, K

u = Plume velocity at any point in the plume in the direction of the tangent to the plume axis, m/s

u^* = Plume velocity on the plume axis in the direction of the tangent to the plume axis, m/s

u' = Entrainment velocity due to atmospheric turbulence, m/s

u_a = Wind velocity, m/s

u_v = Venting speed, m/s

ρ' = Plume density at any point in the plume, kg/m^3

ρ_a = Density of air, kg/m^3

ρ_{ao} = Density of air at release point, kg/m^3

ρ_g = Density of gas, kg/m^3

$\dot{\rho}$ = Density difference between plume and atmosphere, kg/m^3

α_1 = Entrainment coefficient of a free jet

α_2 = Entrainment coefficient due to thermal stratification

α_3 = Entrainment coefficient due to atmospheric turbulence

λ = Turbulent Schemedit number

ϕ = Angle between plume axis to horizontal component

δ = Length of transition zone, m

Q_f = Dimensional number

REFERENCES

1. Blewitt, D N, Yohn, J F, Koopman, R P, and Brown, T C, (1987). *AIChE Int. Conf. on vapour cloud modelling*, Boston, Massachusetts, New York.

2. Bodurtha, F T, (1961). The behaviour of dense stack gases, *J. Air Pollution Contr. Asso.*,**11**, 431.

3. Khan, F I, and Abbasi, S A, (1997). Modelling of dispersion of heavy gas based on modification in Plume Path Theory, *Atmos Environ.*, (in press).

4. Krogstad, P,A, and Jacobsen, j. (1991) Dispersion of heavy gas (Air pollution control), *Elsevier Publication,* 63-678.

5. McQuaid, J, (1986). Refinement of estimates of consequence of toxic vapour release, *Procd. IChmE Sym.*, Manchester.

6. Moore, G E, Milich, L B, and Liu, M K, (1988). Study on Plume behaviour using lidar and SF_6 tracer at flat and heavy site, *Atmos Environ.,* **22,** 1673.

7. Niewstadt, F T M, (1992). A large -eddy simulation of a line source in a convective atmospheric boundary layer -II, Dynamic of a buoyant line source, *Atmos Environ.* **26 A,** 499.

8. Ooms, G, (1972) . A new method for the calculations of the plume path of gases emitted by stack, *Atmos Environ,* . **6** , 899.

9. Ooms, G, and Mahiue, A P, (1974). The plume path of vent gases, *Loss prevention and safety promotion in process industries*, Elsevier New York USA

10. Ooms, G, Mahiue, A P, and Zelis, F, (1974). The plume path theory of vent gases heavier than air, *Proceeding of the first International loss prevention symposium*, Delft, The Netherlands

11. Ooms, G, and Duijm, N J, (1983). Dispersion of stack plume heavier than air, *IUTAM Sym on Atmospheric Dispersion of Heavy Gases and Small particles*, Delft, The Netherlands.

12. Rottman, J W, Simpson, J E, Hunt, J C R, and Bitter, R E, (1985). *Hazardous Materials*, **11**, pp 325.

13. Weil, J C, (1988). Plume rise (Eds : Venkatram and Wyngaard) , *Amer Metr Soci*., Boston USA.

9

HAZDIG : A NEW SOFTWARE PACKAGE FOR ASSESSING THE RISKS OF ACCIDENTAL RELEASE OF TOXIC CHEMICALS*

HAZDIG (HAZardous DIspersion of Gases) is a user-friendly PC based software for generating scenarios for the emissions and gaseous dispersion of hazardous chemicals. It can simulate accidental as well as normal release but has been specifically developed as a tool for studying accidental release of hazardous chemicals and its consequences. HAZDIG is made-up of five main modules - data, release scenario generation, dispersion, characteristics estimation, and graphics.

HAZDIG incorporates latest models for estimating atmospheric stability (Van Ulden and Hostlag, 1985; Hsu, 1992; Erbink, 1995) and dispersion (Pasquill and Smith, 1983; Van Ulden, 1988; Erbink, 1993; Khan and Abbasi, 1997a). The data needed to run the models is easy to obtain and feed - properties of chemicals, operating conditions, ambient temperature, and a few commonly available meteorological parameters. A database containing various proportionality constants and complex empirical data has been built into the system. The graphics module enhances the user friendliness of the software, and enables presentation of the results in an easy-to-understand and visually appealing manner. The output of the software is so formatted that it can be directly used for reporting the results without the need of editing.

Key words : Consequence analysis, dispersion of gases, industrial accidents, hazard assessment

INTRODUCTION

Dispersion modelling of likely accidental releases of hazardous chemicals is an integral part of the risk assessment and management process. It forms the critical link between the hypothesised equipment failures or release scenarios in terms of loss of lives and property if accident do takes place. The dispersion analysis provides the means by which hazardous chemical vapour concentrations can be estimated, both within and beyond plant boundaries, to provide a basis for the quantification of the risk.

The physical processes involved in the emission and dispersion of many hazardous chemicals are very complex, and often not very well understood. Much of this complexity stems from the vast array of possible release and dispersion scenarios that can exist in a given industry. Even dispersion of pollutants emitted from a well-defined and fairly steady-state source, such as a power plant stack, is difficult to accurately model. In contrast hazardous chemical

* Reproduced from *Journal of Loss Prevention in* Process Industries, UK.

releases typically are not well defined and are transient in nature. They consequently pose much greater challenges to the modeller. The release may be instantaneous or continuous from a vessel or pipe involving pressurised gases, refrigerated or pressurised liquids, or liquids at ambient pressure and temperature, resulting in vapour emissions that may or may not be heavier than air. The vapour emissions may be relatively steady-state or may vary with time if released from a pressurised vessel or from an evaporating pool of liquid. The release may involve phase changes and thermodynamic interactions with the environment, with possible rain-out of liquid droplets from the plume. Plant structures and irregular terrain may significantly affect the fate of released chemicals, which may further complicate the assessment process (Pasman *et al.* 1992; Greenberg and Crammer, 1992).

In order to estimate the effects of such accidental releases, a number of components of consequence analysis need to be employed. These include calculations of:

i) release rate,

ii) liquid spreading and evaporation rate,

iii) pressurised liquefied gas release,

iv) gas dispersion,

v) toxic load effects.

The depth and breadth of the problems associated with the assessment of accidental release and dispersion of hazardous chemicals has necessitated the development of a number of techniques and methodologies. There are more than 100 mathematical models of varying degrees of sophistication that attempt to address most of the physical processes that can potentially be involved in postulated accident scenarios (Lees, 1996; Khan and Abbasi, 1995;1996;1997b). Many of the software based on these models are operable on micro computers : WHAZAN, HASTE, CHARM, CARE, MIDAS. A few require mainframes DENZ, DEGADIS. Most of these software require a great deal of expertise in their application to a particular problem, as well as technical background in chemical processes, thermodynamics, and turbulent diffusion theory. This limits the software's user-friendliness. Moreover most of these software are unable to handle such accidental release situations as emissions of large quantities of chemicals with great force which may effect the existing atmospheric conditions.

In this context these authors have developed a software package capable of performing consequence analysis of normal as well as accidental release of chemicals. The package can handle myriad factors effecting the dispersion : density (lighter-than/lighter-as/heavier-than-air), convection, buoyancy and momentum. The main objectives behind the development of this software are:

a) *wider applicability*- HAZDIG incorporates larger number of models than existing packages dealing with accident simulation, to handle larger variety of situations with minimum data inputs.

b) *greater sophistication*- HAZDIG incorporates more precise, accurate, and recent models than handled by existing packages;

c) *greater user-friendliness* - HAZDIG is easier to run, and has a comprehensive database built into it.

ALGORITHM AND STRUCTURE OF HAZDIG

In essence, HAZDIG is a tool for consequence analysis, and performs assessment of likely consequences if an accident involving release of chemical occurs. The consequences are quantified in terms of damage radii or the radii of the area which shall be most susceptible to damage. HAZDIG computes likely impacts in terms of direct physical damage (shattering of window panes, caving of buildings) deaths due to blast wave injuries as well as toxic effects (chronic/acute toxicity, mortality). HAZDIG makes use of a wide variety of mathematical models (Table 1). For example, source models are used to predict the rate of release of hazardous materials, the degree of flashing, and the rate of evaporation. The impact intensity models are used to predict human response to different levels of exposures to toxic chemicals. HAZDIG handles several types of release and dispersion scenarios: liquid release, vapour release, gas release, two phase release, dispersion of lighter-than-air gases, buoyant dispersion, non-buoyant dispersion, and

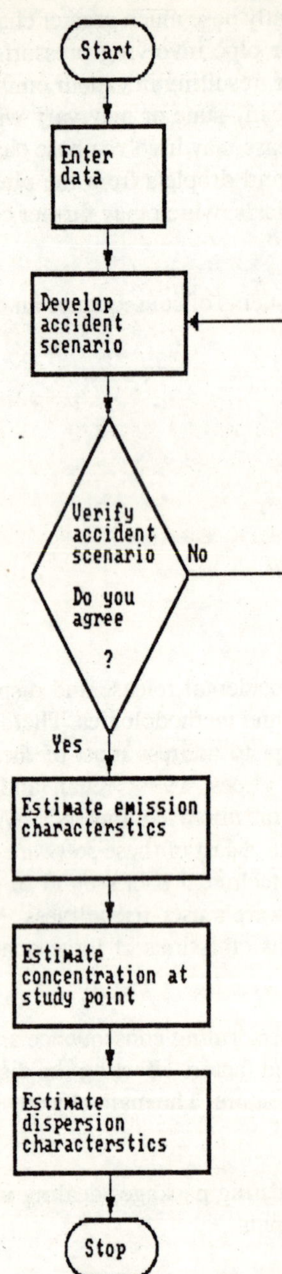

Figure 1. Algorithm of HAZDIG

momentum driven dispersion. A special feature of HAZDIG is that it is able to handle dispersion of heavy (heavier-than-air) gases, and momentum driven dispersion with minimal input of data.

HAZDIG has been developed in object-oriented architecture using C++ as a coding tool. The software is compatible with DOS as well as WINDOWS operating environments. It is operable on computers with a minimum of 8 MB RAM and 80 MB ROM. The algorithm of HAZDIG is shown in Figure 1.

Details of the HAZDIG Modules

As seen in Figure 2, HAZDIG consists of five main modules (Set of objects): data, release scenario generation, dispersion, characteristics estimation and graphics interface. Each module consists of two to three sub-modules (objects). These sub-modules depend on their parent modules as well as on other modules. A schematic diagram showing flow of information and dependency of different sub-modules to the main modules is presented in Figure 2.

DATA module

The main purpose of this module is to collect all relevant informations needed for the execution of other modules. The module consists of three main sub-modules derived from the main DATA module : release, dispersion and characteristics, and site specific. The dispersion and characteristic sub-module is further divided into sub-modules such as, lighter gas, heavy gas and momentum driven dispersion. The release sub-module branches into instantaneous, continuous, jet, and two-phase release.

Each sub-module needs a set of data necessary for the analysis of that particular option. This is illustrated in Table 2 which shows the data list related to a continuous release accident scenario. Most of the options require data pertaining to chemical properties, operating conditions, and release conditions besides synoptic meteorological data. To cater this need, the requisite data base has been built into the software.

Scenario generation module

In this module release scenarios are generated for the unit under study. It is a very important input for the subsequent steps, as the accuracy of the forecast of the type of accident is directly influenced by the realism of the release scenario. Consequently all the subsequent steps are also strongly influenced.

Each release scenario is basically a combination of different likely events that may occur in an industry. Such scenarios are generated based on the properties of chemicals handled by the industry, physical conditions under which reactions occur or reactants/products are stored, geometries and material strength of vessels and conduits, etc. External factors such as site characteristics (topography, presence of trees, ponds, rivers in the vicinity, proximity to other industries or neighbourhoods etc.) and meteorological conditions are also considered. In the available software packages such as WHAZAN (Technica,1992), EFFECTS (TNO, 1991), RISKIT (VTT, 1993), and SAVE (TNO, 1992), these aspects have been used to some extent. But the level of sophistication needs to be enhanced substantially by using advanced models of thermodynamics, heat transfer, and fluid dynamics to generate more realistic release scenarios. Furthermore, the user-friendliness of these packages have some limitations as a result of which several

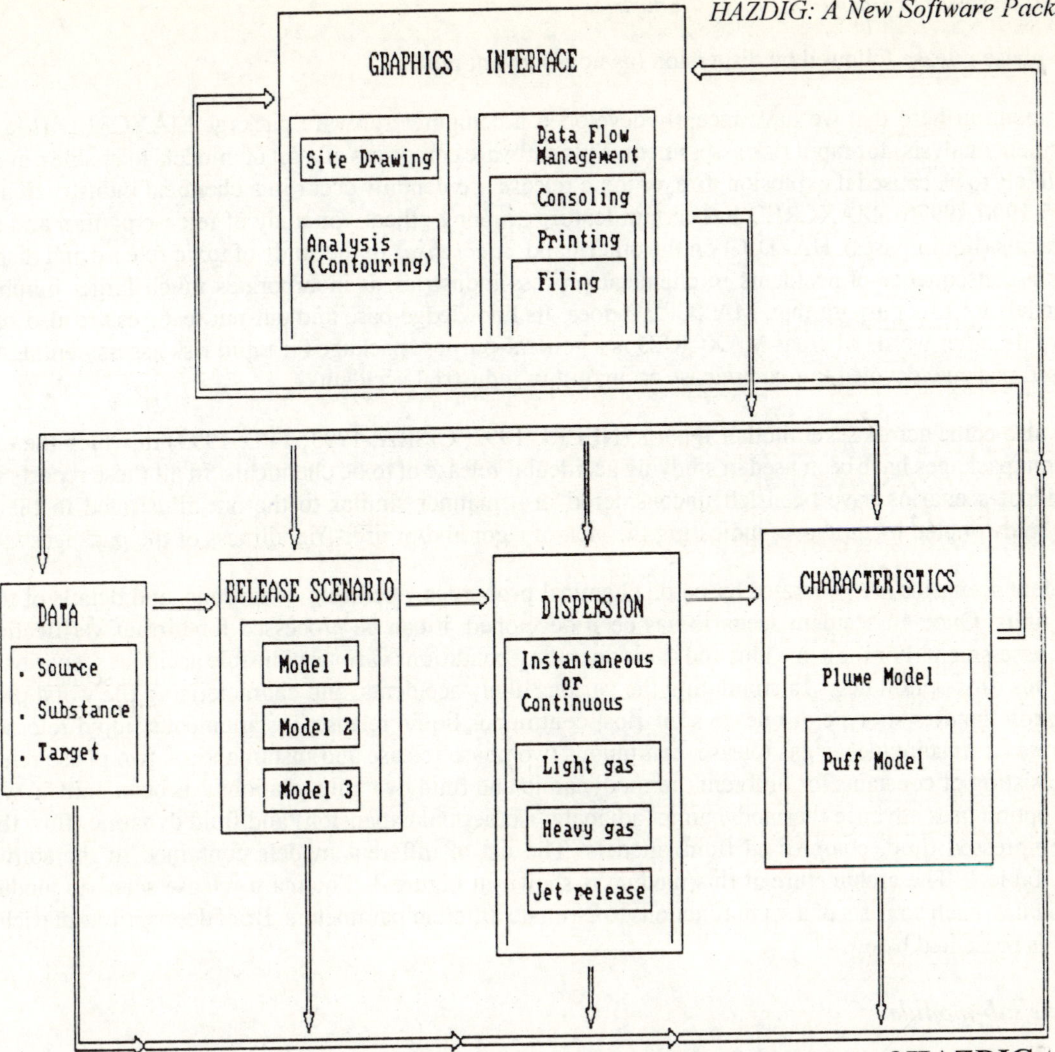

Figure 2. Hierarchical structure and message flow sequence of HAZDIG

real-life studies conducted on the basis of these packages seem to have major lacunae. This is illustrated by the following example.

A multinational project involving 11 institutions was operated (Contini *et al.* 1991) to study the accidental release and dispersion of ammonia from a pressurised tank. The teams utilised commercially available packages CRUNCH, DEGADIS, DENZ, HEAVY-PLUME, RISKIT, WHAZAN, SAFETI, EFFECTS, and DECARA (Contini *et al.* 1991) .

One of the basic aims of this study was to evaluate the efficacies of these packages and to set a benchmark for studies to be conducted in future. A total of five different accident scenarios were generated using these packages. Among these, the most common and worst disastrous accident scenarios invoked by the packages are:

- catastrophic failure of a pressurised storage tank,
- release of ammonia through a large hole on the roof. The scenario relevant to toxic dispersion is the second one. The packages mentioned above modelled the second scenario as instantaneous two-phase release followed by denser-than-air-gas dispersion.

Table 3 presents a comparison of various models available with the different software used by the teams to study this scenario. It is seen that total of eleven different models are available in HAZDIG relevant to the study of the above mentioned problem, whereas *MAXCRED* (Khan and Abbasi, 1997c) has 6 models and other packages such as RISKIT and SAFETI have only 4 models. Moreover, only HAZDIG generates the scenario of two-phase release followed by flashing, evaporation and dispersion (initially momentum driven dispersion with density effect) while others just identify two-phase release followed by dispersion (as non-buoyant puff).

We may mention here that we have recently developed a computer software package MAXCRED (Maximum Credible accident analysis) for rapid risk assessment. This software comprises of a set of models to enable rapid study of damages likely to be caused if explosion, fire, or toxic release accidentally occur in a chemical industry (Khan and Abbasi, 1995;1996;1997b). MAXCRED has certain features, among others, for study of release pattern and dispersion of chemicals (liquid/gases). HAZDIG, on the other hand, *specialises* in the study of toxic release and dispersion occurring as a consequence of accidents in chemical process industries. It incorporates much larger number and variety of models for this purpose than MAXCRED does. Its knowledge-base and out-put features are also substantially superior. In other words whereas MAXCRED is a general-purpose package for rapid risk assessment, HAZDIG is a specialised package devoted to toxic release occurring in industrial accidents.

We have also come across several other reports (NEERI, 1992; CISRA, 1993; TPL, 1993) in which the existing risk assessment packages have been used in studying accidental release of toxic chemicals. In all these reports several credible accident scenarios have been left unconsidered in a manner similar to the one illustrated in the multi-institutional study quoted by us above, indicating the lack of rigor and/or user-friendliness of the packages used.

The accident scenarios are generated based on chemical properties, operating conditions, and details of the process/storage units. Once an accident scenario has been developed, it can be processed for further verification and consequence assessment. For the same unit and same operating conditions various plausible accident scenarios can be visualised. Thus, this option helps in simulating the various likely accidents, and characterising the worst plausible ones. The option handles six type of release scenarios; continuous liquid release, instantaneous liquid release, continuous gas release, instantaneous gas release, continuous two phase release and instantaneous two phase release. A data-base consisting of constants for different thermodynamic and fluid dynamic relations has been built-in with the option. This option uses advance thermodynamic (adiabatic/isothermal expansion) and fluid dynamic (flow through orifice, uncompressed fluid, compressed fluid) models. The list of different models contained in the software is presented in Table 1. The architecture of this module is shown in Figure 3. The main release scenario module has three sub-modules, each consists of a set of functions to estimate different parameters. Brief descriptions of each of the sub-modules is presented below.

Liquid release sub-module

If a crack occurs in the liquid portion of a pressurised or refrigerated storage vessel, the discharge rate is dependent on the pressure inside the tank, the liquid head, and the size of the puncture. This sub-module works out release pattern of the chemical on the basis of storage/process conditions. It first identifies whether the release is continuous or instantaneous. It then characterises the release as normal liquid release, superheated liquid release, or refrigerated liquid release. This option calculates the release rate, quantity of the liquid flashed to vapour, rate of evaporation, and other relevant parameters.

Gaseous release sub-module

Purely gaseous releases from pressurised vessels or pipes generally occur in the form of a jet that can be characterised as critical or sub-critical flow. The occurrence of critical or "choked" flow, which has a maximum exit velocity as that of the speed of sound, is dependent on the ratio of storage pressure to atmosphere pressure.

This sub-module characterises the release of different types of gases. It identifies the release scenarios as instantaneous gaseous release (due to rupture of tanker unit, sudden opening of safety relief valve, etc.) with or without explosion, or continuous gas release. A continuous release is further characterised as sub-sonic or sonic release depending upon the property of the gas and the orifice of release.

Two-phase release sub-module

This type of release is characterised by sudden or continuous release of volatile chemical stored or processed above the normal conditions. The pattern of release depends on the properties of the concerned chemical and the storage or process conditions. This sub-module estimates the release rate and the percentage of liquid droplets going in the out flow.

The conditions necessary and sufficient to cause the above mentioned release scenarios (gas, liquid or two phase) have been incorporated as a knowledge-base which is a system of rules in terms of if-and-else structure. This is linked with the main release scenario module. When the user keys in information on operating conditions and properties of chemicals, the software works out appropriate release scenario which it then verifies and uses in dispersion and characteristics modules for further analysis.

Table 1. List of various models in-built in HAZDIG

Event	Model Incorporated	References
EMISSION		
Liquid release		
Continuous		
normal	flow through orifice	Coullson and Richardson, 1977; Pilborough, 1989
refrigerated	flow and heat transfer model	Clancey, 1974; Drake and Reid, 1975; Drivas, 1982
superheated	thermodynamic and flow model	Kletz, 1984; Leung and Epstein, 1990
Instantaneous		
normal	rupture of vessel model	Hess et al., 1974; Lees, 1996; Reed and Clark, 1983
refrigerated	heat transfer and evaporation model	Clancey, 1974; Foster, 1981; Woodward and Mudan, 1991
superheated	thermodynamic and evaporation model	Kletz, 1984; Picard and Bishnoi, 1988 Greenbook, 1992; Shaw and Brisco, 1976
Gaseous release		
Instantaneous	thermodynamic model	Cox and Comer, 1980; Drivas et al., 1983; Nolan et al., 1990
explosively	boiling liquid expanding vapor explosion	Prugh, 1991; Kayes, 1986; Kletz, 1984 Vernart et al., 1993
Continuous		
sub sonic	fluid dynamic model	Greenbook, 1992; Lees, 1996; Woodward, 1990
sonic	fluid dynamic model	Coullson and Richardson, 1977; Woodward and Mudan, 1991
Two phase release		
refrigerated	thermodynamic and heat-transfer model	Fauske, 1964;1988; Fauske et al., 1984; Hague and Pepe, 1990 Kern, 1985, Perry et al., 1984; Kayes, 1986
superheated	thermodynamic and heat-transfer model	Greenbook, 1992; Sumipathala et al., 1990 Perry et al., 1984; Leung, 1990
Atmospheric Stability	boundary layer and macro-meteorological parameters based models	Van Ulden and Holtslag, 1985; Hsu, 1992 Erbink, 1995
DISPERSION		
Light gas dispersion	Pasquill, Gifford and-Turner model	Pasquill and Smith, 1983; Gifford, 1961 Turner, 1970;1985
	Robert model	Robert et al., 1992; Erbink, 1993
	Sutton model	Sutton, 1948,
Heavy gas dispersion	BOX, PLUME and SLAB model	Van Ulden, 1974;1988; Deaves, 1992 Khan and Abbasi, 1997a; Predikanis et al., 1994 Earmak and Chan, 1986;1988
Jet dispersion	Jet release and dispersion model	Mahieu and Oomes, 1974; Brown et al., 1993 Khan and Abbasi, 1997a; Lees, 1996
CHARACTERISTICS		
Continuous release	Plume model Khan and Abbasi, 1997a;	Mahieu and Oomes, 1974; Lees, 1996 Ooms and Tennekes, 1984
Instantaneous release	Puff model	Greenberg and Cramer, 1992; Deaves, 1992 Ooms and Tennekes, 1984; Van Ulden, 1992
DAMAGE ESTIMATION		
Continuous and instantaneous	Probit model	Essienberg et al., 1975; Greenbook, 1992 Clancey, 1977; Pietersen, 1990; CCPS, 1989

Table 2. The set of input data required to run different options of HAZDIG

Parameters	Values, units	
PERTAINING TO SUBSTANCE		
specific heat at constant pressure	0.39470	cal/g/c
specific heat at constant volume	0.29237	cal/g/c
diffusion constant	0.00045	
specific heat ratio	1.35000	
kinematic velocity	0.00034	sq m/s
molecular weight	17.00000	
liquid density	1073.46000	kg/cu m
vapor density	0.60000	kg/cu m
boiling point	-33.00000	C
heat of vaporization	1.37226	kJ/kg
PERTAINING TO SOURCE		
release Instantaneous/continuous	C	
release type 0: gas, 1: liquid, 2: two phase	0	
discharge coefficient	0.03500	
height of source	12.00000	m
liquid head	15.00000	m
total liquid/vapor mass	5.00e06	m
atmospheric pressure	1.01e05	Pa
processing pressure	3.01e05	Pa
saturation pressure	5.00e05	Pa
gas release rate	2.00000	kg/s
radius of puncture	0.02500	m
ambient temperature	25.0000	C
process temperature	5.0000	C
PERTAINING TO TARGET		
x distance from source	500.0000	m
Y distance from source	50.0000	m
Z distance from source	10.0000	m
wind speed	5.0000	m/s
duration of release	250.0000	s

The module pertaining to verification of release scenario

This feature is one of the specialities of HAZDIG. It verifies the plausibility of the proposed scenario. For example, if the scenario envisages two phase release of chemical on the basis of the characteristics of the chemical and conditions in which it is employed, this step checks whether the set of input conditions would indeed lead to the envisaged release. For example, a non-liquefied chemical may not exit in a two-phase mode, if the storage/process conditions are normal but for the same chemical there would be a high probability of two-phase release if the storage is under refrigerated or pressurised conditions. When chemical escapes from such a vessel, its mixing with the ambient air would be inefficient leading to build-up of the concentration of the chemical in the atmosphere, which subsequently may lead to severe consequences.

If HAZDIG finds that an envisaged scenario is not within the realms of probability, it modifies the scenario to the extent that it become plausible.

Dispersion module

This module consists of up-to-date mathematical models for simulating the accidents chosen as credible in the previous step. This module works out the dispersion characteristics profile, percentage of lethality, and damage radii of the release chemical. The output of this module quantifies impacts such as concentration at particular location, concentration profile, toxic dosage, damage radii of different impacts, and probabilities of causing lethality. The output of this object has been so formatted that it can be directly used in reports without having to do any editing. Moreover, using these results it is very easy to draw damage/risk contours.

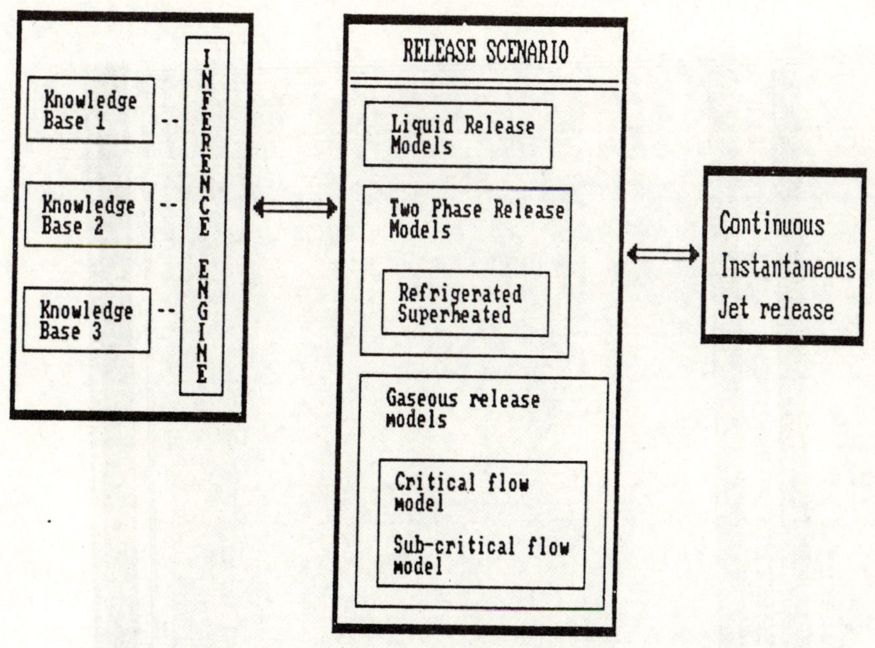

Figure 3. Structure of scenario generation module

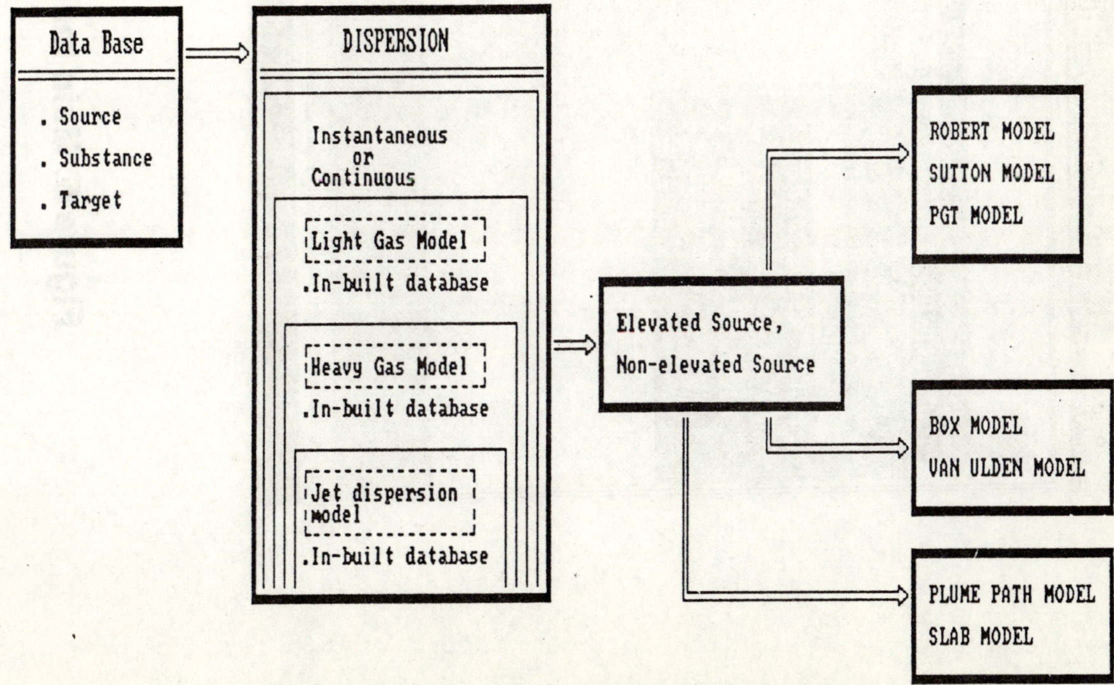

Figure 4. Structure of dispersion module

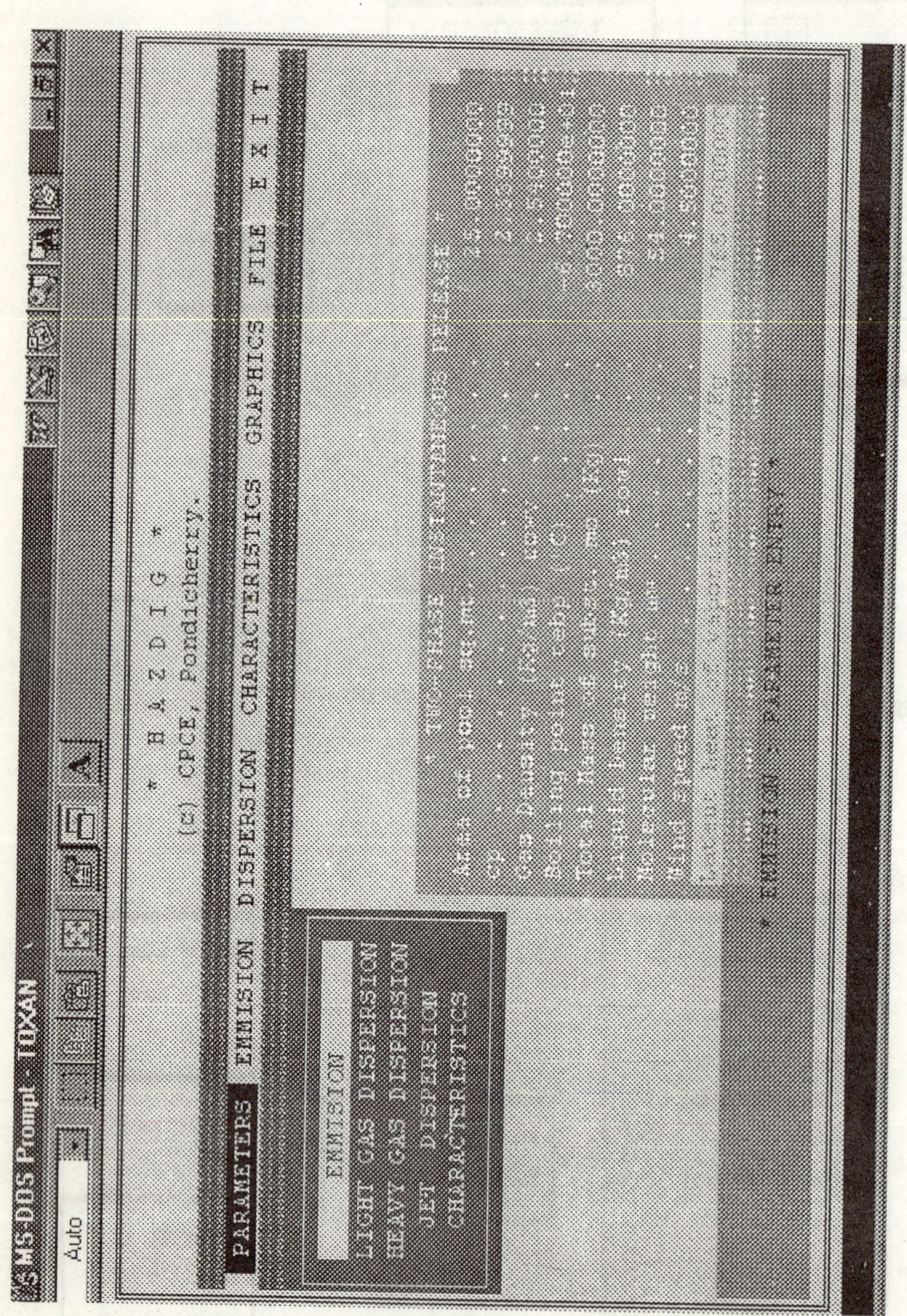

Figure 5. Main menu and available options in *HAZDIG*

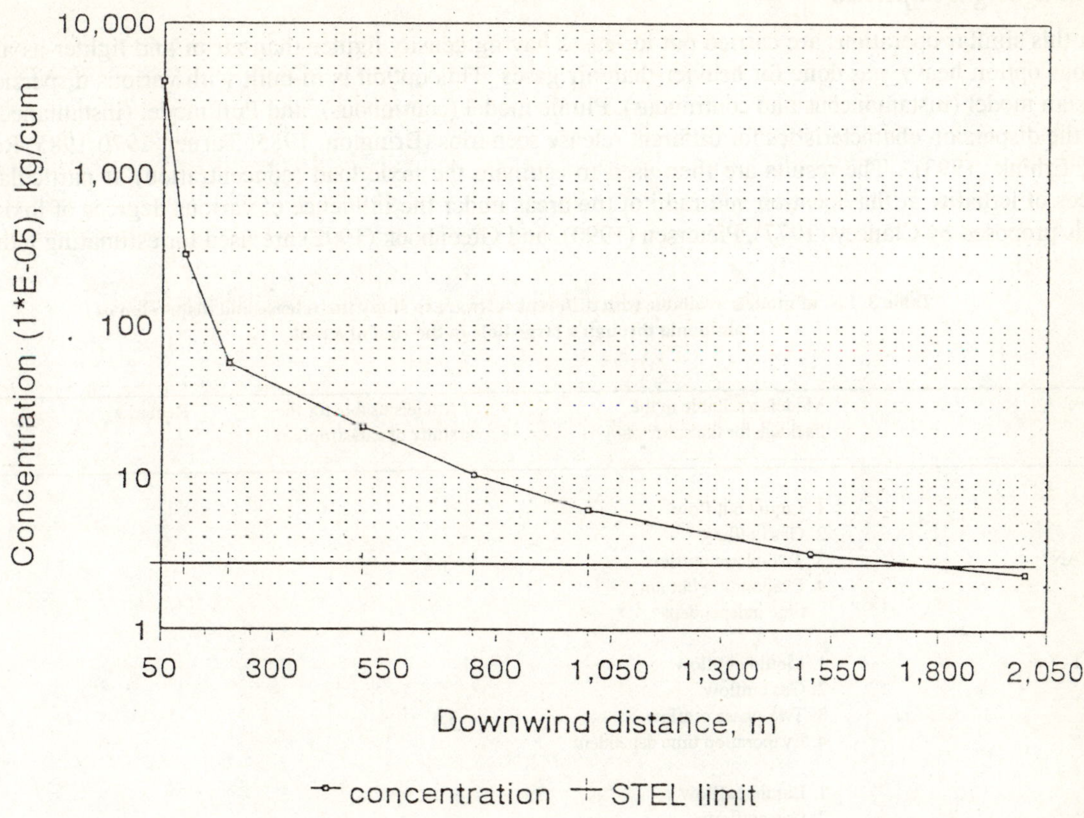

Figure 6. Concentration profile for the accidental release of ammonia

The mathematical models used in this module are listed in Table 1. Brief explanatory notes on the phenomena simulated by these models are presented below.

This module assesses the consequences of release and dispersion of toxic gas/vapour. It simulates different types of release scenarios such as; continuous release, two-phase release, and instantaneous release. In conducting dispersion studies it takes into consideration the densities of the gases or gas-air mixtures (because of the pronounced influence density exerts on the shape of the plume) and momentum of release. The models can thus simulate dispersions of heavier-than-air, lighter-as-air and lighter-than-air gases/gas-air plumes. This module first estimates the concentration profile of the toxic gas that would develop consequent dispersion under the given meteorological conditions. It then works out the areas of toxic impact and the *extents* of toxicity that would be caused on the basis of exposure-based-toxicity data.

This module can handle the following options: heavy_gas dispersion, light_gas dispersion, momentum driven dispersion. The structure of this module is shown in Figure 4 and brief description of these options is presented below.

Option heavy_gas dispersion

This option estimates dispersions characteristics (concentration profile, distance travelled by the cloud/plume, and the dimensions of the cloud/plume) of the gases having effective density higher-than-air. It uses BOX model for instantaneous release (Van Ulden, 1974; Van Ulden and Hostage, 1985; Deaves, 1992; Erbink, 1993) and PLUME and SLAB model (heavy gas) for continuous release (Ermak and Chan , 1986;1988; Predikanis *et al.* 1994; Langlo and Schatzmawn, 1991; Khan and Abbasi, 1996) to estimate gas concentrations and other dispersion characteristics. The results are then passed on to damage estimation options to calculate the percent likelihood of lethality and area under influence for various degrees of toxicity.

Option light_gas dispersion

In this similar operations are carried out for gases having density lighter-than-air or/and lighter-as-air as in the previous option heavy_gas done for heavier-than-air gases. This option is in-built with various dispersion models: Gaussian model (instantaneous and continuous), Plume model (continuous), and Puff model (instantaneous) to estimate the dispersion characteristics for different release scenarios (Brington, 1985; Turner, 1970;1985; Robert *et al.* 1992; Erbink, 1993) . The results are then used to estimate the toxic load (concentration) at particular location, chances of lethality at that location and radii of the areas under the influence of various degrees of toxicity. Probit models proposed by Clancey (1977), Pietersen (1990), and Greenbook (1992) are used for estimating lethality.

Table 3. List of models available with different software to study the release and dispersion of ammonia through a large hole in the roof of a tank

Software	Models available in the package for the study of@	Models usable for the study of catastrophic	Remarks
WHAZAN	1. Liquid out flow 2. Gas outflow 3. Two-phase outflow 4. Evaporation but not time independent	3,4	
SAFETI	1. Liquid out flow 2. Gas outflow 3. Two-phase outflow 4. Evaporation time dependent	3,4	
RISKIT	1. Liquid outflow 2. Gas outflow 3. Two-phase outflow 4. Heavy gas dispersion	3,4	
EFFECTS	1. Liquid outflow 2. Vapor outflow 3. Gas outflow 4. Two-phase outflow 5. Evaporation but not time dependent	4,5	
MAXCRED	1. Liquid release 2. Gaseous release 3. Two-phase release 4. Evaporation but not time dependent 5. Light gas dispersion 6. Heavy gas dispersion	3,4,6	Two phase release of ammonia followed by the evaporation and heavy gas dispersion.
HAZDIG	1. Momentum release 2. Liquid release 3. Gaseous release 4. Two-phase release 5. Flashing of vapor 6. Evaporation but not time dependent 7. Light gas dispersion 8. Heavy gas dispersion 9. Jet release and dispersion 10. Plume characteristics 11. Puff characteristics	4,5,6,8,10	Two-phase release followed by flashing of vapor and subsequent evaporation of remaining liquid ammonia followed by heavy gas dispersion and puff characteristics estimation.

@ As listed in Contini et al. (1991)

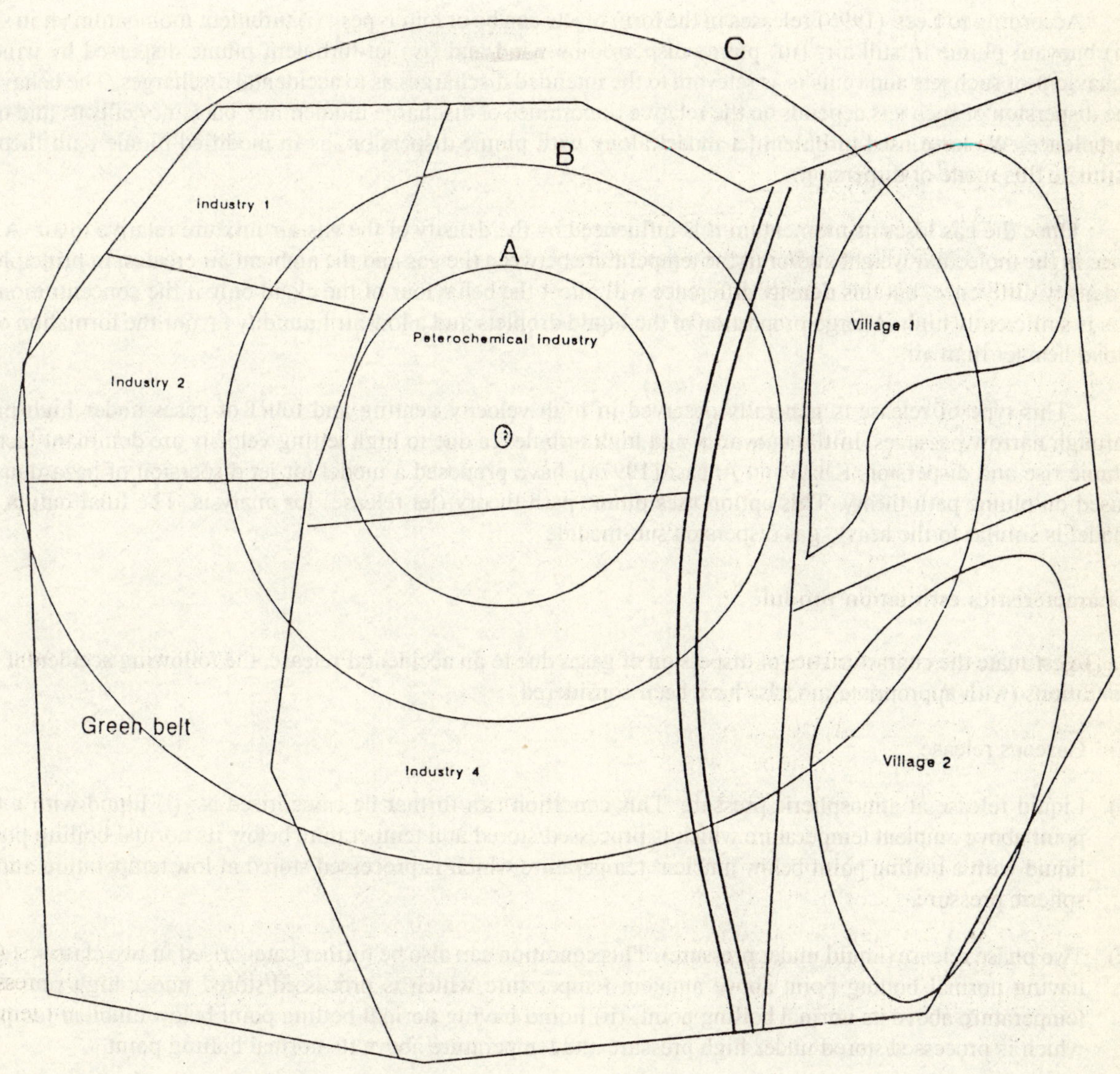

Figure 7. Risk contours for accidental release of ammonia; (A) represents severe risk contour, (B) high risk contour and (C) Low risk contour

Option momentum_driven dispersion

As long as the momentum of the escaping gas is significant the density factor does not become operative but as soon as the momentum dies down to a level where the ambient air movements could effect dispersion, the density factors take over to influence the shape of the plume.

When the gas escapes at high velocity as from a jet or a vent, the momentum effect is more prominent and lasts longer (due to higher velocity of release) than when the release velocity (venting velocity) is low.

According to Lees (1996) releases in the form of jets can be of four types : (i) turbulent momentum jet in still air, (ii) buoyant plume in still air; (iii) plume dispersed by wind and (iv) jet-turbulent plume dispersed by wind. The behaviour of such jets and vents is as relevant to the intended discharges as to accidental discharges. The behaviour of the dispersion of such jets depends on the relative importance of discharge momentum, buoyancy effects, and of wind turbulence. We have used turbulent jet model along with plume dispersion, as in modified plume path theory to estimate this mode of dispersion.

Once the gas loses its momentum it is influenced by the density of the gas-air mixture relative to air. A difference in the molecular weight and/or in the temperature between the gas and the ambient air creates, in principle, such a density difference, but this density difference will affect the behaviour of the cloud only if the concentration of the gas is sufficiently high. A large proportion of the liquid droplets and a low air humidity favour the formation of a gas cloud heavier than air.

This type of release is generally observed in high velocity venting and relief of gases under high pressure through narrow passages. Initial buoyancy and high turbulence due to high jetting velocity are dominant factors for plume rise and dispersion. Khan and Abbasi (1997a), have proposed a model for jet dispersion of hazardous gases based on plume path theory. This option uses plume path theory (jet release) for analysis. The final output of this model is similar to the heavy_gas dispersion sub-module.

Characteristics estimation module

To estimate the characteristics of dispersion of gases due to an accidental release, the following accidental release conditions (with appropriate models) have been considered.

a) Gaseous release.

b) Liquid release at atmospheric pressure. This condition can further be categorised as: (i) liquid with a boiling point above ambient temperature which is processed/stored at a temperature below its normal boiling point; (ii) liquid with a boiling point below ambient temperature which is processed/stored at low temperature and atmospheric pressure.

c) Two phase release (liquid under pressure). This condition can also be further categorised in two classes: (i) liquid having normal boiling point above ambient temperature which is processed/stored under high pressure and temperature above its normal boiling point; (ii) liquid having normal boiling point below ambient temperature which is processed/stored under high pressure and temperature above its normal boiling point.

According to the mode of release this object consists of two sub-objects (options).

Plume_characteristics sub-module

A continuous release of gas/vapour (light, heavy, jet release) gives rise to a *plume*. By using the plume path theory of dispersion (Mahieu and Oomes, 1974; Khan and Abbasi, 1997a) for light and heavy gases the characteristics of plume can be computed. This includes dimension of the plume, rise of the plume, maximum concentration in the plume at ground level, and distance from the exit point at which maximum concentration would be observed. It takes into account atmospheric stability and release conditions to compute these parameters.

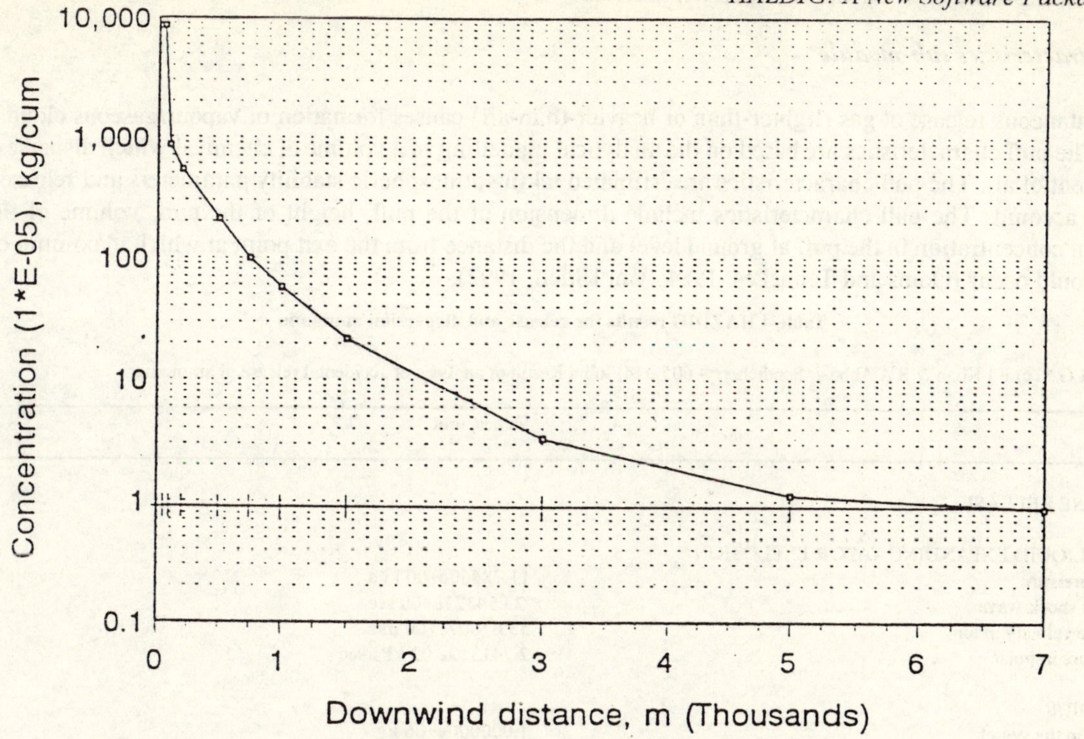

Figure 8. concentration profile for the accidental release of chlorine

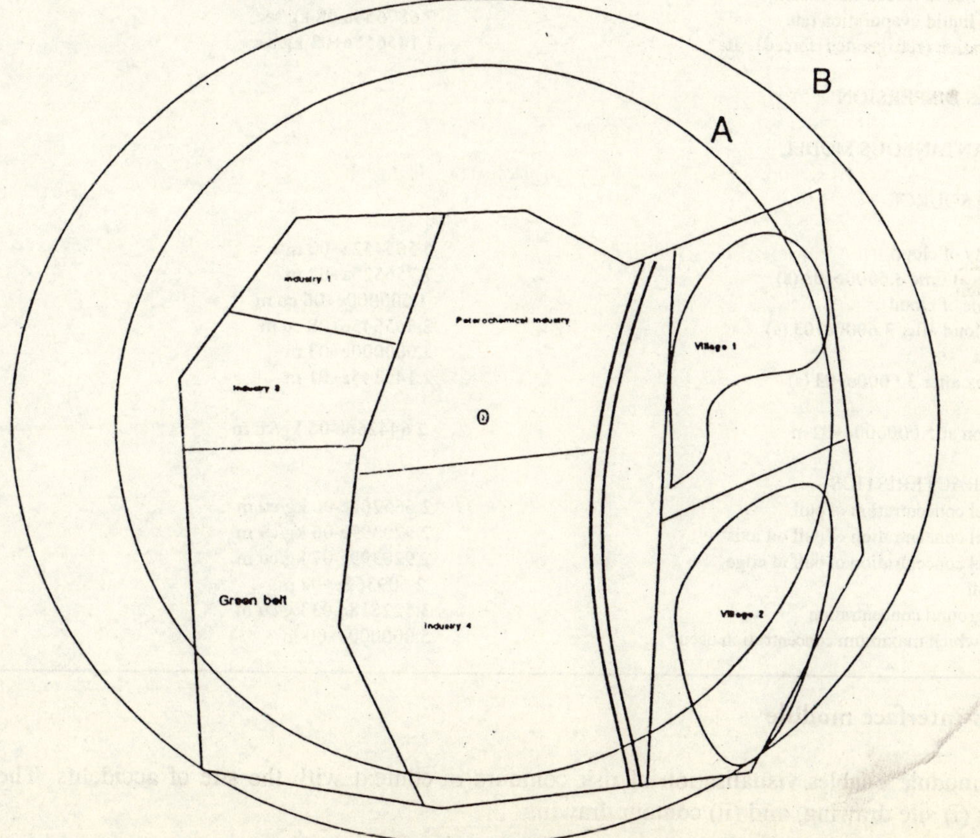

Figure 9. Risk contours for the accidental release of chlorine; (A) severe risk contour, and (B) high risk contour

Puff_characteristics sub-module

Instantaneous release of gas (lighter-than or heavier-than-air) causes formation of vapour/gaseous cloud known as *puff*. The puff characteristics are based on the analytical modelling of a volume of chemical which disperses due to entrainment of air. The puff characteristics are estimated taking atmospheric stability parameters and release condition into account. The puff characteristics include dimension of the puff, height of the puff, volume of the puff, maximum concentration in the puff at ground level and the distance from the exit point at which maximum concentration would occur (Ooms and Tennekes, 1984; Van Ulden, 1992).

Table 4 HAZDIG results for release and dispersion ammonia

* H A Z D I G * (c) F I Khan & S A Abbasi, Pondicherry- 605 014, India Result of analysis of accidental release of ammonia

Parameters	Values, unit
TWO PHASE RELEASE	
BOILING LIQUID EXPANDING VAPOR EXPLOSION	
Peak over pressure	11.78460e+00 kPa
Duration of shock wave	23.54321e+00 sec
Shock wave velocity in air	53.67607e+00 m/s
Over pressure impulse	2.741312e-02 kPa/sec
PUFF RADIUS	
Total mass in the vessel	1.000000e+06 kg
Mass of vapor flashed	7.754567e+04 kg
Radius of puff	6.354876e+01 m
VAPOR GENERATION RATE	
Area of liquid pool	1.192651e+04 sq m
Evaporation due to forced circulation	1.145655e+03 kg/sec
Refrigerated liquid evaporation rate	7.687654e-08 kg/sec
Total evaporation (refrigerated+forced) rate	1.145655e+03 kg/sec
HEAVY GAS DISPERSION	
BOX INSTANTANEOUS MODEL	
ELEVATED SOURCE	
Front velocity of cloud	5.565452e+00 m/s
Cloud radius at time 3.6000e+03 (s)	7.756525e+02 m
Initial volume of cloud	1.000000e+06 cu m
Volume of cloud after 3.6000e+03 (s)	2.565645e+08 cu m
Initial height	5.000000e+03 m
Height of box after 3.6000e+03 (s)	2.145345e+01 m
Concentration at 5.000000e+02 m	2.644266e-06 kg/cu m
PUFF CHARACTERISTICS	
Ground level concentration of puff	2.665262e-06 kg/cu m
Ground level concentration of puff on axis	2.920399e-06 kg/cu m
Ground level concentration of puff at edge	2.920399e-07 kg/cu m
Width of puff	2.509362e+02 m
Maximum ground concentration	3.522818e-03 kg/cu m
Distance at which maximum concentration occur	5.000000e+00 m

Graphics-interface module

This module enables visualisation of risk contours in context with the site of accidents. The option has two facilities: (i) site drawing, and (ii) contour drawing.

The site drawing option enables the user to draw any industrial site/layout using freehand drawing or using any already defined drawing tool. The contour drawing option has the facility for drawing various damage/risk contours over the accident site. The contours can be drawn in different shapes and sizes as per the requirement of the user.

The module also deals with handling of different files such as: data file, scenario file, output file, graphic file, and flow of information. This object works as 'information manager': it provides the necessary information to each module and sub-module to carry out desired operations, and stores the results in different files. Besides this, it also provides all commonly used file operations such as copying, deleting, consoling and printing.

The main menu and different options available at each module are shown in Figure 5. The applicability of the software is demonstrated with a case study presented below.

Table 5 HAZDIG results for release and dispersion of chlorine

* H A Z D I G * (c) F I Khan & S A Abbasi, Pondicherry- 605 014, India Result of analysis of accidental release of chlorine

Parameters	Values, unit
TWO PHASE RELEASE	
PUFF RADIUS	
Total mass in the vessel	5.000000e+05 kg
Mass of vapor flashed	2.347187e+04 kg
Radius of puff	1.308699e+01 m
LIQUID EMISSION RATE	
Area of puncture	1.963495e-03 sq m
Liquid emission rate through the puncture	4.335294e+01 kg/sec
Total time of spill	1.153324e+04 sec
Area of liquid pool after 6.000e+01 (s)	1.192651e+04 sq m
VAPOR GENERATION RATE	
Area of liquid pool	1.192651e+04 sq m
Evaporation due to forced circulation	8.915990e+02 kg/sec
Refrigerated liquid evaporation rate	2.637018e-10 kg/sec
Total evaporation (refrigerated+forced) rate	8.915990e+02 kg/sec
HEAVY GAS DISPERSION	
PLUME CONTINUOUS MODEL	
Front velocity of cloud	2.200992e+00 m/s
Cloud radius at time 3.6000e+03 (s)	2.642137e+02 m
Initial volume of cloud	2.000000e+05 cu m
Volume of cloud after 3.6000e+03 (s)	1.056855e+07 cu m
Initial height	2.546479e+03 cu m
Height of box after 3.6000e+03 (s)	4.818977e+01 m
Concentration at 5.000000e+02 (m)	5.405993e-06 kg/cu m
PLUME CHARACTERISTICS	
Ground level concentration of plume	5.470422e-06 kg/cu m
Ground level concentration of plume on axis	5.994085e-06 kg/cu m
Ground level concentration of plume at edge	5.994085e-07 kg/cu m
Width of plume	2.509362e+02 m
Maximum ground level concentration	5.141720e-04 kg/cu m
Distance at which maximum concentration occur	3.500000e+01 m

CASE STUDY

Problem statement 1

Catastrophic rupture of a vessel storing ammonia at refrigerated condition. The incident occurs during early evening.

Analysis

The problem has been identified as instantaneous release (boiling liquid expanding vapour explosion-BLEVE) of ammonia under slightly stable conditions (using macro meteorological data). Eventhough ammonia vapour has density lighter-than-air, light gas dispersion model can not be used because in the present case study, ammonia is stored in refrigerated condition and an instantaneous release (as BLEVE) would lead to the formation of vapour cloud consisting of liquid ammonia droplets. Thus the effective density of the cloud will be higher-than-air. HAZDIG also confirms this phenomenon and suggests two phase release with shock wave development and non-buoyant dispersion.

Table 4 shows the output of HAZDIG; it specifies accidental release scenario as-*instantaneous two phase release of gas* (flashing followed by evaporation) under sub-normal condition. It also presents the output of dispersion of heavy-gas module using BOX model. It suggests that at a distance of 500 meter from the accident site the concentration of gas would be 2.64E-06 kg/m^3, which is a lethal dose considering that STEL (short term exposure limit) lethality concentration 0.027*E-09 kg/m^3 (Fowcett and Wood, 1993). The concentration profile for ammonia with distance, shown in Figure 6, suggests that up to a distance of 1500 meters the concentration of ammonia would be above permissible limit vis a vis STEL (15 minutes exposure) for instantaneous exposure.

The puff characteristics of release and dispersion scenario can be interpreted from Table 4 which is an output of HAZDIG. It suggests that after 1 hour of release the puff would be around 250 meter in radius and about 10 meter high from the ground level. The maximum concentration of ammonia, 3.5*E-03 kg/m^3, would occur at a distance of 5 meters from the release point. Figure 7 presents the damage contours of lethal dose over the area. It is clear that lethal concentration shall occur only within the industry's periphery (400 meter). However, high risk contour (representing 50% probability of lethality, estimated using probit function) would cover large area (1200 meter) which encompasses populated areas. Thus, the consequences due to release of toxic NH_3 have high risk (50% probability of lethality) to surrounding and for the populated areas near to the industrial site.

Problem Statement 2

Chlorine, stored under high pressure, is accidentally released from a storage vessel due to failure of flange in the forenoon in industrial area on a clear sun-lit day.

Analysis

We have defined the problem as *continuous release of chlorine under unstable meteorological conditions*. As chlorine is a 'heavy' (denser-than-air) gas and is released at high pressure (above vapour pressure) heavy-gas continuous model is used by HAZDIG to forecast the dispersion profile.

Table 5 presents the output of HAZDIG for chlorine release. It provides the accident release scenario as continuous two phase release of chlorine (flashing followed by evaporation) under pressurised condition. Table 5 also presents the output of heavy gas module using plume path model. It suggests that at a distance of 500 meter from industrial site the concentration of gas would be 5.409E-06 kg/m^3, which is above the lethal limit as per the STEL of 9.0E-09 kg/m^3. The concentration profile of chlorine with distance is shown in Figure 8; it indicates that over a distance of 4500 meter the concentration of chlorine would be above permissible limit vis a vis STEL for instantaneous exposure (15 minutes).

The plume characteristics as per this release scenario can be interpreted from Table 5. The plume, after 1 hour of the accidental release would be ~250 meter in radius and shall be, ~7.5 meter above the ground level. The maximum concentration (5.147E-04 kg/m^3) would occur at a distance of 35 meter from the release point. Figure 9 presents the damage contours over the area. It is evident from Figure that severe risk contour (contour representing having more than 75% probability of lethality) would envelop large area (3000 meter radius) and densely populated areas are coming under the severe damage threat (severe risk).

CONCLUSION

HAZDIG is a computer software specifically developed to estimate the consequences (damage potentials and risks) due to release of toxic chemicals, accidentally or voluntarily. The modular structure of HAZDIG (developed in object oriented environment) enables swift processing of data and computation of result. It is also easy to maintain and up-grade. HAZDIG incorporates the latest available models for atmospheric stability estimation, release of chemicals (gases, liquid, two-phase, jet) and dispersion. It is capable of handling various types of release and dispersion scenarios: two phase release followed by dispersion, momentum release followed by dispersion, dispersion of heavier-than-air gases, etc. The Graphics option enables the user to draw any industrial site/layout using freehand drawing or using any already defined drawing tool. The contour drawing option has the facility for drawing various damage/risk contours over the accident site. The contours can be drawn in different shapes and sizes as per the requirement of the user.

All-in-all HAZDIG is superior to other commercially available packages for studying accidental release of gases in following terms:

i) *wider applicability* - HAZDIG incorporates larger number of models to handle, larger variety of situations with minimum data inputs;

ii) *greater sophistication* - more precise, accurate, and recent models have been incorporated in HAZDIG than handled by existing packages;

iii) *greater user-friendliness* - easy to run, has an extensive data-base built-in, generates output which can be directly used in reports, and enables visual comprehension of likely consequences.

Software availability: those interested in the software may contact Director, Centre for Pollution Control & Energy Technology, Pondicherry University, Pondicherry -605 014, India.

REFERENCES

1. Brington, P W, (1985). Evaporation from a plane liquid surface into a turbulent boundary layer, *J of Fluid Mech.*, **159**, 323.

2. Brown, M J, Pal Arya, S, and Snyder, W H, (1993). Dispersion from surface and elevated release an investigation of non-plume model, *J.Appl.Metr*, **32**, 490.

3. CCPS (1989). Guidelines for chemical process quantitative risk analysis, *Center for Chemical Process Safety*, **Publication number G-8**, AIChE, Washington, D C.

4. CISRA (1993). Risk assessment of Chloralkali industry, Cell for Industrial Safety and Risk Analysis, *CLRI,* Madras, India.

5. Clancey, V J, (1974). The evaporation and dispersion of flammable liquid spillage's. *Chemical Process Hazards*, **5**, 80.

6. Clancey, V J, (1977). Dangerous clouds, their growth and explosive properties, *Chemical Process Hazards*, **6**, 111.

7. Clancey, V J, (1974). The evaporation and dispersion of flammable liquid spillage's. *Chemical Process Hazards*, **5**, 80.

8. Contini, C A, Amendal, A., and Ziomas, I, (1991). Benchmark study on major hazard study, *JRC-ISPRA*, 134, Amestradam.

9. Coullson, J M, and Richardson, J F, (1977). *Chemical Engineering* (SI ed), Oxford: Pergamon press, London

10. Cox R A, and Comer, P J, (1980). Containment failure discharge and vapour cloud formation, *Safety promotion and loss prevention in the process industries*, Oyez, London.

11. Deaves, D M, (1992). Dense gas dispersion modelling, *Journal of Loss Prev in Process Ind*, **5,** 219.

12. Drake, E M, and Reid, R C, (1975). How LNG boils on soils. *Hydrocarbon Processing*, **54**(5), 191.

13. Drivas, P J, (1982). Calculation of evaporative emissions from multi-component liquid spills, *Environ. Sci.*

Tech., **16**, 726.

14. Drivas, P J, Sabnis, J S, and Teuscher, L H, (1983). Model simulates pipeline, storage tank failures. *Oil Gas J.*, **September** , 162.

15. Eissenberg, N A, Lynch, C J, and Breeding, R J, (1975). Vulnerability Model: A Simulation System for Assessing Damage Resulting from Marine Spills, *Report CG-D-136-75 (Enviro control)*, Rockville M D., USA.

16. Erbink, J J, (1993). The advanced Gaussian model STACKS, Procd. of ERCOFTAC, *Work shop on Inter comparison of Advanced Practical Short range Atmospheric Dispersion Modelling*, Manno, Switzerland.

17. Erbink, J J, (1995). Turbulent diffusion model from tall stacks, *Ph.D. thesis submitted to VRIJ University*, The Netherlands.

18. Ermak, D L, and Chan, S T, (1986). A study of heavy gas effects on the atmospheric dispersion of dense gases, *Air Pollution Modelling and its Application, (Ed: Wispleasere et al., 1986)*, Plenum Press.

19. Ermak, D L, and Chan, S T, (1988). Recent development on the FEM3 and SLAB atmospheric dispersion models, *Stable Stratified Flow and Dense Gas Dispersion (Ed: Puttok, J.S.)*, Clarendon Press.

20. Fauske, H K, (1964). The discharge of saturated water through tubes. Seventh Nat. Heat transfer Conf., *Inst. Chem. Engrs*, New York, 210.

21. Fauske, H K, (1988). Emergency relief system design for reactive and non-reactive systems: extension of the DIERS methodology. *Plant/Operations Prog.*, 7, 153.

22. Fauske, H K , Grolmes, M A, and Leung, J C, (1984). Multiphase flow considerations in sizing emergency relief systems for runaway chemical reactions. *In Multi-phase Flow and Heat Transfer III, Pt B: Applications, ed;. T.N. Veziroglu and A.E. Bergles,* Elsevier, Amsterdam, 899.

23. Foster, T C, (1981). Time required to empty a vessel. *Chem. Engr,* **88**, 105.

24. Fowcett, H H, and Wood, W S, (1993). *Safety and accident prevention in chemical operation (third ed.),* John willey, New York.

25. Gifford, F A, (1961). Use of routine meteorological observation for estimating atmospheric diffusion, *Nuclear safety*, **20**, 4.

26. Greenberg, H R, and Crammer, J J, (1992). *Risk Assessment and risk management in chemical process industries*, Van Norstand Reinhold, New York.

27. Greenbook, (1992). Methods for determining of possible damage to people and objects resulting from release of hazardous materials, **Report CPR-16E**, Voorburg, Warrington, UK.

28. Hague, W J, and Pepe, W, (1990). Flow chamber simulations of aerosol formation and liquid jet break-up for pressurised releases of hydrogen fluoride. *Plant/Operations Prog.*, **9**, 125.

29. Hess, K, Hoffmann, W, and Stoeckel, A, (1974). Propagation processes after the bursting of tanks filled with liquid propane - experiments and mathematical model. *Loss prevention and safety promotion,* **1**, 227.

30. Hsu, S A, (1992). An overwater stability criterion for the offshore and coastal dispersion model, *Boundary Layer Meteorology,* **60**, 397.

31. Kayes, P J, (1986). *Manual of industrial hazard assessment technique*, Technica Ltd., London.

32. Kern, D Q, (1985). *Process heat transfer*, McGraw Hill publication, New York.

33. Khan, F I, and Abbasi, S A, (1995). Anatomy of industrial accidents, *Chemical Engineering World*, September, Bombay.

34. Khan F I, and Abbasi, S A, (1996). Accident simulation in CPI using MAXCRED, *Indian Journal of Chemical Technology*, **3**, 338.

35. Khan, F I, and Abbasi, S A, (1997a). Modelling and Simulation of Heavy gas dispersion on the basis of modifications in modified plume path theory, *Atmospheric Environment* (communicated) .

36. Khan, F I, and Abbasi, S A, (1997b). Risk analysis of epichlorohydrin industry using computer automated tool MAXCRED, *J. of Loss Prev. Process Ind.*, **10**, 11.

37. Khan, F I, and Abbasi, S A, (1997c). MAXCRED- A software package for quantitative risk analysis, Report No CPCE/R&D 5/94, Pondicherry University, Pondicherry, (1994); Environmental Modelling and Software (in press).

38. Kletz, T A, (1986). *What went wrong*, Gulf Publication, London.

39. Kletz, T A, (1984). The prevention of major leaks - better inspection after construction? *Plant/Operations Prog.*, **3**, 19.

40. Langlo Koing, G, and Schatzmawn, (1991). Wind tunnel modelling for heavy gas dispersion", *Atmospheric Environment*, **25 A**(7), 1188.

41. Lees, F P, (1996). *Loss prevention in the process industries*, **1**, Butterworths publication, 15/300.

42. Leung, J C, (1990). Similarity between flashing and non-flashing two-phase flows. *AIChE J.*, **36**, 797.

43. Leung, J C, and Epstein, M. (1990). The discharge of two-phase flashing flow from an inclined duct., *J.Heat Transfer*, **112**, 524.

44. Mahieu, A P, and Ooms, G, (1974). The plume path of vent gases, *Loss Prevention & Safety promotion in process industries*, Elsevier, New York, USA.

45. NEERI (1992). Risk assessment of Reliance petrochemical complex, *National Environmental Research Institute*, Nagpur, India.

46. Nolan, P F, Petty, G N, Hardy, N R, and Bettis, R J, (1990). Release conditions following loss of containment. *J. Loss Prev. in Process Ind.*, **3**(1), 97.

47. Ooms, G, and Tennekes, H, (eds) (1984). *Atmospheric dispersion of heavy gases and small particles*, Springer, Berlin

48. Pasquill, F, and Smith, F B, (1983). *Atmospheric diffusion, (third edition)*, John whiley, New York, .

49. Pasman, H J, Duxbury, H A and Bjordal, E N, (1992). Major hazards in the process industries : achievements and challenges in loss prevention, *Journal of Hazardous Materials*, **30**, 1.

50. Perry, R H, Green, D W, and Maloney, J O, (1984). *Perry's chemical engineering handbook*, McGraw Hill publication (6th edition), New York.

51. Pietersen, C M, (1990). Consequence of accidental release of hazardous materials, *Journal of Loss Prev. in Process Ind*, **3**, 136.

52. Picard, D J, and Bishnoi, (1988). The importance of real-fluid behaviour and non-isentropic effects in modelling decompression characteristics of pipeline fluids for application in ductile fracture propagation analysis, *Canadian J. of Chemical Engineering*, **66**, 3.

53. Pilborough, L, (1989). *Inspection of industrial plant, 2nd ed.*, Hampshire: Gower Technical, Aldershot.

54. Predikanis, G A, and Mayinego, Franz, (1994). Numerical simulation of heavy gas cloud dispersion within topographical complex terrain, *J. Loss Prevention. in Process Ind.*, **7**, 391.

55. Prugh, R W, (1991). Quantitative evaluation of BLEVE hazards, *Journal of Fire Protection Engineers*, **3**(1), 9-24.

56. Reed, R P, and Clark, A F, (1983). *Materials at low temperatures* , Amer. Soc. of Materials, Ohio, 395.

57. Roberts, C S, Timmis, R J, Hackman, M P, and Willianus, M L, (1992). *Proc of the 19th International technical meeting of NATO-CCMS on Air Pollution Modelling and its application (eds H Van Dop and G. Kalleos),* Plenem Press, New York, USA.

58. Shaw, P and Brisco, F, (1976). *Evaporation from spills of hazardous liquids, United Kingdom atomic energy report,* Report **SRD-100**, UK.

59. Sumathaipala, K, Venart, J E S, and Steward, F R, (1990b). Two-phase swelling and entrainment during pressure relief valve discharges. *J. Hazardous Materials*, **25**(1/2), 219.

60. Sutton, O G, (1948). The theoretical distribution of air borne pollution from factory chimneys, *J.Royl.Met.Soc.*, **73**,426.

61. Technica, (1992). *WHAZAN : A software for hazard assessment*, Technica Ltd., London.

62. TNO, (1991). *EFFECTS : A software for hazard assessment*, TNO Prins Mauritis Research Laboratory, The Netherlands.

63. TNO, (1992). *SAVE : A software for hazard assessment*, TNO Prins Mauritis Research Laboratory, The Netherlands.

64. TPL, (1993). Risk analysis of storage unit of chemical process industry, *Tamilnadu Petrochemical Ltd.*, Manali, Madras, India.

65. Turner, D B, (1970). Workbook of atmospheric dispersion estimates reports AP-26, *U S Env. Prot. Agency report no -NC 277111*, Qeseach Triangle park.

66. Turner, D B, (1985). Proposed pragmatic methods for estimating plume rise and plume penetration through atmospheric layers, *Atmospheric Environment*, **19**, 1215-1218, .

67. Van Ulden, A P, and Hostlag, A A, (1985). Estimation of atmospheric boundary layer parameters for diffusion application, *Journal of Climate and Applied Meteorology*, **24**, 1196 .

68. Van Ulden, A P, (1988). The spreading and mixing of a dense cloud in still air. *In Puttock, J.S. 1988b*, 141.

69. Van Ulden, A P, (1992). A surface-layer similarity model for the dispersion of a skewed passive puff near the ground, *Atmospheric Environment*, **26A**, 681.

70. Van Ulden, A P, (1974). The spreading of a heavy gas released near the ground, *Loss Prevention*, **1**, 221.

71. Vernart, J E S, Rutledge, G.A., Sumathipala,K. and Sollows, K., (1993). To BLEVE or not to BLEVE ; Anatomy of Boiling Liquid expanding vapour Explosion, *Process Safety Progress*, **2**, 112.

72. VTT, (1993). RISKIT : a software for risk assessment, *The Technical Research Centre of Finland*, Tempere, The Finland.

73. Woodward, J L, (1990). An integrated model for discharge rate, pool spread, and dispersion from punctured vessels. *J.Loss Prev. in Process Ind.*, **3,** 33.

74. Woodward, J L, and Mudan, K S, (1991). Liquid and gas discharge rates through holes in process vessels, *J.Loss Prev. in Process Ind.*,**4**, 161.

¨ Reproduced from *Journal of Loss Prevention in Process Industries*, UK

10

MOSEC (MODELLING AND SIMULATION OF FIRES AND EXPLOSIONS IN CHEMICAL PROCESS INDUSTRIES): A Tool for Consequence Analysis*

A computer-automated tool (software package) has been developed for the modelling and simulation of fires and explosions in chemical process industries. In this paper the concepts, techniques, and methodologies, including the software engineering which forms the basis of the package have been described. The special attributes of the package include a) wide range of applications - achieved by incorporating models capable of handling all types of industrial fires and explosions, b) sophistication - brought about by including state-of-the-art models developed by these authors and others, c) user-friendliness - achieved by incorporating on-line help, graphics, carefully formatted output, and, above all, an automatic module with which even a lay user can conduct risk assessment. The entire package, especially its automatic module, is supported by an extensive knowledge-base built into the software.

The efficacy of the software has been illustrated by describing its successful use in conducting risk assessment in a real-life situation (of a storage unit in a typical petroleum refinery).

Key words : Industrial fires, industrial explosions, risk assessment, hazard assessment, industrial accidents

INTRODUCTION

Likelihood of fires and explosions are two of the major hazards associated with chemical process industries.

Explosions may be caused by several factors:

a) Pressure in a vessel or a pipe rising above critical limits due to excessive inflow of chemicals caused by a malfunctioning of flow controls - as happened at Flixborough(Less, 1996; Khan and Abbasi, 1997a; Marshall, 1987).

b) Leakage of flammable material, which may then mix with air, and form a vapour cloud. The cloud may drift until meeting a source of ignition and exploding.

* Reproduced from Process Safety Progress, USA.

c) Pressure in an equipment rising above critical limits due to runaway reaction (generation of gases and/or heat).

d) Ignition of a flammable chemical in confinement causing building of pressure (due to heat load and combustion products) far above safety pressure.

e) Boiling of chemical in the confinement due to absorption of external heat, thereby generating overpressure.

f) Failures of chemical storage vessels due to fracture, development of cracks, or corrosion.

g) Release of highly pressurised fluid through a narrow opening (crack, leak from joints, leakage of gasket, etc.) causing sudden phase change which may develop overpressure and generate shock waves.

Fires occur more frequently in chemical process industries than other types of accidents eventhough a large number of them are put off before significant damage is done. But major fires can be very destructive. Fires are also among the most frequent causes of explosions.

Fires can break out for various reasons:

i) ignition of flammable chemical exiting from an opening (valve or crack);

ii) continuous/instantaneous release of flammable gas which on meeting a source of ignition catches fire;

iii) continuous/instantaneous release of liquid flammable chemical either through regular openings such as valves or through irregular opening such as leaks or cracks, creating pools of liquid which on ignition catch fire.

The destructive impact of explosion generally covers wider area than the region-of-impact of a fire. Secondly, except in certain cases when ambient conditions conspire to enable very rapid spread of a fire, most fires take time to consolidate. If emergency preparedness measures are in place, this time proves crucial in enabling to control the fire. On the other hand, when an explosion takes place it does so instantly, giving no time to escape from it.

In very large situations, explosions in chemical process industries are either caused by fire, or lead to a fire. It is therefore necessary to study explosions and fires together eventhough they are essentially two very different types of events.

MECHANISMS OF THE DAMAGE CAUSED BY EXPLOSIONS AND FIRES

An explosion in air is a sudden release of energy accompanied by the production of a shock wave and loud noise. It has the potential to injure living systems and damage assets such as buildings and the environment. The violence of an explosion depends on the rate at which energy is released.

Explosions in chemical process industries are associated with sudden release of physical energy, chemical energy, or both.

Physical energy is manifested as pressure energy in gases, strain energy in metals or electrical energy. Examples of the violent release of physical energy are the explosion of a vessel due to high gas pressure and the sudden rupture of a vessel due to brittle fracture (Lees, 1991). In such explosions, the violence of which depends upon the internal pressure, damage may be caused by a blast wave from the expanding gas or by portions of the disrupting container. At times parts of such a vessel may be shot away to hundreds of meters. Explosions often occur if pressure on a liquefied gas (which seldom exceeds 40 bars as this is the critical pressure of most common liquefied gases) is suddenly released (Marshall, 1987).

Chemical explosions involve energy derived from a chemical reaction. Explosion of a vessel due to combustion of flammable gas, and explosion of a reactor caused by decomposition of reaction products in a runaway chemical reaction, are examples of accidents involving chemical energy.

As stated, an explosion may involve both kinds of energy and thus it is important to study the role of both types of energies singly and in combination in order to understand (and the control) the mechanism of industrial explosions.

Deflagration and detonation

Combustion of flammable gas may lead to two kinds of explosions: deflagration or detonation. In a deflagration the flammable mixture burns relatively slowly. For hydrocarbon-air mixtures the deflagration velocity is typically of the order of 1 m/s.

In a detonation the flame front travels as a shock wave followed closely by a combustion wave which releases the energy to sustain the shock wave. The detonation front may reach velocities of the order of the velocity of sound and the hot products of combustion may have supersonic velocities. For hydrocarbon-air mixtures the detonation velocity is typically of the order of 2000-3000 m/s.

A detonation generates greater pressures and is more destructive than a deflagration. But, a deflagration may turn into a detonation, particularly when travelling down a long pipe. Where a transition from deflagration to detonation is occurs, the deflagration velocity naturally exceeds that quoted above.

Types of explosion

Explosions in the storage or process units can be categorised in four main groups, according to their mode of occurrence and damage potential:

- confined vapour cloud explosion-CVCE, (Baker *et al.*, 1983; WHO, 1984; Lunn, 1989, Catlin, 1991; Greenbook, 1992)
- vapour cloud explosion-VCE, (Kletz, 1977; Prugh, 1987; Pietersen, 1990; Van den Berg, 1985; Van den Berg and Lennoy, 1993; Van den Berg, 1984);
- boiling liquid expanding vapour explosion-BLEVE, (Birk and Cunningham, 1994; CCPS, 1989; Prugh, 1991; Venarat *et al.*, 1993);
- vented explosion (Catlin, 1991; Harrison and Keyre, 1987; Cates and Bimson, 1991; Kalghatgi, 1983).

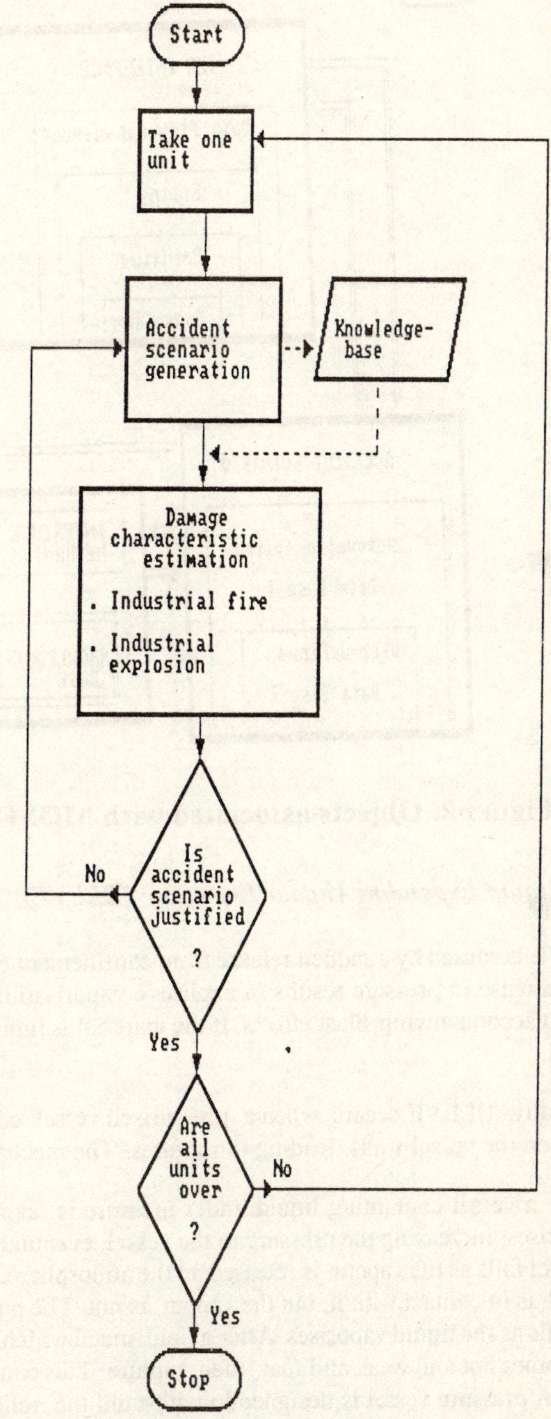

Figure 1. The algorithm of MOSEC

These explosions are initiated either by the thermal stratification of the liquid and vapour or by such high explosion shock waves, which have sufficient strength to rupture the reaction/storage vessels or conduits. An explosion may or may not be accompanied with fire; it depends upon the type of explosion and the chemical involved in the explosion. A brief description of each type of explosion is presented below.

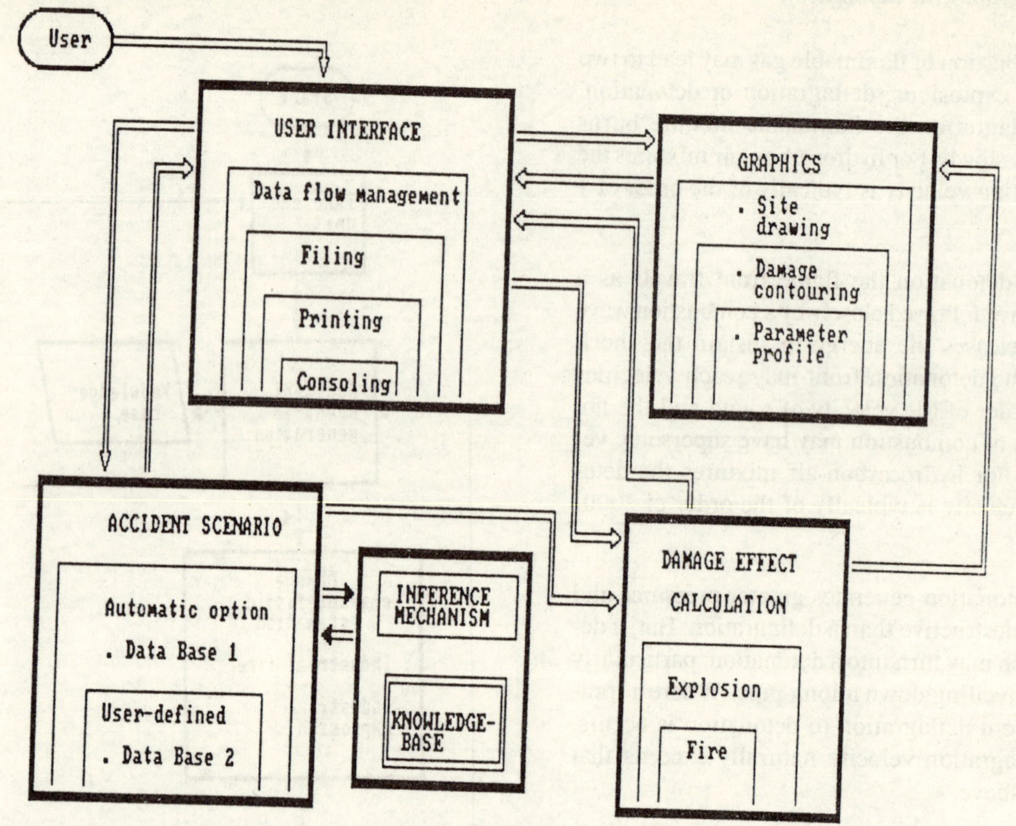

Figure 2. Objects associated with MOSEC and the message flow across them.

Boiling Liquid Expanding Vapour Explosion (BLEVE)

BLEVE is caused by a sudden release from confinement of a liquid at a temperature above its boiling point. The sudden decrease in pressure results in explosive vaporisation of a fraction of the liquid and a cloud of vapour and mist, with accompanying blast effects. If the material is flammable and an ignition source is present, a fire ball may be formed.

Generally, BLEVE occurs when a pressurised vessel containing a flammable liquid is exposed to fire which may weaken the vessel walls, leading to ruptures. The mechanism is as detailed below:

When a vessel containing liquid under pressure is exposed to fire, the liquid heats up and the vapour pressure rises, increasing the pressure in the vessel, eventually activating the pressure relief valve. The liquid level in the vessel falls as the vapour is released to the atmosphere. The liquid is effective in cooling that part of the vessel wall which is in contact with it, but the vapour is not. The portion of the vessel wall which has the benefit of liquid cooling falls as the liquid vaporises. After a time, metal which is not cooled by liquid becomes exposed to the fire; the metal becomes hot and weak and may then rupture. This can occur eventhough the pressure relief valve is operating correctly. A pressure vessel is designed to withstand the relief valve set pressure, but only within the design temperature conditions. If the metal has its temperature raised, it may lose strength sufficiently to and get ruptured.

A BLEVE of a vessel containing a flammable liquid gives rise to the following effects: (1) blast wave, (2) fragments and (3) fireball.

Vapour Cloud Explosion (VCE)

The delayed spontaneous ignition of a vapour cloud of flammable chemical in a unconfined or semi-

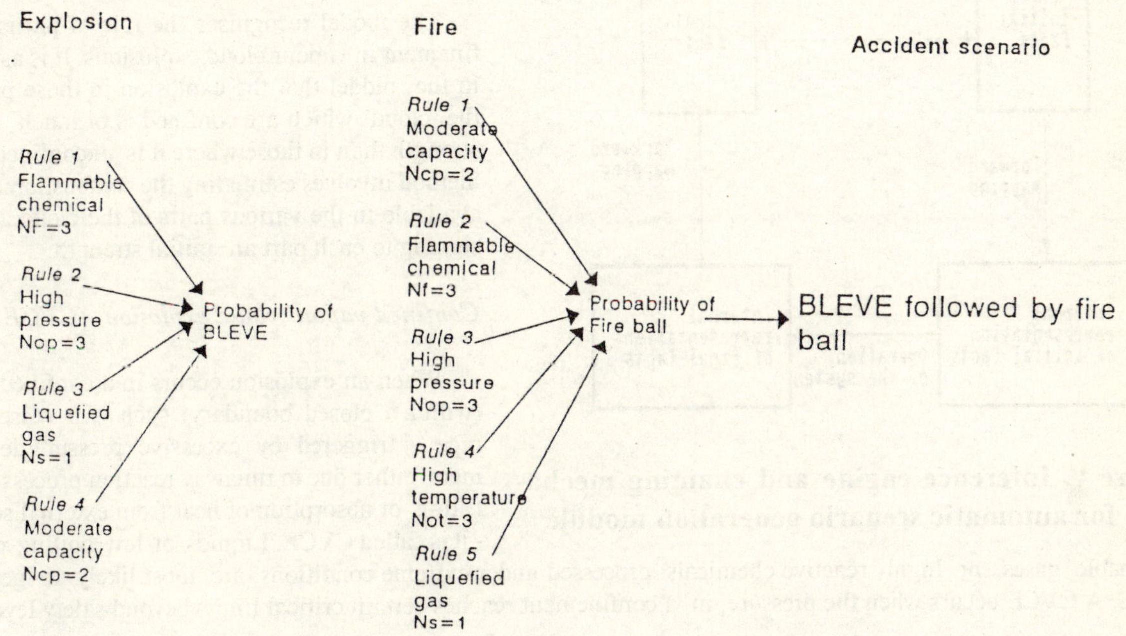

Figure 3. Rule network for the accident scenario BLEVE followed by fire ball

unconfined (congested boundary) space results in vapour cloud explosion (VCE) or unconfined vapour cloud explosion (UVCE). Until the early 1980s a vapour cloud explosion (VCE) was generally referred to as an unconfined vapour cloud explosion (UVCE). However, since in combustion of a vapour cloud the overpressure tends to occur due to the presence of structures and obstacles and of partial confinements, the term 'unconfined' is now generally omitted.

A vapour cloud explosion is one of the most serious hazards in the process industries because a vapour cloud may drift some distance from the point where the leak has occurred before exploding; it may thus threaten areas lying far away from the source of the vapour cloud.

The importance of the vapour cloud explosion hazard has grown in recent years. Whereas in earlier times the major disasters tended to be those caused by explosives, including ammonium nitrate, many of the recent disasters have been due to vapour cloud explosions.

Two approaches are used to assess vapour cloud explosions: one is the TNT equivalent model and the other is multi-energy method (Van den Berg and co-workers, 1984, 1985, 1991, 1993). They are briefed here.

In the TNT equivalent model the explosion is taken to be equivalent to that of a TNT explosion. This model is empirical but, within its limitations, has served the study of explosions rather well.

The TNT equivalent model is based on a single parameter: the mass of TNT. It is made more flexible by taking into consideration a second parameter -the height above ground at which the explosion occurs. Higher the point of explosion lower is the overpressure near the epicentre. The use of an arbitrary assumed explosion height helps in obtaining better fits to overpressure assessed from damage in actual explosion.

The TNO vapour cloud explosion model is the multi-energy (ME) model described by Van den Berg (1984), Van

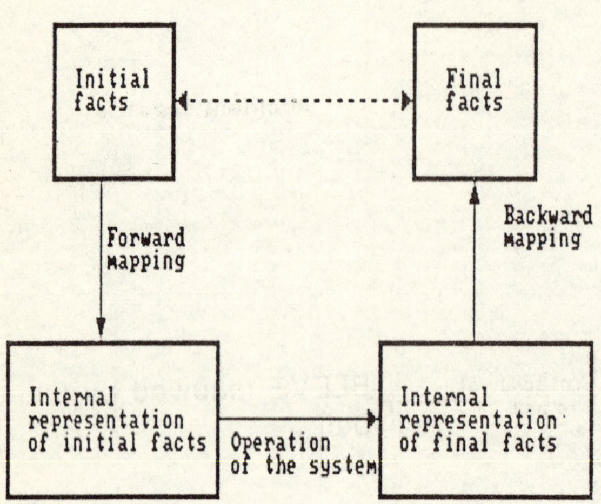

Figure 4. Inference engine and chaining mechanism for automatic scenario generation module

den Berg, (1985), Van den Berg *et al.*, (1991), Van den Berg and Lennoy (1993). This model allows the peak overpressure, peak dynamic pressure and duration time to be estimated.

The model recognises the role of partial confinement in vapour cloud explosions. It is assumed in the model that the explosion in those parts of the cloud which are confined is of much higher strength than in those where it is unconfined. The method involves estimating the combustion energy available in the various parts of the cloud and assigning to each part an initial strength.

Confined vapour cloud explosion (CVCE)

When an explosion occurs in a confined space (within a closed boundary) such as a vessel or a pipe - triggered by excessive pressure development either due to runaway reaction process, overfilling, or absorption of heat from external sources - it is called CVCE. Liquids of low boiling points, flammable gases, or highly reactive chemicals processed under extreme conditions, are most likely to generate CVCE. A CVCE occurs when the pressure in a confinement reaches certain critical limits beyond safety level.

The explosion energy leading to the bursting of a vessel is a function of the initial pressure, which in turn depends on the failure scenario. The higher the pressure, the stronger the explosion.

If the vessel fails due to build up of pressure inside it beyond critical levels, and because the pressure relief valve has failed, the vessel will burst at a pressure which is some multiple of the design pressure.

If the vessel fails due to material defect, wear-and-tear, or corrosion, or powerful impact, the burst pressure will be the operating pressure.

If fire engulfment occurs, but with the pressure relief operating, the pressure at the moment of vessel rupture will be the accumulation pressure. This is the typical scenario of a BLEVE. In principle, the energy available will be partitioned as energy in (1) vessel expansion, (2) vessel rupture, (3) blast, and (4) fragments.

The impact of CVCE can be observed over a much larger distance than UVCE. Due to its large area of impact and more severe shock waves CVCE also has greater potential of causing secondary, tertiary and higher order accidents (domino / cascading effects).

Vented explosion

Vented explosion is a phenomenon observed because of the formation of fire torch in a vessel due to ignition of a flammable chemical (gas or liquid) at release point. In this situation the flame front may move backwards in the vessel with high speed and ignite the contents of the vessel resulting in excessive pressure development leading to an explosion. In vented explosion flame front speed may reach over 50 m/s. It is differentiated from CVCE by its mode of initiation and its damaging effects. Eventhough vented explosion also generates shock wave, over pressure, heat load, and missiles, its damaging effects are generally confined to smaller areas than the impacts of CVCE. The intensity of the damaging effects are also lower: a vented explosion typically generates shock (blast) wave of 330 to 500 m/s and overpressure of 0.3 to 10 atm.

Fire

Fire occurs when a source of heat comes in contact with a combustible material. If a combustible liquid or solid is

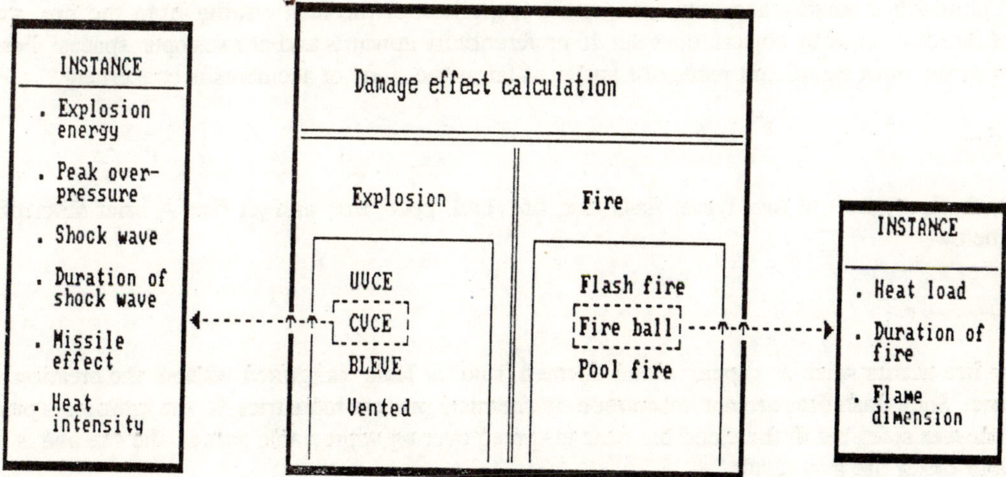

Figure 5. The internal architecture of damage effect calculation module

heated it evolves vapour, and if the concentration of vapour is high enough it forms a flammable mixture with the oxygen of the air. If this flammable mixture is then heated further to its ignition point, combustion starts. Similarly, a combustible gas or vapour burns if it is heated to a sufficiently high temperature.

Three components must be present if fire is to occur: (1) fuel, (2) oxygen, and (3) heat. These components are often called as 'the fire triangle'. If one of the components is missing, fire does not occur and if one of them is removed, fire is extinguished.

Fire is generally initiated by an external source (such as a spark). It is then perpetuated and intensified by the combustion process itself. The three components essential for a fire also provide us the clue on how to model the fire, indeed how to fight it.

The first step towards stopping a fire is to cut off the fuel. This is particularly relevant for fires caused by leaks in process plant. The second method is to remove heat. This is usually done by putting water on the fire. The third method is to stop the supply of oxygen. This may be effected in various ways, including the use of foam or inert gas.

When fire reaches close to a vessel or it transfers to it a heat load which may be large enough to overcome the creep of the material of construction of the vessel or overheat its contents generating excessive pressure, an explosion may result. Important aspects of modelling fire -related accidents are: flame height, flame merging phenomena in fires in close proximity, the effect of wind on flame tilt and length, and heat load.

Fire is among the most common accident that occurs in chemical industries; it is estimated that fire of large or small magnitude occurs at least once a year. There is considerable possibility that one among ten fires can generate heat load large enough to precipitate a significant accident.

In a fire, the heat is not uniformly distributed. In some parts, particularly near the edge of the fire, the heat balance may be only just positive. The fire extinguishers should be directed to those parts of the fire so as to hit it at its weakest points.

Fire normally grows and spreads by direct burning, which results from impingement of the flame on combustible materials, by heat transfer or by movement of the burning material.

All the three modes of heat transfer -conduction, convection, and radiation are significant in heat transfer from fires. Conduction is important particularly in allowing heat to pass through a solid barrier and ignite material on the other side. Most of the heat transfer from fires, however, is by convection and radiation. It is estimated that in most fires some 75% of the heat emanates by convection. The hot products of combustion rising from a fire typically have a temperature in the range 800-1200°C and density a quarter that of air. Radiation is the other main mode of heat transfer. Although it usually accounts for a small proportion of the heat issuing from the fire, radiated heat is transferred directly to nearby objects, does not go preferentially upwards and crosses open spaces. For these reasons it is generally the most significant mode of transfer as far as the study of accidents is concerned.

Types of fire

Industrial fires are of four types: flash fire, fire ball, pool fire, and jet fire. A brief description of each is presented below.

Flash fire

A flash fire occurs when a vapour cloud, formed from a leak, is ignited without the creation of significant overpressure. Such flash fires are not uncommon in chemical process industries. If the ignition is prompt the cloud may be modest in size, but if the cloud has time to spread over an appreciable part of the site and is then ignited, a major vapour cloud fire may result.

Flash fire is modelled by considering dispersion of the vapour cloud and its ignition. One of the first such models was by Eisenberg *et al.* (1975) in which the vapour cloud was assumed to be a half ellipsoid. In another model of Raj and Emmons (1975), the speed of the flame propagating through the vapour cloud is taken into account. It is assumed that during the combustion of a vapour cloud there is a turbulent flame front propagating into the unburned cloud at constant velocity which is roughly proportional to the wind speed, and that at high gas concentrations there is a tall flame plume at the edge of the unburned cloud. A modified version of this model has been recommended for use by CCPS (1994) (centre for chemical process safety) in their guidelines (1994). Considine and Grint (1985) have developed graphs linking distance from flash fire to fatal injury.

Fire balls

A spontaneous ignition of vapour cloud not having sufficient energy to explode leads to *fire ball.* This phenomenon is generally observed for high boiling yet highly flammable liquids stored or processed at extreme conditions of temperature and pressure. Most treatments of fireballs relate to liquefied gas. A distinction must be made between a fireball resulting from the bursting of a pressure vessel and the one resulting from the formation of a vapour cloud. In the former the bursting may be caused by a fire and can be part of a BLEVE or it may occur in the absence of fire. In such cases momentum forces predominate. But in the latter case buoyancy forces play dominant role. The destructive ability of fire ball is very high as the heat load generated by it is of the order of 1000 kJ/m^2. The fire ball radii generally vary from 100 meter to 300 meter and its impact duration from few seconds to few minutes.

The modelling of fireballs involves consideration of : (1) the fireball regime, (2) the mass of fuel in the fireball, (3) the fireball development and time scales, (4) the fireball diameter and duration, (5) the heat radiated and (6) the view factor. A fireball may be of a relatively short duration, but it passes in its life cycle through several distinct stages which need to be carefully defined if confusion is to be avoided(Roberts, 1982).

Pool fire

When a flammable liquid spills onto the ground and is ignited, a pool fire results. A fire in a liquid storage tank is also a form of pool fire, as is a trench fire. A pool fire may also occur on the surface of flammable liquid spilled onto water.

A pool fire burns with a flame which is often taken to be a cylinder with a height twice the pool diameter. In still air the flame is vertical, but in wind it tilts. Wind also causes the base of the flame to extend beyond the downwind edge of the pool, thus exhibiting flame drag. In some pool fires blowout can occur at a wind speed of about 5 m/s.

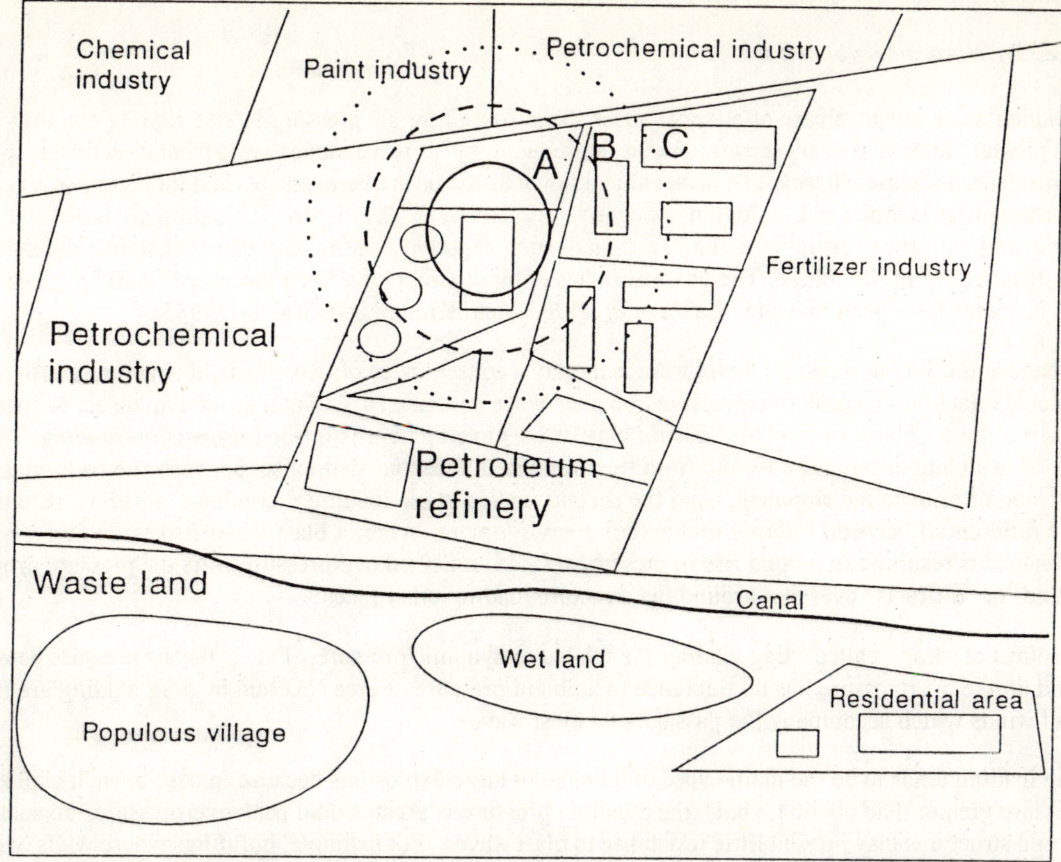

Figure 6. Damage contours indicating the impact area of an accident in LPG storage vessel; 75% probability of damage (A), 50% probability of damage (B), and 10% probability of damage (C)

The characteristics of a pool fire depend on the pool diameter. The liquid burning rate increases with diameter until for large diameters it reaches a fixed value. The heat radiated from the flame behaves similarly.

In modelling pool fires the following aspects have to be taken into account (1) flamc geometry, (2) liquid burning rate, (3) flame characteristics, (4) heat radiated and (5) view factor.

Jet fire

Burning of a flammable gas issuing from a pipe or other orifice at the point of exit leads to jet fire. Jet flames have been involved in a number of accidents. Perhaps the most dramatic were the large jet flames from the gas riser at Piper Alpha(Less, 1996; Lees, 1991).

Jet flame can occur in chemical process industries, either by design or by accident. They occur intentionally in burners and flares. Ejection of flammable fluid from a vessel, pipe or pipe flange can give rise to a jet flame if the material ignites. An intermediate situation, and one which particularly concerns the designer, is where the jet flame results from ignition of flammable material vented from a pressure relief valve. Scenarios involving jet flames are not easy to handle, since a large jet flame may have a substantial 'reach', sometimes up to 50 m or more.

Compared to pool fire and fire balls, jet flames can occur in more diverse ways. The scenario most often considered is that of a vertical flame or an upward pointing jet, in calm conditions or in wind. But a jet may point upwards not vertically but at an angle, in such a case there may be a variety of wind directions, confluent with, opposed to or across the jet. There can also be a horizontal jet too, on which the wind may act in tandem, opposed to, or across it.

IMPACT OF EXPLOSIONS AND FIRES

Overpressure/Blast waves/Shock waves

A sudden and violent release of energy causes the surrounding air pressure to rise rapidly creating a region of positive pressure known as *overpressure*. As the consequent 'blast' wave moves away from its source at high velocity the overpressure increases sharply to a peak value, known as the peak overpressure, and then gradually recedes. The overpressure phase is followed by a region of negative pressure or underpressure. This pressure is generally insignificant compared with the overpressure phase, although such negative pressure can cause moderate damage especially at close distances from the charge. The characteristics of blast waves have been discussed briefly by Lees (1996) and detailed accounts have been given by Baker *et al.* (1983), and Kinney and Graham (1985).

Damage and injury as a result of explosion is largely a consequence of two effects, diffraction and drag. Diffraction effect is related to the peak overpressure of a blast wave as it passes over and around an object or structure. The force exerted on an object or structure during blast wave envelopment is termed *diffraction loading*. The loading consists of two components: one results from the pressure differential that exists between the front and back of an object/structure prior to envelopment, and the second -called static loading ("crushing" forces) - results from the pressure differential between internal and external environment. When a blast wave strikes an object or structure, reflection occurs resulting in a rapid rise in pressure termed 'reflected overpressure'. As the pressure drops the blast wave bends or "diffracts" over and around the structure loading other faces.

The effect of 'drag', called 'drag loading', is related to dynamic pressure. This is the air pressure behind a shock front and unlike overpressure has no reference to ambient pressure. Forces exerted by drag loading are the result of transient winds which accompany the passage of a blast wave.

Drag loading tends to be the main cause of damage in large explosions because in case of such explosions (peak overpressure greater than about 4.8 bar), the dynamic pressure is greater than peak overpressure. In such situations objects and structures may present little resistance to blast waves. For example, buildings whose walls, windows and doors rapidly fail during blast wave interaction cause prompt equalisation of interior and exterior environments. This in turn can reduce the duration and magnitude of diffraction loading to a negligible level.

All objects and structures simultaneously suffer both diffraction and drag loading because overpressure and dynamic pressure both exist during a blast and cannot be separated. The relative importance of each load type is largely dependent on size, shape, weight and resistance of objects and structures. Closed or semi-closed structures, such as buildings with small openings or large tanks, etc. are vulnerable to diffraction loading, whereas, tall thin objects and buildings with large openings are vulnerable to drag loading.

In the modelling of blast wave damage, recourse is most often taken in assessing overpressure. This is probably due to its ease of measurement and estimation compared with other damage-relation criteria. However, blast wave damage is also a function of rate of pressure rise and wave duration, and these factors are also considered in some models. An impulse is also used as measure of blast damage. Impulse is a function of both overpressure and wave duration. It is often considered a better measure of blast wave damage.

Missile

Objects or their fragments may be turned to missiles as a result of energy delivered to them by an explosion and can cause significant damage to the bodies they hit.

The missiles are characterised by velocity, range and penetration. The missiles may be either primary or secondary. Primary missiles consist of casing and/or container fragments from the exploded unit, whereas secondary missiles consist of fragments from objects located close to the explosion source which have interacted with the blast wave.

The missiles generated from cased charges have initial energy of the order of 20% - 60% of the explosion energy. The initial velocity of the missile can be calculated from.

$$E = 1/2*M*V^2$$

Where, E denotes energy associated with fragments (J), M is mass of fragment (kg), and V is velocity of missile (m/s).

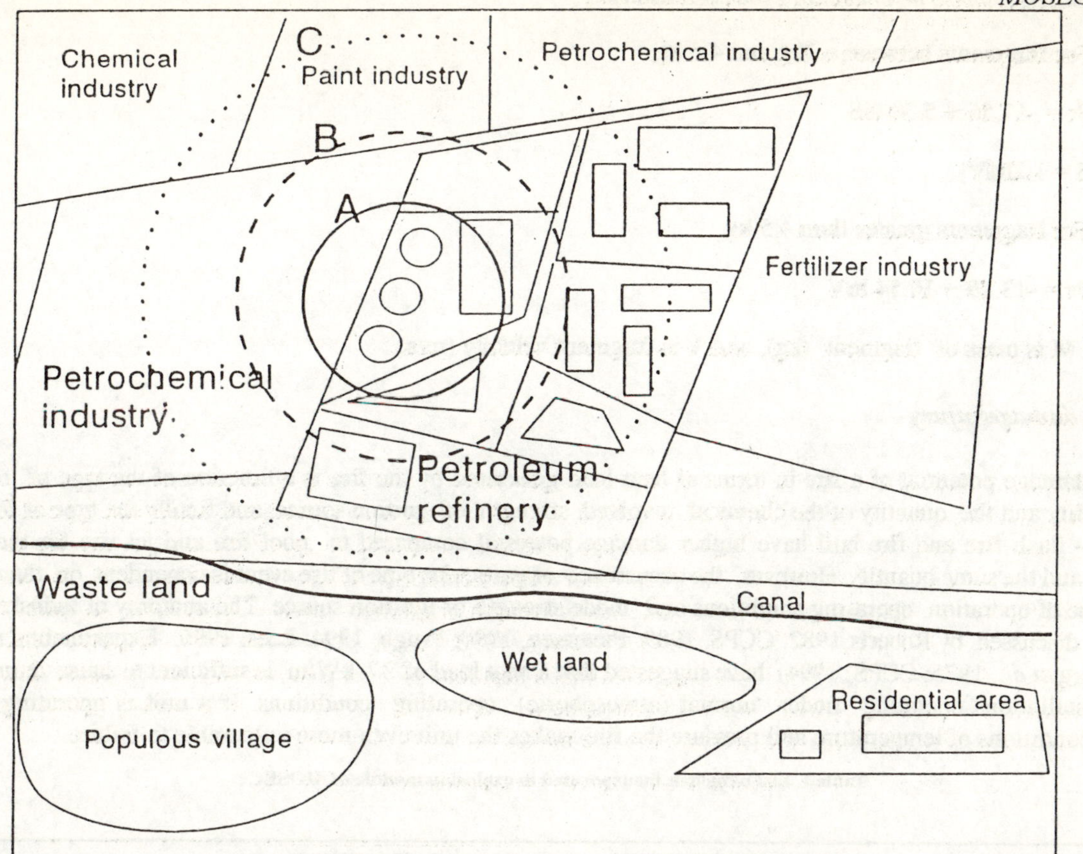

Figure 7. Damage contours indicating the impact area of an accident in ethylene storage vessel; 75% probability of damage (A), 50% probability of damage (B), and 10% probability of damage (C)

The range of a missile is calculated using an empirical equation (CCPS, 1989; CCPS, 1994; Davies, 1993).

$$X = (W^{1/3}/kCd) (\ln U/V)$$

Where X denotes the range (m), W fragment mass (kg), U initial fragment velocity (m/s), V fragment velocity (m/s), k is a constant (0.002 velocity supersonic, 0.0014 velocity subsonic) and Cd is the drag coefficient.

Depending on the momentum they carry when they hit an object, the missiles may cause damage varying from the superficial to the devastating. According to Explosives Storage and Transport Committee (ESTC), UK, missile with ~80 J of kinetic energy may prove lethal to humans Davies (1993). The ESTC suggests that one fragment per 56 square meters provides individuals who are out in the open with a 1% chance of being hit. Buildings and other relatively large objects can be crushed or penetrated by missiles leading to minor hazards, such as, falling debris and glass breakage. However, impulsive loading during impact, especially from large heavy missiles, presents the greatest indirect hazard. This is because impulsive loads may instigate or encourage collapse of structures and/or escalate the amount and rate of falling debris and glass breakage. The missile may also lead to the initiation of domino effects (Khan and Abbasi, 1997b; 1997c), so much so that the secondary or higher order accidents thus caused may generate more damage than the primary event.

The department of industrial safety, The Netherlands has proposed equations relating the probability of fatality to skin penetration based on fragment velocity and mass (Pasman *et al.*, 1992).

For fragments of less than 0.1 kg.

$$Pr = -29.15+2.10 \ln S$$

where S equals $MV^{5.115}$

For fragments between o.1kg and 4.5 kg,

$$Pr = -17.56 + 5.30 \ln S$$

$$S = 1/2MV^2 ,$$

For fragments greater than 4.5 kg,

$$Pr = -13.19 + 10.54 \ln V$$

where M is mass of fragment (kg), and V is fragment velocity (m/s).

Thermal damage/injury

The damage potential of a fire in terms of heat load generated by the fire is a function of the type of release, flammability and the quantity of the chemical involved, strength of ignition source, and finally the type of fire. For example - flash fire and fire ball have higher damage potential compared to pool fire and jet fire for the same chemical and the same quantity. However, the occurrence of particular type of fire event is dependent on the release mode, type of operation, operating conditions and mode/strength of ignition source. The anatomy of industrial fire has been discussed by Roberts,1982; CCPS, 1989; Pietersen, 1990; Prugh, 1994; Lees, 1996. Experimental studies (Eissenberg *et al.*, 1975; CCPS, 1994) have suggested that a heat load of 37 kW/m^2 is sufficient to cause damage to other installations operating under normal (atmospheric) operating conditions. If a unit is operating under extreme conditions of temperature and pressure the fire makes the unit even more vulnerable to failure.

Table 1. List of models incorporated in explosion module of MOSEC

Event	Models name/type	Important references
CVCE	Isothermal and adiabatic expansion,combustion in confinement, and heat transfer models	Lunn6,1989; Kayes50, 1986; Davenport51,1986; Phylaktou & Andrews48,1991; Pietersen11,1990; Scheuermann49,1994; CCPS16,25; Singh52, 1988;
UVCE	Releases and dispersion models, TNT equivalent and multi energy models	Baker et al4,1983; Scilly and High53,1986; Prugh10,1987; Van den Berg and co-workers12-14,22, 1984,1985,1989,1993; Van Wingerden and co-workers53,54, 1989,1994
BLEVE	Thermodynamic and heat transfer models, empirical models	CCPS16,25; Prugh17,1991; Johnson and Pritchard55,1991; Singh52,1988; Venart et al18,1994; Birk and Cunningham15,1994;
Vented explosion	Release with momentum, combustion model, flame propagation, adiabatic expansion, and heat transfer models	Harrison and Cyre19, 1987; Cates and Samules56,1991; Cates and Bimson20, 1992; Greenbook8,1992;
Missile effect	Momentum and energy balance models, empirical models	Munday57,1980; Holden and Reeves58,1985; Hart and Croft59,1988; Scilly and Crowther60,1992; Pasman et al33,1992; Khan and Abbasi32,1997
Blast wave effect	Overpressure impulse models, peak dynamic pressure model,charge distance model, and thermodynamic model	Dangreaux61,1986; Davenport51,1986; Esparza62,1986; Prugh17,1991; Davies30,1993; Greenbook8,1992

Vis a vis impacts on humans, correlations for both fatal and non-fatal burn injuries have been derived by Eisenberg *et al.* (1975). Such impacts depend very much on the source of radiation. One such source which is of long-standing interest is a flare. Another source of thermal radiation which has received increasing attention is a fireball. A fireball is better defined than most other types of fire to which people may be exposed; it is also one of the fire hazards most likely to give rise to a large number of serious injuries.

Besides scorching, fire may also induce lethality by causing rapid depletion of oxygen in the atmosphere due to the consumption of oxygen in the combustion process. This impact is generally limited to the immediate vicinity of the fire. Of importance also are the health effects arising from exposure to the fumes generated as a result of fire. These fumes may include toxic gases, such as sulphur dioxide from the combustion of carbon disulphide and nitrous oxides from a fire involving ammonium nitrate.

When the thermal radiation load on a process vessel becomes intense (greater than 37 kW/m^2), the pressure and temperature inside the vessel increase rapidly. Normally, the pressure relief valve opens when the corresponding set pressure is reached. It may open and close several times and may eventually remain open if the thermal inflow to the tank is sufficient to maintain the necessary level of vaporisation. If the thermal radiation inflow continues unchecked, the shell temperature and vapour space pressure increase to levels that weaken the materials of construction and a rupture ensues with a large energy release. Under such circumstances, high velocity fragments of the vessel can be propelled over long distances.

MOSEC (MODELLING AND SIMULATION OF FIRES AND EXPLOSIONS IN CHEMICAL PROCESS INDUSTRIES)

Among the available software packages specialising in assessment of risk due to explosion and fires are BLAST (Van den Berg, 1980), FIRE2 (Pritchard and Binding, 1992), REAGAS (Van den Berg, 1989), SAFETI (Pitbaldo and Nalpanis, 1989), SAVE (TNO, 1992), EFFECTS (TNO, 1991), RISKIT (VTT, 1993), CMBWAT (Madsen and Wagner, 1994). MOSEC has aimed to substantially improve upon these in terms of:

- *greater applicability* - achieved by incorporating large number of models and modules for studying a wider range of situations;
- *greater sophistication* - achieved by incorporating the most refined and recent models and methodologies; also by using one of the most advanced coding tool viz C++;
- *greater user-friendliness* - achieved by adding features such as 'automatic module' so that even a person not well-versed in chemical engineering or risk assessment can gainfully use the tool. The architecture, internal contents, and capabilities of MOSEC are described below.

Structure

MOSEC (Figure 1) has four main modules namely, i) accident scenario generation, ii) damage effect calculation, iii) graphics interface and iv) user interface. The hierarchy of these modules is shown in Figure 2. Each module has its own sub-modules, function, and attributes.

Accident scenario generation module

This module helps the user to generate credible scenario of all likely ways in which fire and/or explosion may occur in an industry. This step is of overwhelming importance because the more realistic an accident scenario, the more accurate is forecasting of the type of accident, its consequences, and associated risks. Consequently this step holds the key to development of the most appropriate and effective strategies for crisis prevention and management.

Each accident scenario is basically a combination of different likely accidental events that may occur in an industry. Such scenarios are generated based on the properties of chemicals handled by the industry, physical conditions under which reactions occur or reactants/products are stored, geometries and material strengths of vessel and conduits, valves and safety arrangements etc. External factors such as site characteristics (topography, presence of trees, ponds, rivers in the vicinity, proximity to other industries or neighbourhoods etc.) and meteorological conditions are also considered. In the available software packages such as BLAST (Van den Berg, 1980), FIRE2 (Pritchard and Binding, 1992) this concept of risk assessment has been used to some extent. But the level of sophistication needs to be enhanced substantially by using advanced models of thermodynamics, heat transfer, and fluid dynamics to generate more realistic accident scenarios. Furthermore, the user-friendliness of these packages have some limitations.

Table 2. List of models incorporated in fire module of MOSEC.

Event	Models name/type	Important references
Flash fire	Spontaneous combustion, isothermal expansion, heat transfer, and damage distance model	Considine and Grint26,1985; Kayes50,1986, CCPS25; Lees1,1996; de Faveri et al63,1985
Fire ball	Spontaneous combustion turbulence and heat transfer, empirical models for fire ball dimension and duration	Moorehouse and Pritchard64,1982; Roberts27,1983; Marshall3,1987; CCPS16,25; Prugh34,1994; Lees65,1994
Pool fire	Release, vaporization combustion models, and vulnerability models	Moorehouse66,1982; Considine35,1984; Kayes50,1986; Crocker and Napier67,68,1986;1989; Greenbook62,1992
Jet fire	Flare,fire torch models thermodynamic heat transfer models, and vulnerability models	Kalaghatgi21,1983; de Faveri et al63,1985; Crocker and Napier68,1986; Cowley and Pritchard69,1991; Johnson et al70,1994

For example Olaniya *et al.* (1996) have presented a risk assessment case study of a fertilizer plant. A number of accident scenarios have been visualised in various units of the plant using software SAFETI (Pitblado and Nalpanis, 1989) and EFFECT (TNO, 1991). Almost all accidents have been visualised as one-likely-mode leading to one-likely consequence. For example rupture of secondary reformer has been visualised only as a vapour cloud explosion (VCE), instantaneous hydrogen release also only as VCE; failure of associated gas pipe line also as VCE, and leak in methanator as flare (flash fire). However, storing or processing large quantities of chemicals under extreme conditions of temperature and pressure may generate diverse possibilities of accidents in each situation. For example rupture of secondary reformer would indeed cause explosion as visualised by Olaniya *et al.* (1996) but there would also be sufficient unburned chemical which may lead to fire. Hence one of the credible scenarios would be VCE followed by fire. Unless the software tool is versatile enough to lead the user to all likely situations, such credible accident scenarios may be omitted thereby seriously effecting all subsequent steps in risk analysis and management.

In MOSEC all credible accident scenarios are carefully generated based on the properties of chemicals, operating conditions, and details of the process/storage units. Once accident scenarios have been developed, they are processed for further verification and consequence assessment. For the same unit and same operating conditions several plausible accident scenarios are visualised. All-in-all this option helps in simulating the various likely accidents, and characterising the worst plausible ones.

Automatic scenario generation sub module (option):

To help a user not well-versed with risk assessment, a knowledge-based expert submodule (automatic scenario generation option) has been included to help the user in developing accident scenarios.

This is a derived object from the main accident scenario object. It deals with the knowledge-base which decides the accident scenario for a set of information provided by the user. The knowledge base is a compendium of conditions (frames) and facts stored in as if-and-else reasoning sequences (rule network).

The combination of rules has been designed keeping the following aspects in view.

a) the output of one rule provides the input to another,

b) several rules lead to a single hypothesis,

c) the same top event (in this case an accident scenario) may occur via different routes taken by different combina tions of causative factors.

Table 3. The output of MOSEC for accident scenario CVCE followed by fire ball

MOSEC (c) Khan & Abbasi, Pondicherry-605 014, India

Parameters	Values
CONFINED VAPOR CLOUD EXPLOSION	
Explosion characteristics	
Total energy released	(kJ) = 5.6E+07
Adiabatic energy lost due to expansion of gas	(kJ) = 2.0E+06
Energy associated with shock wave	(kJ) = 2.5E+07
Energy lost in fracture/plastic deformation of material	(kJ) = 7.6E+04
Energy available for bursting	(kJ) = 4.3E+07
Energy released as heat	(kJ) = 2.8E+07
Radiation heat flux	(kJ/sq.m) = 5.0E+01
Shock wave characteristics	
Peak over pressure	(kPa) = 339.8
Duration of shock wave	(ms) = 34.9
Variation of over pressure with time	(kPa/s) = 4.3E-04
Shock wave velocity in air	(m/s) = 640.3
Particle velocity behind the shock wave	(m/s) = 3.9E+02
Dynamic pressure	(dimensionless) = 2.6E+02
Reflected overpressure	(kPa) = 1.3E+03
Over pressure impulse (positive phase)	(kPa/s) = 8.5E+02
Missile characteristics	
Mass of the fragment	(kg) = 5.0
Initial velocity of fragment	(m/s) = 2.1E+02
Kinetic energy associated with fragment	(kJ) = 1.1E+05
Fragment velocity at 250 m from epicentre	(m/s) = 1.27E+02
Penetration ability (estimated using empirical models)	
Penetration ability on concrete structure	(m) = 6.2E-02
Penetration ability on brick structure	(m) = 4.9E-02
Penetration ability on steel structure	(m) = 1.3E-02
FIRE BALL	
Radius of fire ball	(m) = 384.2
Duration of fire ball	(s) = 157.0
Energy released by fire ball	(kJ) = 6.7E+11
Area of fire ball	(sq.m) = 1.8E+06
Radiation heat intensity	(kJ/sq.m) = 4.1E+05

The information provided by the user is passed on to the knowledge base which examines whether the information satisfies the conditions necessary for a credible accident; the latter is defined as the accident which is within the realm of possibility (i.e, probability higher than 1*E-06 /yr) and has *a propensity to cause significant damage (at least one fatality)*. This concept comprises of both probable damage caused by an accident and probability of its occurrence (Less, 1996; Ale, 1991; Hagon, 1984, HSE, 1988). There may be a type of accident which may occur very frequently but would cause little damage. And there may be another type of accident which may cause great damage but would have very low probability of occurrence. Both are not credible. But accidents which have appreciable probability of occurrence as well as significant damage potential (as quantified above) come under the category of *credible accidents*. The rule network to arrive at this conclusion is shown in Figure 3.

The knowledge base has been developed in object-oriented architecture without using any expert shell, and by using heuristic and if-and-else reasoning. Forward chaining has been used to retrieve the information from the knowledge base while backward chaining is used to justify or check the retrieved information. The set of conditions on the basis of which the package decides whether an accident would occur or not for a given set of input parameters have been based on the reports of past accidents(Less, 1996; Khan and Abbasi, 1997a; Marshall, 1987) and data generated by controlled experiments simulating accidents.

Table 4. The output of MOSEC for accident scenario BLEVE followed by fire ball

MOSEC (c) Khan & Abbasi, Pondicherry-605 014, India

Parameters	Values
BOILING LIQUID EXPANDING VAPOR CLOUD EXPLOSION	
Shock wave characteristics	
Peak over pressure	(kPa) = 105.5
Duration of shock wave	(ms) = 34.9
Variation of over pressure with time	(kPa/s) = 1.3Ee-04
Shock wave velocity in air	(m/s) = 454.0
Particle velocity behind the shock wave	(m/s) = 1.7E+02
Dynamic pressure	(dimensionless) = 3.4E+01
Reflected overpressure	(kPa) = 2.9E+02
Over pressure impulse (positive phase)	(kPa/s) = 2.6Ee+02
Missile characteristics	
Mass of the fragment	(kg) = 5.0
Initial velocity of fragment	(m/s) = 6.2E+02
Kinetic energy associated with fragments	(kJ) = 3.4E+05
Fragment velocity at 250 m from epicentre	(m/s) = 3.7E+02
Penetration ability (estimated using empirical models)	
Depth of penetration on concrete structure	(m) = 2.4E-01
Depth of penetration on brick work structure	(m) = 3.1E-01
Depth of penetration on mild steel structure	(m) = 3.8E-02
FIRE BALL	
Radius of the fire ball	(m) = 244.1
Duration of the fire ball	(s) = 99.7
Energy released by fire ball	(kJ) = 1.3E+10
Area of the fire ball	(sq.m) = 7.4E+05
Radiation heat flux	(kJ/sq.m) = 8.1E+03

Inference mechanism

The goal of the knowledge-based system is to formulate accident scenarios for a set of chemicals, equipment, operating conditions, ambient conditions, etc. The flow of control in the scenario inference engine of this knowledge based system is outlined in Figure 4.

As discussed in earlier sections, the knowledge base has been developed in the form of a frame, and a rule network (if-and-else reasoning). An internal inference mechanism is used to propagate the faults through these frames to the network till the final set of results are arrived at. The frame system is organised into a hierarchy which supports inheritance of the common attributes. The mapping starts from the initial object identification to estimation of explosion (elements of explosion object domain) and fire (elements of fire object domain). The algorithm incorporated here for rule justification (attributes with conditions) is based on the criteria of minimum condition satisfaction. This is applied throughout the system, from beginning of mapping to final state (forward chaining). Once this mapping is complete, the results are checked by backward chaining to identify any discrepancy and to verify the logical sequence. The combination of these two mapping techniques (forward and backward) make the inference engine more reliable, in terms of quality of results.

User-defined scenario generation sub module (option):

In this option the user defines the accident scenario on the basis of his/her knowledge and experience. For example, failure of a liquefied petroleum gas storage vessel can be visualised through various accident scenarios such as: leakage followed by UVCE, fire accompanied by CVCE, jet fire, etc.

The user considers these possibilities and chooses one or more of the likely modes of accidents. These decisions become inputs to the subsequent analysis by MOSEC. For example; accidental release of propylene under pressure may be visualised by following accident scenarios;

i) CVCE followed by flash fire or fire ball.

ii) VCE followed by pool fire or flash fire.

iii) BLEVE followed by fire ball.

iv) Fire ball.

Of these accident scenarios, the first one has the maximum damage potential. The probability of consequent damage can be made low by: a) providing high pressure safety valve, b) making provision for the availability of sufficient quantity of inert gas in times of emergency to dilute the concentration of propylene in atmosphere, and c) providing means for rapid cooling of the vessel when such need arises. The other three scenarios can likewise be developed and studied for evolving appropriate damage prevention/control strategies.

Damage effect calculation module

This module consists of state-of-the-art mathematical models for simulating the accidents chosen as credible in the previous step. This module works out the scale and the characteristics (type of accident, damage potential, percentage of lethality, and damage radii) of the accidents, the types of damaging impacts (shock waves, heat loads, missiles, etc.) they may cause, and their area of impact. The output of this module quantifies impacts such as peak overpressure, shock wave velocity, shock wave duration, heat load, missile velocity, damage radii of different impacts, and probabilities of causing lethality. The output of the consequence analysis has been so formatted that it can be directly used in report without editing. Moreover, using these results it is very easy to draw damage/risk contours. The main module consists of two sub modules, one each devoted to explosion and fire (Figure 5). The mathematical models used in these submodules are listed in Tables 1 and 2.

Graphic interface module

This module enables visualisation of risk contours in context of the site of accidents. The option has two facilities: (i) site drawing, and (ii) contour drawing.

The site drawing option enables the user to draw any industrial site layout using freehand drawing or using any already defined drawing tool. The contour drawing option has the facility for drawing various damage/risk contours over the accident site. The contours can be drawn in different shapes and sizes as per the requirement of the user.

Table 5. Accident scenarios generated by user-defined accident scenario generation option

Chemical	Accident scenarios as per the user-defined accident scenario option	Probability of occurrence (relative percent*)	Damage potential (in terms of damage radii#)	Most credible scenario (based on damage potential and probability)
Ethylene	BLEVE	17	55	BLEVE followed
	BLEVE followed by fire ball	17	125	by fire ball
	BLEVE followed by flash fire	04	110	
	UVCE followed by flash fire	07	65	
	CVCE followed by fire ball	14	185	
	CVCE	14	135	
	Fire ball	27	70	
LPG	BLEVE followed by fire ball	34	105	CVCE followed
	CVCE followed by fire ball	08	150	by fire ball
	CVCE	04	85	
	UVCE followed by pool fire	11	45	
	UVCE	15	25	
	Fire ball	28	45	

$$* \text{ Relative percent} = \frac{\text{frequency occurrence of particular scenario}}{\text{sum of the probabilities of different accidental event}}$$

User interface module

This module deals with the handling of data file, scenario file, output file and flow of information. This module also works as 'information manager': it provides the necessary information to each module/submodule for carrying out desired operations, and stores the results in different files. Besides this, it also provides all commonly used file operations such as copying, deleting, consoling and printing.

This option also provides facility for modification or upgradation of knowledge base according to the need and experience of the user.

Application of MOSEC : an illustration

MOSEC has been applied to the study of a storage unit in a typical refinery. Accident scenarios leading to fire and explosion have been generated for the unit storing ethylene and liquefied petroleum gas (LPG).

Analysis using automatic scenario generation option

Using the automatic option, accident scenarios (one for each chemical) were generated and subsequently passed to the next option to estimate the damage characteristics.

Ethylene is a highly flammable chemical having low autoignition temperature. A high pressure build up either due to autoignition or due to sudden boil up of liquid in the vessel results in a CVCE. The released unburned cloud of chemical on ignition becomes a fire ball.

An instantaneous release of LPG either through vent valve or through any other accidental opening causes the vessel to explode in the manner of a BLEVE. As the released chemical is highly flammable it turns in to a fire ball on meeting an ignition source. The forecasts of MOSEC for these accidents are presented in Tables 3 and 4.

Analysis using user-defined scenario generation option

The same unit was also studied with the user-defined scenario generation option. Table 5 presents the list of plausible accident scenarios obtained from this option and the scenarios are termed most credible on the basis of probability of occurrence and damage potential. It is evident from the table that the most credible accident scenarios anticipated by this option are the same as anticipated by the automatic scenario generation option. This indicates the efficacy of the automatic option.

Graphics

The industrial layout and damage contours have been drawn (Figures 6 and 7) using the graphics option. The figures reveal that the damage potential of ethylene is higher than that of LPG and its consequences would extend beyond the industry's boundary.

SUMMARY and CONCLUSIONS

Likelihood of fires and explosions are two of the major hazards associated with chemical process industries. Fires occur more frequently in chemical process industries than other types of accidents eventhough a large number of them are put off before significant damage is done. But major fires can be very destructive. Fires are also among the most frequent causes of explosions. The destructive impact of explosion generally covers wider area than the region-of-impact of a fire. Secondly, except in certain cases when ambient conditions conspire to enable very rapid spread of a fire, most fires take time to consolidate. If emergency preparedness measures are in place this lead time proves crucial in enabling the control of the fire. On the other hand when an explosion takes place it does so instantly, giving no time to escape from it. It is therefore necessary to study explosions and fires together eventhough they are essentially two very different types of events.

To enable such study, these authors have developed a computer-automated tool (software package) for modelling and simulation of fires and explosions in chemical process industries and named it MOSEC (Modelling and Simulation of fires and Explosions in Chemical process industries). MOSEC has been aimed to substantially improve upon the existing software in terms of: *greater applicability* - achieved by incorporating large number of models and modules for studying a wider range of situations; *greater sophistication* - achieved by incorporating the most refined and recent models and methodologies; also by using one of the most advanced coding tool viz C++; and *greater user-friendliness* - achieved by adding features such as on-line help, graphics, and 'automatic module' so that even a person not well-versed in chemical engineering or risk assessment can gainfully use the tool.

REFERENCES

1. Ale, B J M, (1991). Risk analysis and risk policy in the Netherlands and EEC, *J Loss Prevention in Process Industries*, **4(1)**, 58.

2. Baker, W E, Cox, P A, Westin, P S, Kulesz, J J, and Strelow, R A, (1983). Explosion hazard and evaluation, *Elesvier*, Amsterdam.

3. Birk, A M, and Cunningham, M H, (1994). The boiling liquid expanding vapour explosion, *J. Loss Prevention in Process Industries*, 7, 474.

4. Cates, A T, and Bimson, S J, (1991). Fuel and obstacle dependency in pre-mixed transient deflagration, *13th ICODERS*, Nagoya, Japan.

5. Cates, A T, and Samuels, B, (1991). A simple assessment methodology for vented explosions. *J. Loss Prevention in Process Industries*, **4**, 287.

6. Catlin, C A, (1991). Scale effects on the external combustion caused by venting of a confined explosion, *Combustion Flame*, 83, 399.

7. CCPS, (1989). Guidelines for chemical process quantitative risk analysis, *Centre for Chemical Process Safety, AIChE*, New York.

8. CCPS, (1994). re and explosion guidelines, Centre for Chemical Process Safety, *AIChE*, New York.

9. Considine, M, (1984). Thermal radiation hazards ranges from large hydrocarbon pool fires, *SRD report number R297*, U K atomic energy authority.

10. Considine, M, and Crint, G C, (1985). apid assessment of the consequences of LPG releases. *Gastech,* **84**, 187.

11. Cowley, L T, and Pritchard, M J, (1991). Large-scale natural gas and LPG jet fires and thermal impact on structures, *Gastech 90*, 3.6.

12. Crocker, W P, and Napier, D H, (1986). Thermal radiation hazards of liquid pool fires. In *Hazards*, **IX**, 159.

13. Crocker, W P, and Napier, D H, (1988). Mathematical models for the prediction of thermal radiation from jet fires, *Preventing Major Chemical and Related Process Accidents*, 331.

14. Dangreaux, J, (1986). Destructive explosion effects, *Los Prevention and Safety Promotion,* **5**, 9.1.

15. Davenport, J A, (1986). Hazards and protection of pressure storage of liquefied petroleum gases. *Loss Prevention and Safety Promotion,* **5,** 22.1.

16. Davies, P A, (1993). A guide to the evaluation of condensed phase explosion, *Journal of Hazardous Materials,* **33**, 1.

17. de Faveri, D M, Fumarola, G, Zonato, C, and Ferraiolo, G, (1985). Estimate flare radiation intensity. *Hydrocarbon Process.*, **64**(5), 89.

18. Eissenberg, N A, Lynch, C J, and Breeding, R J, (1975). Inerability Model: A Simulation System for Assessing Damage Resulting from Marine Spills, *Report CG-D-136-75(Enviro control),* Rockville M D., USA.

19. Esparza, E D, (1986). Blast measurements and equivalency for spherical charges at small scaled distances. *Int. J. Impact Engineering*, **4**, 23.

20. Greenbook, (1992). Methods for determining of possible damage to people and objects resulting from release of hazardous materials, *Report CPR-16E*, Voorburg, Warrington, UK.

21. Hagon, D O, (1984). Use of frequency-consequence curves to examine the conclusion of published risk analysis and to define broad criteria for major hazard installations, *Chem Engng Res Dev*, **62**, 381.

22. Harrison, A J, and Keyre, J A, (1987). 'External explosions' as a result of combustion venting. *Combustion Science Technology.*, **52**, 91.

23. Hart, D, and Croft, T, (1988). Modelling with Projectiles, *Ellis Horwood*, Chichester.

24. Holden, P I, and Reeves, A B, (1985). Fragment hazards from failures of pressurised liquefied gas vessels, IN *The Assessment and Control of Major Hazards,* IChEM, Rugby 205.

25. HSE, (1988). The tolerability of risks formation from nuclear power stations, *Health and Safety Executive* , HM Stationary Office, London.

26. Johnson, A D, Brightwell, H M, and Carsley A J, (1994). A model for predicting the thermal radiation hazards

from large-scale horizontally released natural gas jet fires. *Hazards*, **XII**, 123.

27. Johnson, D M, and Pritchard, M J, (1991). Large scale experimental study of boiling liquid expanding vapour explosions (BLEVEs). *Gastech 90*, 3.3.

28. Kalghatgi, G T, (1983). The visible shape and size of a turbulent hydrocarbon jet diffusion flame in a cross wind. *Combust. Flame*, **52**, 91.

29. Kayes, P J, (1986). Manual of industrial hazard assessment technique, *Technica Ltd.*, London.

30. Khan, F I, and Abbasi, S A, (1997a). Risk analysis of epichlohydrin manufacturing industry using new computer automated tool MAXCRED, *J Loss Prevention in Process Industries*, **10**(2), 91.

31. Khan, F I, and Abbasi, S A, (1997c). Models of Domino effect analysis in chemical process industry, *Process Safety Progress*, (in press).

32. Khan, F I, and Abbasi, S A, (1997b). Risk analysis of a cloralkali industry situated in densely populated area, *Process Safety Progress*, **16**(3), 172.

33. Kinney, G F, and Graham, K J, (1985). Explosives Shocks in Air, 2nd ed, *Springer*, Berlin,.

34. Kletz, T A, (1977). Unconfined vapour cloud explosions, *AIChE Loss Prevention*, **11**, 5.

35. Lees, F P, (1991). Piper Alpha and the plant engineer, *Plant Engr*, **35**, 33.

36. Lees, F P, (1994). The assessment of major hazards: a model for fatal injury from burns, *Process safety and Enviroment.*, **72B**, 127.

37. Lees, F P, (1996). Loss prevention in CPI, *Butterworths*, London.

38. Lunn, G A, (1989). Methods for sizing dust explosion event areas: a comparison when reduced pressures are low. *J. Loss Prevention in Process Industries*, **2**(4), 200.

39. Madsen, W W, and Wagner, R C, (1994). An accurate method for modelling the characteristics of explosion effects. *Process Safety Progress.*, **13**, 171.

40. Marshall, V C, (1987). Major chemical hazards, *John Wiley & Sons*, New York.

41. Moorehouse, J, (1982). Scaling criteria for pool fires derived from large scale experiment, In *The Assessment of Major Hazards*, IChEM, Rugby, 165.

42. Moorehouse, J, and Pritchard, M J, (1982). Thermal radiation hazards from large pool fires and fireballs - a literature review, In *The Assessment of Major Hazards*, IChEM, Rugby, 123.

43. Munday, G, (1980). Initial velocities attained by plant-generated missiles, *Nuclear Engineering*, **19**, 165.

44. Olaniya, R S, Mathurkar, H N, and Deshpande, A W, (1996). Probabilistic risk assessment of fertilizer plants, 3 87-94.

45. Pasman, H J, Duxbury, H A, Bjordal, P, (1992). Major hazards in the process industries, : achievements and challenges in loss prevention, *J Hazardous Materials*, **33**, 1.

46. Phylaktou, H and Andrews, G E, (1991). Gas explosions in long closed vessels. *Combust. Sci. Technol.*, **77**, 27.

47. Pietersen, C M, (1990).Consequence of accidental release of hazardous materials, *J. of Loss Prevention in Process Industries*, **3**, 136-141.

48. Pitblado, R M, and Nalpanis, P, (1989). Quantitative assessment of major hazard installations: 2, Computer programs., (eds Lees, and Ang), *Butterworths*, London.

49. Pritchard, M J, and Binding, T M, (1992). FIRE2 ; a new approch for predicting thermal radiation levels from hydrocarbon pool fires, *Major hazards onshore and offshore,* 491.

50. Prugh, R W, (1987). Evaluation of unconfined vapour cloud explosions, *Proceedings of International Conference of Vapour Cloud Modelling*, Boston.

51. Prugh, R W, (1991). Quantitative evaluation of BLEVE hazards, *Journal of Fire Protection Engineers*, **3**(1), 9-24.

52. Prugh, R W, (1994). Quantitative evaluation of fire ball hazards, *Process Safety Progress*, **13**(2), 83.

53. Raj P P K, and Emmons, H W, (1975). the burning of a large flammable vapour cloud. Combustion Inst., *Joint Tech. Mtg of the Western and Central State Sections*) , Pittusberg.

54. Roberts, A P, (1983). Thermal radiation hazard from release of LPG from pressurised storage, *Fire & Safety Journal*, **4**, 197.

55. Scheuermann, K P, (1994). Studies concerning the influence of turbulence on the course of explosions. *Process Safety Progress*, **13**, 219.

56. Scilly, N F, and Crowther, J H, (1992). Methodology for predicting domino effects from pressure vessel fragmentation :Hazard Identification and Risk Analysis, *Human Factors and Human Reliability in Process Safety*, **1**.

57. Scilly, N F, and High, W G, (1986). The blast effects of explosions, *Loss Prevention and Safety Promotion* ,**5,** 39.

58. Singh, J, (1988). Explosion propagation in non-spherical vessel: simplified equations and applications, *J Loss Prevention in Process Industries*, **1**(1), 39.

59. TNO, (1991). EFFECTS : a software for hazard assessment, *TNO Prins Mauritius Research Laboratory*, The Netherlands.

60. TNO, (1992). SAVE : a software for hazard assessment, *TNO Prins Mauritius Research Laboratory*, The Netherlands.

61. Van den Berg, A C, (1980). "BLAST" - A 1-D Variable Flame Speed Blast simulation Code using a Flux-corrected-transport Algorithm. *Report PML* 1980-162. Prins Maurits Lab., TNO, Rijswijk, The Netherlands.

62. Van den Berg, A C, (1984). Blast effects from vapour cloud explosion, *Ninth Int. Sym. on The Prevention of Occupational Accidents and Diseases in the Chemical Industry*, Lucerne.

63. Van den Berg, A C, (1985). The multi-energy method. A framework for vapour cloud explosion blast prediction. *J. Hazardous Materials*., **12**(1), 1.

64. Van den Berg, A C, and Lennoy, A, (1993). Methods for vapour cloud explosion blast modelling, *J Hazardous Materials*, **34**, 171.

65. Van den Berg, A C, Van Wingerden, C J M, and The, H G, (1991). vapor cloud explosion : experimental investigation of key parameters and blast modelling, *Trans I Chem Engg*, **69(B)**.

66. Van den Berg, AC, (1989). REAGAS - A Code for Numerical Simulation of 2-D Reactive Gas Dynamics. *Rep. PML-1989-in-48*, TNO Prins Maurits Lab. Rijswijk, The Netherlands.

67. Van Wingerden, C J M, (1989). Experimental investigation into the strength of blast waves generated by vapour cloud explosions in congested areas, *Loss Prevention and Safety Promotion*, **6**, 26.

68. Van Wingerden, K, Peterson, G H, and Wilkins, B A, (1994). Turbulent flame propagation in gas mixtures, *Hazards*, **XII**, 249.

69. Vernart, J E S, Rutledge, G A, Sumathipala, K and Sollows, K, (1993). To BLEVE or not to BLEVE ; Anatomy of Boiling Liquid expanding vapour Explosion, *Process Safety Progress*, **2**, 112.

70. VTT, (1993). RISKIT : a software for risk assessment, *The Technical Research Centre of Finland*, Tempere, The Finalnd.

71. WHO, (1984). Major Hazard Control : A practical manual, *International Labour Office*, Geneva.

¨ Reproduced from *Process Safety Progress*, USA,

Part IV

Qualitative Methods of Risk Assessment-II : Rapid risk assessment

Risk assessment (RA) involves steps such as HAZOP (Hazard and Operability study) and FTA (Fault Tree Analysis) which are expensive in terms of time as well as money. In order to achieve thoroughness, all industries must carry out total risk assessment involving all these essential steps. Yet, we often encounter situations when it is required to conduct risk assessment quickly and inexpensively. These are situations when a certain degree of imprecision (which would come because of lesser thoroughness) is tolerable. For example in a reconnaissance of risks associated with a large industrial complex, rapid risk assessment (RRA) can be used to zero down on units requiring more elaborate RA. In this sense RRA is a methodology of which the sophistication, accuracy, and precision fall in-between index-based screening and total risk assessment.

RRA can be used for taking interim measures while a total RA is awaited. It is also very useful in choosing between alternative sites for a future industrial unit.

In this part we present a computer-automated tool MAXCRED developed by us for RRA (Chapter 11). The applications of MAXCRED are illustrated in Chapters 12 and 13.

11

MAXCRED - A NEW SOFTWARE PACKAGE FOR RAPID RISK (ASSESSMENT IN CHEMICAL PROCESS INDUSTRIES*)

A new software package for conducting rapid risk assessment (RRA) in chemical process industries and the system of methodologies on which it is based are described.

The objectives behind the development of the package are to achieve greater breadth and depth, sophistication, and user-friendliness in conducting RRA. In pursuance of these objectives we have incorporated in the package state-of-the-art models for generating accident scenarios and assessing their consequences. The package has been coded in C++ using the concepts of object oriented programming to enhance the tool's speed of execution and ease of use. The paper also demonstrates the applicability of MAXCRED with an illustrative example of a RRA conducted with its help.

Key words: Hazard assessment, consequence analysis, risk assessment, quantitative risk assessment.

SOFTWARE AVAILABILITY

Name of the Product	:	**MAXCRED**
Developed by	:	**Faisal I Khan and S A Abbasi**
Contact address	:	S A Abbasi, Director, Centre for Pollution Control & Energy Technology, Pondicherry University, Pondicherry, 605 014, India
Phone	:	+91 413 65267/65262
Fax	:	+91 413 65227/65263
Available since	:	1997
Coding language	:	C++
Hardware requirement	:	IBM PC AT 586 or equivalent

INTRODUCTION

Chemical industries which often handle hazardous chemicals and operate reactors/storage vessels under extreme

* Reproduced from *Journal of Environmental Modelling and Software, The Netherlands*

conditions of temperature and pressure are susceptible to accidents. These accidents may be triggered by material failure. The increasing density of industries coupled with increasing density of human population have not only increased the frequency of accidents but also the extent of damage caused by the accidents. The most gruesome example is the Bhopal gas tragedy - which claimed over 20,000 lives.

The science of risk analysis has emerged to forecast the likelihood of accidents, assess the consequences of the likely accidents, work out the strategies to prevent the accidents and also to cushion the adverse impacts if an accident does occur.

A total risk assessment exercise covering all steps (Greenberg and Crammer, 1992; Khan and Abbasi,1995a) exhaustively from beginning to end is expensive in terms of time as well as monetary and personnel inputs. It often becomes necessary to conduct *rapid risk assessment* (RRA) to draw the same conclusions that a full fledged risk assessment would lead to, albeit with lesser (yet practicable) accuracy and precision.

In this paper we describe a software package, and the system of methodologies on which the package is based, for conducting RRA in chemical process industries. The package is named MAXCRED (MAXimum CREDible accident analysis) and is coded in C++.

In the past, software packages have been offered by others for RRA; notably among these are *WHAZAN* (Technica,1992), *RISKIT* (VTT,1993), SAVE (TNO,1992) and *EFFECTS* (TNO,1991). MAXCRED improves upon the existing packages in the following areas :

a) *wider applicability*; MAXCRED incorporates a larger number of models to handle a larger variety of situations;

b) *greater sophistication*; more precise, accurate, and recent models have been incorporated in MAXCRED than handled by existing packages;

c) *greater user-friendliness*;

d) *scope for assessing second and higher order accidents*; whereas the existing RRA packages are capable of handling only the primary accidents, MAXCRED has provision for assessing the likelihood as well as magnitude of secondary and higher order accidents triggered by the primary event.

The paper also illustrates the applicability of the new package in a real-life situation.

METHODOLOGY OF MAXCRED

MAXCRED enables accident simulation and damage potential estimation. The software has been developed in object-oriented architecture using C++ as a coding tool. The software is compatible with DOS as well as WINDOWS operating environments. It is operable on computers with a minimum of 4MB RAM and 7 MB ROM.

The sequence of actions or main steps involved in MAXCRED, its object architecture, and information pathways are depicted in Figures 1-4. Figure 1 represents the sketch of main menu and available options of MAXCRED and Figure 2 shows the object oriented architecture of MAXCRED. Figure 3 depicts five essential steps of MAXCRED, briefly described as follows.

The accident scenario generation step

In this step accident scenarios are generated for the unit under study. It is a very important input for the subsequent steps. The more realistic the accident scenario, the more accurate is forecasting the type of accident, its consequences, and associated risks. This would help in development of more appropriate and effective strategies for crisis prevention and management.

Each accident scenario is basically a combination of different likely accidental events that may occur in an industry. Such scenarios are generated based on the properties of chemicals handled by the industry, physical conditions under which reactions occur or reactants/products are stored, geometries and material strengths of vessel and conduits, in-built valves and safety arrangements etc. External factors such as site characteristics (topography, presence

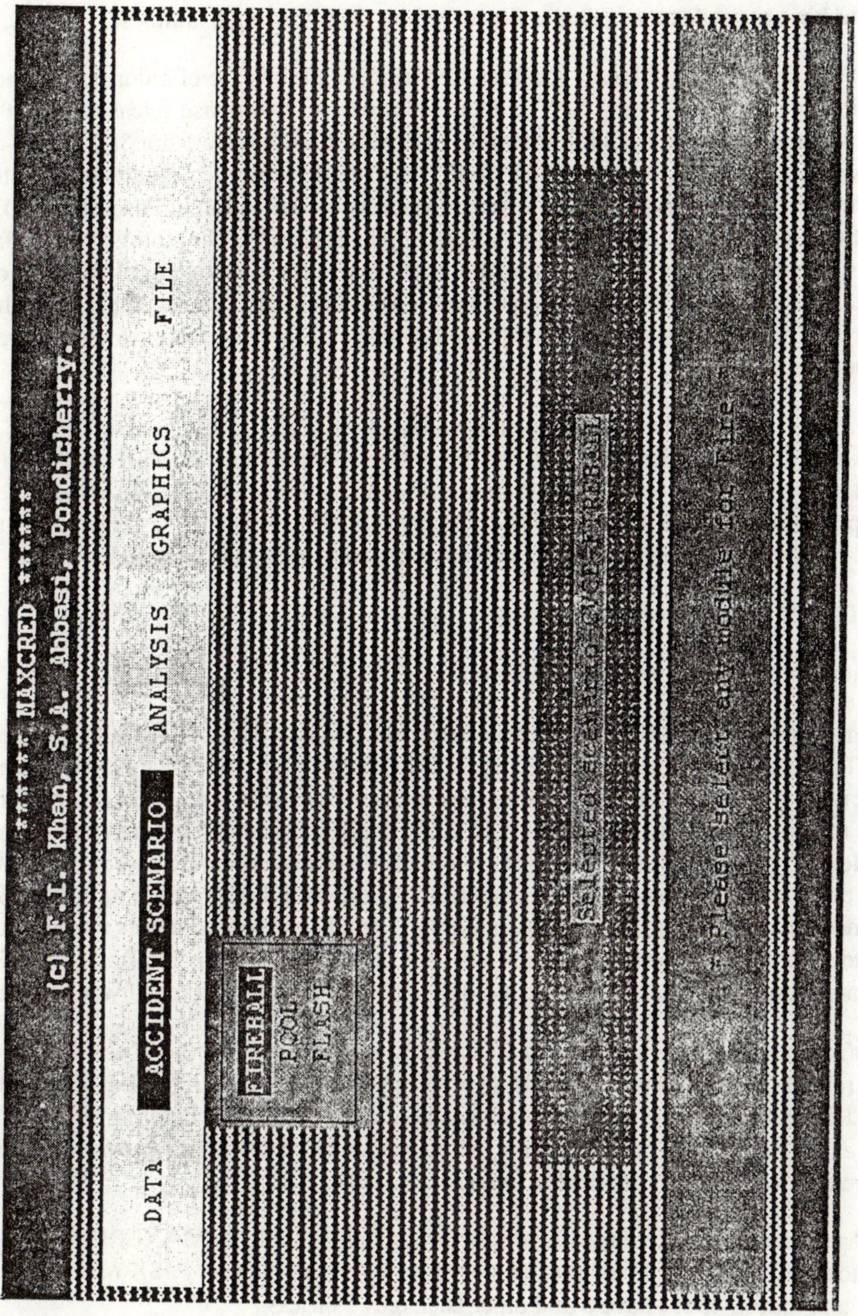

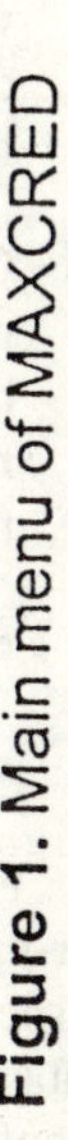

Figure 1. Main menu of MAXCRED

of trees, ponds, rivers in the vicinity, proximity to other industries or neighbourhoods etc.) and meteorological conditions are also considered. In the available software packages such as WHAZAN (Technica ,1992), EFFECTS (TNO,1991), RISKIT (VTT,1993), and SAVE (TNO,1992), this concept of risk assessment has been used to some extent. But the level of sophistication needs to be enhanced subsequently by using advanced models of thermodynamics, heat transfer, and fluid dynamics to generate more realistic accident scenarios. Furthermore the user-friendliness of these packages have some limitations as a result of which several real-life studies conducted on the basis of these packages are seem to have major lacunae. This is illustrated by the following examples.

a) Chary *et al.* (1995) studied two different accident scenarios for the release of chlorine (stored in vessels under high pressure in liquefied state) using SAVE. The scenarios are, two-phase release from 10 mm copper tube connected to a storage vessel (under high pressure) and two-phase release from 3/8" liquid chlorine line connected to the same vessel. The study considers only toxic dispersion effect generated when the atmospheric stability is in the 'D' category (as per the atmospheric stability classification of Pasquill,1971). The package has not led the user to study another major risk, of sudden drop in pressure in the storage vessel if an accidental leak takes place. In such situations, of which the probability of occurrence is as high as of the other accidents, storage vessel may develop a major rupture, the extent of which would depend upon the capacity of the vessel, material of construction, and internal pressure. Such catastrophic failure of chlorine vessel would generate shock waves of high damage potential.

b) Contini *et al.* (1991) reported a benchmark exercise undertaken with the aim of assessing the state-of-the-art in risk analysis. A study of the accidental release and dispersion of ammonia from a pressurised tank was performed by 11 different risk assessment teams drawn from different countries. The teams used different software for release and dispersion estimation. A total of five different accident scenarios were generated by the teams. Among these, the most common and most disastrous accident scenarios invoked by the packages are:

- catastrophic failure of a pressurised storage tank,
- release of ammonia through a large hole on the roof.

The first accident scenario has been modelled as a two-phase release of ammonia in bulk followed by denser-than-air-gas dispersion. The second scenario is modelled as continuous two-phase release followed by denser-than-air-gas dispersion. However, in the opinion of the authors the two worst accident scenarios can be refined further. The catastrophic failure of vessel will occur only through BLEVE (boiling liquid expanding vapour explosion) or CVCE (confined vapour cloud explosion) because ammonia is stored under high pressure in liquefied state. The explosive release will lead to overpressure and shock-wave generation. These would create high turbulence in the atmosphere and strongly influence the process of dispersion of ammonia. The adverse consequences would be over pressure, and toxic dispersion under changed atmospheric conditions. But the study team has totally neglected the overpressure effect and change in atmospheric conditions evidently due to the inadequacy of the software used by them.

A comparison of various models available with the different software used by the 11 teams (Contini *et al.* 1991) to study the accident release of ammonia (*scenario* 1) is presented in Table 1. A total of seven different models are available in MAXCRED relevant to the study of the above mentioned problem, whereas software such as RISKIT and SAFETI (Pitblado *et al.* 1990) have only 4 models. Moreover, only MAXCRED generates the scenario BLEVE, followed by toxic release while others are unable to do so.

A list of features available in different software are presented in Table 2. MAXCRED is revealed as the most versatile of the packages as it has 11 of the 14 possible features whereas RISKWIT has 9, WHAZAN and DEGADIS(Havens and Spicer, 1985) have 8 and other packages 7 or less.

c) Raghvan and Mallikarjunan (1988) presented a risk assessment study of a chemical industrial complex dealing with hazardous chemicals such as liquefied petroleum gas (LPG), ammonia, propylene, ethylene oxide, and naphtha. The damage potential of different units and chemicals was assessed only for vapour cloud explosion. Such other effects as explosive release of these chemicals either through BLEVE or CVCE followed by ignition leads to flash fire or fire ball were neglected. Similarly the likely accident involving NH_3 has been analysed only in terms of the gas dispersion. But instantaneous release of NH_3 under high pressure may cause pronounced overpressure and shock-waves leading to significant damage. Further explosive release of NH_3 would influence

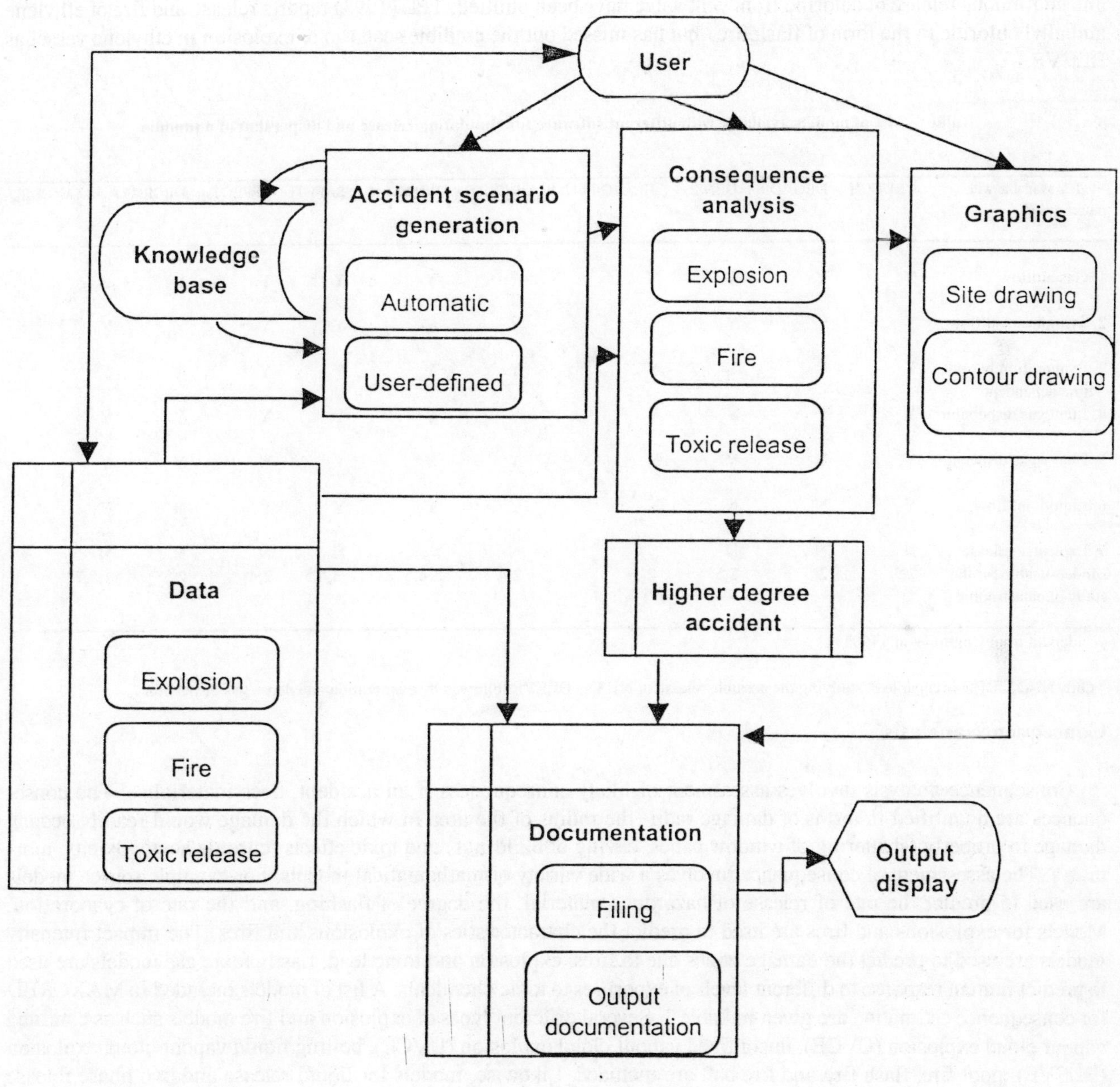

Figure 2. Object-oriented architecture of MAXCRED

the dispersion process as well.

We have also come across several other reports (NEERI,1992; CISRA,1993; TPL,1993) in which one of the existing risk assessment packages have been used. In all these reports several credible accident scenarios have been left unconsidered indicating a lack of rigor and/or user-friendliness of the packages. For example in NEERI (1992), which has considered jet fire in fuel storage vessel, and fire ball formation due to rupture of propylene storage vessel, BLEVE in fuel storage vessel, and CVCE/BLEVE followed by fire ball in propylene storage vessel have been overlooked. In CISRA (1993), which has dealt with instantaneous release of chlorine, and fire ball due to release of hydrogen from the storage vessel, the scenarios pertaining to BLEVE followed by fire ball due to release of hydrogen and continuous release of chlorine from vent valve have been omitted; TPL (1993) reports release and fire of ethylene and allyl chloride in the form of flash fire, but has missed out the credible scenario of explosion in ethylene vessel as BLEVE.

Table 1. List of models available with different software for simulating release and dispersion of ammonia

Models available with packages@	CRUNCH	DEGADIS	DENZ	HEAVG-PLUME	RISKIT	WHAZAN	SAFETI	EFFECTs	DECRARA	MAXCRED
1. Gas outflow	Y	Y	Y	Y	Y	Y	Y	Y	Y	I.C
2. Two-phase outflow	Y	Y	Y	Y	Y	Y	Y	Y	Y	Y
3. Evaporation but not time dependent	Y	Y	Y	Y	Y	Y	Y	Y	Y	Y
4. Light gas dispersion	Y	Y	Y	Y	Y	Y	Y	Y	Y	Y
5. Heavy gas dispersion	Y	Y	Y	Y	Y	Y	Y	N	Y	Y
6. Liquid out flow	Y	N	N	N	Y	Y	Y	Y	N	Y
7. Explosive release	N	N	N	N	N	N	N	N	N	N
Models usable for the study of catastrophic	2,5	2,5	2,5	2,5	2,4	3,4,5	3,4,5	2,4	2,5	1,5,7*

@ adopted from Contini et al. (1991)

* Only MAXCRED is capable of studying the possible release of NH3 as BLEVE followed by evaporation and dense gas dispersion

Consequence analysis

Consequence analysis involves assessment of likely consequences if an accident, does materialise. The consequences are quantified in terms of damage radii (the radius of the area in which the damage would readily occur), damage to property (shattering of window panes, caving of buildings) and toxic effects (chronic/acute toxicity, mortality). The assessment of consequence involves a wide variety of mathematical models. For example source models are used to predict the rate of release of hazardous material, the degree of flashing, and the rate of evaporation. Models for explosions and fires are used to predict the characteristics of explosions and fires. The impact intensity models are used to predict the damage zones due to fires, explosion and toxic load. Lastly toxic gas models are used to predict human response to different levels of exposures to toxic chemicals. A list of models included in MAXCRED for consequence estimation are given in Table 3. Several different types of explosion and fire models such as confined vapour cloud explosion (CVCE), unconfined vapour cloud explosion (UVCE), boiling liquid vapour cloud explosion (BLEVE), pool fire, flash fire and fire ball are included. Likewise, models for liquid release and two phase release have been incorporated. A special feature of MAXCRED is that it is able to handle dispersion of heavy (heavier-than-air) gases, as-light-as-air and lighter-than-air gases. A brief description of different types of accident events is presented in a subsequent section.

Verification of accident scenario

This feature is one of the specialities of MAXCRED. It verifies the plausibility of the proposed scenario. For example if the scenario envisages release of a highly flammable chemical on the basis of the characteristics of the chemical and quantities in which it is employed, this step checks whether the set of input conditions would indeed lead to the envisaged accident. For example the release of a flammable chemical may not lead to UVCE, if the meteorological conditions are unstable (highly turbulent atmosphere making dilution of gas faster) but the same type of release would have a high probability of causing UVCE if the atmospheric conditions are stable. Under such stable conditions mixing of the escaping chemical with ambient air would be inefficient leading to build-up of the concentration of the chemical to the point of explosion.

If MAXCRED finds that an envisaged scenario is not within the realms of probability, it modifies the scenario to the extent that it becomes plausible. For example, user envisaged an accident scenario as CVCE followed by fire ball, however MAXCRED does not verify the same because the minimum conditions (limiting conditions) of CVCE occurrence are not satisfied. It further recommends the scenario to be modified as BLEVE, fire ball, or a combination of these according to the existing situation (data input to MAXCRED).

Table 2. Comparison of features available with different software

Models available with packages@	CRUNCH	DEGADIS	DENZ	HEAVG-PLUME	RISKIT	WHAZAN	SAFETI	EFFECTs	DECRARA	MAXCRED
Different types of release (I,C,V)	Y	Y	N	N	N	Y	Y	Y	Y	Y
Dense cloud	Y	Y	Y	Y	Y	Y	Y	N	Y	Y
Jet	N	N	N	Y	Y	Y	Y	Y	N	Y
Neutral cloud	Y	Y	Y	Y	Y	Y	Y	Y	Y	Y
Buoyant cloud	N	N	N	N	Y	Y	Y	N	Y	Y
Surface roughness	Y	Y	Y	Y	Y	Y	Y	Y	Y	Y
Complex terrain	N	N	N	N	N	N	N	N	N	N
Wind variation in time and space	N	N	N	N	N	N	N	N	N	Y
Advent dispersion model (B,G,K)	Y	Y	Y	Y	Y	Y	Y	Y	Y	Y
Along-wind dispersion	N	Y	Y	N	N	N	N	Y	N	Y
Vertical wind shear	Y	Y	Y	Y	Y	N	N	Y(*)	Y	
Dry or jet deposit	N	N	N	N	Y	N	N	N(*)	N	N
Distance limit	Y	N	N	N	N	Y	N	N	N	N
Evaluation	Y	Y	Y	N	Y	N	N	N	Y	

I = instantaneous B = box * = possible extension
C = continuous G = gaussian
V = variable K = numerical
S = semicontinuous

@ adopted from Contini et al. (1991)

Checking for higher degree of accidents

An accident in a unit caused by another accident in another unit is termed as a 'second order accident' or 'secondary accident'. If the secondary accident causes another accident in a third unit such an accident is termed

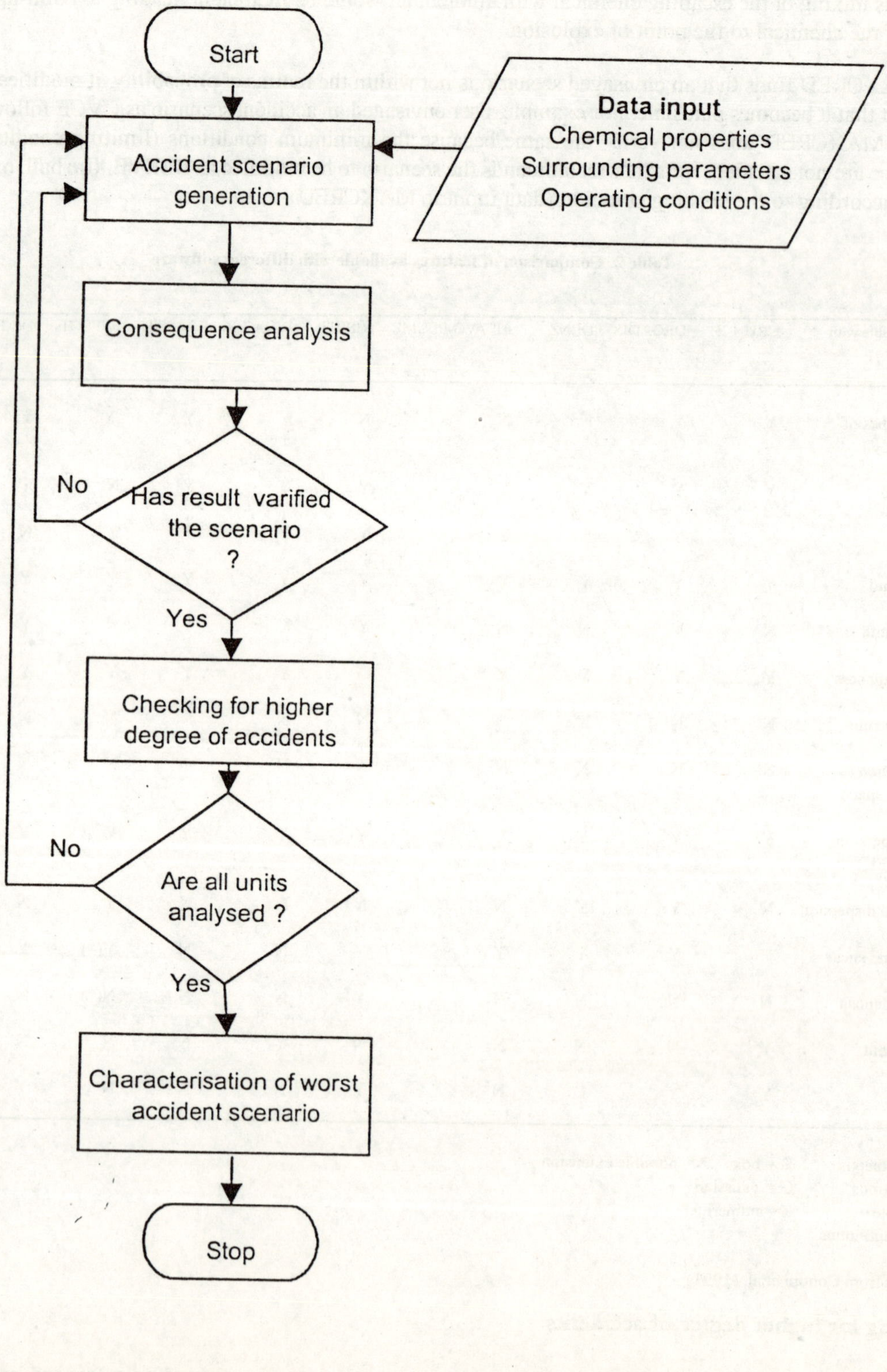

Figure 3. The MAXCRED algorithm

'third order' or 'tertiary' accident. It is a speciality of MAXCRED that the package is capable of simulating second and higher order accidents. To do this, it uses models developed by Pietersen (1985, 1990), Clancey (1977), Eissenberg *et al.* (1975), Fowcett and Wood (1993) and Khan & Abbasi (1996). If the probability of occurrence of secondary accident is higher than a minimum value, the package will estimate the damage potential of the secondary accident and its likelihood of causing a third degree accident, and so on. To estimate the probability of occurrence and damage characteristics, the package uses information related to operating condition of secondary unit, chemical properties and topological parameters (wind velocity, roughness, obstruction etc.).

Table 3. List of different models used in MAXCRED

Event	Model incorporated	Reference
Toxic release		
Light gas dispersion	Gaussian dispersion model with Erbink modification	Pasquill and Smith,1983; Gifford,1961 Turner,1970,1985; Erbink,1993
Heavy gas dispersion	Box model, modified plume path theory for heavy gas	Van Ulden,1974,1985; Deaves,1992 Erbink,1995; Khan and Abbasi,1997b
Explosion		
BLEVE	thermodynamic and heat transfer model	Baker et al.,1983; Martinsen et al.,1986; Prugh,1991; Vernart et al.,1993
UVCE	condensed vapor cloud explosion	Kletz,1977; Lees,1996; Prugh,1987
CVCE	vapor cloud explosion in confinement (vessel or building)	Lees,1996; Baker et al.,1983 Fowcett and Wood,1993; Van den Berg et al.,1991
Fire		
Flash fire	flare model, fire torch and spontaneous combustion	Kayes,1986; Greenberg and Crammer,1992 Fowcett and Wood,1993
Pool fire	combustion of liquid pool	Kayes,1986; Baker et al.,1983; Davies,1993
Fire ball	spontaneous combustion of vapor cloud	Kayes,1986; Roberts,1983; Baker et al.,1983; Davies,1993.

Characterisation of worst accident scenario

Arriving at worst accident scenario is the last step in the MAXCRED algorithm. The step determines the worst accident scenario based on the results of consequence analysis. This step holds the key to the final objective of the risk analysis excessive -devising strategies to avert a crisis or to minimise its adverse impact if the crisis does take place. It is possible that more than one 'worst accident scenario' emerges from the MAXCRED analysis because more than one sequence of events can lead to identical magnitudes of 'worst' damage. In such situations the control strategies would be developed by keeping all the 'worst' scenarios in the view.

DESIGN AND APPLICATION OF MAXCRED

In the following section MAXCRED is described in detail vis a vis design and application.

Data module

The main purpose of the module is to collect all relevant information needed for the execution of other modules. This module consists of three main objects derived from the main DATA object: toxic release, fire, and explosions. The explosion object is further divided into sub objects such as BLEVE, CVCE and UVCE. The fire object branches into flash fire, pool fire and fire ball. The object dependency and message flow of the DATA module is shown in Figure 4.

Accident scenario module

This module, dealing with the generation of accident scenarios, is based on the advanced concepts of hazard assessment proposed by Arendt (1990), Papazoglou *et al.* (1992), Vernart *et al.* (1993) and Khan and Abbasi (1995b,1995c). The accident scenarios are generated based on chemical properties, operating conditions, and details of the process/storage units. Once an accident scenario has been developed, it can be processed for further verification and consequence assessment. For the same unit and same operating conditions various plausible accident scenarios can be visualised. Thus, this option helps in simulating the various likely accidents, and characterising the worst plausible ones. This module consists of two submodules (objects) - *automatic* and *user defined.*

The automatic submodule

This is a derived object to the main accident scenario object. It deals with the knowledge base which decides the accident scenario for a set of information provided by the user. The knowledge base is a compendium of conditions and facts stored in if-and-else reasoning sequences. The information provided by the user is passed on to the knowledge base which examines whether the information satisfies the conditions necessary for a 'credible accident'; the latter is defined as 'the accident which is within the realm of possibility (*i.e,* probability higher than 1*e^{-06} /yr) and has a propensity to cause significant damage (at least one fatality)'. This concept (Hagon, 1984; HSE,1988; Ale 1991; Lees, 1996) comprises of both *probable damage* caused by an accident and *probability* of its occurrence. There may be a type of accident which may occur very frequently but would cause little damage. And there may be another type of accident which may cause great damage but would have very low probability of occurrence. Both are not 'credible'. But accidents which have appreciable probability of occurrence as well as significant damage potential (as quantified above) come under the category of 'credible accidents'. For example the package tells us that the accident scenario for LPG storage under pressure is likely to be BLEVE followed by fire ball. This decision is arrived at as shown below:

if(release: instantaneous)

if(pressure>3.0*vapor pressure)

if(pressure>10*atmospheric pressure)

if(capacity >7000)

100% chances of BLEVE

if(chemical flammable)

80% chances of fire ball

The knowledge base has been developed in object-oriented architecture without using any expert shell, and by using heuristic and if-and-else reasoning. Forward chaining has been used to retrieve the information from the knowledge base while backward chaining is used to justify or check the retrieved information. The set of conditions on the basis of which the package decides whether an accident would occur or not for a given set of input parameters have been based on the reports of past accidents (Lees,1996; Pietersen,1985) and data generated by controlled experiments simulating accidents.

The user defined submodule

In this option the user defines the accident scenario on the basis of his/her knowledge and experience. For example, failure of a liquefied chlorine storage vessel can be visualised through various accident scenarios such as; BLEVE followed by dispersion, continuous release and dispersion, and instantaneous release and dispersion. The user considers these possibilities and chooses one or more of the likely modes of accident. These decisions become inputs to the subsequent analysis by MAXCRED. This option is very helpful for accident simulation study as a number of different accident scenarios can be generated for the failure of a unit, and on the basis of consequence analysis results, the most credible, accident scenario can be identified. For example, in the previous example (failure of Cl_2 storage vessel) among the various scenarios, BLEVE followed by dispersion would be the most credible one.

Table 4. Characteristics of the storage vessels of which risk assessment was conducted with MAXCRED

Variables	Magnitude
Chemical : Sulfur dioxide	
Storage capacity of the unit	7-5 ton
Actual chemical stored in the unit	5-0 ton
Storage pressure	6.5 atm
Storage temperature	-55 oC
Physical state of the Chemical	Liquefied gas
Type of the vessel	Pressurized cylinder
Design pressure of the vessel	7.25 atm
Material of construction of the vessel	Mild steel
Percent degree of conjuction on-site	30%
Type of hazard present	Toxic release
Chemical: Butadiene	
Storage capacity of the unit	13-5 ton
Actural chemical	100 ton
Storage pressure	3.5 atm
Storage temperature	-25oC
Physical state of the Chemical	Liquefied gas
Type of the vessel	Pressurized cylinder
Design pressure of the vessel	5.5 atm
Material of construction of the vessel	Mild steel
Percent degree of conjuction on-site	30%
Type of hazard present	Fire and explosion

Consequence analysis module

This module consists of state-of-the-art mathematical models for simulating the accidents chosen as credible in the previous step (Figure 5). This module works out the scale and the characteristics (type of accident, damage potential, percentage of lethality, and damage radii) of the accidents, the types of damaging impacts (shock-waves, heat loads, missiles, toxic dispersion etc) they may cause, and their area of impact. The output of this module quantifies impacts such as peak overpressure, shock-wave velocity, shock wave duration, heat load, missile velocity, toxic load, damage radii of different impacts, and probabilities of causing lethality. The output of the consequence analysis has been so formatted that it can be directly used in reports without editing. Moreover, using these results makes it easy to draw damage/risk contours.

The mathematical models used in this module are listed in Table 3. Brief explanatory notes on the phenomena simulated by these models are presented below.

Toxic release submodule

This submodule assesses the consequences of release of toxic gas/vapour. It simulates different types of release scenarios such as; continuous release, two-phase release, and instantaneous release. In conducting dispersion studies it takes into consideration, the densities of the gases or gas-air mixtures (because of the pronounced influence density exerts on the shape of the plume). The models can thus simulate dispersions of heavier-than-air, as light as air, and lighter-than-air gases/gas-air plumes. This module first estimates the concentration profile of the toxic gas that would develop consequent dispersion under the given meteorological conditions. It then works out the areas of toxic impact and the extents of toxicity that would be caused on the basis of exposure-based-toxicity data.

This submodule can handle the following options: heavy gas dispersion, light gas dispersion, lethality estimation and, damage estimation. Brief descriptions of these options are presented below.

Option heavy gas

This option estimates dispersion characteristics (concentration profile, distance travelled by the cloud/plume, and the dimensions of the cloud/plume) of gases having effective density higher-than-air. It uses BOX model for instantaneous release and PLUME (heavy gas) model for continuous release (Bington,1986; Van Ulden,1974,1985; Deaves,1992; Erbink,1995; Khan and Abbsi,1997) to estimate gas concentrations and other dispersion characteristics. The results are then passed on to damage estimation options to calculate the percent likelihood of lethality and area under influence for various degrees of toxicity.

Table 5. Impacts of scenario 1 at a distance of 500 meter from accident epicentre

Parameter	Magnitude
UVCE	
Peak over pressure (kpa)	21.05
Duration of shock wave (ms)	41.09
Shock wave velocity in air (m/s)	358.1
Over pressure impulse (kpa/sec)	0.693
Area covered by explosive mixture(sqm)	253.3
Volume of vapor cloud (cu.m)	20265.0
Total heat released by UVCE (kJ)	1.3E+06
Radiant heat intensity (kW/sq.m)	0.258
POOL FIRE	
Mass release rate (kg/s)	73.79
Area of pool fire (sq.m)	69.97
Burning area (sq.m)	15372.8
Flame velocity (m/s)	1.64
Heat flux (kJ/sq.m)	20.8
NO MISSILE	
TOXIC LOAD	
Box continous model	
Elevated source	
Concentration (kg/cu.m)	6.65E-05
Heavy gas plume Characteristics	
Ground level conc. of plume(kg/cu.m)	6.61E-05
Ground level conc. of plume on axis(kg/cu.m)	7.24E-05
Width of plume (m)	2.50E+02
Maximum ground level concentration (m)	3.49E+01
Distance at which maximum concentration occur(m)	10.0
Secondary Accident	
The probability of leading secondary accident	0.23

Option light gas

In this, similar operations are carried out for gases having density lighter-than-air or/and as light as air in the previous option heavy gas done for heavier-than-air gases. This option incorporates with various dispersion models: Gaussian model (instantaneous and continuous), Plume model (continuous), and Puff model (instantaneous) to estimate the dispersion characteristics for different release scenarios (Pasquill and Smith,1983; Turner,1985; Erbink,1993). The results are then used to estimate the toxic load (concentration) at particular location, chances of lethality at that location and radii of the areas which are under the influence of varying degrees of toxicity. Probit models proposed by Pietersen (1990), Greenbook (1992) and Clancey (1977) are used for estimating lethality.

Explosion submodule

An explosion is defined as sudden and violent release of energy. According to mode of occurrence and conse-

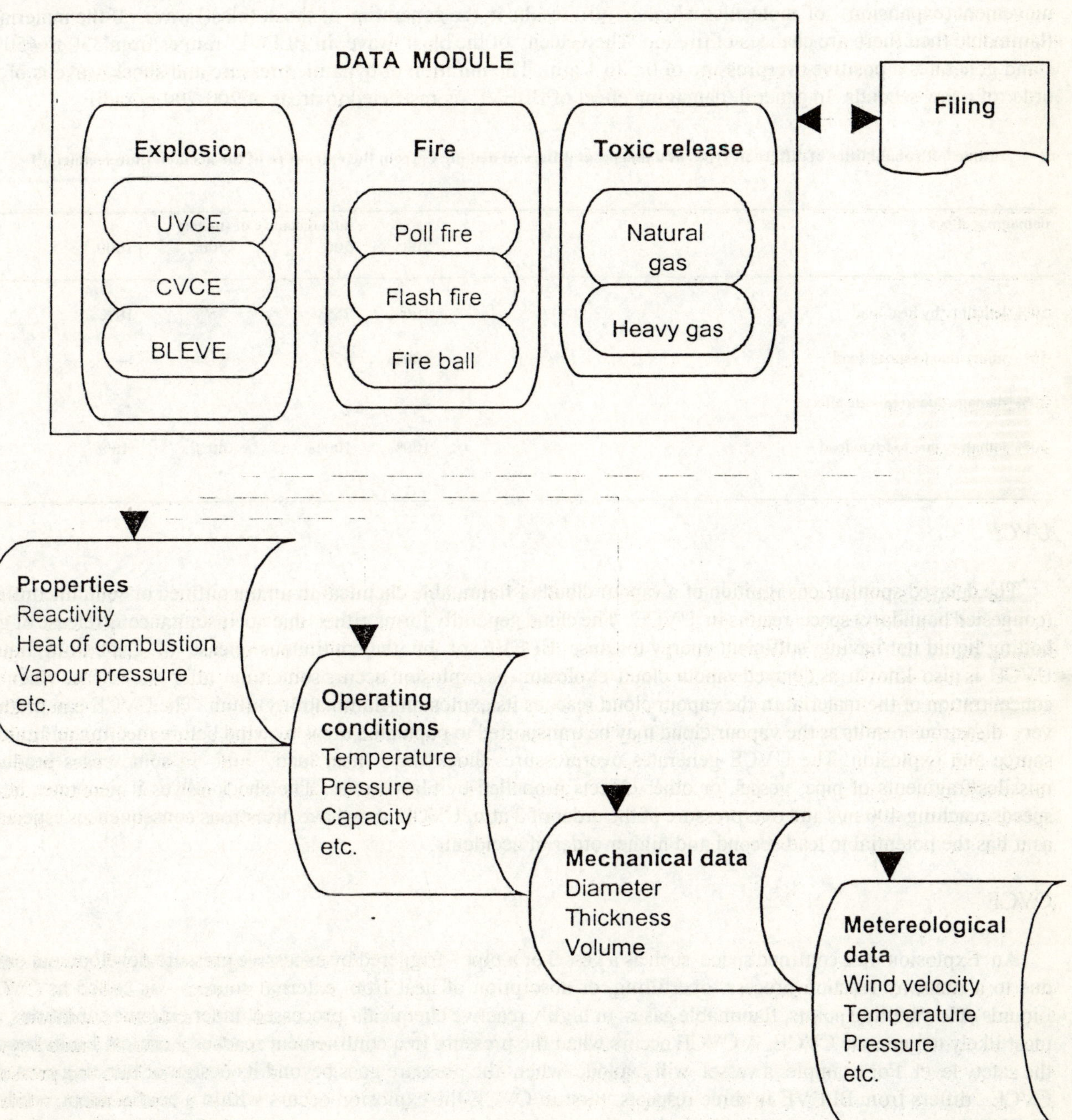

Figure 4. Object-oriented architecture of Data Module

quence, explosions have been further categorised as - boiling liquid expanding vapour explosion (BLEVE), confined vapour cloud explosion (CVCE) and unconfined vapour cloud explosion (UVCE).

BLEVE

A sudden release of pressurised gas or boiling liquid processed or stored under high pressure leads to BLEVE. As highly energised molecules (due to high pressure) have high tendency to escape, a sudden release leads to a very fast movement (expansion) of molecules which in turn results in the generation of shock (blast) waves. If the material is flammable then there are chances of fire too. The velocity of the blast wave in BLEVE ranges from 330 to 450 m/s and generates a positive overpressure of 0.5 to 1 atm. The duration of dynamic pressure and shock-wave is of the order of a few seconds. In general, damaging effect of BLEVE is restricted to areas of 200-700 m radii.

Table 6. Probabi lities of differe nt types of damages at differe nt distanc es from the epicent re of the acciden t for scenari o 1

damagin g effect	at a distanc e of (meter)			
	200	500	700	1000
50% lethali ty by heat load	100%	75%	35%	10%
50% injury due to shock load	100%	85%	11%	--
50% damage due to missile effect	--	--	--	--
50% lethali ty due to toxic load	100%	100%	40%	16%

UVCE

The delayed spontaneous ignition of a vapour cloud of flammable chemical in an unconfined or semi unconfined (congested boundary) space results in UVCE. The cloud generally forms either due to instantaneous release of gas/boiling liquid not having sufficient energy to cause BLEVE or by the continuous release of gas/boiling liquid. UVCE is also known as delayed vapour cloud explosion as explosion occurs some time after the release when the concentration of the material in the vapour cloud reaches its explosion (flammability) limit. The UVCE can produce very disastrous results as the vapour cloud may be transported to populated areas by wind before meeting an ignition source and explosion. The UVCE generates overpressure, shock-wave, heat load, and in some cases produces missiles/fragments of pipe, vessel, or other objects propelled by blast waves. The shock-waves it generates attain speeds reaching 400 m/s and overpressure of the order of 2 atm. UVCE may have disastrous consequences especially as it has the potential to lead second and higher order of accidents.

CVCE

An Explosion in a confined space such as a vessel or a pipe - triggered by excessive pressure development either due to a runaway reaction process, overfilling, or absorption of heat from external sources - is called as CVCE. Liquids of low boiling points, flammable gases, or highly reactive chemicals processed under extreme conditions, are most likely to generate CVCE. A CVCE occurs when the pressure in a confinement reaches a critical limits beyond the safety level. For example, a vessel will explode when the pressure goes beyond its design or bursting pressure. CVCE differs from BLEVE in three respects. First in CVCE the explosion occurs within a confinement, while in BLEVE the material expands outside the boundary of the confinement (vessel) and can drift away before exploding. Secondly CVCE occurs at very high pressure, quite higher than the pressures adequate for BLEVE. Lastly CVCE could be more disastrous than BLEVE as it generates shock-waves of higher speeds and greater overpressure. The impact of CVCE can be observed over a much larger distance (1 to 3 km). Due to its large area of impact and more severe shock-waves CVCE has a greater potential of causing secondary, tertiary and higher order accidents.

Fire submodule

Uncontrolled combustion of any chemical in the presence of air is termed as fire. According to the mechanism of

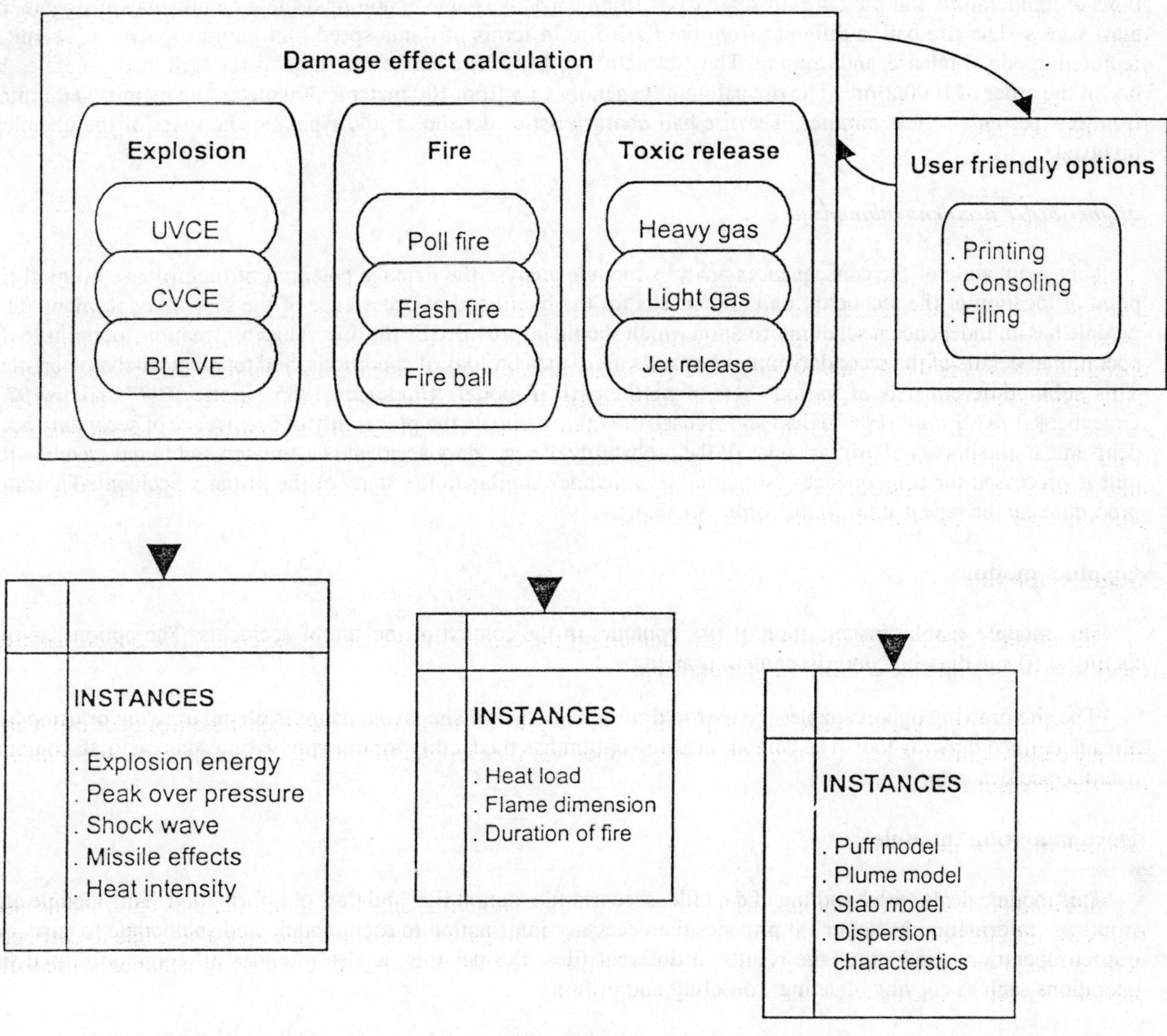

Figure 5. Internal architecture for Consequence Analysis Module

formation and the broad shapes it attains, the fire can be classified into three main types: pool fire, flash fire, and fire ball.

Release of low boiling/non boiling liquid from a vessel may give rise to a pool of liquid which on ignition would yield *pool fire*. In certain situations a pool fire may also generate an explosive vapour cloud by supplying the required heat of evaporation to a liquid pool. However, possibility of occurrence of this phenomenon is limited to the boiling liquid processed / stored under liquefied or refrigerated conditions. There may be different ways of initiation of a pool fire but the ultimate destructive impact of a pool fire is caused by its heat load.

An instantaneous combustion of flammable gas or high boiling liquid (liquid of high vapour pressure) on ignition causes *flash fire*. Flash fire generally occurs when the quantity of chemical is not high enough to form an explosive cloud. The low flammability characteristics and rate of release of the chemical restrict flame speed precluding generation of a blast wave. However, the heat load generated by flash fire is quite high and its damaging effect can be observed over long distances. According to the different modes of release and ignition, flash fires can be characterised as *flare*, *fire torch* etc.

A spontaneous ignition of vapour cloud not having sufficient energy to explode leads to a *fire ball*. This phenomenon is generally observed for high boiling yet highly flammable liquids stored or processed under extreme conditions of temperature and pressure. In some cases (high capacity, stable conditions) these clouds may also generate blast waves. The fire ball is different from the flash fire in terms of flame speed, minimum capacity of chemical required, mode of release, and ignition. The destructive ability of fire ball is very high as the heat load generated by it is of the order of 1000 kJ/m^2. The fire ball radii generally vary from 100 meter to 300 meter and its impact duration from few seconds to few minutes. The fire ball characteristics depend on the type and the mass of the chemical involved.

Higher order accident submodule

This submodule of the consequences analysis module analyse the damage potential of the primary event at the point of location of the secondary unit and checks for the likelihood of occurrence of the secondary accident. This module has an independent set of information which should be provided by the user. This information, pertains to the operational details of the secondary unit, chemicals used, meteorological conditions, and topological characteristics. This submodule consists of various sets of mathematical models (Pietersen,1985; Clancy,1977; Kletz,1977; Greenbook,1992; Prugh, 1987; Khan and Abbasi,1997a) to estimate the probability of occurrence of secondary accidents due to the impact of primary ones. If the probability of secondary accident is estimated and found credible, the unit is processed for consequences estimation in a manner similar to the study of the primary accident. The same procedure can be repeated for higher order accidents.

Graphics module

This module enables visualisation of risk contours in the context of the site of accidents. The option has two facilities: (i) site drawing, and (ii) contour drawing.

The site drawing option enables the user to draw any industrial site layout using freehand drawing or using any already defined drawing tool. The contour drawing option has the facility for drawing various damage/risk contours over the accident site.

Documentation module

This module deals with handling of data file, scenario file, output file, and flow of information. This module also works as 'information manager': it provides the necessary information to each module and submodule to carry out desired operations, and stores the results in different files. Besides this, it also provides all commonly used file operations such as copying, deleting, consoling and printing.

The applicability of the software is demonstrated with an illustrated example of its use in RRA as follows.

AN ILLUSTRATIVE EXAMPLE OF APPLICATION OF MAXCRED IN RRA

Problem Statement

Risk assessment study has been carried out for a typical chemical industry situated in an industrial area at Harmoli, Madya Pradesh, India. The industry primarily manufactures sulfolene which is a solvent used for the extraction of hydrocarbon; and is also used as feedstock for many chemical and petrochemical industries. The industry handles several hazardous chemicals such as butadiene, sulfur dioxide (SO_2), catechol, and sulfolene.

Sulfolene is prepared by a reaction of butadiene and sulfur dioxide (SO_2). The reaction is exothermic and is carried out in liquid phase under high pressure. If the reaction temperature goes even slightly above normal, it leads to undesirable side reactions (which cause further increase in the temperature and pressure in the reactor). The process also necessitate maintaining butadiene : sulfur dioxide concentration in the ratio 1:8 otherwise side reactions may occur generating high pressure and temperature in the reactor. Thus, precise control of material flow, temperature, and pressure are essential to prevent unwanted side reaction. Some other units in the industry, notably evaporation, stripping compressor and storage units prone to accidents. Of these the storage units (for butadiene and sulfur dioxide) are the most hazardous. Thus, a detailed risk assessment for the butadiene and sulfur dioxide storage units have been conducted. The set of data used in the present study is given in Table 4.

Table 7. Impacts of scenario 2 at a distance of 500 meter from accident epicentre

Parameter	Magnitude
CVCE	
Peak over pressure (kpa)	206.11
Duration of shock wave (ms)	41.09
Shock wave velocity in air (m/s)	546.56
Over pressure impulse (kpa/sec)	6.78
Total energy available (kJ)	2.30E+08
Net energy available for bursting (kJ)	1.51E+08
Energy released by CVCE (kJ)	1.59E+07
Heat intensity (kW/sq.m)	9.167
MISSILE	
Initial velocity of fragment(1kg) (m/s)	305.45
Kinetic energy associated with fragment (kJ)	6.3E+03
Penetration st. of mild steel at 500 m, (m)	0.0045
FLASH FIRE	
Volume of vapor cloud (cu.m)	16330.5
Area under the fire effect (sq.m)	280993.0
Heat generated (kJ)	1.24E+06
Effective time of fire (sec)	51.16
Radiation heat intensity (kW/sq.m)	15.96
TOXIC LOAD	
Box instantaneous model	
Elevated source	
Concentration (kg/cu.m)	3.45E-07
Heavy gas puff Characteristics	
Ground level conc. of plume(kg/cu.m)	5.22E-07
Ground level conc. of plume on axis(kg/cu.m)	7.43E-07
Cloud radius (m)	1.16E+02
Maximum distance traveled by the cloud (m)	7.87E+02
Maximum ground level concentration (m)	4.34
Secondary Accident	
The probability of leading secondary accident	0.54

*** MAXCRED *** (c) F.I. Khan & S.A. Abbasi, Pondicherry-605 014, India

Accident scenario generation

The storage units pose the following three types of hazard: explosion hazard (due to butadiene and sulfur dioxide), fire hazard (due to butadiene), and toxicity hazard (due to sulfur dioxide). The plausible accident scenarios are:

***Scenario 1**: A UVCE followed by pool fire in butadiene tank which may damage the SO_2 tank , in turn causing toxic release.*

A continuous release of butadiene forms an explosive vapour cloud which on ignition leads to *UVCE*. The unexploded chemical in the dike or in the vessel burns as *pool fire*. Due to the consequent heat and overpressure load the other tank (containing SO_2) is damaged causing the release of toxic gas.

***Scenario 2**: A CVCE followed by flash fire in butadiene tank which may later trigger and cause toxic release from the (SO_2) tank.*

An instantaneous, explosive, release of butadiene under very high pressure sets off *CVCE*. The released chemical is ignited as a *fire ball*. As the heat and overpressure loads are very high the SO_2 storage tank is damaged causing the release of its toxic contents.

Scenario 3: A BLEVE followed by fire ball .

A sudden release of butadiene as *BLEVE* on ignition turns into a fire ball. As the damage potential of a *BLEVE* is (generally) lesser than of *CVCE* or *UVCE*, the SO_2 storage tank is not affected.

Scenario 4: Toxic release of SO_2

A continuous release of SO_2 from the SO_2 storage tank.

Table 8. Probabi lities of differe nt types of damages at differe nt distanc e from the epicent re of the acciden t for scenari o 2

damagin g effect	at a distanc e of (meter) 200	500	700	1000
50% lethali ty by heat load	100%	100%	85%	65%
50% injury due to shock load	100%	100%	75%	45%
50% damage due to missile effect	50%	22%	3%	--
50% lethali ty due to toxic load	100%	100%	80%	65%

Table 9. Impacts of scenario 3 at a distance of 500 meter from accident epicentre

Parameter	Magnitude
BLEVE	
Peak over pressure (kpa)	11.78
Duration of shock wave (sec)	23.54
Shock wave velocity in air (m/s)	53.67
Over pressure impulse (kpa/sec)	2.74E-02
FIRE BALL	
Radius of fire ball (m)	98.56
Duration of fire ball (sec)	10.89
Heat generated (kJ)	1.05E+06
Radiation heat intensity (kW/sq.m)	11.45
Secondary Accident	
The probability of leading secondary accident	0.023

*** MAXCRED *** (c) F.I. Khan & S.A. Abbasi, Pondicherry-605 014, India

Results

The output of MAXCRED for *scenario* 1 is shown in Table 5. It is seen that lethal heat load and severely intense overpressure load would occur over an area of ~500 m radius. Lethal toxic load due to release of SO_2 (secondary accident) would occur over an area of ~700 m radius. The probability of secondary accident (release of SO_2) is estimated as 23%. The damage potential (in terms of percentage damage) of various accidental events are presented in Table 6. It is evident that an area of ~500 m radius is under high risk (individual risk factor greater than $1*10^{-3}$ /yr) due to lethal overpressure and toxic load.

The MAXCRED output for *scenario* 2 is shown in Table 7. Up to a radial distance of ~500 m from the accident epicenter, lethal heat load as well as damage causing shock-waves (overpressure) would be encountered. The probability of a secondary accident (release of SO_2) is high : over 50%. The damage potentials of various impacts over different areas are shown in Table 8. An area of ~700 m radius would be at high risk.

The MAXCRED outputs of *scenarios* 3 and 4 are presented in Tables 9 and 10 respectively. Table 9 reveals that a moderately intense heat load having 50% probability of first degree burn as well as damage causing shock-waves would occur over an area of ~150 m radius. As per *scenario* 4 (Table 10), a lethal toxic load would be persistent over an area of ~500 m radius. The probability of secondary impacts is low in both the scenarios. The damage potential of *scenarios* 3 and 4 as a function of distance from accident epicenter are presented in Tables 11 and 12 respectively. Severe damage due to overpressure and heat load as per *scenario* 3 would be limited to less than 200 m radius while the toxic load as per *scenario* 4 would extend beyond 500 m radius.

Table 10. Iiapacts of scenario 4 at a distance of 500 meter from accident epicentre

Parameter	Magnitude
TOXIC LOAD	
Box instantaneous model	
Elevated source	
Concentration (kg/cu.m)	1.13E-06
Heavy gas puff Characteristics	
Ground level conc. of plume(kg/cu.m)	2.85E-06
Ground level conc. of plume on axis(kg/cu.m)	1.23E-06
Cloud radius (m)	2.28E+02
Maximum distance traveled by the cloud (m)	1.15E+03
maximum concentration at ground level (kg/cu.m)	6.72
Secondary Accident	
The probability of leading secondary accident	0.00

DISCUSSION

The MAXCRED forecasts consequence of the scenario for the release of butadiene (UVCE followed by pool fire) reveal that the likely damage due to this event in terms of shock waves, missile, and heat load would be intense. It is evident from MAXCRED results (Tables 5 and 6) that even at a distance ~500 m away from the accident epicenter the intensity of shock waves and heat load would be severe enough to cause lethal damage. The high risk contour (individual risk factor > 1*e-03) for more than 50% probability of damage/lethality would be extended over an area of ~500 m radius (Table 6). This scenario has 23% probability of causing secondary accident (release of sulfur dioxide), which could propel the gas in lethal concentrations over an area of ~500 m radius.

The CVCE in butadiene tank as per *scenario* 2 would generate shock waves and missile effects (Table 7). The damage potential due to these shock waves and the missiles would cover wider area than likely as per *scenario* 1 (Table 8). The released butadiene from the vessel would form a vapour-air mixture which on ignition would cause flash fire lethally effecting an area of ~700 m. The probability of a secondary accident (release of sulfur dioxide) due to this accident is about 54%. The secondary accident would cause toxic build-up of SO_2 over a wide area. All-in-all a region of ~700 m radius would be at great risk due to heat load, shock waves, and toxic load.

Compared to accident *scenarios* 1 and 2, the forecasts as per *scenario* 3 reveal moderate impacts; limited to within a periphery close to the accident site (Tables 9 and 11). The probability of secondary accident is negligible.

The results of accident *scenario* 4 (release of SO_2) reveal build-up of lethal toxic concentration over an area of ~500m radius (Tables 10 and 12) with near-zero probability of secondary accident.

In summary *scenario* 2 represents the worst likely disaster within the realm of credibility. It has the largest area-of-lethal-impact (shock waves, lethal heat load, and lethal concentration of SO_2 over an area of ~700 m). Further, the most thickly populated areas (including neighbourhoods) lie within its range. This scenario is also the one most likely to cause domino effects as missiles, shock waves, and radiation loads would be generated simultaneously and units dealing with hazardous chemicals (flammable and toxic materials) are situated within the striking distance of the impact area of this scenario. Similar to *scenario* 2, *scenario* 1 is also likely to cause secondary accidents. In conclusion *scenario* 2 is the worst as far as the largeness of its impact area is concerned as well as in terms of its potentiality of causing secondary accidents.

Table 11. Probabi lities of differe nt types of damages at differ ent distanc es from the epicent re of the acciden t for scenari o 3

damagin g effect	at a distanc e of (meter) 200	500	700	1000
50% lethali ty by heat load	65%	38%	22%	8%
50% injury due to shock load	25%	8%	--	--
50% damage due to missile effect	--	--	--	--
50% lethali ty due to toxic load	--	--	--	--

Table 12. Probabi lities of differe nt types of damages at differ ent distanc es from the epicent re of the acciden t for scenari o 4

damagin g effect	at a distanc e of (meter) 200	500	700	1000
50% lethali ty by heat load	--	--	--	--
50% injury due to shock load	--	--	--	--
50% damage due to missile effect	--	--	--	--
50% lethali ty due to toxic load	100%	80%	60%	45%

*** MAXCRED ***

CONCLUSION

A new software package MAXCRED (MAXimum CREDible accident analysis) has been developed as a comprehensive and user-friendly tool for rapid risk assessment in the chemical process industries. The package, coded in C++, has the following attributes:

i) it incorporates larger number of models to handle larger variety of situations useful in RRA;

ii) it includes more precise, accurate, and recent models than handled by existing commercial packages;

iii) greater user-friendliness;

iv) ability to forecast whether second or higher order accidents may occur.

The applicability of MAXCRED has been demonstrated with an illustrative example of RRA conducted in the storage unit of a typical chemical process industry. MAXCRED generated scenarios of four credible accidents and helped in assessing their consequences. It revealed that the scenario which forecasts a CVCE (confined vapour cloud explosion) followed by flash fire would be the worst of all as it would lethally effect the largest area as also would have the largest probability of triggering secondary, tertiary, and higher order accidents. The least harmful of four credible accidents was the scenario as per which a BLEVE (boiling liquid expanding vapour explosion) would occur followed by the formation of fire ball.

REFERENCES

1. Ale, B J M, (1991). Risk analysis and risk policy in the Netherlands and EEC, *J Loss Prevention in Process Industries*, **4**(1), 58.

2. Arendt, J S, (1990). Using quantitative risk assessment in the chemical process industries, *Reliability Engineering and System Safety*, **29**, 133-149.

3. Baker, W E, Cox, P A, Westin, P S, Kulesz, J J, and Strelow, R A, (1983). Explosion hazard and evaluation, *Elesvier*, Amsterdam.

4. Bington, P W M, (1986). Heavy gas dispersion from source inside building or in wake, *Proceeding IChemE Symposium on refinement of estimate of the consequence of heavy toxic release*, Manchester.

5. Chary, S V, Suryanarayana, G, Rao, K C K, (1995). Risk assessment in pesticide industry- a case study, *Journal of IAEM*, **2**3,27-35.

6. CISRA, (1993). Risk assessment of Chloralkali industry, *Cell for Industrial Safety and Risk Analysis*, CLRI - Madras, India.

7. Clancey, V J, (1977). Dangerous clouds, their growth and explosive properties, *Chemical Process Hazards*, **6**, 111-123.

8. Contini, C A, Amendal, A, and Ziomas, I, (1991). Benchmark study on major hazard study, *Joint Research Centre -ISPRA*, 134, Amsterdam.

9. Davies, P A, (1993). A guide to the evaluation of condensed phase explosion, *Journal of Hazardous Materials*, **33**, 1-33.

10. Deaves, D M, (1992). Dense gas dispersion modelling (HEAVG-PLUME), *Journal of Loss Prevention Process Industries*, **5**(4), 219-222.

11. Eissenberg, N A, Lynch, C J, and Breeding, R J, (1975). Vulnerability Model: A Simulation System for Assessing Damage Resulting from Marine Spills, *Report CG-D-136-75 (Enviro control)*, Rockville M D., USA.

12. Erbink, J J, (1993). The advanced Gaussian model STACKS, *Procd. of ERCOFTAC work shop on Inter comparison of Advanced Practical Short range Atmospheric Dispersion Modelling*, Manno, Switzerland.

13. Erbink, J J, (1995). Turbulent diffusion model from tall stacks, *Ph.D. thesis submitted to VRIJ University*, The Netherlands.

14. Fowcett, H H, and Wood, W S, (1993). Safety and accident prevention in chemical operation, (third ed.), *John willey*, New York.

15. Gifford, F A, (1961). Use of routine meteorological observation for estimate atmospheric diffusion, *Nuclear Safety*, **24**, 67.

16. Greenberg, H R, and Crammer, J J, (1992). Risk Assessment and risk management in chemical process industries, *Van Norstand Reinhold*, New York.

17. Greenbook, (1992). Methods for determining of possible damage to people and objects resulting from release of hazardous materials, *Report CPR-16E*, Voorburg, Warrington, UK.

18. Hagon, D O, (1984). Use of frequency-consequence curves to examine the conclusion of published risk analysis and to define broad criteria for major hazard installations, *Chem Engng Res Dev*, **62**, 381.

19. Havens, J A, and Spicer, T O, (1985). (DEGADIS) Development of an atmospheric dispersion model for heavier-than-air gas mixtures, *Report number CG-D-23-85*, U S Coast Guard, Washington, D C.

20. HSE, (1988). The tolerability of risks formation from nuclear power stations, Health and Safety Executive , *HM Stationary Office*, London.

21. Kayes, P J, (1986). Manual of industrial hazard assessment technique, *Technica Ltd.*, London.

22. Khan, F I, and Abbasi, S A, (1995a). Risk Analysis : An optimum approach, *research report to CPCE /RA 011/ 95*, Pondicherry University.

23. Khan, F I, and Abbasi, S A, (1995b). Anatomy of industrial accidents, *Chemical Engineering World*, September, Bombay.

24. Khan, F I, and Abbasi, S A, (1995c). Accident simulation in CPI using MAXCRED, *Indian Journal of Chemical Technology*, **3**, 338-344.

25. Khan, F I, and Abbasi, S A, (1997a). Models for domino effect analysis in chemical process industries, *Process Safety Progress (accepted; in press).*

26. Khan, F I, and Abbasi, S A, (1997b). Modelling and simulation of heavy gas dispersion on the basis of modification in plume path theory, *Atmospheric Environment*, (in press).

27. Kletz, T A, (1977). Unconfined vapour cloud explosions, *AIChE Loss Prevention*, **11**, 50.

28. Lees, F P, (1996). Loss prevention in CPI, *Butterworths*, London.

29. Martinsen, W E, Johnson, D W, and Terell, W F, (1986). BLEVE : Their causes effects and prevention, *Hydrocarbon Processing*, **65**(11), 141.

30. NEERI (1992). Risk assessment of Reliance petrochemical complex, *National Environmental Research Institute*, Nagpur, India.

31. Papazoglou, I A, Nivoliantou, Z, Aneziris, O, and Christou, M, (1992). Probabilistic safety analysis in chemical process industries, *Journal of Loss Prevention Process Industries*, **5**, 3-15.

32. Pasquill, F, (1971). Atmospheric dispersion of pollutants, *J of Royal Meteorological Society*, **97**, 369-395.

33. Pasquill, F, and Smith, F B, (1983). Atmospheric diffusion, *John willey*, New York.

34. Pitblado, R M, Shaw, S J, and Stevens, G C, (1990). The SAFETI risk assessment package and case study application, *Safety and loss prevention in the chemical and oil industries*, 51.

35. Pietersen, C M, (1985). Analysis of the LPG-incident in San Juan Ixhuasapec- Mexico city, *TNO report*, The Netherlands.

36. Pietersen, C M, (1990). Consequence of accidental release of hazardous materials, *Journal of Loss Prevention Process Industries*, **3**, 136-141.

37. Prugh, R W, (1987). Evaluation of unconfined vapour cloud explosions, *Proceedings of International Conference of Vapour Cloud Modelling*, Boston.

38. Prugh, R W, (1991). Quantitative evaluation of BLEVE hazards, *Journal of Fire Protection Engineers*, **3**(1), 9-24.

39. Raghvan, K V, and Mallikarjunan, M M, (1988). An approach to Maximum Credible Accident Analysis of cluster of industries, *Procd. Envirotech International conference*, Bombay.

40. Roberts, A P, (1983). Thermal radiation hazard from release of LPG from pressurized storage, *Fire & Safety*

Journal, **4**, 197-212.

41. Technica, (1992). *WHAZAN* : A software for hazard assessment, *Technica Ltd.*, London.

42. TNO, (1991). *EFFECTS* : a software for hazard assessment, *TNO Prins Mauritis Research Laboratory*, The Netherlands.

43. TNO, (1992). SAVE : a software for hazard assessment, *TNO Prins Mauritis Research Laboratory*, The Netherlands.

44. TPL, (1993). Risk analysis of storage unit of chemical process industry, *Tamilnadu Petrochemical Ltd.*, Manali, Madras, India.

45. Turner, D B, (1970). Workbook on atmospheric dispersion estimates report Ap-26, *US EPA*, Qeseach Triangle park, NC.

46. Turner, D B, (1985). Pragmatic method for the estimating boundary layer parameter for diffusion calculation, *Boundary Layer Metrology*, 8, 93-100.

47. Van den Berg, A C, Van Wingerden, C J m, and The, H G, (1991). Vapour cloud explosion : experimental investigation of key parameters and blast modelling, *Trans I Chem Engg*, **69**B.

48. Van Ulden, A P, (1974). On spreading of a heavy gas cloud released near ground, *Loss Prevention and Safety Promotion*, **1**, 221.

49. Van Ulden, A P, (1985). Estimate of atmospheric boundary layer parameters for diffusion application, *Journal of Climatology and Applied Meteorology*, **25**, 1609.

50. Vernart, J E S, Rutledge, G A, Sumathipala,K, and Sollows, K., (1993). To BLEVE or not to BLEVE ; Anatomy of boiling liquid expanding vapour explosion, *Process Safety Progress*, **2,** 112-123.

51. VTT, (1993). *RISKIT* : a software for risk assessment, *The Technical Research Centre of Finland*, Tempere, The Finalnd.

¨ Reproduced from *Journal of Environmental Modelling and Software*, The Netherlands

12

RISK ANALYSIS OF AN EPICHLOROHYDRIN MANUFACTURING INDUSTRY USING: The New Computer Automated Tool Maxcred**

Studies pertaining to risk analysis, conducted on the storage units of a typical chemical industry engaged in the manufacture of epichlorohydrin, are described. A comprehensive software package MAXCRED (MAXimum CREDible accident analysis) recently developed by us has been utilized for the purpose. Eight different scenarios, one for each storage unit, have been studied. It is observed that the accident scenario for chlorine (BLEVE followed by dispersion) leads to the largest area-under-lethal-impact while the accident scenario for propylene (CVCE followed by fire ball) forecasts the most intense damage per unit area. The accidents involving propylene, epichlorohydrin and fuel oil have high possibility of causing domino/secondary accidents as their destructive impacts (shock waves, heat load) would envelope other storage and process units.

Besides demonstrating the utilizability of MAXCRED, this study also focuses attention on the need to bestow greater effort towards risk assessment/crisis management. The authors hope that these studies would highlight the severity of risk posed by the industry and would thus generate safety consciousness among plant managers. The studies may also help in developing accident-prevention strategies and installation of damage control devices.

INTRODUCTION

Serious accidents can take place in chemical process industries - in the form of explosions, fires and release of toxic chemicals. Such accidents can take heavy toll in terms of loss of property and human lives. The accidents - if they involve release of large quantities of toxic chemicals - can also contaminate large areas and render them useless for several years.

Accidents in process industries are generally caused by the following factors :

a) Cracks in storage or reaction vessels leading to rupture

b) Malfunctioning of control equipment such as valves

c) Other type of failures in instruments and piping

d) Human errors

e) A combination of two or more of the above factors.

We have given in chapter 11a review of some of the accidents occurred in different industries is presented below to illustrate the myriad ways in which human or equipment failure can cause an accident leading to loss of lives and property. A few more case studies are presented below.

At a refinery in France, a spillage occurred on 4 January 1996 when an operator was draining water from a 1200 m pressurized propane sphere. The propane vapor spread over a radius of 150 m and was ignited by a car on the road. The pool of propane below the sphere engulfed the vessel in flames. The resultant boiling-liquid-expanding-vapor explosion (BLEVE) killed the fireman and 17 others. The conflagration took 48 hours to control and caused extensive damage to the refinery.

On 22 June 1974 a 16" elbow of a pipe carrying potassium carbonate solution in a fertilizer plant at Tamilnadu, India, ruptured suddenly, splashing the hot solution into the nearby control room. The toughened glass panes shattered; 8 persons died in the control room instantaneously, one died in the hospital and another sustained grievous injuries.

On 8 March, 1984, an explosion in a refinery at Kerala destroyed fire tender along with the shed wherein it was housed, besides a chemical warehouse, cooling tower and other facilities. Later investigations revealed many short-comings in the plant layout.

On 12 December, 1987, a crude oil storage tank in a refinery at Maharashtra, India, started boiling over, spilling the contents on the dike around it. Emergency services and fire brigades, who were alerted, tried to evacuate the contents. After 4 hours of pumping out, the tank caught fire and exploded, spilling the contents. Eight hours of vigorous fire fighting had to be carried out before the fire could be controlled. There was extensive damage to the property. A liberal sizing of the dike and providing a separate dike for a large tank like this would have helped to prevent the spread of fire to other tanks.

On 5 November, 1990, an explosion at the offside battery of compressors at a gas cracking plant in Maharashtra, India, killed 35 persons, besides causing heavy damages to property and business interruption losses. Among the deficiencies in the layout, identified after the disaster, was the location of a contractor's shed dangerously close to the gas compressors. Less publicized, but perhaps of greater consequence, was the lack of facility to shut down the flow of hydrocarbon at the site itself. The plant personnel had to run to the control room faster than the vapor that followed them to close the feed valve.

An accident took place on 18 April, 1989, in a 14" natural gas pipeline in a gas company in India. The pipeline was carrying compressed natural gas at a pressure of about 295 - 298 psig from the compressor station to various consumers. The spot of the accident was about 730 ft. from the compressor station. A security personnel heard a loud sound at about 0950 hrs and saw a huge cloud of black smoke emanating from the ruptured pipeline which caught fire immediately. The flame rose as high as 150 ft during the initial stage.

The fire damaged buildings consisting of the general stores and the office of the materials department. Two employees died and six others received burn injuries. Investigations revealed that the portion of the pipeline which had blown off was extensively corroded as compared to other portions of the pipeline. The underground pipeline was close to the materials department where old lead cells were stored. The corrosion could be due to the leakage of spent weak acid which seeped through the ground and corroded the buried pipeline.

Bhopal disaster : The worst-ever disaster in the history of the chemical industry occurred in Bhopal, India, on December 3, 1984. A leak of methyl isocyanate from a chemical plant, where it was used as an intermediate in the manufacture of a pesticide, spread beyond the plant boundary and caused death by poisoning of over 2,500 people - injuring about 10 times as many .

Methyl isocyanate boils at about 40 C at atmospheric pressure. According to press reports, the contents of the storage tank got overheated and boiled, causing the relief valves to lift. The discharge of vapor - about 25 tons - was too great for the capacity of the scrubbing system. The escaping vapor spread beyond the plant boundary where a shanty town had sprung up. The cause of the overheating was contamination of the methyl isocyanate, by water or other materials, and several possible mechanisms were suggested. According to some reports cyanide was produced.

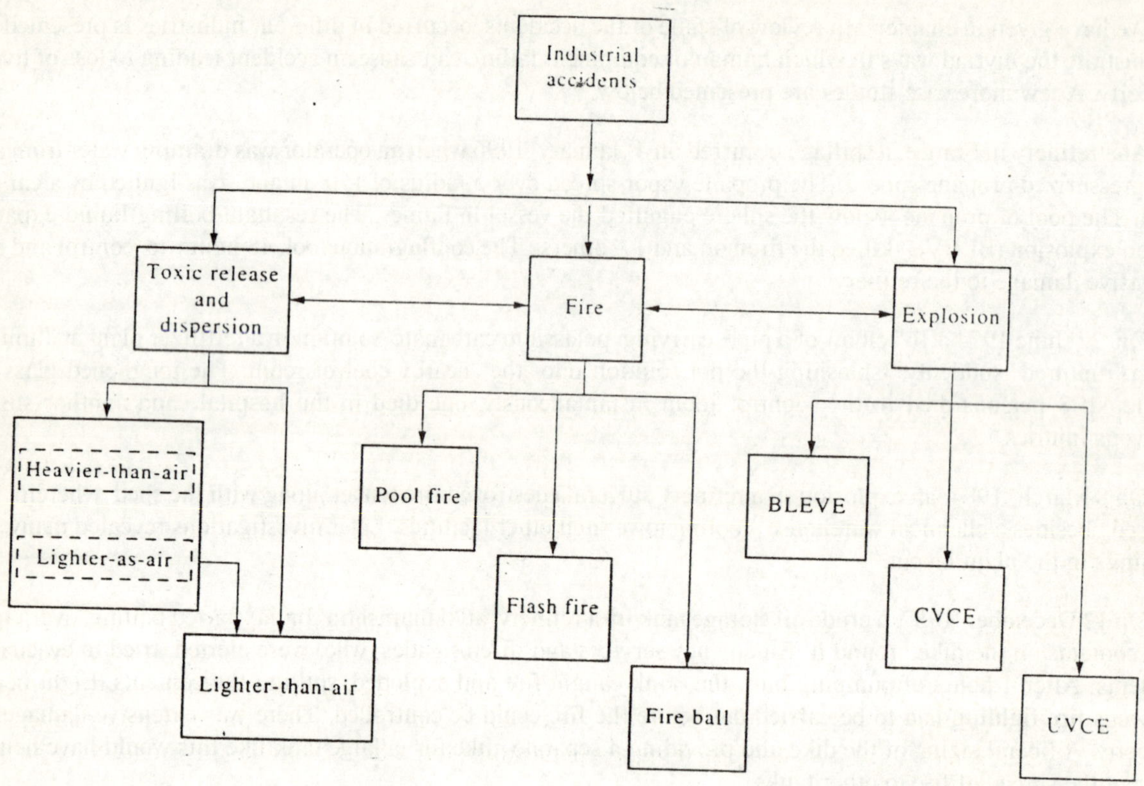

Figure 1. Tree diagram showing different accidental events and their interdependency

Had Union Carbide conducted risk analysis, (specifically maximum credible accident analysis) during the design of the MIC system or even later, it would have learnt that in the event of a MIC leak the scrubbing system would be inadequate. This would have enabled the industry to install better emergency handling systems, thereby saving thousands of lives.

Pepcon explosion : On May 4, 1988, a massive explosion destroyed Pacific Engineering and Production Company, (PEPCON) plant near Henderson, about 12 miles south of Las Vegas, USA.

PEPCON was one of the only two plants in USA that produced ammonium perchlorate (AP); the other was the Kerr-Mc Gee plant, also located in Henderson about 2 miles from PEPCON plant. PEPCON reportedly produced about one-third of the AP used as an oxidizer and propellant in solid, composite rocket fuels for NASA's space shuttle and missiles.

Although a fire started the PEPCON explosion, the cause of the fire was not easy to explain. After the explosion, PEPCON blamed the fire on a leaking underground pipeline of Southwest Gas Company that traversed PEPCON'S property. But the natural gas pipeline had been installed about 10 years before PEPCON's plant, and although ruptured, it only contributed to the fire and heat required to detonate the second and the largest explosion.

The fire was also attributed to a welder's torch but one of the reports absolved the welder of the blame. Some blamed the batch dryer's fiber glass insulation which had a history of AP spills into the combustible insulation.

The following were the tell-tale conditions in and around PEPCON.

a) lack of proper storage;

b) combustible fiber glass insulation and sources of fire;

c) glass panel walls in the batch house;

d) inadequate spacing between adjacent process vessels and product storage tanks;

e) no alarm to warn plant personnel, fire departments or Henderson's other citizens;

f) no dependable fire-fighting arrangement with sprinklers and deluge system;

g) no modern, dependable, radio system to back-up damaged telephone lines needed to call for help, coordinate response teams and warn the community;

h) lack of an effective emergency response plan at PEPCON, within the surrounding industrial complex and within the town of Henderson.

The explosion caused about $ 100 million in damages to the surrounding community and completely destroyed a neighboring marshmallow plant. About 350 persons were injured. Two persons died - the plant manager and the controller.

The Phillips explosion : The explosion at the Phillips petrochemical (similar to the present case study) plant in Pasadena, Texas, on 23 Oct 1989 is one of the worst industrial accidents of the last 10 years.

Table 1. The main units of epichlorohydrin (EPI) plant

Units	Reference used in Figure 2	Operation
Propylene purification	A	Fractionation
Propylene chlorination	B	Reaction
AllylChloride purification	C	Fractionation
Chlorine absorption in water	D	Absorption
Chlorohydrination	E	Reaction
Hydrolysis and EPI purification	F	Reaction & Distillation
Quenching	G	Heat transfer
Vent scrubbing	H	Separation
Propylene bullets	I	Storage
EPI tanks	J	Storage
Fuel oil tanks	K	Storage
Chlorinated organic tanks	L	Storage
Chlorine storage	M	Storage

The immediate cause was simple: a length of pipe was opened up to clear a choke without bothering to see that the isolation valve (which was operated by compressed air) had not been duly closed. The air hoses which supplied power to the valve were connected up the wrong way round so the valve was open when its actuator was in the closed position. Identical couplings were used for the two connections so it was easy to reverse them. According to company procedure they should have been disconnected during maintenance but they were not. The valve could be locked open or closed but this hardly mattered as the lock was missing. The explosion occurred less than 2 minutes after the leak started and two iso-butane tanks exploded 15 minutes later.The explosive force was equivalent to 2.4 tones of TNT; 23 people- all employees - were killed and over 130 injured. Nearly 40 tones of ethylene gas leaked and exploded.

The Siberian accident : Perhaps the most macabre accident - next only to Bhopal gas tragedy (chapter 11) in its severity - occurred on June 3,1989, near Nizhnevartovsk in Western Siberia. Engineers stationed there noticed a sudden drop in pressure at the pumping end of an LPG pipeline. The pipeline was commissioned in 1985 to carry mixed LPG to feed the industrial city of Ufa. Instead of investigating the trouble, the engineers responded by increasing the pumping rate in order to maintain the required pressure in the pipeline. The actual leakage point was about 890 miles downstream between the towns of Asma and Ufa where the pipeline was installed about 1/2 mile away to the side of the Trans Siberian Railway. The smell of escaping gas was reported from the valley settlements in the area but no one did anything about it. The escaping liquefied gas formed two large pockets in the low lying areas along the railway line. The gas cloud then drifted for a distance of 5 miles. Some hours later, after the main leakage had started, a train from Nizhnevartovsk destined for the Red Sea resort of Alder was approaching the leakage area when the driver noticed a fog in the area that had a strong smell. The driver of another train approaching from the opposite direction (Alder to Nizhnevartovsk) saw much the same as he approached the West bound train. Both trains were packed, with a total of 1168 people on board, and as they approached the area, the turbulence caused by them mixed up LPG mist and vapor with the overlying air to form a flammable cloud. One or the other train ignited the cloud. Several explosions took place in quick succession followed by a ball of fire that was about 1 mile wide and which raced down the railroad tracks in both directions. Trees were flattened within a radius of 2 1/2 miles of the epicentre of explosions and windows were broken upto 8 miles away. The accident left 462 dead and 796 hospitalized with 70% to 80% burn injuries.

Table 2. Operating conditions of different storage units

Hazardous chemicals	No. of Tanks	Capacity of each tank (Ton/m3)	Operating pressure (atm)	Operating temperature (oC)
Propylene	2	60 T	15.20	40
Chlorine	2	100 m3	4.25	20
Allylchloride	2	50 m3	1.00	35
Epichlorohydrin	2	450 m3	2.25	40
Fuel oil	1	400 m3	1.00	40
Chlorohydrine	1	51 m3	1.22	40
Chlorinated organics	1	100 m3	1.00	40

Prevention/Control of accidents

Considering the serious and ever - increasing risk posed by the chemical process industries as elucidated above, it is necessary to conduct risk assessment and develop strategies to prevent the accidents or, if preventive measures fail, to cushion their adverse impacts.

As detailed in chapter 11, such exercises in risk assessment would involve the following essential steps :

a) to identify vulnerable spots or 'high risk' points in an industry;

b) to simulate accidents and assess the damage they may cause;

c) to use the results of the previous step in identifying the priority areas where preventive measures need to be introduced;

d) to develop disaster management plans based on 'b' & 'c' above.

It is evident that the step 'b' is very important in quantifying the risk posed. We have, therefore, developed a software package MAXCRED. The package incorporates state-of-the-art mathematical models, including some developed or modified by the authors, for rapid quantitative and comprehensive risk assessment. A brief description of MAXCRED is presented here.

THE PACKAGE MAXCRED

MAXCRED is a software package developed at Risk Assessment Division of Centre for Pollution Control & Bio-Waste Energy . The package enables simulation of accidents and estimation of their damage potential. The software is written in C++ language and is compatible with DOS as well as WINDOWS working environments. The software is operable on personal computer requiring a minimum of 1 MB RAM and 1.5 MB ROM space.

The software has four main modules (options) : scenario generation, consequence analysis, file, and graphics. The scenario generation module enables the development of accident scenarios based on the properties of chemicals, operating conditions and likely ways of malfunctioning that would cause accidental releases. The consequence analysis module uses the previously developed accident scenarios and advanced models of thermodynamics, heat transfer and fluid dynamics to forecast the nature of the accidents, and their potentialities to cause damage. This module also enables the estimation of the damage radii and the probabilities of degrees of damage. The file option enables the user to handle input/output information and the graphics with ease. With the last-graphics option, visual scenarios of accidents are generated. All-in-all MAXCRED is a versatile tool for risk assessment and is envisaged to be self contained in the sense that it does not need other packages for data analysis or graphics support.

In this paper, MAXCRED has been used to visualize different accident scenarios in a typical chemical industry's storage unit. The industry is a part of large industrial complex situated near Muzzafarnagar, Uttar Pradesh, India. The results have been represented in the terms of risk (damage*probability) contour maps over the accident site to enable easy and swift assessment of maximum credibility scenario.

Table 3. The output of MAXCRED for scenario 1

MAXCRED
F.I. Khan & S.A. Abbasi, Pondicherry- 605 014

Parameters	Values
Distance from accident epicenter	(m) : 200
Explosion : CVCE	
Energy released during explosion	(kJ) : 1.733260e+8
Peak over pressure	(kPa) : 5230.851562
Variation of over pressure in air	(kPa/s) : 2339.458984
Shock velocity of air	(m/s) : 1978.708984
Duration of shock wave	(s) : 33.019657
Missile characteristics	
Initial velocity of fragment	(m/s) : 1098.601074
Kinetic energy of fragment	(kJ) : 7.860266e+05
Fragment velocity at study point	(m/s) : 984.562378
Peneration ability at study point	
Concerete structure	(m) : 0.975414
Brick structure	(m) : 0.992585
Steel structure	(m) : 0.094620
Fire : Fire ball	
Radius of the fire ball	(m) : 278.059906
Duration of the fire ball	(s) : 113.623726
Energy released by fire ball	(kJ) : 2.468228e+10
Radiation heat intensity	(kJ/sq.m) : 23570.539062

NATURE OF LIKELY ACCIDENTS

In general, an industry may have four types of accidents -namely (i) fire, (ii) explosion, (iii) toxic release and dispersion, and (iv) a combination of i, ii, and iii. The logical sequence and dependency of most likely accidents that may occur in an industry is presented in Figure 1.

CASE STUDY

A risk assessment study has been carried out for a typical chemical industry situated in a congested industrial complex (Figure 2)and engaged in manufacturing of epichlorohydrin (EPI). EPI is a chemical which can cause fire as well as toxicity. Moreover, during the manufacture of EPI industry deals with various hazardous chemicals such as propylene, chlorine, and allylchloride at elevated temperatures and pressures. The industry and nearby areas are threatened because of different type of hazards (explosion, fire , toxic gaseous release, and corrosive liquid release) present in the industry.

Process summary

Purified propylene in gaseous phase reacts with chlorine to give allylchloride. The crude allylchloride is purified by passing through fractionating column. The purified chemical subsequently passes through chlorohydration process at nearly ambient temperature to yield glycerol dichlorohydrin (GDH). GDH is further subjected to hydrolysis at 10 °C using lime as saponification agent. The crude EPI thus produced by hydrolysis passes through the fractionating column to yield pure EPI, which is then stored in tanks. The main units of EPI plant are listed in Table 1.

We have conducted risk analysis of the complete plant. In order to optimize the time and effort, a hazard identification and ranking exercise was first carried out. The exercise is meant to identify the type of hazards present and a rough estimation of their hazard potential. The units are accordingly characterized and ranked in priority for the comprehensive study. Dow's Fire & Explosion Index has been used for this step and a summary of results thus obtained are presented in Figure 3. It is clear from the figure that storage of propylene and chlorine are the most hazardous, followed by the storage of fuel oil, and allylchloride. Other process units: chlorination, chlorohydration and quenching, are comparatively less hazardous. All these units have been further subjected to MAXCRED for hazard assessment and damage potential estimation.

For the sake of brevity, the present paper gives details of the study of only the most hazardous units in the plant (storage unit).

The storage unit comprises of the vessels storing various chemicals at elevated temperature and pressure (Table 2). Each storage vessel (for each hazardous chemical) has been subjected to MAXCRED for hazard assessment and damage potential quantification. To felicitate understanding of the use of MAXCRED, the results of the study are presented in steps that follow the algorithm of MAXCRED.

Table 4. The output of MAXCRED for scenario 2

MAXCRED
F.I. Khan & S.A. Abbasi, Pondicherry- 605 014

Parameters	Values
Distance from accident epicenter	(m) : 200
Explosion : BLEVE	
Total energy released	(kJ) : 5.786538e+05
Peak over pressure	(kPa) : 134.8982
Variation of over pressure in air	(kPa/s) : 57.98675
Shock velocity of air	(m/s) : 343.9556
Duration of shock wave	(s) : 33.48331
No missile effect	
Toxic release & dispersion	
Light gas dispersion characteristics	
Gaussian instantaneous: model	
Concentration at distance 200 m	(kg/cu.m) : 1.845254e-04
Concentration at cloud axis	(kg/cu.m) : 1.345267e-02
Value of source height	(m) : 5.000000
Puff characteristics:	
Puff concentration at centre of cloud	(kg/cu.m) : 8.169945e-04
Concentration at cloud edges	(kg/cu.m) : 8.139317e-04
Distance along downwind	(m) : 200.000000
Dosage at study point	(kg/cu.m) : 0.078989

Generation of accident scenarios

Based on the history of major accidents in process industries and the authors' experience, following scenarios have been visualized for accidents in different storage units.

Table 5. The output of MAXCRED for scenario 3

MAXCRED
F.I. Khan & S.A. Abbasi, Pondicherry- 605 014

Parameters	Values
Distance from accident epicenter	(m) : 200
Explosion : UVCE	
Total energy released by explosion	(kJ) : 6.628088e+05
Peak over pressure	(kPa) : 115.6722
Variation of over pressure in air	(kPa/s) : 42.56866
Shock velocity of air	(m/s) : 453.5449
Duration of shock wave	(s) : 21.90854
Missile characteristics:	
Initial velocity of missile	(m/s) : 876.561
Kinetic energy associated with missile	(kJ) : 1988426.3750
Fragment velocity at study point	(m/s) : 234.740
Penetration ability at study point	
Concerete structure	(m) : 0.2165
Brick structure	(m) : 0.2456
Steel structure	(m) : 0.0021
Fire : Pool fire	
Instantaneous model	
Radius of the pool fire	(m) : 5.000000
Burning area	(sq.m) : 78.53749
Burning rate	(kg/s) : 38.42223
Heat intensity	(kJ/sq.m) : 1160.191
Toxic release & dispersion	
Light gas dispersion characteristics	
Gaussian instantaneous: model	
Concentration at distance 200 m	(kg/cu.m) : 6.642933e-07
Concentration at cloud axis	(kg/cu.m) : 5.335456e-05
Puff characteristics:	
Puff concentration at centre of cloud	(kg/cu.m) : 2.932708e-05
Concentration at cloud edges	(kg/cu.m) : 2.972075e-05
Distance along downwind	(m) : 200.000000
Dosage at study point	(kg/cu.m) : 0.0008844

Scenario 1

An excessive pressure development in the storage vessel of propylene (under high pressure and temperature) leads to confined vapor cloud explosion (CVCE). The vapor cloud generated by CVCE on ignition turns into a fire ball and consequently damages the other storage vessels (chlorine, allylchloride, epichlorohydrin, fuel oil).

Scenario 2

A sudden release of pressurized chlorine triggers a boiling liquid expanding vapor explosion (BLEVE) and dispersion of toxic vapor cloud; in other words explosive release followed by toxic dispersion.

Table 6. The output of MAXCRED for scenario 4

MAXCRED
F.I. Khan & S.A. Abbasi, Pondicherry- 605 014

Parameters	Values
Distance from accident epicenter	(m) : 200
Fire : Pool fire	
Continuous model	
Burning area	(sq.m) : 75.0000000
Burning rate	(kg/h) : 15042.8281
Heat intensity	(kJ/sq.m) : 986.848602

Table 7. The output of MAXCRED for scenario 5

MAXCRED
F.I. Khan & S.A. Abbasi, Pondicherry- 605 014

Parameters	Values
Distance from accident epicenter	(m) : 200
Fire : Pool fire	
Instantaneous model	
Radius of the pool fire	(m) : 5.000000
Burning area	(sq.m) : 78.53749
Burning rate	(kg/s) : 38.42223
Heat intensity	(kJ/sq.m) : 1160.191

Scenario 3

Unconfined vapor cloud explosion (UVCE) occurs in the epichlorohydrin unit accompanied by a pool fire. This shall happen if a small leak in the storage vessel releases material at moderate flow rate and forms a vapor cloud in the atmosphere which on ignition leads to UVCE. Due to the heat generated by UVCE or by external source of ignition the remaining material in the vessel or duke catches fire causing a pool fire. A UVCE followed by pool fire can damage neighboring vessels, due to excess shock waves and heat load and trigger secondary and higher order accidents.

Scenario 4

Instantaneous release is followed by pool fire in the allylchloride storage unit.

Scenario 5

There is a pool fire in the fuel oil storage unit.

Scenarios 6 and 7

Toxic release of chlorine and chlorinated organic is followed by evaporation and dispersion.

These scenarios have been processed for damage estimation through MAXCRED. A brief note on the damage-effect calculation models used for the detailed study is presented below.

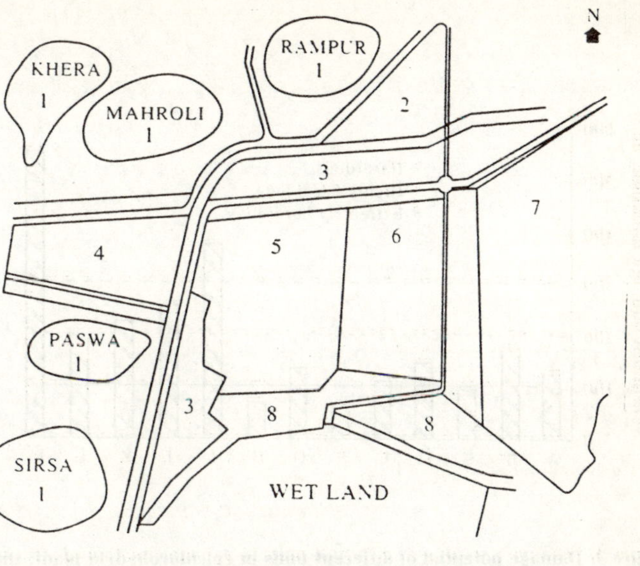

Figure 2. Layout of the study area showing location of industries and their surroundings. 1: Populous villages; 2: residential buildings; 3: green belt; 4: chemical industry; 5: fertilizer industry; 6: petroleum refinery; 7: petroleum refinery; 8: waste lands

Damage effect calculations for the accident scenarios

The explosion, fires and toxic dispersions eventually cause damage in four ways. The potential of these effects can be expressed in terms of probit function , which relates percentage of the people affected in a bounded region due to a particular accident event by a normal distribution function.

1) Heat radiation effect

The probit function for 100% lethality for heat radiation is given as :

$$pr = 36.38 + 2.56*\ln [t*q^{4/3}]$$

Where q is defined as thermal load (kw/m); t is time of exposure (s); and Pr is probit value.

2) Toxic effect

Lethality of a toxic load is expressed in terms of probit function as :

$$Pr = a + b \ln (C^n * t)$$

Where a, b, n, are constants; C is concentration in ppm, and t is time of exposure (s). The values of the constants for different gases are available in literature .

3) Pressure and shock wave effect

The probit equation for likelihood of death due to shock wave(lung rupture) is given by

$$Pr = -77.1 + 6.91 * \ln Po$$

For injury , the equation is

$$Pr = -15.6 + 1.93 \ln Po$$

Where Po is peak overpressure(N/m2).

4) Missile effect

The probit function for fatality in human beings or damage to vessels is expressed as:

$$Pr = -17.50 + 5.30 \ln S$$

Where, S is the kinetic energy of the missile (J).

Hazard quantification

The results of the calculations for different accident scenarios are summarized below.

Table 3 presents the summary of calculation (output of MAXCRED) for scenario 1. The missiles generated by CVCE may hit nearby targets and can lead to secondary explosions or toxic releases. The vapor cloud generated by CVCE on ignition may cause a fire ball and hence severe heat radiation effect. The shock wave generated due to CVCE can cause injury as well as second order accidents by seriously damaging other vessels. It has been estimated that shock waves with 50% probability of causing injury would be observed over an area of 500 m radius. The heat radiation effect with 100% probability of lethality would be observed over an area of 300 m radius and missile effects with 50% chances of damage would be observed across 750 m radius.

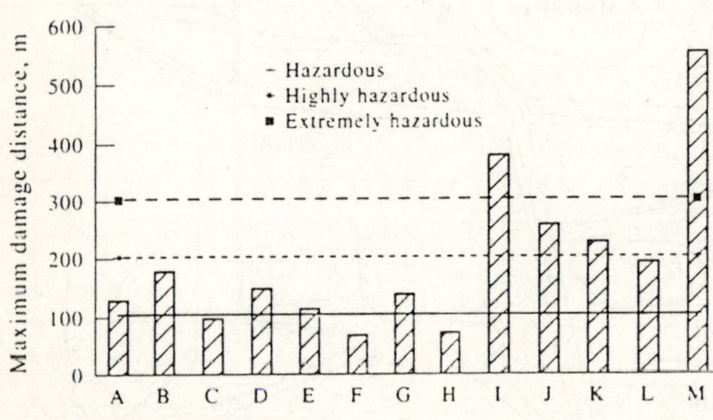

Figure 3. Damage potential of different units in epichlorohydrin plant; the elaborations of A,B,... M are given in Table 1

The sudden release of chlorine and the consequent BLEVE as per scenario 2 would lead to severe shock waves, and toxic releases (Table 4). In this scenario the damage potential of the shock waves is estimated to be comparatively lesser than scenario 1. 100% damage -causing shock wave would be operative over an area of 400 m radius. As chlorine is non-combustible, no heat radiation effects would be observed, but a build-up of lethal concentration would take place over an area of 1500 m radius.

An UVCE as per scenario 3 would give rise to heat radiation effects, shock waves, and missile effects. In addition there would be secondary impact of burning of released material in the dike/vessel which would again lead to additional heat load. In scenario 3, missile effect is not significant (Table 5). However, shock waves of intensity high enough to damage all objects coming in their way would be persistent in an area of 300 m radius. The combined impact of heat radiation, UVCE, and pool fire would be lethal over an area of 600 m radius. Due to intense heat load some of the chemical would evaporate and disperse causing its build up to a lethal concentration over an area of 200 m radius.

The model results for scenario 4 are presented in Table 6. Lethal heat load would be observed over the study area; the maximum damage distance would envelope an area of 400 m radius.

The output of MAXCRED for scenario 5 (fuel oil) is tabulated in Table 7. Lethal heat load would be observed over an area of 350 m radius.

The results of scenarios 6 and 7 have been presented in Table 8 and 9 respectively. In both cases the lethal concentration (100% chances of fatality) is confined to an area of 200 m radius.

Table 8. The output of MAXCRED for scenario 6

MAXCRED
F.I. Khan & S.A. Abbasi, Pondicherry- 605 014

Parameters	Values
Distance from accident epicenter	(m) : 200
Fire : Pool fire	
Continuous model	
Burning area	(sq.m) : 75.00000
Burning rate	(kg/h) : 11842.82
Heat intensity	(kJ/sq.m) : 336.84860

Table 9. The output of MAXCRED for scenario 7

MAXCRED
F.I. Khan & S.A. Abbasi, Pondicherry- 605 014

Parameters	Values
Distance from accident epicenter	(m) : 200
Fire : Pool fire	
Continuous model	
Burning area	(sq.m) : 75.0000000
Burning rate	(kg/s) : 13304.3451
Heat intensity	(kJ/sq.m) : 456.848602

Risk estimation

Using the results obtained by MAXCRED and the probability of occurrence of the accident scenarios, individual fatal risk factors have been estimated. The probability of occurrence of an individual event has been adopted from literature[13-17]. The risk factor is a direct representation of the threat (taking into consideration both damage potential and probability of occurrence) to an individual in an area.

In order to enable visualization of accident scenarios, their risk contours have been drawn over the study area (Figures 4-8). It may be seen that the risk contours for scenarios 1-3 (Figures 4-6) are extending beyond the boundaries of the industry and enveloping other industries and nearby populated areas. The risk contours for other scenarios are confined to the campus of the EPI plant but the risk contours for scenarios 4 and 5 extend upto other storage vessels in the factory (Figures 7 and 8). This may cause secondary accidents, the impacts of which may go beyond the factory confines.

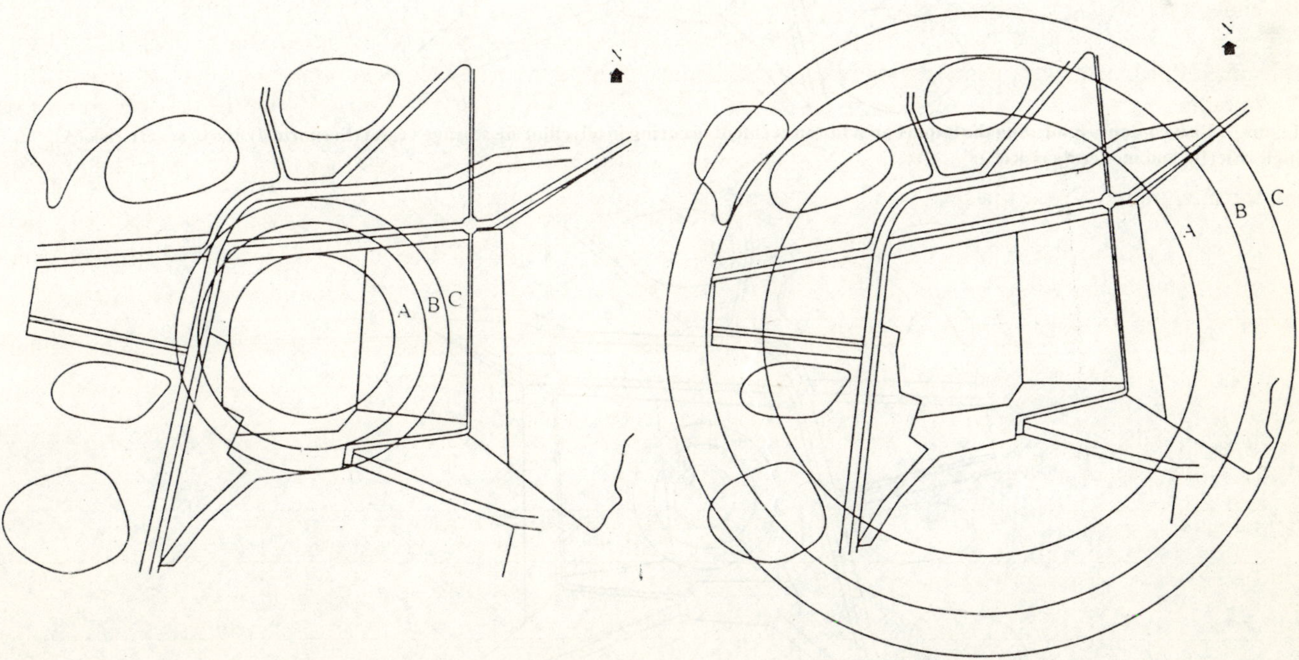

Figure 4. Risk contours indicating the impact area for an accident occuring in propylene storage vessel (Scenario 1) due to severe risk (A), high risk (B), and moderate risk (C)

Figure 5. Risk contours indicating the impact area for an accident occuring in propylene storage vessel (Scenario 2) due to severe risk (A), high risk (B), and moderate risk (C)

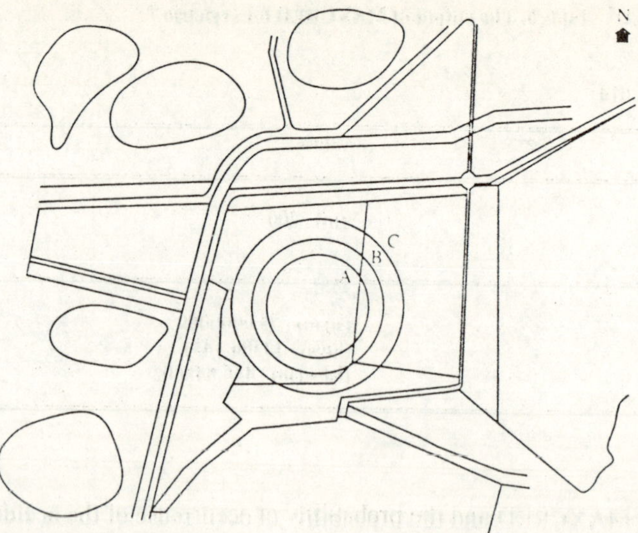

Figure 6. Risk contours indicating the impact area for an accident occuring in epichloropydrin storage vessel (Scenario 3) due to severe risk (A), high risk (B), and moderate risk (C)

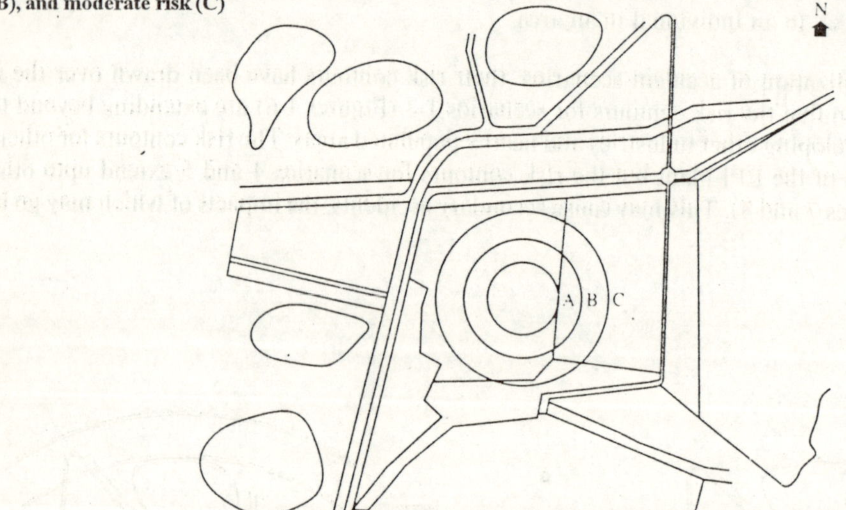

Figure 7. Risk contours indicating the impact area for an accident occuring in allychloride storage vessel (Scenario 4) due to severe risk (A), high risk (B), and moderate risk (C)

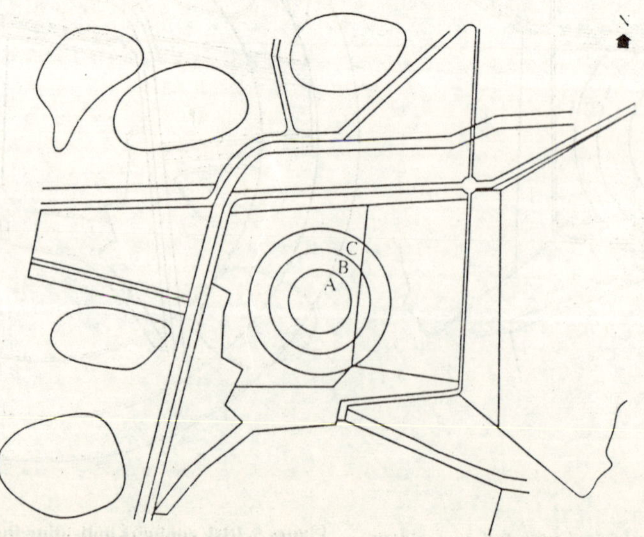

Figure 8. Risk contours indicating the impact area for an accident occuring in oil storage vessel (Scenario 5) due to severe risk (A), high risk (B), and moderate risk (C)

In summary scenario 2 represents the worst likely disaster within the realm of credibility. It has the largest area-of-lethal-impact (shock wave over an area of radius 500 m and lethal concentration across an area of radius 1500 m). Further, the most thickly populated areas (including residential areas of Mahroli and Rampur) lie within its range. If one considers the cumulative effects, the scenario 1 would come out as the worst, as more intense impacts (in terms of heat radiation,shock waves,missiles) are observed per unit area in this scenario. Of the eight scenarios, scenario 1 is the most likely to cause cascading effects as missiles, shock waves, and radiation effects would be generated simultaneously and other industries or units dealing with flammable and toxic materials are situated within the striking distance of the primary accident of scenario 1. Scenarios 3, 4 and 5 also have the potential to lead to secondary accidents as severe heat load generated in these would encompass other storage vessels. All-in-all, scenario 2 is the worst as far as primary effects are concerned whereas scenario 1 is the worst in terms of its potentiality of causing cascading (domino) effects.

CONCLUSIONS

This paper demonstrates the applicability of software package MAXCRED for performing quantitative risk analysis. The package generates different credible accident scenarios, and quantifies the damage they cause. This information can then be used in developing strategies for preventing accidents and to dampen their adverse impacts if the accidents do take place. The applicability has been illustrated with a case study of a typical chemical industry situated in Muzzafarnagar, Uttar Pradesh, India.

In the first step - hazard identification and ranking - storage and process units involving chlorination, chlorohydration, and quenching were identified as the most vulnerable vis a vis propensity of causing accidents. A detailed study of the credible accidents in storage units and their impacts was then carried out with the help of MAXCRED. The studies reveal that the storage units of propylene, chlorine and epichlorohydrin are the most hazardous, and accidents in these units may cause severe damage to the factory and its surroundings.

To reduce the hazards associated with the storage of chlorine, propylene and epichlorohydrin, proper hazard minimization/mitigation measures should be taken. A few suggestions are made in this context :

i) Instead of one or two large-capacity vessels several vessels of smaller capacity should be used for storage.

ii) Adequate space should be kept between the storage vessels and buffers provided between them so that adverse consequences of failure in one of them do not cause second or higher order accidents.

iii) Sensitive gas-detecting devices for flammable and toxic gases should be installed in the premises of storage area and other units.

iv) There should be regular and thorough inspections of electronic control equipment followed by meticulous maintenance.

v) Sufficient quantities of inert gases should be readily available to dilute the concentrations of toxic/flammable gases if they escape to the atmosphere, and to control fire.

vi) A thorough emergency preparedness strategy should always be kept in position, fortified by periodic drills or 'dry runs' so that the damage is contained if an accident does occur.

REFERENCES

1. Abbasi, S A and Venilla, V, Risk Assessment, Encyclopedia for environmental engineering, (Enviro Media, Karad), (1994).

2. Khan, F I and Abbasi, S A, Anatomy of Industrial Accidents, Report No. CPCE\R&D 1\ 94, Pondicherry University, Pondicherry, (1994).

3. Lees, F P, Loss prevention in the process industries, (Butterworths, London), volume 1, (1980).

4. Kletz, T A, What went wrong, (Gulf Publication, London), (1986).

5. Khan, F I and Abbasi, S A, Major accident case studies in chemical process industries, Chemical Engineering world September, 1996.

6. Khan, F I and Abbasi, S A, Risk Analysis: an optimum scheme for hazard identification and assessment, Proceeding of National system conference, Coimbatore, (1995).

7. Greenberg, H R and Crammer, J J Risk assessment and management for chemical process industries, (Van Nostrand Reinhold), New York, (1991).

8. Khan, F I and Abbasi,S A, MAXCRED- A software package for quantitative risk analysis, eport No CPCE/R&D 5/94 Pondicherry University,Pondicherry,(1994); Environmental software (in press).

9. Dow Chemical Company Dow fire and explosion index, azard Classification Guide (6th edition) (1980).

10. Mallikarjunan, M M and Raghvan, K V, Risk assessment techniques and their application, Proceeding of National conference of safety system New Delhi, (1989).

11. Pitersen, C M, Consequences of accidental release of hazardous material, Journal of Loss Prevention Process Industries, 3, 136-141, (1990).

12. Kayes,P J, World bank manual of industrial hazard assessment techniques, (Technica Ltd., London), (1985).

13. Contini, S, Amendola, A and Ziomas, I, Benchmark exercise on major hazard analysis, Joint Research Centre-ISPRA, (1991).

14. Lees, F P, Loss prevention in the process industries: Failure and event data, (Butterworths, London), volume 2, (1980).

15. Reliability Directorate, Failure frequency of hardware components, Report No. 87-2981R.27/NVE, Reliability directorate, (1992).

16. European Community, council direction on the major accident hazardous of certain industrial activities, Report No. 82/50/501 EEC, London (1992).

17. Khan, F I and Abbasi, S A, Accident simulation in chemical process industries using software MAXCRED, Indian Journal of Chemical Technology, 3, 339-344, 1996.

13

*RISK ANALYSIS OF A CHLORALKALI INDUSTRY SITUATED IN A POPULATED AREA USING THE SOFTWARE PACKAGE MAXCRED-II**

Risk assessment, based on quantitative maximum credible accident analysis (MCAA), has been conducted for a chloralkali industry situated in the midst of densely populated coastal villages. The study has made use of a software package MAXimum CREDible accident analysis version 2 (henceforth referred as MAXCRED-II) recently developed by us.

Among the six different most credible accident scenarios developed using MAXCRED-II, the one envisaging 'confined vapor cloud explosion followed by fire ball' (in the hydrogen storage vessel) comes out to be the worst in terms of the highest propensity for damage (overpressure, missile, heat load). It also has the potential of causing domino effect (chain of accidents). The scenario of 'continuous release of chlorine from storage vessel' is the second most disastrous, in terms of lethal toxic load likely over a large distance (3252 meters). In summary, the study reveals that given the masses of materials stored, and the conditions in which they are stored, there is a live risk of accidents in the storage vessels that would have far-reaching consequences. The industry thus poses a great risk to large areas of surrounding including densely populated villages (particularly Chinnakalapet and Kalapet) and the campuses of Pondicherry University and Pondicherry Engineering College.

The paper demonstrates the utilizability of MAXCRED-II and also focuses attention on the need to bestow greater effort towards risk assessment. It is hoped that these studies would make plant managers conscious of the serious consequences that accidents in their vulnerable units can have. This appreciation of the risk, we hope, would prompt them to develop accident prevention strategies and to put in position emergency preparedness plans to cushion the adverse impacts if accident do occur.

INTRODUCTION

A large number of chemical process industries either use hazardous materials or operate reactors under conditions of high temperature and pressure. Such industries are prone to accidents in which hazardous material can leak out of the storage/reaction vessels and contaminate the environment or reactors may crack/explode leading to shock waves, fires or both. There have been numerous accidents of this type all over the world resulting in massive losses of monetary resources and human lives; illustrative examples of a few accidents are presented in Table 1.

Over the last few years a new branch of science -risk assessment in chemical process industries (RACPI) - has emerged to deal with the hazards faced by a chemical process industry. RACPI aims to develop techniques and tools with which an industry can anticipate the likelihood of accidents, identify 'soft spots' or 'danger zones' in its produc-

* Reproduced from *Process Safety Progress, USA, 16 (3), 172-184, 1997.*

tion system, work out probabilities of failures that may occur in its equipment or the mistakes in the handling of the equipment, assess the damage potential of likely accidents, work out preventive steps and, finally, develop crisis management strategies (if an accident does occur inspite of all precautions).

One of the most potent branches of RACPI is quantitative risk assessment (QRA) of which a major component is maximum credible accident analysis (MCAA). In MCAA4,5 we identify hazardous situations, develop different accident scenarios and estimate damage potential of likely accidents. MCAA comprises of the following main steps : (i) study of the plant to identify hazardous materials and their capacities; (ii) identification of vulnerable sections; (iii) visualization of different accident scenarios; (iv) damage calculation through mathematical modeling; (v) delineation of maximum credible accident scenario.

Thus so far no indigenous package of adequate sophistication or user-friendliness was available in India to conduct MCAA. This had compelled the industries and consultancy firms to depend on imported packages such as WHAZAN9 offered by Technica limited, RISKWIT 10 offered by VTT Technical Research Centre of Finland and EFFECTS11 offered by TNO-Mauris Laboratory, The Netherlands. To overcome this gap as also to increase the level of sophistication (as also user-friendliness) a package MAXCRED (MAXimum CREDible accident analysis)12 has been developed by us based on MCAA. The package incorporates state-of-the-art mathematical models, including some developed or modified by authors for rapid quantitative and comprehensive MCAA. We have recently modified MAXCRED and the higher version MAXCRED-II is now available13. A brief description of MAXCRED-II is presented below.

The package MAXCRED-II

MAXCRED-II is an improved version of the software package MAXCRED (ver 1)12 which was developed by us in 1994. The package is coded in C++ language and is compatible with DOS as well as WINDOWS working environments. The software is operable on personal computer requiring a minimum of 1MB RAM and 1.5 MB ROM. The MAXCRED-II algorithm is presented in Figure 1.

The software has four main options (modules) : data, scenario generation, consequence analysis and file processing. The data option handles general information related to the properties of the various chemicals, operations, and the surrounding, needed for the execution of different models. The scenario generation module enables development of accident scenarios based on the properties of the chemicals involved, operating conditions and the likely ways of malfunctioning of the equipment or process that would cause an accident. The scenario generation option has two further options a) user defined and b) automatic. In the former, the user can define define the accident scenario as per his/her own judgment. In the later, scenarios are generated by MAXCRED-II on the basis of the knowledge base attached to the it. The consequence analysis module takes the study of its next logical step, i.e. to forecast the nature and the severity of the accident using advanced models of thermodynamics, heat transfer, and fluid dynamics. The file option enables the user to handle input-output information. It also provides facilities such as consoling, printing, copying etc. All-in-all MAXCRED-II is a versatile tool for QRA and in envisaged to be self-contained in the sense that it does not need other packages for data analysis or graphics. A detailed description regarding internal structure and working of MAXCRED-II is available with the authors.

In this paper, MAXCRED-II has been used to study quantitative risk analysis of a typical hazardous industry - chloralkali. The industry is situated on the coastal line (Bay of Bangal) and surrounded by densely populated areas (villages - Chinnakalapet, Kalapet, university hostels etc.). The results of the study have been represented in terms of risk (damage*probability) contour maps on the accident site to enable easy and swift assessment of maximum credible scenario and damage potential.

NATURE OF LIKELY ACCIDENTS

Explosions and fires

Explosions in the storage or process units can be categorized in three main groups, according to mode of occurrence and damage potential14-17. These explosions are initiated either by the thermal stratification of the liquid and vapor or by such high explosion shock waves, which have sufficient strength to rupture the reaction/storage vessels or conduits. An explosion may or may not be accompanied with fire; it depends upon the type of explosion and the chemical involved in the explosion.

Table 1. Some major accidents in the process industries during last twenty years

Year	Location	Chemical	Event	Deaths	Financial loss@
1971	Houston, USA	Vinyl chloride monomer	BLEVE*	1	145 million $
1972	Brazil	Butane	UVCE**	37	90 million $
1972	West Virginia, USA	Gas	CVCE***	21	110 million $
1973	Potchefstroom, South Africa	NH_3	Toxic release	18	95 million $
1973	State Island, USA	LNG	Fire in empty storage tank	40	350 million $
1974	Flixborough,UK	Cyclohexane	UVCE**	28	450 million $
1976	Seveso, Italy dibenzo-paradioxin	Tetra chlora	Toxic release	-	35 million $
1977	Columbia	NH3	Toxic release	30	35 million $
1978	Waverly, USA	Propane	BLEVE	12	47 million $
1981	Montanas, Mexico	Chlorine	BLEVE	29	103 million $
1982	Spencer, USA	H2O	BLEVE	7	8 million $
1983	Houston, USA	Methyl bromide	BLEVE	2	10 million $
1984	Mexico city, Mexico	Propane	BLEVE	650	50 million $
1984	Bhopal, India	Methyl-iso -cyanate	Toxic release	2500	350 million $
1986	Kennedy Space Center, USA	Hydrogen	BLEVE	7	250 million $
1987	Piper Alpha, UK	Hydrogen	Explosion & Fire	167	300 million $
1988	Illinois, USA	Propane	BLEVE	15	835 million $
1989	Pasadena, USA	Iso-butane	BLEVE	23	255 million $
1989	Antwerp, Belgium	Ethylene oxide	UVCE	20	700 million $
1989	Ufa, USSR	Ammoniya	Explosion & Toxic release	7	570 million $
1990	Bombay, India	Hydrocarbon	Fire & Explosion	35	30 million $
1990	Porto de Leixoes, Portugal	Propane	Fire & Explosion	14	65 million $
1990	Bangkok, Thailand	Hydrocarbon	Fire & Toxic release	17	55 million $
1993	Panipat, India A	mmoniya	Explosion & Toxic release	3	75 million $
1994	Dronka, Egypt	Chlorinated gas	Toxic release	4	25 million $
1995	Madras, India	Bengene	Explosion &	150	45 million $

{Cont.}

			Fire		
1995	Gujrat, India	Natural gas	Fire	2	10 million $
1996	Mumbai, India	Hydrocarbon	Fire	2	15 million $

* Boiling liquid expanding vapor explosion
** Unconfined vapor cloud explosion
*** Confined vapor cloud explosion
@ approximated loss in terms of US $

Confined vapor cloud explosion (CVCE)

CVCE[14] as the name suggests, is condensed phase explosion occurring in confinement (equipment, building or/and congested surrounding). Explosions in vessels and pipes, processing or storing reactive chemicals at elevated conditions are examples of CVCE. The excessive build-up of pressure in the confinement leads to this type of explosions leading to high overpressure, shock waves and heat loads (if chemical is flammable and get ignited). The fragments of exploded vessels and other objects hit by blast waves, become airborne and act as missiles. These missiles can lead to further accidents by ramming into other process units. The damage potential of the missiles is assessed on the basis of the momentum they attain. The extent of damage caused by a CVCE depends on the mass of the chemical and the explosion pressure.

Unconfined vapor cloud explosion (UVCE)

UVCE[14,16] generally occurs when sufficient amount of flammable material (gas or liquid having high vapor pressure) gets released and mixes with air to form a flammable cloud such that the average concentration of the material in the cloud is higher than the lower limit of explosion. The resulting explosion has high potential of damage as it occurs in an open space covering large areas. The intensity of explosion mainly depends on the quantity of material released and the strength of the ignition source.

The explosive power of a CVCE and UVCE can be expressed in terms of blast wave characteristics (overpressure, overpressure-impulse, reflected pressure, duration of shock, etc.). The overpressure is a very important parameter; its magnitude depends on the speed of flame propagation. Any obstruction in the flame propagation enhances the blast effect.

Boiling liquid expanding vapor explosion (BLEVE)

BLEVE[15] is caused by a sudden release from confinement of a liquid at a temperature above its atmospheric pressure boiling point. The sudden decrease in pressure results in explosive vaporization of a fraction of the liquid and a cloud of vapor and mist, with accompanying blast effects. If the material is flammable and an ignition source is present, a fire ball may be formed. The broad definition of BLEVE, as used by the Prugh[15] (1991) is used here. According to this definition any liquefied vapor, flammable or non-flammable, can produce a BLEVE. A fire ball/flash fire is not a part of this definition, since a fire (fire ball/flash fire) would result only if the material released is flammable and thus ignition occurs. Nevertheless, it is a historical fact that most BLEVEs involve flammable liquids, and most of these BLEVE releases are ignited by a surrounding fire, resulting in a fire ball/flash fire.

Fires

Spillage of flammable material (liquid/gas) may lead to fire[14,17] which could be triggered by any of these ignition sources: (a) an electric spark; (b) a momentary flame due to welding operation; (c) atmospheric friction; (d) burning of match stick. In case of highly flammable materials the fire may be started even by the mild friction caused by atmospheric disturbances. Generally the fire effects are limited to areas close to the source of fire (approx. ~200 m radius). However industrial fires can have a greater pervasive effect. The industrial fires are mainly characterized in three groups, described below.

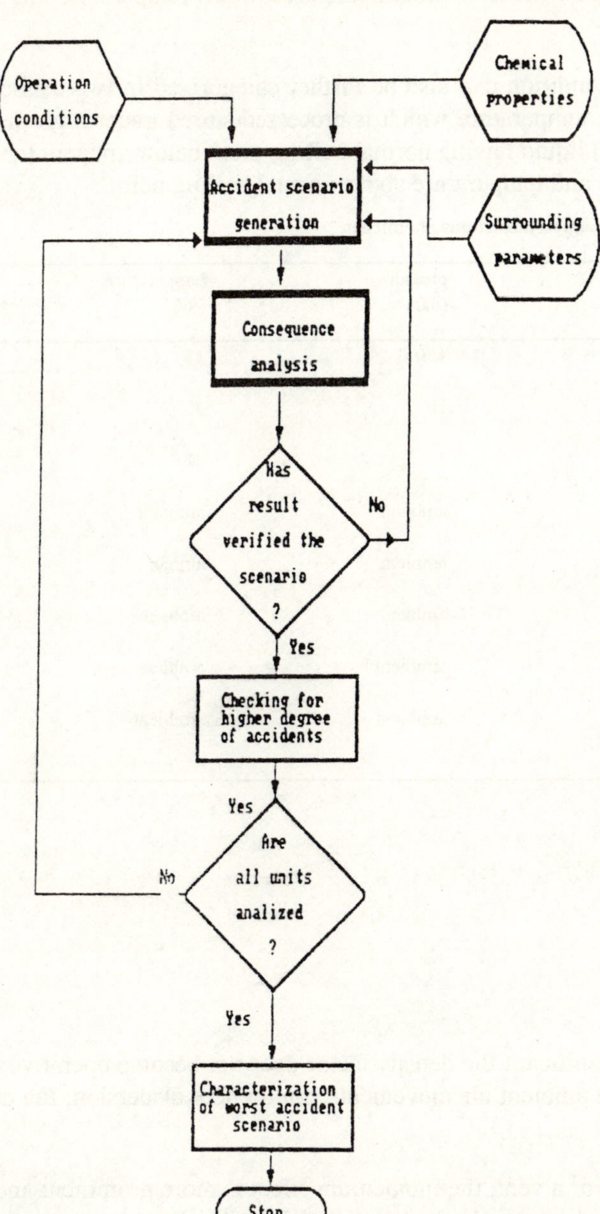

Figure 1. The MAXCRED-II algorithm.

Pool fire

Continuous or instantaneous release of flammable liquid on ignition results in a pool fire. Pool fire characteristics mainly depend on the duration of release, saturation pressure, and the flammable properties of materials.

Flash fire

Instantaneous ignition of a vapor cloud having concentration above lower flammability limit gives a flash fire but doesn't explode. It occurs only with flammable chemical having boiling point lower than ambient temperature. It is different from fire ball in terms of flame propagation, duration of fire, and heat load generated. Flash fire occurs with highly flammable chemical stored or processed at ambient conditions. Damage associated with flash or pool fire is assessed on the basis of the dose of heat radiation load received for a particular/given time interval.

Fire ball

Instantaneous combustion of flammable vapor cloud due to radiation exposure above material threshold levels or missile and blast wave interaction is characterized as fire ball. The fire ball is generally observed for highly flammable chemicals processed or stored under extreme conditions. Evaluation of the consequences of a fire ball requires the quantification of fire ball temperature, fire ball duration and fire ball size. Fire ball temperature is dependent on the heat capacity of the fuel consumed and the means of combustions. The fire ball temperature may vary from 1350 K for flammable gases to 5000 K for chemical explosives.

Toxic release and dispersion

Vapor clouds from industrial installations arise principally from the accidental release of gases, flashing liquefied gases or evaporation of spilled liquids. The toxic vapor (gas) cloud is likely to be dangerous even at much greater distance from the point of release than their flammable counterparts. This is mainly due to the ease of their dispersion and the high probability of coming in direct contact with the living systems.

Release conditions

To estimate the characteristics of dispersion of gases due to an accidental release, the following accidental release conditions (with appropriate models) havc been considered[3,18-20].

a) Gaseous release.

b) Liquid release at atmospheric pressure. This condition can further be categorized as : (i) liquid with a boiling point above ambient temperature which is processed/stored at a temperature below its normal boiling point; (ii) liquid with a boiling point below ambient temperature which is processed/stored at low temperature and atmospheric pressure.

c) Two phase release (liquid under pressure). This condition can also be further categorized in two classes : (i) liquid having normal boiling point above ambient temperature which is processed/stored under high pressure and temperature above its normal boiling point; (ii) liquid having normal boiling point below ambient temperature which is processed/stored under high pressure and temperature above normal boiling point.

Table 2. Storage deatails of hazardous chemicals

Chemical	number of tanks	capacity (m3)	pressure (bar)	temperature (oC)
Hydrogen	1	150	150	31
Chlorine	1	50 MT	10	30
Furnace oil	1	15	1	35
Sulfuric acid	2	10.2	ambient	ambient
HCL	2	125	ambient	ambient
NaOH (33%)	3	325	ambient	ambient
NaOH (48%)	1	325	ambient	ambient
Calcium hyper-chlorate	2	15	ambient	ambient

Dispersion

Dispersion is primarily governed by two facts:

a) Momentum of release.

b) Density of the gas relative to air.

As long as the momentum of the escaping gas is significant the density factor does not become operative but as soon as the momentum dies down to a level where the ambient air movements could effect dispersion, the density factors take over to influence the shape of the plume.

When the gas escapes at high velocity as from a jet or a vent, the momentum effect is more prominent and lasts longer (due to higher velocity of release) than when the release velocity (venting velocity) is low.

According to Lees[2] (1996) releases in the form of jets can be of four types : (i) turbulent momentum jet in still air, (ii) buoyant plume in still air; (iii) plume dispersed by wind and (iv) jet-turbulent plume dispersed by wind. The behavior of such jets and vents is as relevant to the intended discharges as to accidental discharges. The behavior of the dispersion of such jets depends on the relative importance of discharge momentum, buoyancy effects, and of wind turbulence. We have used turbulent jet model along with plume dispersion, as in modified plume path theory18 to estimate this mode of dispersion.

Once the gas loses its momentum it is influenced by the density of the gas-air mixture relative to air. A difference in the molecular weight and/or in the temperature between the gas and the ambient air creates, in principle, such a density difference, but this density difference will affect the behavior of the cloud only if the concentration of the gas is sufficiently high. A large proportion of the liquid droplets and a low air humidity favor the formation of a gas cloud heavier than air.

A heavy cloud behaves differently from one of neutral density in several important aspects. It spreads not only downwind but also upwind, it is flatter in shape and the mechanisms of mixing with the air are different. Compared to dispersion of lighter-than-air or as-dense-as-air gases, heavy gas dispersion has been studied to a much lesser degree. Only a handful of models are available to handle heavy gas dispersion18,20. We have adopted Box model20 for heavy gas dispersion.

Dispersion of gases (gas-air mixture) having density equal or less than air under the influence of ambient air movements is characterized by neutral buoyancy dispersion. Even a heavy gas acquires a dispersion pattern akin to that of neutral buoyancy dispersion when density- driven turbulence becomes weak (in other words density difference between air-gas mixture and air become negligible) as more and more ambient air is entrained in the cloud causing atmospheric turbulence to dominate the dispersion process. We have used Gaussian plume and puff models for continuous and instantaneous release conditions respectively to predict the behavior of neutral dispersion.

CASE STUDY

ChemFab Alkalis Limited[21] (CAL) is a Chloralkali industry situated about 11 km North of Pondicherry on the East Coast on Indian Peninsula. It is engaged in the manufacture of chloralkali products such as; caustic soda, liquid chlorine, hydrogen, and hydrochloric acid. The industry lies in the midst of densely populated villages (Chinnakalapet, Kalapet, Pillaichavady, and Kanagachettykulam). Several educational institutions including Pondicherry University, Pondicherry Engineering College, and several schools are situated in close proximity of the industry (Figure 2).

We have subjected the entire CAL plant to MCAA. In the initial step of the study we have identified the set of storage units (central tank farm) as the most vulnerable part of the plant. The farm stores large quantities of hazardous chemicals under high pressure; a list of such chemicals with capacity and storing conditions of each is presented in Table 2.

We have conducted MCAA for each of the storage vessels with MAXCRED-II but for the sake of brevity we present below the results of the study of the accidents involving three most hazardous chemicals (hydrogen, chlorine, and furnace oil).

Accident scenarios

Based on the history of major accidents in the chloralkali industries14,22,23 and authors' experience, following scenarios have been visualized for accidents in the vessels storing different chemicals.

Table 3. Values of the constants a,b,n14,24 of equation 2 for different chemicals

Chemical (gas/vapor)	a	b	n
Acroline	-9.93	2.05	1.0
Ammonia	-12.4	1.0	2.0
Bromine	-12.4	1.0	2.0
Chlorine	-5.3	0.5	2.7
Hydrogen floride	-26.4	3.35	1.0
Hydrogen chloride	-21.76	2.65	1.0
Methyl bromide	-19.92	5.16	1.0
Methyl-isocyanate	-1.2	1.0	0.7
Nitrogen oxide	-18.6	1.0	3.7
Phosgene	-0.80	1.0	0.9
Sulfur dioxide	-19.2	1.0	2.4

Hydrogen

Scenario 1

An excessive high pressure development in the storage vessel of hydrogen leads to CVCE. The unburnt vapor cloud released due to explosion on ignition leads to fire ball.

Table 4. Result of MAXCRED Simulation for Accident Scenario-CVCE and Fire Ball

MAXCRED
(c) F I Khan & S A Abbasi, Pondicherry -605 014, India

File: HYd1.out

Results of MAXCRED simulation for accident scenario -CVCE and fire ball

Parameters	Values
Explosion : CVCE	
Energy released during explosion	(kJ) : 8.8E+08
Peak overpressure	(kPa) : 782.5
Variation of overpressure in air	(kPa/s) : 806.8
Shock velocity of air	(m/s) : 1079.4
Duration of shock wave	(ms) : 233.1
Missile result	
Initial velocity of fragment	(m/s) : 665.6
Kinetic energy of fragment	(kj) : 133668.2
Fragment velocity at 200 m	(m/s) : 308.0
Penetration ability at 200 m (based on empirical models)	
Concrete structure	(m) : 0.071
Brick structure	(m) : 0.091
Steel structure	(m) : 0.015
Damage radii (DR) for various degrees of damage due to overpressure	
DR for 100% complete damage	(m): 975
DR for 100% fatality or 50% complete damage	(m): 1315
DR for 50% fatality or 25% complete damage	(m): 1934
Damage radii (DR) for the various degree of damage due to missile	
DR for 100% damage or 100% fatality	(m) : 1845
DR for 50% damage or 100% fatality	(m) : 1931
DR for 100% fatality or 10% damage	(m) : 2007
Fire : Fire ball	
Radius of fire ball	(m) : 89.5
Duration of fire ball	(s) : 54.3
Energy released by fire ball	(kJ) : 2.2E+07
Radiation heat intensity	(kJ/sq.m) : 217.5
Damage radii due to thermal load	
Damage radii for 100% fatality/damage	(m) : 125
Damage radii for 50% fatality/damage	(m) : 175
Damage radii for 100% third degree of burns	(m) : 229
Damage radii for 50% third degree of burns	(m) : 276

Scenario 2

A high pressure development or a leak in the vessel leads to release of flammable hydrogen vapor, which forms a vapor cloud. The vapor cloud on instantaneous ignition yields UVCE. The remaining unburnt vapor cloud having concentration below the low explosive limit on ignition gives rise to flash fire.

Chlorine

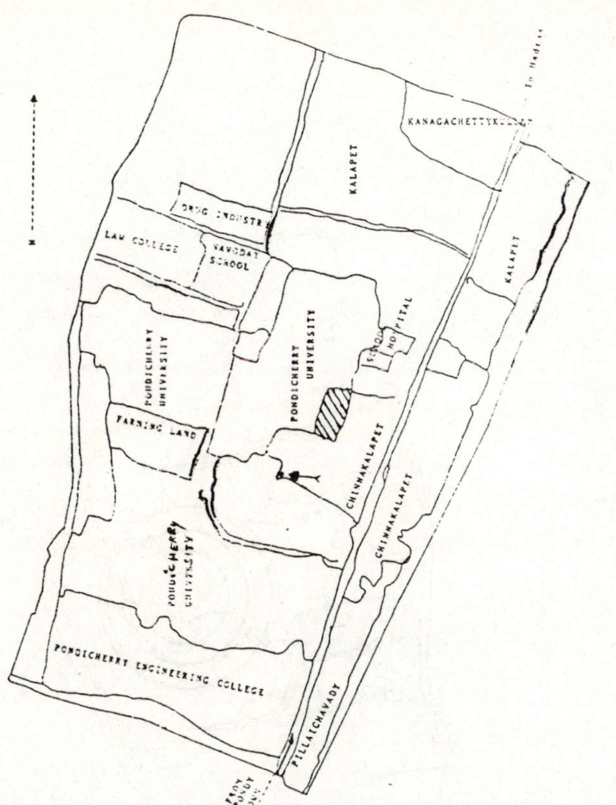

FIGURE 2 Layout of the study area showing the location of CAL (Chem-Fab Alkalies Limited—marked with slanted lines). The location of authors' research centre is marked with an arrow.

Scenario 3

Build up high pressure in the vessel leads to sudden release of liquid chlorine as BLEVE. The released chemical disperse in the atmosphere under slightly stable atmospheric condition (occurs most frequently, around 65% in a year). As release is of two phase and density of gas is higher than air, heavy gas dispersion model under coastal meteorological conditions is operative.

Scenario 4

A continuous release and dispersion of chlorine. In this case also heavy gas dispersion model with coastal effects should be used.

Furnace oil

Scenario 5

An instantaneous release of furnace oil (high density liquid fuel) on ignition leads to pool fire (instantaneous model).

Scenario 6

A continuous release of furnace oil on ignition leads to pool fire (continuous model). These scenarios have been processed for damage estimation through MAXCRED-II. A brief note on the damage-effect calculation models used for the detailed study is presented below.

Damage effect calculations for the accident scenarios

The explosion, fires and toxic dispersions eventually cause damage in four ways. The potential of these effects can be expressed in terms of probit function[2,22-24], which relates percentage of the people affected in a bounded region due to a particular accident event by a normal distribution function.

1) Heat radiation effect

The probit function for 100% lethality for heat radiation is given as[2]:

$$pr = 36.38 + 2.56*\ln[t*q^{4/3}] \qquad (1)$$

Where q is defined as thermal load (KW/m^2); t is time of exposure (s); and Pr is probit value.

2) Toxic effect

Lethality of a toxic load is expressed in terms of probit function as[22-24]:

$$Pr = a + b \ln (C^n*t) \qquad (2)$$

Where a, b, n, are constants; C is concentration in ppm, and t is time of exposure (s). The values of the constants

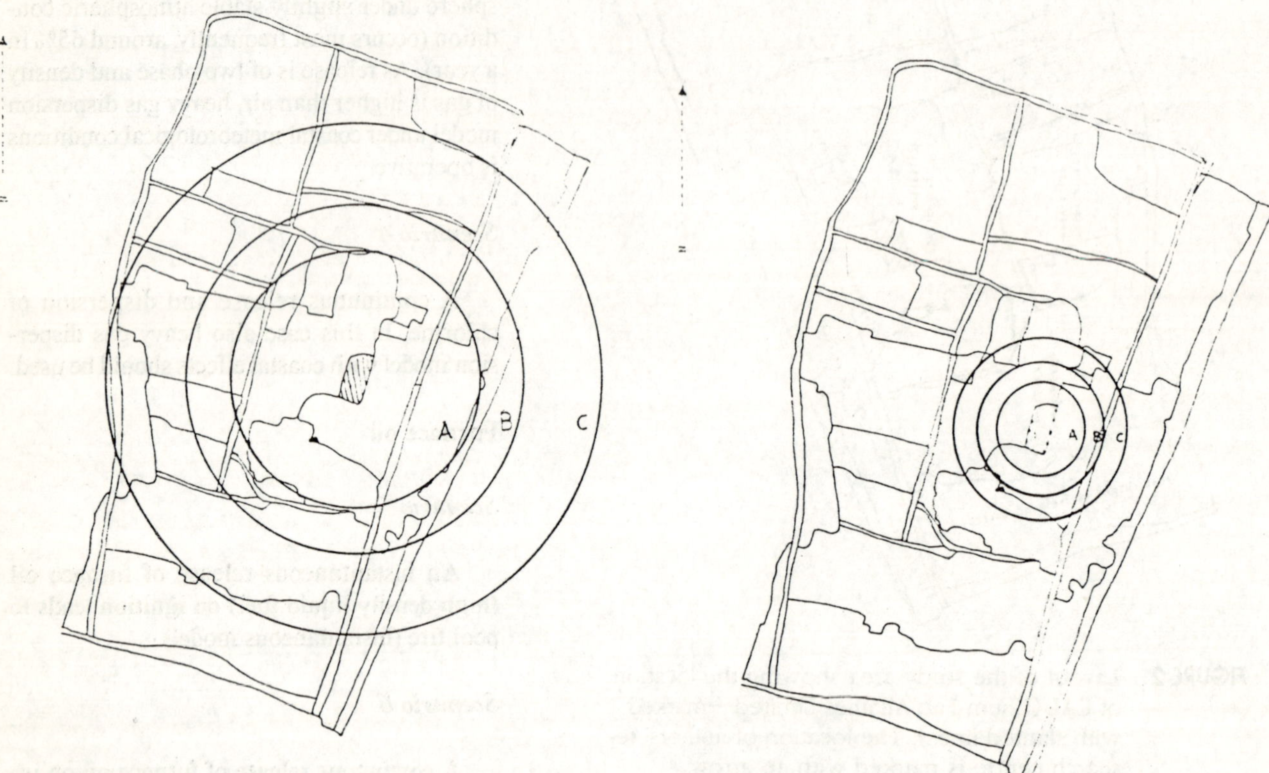

Figure 3. Risk contours indicating the impact area for an accident occuring in hydrogen storage vessel (Scenario 1) due to severe risk (A), high risk (B), and moderate risk (C).

Figure 4. Risk contours indicating the impact area for an accident occuring in hydrogen storage vessel (Scenario 2) due to severe risk (A), high risk (B), and moderate risk (C).

for different gases are presented in Table 3.

3) Pressure and shock wave effect

The probit equation for likelihood of death due to shock wave(lung rupture) is given by[23]

$$Pr = -77.1 + 6.91 * \ln Po \qquad (3)$$

For injury , the equation is

$$Pr = -15.6 + 1.93 * \ln Po \qquad (4)$$

Where Po is peak overpressure (N/m^2).

4) Missile effect

The probit function for fatality in human beings or damage to vessels is expressed as[23]:

$$Pr = -17.50 + 5.30 * \ln S \qquad (5)$$

Where, S is the kinetic energy of the missile(J).

DISCUSSION

The results of the calculations for different accident scenarios are presented below. Table 4 represents the output of MAXCRED-II for scenario 1. Lethal overpressure load, as well as missiles would be observed over areas of ~975 and ~1845 meters respectively. The vapor cloud generated by CVCE on ignition would lead to a fire ball which would cause scorching. Such lethal heat load would be observed over an area of 125 meters radius. The shock waves and heat load would also trigger secondary accidents by seriously damaging other vessels. It is evidenced from Table 4, this scenario has very high damage potential (shock waves, missile and heat load) over an area of ~300 meters radius and as other storage units (chlorine, HCl, NaOH) are situated within this range, hence, there is a high probability of second or high order (domino effect) accidents. Moreover, an area of around ~1000 meters radius from the site of accident, which contains densely populated pockets, comes under the range of lethality.

Table 5. Results of MAXCRED Simulation for Accident Scenario-UVCE and Flash Fire

Parameters	Values
Explosion : UVCE	
Total energy released by explosion	(kJ) : 2.0E+06
Peak overpressure	(kPa) : 414.8
Variation of overpressure in air	(kPa/s) : 438.5
Shock velocity of air	(m/s) : 751.9
Duration of shock wave	(ms) : 94.7
Missile characteristics	
Initial velocity of missile	(m/s) : 379.3
Kinetic energy associated with missile	(kJ) : 359102.5
Fragment velocity at 200 m	(m/s) : 174.9
Penetration ability at 200 m (based on empirical models)	
Concrete structure	(m) : 0.015
Brick structure	(m) : 0.019
Steel structure	(m) : 0.005
Damage radii (DR) for various degrees of damage due to overpressure	
DR for 100% complete damage	(m) : 600
DR for 100% fatality or 50% complete damage	(m) : 920
DR for 50% fatality or 25% complete damage	(m) : 1360
Damage radii (DR) for the varying degree of damage due to missile	
DR for 100% damage or 100% fatality	(m) : 865
DR for 50% damage or 100% fatality	(m) : 1089
DR for 100% fatality or 10% damage	(m) : 1324
Fire : Flash fire	
Volume of vapor cloud	(cu.m) : 173956.0
Effective time of fire	(s) : 345.9
Effective thermal load	(kJ/sq.m) : 234.3
Damage radii due to thermal load	
Damage radii for 100% fatality/damage	(m) : 45
Damage radii for 50% fatality/damage	(m) : 76
Damage radii for 100% third degree of burns	(m) : 105
Damage radii for 50% third degree of burns	(m) : 121

Figure 3 represents risk contours over the site of accident. The risk contours have been plotted on the basis of frequency of occurrence of particular event (taken from literature2,24-26) and damage potential calculated by

MAXCRED-II. The 'severest risk contour' (risk factor >1*10-4) has been observed over an area of around ~1050 meters radius, while 'high risk contour' (risk factor >1*10-5) and 'moderate risk contour' (risk factor >1*10-6) have been observed over areas of ~1750 and ~2200 meters radii respectively.

The results for scenario 2 (UVCE followed by flash fire) are presented in Table 5. In this case the damage potential of the shock waves and missiles is lower compared to the scenario 1. The unburnt mixture of vapor-air having concentration lower than its explosive limits would lead to flash fire. Lethal overpressure load would be generated upto a radial distance of ~600 meters, while missiles would cause damage upto ~865 meters (without considering the probability of impact of missile) all round the epicenter of the accident. The lethal heat load would encompass an area of ~45 meters radius. This scenario is less likely to cause secondary accidents as its zone of influence is smaller. However, the probability of occurrence of this scenario is 12 times greater than that of scenario 1. The risk contours for scenario 2 are shown in Figure 4. The severest risk contour is extended upto ~215 meters radius while high and moderate risk contours extend upto ~345 and ~575 meters radii respectively.

A BLEVE as per scenario 3 would lead to overpressure, and instantaneous toxic release. As the chemical is non-flammable no heat load would be observed but toxic dispersion would occur. The output of MAXCRED-II for this scenario, presented in Table 6, shows that lethal overpressure load would be observed over an area of ~323 meters radius, while lethal toxic load (as per short term exposure limit, STEL) would be observed over an area of ~2529 meter radius. The risk contours for this scenario are presented in Figure 5; the 'severest risk contour' extends upto ~1150 meters (due to toxic load) while 'high' and 'moderate' risk contours extend upto ~1910 and ~2750 meters radii respectively. The severest risk contour envelopes the densely populated villages (Chinnakalapet and Kalapet) as well as residential academic institutions (Pondicherry University campus and schools).

The output of MAXCRED-II for the continuous release of toxic gas chlorine is presented in Table 7. Lethal toxic load would be observed over an area of ~3252 meters radius, which covers four villages (Chinnakalapet, Kalapet, Pillaichavady and Kanagachettykulam) with a total population of around 20,000. The frequency of occurrence (4.5*10-5 /yr) of this scenario is 8 times higher than that of scenario 2. The 'severest risk contour' (Figure 6) extends upto ~3500 meters radius, while 'high' and 'moderate' risk contours extends upto areas of ~4750 and ~6530 meters radii.

The output from MAXCRED-II for instantaneous pool fire of furnace oil (scenario 5), given in Table 8, reveals that lethal heat load would be observed over an area of around 188 meter radius. This area encompasses parts of the nearby academic institution (Pondicherry university) and the village Chinnakalapet. The 'severest risk contour' (Figure 7) extends upto 300 meters radii, while 'high' and 'moderate' risk contours envelop areas with radii of ~450 and ~600 meters respectively. This scenario also bespeaks of the threats to nearby storage vessels by secondary accidents.

The results of scenario 6 are presented in Table 9. In this scenario, severest risk contour would be confined to ~134 meters radius and the high and moderate risk contours would extend upto circles of ~250 and ~475 meters radii respectively (Figure 8).

In summary scenario 1 has the highest risk factor (Table 10) and represents the worst disaster. It has the largest area-of-lethal-impact (overpressure zone of ~975 meters radius, missile zone of 1845 meters radius, and heat load zone of ~125 meters radius). Densely populated areas (four villages) and sensitive locations (two academic institutes) would come under its lethal impact range. The next most undesirable likely event is scenario 4, it has the largest damage area (due to likely lethal toxic load) of around ~3252 meters radius, but there is low probability of other types of accidents (domino effect) in this scenario, and the overall risk factor is lesser than scenario 1. Furthermore, Scenario 1 would be the most likely to cause cascading effects as missile, shock wave, and radiation impacts would be occurring simultaneously. Several other vessels storing flammable, toxic, and corrosive materials are situated within the striking distance of the area of influence of this scenario.

CONCLUSIONS

This paper demonstrates the applicability of software package MAXCRED-II for performing quantitative MCAA. The package can be used to generate different accident scenarios and simulate likely accidents. The output of the package can be used in developing strategies for hazard prevention and mitigation .

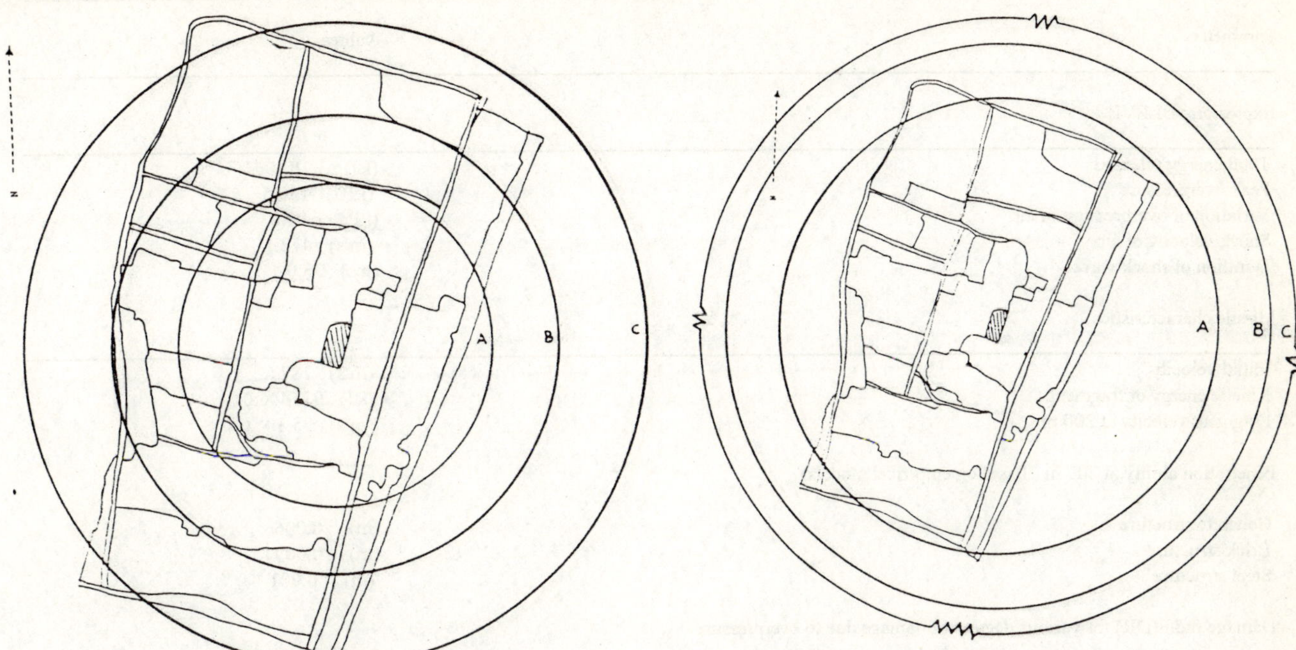

Figure 5. Risk contours indicating the impact area for an accident occuring in chlorine storage vessel (Scenario 3) due to severe risk (A), high risk (B), and moderate risk (C).

Figure 6. Risk contours indicating the impact area for an accident occuring in chlorine storage vessel (Scenario 4) due to severe risk (A), high risk (B), and moderate risk (C).

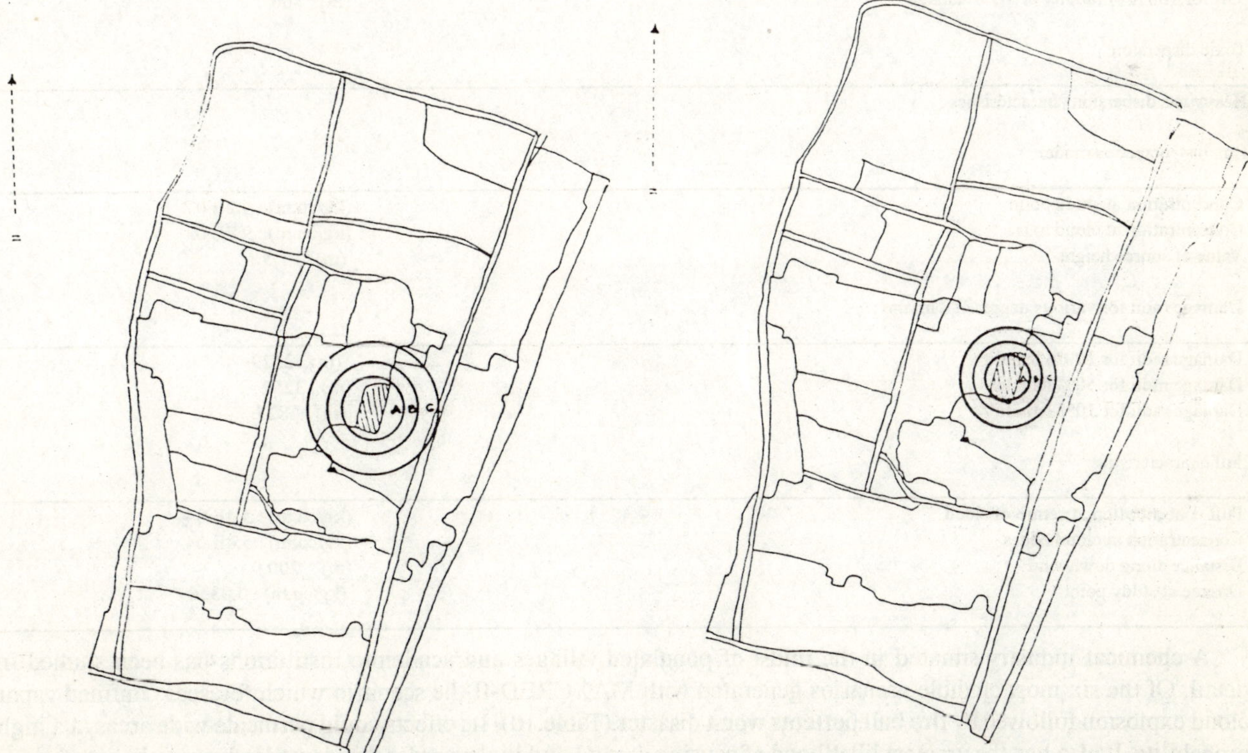

Figure 7. Risk contours indicating the impact area for an accident occuring in furnace oil storage vessel (Scenario 5) due to severe risk (A), high risk (B), and moderate risk (C).

Figure 8. Risk contours indicating the impact area for an accident occuring in furnance oil storage vessel (Scenario 6) due to severe risk (A), high risk (B), and moderate risk (C).

Table 6. Results of MAXCRED simulation for accident scenario-BLEVE and toxic release

Parameters	Values
Explosion : BLEVE	
Total energy released	(kJ) : 3.2E+06
Peak overpressure	(kPa) : 150.5
Variation of overpressure in air	(kPa/s): 99.0
Shock velocity of air	(m/s) : 472.1
Duration of shock wave	(ms) : 33.0
Missile characteristics	
Initial velocity	(m/s) : 287.6
Kinetic energy of fragment	(kJ) : 975446.0
Fragment velocity at 200 m	(m/s) : 95.1
Penetration ability at 200 m (based on empirical models)	
Concrete structure	(m) : 0.006
Brick structure	(m) : 0.007
Steel structure	(m) : 0.001
Damage radii (DR) for various degrees of damage due to overpressure	
DR for 100% complete damage	(m) : 323
DR for 100% fatality or 50% complete damage	(m) : 494
DR for 50% fatality or 25% complete damage	(m) : 731
Damage radii (DR) for the various degree of damage due to missile	
DR for 100% damage or 100% fatality	(m) : 498
DR for 50% damage or 100% fatality	(m) : 683
DR for 100% of fatality or 10% damage	(m) : 860
Toxic dispersion	
Heavy gas dispersion characteristics	
Box instantaneous model	
Concentration at study point	(kg/cu.m) : 4.2E-07
Concentration at cloud axis	(kg/cu.m) : 9.7E-03
Value of source height	(m) : 7.5
Damage radii for various degree of damage :	
Damage radii for 100% lethality	(m) : 2529
Damage radii for 50% lethality	(m) : 3252
Damage radii for 10% lethality	(m) : 5825
Puff characteristics:	
Puff concentration at centre of cloud	(kg/cu.m) : 5.4E-04
Concentration at cloud edges	(kg/cu.m) : 5.4E-04
Distance along downwind	(m) : 200.0
Dosage at study point	(kg/cu.m) : 0.0356

A chemical industry situated in the midst of populated villages and academic institutions has been studied in detail. Of the six most credible scenarios generated with MAXCRED-II the scenario which foresees confined vapor cloud explosion followed by fire ball portents worst disaster (Table 10). Its effects could permeate wide areas at a high probability. It also has the greatest likelihood of causing second and higher order accidents leading to chain reactions or 'domino' effects. Another scenario (number 4) which focuses on the release of chlorine has the highest likely damage radius of all the scenarios even though its overall risk factor is lesser than of scenario 1 (Table 10) due to lesser probability of occurrence. Other three scenarios, which all are very much within the realms of possibility, also have significantly high risk potential.

All-in-all the study reveals that the university campus and the villages (particularly Chinnakalapet and Kalapet) are at very high risk due to the presence of CAL's storage units.

Table 7. Results of MAXCRED simulation for accident scenario -toxic release

Parameters	Values
Toxic dispersion	
Heavy gas dispersion characteristics	
Box continuous model	
Value of wind speed	(m/s) : 3.5
Ground level X concentration	(kg/cu m) : 0.0023
Damage radii for various degree of damage	
Damage radii for 100% lethality	(m) : 3252
Damage radii for 50% lethality	(m) : 4615
Damage radii for 10% lethality	(m) : 10404
Plume characteristics	
Ground level conc of plume	(kg/cu m) : 0.0027
Ground level conc of plume on axis	(kg/cu m) : 0.0044
Ground level conc of plume at border	(kg/cu m) : 0.0004
Width of plume	(m) : 112.0
Cloud concentration	(kg/cu m) : 0.0042
Maximum ground level concentration (kg/cu m) : 0.0505	

Table 8. Results of MAXCRED simulation for accident scenario -pool fire

MAXCRED
(c) F I Khan & S A Abbasi, Pondicherry -605 014, India

Parameters	Values
Fire : Pool fire	
Instantaneous model	
Radius of pool fire	(m) : 5.0
Burning area	(sq.m) : 78.5
Burning rate	(kg/s) : 6.1
Heat flux	(kJ/sq.m) : 965.6
Damage radii due to thermal load	
Damage radii for 100% fatality/damage	(m) : 188
Damage radii for 50% fatality/damage	(m) : 236
Damage radii for 100% third degree of burns	(m) : 273
Damage radii for 50% third degree of burns	(m) : 350

Table 9. Results of MAXCRED simulation for accident scenario -pool fire

MAXCRED
(c) F I Khan & S A Abbasi, Pondicherry -605 014, India

File: Fur2.out

Parameters	Values
Fire : Pool fire	
Continuous model	
Radius of the pool fire	(m) : 5.0
Burning area	(sq.m) : 13060.8
Burning rate	(kg/s) : 1016.7
Heat intensity	(Kj/sq.m) : 675.9
Damage radii due to thermal load	
Damage radii for 100% fatality/damage	(m) : 134
Damage radii for 50% fatality/damage	(m) : 243
Damage radii for 100% third degree of burns	(m) : 349
Damage radii for 50% third degree of burns	(m) : 563

Table 10. Risk factors for different scenarios

Scenario	Maximum damage distance, MDD (meters)	Probability@ (year-1)	Individual risk factor at MDD
1	975	4.5e-05	3.214e-04
2	600	1.0e-03	1.562e-06
3	2529	1.0e-05	7.424e-05
4	3252	1.0e-05	1.124e-04
5	300	5.0e-03	3.497e-05
6	250	5.0e-03	5.077e-06

@ values are adopted from Lees (1996) and Continis (1991) at normal operating conditions

LITERATUE CITED

1. Kletz, T.A., "What Went Wrong", Gulf Publication, London, (1986).

2. Lees, F.P., "Loss Prevention in the Process Industries", Volume 1-3, Butterworths, London, (1996).

3. Khan, F.I. and S.A. Abbasi, "Disaster Forecasting and Consequence Analysis (Risk assessment) in Chemical Process Industries", XXIX National Conference on Environmental Genotoxins, pp. 54-59 (February 1996)

4. Mallikarjunan, M.M. and K.V. Raghvan, "Risk Assessment Techniques and their Application", Proceeding of National Conference of Safety System, New Delhi, (1989).

5. Greenberg, H.R. and J.J. Crammer, "Risk Assessment and Management for Chemical Process Industries", Van Nostrand Reinhold, New York, (1991).

6. Khan, F.I. and S.A. Abbasi, "Risk Analysis: A Systematic Method of Hazard Assessment and Control", Jr. of

Industrial Pollution Control, 11(2), pp. 89-98 (1995).

7. Van Sciver, G.R., "Quantitative Risk Analysis in the Chemical Process Industries", Reliability Engineering & System Safety, 29, pp. 55-68 (1990).

8. Arendt, J.S., "Management of Quantitative Risk Assessment in the Chemical Process Industry", Plant/Operation Progress, 9(4), pp. 262-268 (1990).

9. WHAZAN, Technica Limited, London (1990).

10. RISKWIT, VTT - The Technical Research Centre of Finland, Tempere, (1994).

11. EFFECTS, TNO-Prins Maurits Laboratory, Rijswijk, (1992).

12. Khan, F.I. and S.A. Abbasi, "MAXCRED- A Software Package for Quantitative Risk Analysis", Report No CPCE/R&D 5/94, Pondicherry University, Pondicherry, (1994); Environmental Software (in press).

13. Khan, F.I. and S.A. Abbasi, "MAXCRED-II: An Advanced Version of MAXCRED", Report No CPCE/R&D 14/96, Pondicherry University, Pondicherry, (1996).

14. Pitersen, C.M., "Consequences of Accidental Release of Hazardous Materials", J. of Loss Prevention Process Industries, 3, pp. 136-141 (1990).

15. Prugh, R.W., "Quantitative Evaluation of "BLEVE" Hazards", Fire Prot Engg, 3(1), pp.3-9 (1991).

16. Scielly, N.F. and W.G. High, "The Blast Effects of Explosions", in Proceeding of Fifth International Symposium on Loss Prevention and Safety Promotion, Cannes, (1986).

17. Roberts, A.F., "Thermal radiation hazards from releases of LPG from pressurized storage", Fire Safety Journal, 4, pp. 197-212 (1982).

18. Khan, F.I. and S.A. Abbasi, "Modeling of Heavy Gas Dispersion using Modified Plume Path Theory", Atmospheric Environment (in press), (1997).

19. Van Ulden, A.P., "A New Bulk Model for Dense Gas Dispersion : Two Dimensional Spread in Still Air", IUTAM Symposium on Atmospheric Dispersion of Heavy Gas and Small Particles, Delft, (1983).

20. Weatley, C.J. and D.M. Webber, "Aspects of the Dispersion of Denser-than-Air Vapors Relevant to Gas Cloud Explosions", SRD report ST/007/80/UK/H, Safety and Reliability Directorate, Warrington, (1984).

21. ChemFab Alkalis Ltd, "Risk analysis for the Chloralkali plant", Cell for Industrial Safety and Risk Analysis, pp. 5-102 (1993).

22. Khan, F.I. and S.A. Abbasi, "Accident Simulation in Chemical Process Industries using Software MAXCRED", Indian Journal of Chemical Technology, 3, pp. 339-344 (1996).

23. Pasman, H.J., et al., "Major Hazards in the Process Industries : Achievements and Challenges in Loss Prevention", Journal of Hazardous Materials, 30, pp. 1-38 (1992).

24. Contini, S., et al., "Benchmark Exercise on Major Hazard Analysis", Joint Research Centre, Institute of Systems Engineering & Informatics, Ispra, (1991).

25. Reliability Directorate, "Failure Frequency of Hardware Components", Report No. 87-2981R.27/NVE, Reliability Directorate, (1992).

26. European Community, "Council Direction on the Major Accident Hazards of Certain Industrial Activities", Report No. 82/50/501 EEC, London (1992).

¨ Reproduced from *Process Safety Progress*, **16**(3), 172-184, 1997

Part V

Quantitative Methods of Risk Assessment-III : Probabilistic hazard assessment

Like HAZOP (HAZard and Operability study), FTA (fault tree analysis) is one of the classical methodologies used in risk assessment and like HAZOP it, in its conventional form, is a tedious, lengthy, and costly endeavour.

We have formulated a quantitatiave methodology for conducting probabilistic fault tree analysis, and have developed a software package PROFAT (PRObabilistic FAult Tree analysis) to facilitate the use of the methodology. Some success has been achieved in increasing resilience towards inadequacies in the input data, swifter processing, and lesser requirements of computation time. The details are presented in the pre-print of the research paper PROFAT: a user-friendly system for probabilistic fault tree analysis due for publication in Journal of Loss Prevention in Process Industries.

14

PROFAT: A USER FRIENDLY SYSTEM FOR PROBABILISTIC FAULT TREE ANALYSIS*

A methodology has been developed to conduct probabilistic fault tree analysis during risk assessment in chemical process industries. The methodology is based on a system involving a) development of fault tree, b) determination of minimum cutsets or shortest pathways leading from initiating events (malfunctioning) to the top event (the major accident), c) probability analysis, and d) working out improvement index values. To this end techniques of Boolean algebra, structure modulling, analytical method of cutsets finding (top-to-bottom algorithm), Monte-Carlo simulation, optimisation technique and fuzzy probability set have been used. The methodology has been termed by us analytical -simulation methodology (ASM) and a software package PROFAT (PRObabilistic FAult Tree analysis) has been developed by us to facilitate the use of the methodology in a rapid and effective, yet user-friendly manner. PROFAT enables the user to find out, in an industry, i) initiating events which may eventually lead to a major accident, ii) minimum cutsets (a series of initiating events aiding each other in causing the accident), iii) the probabilities of occurrence of such initiating events, iv) relative contributions of each of the initiating event and, finally, v) identifying initiating events with the greatest potential to cause the top event (major accident) so that accident prevention strategies and emergency preparedness plans can be focused on them. The noteworthy attributes of the system are: resilience towards lack of precision in the basic data, swift processing with moderate requirements of computation capacity (sophistication of computers needed), ease of use, and directly utilizable output. The applicability of PROFAT has been demonstrated with a case study of a sulfolane manufacturing unit.

Key words: Fault tree analysis, probabilistic risk assessment, hazard assessment, risk analysis.

INTRODUCTION

Fault tree analysis (FTA), and its derivative probabilistic fault tree analysis (PFTA), are among the popular techniques used in identifying hazards in a chemical process industry. FTA/PFTA are normally used in conjunction with other techniques such as hazards and operability (HAZOP) studies, maximum credible accident analysis (MCAA), etc. in conducting risk assessment (Guymer, 1987; Lees, 1996; Khan and Abbasi, 1995; 1997).

As conventionally done (Lapp and Power, 1976; 1979; Vesely *et al.* 1981; Prugh 1981; Taylor, 1982; Moetin Solis *et al.* 1982; Hauptmanns *et al.* 1982; Hauptmanns and Yllera, 1983; Doelp *et al.* 1984, Henley *et al.* 1985; CCPS, 1989; Hauptmanns and Werner, 1990; Lap, 1991; Lees, 1996), FTA involves several steps which require large inputs of experts time, rcliable data, and computational capabilities. For example a typical FTA consists of the following:

* Reproduced from *Chemical Engineering Progress, USA*

I. familiarisation with the system using process description, piping and instrumentation diagrams and the information obtained from the plant personnels;

II. definition of the undesired or accident-initiating events using material information, checklists, historical evidence, etc.;

III. development of the fault tree(s);

IV. obtaining probabilities for the failure of various technical components and human error;

V. evaluation of the fault tree(s);

VI. analysis of the results, ratting of the proposals for system improvement, if necessary, corresponding changes of the fault tree(s), and renewed fault tree evaluation,

VII. repeat I-VI in case VI is not satisfactory.

Each of these steps is costly in terms of money and time. Step V is of particular concern as it more often than not requires Monte-Carlo simulation. This is because a range of probabilities rather than a single value of probability is normally associated with most events of a fault tree. In other words the probability of most failures is not characterised by a point value but a probability density function (PDF). And since the probability of most events up a fault tree are expressed as PDFs, the probability of the top event (the accident) is also expressed as a PDF. This enormously increase the computational time required in conducting simulation because the number of trials needed to get accurate results increase with the inverse of the square of the value of the top-event probability.

ANALYTICAL-SIMULATION METHODOLOGY

We have developed a methodology, termed by us as Analytical-Simulation Methodology (ASM) to drastically cut short the monetary and other costs (including time inputs) in conducting FTA. The methodology is built around several techniques independently proposed by different authors (Noma *et al.* 1981; Camarinpoulous and Yllera, 1985; Yllera, 1988; Shafaghi,1988; Hauptmanns, 1988; Lai *et al.* 1988; CCPS, 1989; Beckjord *et al.*, 1993; Vincoli,1993). These techniques have been suitably modified/adopted by us and woven together in a cogent system. The algorithm of ASM is presented in Figure 1. The resulting procedure consists of the following steps:

i) *fault tree development* - based on the detailed study of the process, control arrangement, and behaviour of components of the unit/plant the top event (most undesirable situation) is identified. Further a logical dependency between the causes leading to the top event is developed and represented in terms of a fault tree. Such a fault tree can be developed for an individual unit or a combination of units, depending upon the convenience of the user.

ii) *Boolean matrix creation* - the fault tree developed as above is transformed to a Boolean matrix. If the dimension of the Boolean matrix happens to exceed the processing ability of the computer available with the user, structural modulling technique may be applied (Shafaghi, 1988; Yllera, 1988). This technique proposes modulling of the fault tree into a number of smaller sub-modules with a dependency relation among them. This reduces the memory allocation problem as well as make the computation faster (Bossche, 1991).

iii) *finding of minimum cutsets and optimisation* - the Boolean matrix is then solved using analytical method for minimum cutsets (Camarinpoulous and Yllera, 1985; Khoda and Henley, 1988; Papazoglou *et al.* 1992 ; Greenberg and Slater, 1992). If the problem has been structurally modulled, then each module is solved independently, and the results thus occurred are combined. The minimum cutsets which result may be optimised using any appropriate technique. These authors have found the modified Fibonaci method a good option. Optimisation is necessary in order to eliminate the unimportant paths (cutsets).

iv) *probability analysis* - the already optimised minimum cutsets are processed for probability estimation. These authors recommend the use of Monte-Carlo simulation method (Soon Chang *et al.* 1985; Worrel and Stack, 1990; James *et al.* 1992; Rauzy, 1993) for this purpose instead of direct estimation because, simulation method not only gives the probability of the top event but it also provides information on the sensitivity of the results. Further, simulation is helpful in studying the impact of each of the initiating events. To increase the accuracy of

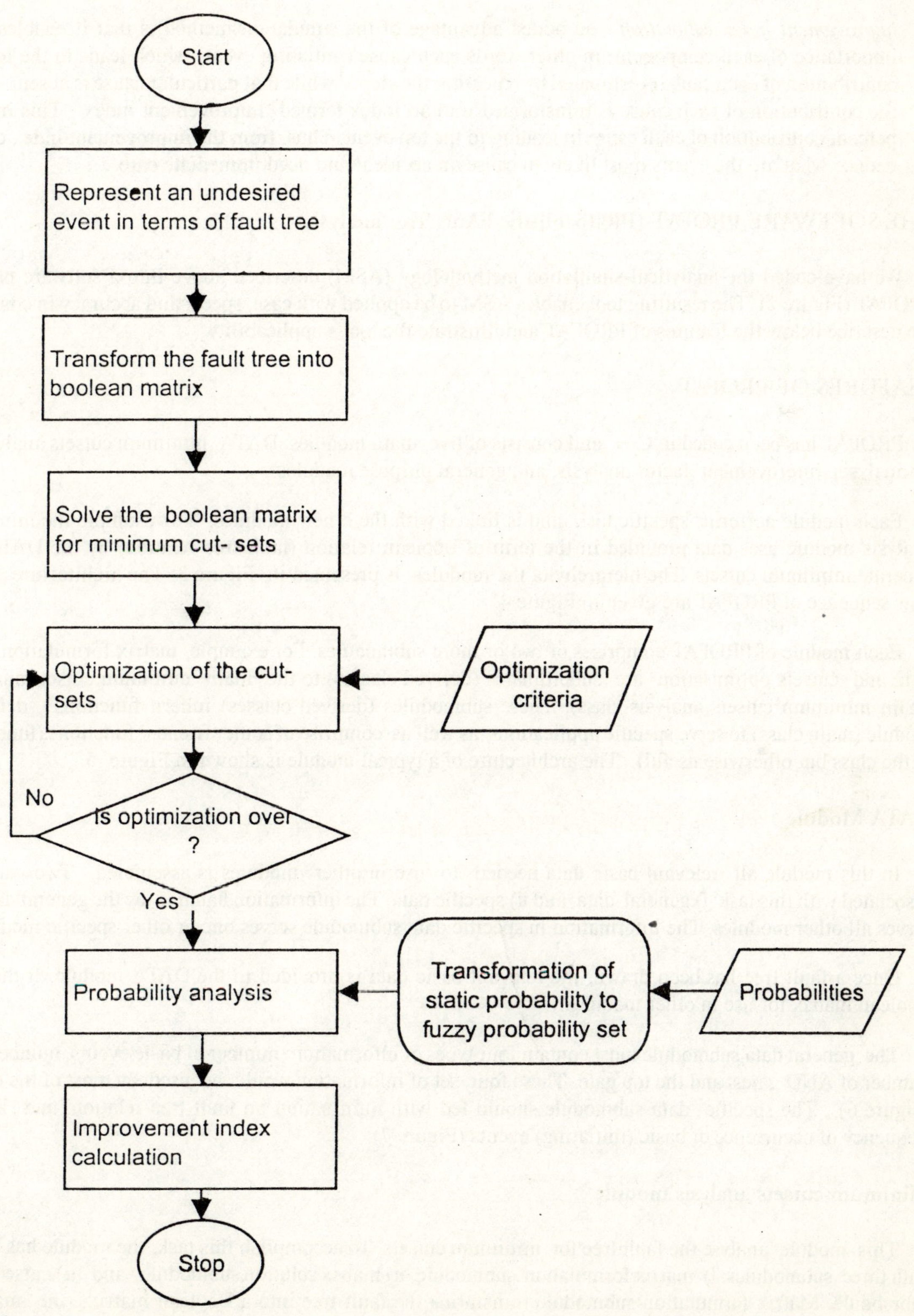

Figure 1. Algorithm of analytical-simulation methodology

the computations and reduce the margin of error due to inaccuracy involved in the reliability data of the basic events (initiating events), authors recommend the use of fuzzy probability set (Dubois and Prade, 1980; Noma *et al.* 1981; Tanaka *et al.* 1983, Lai *et al.* 1988; Prugh, 1992).

v) *improvement index estimation* - an added advantage of the simulation method is that it enables study of the importance of each component; in other words each cause (initiating event) which leads to the top event. The contribution of each cause is estimated by repeating the step V while that particular cause is absent. Subsequently the contribution of each cause is transformed into an index termed 'improvement index'. This index signifies percent contribution of each cause in leading to the top event. Thus, from the improvement index one can easily deduce what are the events most likely to cause an accident and need immediate care.

THE SOFTWARE PROFAT (PRObabilistic FAult Tree analysis)

We have coded the analytical-simulation methodology (ASM) described above into a software package called PROFAT (Figure 2). The resulting tool enables ASM to be applied with ease, speed, and accuracy in conducting FTA. We describe below the features of PROFAT and illustrate the tool's applicability.

FEATURES OF PROFAT

PROFAT has been coded in C++ and consists of five main modules: DATA, minimum cutsets analysis, probability analysis, improvement factor analysis, and general purpose modules.

Each module performs specific task, and is linked with the other modules. For example the minimum cutsets analysis module uses data provided in the form of Boolean relation (fault tree relation) by the DATA module, to generate minimum cutsets. The hierarchy of the modules is presented in Figure 3. The architecture and message flow sequence of PROFAT are given in Figure 4.

Each module of PROFAT comprises of two or more submodules. For example, matrix formulation, matrix solution, and cutsets optimisation are subordinates (derived classes) to the main minimum cutsets analysis module (main minimum cutsets analysis class). These submodules (derived classes) inherit functions defined in main module (main class) to serve specific applications as well as comprise of some 'friends' functions (functions not part of the class but otherwise useful). The architecture of a typical module is shown in Figure 5.

DATA Module

In this module all relevant basic data needed to use in other modules is assembled. Two submodules are associated with this task: i) general data, and ii) specific data. The information handled by the general data submodule serves all other modules. The information in specific data submodule serves one or other specific module.

Once a fault tree has been drawn, the relevant basic data is provided to the DATA module. It then develops a Boolean matrix for use in other modules.

The general data submodule must contain four types of information: number of basic events, number of OR gates, number of AND gates, and the top gate. These four set of information would be used by most of the other modules (Figure 6). The specific data submodule should fed with information on fault tree relation, and ii) probability/frequency of occurrence of basic (initiating) events (Figure 7).

Minimum cutsets analysis module

This module analyse the fault tree for minimum cutsets. To accomplish this task, the module has been provided with three submodules: i) matrix formulation submodule, ii) matrix solution submodule, and iii) cutsets optimisation submodule. Matrix formulation submodule transforms the fault tree into a Boolean matrix, the matrix solution submodule solves the Boolean matrix for minimum cutsets. Lastly the optimisation submodule does the optimisation of minimum cutsets.

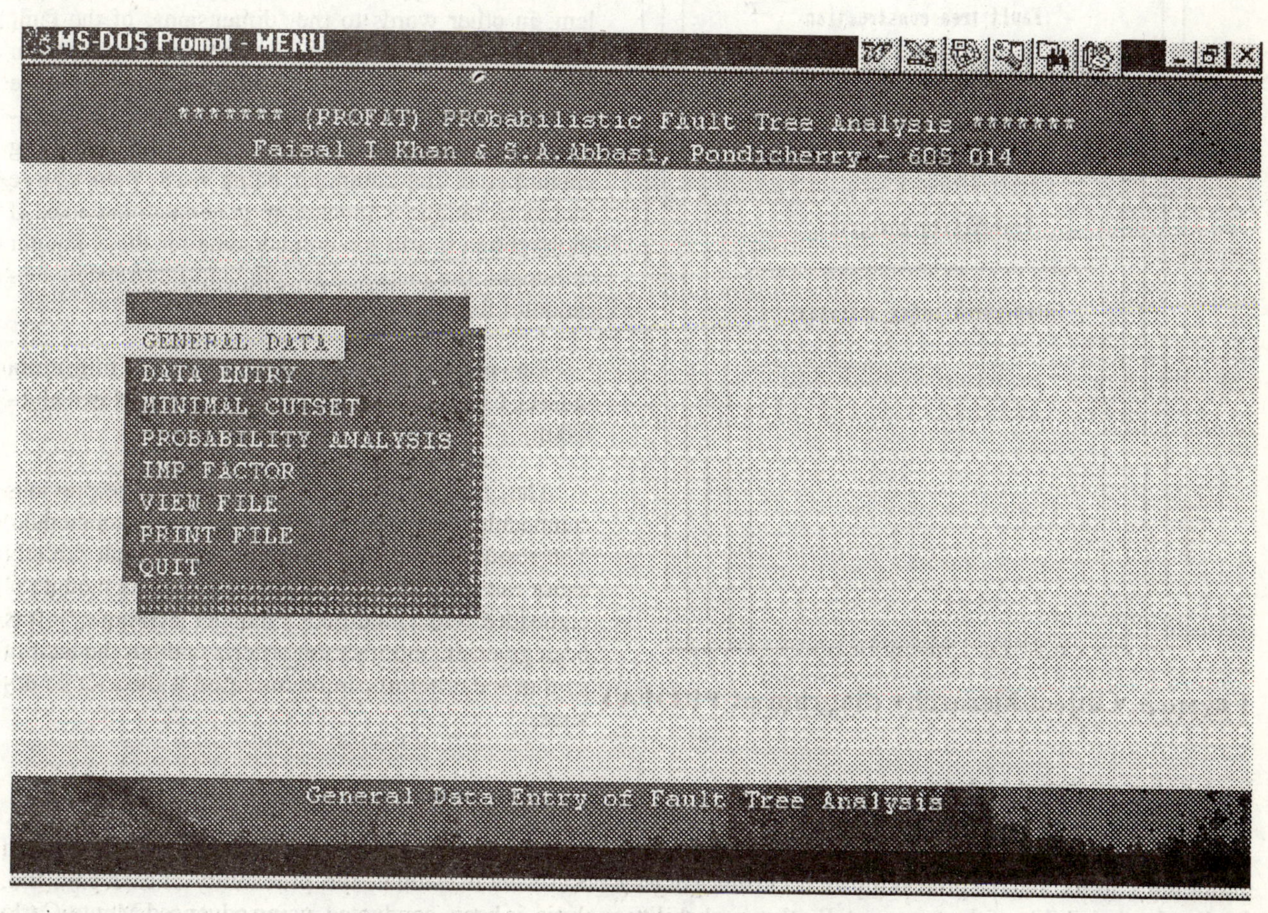

Figure 2. Main menu of PROFAT

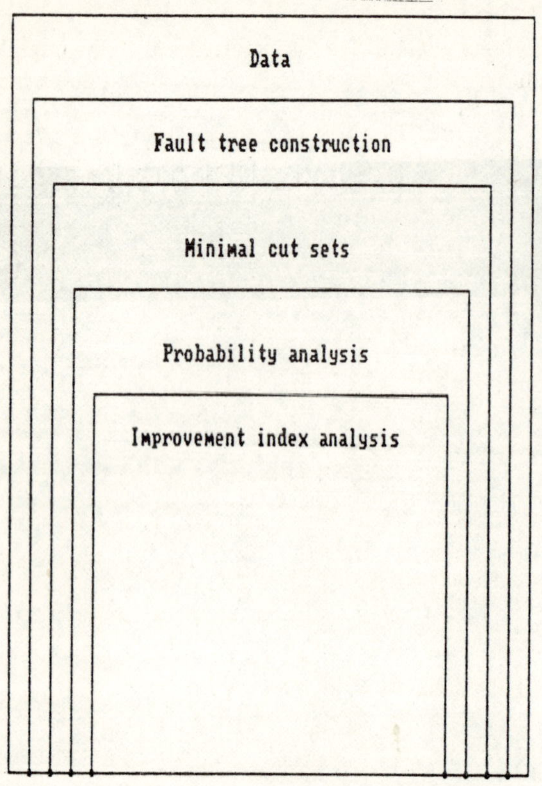

Figure 3. Object hierarchy diagram of PROFAT

Development of Boolean matrix is the starting of fault tree evaluation procedure and needs utmost care because the efficacy of further operations is strongly influenced by the matrix. The dimension of the matrix is dependent on the complexity of the problem; in other words to the 'dimensions' of the fault tree. Different techniques have been incorporated in the module to handle the complexity and to minimise the memory allocation problem. For example; if matrix dimension happens to go beyond the processing capability of the computer being used, then spurge matrix technique is invoked to generate the matrix. If the problem is still too cumbersome for the computer to handle, the matrix gets split into interrelated submodules for processing.

The matrix is eventually solved for minimum cutsets, using an analytical method (top-to-down algorithm).

The minimum cutsets developed in the previous submodule are passed on to the optimisation submodule. The resulting cutsets represent paths which directly cause the top event. The optimisation submodule is embedded with modified Fibonaci technique. It has been given an optimisation criteria and has the facility so that the criteria, can be modified if the user so desires.

Probability analysis module

This module conducts probability analysis of the already developed and solved fault tree. It uses optimum minimum cutsets and the probability of occurrence of each basic event to estimate the probability of each path and, finally, the probability of the top event. Further probability analysis is been conducted using advanced Monte-Carlo simulation technique (Bossche, 1991; Rauzy-1993; Vincoli, 1993) with fuzzy probability sets. The latter reduce the margin of error which may originate from the input reliability data. Thus, fairly good accuracy can be obtained even when the probability of the basic causes (initiating events), had been approximated. This is more so for situations in which reliable data were not available. The probability of occurrence of the top event represents the frequency of occurrence of the undesired event when all initiating events actually take place.

The probability analysis module consists of three submodules: i) fuzzy set conversion submodule, which transforms the static probabilities to fuzzy probability sets, ii) probability analysis submodule: it estimates the probability of each path and the probability of top event, and iii) static submodule: it transforms the fuzzy probability to static probability.

Improvement analysis module

Improvement analysis module is also based on the Monte-Carlo simulation technique. In it, simulation is conducted for each event (that particular event is made under full control position or in other words functioning properly). Subsequently, using this probability and the probability when all events are occurring, improvement factor is calculated. Finally the improvement factors are transformed into the 'improvement index'. This index represents direct contribution (in percentage) of an event in leading the system to the undesired condition (top event to occur). Higher the improvement index, more potent the initiating event vis a vis its role in the eventual accident.

General purpose module

This module deals with handling of data files, output files, and general flow of information. This module also works as 'information manager': it provides the necessary information to each module and submodule to carry out desired operations, and stores the results in different files. It also provides all commonly used file operations such as copying, deleting, consoling and printing.

Table 1. List of the basic (initiating) events and their frequency of occurrence.

Event Number	Basic Event description	Probability of occurrence/10000 yr
1	Pump P1 fail to run	0.2628
2	Flow control FRC1 fail	0.3813
3	Leak in line L1	0.4130
4	Pump P2 fail to run	0.2628
5	Flow control FRC2 fail	0.3650
6	Leak in second line L2	0.4130
7	Pump P5 fail to run	0.2628
8	Temperature control TCSF fail	0.3813
9	Pressure control PCF1 fail	0.3245
10	Cooling water not available	0.0630
11	Cooling liquid valve VC closed	0.0365
12	Cooling jacket fouled	0.1973
13	Ratio control RCF1 fail	0.3654
14	Change in Set Point STP1	0.5084
15	Volume of reactor decreased	0.0413
16	Transformer TRNS1 fail	0.0473
17	Strirrer speed regulator fail	0.0378
18	Power supply is off	0.3481
19	Strirrer motor STRM fail	0.4730
20	Leak in Vessel	0.0263
21	Pressure control in reactor fails	0.3813
22	Decrease in reactant pressure	0.1331
23	Leak in pump P1	0.1971
24	Leak in pump P2	0.1971
25	Water ingress into reactor due to leak in cooling jacket	0.0085
26	Solvent is not pure	0.0367
27	Human error in adding solvent	0.7321

HARDWARE AND SOFTWARE REQUIREMENTS OF PROFAT

PROFAT is a PC based system. It needs about 8 MB RAM and ~60 MB ROM. It is operable on DOS as well as on WINDOWS environments.

It does not need any other hardware or software to input the data or to prepare final reports based on the output. The output is so formatted that it can be directly used in filling reports. Further PROFAT is easy to operate and has on-line help available for each step. Even those not well-versed with the analytical and simulation techniques employed in PROFAT can gainfully use the software.

APPLICATION OF PROFAT - an example

A probabilistic fault tree analysis study was conducted for a sulfolane manufacturing plant (Khan, 1992). The objectives of the study were a) to identify the different events which may cause an accident (explosion in the sulfonation reactor), b) assess the probability of occurrence of the accident and the contribution of each event in causing it.

Table 2. The Boolean matrix showing the optimal minimal cutsets

PROFAT
Khan, F.I. & Abbasi, S A, Pondicherry-605 014

Boolean matrix

000000000000000000000000100
000101000000000000000000000
000100000000000000000000000
010100000000000000000000000
101000000000000000000000000
100000000000000000000000000
000010000000000000000000000
000001000000000000000000000
000000100000000000000000000
010010000000000000000000000
010001000000000000000000000
010000100000000000000000000
010000000000000000000000000
001000000000000000000000000
000000000000000000010000000
000000000000000000000011000
000000010000000000000000000
000000000000100000000000000
000000000000001000000000000
000000000000000001000000000
000000000000000000000000010
000000000000000000001000000
000000000000000000000100000
000000000000010000000000000
000000001000000000000000000
000000000001000000000000000
000000000000000110000000000
000000000000000000100000000
000000000000000000000000001
110000000000000000000000000
000000000100000000000000000
000000000010000000000000000

Process summary

Sulfolane (tetra hydrothiophene 1-1 dioxide) is prepared in two steps. First sulfolene (2,4, dimethyl thiophene) is prepared by a reaction of butadiene and sulphur dioxide (SO_2); the product is then hydrogenated in the presence of Nickle(Ni) catalyst to yield sulfolane.

The reaction producing sulfolene is highly exothermic and is carried out in liquid phase under high pressure. A condition of slightly above normal reaction temperature favours undesirable side reactions which further increase the temperature and pressure in the reactor. Moreover, concentration of butadiene and sulphur dioxide should be maintained in a proportion of 1:8 otherwise the undesirable side reactions may occur generating high pressure and temperature in the reactor. Thus, precise measurement and accurate control of material flow, temperature, and pressure are essential to control the unwanted reaction. Otherwise accident may occur, the probability of which is dependent upon the reliability of the temperature/pressure/flow control systems.

Basically sulfonation reactor is a three stage cascade type continuous stirred tank with cooling jacket to remove the excess heat. The schematic diagram of reactor along with control configuration is shown in Figure 8.

Problem formulation and fault tree development

The top event was identified as unwanted side reaction in the sulfolanation reactor leading to explosion. There are twenty seven basic events (initiating events) which may contribute directly and/or indirectly to the failure of

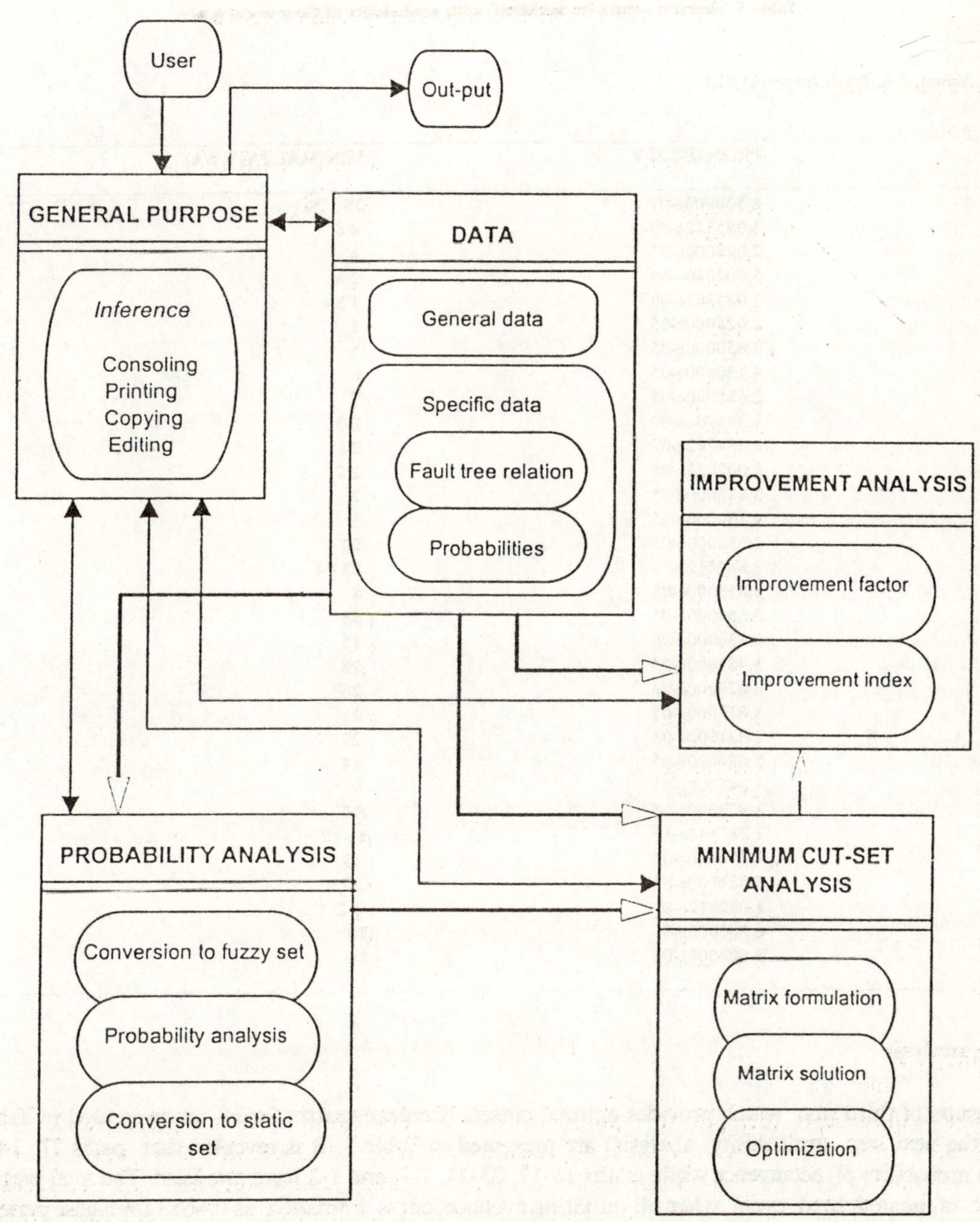

Figure 4. Architecture and message flow sequence of PROFAT

the reactor. A list of the identified basic events with their frequency of failure is given in Table 1. As the industry is yet to be commissioned, precise industry-specific data is not available. Therefore, we have taken the relevant data from literature (Thangamani, 1992; Lees, 1996). Thus, some 'uncertainty' is associated with this data as it does not actually pertain to the industry we have studied with PROFAT.

Based on the process description and the detailed study of the reactor, fault tree was developed (Figure 9).

Table 3. Shortest routes (to accident) with probability of their occurrence

PROFAT
Khan, F.I. & Abbasi, S A, Pondicherry-605 014

PROBABILITY	MINIMAL PATHWAY
8.500000e-07	25
1.085312e-09	4 6
2.628000e-05	4
1.002010e-09	2 4
1.085301e-09	1 3
2.628000e-05	1
3.650000e-05	5
4.130000e-05	6
2.628000e-05	7
1.391701e-09	2 5
1.574712e-09	2 6
1.002012e-09	2 7
3.813000e-05	2
4.130000e-05	3
2.630000e-05	20
3.884412e-10	23 24
3.813000e-05	8
3.654000e-05	13
4.130000e-06	15
3.481000e-05	18
3.670000e-06	26
3.813000e-05	21
1.331000e-05	22
5.084000e-05	14
3.245000e-05	9
1.973000e-05	12
1.787941e-11	16 17
4.730000e-05	19
7.321000e-05	27
1.002012e-09	1 2
6.300000e-06	10
3.600000e-06	11

Fault tree analysis

The results of third step, which provides optimal cutsets (Boolean matrix form), are presented in Table 2. The results of the next step (probability analysis) are presented in Table 3. It is revealed that paths 27, 14 have the maximum probability of occurrence while paths 16-17, 23-24, 1-3, and 1-2 have the least. The total probability of occurrence of the undesired event when all initiating events occur is estimated as 0.6653 for a base period of 1000 years.

The improvement factor analysis (fifth step of ASM) suggests that event 27 would have the largest contribution (about 11%) to the probability of the eventual accident. Table 4, which summarises the results of improvement analysis indicate that events which would have the lowest contribution towards the undesired event are 23-24, 16-17, 1-2, 2-4, and 2-7.

The study concludes that to control, particular attention must be paid to the events 27, 14, 19, 3, and 6 which are most likely to lead to the eventual accident (top event). Events 23, 24, 16, and 17 are less likely to precipitate the top event.

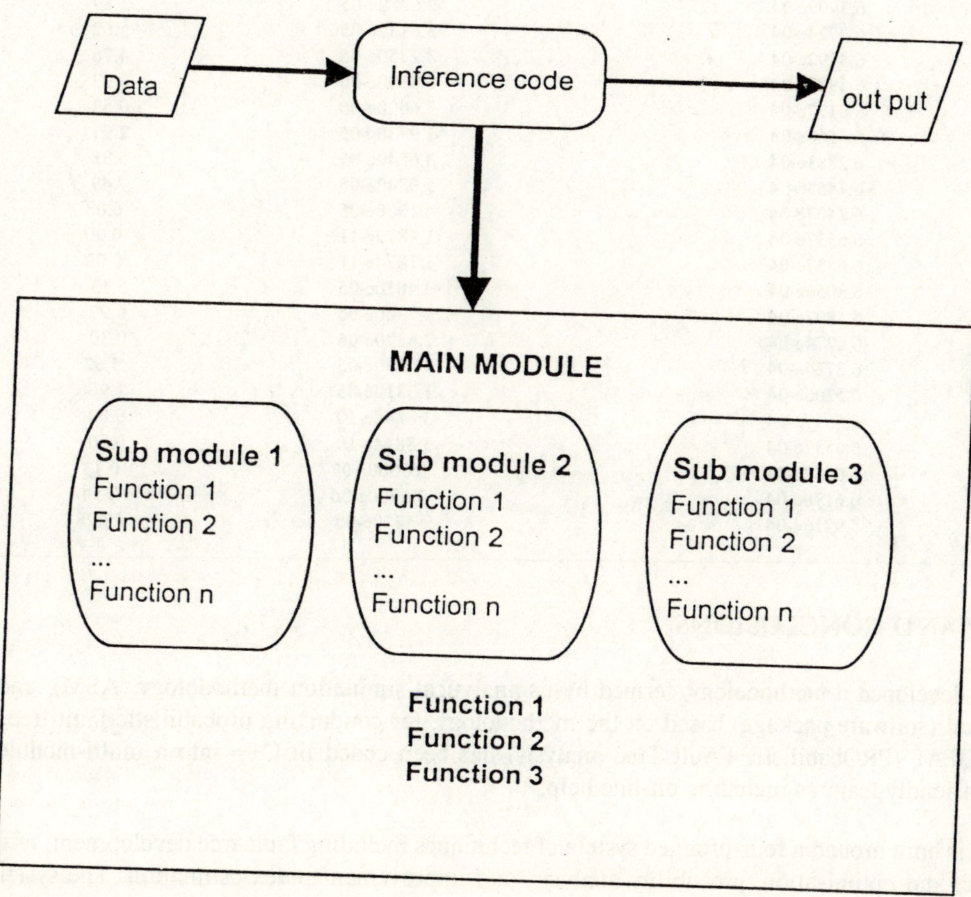

Figure 5. Internal architecture of a typical module

Table 4. Improvement factors and improvement indices for different events

PROFAT
Khan, F.I. & Abbasi, S A, Pondicherry-605 014

Event not-	Probability occurring	Improvement factor	Improvement index
0	6.6537e-04	0.0000e+00	0.00
1	6.3909e-04	2.6282e-05	3.87
2	6.2727e-04	3.8105e-05	5.61
3	6.2407e-04	4.1301e-05	6.08
4	6.3909e-04	2.6282e-05	3.87
5	6.2887e-04	3.6500e-05	5.38
6	6.2407e-04	4.1301e-05	6.08
7	6.3909e-04	2.6282e-05	3.87
8	6.2724e-04	3.8132e-05	5.62
9	6.3292e-04	3.2450e-05	4.78
10	6.5907e-04	6.3000e-06	0.93
11	6.6177e-04	3.6000e-06	0.53
12	6.4564e-04	1.9730e-05	2.91
13	6.2883e-04	3.6540e-05	5.38
14	6.1453e-04	5.0840e-05	7.49
15	6.2407e-04	4.1300e-05	6.08
16	6.6537e-04	1.7879e-11	0.00
17	6.6537e-04	1.7874e-11	0.00
18	6.3056e-04	3.4810e-05	5.13
19	6.1807e-04	4.7300e-05	6.97
20	6.6274e-04	2.6300e-06	0.39
21	6.2724e-04	3.8130e-05	5.62
22	6.5206e-04	1.3310e-05	1.96
23	6.6537e-04	3.8844e-10	0.00
24	6.6537e-04	3.8844e-10	0.00
25	6.6452e-04	8.5000e-07	0.13
26	6.6170e-04	3.6700e-06	0.54
27	5.9216e-04	7.3210e-05	10.78

SUMMARY AND CONCLUSIONS

We have developed a methodology, termed by us analytical-simulation methodology (ASM), and a computer-automated tool (software package) based on the methodology, for conducting probabilistic fault tree analysis. The package PROFAT (PRObabilistic FAult Tree analysis) has been coded in C++ into a multi-module system with several user-friendly features including on-line help.

PROFAT is built around a four-pronged system of techniques including fault-tree development, minimum cutsets determination and optimisation, probability analysis, and improvement index estimation. The system enables the user to find out, in an industry, i) initiating events which may eventually lead to a major accident, ii) shortest routes (minimum cutsets) a series of initiating events may take while aiding each other in causing the accident, iii) the probabilities of occurrence of such initiating events, iv) relative contributions of each of the initiating event and, finally, v) identifying initiating events with the greatest potential to cause the top event (major accident) so that accident prevention strategies and emergency preparedness plans can be focused on them. The noteworthy attributes of the system are: resilience towards lack of precision in the basic data, swift processing with moderate requirements of computation capacity (sophistication of computers needed), ease of use, and directly utilizable output.

The applicability of PROFAT has been demonstrated with a case study of a sulfolane manufacturing unit.

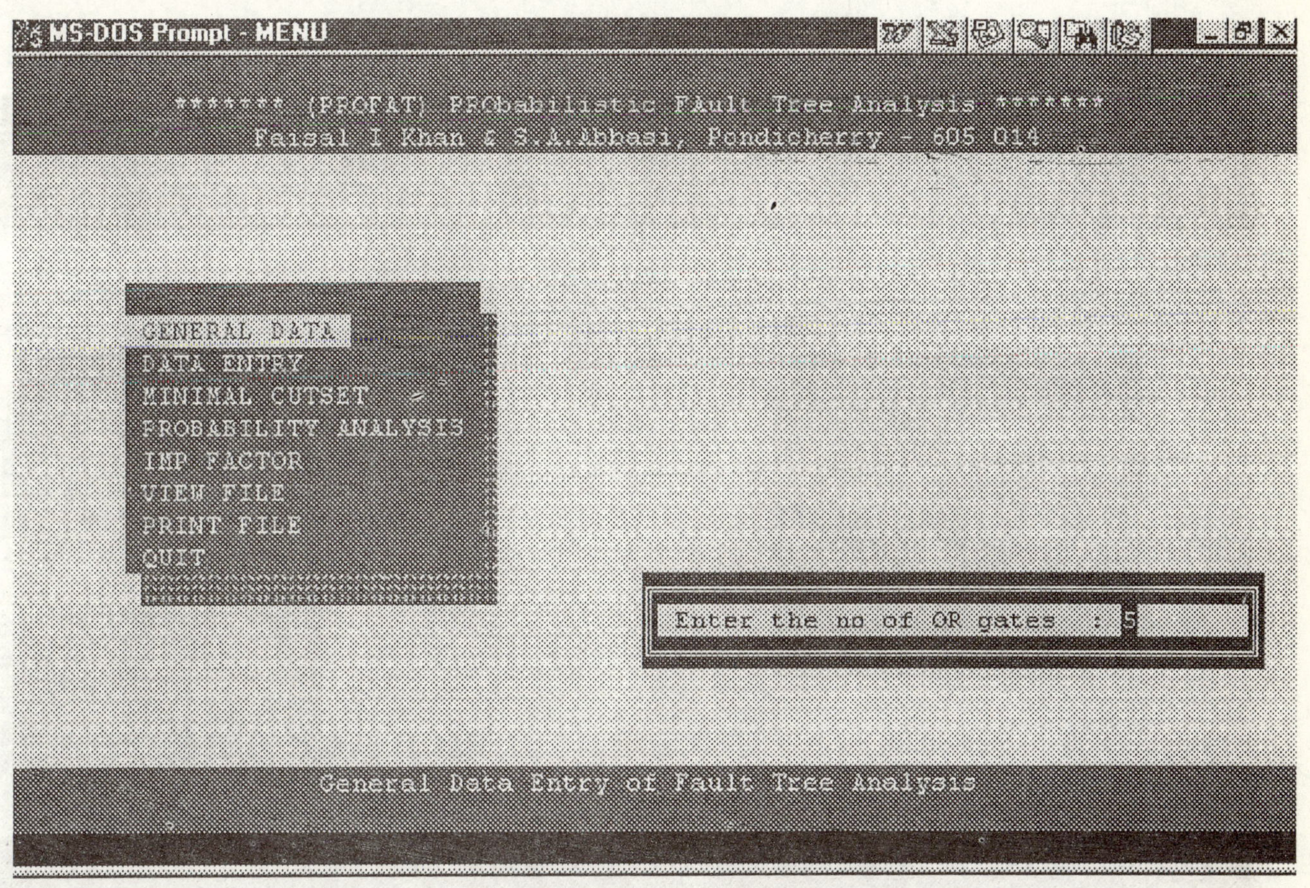

Figure 6. General data entry option

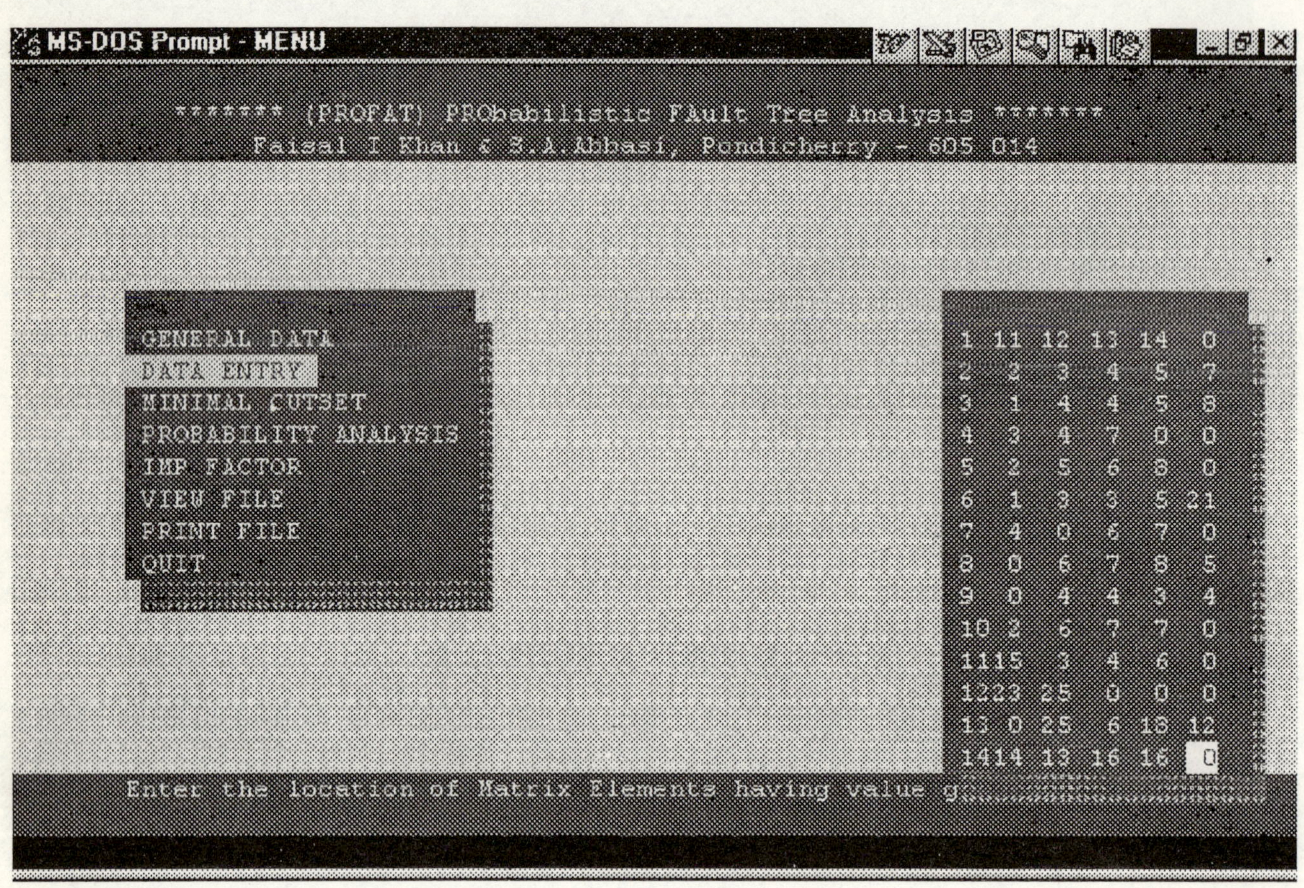

Figure 7. Specific data entry option

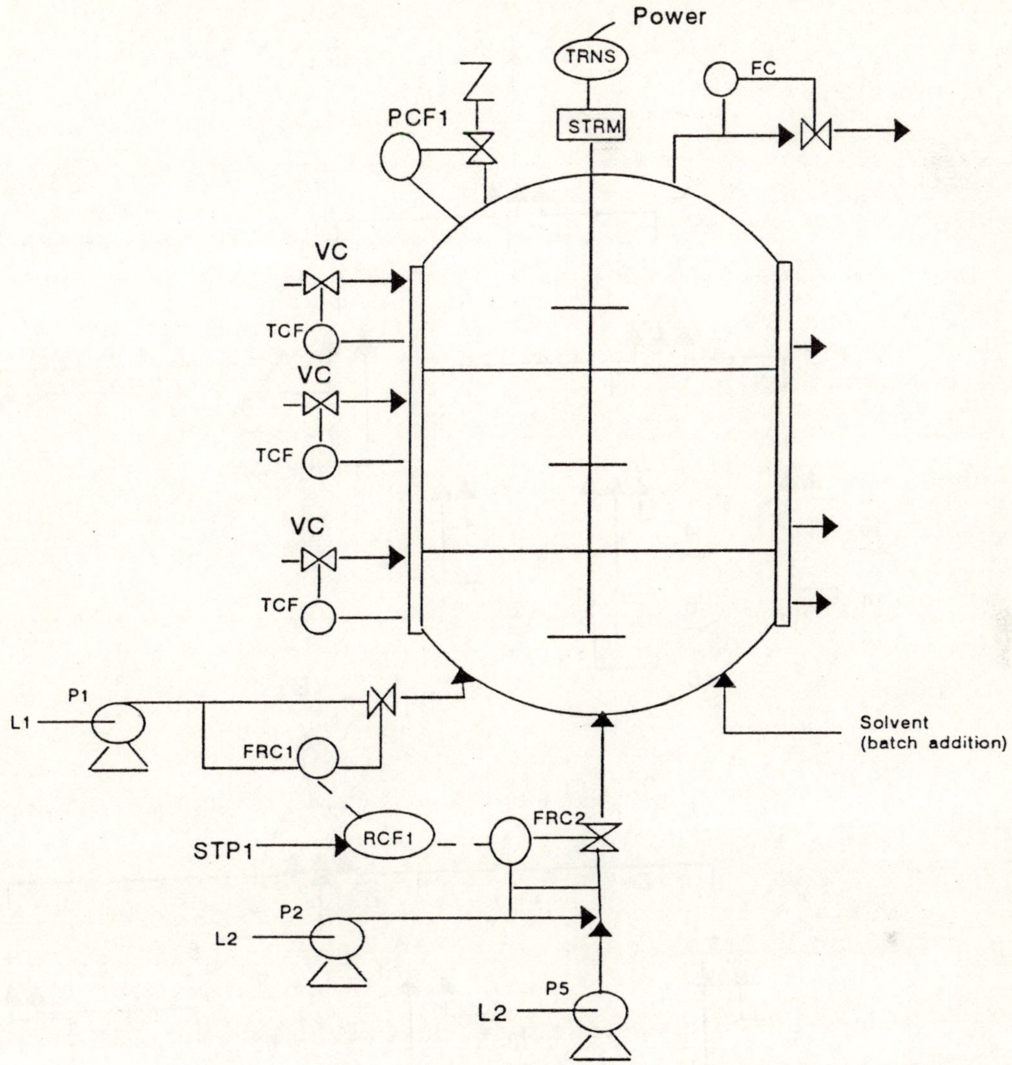

Figure 8. Schematic diagram of sulfonation reactor

REFERENCES

1. Beckjord, E S, Cunningham, M A, and Murphy, J A, (1993). Probabilistic safety assessment development in the United States 1972-1990, *Reliability Engineering & System Safety*, **39**, 159-170.

2. Bossche, A, (1991). Computer Aided Fault tree synthesis; system modelling and causal trees I,II,III real time fault location, *Reliability Engineering and System Safety*, **32 and 33**, 217-241, 1-21, 161-176.

3. Camarinpoulous, L and Yllera, J, (1985). An improved top-down algorithm combined with modularisation as a highly efficient method for fault tree analysis, *Reliability Engineering,* **11** (2), 93.

4. CCPS (1989). Guidelines for technical management of chemical process safety, Centre for chemical process safety , *AIChE,* New York.

5. Doelp, L C, Lee, G K, Linney, R E, and Ormsby, R M, (1984). Quantitative fault tree analysis: gate-by-gate method. *Plant/Operations Progress,* **3**, 227.

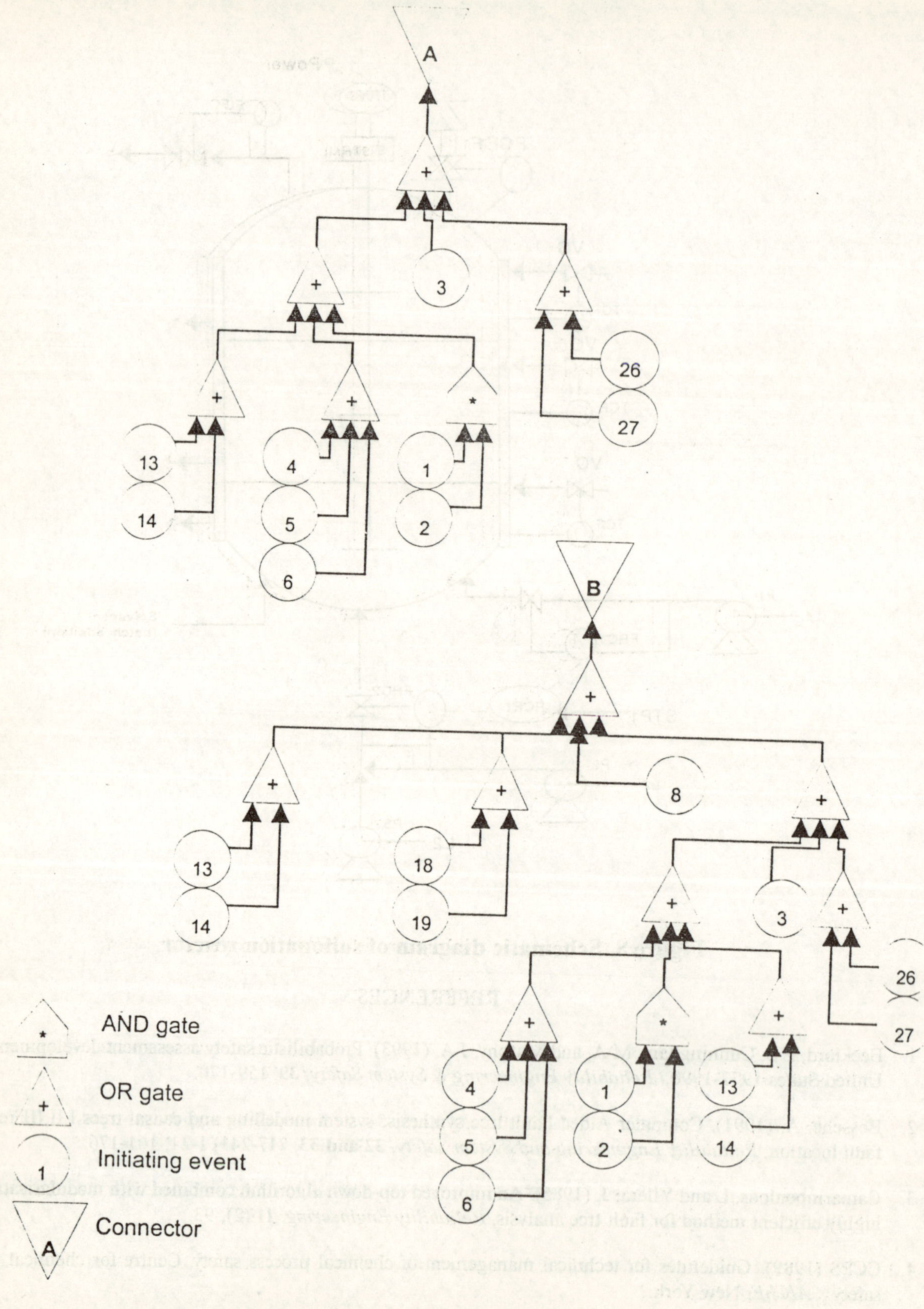

Figure 9. Simplified fault tree diagram for explosion in sulfonation reactor

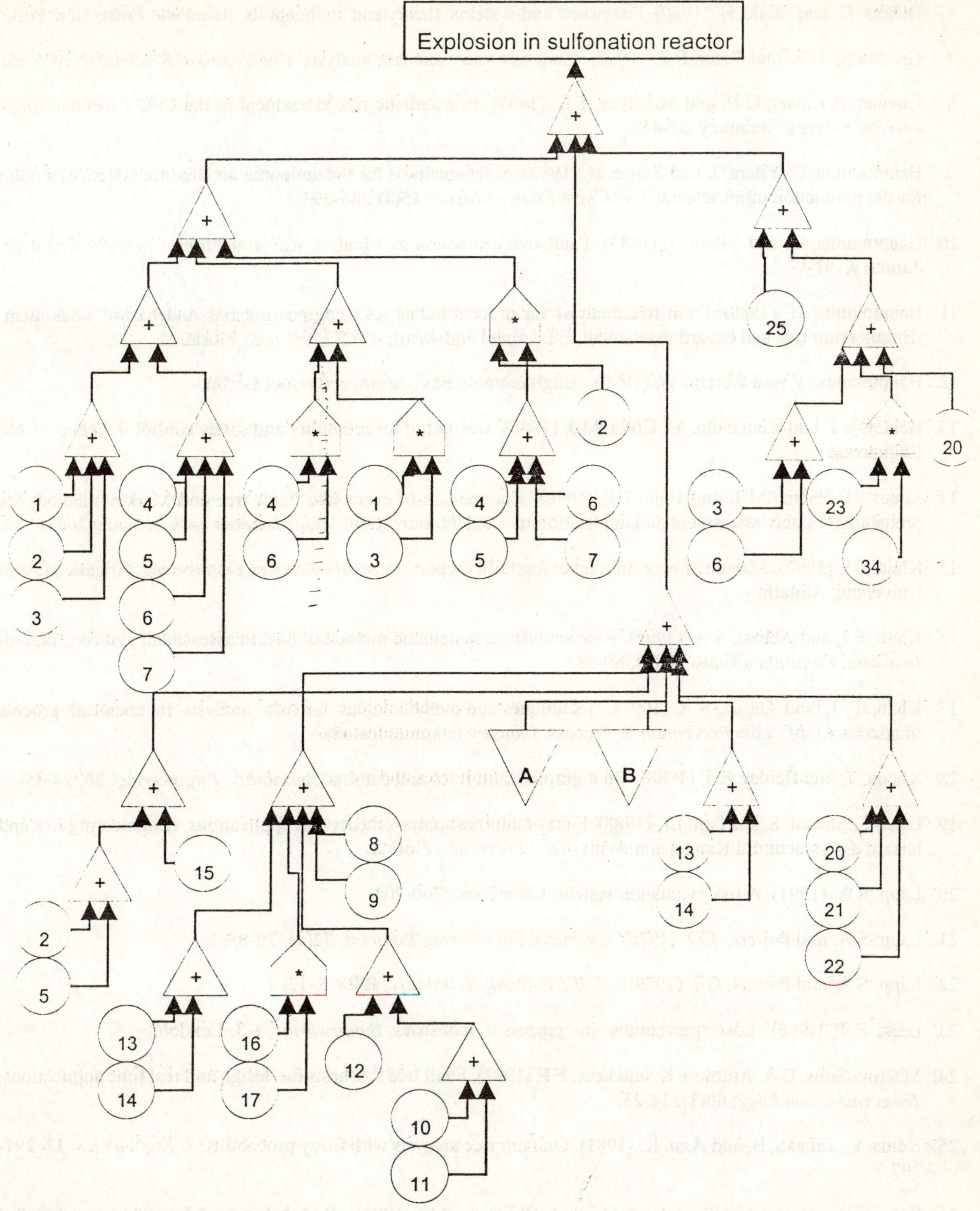

Figure 9. (continue)

6. Dubois, D, and Prade, H, (1980). Fuzzy sets and systems: theory and applications, *Academic Press*, New York.

7. Greenberg, H R, and Slater, B B, (1992). Fault tree and event tree analysis, *Van Nostrand Reinhold*, New York.

8. Guymer, P, Kaiser, G D, and Mckelvey, T C, (1987). Probabilistic risk assessment in the CPI, *Chemical Engineering Progress*, **January**, 37-45.

9. Hauptmanns, U, Yllera, J, and Sastre, H, (1982). Safety analysis for the ammonia air mixture system of a plant for the production of nitric acid, *J. of Chem Engg of Japan*, **15**(4),286-293.

10. Hauptmanns, U, and Yllera, J, (1983). Fault-tree evaluation by Monte-Carlo simulation, *Chemical Engineer*, **January,** 91-97.

11. Hauptmanns, U, (1988). Fault tree analysis for process industries : engineering risk and hazard assessment, (Engineering risk and hazard assessment, Ed:Kandel and Avni), *CRC Press Inc.*, Florida.

12. Hauptmanns, V, and Werner, W, (1990). 'Engineering Risks', *Springer-Verlag*, Berlin,

13. Henley, E J, and Kumanoto, M, Cliffs, M J, (1985). Designing for reliability and safety control, *Printice - Hall*, Englewood.

14. James, H, Harris, M J, and Hall, S F, (1992). Comparison of event tree, fault tree and Markov methods for probabilistic safety assessment and application to accident mitigation, *Major hazards onshore and offshore*, 59.

15. Khan, F I, (1992). Manufacture of Sulfolane: feasibility report, *Dept. of Chemical Engineering*, Aligarh Muslim University, Aligarh,

16. Khan, F I, and Abbasi, S A, (1995). Risk analysis: a systematic method of hazard assessment and control, *J of Industrial Pollution Control*, **11**(2), 89-98.

17. Khan, F I, and Abbasi, S A, (1997). Techniques and methodologies for risk analysis in chemical process industries, *J of Loss Prevention in Process Industry* (communicated).

18. Khoda, T, and Henley, E J, (1988). On digraphs, fault trees and cut sets. *Reliability. Engineering*, **20**, 24-35.

19. Lai, F S, Shenoi, S, and Fan, LT, (1988). Fuzzy fault tree analysis theory and applications, (Engineering risk and hazard assessment, Ed:Kandel and Avni), *CRC Press Inc.*, Florida.

20. Lapp, S A, (1991). A risk evaluation system, *ChemTech.*, 700-704.

21. Lapp, S A, and Powers, G J, (1976).,*Chemical Engineering Progress*, **72**(4), 79-89.

22. Lapp, S A, and Powers, G J, (1979)., *J IEEE Trans. Reliability*, **R-28**, 2-12.

23. Lees, F P, 1(996). Loss prevention in process industries, *Butterworths*, **1-3**, London.

24. Moetin - Solis, G A, Ardow, P K, and Lees, F P, (1982). Fault tree synthesis for design and real time applications, *Trans Inst Chem Engg*, **60**(1), 14-25.

25. Noma, K, Tanaka, H, and Asai, K, (1981). On fault tree analysis with fuzzy probability, *J. Ergonomics*, **17**, 291-297.

26. Papazoglou, I A, Nivoliantiou, A O, and Christou, M, (1992). Probabilistic safety analysis in chemical installation, *J Loss Prevention Process Industries*, **5**(3), 181-191.

27. Prugh, R W, (1981). Application of fault tree analysis, *Loss prevention*, **14**, 1-7.

28. Prugh, R W, (1992). Computer-aided Hazop and fault tree analysis, *J. Loss Prevention. Process Industries*, **5**, 3-14.

29. Rauzy, A, (1993). New algorithms for fault tree analysis, Reliability Engineering and System Safety, **40**, 203-211.

30. Shafaghi, A, (1988). Structure modelling of process systems for risk and reliability analysis, (Engineering risk and hazard assessment, Ed:Kandel and Avni), *CRC Press Inc.*, Florida.

31. Soon H. Chang, Joo Y. Park, and Myung K.Kim (1985). The Monte-Carlo method without sorting for uncertainty propagation analysis in PRA. *Reliability. Engineering*. **10**, 233.

32. Tanaka, H, Fan, L T, Lai, F S, and Toguchi, K, (1983). Fault tree analysis by Fuzzy probability, *IEEE Transactions on Reliability*, **R-32/51**, 453-456.

33. Taylor, J M, 1982. An algorithm for fault tree construction, *IEEE Trans Reliability*, **R-31**, 137-146.

34. Thangamani, K, (1992). Reliability of FCC unit using Monti-Carlo and direct simulation technique, *Reliability Engineering*, **68**, 125-136.

35. Vesely, W E, Goldberg, F F, Roberts, N H, Haas, D F, (1981). Fault tree handbook, *US Nuclear Regulatory Commission*, Washington, DC.

36. Vincoli, J W, (1993). Basic guide to system safety, *Nostrand Reinhold* , New York:.

37. Worrel, R B, and Stack, D W, (1990). 'A SETS user's manual for the fault tree analyst', **SAND77-2051**, Sandia Nat. Lab., Albuquerque, NM.

38. Yllera, J, (1988). Modularisation methods for evaluating fault tree of complex technical system, (Engineering risk and hazard assessment, Ed:Kandel and Avni), *CRC Press Inc*, Florida.

¨ Reproduced from *Chemical Engineering Progress*, USA

Part VI

Studies on Chain of Accidents (DOMINO EFFECTS)

In All the previous chapters we have dealt essentially with accidents occurring in one industry-or even more specifically one of the units in an industry- at a time. But very often accidents do not take place in isolation and an accident in a unit can be the cause of another accident in another unit which, in turn, may lead to a third accident....and so on.

In Part VI we present methodologies developed by us to study such domino effects or chain of accidents. Chapter 15 is a reproduction of a paper accepted for publication in Process Safety Progress. Chapter 16 is the manuscript of a paper presently under review with Environmental Modelling and Software.

15

MODELS FOR DOMINO EFFECT ANALYSIS IN CHEMICAL PROCESS INDUSTRIES*

In the risk assessment parlance, especially with reference to chemical process industries, the term domino effect is used to denote 'chain of accidents', or situations when a fire/explosion/missile/toxic load generated by an accident in one unit in an industry causes secondary and higher order accidents in other units. The multi-accident catastrophe which occurred in a refinery at Vishakhapatnam, India, on 14 September 1997, claiming 60 lives and causing damages to property worth over Rs 600 million, is the most recent example of the damage potential of domino effect. But, even as domino effect has been documented since 1947, very little attention has been paid towards modelling this phenomenon. In this paper, we have provided a conceptual framework based on sets of appropriate models to forecast domino effects, and assess their likely magnitudes and adverse impacts, while conducting risk assessment in a chemical process industry. The utilizability of the framework has been illustrated with a case study.

Key words: domino effect, chain of accidents, risk analysis, industrial safety, consequence analysis.

INTRODUCTION

The biggest industrial accident of the 1990s - the 'HPCL Disaster' (also known as 'The Vishakhapatnam Disaster') which occurred on 14 September 1997 at the HPCL (Hindustan Petroleum Corporation Limited) refinery near the city of Vishakhapatnam, India, has brought into sharp focus the destructive potential of domino effect vis a vis industrial accidents. It was this effect (also variously called 'cascading effect' or 'chain of accidents') which was responsible for a single failure in the HPCL refinery with limited damage potential to escalate into a series of major accidents, eventually claiming over 60 lives, causing damage to property worth over Rs 600 million ($ 20 million), and terrorising a sprawling city of over 2 million inhabitants (Hindu, 1997).

On 14 September 1997 one of the eight Horton spheres, filled with LPG/crude/kerosene and situated near the main gate of the HPCL refinery, caught fire at 6.40 a.m. It then exploded (Figure 1) rocking the entire city and making people think they have experienced an earthquake. The second sphere exploded 15 minutes later and before noon the others also caught fire. The tanks were all full, with crude imports unloaded at the HPCL berth just a few days ago. Fire spread all over the place. People, particularly those living in the vicinity of the refinery, ran for their lives. As the refinery is located in a densely populated industrial belt with several other major industries nearby, a large number of people were directly affected by the happenings at HPCL. Huge tongues of flames and thick black smoke billowed into the sky and joined the hovering monsoon clouds. A sharp shower brought the soot down on the people who saw their white shirts turn black. The rain water flooding the roads was also black and murky.

---

* Reproduced from *Process Safety Progress, USA*

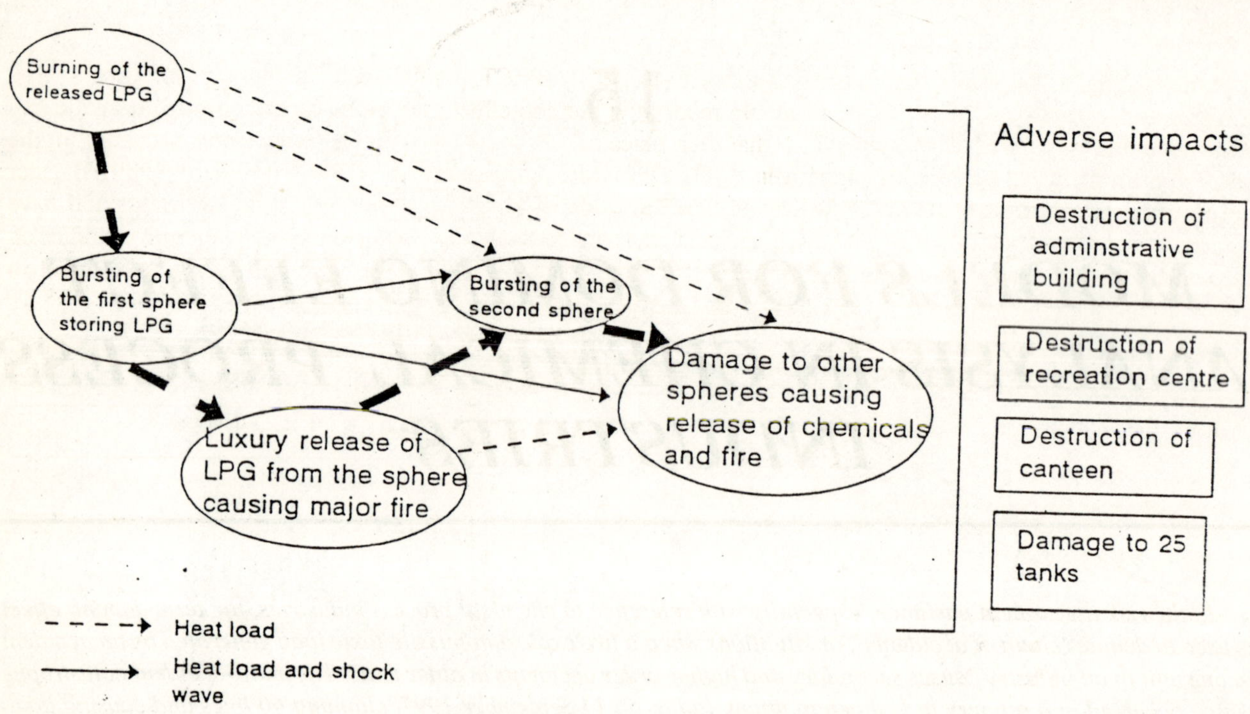

Figure 1. Most probable sequence of events leading to the HPCL's Vishakhapatnam disaster. Thickness of the lines represents the intensity of the heat load impact.

With both the entrances to the refinery blocked by burning tanks, neither the fire tenders nor the officials could enter the premises for several hours. Only when the contents in the tanks were burnt out could they venture in.

It rained again later in the evening preceded by strong winds when the flames lingered low and closer to the ground. This again created panic among the public but soon more rain poured down to provide some relief.

The death toll which eventually crossed 60 would have been higher had the fire started half-an-hour later than it did, when the first shift staff would have come in to relieve the night shift. And Sunday being a holiday, the administrative personnel, who numbered over 200, were saved as they were not on duty (Hindu,1997).

The deep scars on the psyche of the Vishakhapatnam residents that this series of accidents have left can be gauged from what happened 9 days after the catastrophe. A loud sound created by some innocent activity near a naphtha tank in the HPCL confines,, on 23 September 1997 generated such a panic that workers on duty nearby fled from the scene asking safety personnel of HPCL to raise an alarm which they promptly did. This only helped to spread more panic all over the refinery campus and soon the entire Vishakhapatnam city was gripped with fear. People residing near the refinery complex ran helter-skelter, schools abruptly closed down, shops downed shutters and the entire region was plunged into a war-like situation.

Even as the HPCL's Vishakhapatnam disaster is one of the biggest industrial disaster involving domino effect, it is neither the first instance of its type nor the worst ever. Well-documented instances of chain of accidents in chemical process industries have been occurring since 1940s; the worst such accident - in terms of death toll - had occurred in Mexico city on 19 November, 1984. The accident, which also involved petrochemicals claimed 650 lives (Pietersen, 1986). Table 1 presents an illustrative list of some of the major domino accidents that have occurred during the last 30 years.

MODELLING OF DOMINO EFFECTS

In-spite of the destructive potential of domino accidents, and the risk which many industries face from their likelihood all over the world, this phenomenon has received much lesser attention than other aspects of risk assessment.

A thorough scan of primary literature based on CD-ROM, INSPECT, and INDEX searches, as also direct search of books and journals, reveals that the available reports on domino effect are by-and-large confined to qualitative description and interpretations of the events that took place during some of the multiple accidents occurring in the past. For example Kletz (1985,1991), Pietersen (1986,1990), Mallikarajunan *et al.* (1988), Pritchard (1989), Bagster and Pitblado (1991), Prugh (1992), and Lees (1996) have described such past multiple accident events and have discussed the various possible ways in which one accident had led to another. The paucity of quantitative studies on this subject can be gauged from the fact that the 3500-page magnum opus by Lees (1996) on risk assessment in process industries contains barely two-page worth of material on domino effect.

Table 1. List of the important accidents involving domino effect (Lees, 1996)

Location	Chemical	Date	Deaths	Injury
Texas city, USA	Ammonium nitrate	April, 1947	552	3000
Nigata, Japan	Natural gas	June, 1964	3	
Feyzin, France	Propane	January, 1966	18	81
Texas city, USA	Butadiene	October, 1969	13	5
Crescent city, USA	Liquefied petroleum gas (LPG)	June, 1970	0	66
Beek, The Netherlands	Pressurized Naptha	November, 1975	14	104
Westwego, USA	Grain	December, 1977	36	10
Galveston, USA	Grain	December, 1977	15	5
Texas city, Texas	Liquefied petroleum gas (LPG)	November, 1978	7	10
Borger, USA	Light hydrocarbons	January, 1980	0	41
Livingston, USA	Petrochemicals	September, 1982	No details	
Mexico city, Mexico	LPG	November, 1984	650	6400
Antwerp, Belgium	Ethylene oxide	July, 1987	No details	
Antwerp, Belgium	Ethylene oxide	March, 1989	2	5
Pasadena, USA	Isobutane	October, 1989	23	103
Nagothane, India	Ethane and Propane	November, 1990	31	63
Bradford, UK	Azodiisobutyronitrile (AZDN)	July, 1992	No details	
Vishakhapatnam, India	LPG	September, 1997	60	

A rare quantitative study on domino effect has been reported recently by Latha *et al.* (1992). They have focused

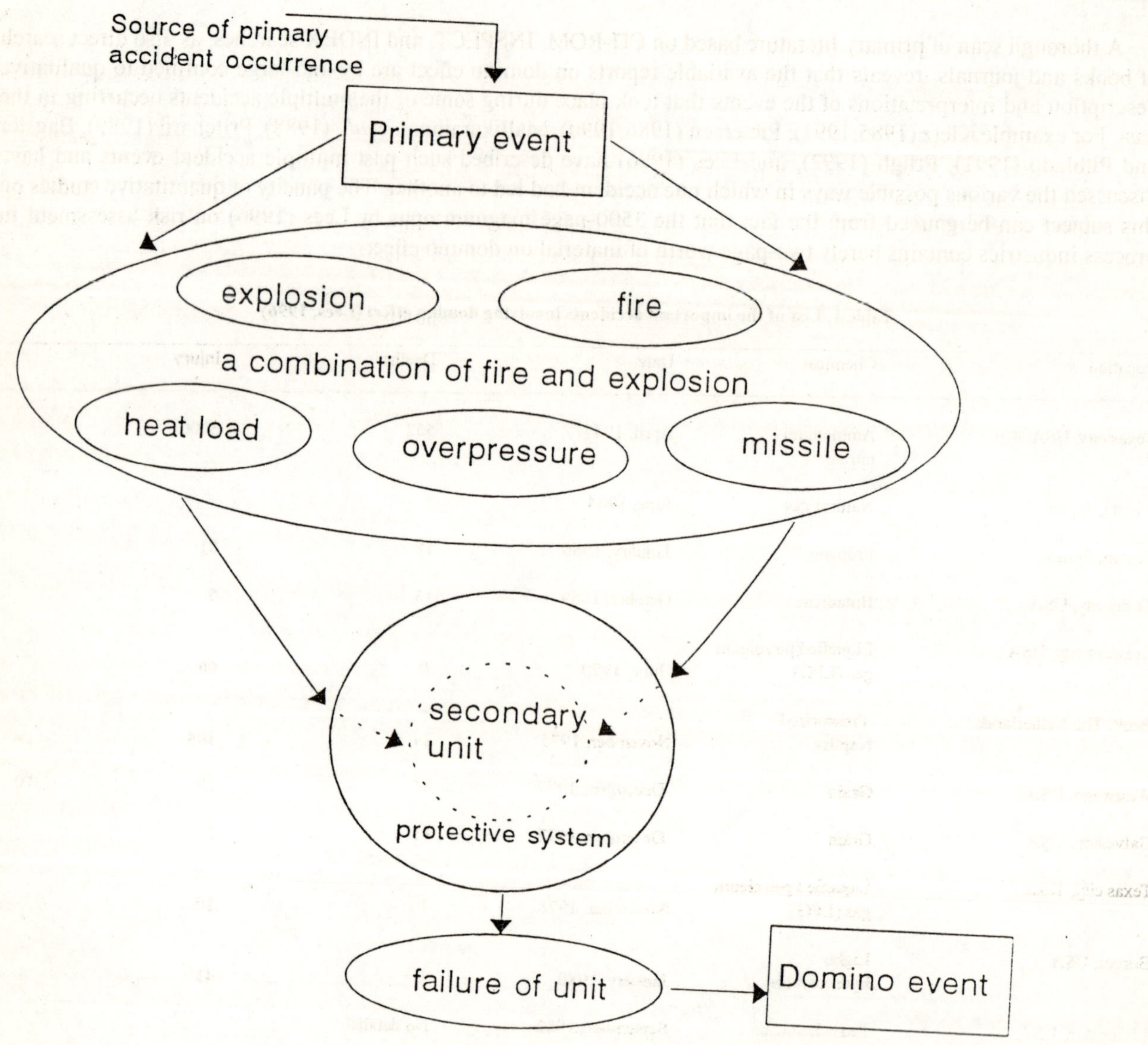

Figure 2. Process sequence in a typical domino event

on chain of accidents initiated by fire and have conceptualised various ways in which a fire can initiate domino effect. They have also tried to quantify the heat loads generated by various types of fires, the 'strengths' of the primary accidents thus caused, and the mechanisms by which heat load would disperse and cause vessel failures. But, useful as this work is, it is confined to only a few aspects of fire-related domino effects. Our careful study of past accidents has indicated that there can be several other accident events beside fires which can trigger a chain of accidents. Indeed some of the explosions are so powerful that they can simultaneously cause more than one chain of accidents to begin.

In this paper we have a) catalogued various types of events which can initiate domino effect, b) presented models for analysing and assessing these events, and c) developed a framework for conducting domino effect analysis in chemical process industries. The applicability of the framework has been demonstrated with an illustrative case study.

EVENTS THAT CAN INITIATE DOMINO EFFECT

We have identified the following events which can trigger domino effect:

I. fire,

II. explosions :

A. blast waves,

B. missiles,

III. toxic release,

IV. simultaneous and interactive impacts of fire and explosion.

To assess the likelihood of occurrence of these events, and their damage potential, and to forecast whether domino effects would occur and in what sequence, deterministic models have to be used in conjunction with probabilistic analysis. The former type of models are useful in quantifying physical and chemical processes such as size of a leak, chemical release mode and rate, dispersion (including cloud formation), type of explosion and its intensity, heat/ missile/shock wave loads generated, etc. The latter type, which are based on careful recapitulation and analysis of past accidents, are needed to work out the probabilities of equipment failure, direction of missiles, direction of fire ball / toxic cloud movement etc.

While choosing the models and conducting analysis based on them one has to be conscious of the following:

a) the computed magnitudes of incident heat and shock-wave effects would have a measure of uncertainty;

b) the stress/strain patterns in vessels effected by fire or fire-explosion combinations would be complex and difficult to quantify with precision;

c) external and transient factors such as wind direction can play a major role;

d) simultaneous occurrence of heat and mass transfer, made complex by transient and rapidly changing nature and magnitudes of the initiating events such as fire due to leakage in a storage vessel, can contribute to the uncertainty.

A typical sequence of a domino accident which indicates the complexities associated with this phenomena, is given in Figure 2.

We now present brief reviews of the events which could initiate domino effects vis a vis accidents in chemical process industries.

Fire as initiating event

Fire is a result of uncontrolled oxidation of chemical in the presence of air liberating heat. Fire in a unit generates heat load, which may be large enough to overcome the creep of the material of construction of the nearby units or build up high pressure in the nearby units due to boiling/heating of the chemicals contained in them. Important aspects of modelling domino effects due to fire include prediction of flame heights, flame merging phenomena in fires in close proximity, the effect of wind on flame tilt and length, and heat load.

Fire is among the most common accident that occurs in chemical industries; it is estimated that fire of large or small magnitude occurs at least once a year. There is considerable possibility that one among ten fires can generate heat load large enough to precipitate a significant accident. Study of past accidents indicates that the affects of major fires are significant upto a distance of 200 m from their point of origin (Kletz, 1983; Roberts, 1983; Kayes, 1986; Davies, 1993; Prugh, 1994) while the spacing between hazardous units is generally kept between 50 to 150 m. It thus becomes very important to model the phenomena of heat load effecting a nearby unit. Several factors would play

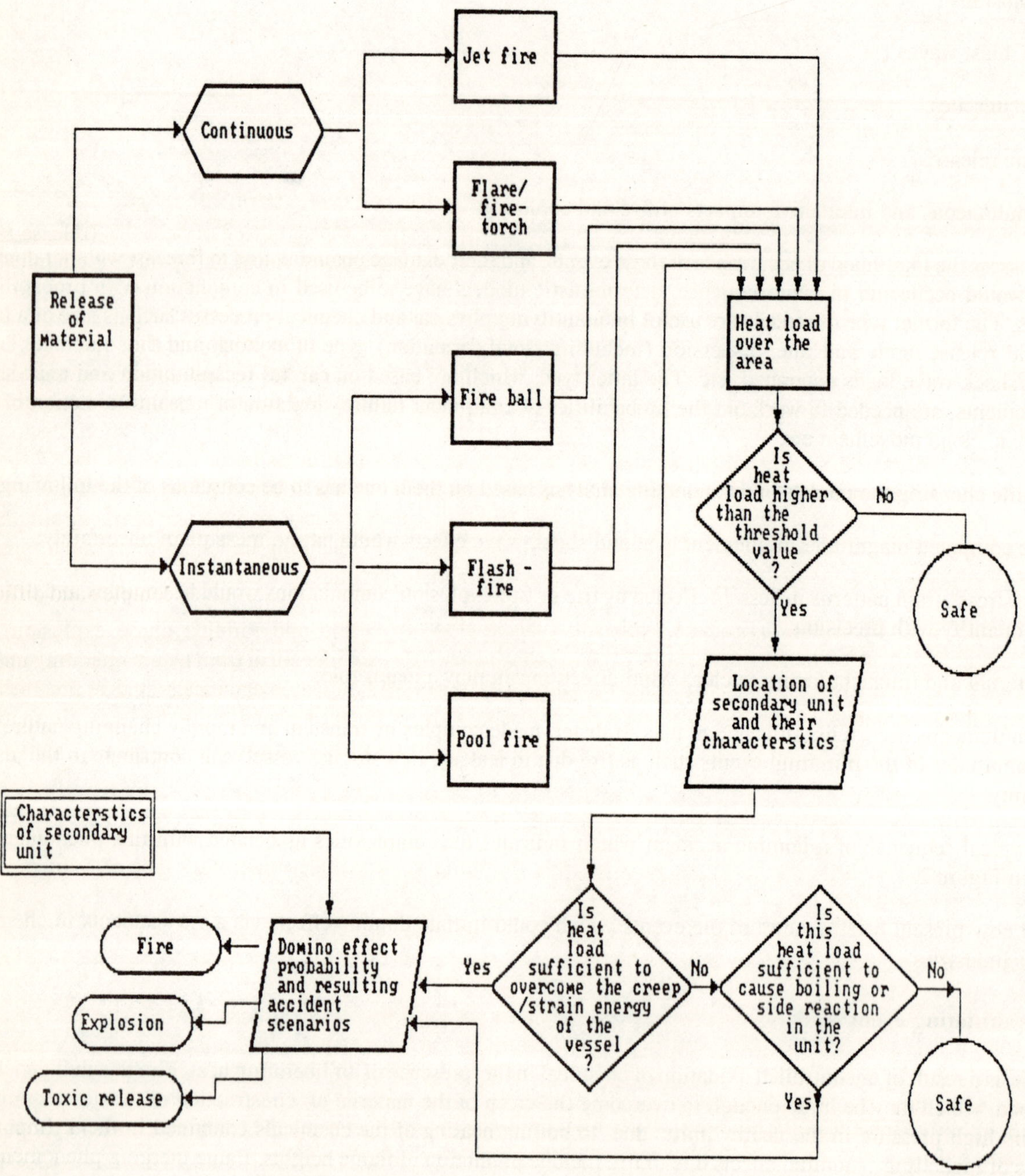

Figure 3. Domino effect model for fire as initiating event

important roles including atmospheric conditions (which would determine the direction of maximum flux and rate of heat loss), flame geometry, position and orientation of the receiving unit, the nature and state of chemical contained in the receiving (target) unit etc.

A conceptual model of domino effect triggered by a fire is presented in Figure 3. The following combination of events can be initiated by a fire.

fire - explosion - release of chemical ...

fire - release of chemical - fire ...

fire - flammable chemical release - explosion - ...

fire - toxic release ...

Which of these combinations would actually occur, would depend upon the source characteristics (release rate, atmospheric conditions, release conditions, etc.) as well as target characteristics (location, operation, chemical in use, etc.).

The severity of fire in terms of heat load is a function of type of release, flammability and the quantity of the chemical involved, strength of ignition source, and finally the type of fire. For example - flash fire and fire ball have higher damage potential compared to pool fire and jet fire for the same chemical and the same quantity. However, the occurrence of particular type of fire event is fully dependent on the release mode, type of operation, operating conditions and mode/strength of ignition source. The anatomy of industrial fire has been discussed by Roberts (1983), CCPS (1989), Pietersen (1990), Prugh (1994), and Lees (1996). Experimental studies (Eisenberg, 1975; Considine, 1984) have suggested that a heat load of 37 kW/m^2 is sufficient to cause damage in other installations operating under normal (atmospheric) operating conditions. If a unit is operating under extreme conditions of temperature and pressure, the fire makes the unit even more vulnerable to failure.

In general, fire is very likely to produce explosion (vapour cloud explosion and rarefied phase explosion) in units handling liquefied flammable gases under high pressure, cause release of chemical from a unit operating under normal conditions, and cause flash fire/fire ball in a unit dealing with flammable chemicals under pressurised conditions. These scenarios can be further refined by detailed analysis of operating conditions and such information as material of constructions of unit, capacity of unit, orientation of the unit, existing heat load etc.

Explosion as initiating event

Next to fire, explosion is the event more capable of initiating domino effect than other type of failures in a chemical process industry.

The explosion process

An explosion is a sudden and violent release of energy. In chemical process industries, the energy thus released may be chemical or physical; the destructive potential of an explosion depends on the rate at which the energy is released.

Examples of the violent release of physical energy are the explosion of a vessel due to high gas pressure and the sudden rupture of a vessel due to brittle fracture. Thermal energy is also very important in this context - it often creates the conditions for an explosion rather than being a direct source of energy for the explosion itself. In particular, thermal energy may lead to superheating of a liquid under pressure which in turn would cause flashing off of the liquid if it is let to come down to atmospheric pressure.

Certain types of chemical reactions may release energy large enough to cause explosion. For example, explosion may be caused by a violent release of chemical energy in a vessel due to combustion of flammable gas or decomposition of reaction products in a runaway chemical reaction.

An explosion in a vessel due to chemical reaction tends to be 'uniform' while similar reaction in a long pipe gives a 'propagating' explosion.

Deflagration and detonation

Combustion of flammable gas may lead to two kinds of explosions: deflagration or detonation. In a deflagration, the flammable mixture burns relatively slowly. For hydrocarbon-air mixtures the deflagration velocity is typically of the order of 1 m/s.

In a detonation, the flame front travels as a shock wave followed closely by a combustion wave which releases the energy to sustain the shock wave. The detonation front may reach velocities of the order of the velocity of sound and the hot products of combustion may have supersonic velocities. For hydrocarbon-air mixtures the detonation velocity is typically of the order of 2000-3000 m/s.

Detonation generates greater pressures and is more destructive than a deflagration. But, a deflagration may turn into a detonation, particularly when travelling down a long pipe. Where a transition from deflagration to detonation is occurring, the deflagration velocity naturally exceeds that quoted above.

Shock / blast waves

The damaging impact of explosions besides missiles is caused by shock wave, or blast wave. Blast wave generates overpressure which may injure people and damage equipment and buildings. The anatomy of blast waves and their damaging effects have been discussed by Maurer (1977), Baker *et al.* (1983), Martinsen *et al.* (1986), Medard (1989), Prugh (1991), Greenbook (1992), Cates and Samuels (1993), Venerate *et al.* (1993), Van den Berg and Lennoy (1993), and Davies (1993),

An explosion in air is accompanied by a very rapid rise in pressure leading to the formation of a shock wave. Such wave always travels outwards (from the epicentre of the explosion) with the higher pressure parts moving at higher velocities. After it has travelled some distance, the shock wave reaches a constant limiting velocity which is greater than the velocity of sound in the air, or in the unburned gas, as in the case of a vapour cloud. The shock wave has a profile in which the pressure rises sharply to a peak value and then gradually tails off. As the shock wave travels outwards the peak pressure at the shock front falls.

At some distance from the explosion centre , the region of positive pressure, or overpressure, in the shock wave, is followed by a region of negative pressure, or under pressure. The underpressure is quite weak and does not exceed above 4 psi.

The peak overpressure p^o, given by the Friedlander equation (Davies, 1993), is related to overpressure at different instants after explosion:

$$p = p^o(1-t/td)\exp(-\alpha t/td) \quad (1)$$

Where p is overpressure, po is the peak overpressure, t is the time, td is the duration time and α is the decay parameter.

A study of past accidents (Clancey, 1972; Eisenberg *et al.* 1975; Pietersen, 1986; Prugh, 1991; Davies; 1993; Khan and Abbasi, 1996b) suggests that an over pressure of 0.7 atm is necessary to cause damage and fatality. In industrial explosions, this order of overpressure is observed over a distance of several hundred meters.

Based on careful studies of past industrial accidents and considering such factors as properties of materials used in the construction of the equipment and the mechanisms of material failure these authors believe that the probabilities of an explosion causing a secondary accident is as much a function of the characteristics of target units, such as material of construction, chemical involved, degree of conjunction, operating conditions, etc., as it is of the overpressure/blast wave (Figure 4). Once we take this into consideration, it would appear that domino effect may occur even when overpressure is less than 0.7 atm if the secondary unit has been weakened in any manner due to corrosion, creep, or fatigue. Recent reports of the continuing post-mortom of the HPCL's Vishakhapatnam disaster (Shankar, 1997), have implicated corrosion as being the prime cause behind the primary accident (vessel failure)

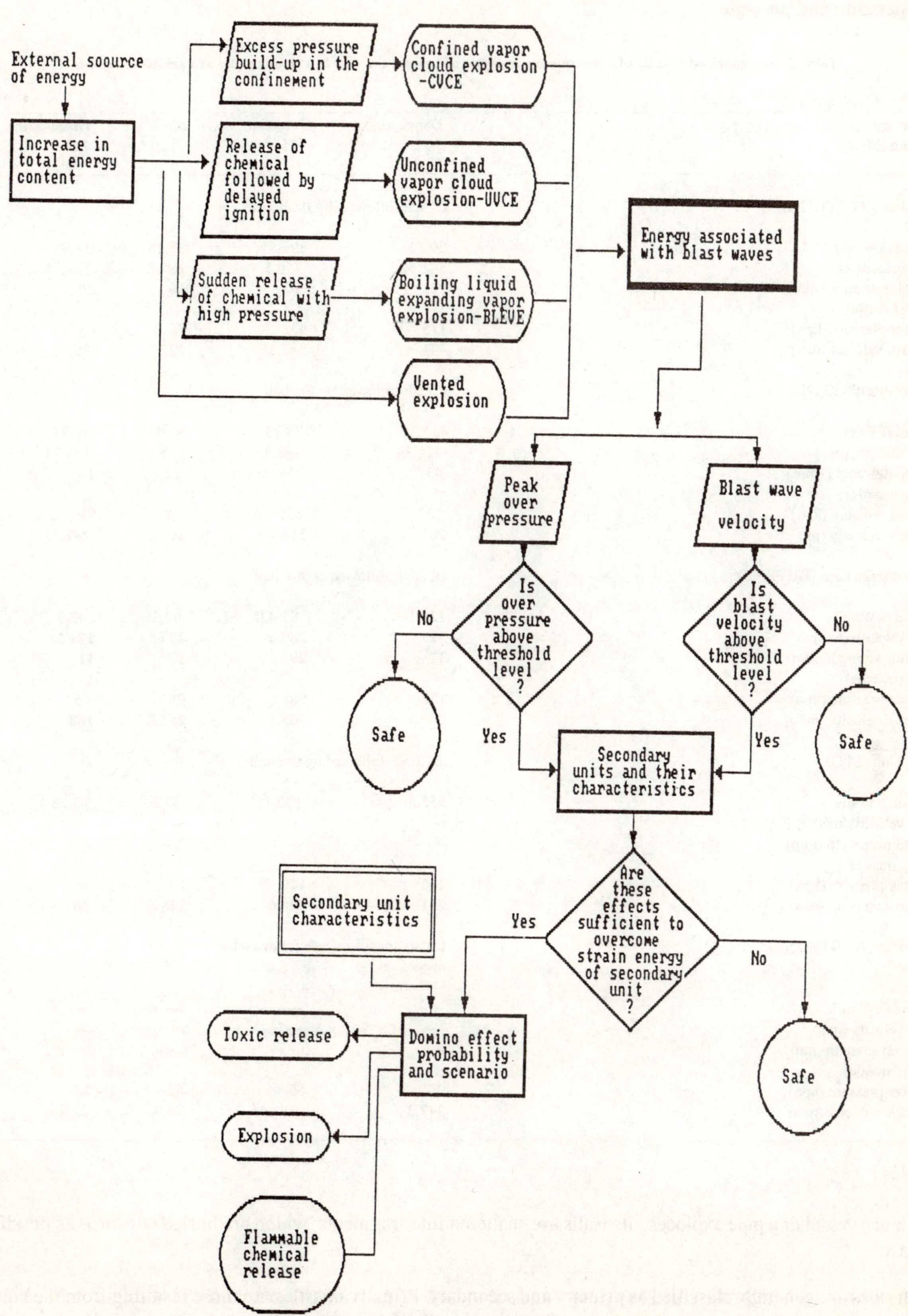

Figure 4. Domino effect model for blast wave as initiating event

leading to domino effect. However, the value of 0.7 atm as the lower limit of damaging overpressure is a useful index because this level of overpressure if reached, would damage an otherwise 'fit' unit operating under normal conditions of temperature and pressure.

Table 2. Summarized results of consequence analysis of primary event in various units at various locations

Unit/Scenario Damaging Effect	Damaging `50	Potential ` `75	at `100	`Distance(m) `125
LDPE plant (ETHYLENE) :	CVCE followed by flash fire			
Heat load (kW/m)	50.55	39.35	27.15	18.73
Missile Velocity (m/s)	341.52	250.1	185.3	138.75
Penetration strength (mm) (for 3 kg missile)	32	24	16	10
Peak Over pressure (kpa)	115	95	75	63
Blast wave velocity (m/s)	471	347.3	222.2	162.6
PP Plant (PROPYLENE) :	CVCE followed by fire ball			
Heat load (kW/m)	115.32	78.23	51.4	39.71
Missile Velocity (m/s)	421.31	348.45	215.3	158.31
Penetration strength (mm) (for 3 kg missile)	43	35	22	14
Peak Over pressure (kpa)	157	129	98	79
Blast wave velocity (m/s)	757	514.2	368.1	247.3
General storage farm (BUTENE):	BLEVE followed by fire ball			
Heat load (kW/m)	128.1	85.42	60.3	42.5
Missile Velocity (m/s)	399.4	287.5	197.1	121.5
Penetration strength (mm) (for 3 kg missile)	37	29	17	11
Peak Over pressure (kpa)	132	98	78	65
Blast wave velocity (m/s)	648.3	368.1	235.2	188.1
Cracker Unit (LPG) :	BLEVE followed by fire ball			
Heat load (kW/m)	155.5	133.1	87.55	73.23
Missile Velocity (m/s)	---	---	---	---
Penetration strength (mm) (for 3 kg missile)	---	---	---	---
Peak Over pressure (kpa)	145	110	81	68
Blast wave velocity (m/s)	701	455.6	287.6	204.4
Caustic Plant (CHLORINE) :	Instantaneous release followed by dispersion			
Heat load (kW/m)	---	---	---	---
Missile Velocity (m/s)	---	---	---	---
Penetration strength (mm) (for 3 kg missile)	---	---	---	---
Peak Over pressure (kpa)	95	65	42	35
Blast wave velocity (m/s)	347.3	188.1	76.6	27.4

Missiles

When a vessel or a pipe explodes, its walls are shattered into fragments, which are hurled outwards as missiles by the blast.

Missiles are generally classified as primary and secondary. Primary missiles are those resulting from the bursting of a containment so that energy is imparted to the fragments which become missiles. Secondary missiles occur due to the passage of a blast wave which imparts energy to objects in its path, turning them into missiles.

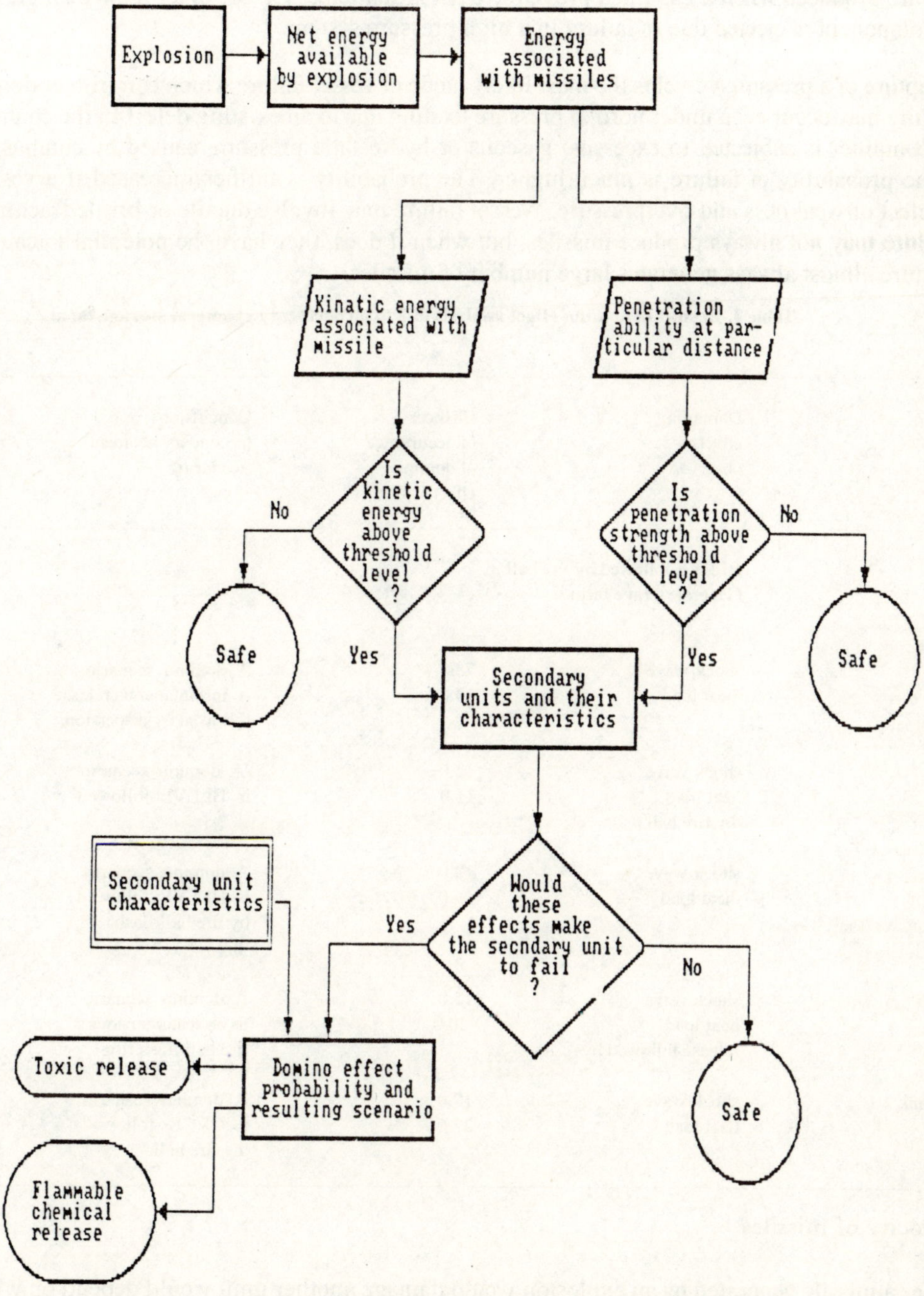

Figure 5. Domino effect model for missile effect as initiating event

Accounts of the source, types and generation of primary missiles include those of Bowen (1980), Porter (1980), Baker *et al.* (1983), and Lees (1996).

Primary missiles are generated in three ways: a) bursting of a vessel into a large number of relatively small fragments; b) separation and rocketing of a vessel or a vessel end; c) ejection of a single item.

The number of missiles formed in an explosion involving rupture of a containment varies widely. Large numbers of missiles are produced when a gas filled pressure vessel is shattered. On the other hand a single missile can result if a valve component is ejected due to failure in a high pressure system.

The rupture of a pressure vessel is the most likely mode of vessel failure which can trigger domino effect (Figure 5). The failure may occur even under normal pressure loading due to an existing defect in the container material. But when the container is subjected to excessive gaseous or hydrostatic pressure, caused by combustion or a runaway reaction, the probability of failure is much higher. The probability is further increased if a vessel is subjected to material defect or weakness and overpressure. Vessel failure may involve ductile or brittle fracture. (Bowen, 1980). Ductile failure may not always produce missiles, but when it does, they have the potential to cause severe damage. Brittle fracture almost always generates large number of missiles.

Table 3. Results of domino effect analysis due to an accident in General storage farm

Unit (Chemicals)	Damaging effects observed	Chances of occurrence of domino effect (%)	Conclusion (secondary accident scenario)	Net probability of occurrence (/yr)
Primary Event : (Butene)	BLEVE followed by fire ball in General storage farm			4.5E-05
Domino Effect :				
Caustic plant (Chlorine)	shock wave heat load	7.0 13.0	A domino scenario is instantaneous release followed by dispersion.	8.5E-06
PP Plant (Propylene)	shock wave heat load by fire ball.	12.0 11.0	A domino scenario is BLEVE followed	9.8E-06
LDPE plant (Ethylene)	shock wave heat load	12.0 15.0	A domino scenario is BLEVE followed by fire ball/flash fire.	1.1E-05
Cracker plant (LPG)	shock wave heat load release followed by	15.0 20.0	A domino scenario is an instantaneous fire ball/flash fire.	1.4E-05
2nd Butene tank (Butene)	shock wave heat load	17.0 23.0	A domino scenario is CVCE followed by fire ball.	1.6E-05

Initial velocity of missiles

Whether a missile generated by an explosion would damage another unit, would depend on whether the momentum of the missile would be high enough to induce failure in the target unit.

The initial velocity of a missile is a function of a) the force or pressure on the missile, b) the transfer of momentum to the missile, and c) the transfer of energy to the missile.

The force acting on a missile depends on the manner of its generation. In case of the rupture of a pressure vessel containing gas, the overpressure may occur due to a slow and gradual rise in pressure or due to a sudden rise as in an

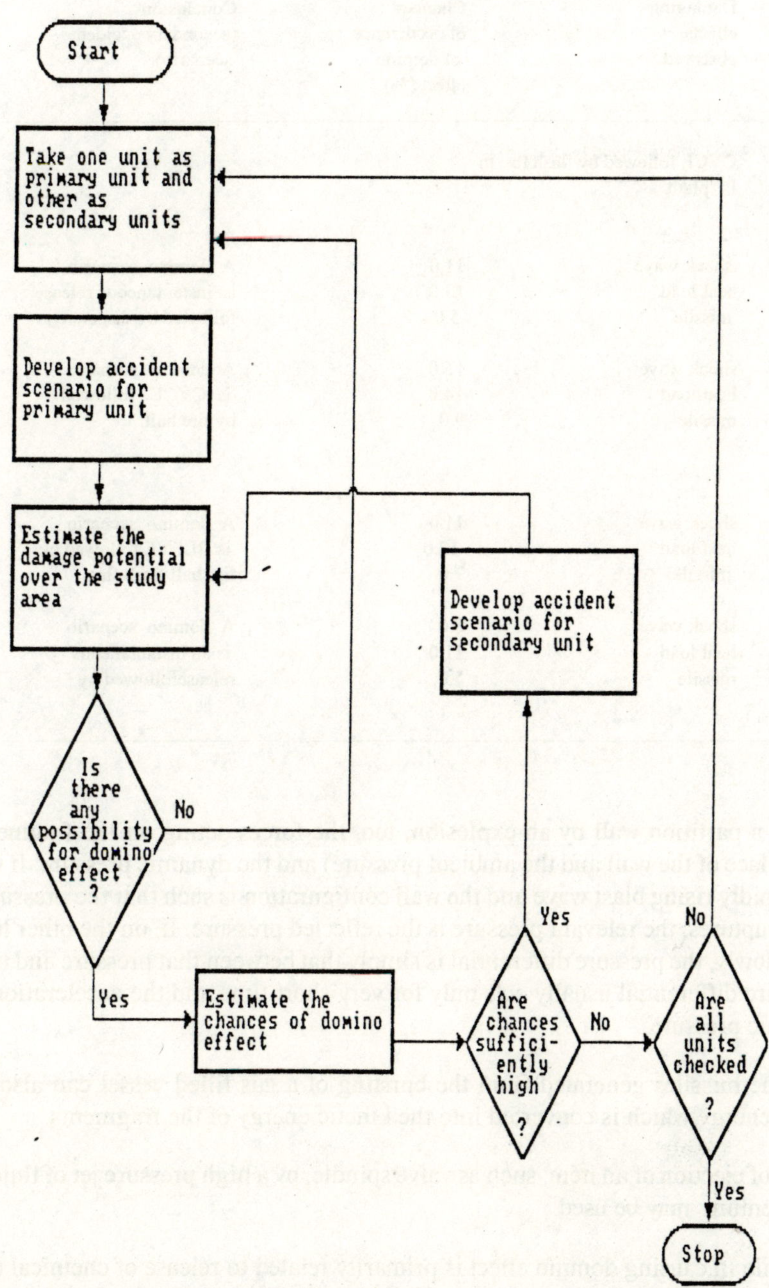

Figure 6. Procedure for domino effect analysis

explosion. Two types of forces act on the fragments to eject them from the vessel. One is the differential between the gas pressure and the ambient pressure. The other is the dynamic pressure, or wind. In practice, the pressure differential acts only for a very short time, and the acceleration of the fragments is essentially due to the dynamic pressure (Lees, 1996; Khan and Abbasi,, 1996b).

Table 4. Results of domino effect analysis due to an accident in PP plant.

Unit (Chemicals)	Damaging effects observed	Chances of occurrence of domino effect (%)	Conclusion (secondary accident scenario)	Net probability of occurrence (/yr)
Primary Event : (Ethylene)	CVCE followed by flash fire in PP plant			5.0E-05
Domino Effect :				
Caustic plant (Chlorine)	shock wave heat load missile	11.0 13.0 5.0	A domino scenario is instantaneous release followed by dispersion	1.3E-05
General storage (Butene)	shock wave heat load missile	15.0 14.0 9.0	A domino scenario is CVCE followed by fire ball.	1.7E-05
LDPE plant (Ethylene)	shock wave heat load missile	11.0 12.0 7.0	A domino scenario is BLEVE followed by fire ball/flash fire.	1.4E-05
Cracker plant (LPG)	shock wave heat load missile	8.0 11.0 5.0	A domino scenario is an instantaneous releasefollowed by	1.1E-05
fire ball/flash fire.				

In case of rupture of a partition wall by an explosion, too, the forces acting on the fragments are the pressure differential (between the face of the wall and the ambient pressure) and the dynamic pressure. If the pressure incident on the wall is that of a rapidly rising blast wave and the wall configuration is such that the pressure differential across it persists until the wall ruptures, the relevant pressure is the reflected pressure. If, on the other hand, the pressure on the wall rises relatively slowly, the pressure differential is simply that between that pressure and the ambient pressure. In either case, the pressure differential usually acts only for very short time and the acceleration of the fragments is mainly due to the dynamic pressure.

The momentum of the missiles generated from the bursting of a gas filled vessel can also be estimated as the fraction of the available energy which is converted into the kinetic energy of the fragments.

To estimate the force of ejection of an item, such as valve spindle, by a high pressure jet of fluid, an approach based on conservation of momentum may be used.

The impact of a missile in causing domino effect is primarily related to release of chemical (Pasman *et al.* 1992; Khan and Abbasi, 1996b; 1997) from the target vessel (Figure 5). However, in conjunction with other effects like blast wave or heat load it may load to explosion, or fire as well. An explosion may simultaneously cause blast wave, heat load, and missiles. Hence the probability of domino effect being caused by an explosion can be quite high eventhough the frequency of occurrence of explosion is lower than that of fire.

Toxic release as an initiating event

In 1995 a runaway plume of acrid gases exiting from a rubber processing factory at Pillaiyarkuppam, Pondicherry,

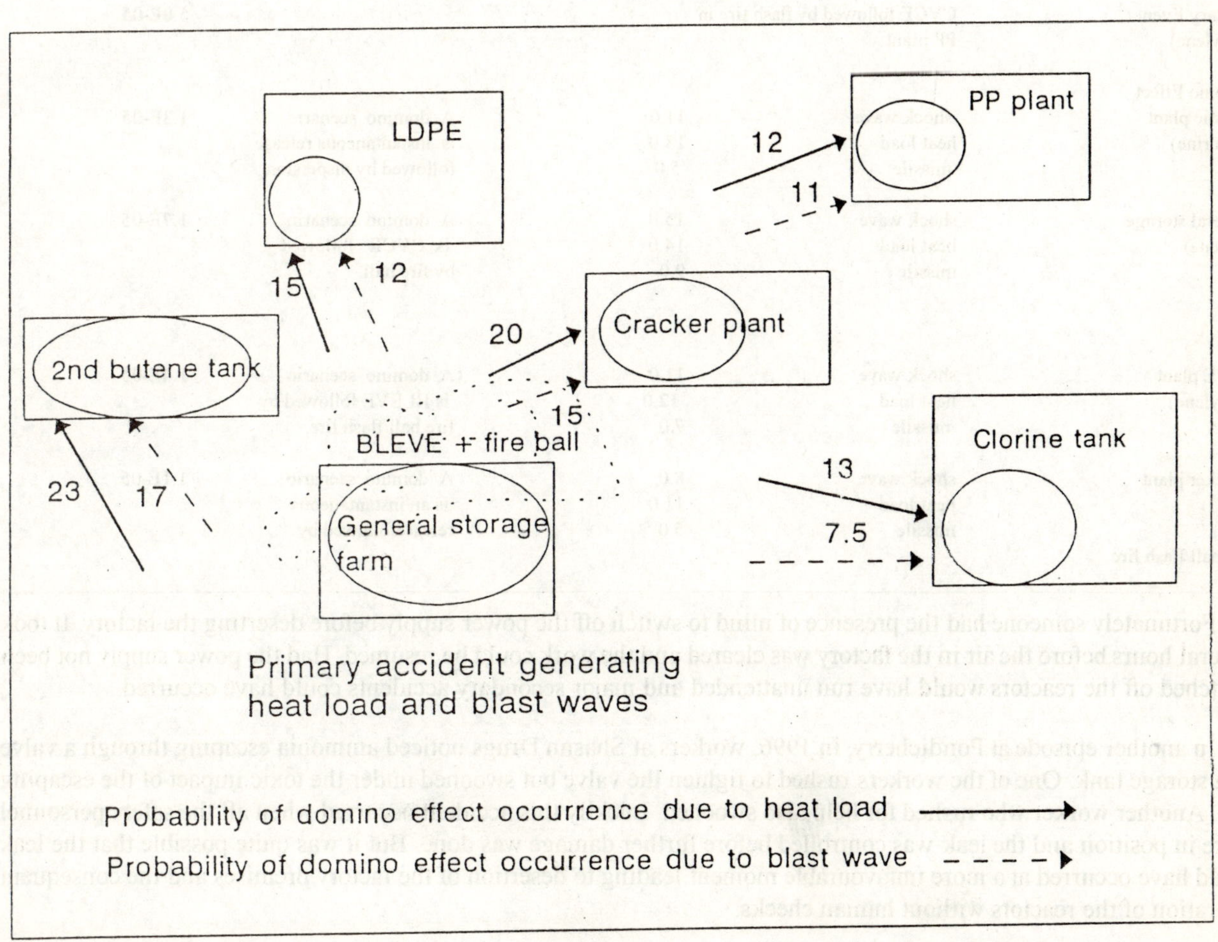

Figure 7. Simplified diagram showing locations of units and impact of primary accident (accident in butene tank) over other units.

India, plunged into a nearby unit engaged in making perfumes. The impact of the acrid plume made the workers in the factory cough and sneeze uncontrollably and when they began to choke, they ran out of the factory premises leaving the giant distillation units unattended.

Table 4. Results of domino effect analysis due to an accident in PP plant.

Unit (Chemicals)	Damaging effects observed	Chances of occurrence of domino effect (%)	Conclusion (secondary accident scenario)	Net probability of occurrence (/yr)
Primary Event : (Ethylene)	CVCE followed by flash fire in PP plant			5.0E-05
Domino Effect :				
Caustic plant (Chlorine)	shock wave heat load missile	11.0 13.0 5.0	A domino scenario is instantaneous release followed by dispersion	1.3E-05
General storage (Butene)	shock wave heat load missile	15.0 14.0 9.0	A domino scenario is CVCE followed by fire ball.	1.7E-05
LDPE plant (Ethylene)	shock wave heat load missile	11.0 12.0 7.0	A domino scenario is BLEVE followed by fire ball/flash fire.	1.4E-05
Cracker plant (LPG)	shock wave heat load missile	8.0 11.0 5.0	A domino scenario is an instantaneous releasefollowed by	1.1E-05
fire ball/flash fire.				

Fortunately someone had the presence of mind to switch off the power supply before deserting the factory. It took several hours before the air in the factory was cleared and the work could be resumed. Had the power supply not been switched off the reactors would have run unattended and major secondary accidents could have occurred.

In another episode at Pondicherry, in 1996, workers at Shasun Drugs noticed ammonia escaping through a valve of a storage tank. One of the workers rushed to tighten the valve but swooned under the toxic impact of the escaping gas. Another worker who rushed for help also swooned. Luckily this accident occurred when all the safety personnel were in position and the leak was controlled before further damage was done. But it was quite possible that the leak could have occurred at a more unfavourable moment leading to desertion of the factory premises and the consequent operation of the reactors without human checks.

Secondary accidents due to the harm caused by toxic release to supervisory staff have not been a common phenomena in the past. But increasing automation, as a consequence of which lesser number of persons are being deployed for supervising process controllers in an industry, toxic release can harm the supervisory personnel to the extent of making them ineffective thereby forcing a situation in which the processes run without human controls. Major chain of accidents can result in such situations. In developing countries like India, the extent of automation has increased but has not reached the stage common in developed countries where process control rooms are carefully constructed and located so as to minimise danger to them from likely accidents.

To quantify the probability of occurrence of domino effect due to the release of toxic chemicals, the following parameters need to be considered in addition to process details, PIDs, etc. required for all other type of initiating events:

i) control systems employed in the various units in the plant;

ii) detailed description of the human duties and their relative positions in the plant;

The probability of occurrence of domino effect due to this event is likely to be far lower than the other initiating events.

Table 6. Results of Domino effect analysis due to an accident in cracker unit

Unit (Chemicals)	Damaging effects observed	Chances of occurrence of domino effect (%)	Conclusion (secondary accident scenario)	Net probability of occurrence (/yr)
Primary Event : (LPG)	BLEVE followed by fire ball in Cracker unit			1.0E-04
Domino Effect :				
Caustic plant (Chlorine)	shock wave heat load	17.0 21.0	A domino scenario is BLEVE followed by dispersion.	3.4E-05
General storage (Butene)	shock wave heat load	19.0 25.0	A domino scenario is BLEVE followed by flash fire.	3.9E-05
PP Plant (Propylene)	shock wave heat load	13.0 17.0	A domino scenario is CVCE followed by fire ball/flash fire	2.8E-05
LDPE plant (Ethylene)	shock wave heat load	10.0 15.0	A domino scenario is CVCE followed by fire ball.	2.4E-05

Combination of initiating events

It has been revealed by various case studies (Kletz, 1985; Marshall, 1987; Raghavan and Swaminathan, 1996; Lees, 1996; Khan and Abbasi, 1995;1997) that a real-life industrial accident is more often than not a combination of different accidental events (explosion, fire and toxic release) rather than a single event. Therefore, in order to study domino effect, probabilities of occurrence of each type of event should be estimated and the final probability of occurrence of domino effect computed accordingly.

PROCEDURE FOR DOMINO EFFECT ANALYSIS (DEA)

As a first step towards DEA, a detailed consequence assessment should be conducted for the primary event (missiles, heat load, overpressure) at the location of secondary unit using latest models for studying the impact generated at the source of the primary event, directional probabilities (in case of missiles and fire jets), damage radii, scenarios of vessel failure etc. The sequence of steps to conduct such a domino effect analysis is presented in Figure 6. This procedure recommends use of computer software to conduct detailed consequence analysis. For this purpose, authors (Khan and Abbasi , 1996a) have developed a software package MOSEC (MOdelling and Simulation of Explosion in Chemical process industries). This software enables the detailed study of damaging characteristics of industrial fires and explosions. The software MOSEC incorporate four different models of explosion namely confined vapour cloud explosion (CVCE), unconfined vapour cloud explosion (UVCE), boiling liquid expanding vapour cloud explosion (BLEVE), and vented explosion. It also incorporates three models for fires, namely flash fire, pool fire, and fire ball. To estimate the damage potential most of these models use multi-energy method (Van den Berg and Lennoy, 1993).

In subsequent steps of DEA, the probability of occurrence of domino effect is estimated on the basis of the location, contents, orientation, and material characteristics of the likely target units. The analysis employs, *inter alia*, vessel failure and probit models (Clancey, 1972; Eisenberg *et al.* 1975; Pietersen, 1986; Greenbook, 1992; Davies, 1993; Lees, 1996; Khan and Abbasi, 1997). If the probability of occurrence of a 'hit' is sufficiently high then an accident scenario for the secondary accident is developed followed by an estimation of its damaging potential. This procedure is repeated till the full chain of likely accidents is covered.

To facilitate DEA we propose a two-tier sequence of studies.

Table 7. Results of domino effect analysis due to an accident in caustic plant

Unit (Chemicals)	Damaging effects observed	Chances of occurrence of domino effect (%)	Conclusion (secondary accident scenario)	Net probability of occurrence (/yr)
Primary Event : (Chlorine)	Instantaneous release followed by dispersion in Caustic soda plant			1.0E-06
Domino Effect : Cracker plant (LPG)	shock wave	3.0	Very low probability of LPG release followed by flash fire.	3.0E-08
General storage	shock wave	1.0	Very low probability of (Butene) butene release followed by flash fire.	1.0E-08
PP Plant (Propylene)	shock wave	7.0	A domino scenario may be propylene release followed by flash fire.	7.0E-08
LDPE plant (Ethylene)	shock wave	0.00	A domino scenario may be ethylene release followed byflashfire.	---

Level I study

In this section a screening is done in order to identify the units which may come under the spell of domino effect. For this purpose threshold values of different damaging effects reported in references Eisenberg *et al.* (1975), Clancey (1972),Pietersen (1986), Pasman *et al.* (1992), Lees (1996), and Khan and Abbasi (1997) are used. For example, it is reported that an overpressure of 0.7 atm can destroy a unit by blast wave impact, a heat load of 37 kW/m^2 is sufficient to induce vessel failure, and a missile (sharp edged) having a velocity higher than 75 m/s has sufficient potential to penetrate the target unit provided that it collides with the unit. If the estimated values of these parameters at the location of the target unit are higher than the threshold values, a detailed analysis or level II study is then performed.

LEVEL II study

At level II, more detailed analysis has to be conducted to verify the existence of domino effect, using the damage potential of the primary event and the characteristics of the secondary unit. The characteristics to be considered are:

- material of construction of the unit,
- process chemicals with operating conditions,
- quantities of chemicals in use,
- properties of the chemicals,

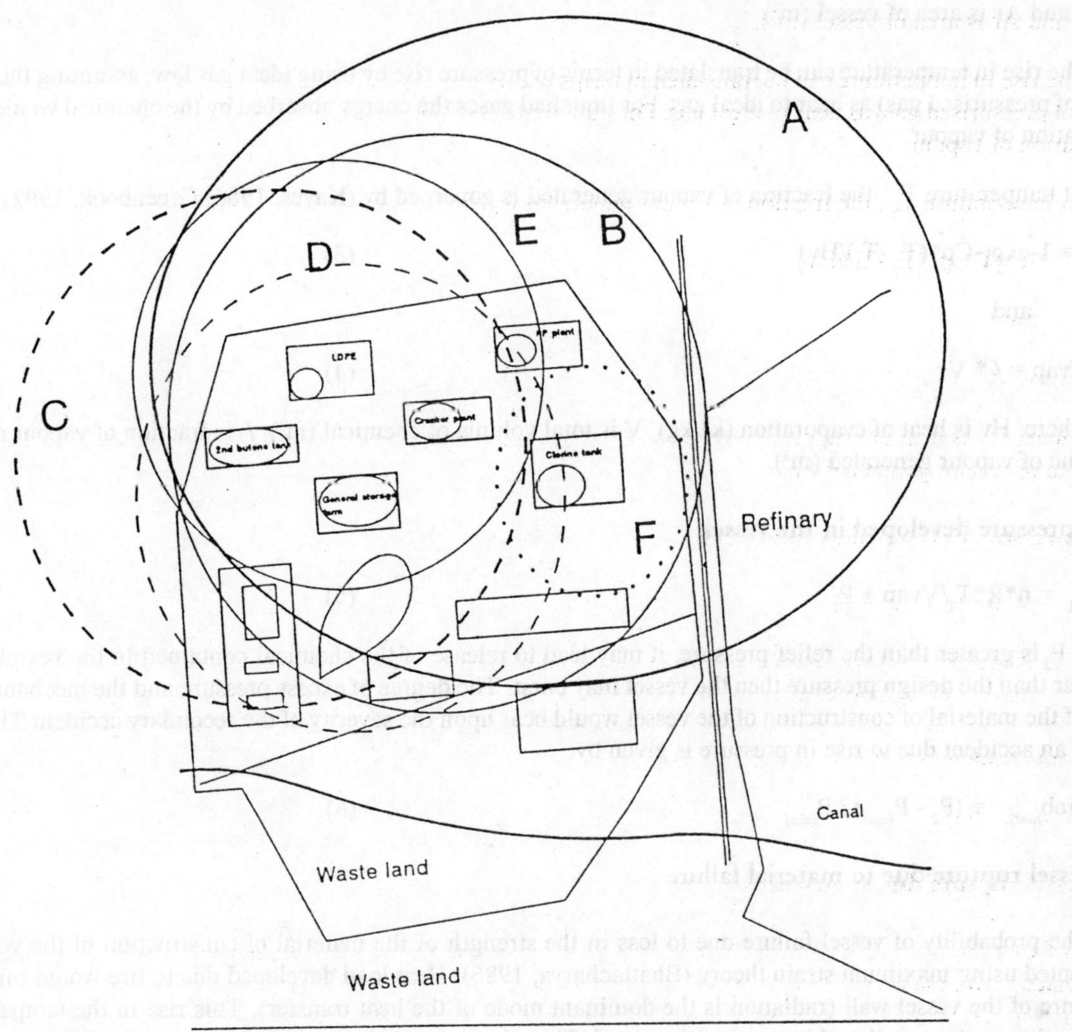

Figure 8. Plot showing severe risk contour due to PP plant (A), Cracker plant (B), General storage farm (C), 2nd butene tank (D), LDPE plant (E), and Chlorine storage vessel (F).

- location of the unit in terms of distance and degree of conjunction, and
- prevailing wind direction.

Using these characteristics and damage potential of primary event, the verification and probability estimation for a secondary event (domino effect) can be worked out as follows.

Heat load

Some 60% of the total heat radiation incident over a vessel would be absorbed by the vessel shell and the remaining 40% would be absorbed by the chemicals in the vessel to raise the temperature/pressure of the contents (Latha *et al.* 1992)

i) Vessel failure due to high pressure build-up

The probability of secondary accident due to heat absorbed by the chemical:

$$0.40*q*Ar = M* Cp *DT \qquad (2)$$

where, Cp represents specific heat of chemical (kJ/m^2/°C), DT is temperature difference, M is mass of chemical (kg), and Ar is area of vessel (m^2).

The rise in temperature can be translated in terms of pressure rise by using ideal gas law; assuming the content (in case of pressurised gas) as near to ideal gas. For liquefied gases the energy absorbed by the chemical would lead to the formation of vapour.

At temperature T_2, the fraction of vapour generated is governed by (Kayes, 1986; Greenbook, 1992).

$$f = 1-\exp(-Cp*(T_2 - T_1)/Hv) \quad (3)$$

and

$$Vvap = f * V \quad (4)$$

where, Hv is heat of evaporation (kJ/kg), V is total volume of chemical (m^3), f is fraction of vapour and Vvap is volume of vapour generated (m^3).

The pressure developed in the vessel:

$$P_2 = n*R*T_2/Vvap + P_1 \quad (5)$$

If P_2 is greater than the relief pressure, it may lead to release of the chemical contained in the vessel and if it is greater than the design pressure then the vessel may burst. The degree of excess pressure and the mechanical properties of the material of construction of the vessel would bear upon the severity of the secondary accident The probability of an accident due to rise in pressure is given by:

$$Prob_{heat2} = (P_2 - P_{relief}) / P_{relief} \quad (6)$$

ii) Vessel rupture due to material failure

The probability of vessel failure due to loss in the strength of the material of construction of the vessel can be computed using maximum strain theory (Bhattacharya, 1986). Heat load developed due to fire would raise the temperature of the vessel wall (radiation is the dominant mode of the heat transfer). This rise in the temperature will reduce the maximum allowable stress of the vessel. This phenomenon is quantified by using the following equations:

$$T_2 = [(\varepsilon*\sigma*T_{fire}^4 - q)/(\varepsilon*\sigma)]^{1/4} \quad (7)$$

In order to quantify the impact of temperature on the maximum allowable stress, these authors have developed an empirical equation taking into consideration a total of 15 common materials of construction over a wide range (50 to 1200°C) of temperature.

Eymax = *function* (temperature)

$$= 1*10^8 (1.858 - 0.0062*T_2 + 1.691E-05 * T_2^2 - 1.959E-08 * T_2^3) \quad (8)$$

Where, Eymax is maximum allowable stress in N/m^2 (property of the material of construction), and T is temperature in °C. The stress developed in the vessel due to rise in the internal pressure of the vessel is quantified using following equation (Bhattacharya,, 1986)

$$Ey = P_2 [(1-\gamma) + 2K (1+\gamma)]/(K^2-1) \quad (9)$$

Where, v denotes Poisson ratio, K denotes diameter ratio, P_2 is Pressure in the vessel in N/m^2.

Subsequently the probability of vessel failure due to failure of the material of construction is estimated as:

$$Prob_{heat2} = Ey_{max}/Ey \quad (10)$$

Finally the probability of secondary accident due to heat load is computed using the function;

$Prob_{heat} = Prob_{heat1} \cup Prob_{heat\,2}$ (11)

$Prob_{heat} = minimum[1, \{1-(1-Prob_{heat1})*(1-Prob_{heat2})\}]$ (12)

Blast load (overpressure)

When a blast wave developed due to an explosion hits an object, it causes a diffraction/drag type of impact. The likely damage due to such impact is measured by effective overpressure at the wave front.

$Pd = Cd * p^{o}$ (13)

$Pe = p^{o} + Pd$ (14)

Where,

Pd is dynamic pressure, p° is peak overpressure, and Cd is drag coefficient (= 0.1 for sphere, 1.2 for cylinder, 2.0 for square; Lees, 1996).

$Pr_{blast} = -23.8 + 2.92 * \ln Pe$ (15)

Using equations 15 and 16 (Pasman *et al.* 1992) the probability of damage due to explosion can be computed:

$Prob_{blast} = fr\ (Pr_{blast})$ (16)

Where *fr* represents probit function (function that transforms probit values to percent chance), and Pe is explosion pressure in Pa.

Missile load

The impact of missiles on the secondary units is assessed using three parameters:

i) **penetration strength, A:**

$Prob_A$=(penetration strength-thickness of vessel)/penetration strength (17)

ii) **impact energy, B:**

As reported by Davies (1993) and Lees (1996) about 40-50% of total impact energy is utilized in raising the temperature of the contents of the secondary unit. Hence

$1/4 * mf * vf^2 = M*Cp*DT$ (18)

$T_2 = T_1 + DT$ (19)

for gases $P_2 / P_1 = T_1 / T_2$ (20)

for liquefied gas $P_2 = n*R*T_2 / Vvap + P_1$, (21)

Where, Vvap = *f**V; *f* represents fraction of vapour, mf the mass of the fragment, and vf the velocity of the fragment.

$Prob_B = (P_2 - P_{relief}) / P_{relief}$ (22)

iii) **Probability of collision, C:**

The probability of a collision can be computed by dividing the volume of vessel by the total volume of the hemisphere of radius equal to distance between the units including diameter of the vessel.

$Prob_C$= volume of vessel/volume of hemisphere (23)

Thus the probability of domino effect due to the impacts of missiles can be computed as:

$$Prob_{missile} = (Prob_A) \cup (Prob_B) \cup (Prob_C) \quad (24)$$

$$Prob_{missile} = minimum\,[1,\{1-(1-Prob_A)*(1-Prob_B)*(1-Prob_C)\}] \quad (25)$$

Finally the probability of occurrence of domino effect will be the sum of the probabilities of each contributing event and can be estimated as;

$$Prob_{domino} = (Prob_{heat}) \cup (Prob_{blast}) \cup (Prob_{missile}) \quad (26)$$

$$Prob_{domino} = minimum[1,\{1-(1-Prob_{hea}t)*(1-Prob_{blast})*(1-Prob_{missile})\}] \quad (27)$$

$$Prob_{domino} = Prob_{domino} \cap Prob_{primary} = Prob_{domino} * Prob_{primary} \quad (28)$$

Where $Prob_{primary}$ represents probability of the primary event occurrence. The applicability of the scheme can be well understood with the help of a case study. Thus, we are presenting a case study of a petrochemical complex in coming section.

APPLICATION OF DEA - AN EXAMPLE

We now illustrate the use of the two-tier DEA procedure with reference to its application to a petrochemical complex situated at Ramgarh, India. It is a multi-product petrochemical industry engaged in the manufacture of low density polymer (LDP), high density polymer (HDP), caustic soda and other related products.

As a prelude to DEA, a screening was carried out of all the units for their hazard potential. This led to the identification of these five units as highly vulnerable units: general storage farm, cracker unit, poly propylene (PP) plant, low density poly ethylene (LDPE) plant, and caustic plant. The screening also helped to identify the five most hazardous chemicals: butene, liquefied petroleum gas (LPG), propylene, ethylene and chlorine. The most credible accident scenarios of the primary event were then developed for each unit and a detailed consequence analysis was carried out. The consequences of the primary event were then visualised at the secondary unit. The summary of the study is presented below.

Primary event : general storage farm (butene)

Butene is highly flammable and as it is stored in a liquid form, the most credible accident scenario visualised for this chemical is BLEVE followed by fire ball. The consequence analysis of this scenario, conducted using the software MOSEC, is presented in Table 2. Similar analysis for other units is also presented in Table 2. The potentiality of damage, if an accident occurs in this unit, to other units situated 50 to 100 meters away has been assessed. The resulting domino effects are described below.

Domino effect triggered by the primary event

Chlorine tank (caustic soda unit situated 70 meters away)

Level I study suggests moderate probability of domino effect due to shock wave and thermal effect.

Level II study verifies the same. The probability of domino effect occurrence due to blast waves is 7.5 % and due to heat load is ~13% (Table 3).

The scenario for the secondary accident has been visualised as a sudden release of chlorine. It is because large quantity of chlorine is stored in liquid form under high pressure, hence a leak or build-up of high pressure would cause the chemical to be released instantly. The resulting damage would be caused by toxic load with slight overpressure.

General storage farm (second butene tank situated 60 meters away)

Level I study suggests high probability of domino effect.

Level II study suggests 17% probability due to blast wave and 23% chances due to thermal effect (Table 3).

The scenario for the secondary accident in this case has been visualised as: confined vapour cloud explosion (CVCE) followed by fire ball. It is because, heat load would create high internal pressure (about 30% higher than the design value) adding to the already high pressure at which the chemical was stored. As the chemical is highly flammable, it would catch fire soon after release, turning into a fire ball.

LDPE Plant (ethylene tank situated 65 meters away)

Level I study suggests moderate probability of domino effect.

Level II analysis suggests that domino effect probabilities due to the blast and the heat load are 12% and 15% respectively (Table 3). The secondary accident would be of a nature similar to the one that may occur in the butene tank: confined vapour cloud explosion followed by fire ball.

PP Plant (propylene tank situated 90 meters away)

Level I study suggests moderate probability of domino effect.

Level II study suggests 12% probability of domino effect due to shock wave and 11% due to heat radiation (Table 3).

The secondary accident scenario likely in the propylene tank is anticipated as; BLEVE followed by fire ball. It is because, the quantity of propylene stored is less and the intensity of damaging events at the location of this unit are also low compared to ethylene but are sufficient to cause sudden release of chemical either through relief valve or through safety valve leading to boiling liquid vapour explosion (BLEVE). The released chemical on meeting an ignition source would lead to fire ball.

Cracker unit (LPG storage situated 60 meters away)

Level I study suggests high probability of domino effect.

Level II study suggests occurrence of domino effect has 15% probability due to shock wave and 20% due to heat load (Table 3).

The domino effect scenario for this unit is visualised as BLEVE followed by fire ball. An intense heat load would develop a high pressure in the LPG bullet and also weaken the strength of vessel which in consequence would lead to sudden release of LPG either through relief valve or through pipe joints as BLEVE. There is lesser probability of CVCE, mainly because in order that a bullet could burst under CVCE excessive pressure must develop in the vessel. This is not possible with the normal storage capacity of a LPG bullet. Of course, the release of LPG on ignition would lead to flash fire or fire ball depending upon the quantity of LPG released.

A simplified block diagram showing the occurrence of domino effect in various units triggered by a primary accident in the butene tank is presented in Figure 7. It is evident that the second butene tank situated near the primary accident site is highly vulnerable. The chlorine tank is comparatively safe.

Similar studies were conducted to analyse the domino effect due to accidents in either one or other of these units PP plant, LDPE plant, cracker unit, and caustic plant. The results are summarised in Tables 4-7.

Consequence analysis covering all the hazardous units reveals that, as far as the primary event is concerned, PP plant has the maximum damage potential as it causes lethal overpressure over the largest area. Risk contours, signifying an individual risk factor greater than $1*10^{-4}$ /yr due to the cumulative effect of the primary and secondary accidents, are plotted over the industry's map in Figure 8. It is evident that an accident in PP plant would endanger an area of more than 300 m radius, while the risk contour for cracker plant would encompass an area of about 200 m radius. An accident in the chlorine storage vessel would bring an area of about 70 m radius under severe risk, the lowest area-of-lethal-impact of the scenarios considered.

In summary, the cracker plant has the potential of causing the most damaging primary accident and *also* has the maximum probability to lead to domino effect. The intensities of blast wave, missiles, and heat load would be lethal over an area of 200 meters radius if an accident occurs in this plant. The plant has several vulnerable units close to it which would facilitate a long chain of accidents. On the other hand an accident in caustic plant has the least damage potential and also the least probability of causing secondary accidents.

SUMMARY and CONCLUSIONS

1. Study of the probability of occurrence of domino effect and forecasting the impacts if such chain of accident occurs, should be an integral part of any risk assessment study. This is borne out by the history of several past accidents including the most recent one — and one of the biggest ever — which occurred at the HPCL's refinery at Vishakhapatnam, India, on 14 September, 1997.
2. Domino effect can be initiated by five types of primary events - fire, overpressure/shock waves, missiles, toxic load, and a combination of one or more of these.
3. In this paper we have presented details of the mechanisms by which domino effect is initiated by the five types of primary accidents mentioned above. We have then presented models for determining the probabilities of occurrence of these events, developing secondary (and higher order) accident scenarios, forecasting their consequences, and developing disaster prevention/management strategies based on these studies.
4. A two-tier procedure for conducting a typical domino effect study has been presented. The applicability of the procedure has been demonstrated with the help of a case study.
5. One of the interesting and revealing observations that emerges from the case study is that it is not necessary that the unit which has the maximum damage potential (if it meets with an accident) would also have the maximum probability of causing domino effect. It is because the probability of occurrence of domino effect depends not only upon the damage potential of the primary accident but also on a number of others factors such as characteristics of the secondary unit, location of the unit, and site characteristics.

NOMENCLATURE

Ar = cross sectional area of the unit, m^2

Cd = drag coefficient

Cp = specific heat of the chemical, $(kJ/m^2/\ ^\circ C)$

DT = temperature difference, °C

Eymax = maximum allowable stress of the material of construction of the unit, N/m^2

Ey = stress developed in unit due to the rise in temperature, N/m^2

f = fraction of vapours

Hv = heat of evaporation (kJ/m^2)

K = diameter ratio

M = mass of the chemical, kg

mf = mass of fragment generated due to explosion, kg

n	= number of moles of chemical
P	= pressure, N/m^2
p^o	= peak over pressure, N/m^2
p	= over pressure, N/m^2
Pr	= Probit value
Prob	= probability (/yr)
q	= heat flux, kJ/m^2
R	= gas constant (N m/°C)
T	= temperature, °C
t	= time , s
td	= decay time, s
V	= volume of the unit, m^3
vf	= velocity of fragment generated due to explosion, m/s
Vvap	= volume of chemical transformed to vapour, m^3

Symbols

ε	= emissivity of the atmosphere
σ	= Stefen-Boltzman's constant
γ	= Poisson ratio
α	= decay parameter

Subscript

1	= initial condition
2	= final condition
blast	= shock wave load
d	= dynamic
e	= explosion
fire	= average fire temperature, K
heat	= heat load
missile	= missile load
relief	= pressure relief condition

REFERENCES

1. Bagster, D F, and Pitblado, R M, (1991). The estimation of domino incident frequencies - an approach, *Process Safety Environ*, **69B**, pp 196-210.

2. Baker, W E, Cox, P A, Westin, P S, Kulesz, J J, Strehlow, R A, (1983). Explosion hazards and evaluations , *Elesevier Science Ltd.*, Amsterdam.

3. Bhattacharya, B C, (1986). Chemical equipment design , *CBC publication*, Delhi, pp 214-216.

4. Bowen, J H, (1980). Missile problems in the chemical and nuclear power industries , *Nuclear Engineering*, **19**, p 149.

5. Cates, A T ,and Samuels, B, (1993). A simple assessment methodology for vented explosions , *J Loss Prevention in the Process Industries*, **4**, pp. 287-296.

6. Centre for Chemical Process Safety, (CCPS), (1989). Guidelines for chemical process quantitative risk analysis , *CCPS Publication G-8*, pp.8, 87, 108, 114, 116, and 123-133.

7. Clancey, V J, (1972). Diagnostic features of explosion damage , *Proc. Sixth International Meeting of Forensic Science*, Edinburgh.

8. Considine, M, (1984). Thermal radiation hazards ranges from large hydrocarbon pool fires , *SRD report number R297*, U K atomic energy authority.

9. Davies, P A, (1993). A guide to the evaluation of condensed phase explosions , *J of Hazardous Materials*, 33, pp 1-18.

10. Eisenberg, N A, Lynch, C J, and Breeding, R J, (1975). Vulnerability model - a simulation system for assessing damage resulting from marine spills , *Report G-D-136-75*, Washington DC.

11. Greenbook , (1992). Methods for determining the possible damage to people and objects resulting from release of hazardous materials , *Rep CPR 16E, Voorburg*, Warrington.

12. Hindu , (1997). Major fire in Vizag refinery , *The Hindu publication*, September 15, pp 1.

13. Kayes, P J, (1986). Manual of industrial hazard assessment technique , *Technica Ltd.*, London.

14. Khan, F I, and Abbasi, S A, (1995). An anatomy of industrial accidents , *Report CPCE/RA 011/95* , Pondicherry University.

15. Khan, F I, and Abbasi, S A, (1996a). MOSEC -Modelling and Simulation of Explosion in Chemical industries , *Report CPCE/RA 013/96*, Pondicherry University.

16. Khan, F I, and Abbasi, S A, (1996b). Accident simulation in chemical process industries using software MAXCRED , *Indian J of Chemical Technology*, **3**, pp. 338-344.

17. Khan, F I, and Abbasi, S A, (1997). Risk analysis of a cloralkali industry situated in densely populated area , *Process Safety Progress*, **16**(3), pp. 172-185.

18. Kletz, T A, (1983). After the investigation of fire . *Fire Prevention*, **162**, pp 16-22.

19. Kletz, T A, (1985). What went wrong , *Gulf Publication Company,* England.

20. Kletz, T A, (1991). Process safety: an achievement , *Jr. of Institution of Mechanical Engineers*, **11**, 34.

21. Latha, P, Gautam, G, and Raghavan, K V, (1992). Strategies for quantification of thermally initiated cascade effects , *J of Loss Prevention Process Industries*, **5**(1),.

22. Lees, F P, (1996). Loss prevention in process industries , *(2nd edition)*, *Butterworths*, **1-3**, London.

23. Mallikarajunan, M M, Raghavan, K V, and Pietersen, C M, (1988). An approach to maximum Credible Accident Analysis of a cluster of Chemical industries , *EnviroTec International Conference*, September 21-24, Bombay.

24. Martinsen, W E, Johnson, D W, and Terrell, W F, (1986). BLEVEs : Their causes, effects and prevention , *Hydrocarbon Processing*, **65**, p 11.

25. Marshall, V C, (1987). Major chemical hazards , *John Wiley & Sons*, New York.

26. Maurer, B, (1977). Modelling of vapour cloud dispersion and deflagration after bursting of tanks filled with liquefied gas , *2nd International Symposium on Loss Prevention in Process Industries*, Heidelberg , pp.VI-305.

27. Medard, L A, (1989). Accidental explosions , *Ellis Horwood*, England.

28. Pasman, H J, Duxbury, H A, Bjordal, P, (1992). Major hazards in the process industries, : achievements and challenges in loss prevention , *J of Hazardous Materials*, **33**, pp. 1-33.

29. Pietersen, C, M, (1986). Analysis of the LPG disaster in Mexico City , *Loss Prevention and Safety Promotion*, **5**, pp. 21.

30. Pietersen, C M, (1990). Consequence of accidental release of hazardous materials , *J of Loss Prevention Process Industries*, **3**, pp. 136-141.

31. Porter, W H L, (1980). Generation of missiles and destructive shock fronts and their consequences , *Nuclear Engineering*, **19**, pp. 171-178.

32. Pritchard, D K, (1989). A review of methods for predicting blast damage from vapour cloud explosions , *J of Loss Prevention Process Industries*, **2**(4), pp.193-199.

33. Prugh, R W, (1991). Quantitative evaluation of BLEVE Hazards , *Chemical Engineering Progress*, **87**(2), pp. 60-71.

34. Prugh, R W, (1992). Modelling and mitigation of the consequence of accidental release of hazardous materials , *Plant Operation Progress*, **11** (1), pp.19-25.

35. Prugh, R W, (1994). Quantitative evaluation of fire ball hazards , *Process Safety Progress*, **13**(2), pp. 83-89.

36. Raghavan, K V, and Swaminathan, G, (1996). Hazard assessment and disaster mitigation in petrochemical industries , *Oxford Publishing Company*, Chennai.

37. Roberts, A F, (1983). Thermal radiation hazards from pressurised storage , *Fire Safety*, **4**, pp.197-212.

38. Scielly, N F and High, W G, (1986). The blast effects of explosion , *Proceeding of International Symposium on Loss Prevention and Safety Promotion*, Cannes.

39. Shankar, R, (1997). Corrosion, *Science Express* : *Indian Express Publication,* pp.1-3, (30 September), Chennai.

40. Van den Berg, A C, and Lennoy, A, (1993). Methods for vapour cloud explosion blast modelling , *J of Hazardous Materials*, **34**, pp 171 -179.

41. Venerate, J E S, Rutledge, G A, Sumathipala, and Sollows, K, (1993). To BLEVE or not to BLEVE: Anatomy of Boiling Liquid Expanding Vapour Explosion , *Process Safety Progress*, **12**(2), pp67-70.

¨ Reproduced from *Process Safety Progress*, USA

16

DOMIFFECT (DOMInio eFFECT) : A USER-FRIENDLY SOFTWARE FOR DOMINO EFFECT ANALYSIS*

Most of the past risk assessment studies deal with accident in a single industry, more so in one of the units of an industry. However, it is always possible that accident in one unit can cause a secondary accident in a nearby unit which in turn may trigger a tertiary accident, and so on. The probability of occurrence and adverse impacts of such domino or cascading effects are increasing day by day due to increasing congestion in industrial complexes and increasing density of human population around such complexes. This is especially glaring in developing countries. The recent disaster at a refinery in Vishakhapatnam, India, which claimed over 60 lives and damaged property worth Rs 600 million, has brought the damage potential of domino effect into sharp focus.

This paper presents a new computer automated tool DOMIFFECT (DOMIno eFFECT) which is the first ever such tool reported for studying domino effects. The package is capable of a) estimating the hazards of fire, explosion, toxic release, or combination of these present in a chemical process industry; b) the damage potential of likely accidents, assessed on the basis of credible scenarios the tool develops; c) the likelihood of second accident being triggered by the first, d) the scenarios of the second accident, their damage potential, and the probability of their causing a third accident (steps similar to a-c above), and so on. The software has been coded in C++ and has the attributes i) wide applicability, ii) sophistication, iii) user friendliness, and iv) flexibility for improvement.

Key words: Domino effect, computer software, risk assessment, hazard assessment, consequence analysis.

INTRODUCTION

We have developed techniques and tools for conducting risk assessment in chemical process industries. These include rapid risk assessment using a computer automated tool MAXCRED (Khan and Abbasi, 1996; 1997a), and its advanced version MAXCRED-II (Khan and Abbasi, 1997b), optimising HAZOP (hazard and operability study) procedure (Khan and Abbasi, 1997c), and safety-based design (Khan and Abbasi, 1997d). All these procedures essentially deal with accidents in a single industry, more so in one of the units of an industry. But it is always possible that a major accident in one unit say an explosion or a fire - can cause a secondary accident in a nearby unit which in turn may trigger a tertiary accident. The probability of such domino or cascading effects occurring is increasing day by day with more new industries coming up in already congested industrial areas.

The extent of the likely adverse impacts of such accidents is also increasing rapidly because of increasing demographic pressure which has been forcing people, especially in developing countries, to live close to industrial complexes.

* Reproduced from *Journal of Environmental Modelling and Software, The Netherlands.*

In this paper we present a computer-automated methodology DOMIFFECT (DOMIno eFFECT) which enables one to know a) whether domino effects are likely to occur in a given setting, b) if they do what would be the likely accident scenarios, and c) what would be the likely impacts of the different scenarios. Finally, the tool guides us towards strategies needed to prevent domino effects.

Illustrative case studies of some past accidents involving domino effect

When an accident in one unit causes accidents in one or more other units, the phenomena is called cascading effect / domino effect / chain of accidents. We present below a few illustrative case studies of chain of accidents.

At Fyzin (France), in 1966, a fire in one of the storage vessels led to a series of fires and explosions in other vessels (Mahoney, 1990).

At a refinery at Pernis (The Netherlands), in 1968, an overflow of hydrocarbon caused a small explosion. This triggered another small explosion which in turn led to a major explosion with fire, extensively damaging an area of about 300 m. Two people were killed and 85 injured (Lees, 1996).

At Texas city, USA, one of the LPG storage vessels in a petrochemical industry suffered overpressure while it was being filled, due to failure of a pressure gauge and also of a relief valve (Mahoney, 1990). It cracked and leaked LPG. The leak ignited into a massive fire ball, which shattered the vessel, propelling its fragments as missiles. During the next 20 minutes five horizontal bullets and four vertical ones were damaged by missiles. The other two vessels were also damaged in this way.

On 3 July 1987 an explosion occurred inside an ethylene oxide purification column at a chemicals factory at Antwerp, Belgium (Lees, 1996). The explosion was due to decomposition of ethylene oxide. It was accompanied by a fire ball, which started a number of secondary fires. These, together with blasts and missiles, caused extensive damage. Fourteen people were injured.

In November 1984, a major fire and a series of explosions occurred at the PEMEX LPG terminal at San Juan Ixhautepec, Mexico City (Pietersen, 1986). Some 500 people were killed and the terminal was destroyed. The main LPG storage capacity of 16000 m^3 consisted of six spheres and 48 horizontal cylinders. Early in the morning of 18 November the plant was being filled from a refinery 400 km away. At 5.30 a.m. a fall in pressure was registered in the control room and also at pipeline pumping station 40 km distant. It was due to leakage of LPG. The release of LPG continued for some 5-10 minutes. There was a slight wind of 0.4 m/s. The wind and the sloping terrain carried the gas towards the south-west. People in the nearby neighbourhood heard the noise of the escape and smelled the gas. When the gas cloud had grown to cover an area, which eyewitnesses put at 250*150 m with a height of 2 m, it caught fire giving a high flame and causing violent ground shock. In another 5 minutes the first BLEVE occurred. About a minute later another explosion occurred. One or two of the smaller spheres suffered BLEVE, giving a fire ball of 300 m diameter. There followed a series of explosions as other vessels, too, had BLEVEs. There were some 15 explosions over a period of an hour and a half. BLEVE occurred of the four smaller spherical vessels and many of the cylindrical vessels. The bursting vessels generated numerous missiles, many of these were heavy (10-14 tons) and went as far as a km away. Fifteen of the 48 cylindrical vessels weighing 20 ton became missiles and rocketed over 100 m.

On 23 October 1989 a release occurred in a polyethylene plant at the Phillips company's chemical complex at Pasadena near Houston, Texas (Khan and Abbasi, 1997a). A vapour cloud formed and ignited, giving rise to a massive vapour cloud explosion. There followed a series of further explosions and a fire. Twenty-two persons were killed on the spot and one later from injuries. The number of injured are variously given as 130 and 300.

The mass of gas released was estimated as some 85200 lb of a mixture of ethylene, isobutane, hexane, and hydrogen, which escaped within seconds. A massive vapour cloud formed and moved rapidly downwind. It soon met with a source of ignition.

The TNT equivalent of the resultant explosion was estimated as 2.4 tons. Two other major explosions followed, one when two 20 000 gallon isobutane storage tanks exploded and the other when another polyethylene plant reactor failed catastrophically, some 10-15 minutes and some 25-45 minutes, respectively, after the initial explosion. According to one witness, 10 separate explosions occurred over a 2-hour period. Debris from the explosions was found upto

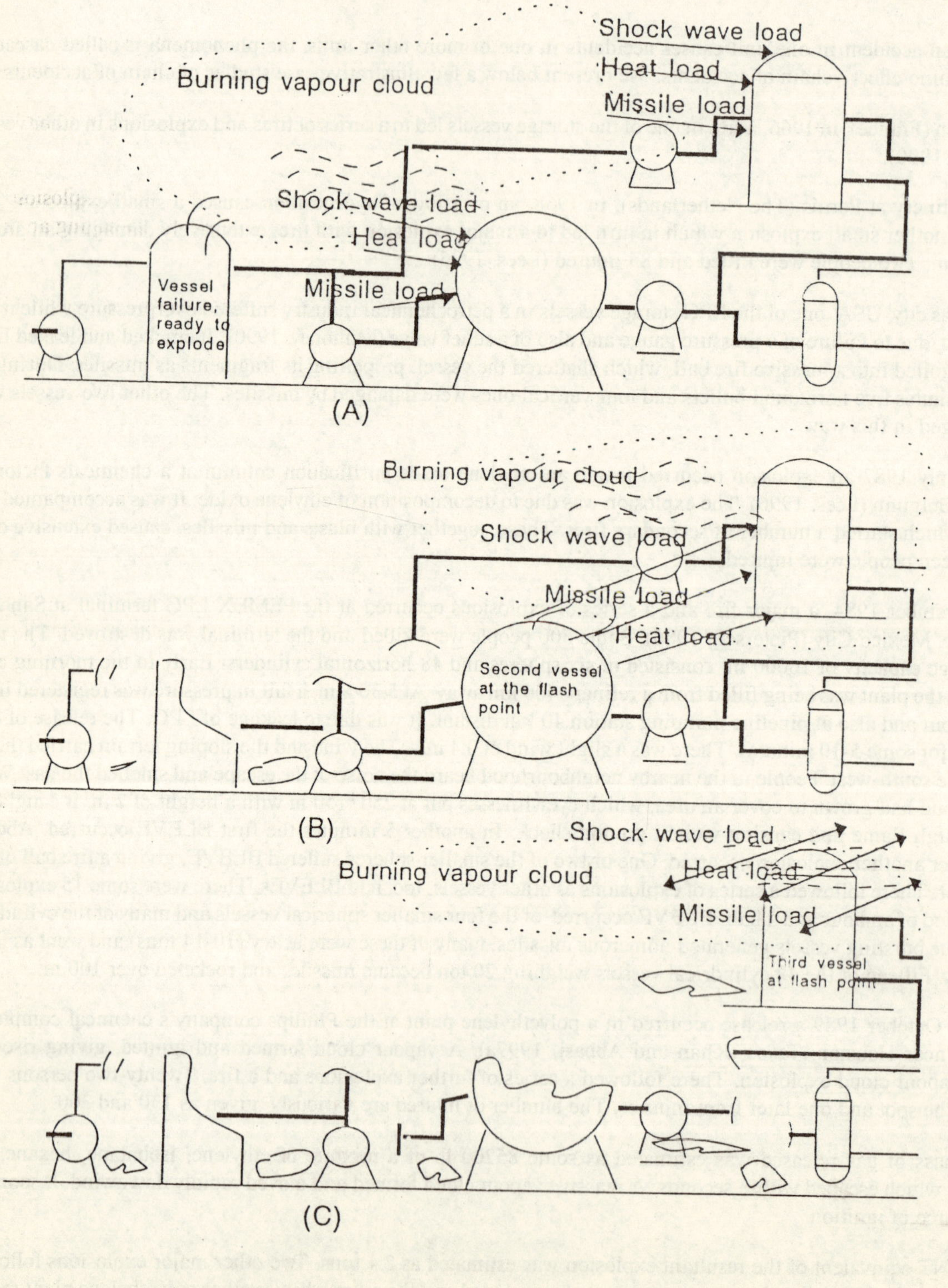

Figure 1. Typical chain of accidents in a chemical process industry

6 miles from the site.

On September 14, 1997 huge fire and explosions devastated the terminals and storage tanks at the refinery of HPCL (Hindustan Petroleum Corporation Limited) unit at Vishakhapatnam in India. More than 55 persons were killed and dozens of others seriously injured (Hindu, 1997).

Two bodies were found on the upper storey of the administrative block which had collapsed while three more were seen in the debris underneath by a team of reporters who ventured in later in the evening. The building housing the recreation club and canteen were also destroyed.

One of the eight Horton spheres or globe tanks, which contained LPG, crude and kerosene tanks separately, near the main gate of the HPCL refinery, caught fire at 6.40 a.m. and exploded rocking the entire Vishakhapatnam city. The storage tanks were all full, with crude imports unloaded at the HPCL berth just a few days ago. The second sphere exploded 15 minutes later and before noon, the others also caught fire. The blaze spread all over the place. Huge tongues of flame and thick black smoke billowed into the sky and joined the hovering monsoon clouds. There was a sharp shower in the morning and people wearing white shirts saw them turn black with soot. The rain water flooding the road also turned black and murky.

With both the entrances to the refinery blocked by burning tanks, neither the fire tenders nor the officials could enter the premises for several hours. Only when the contents in the tanks were burnt out could they venture in. The death toll could have been higher had the fire started half-an-hour later when the first shift staff would have came in.

Even more significantly as the accident occurred on a Sunday which being a holiday, the administrative personnel, who number over a couple of hundred, were not on duty. There were some contract labourers along with the HPCL personnel in the Crude Distilling Unit which was shut down for routine maintenance work. The shock of the initial explosion made people think an earthquake had occurred. They ran helter-skelter leaving their belongings.

Study of domino effect

Domino effect is observed when accident in one of the units in a chemical process industry causes failure in one or more of the other units, setting off secondary or higher order accidents. For such a chain of accidents to occur it is necessary that a) there are sensitive units within 'striking distance' of the missiles or fires generated by an accident, b) the missiles or fires are powerful enough to cause failure in the units they strike, and c) the probability of both the 'hits' occurring, and with sufficient 'destructive potential', is high enough to be significant.

Thus to forecast domino effects it is essential to understand factors such as mechanism of accidents, site characteristics, and such interactions which may initiate a chain of accidents. A typical chain of accidents in a chemical process industry is shown in Figure 1, a-c. Figure 1a shows building-up of high pressure in the vessel which causes explosion and fire, generating heat load, shock waves, and missiles. The nearby unit (sphere, Figure 1b) is damaged, in turn generating fresh heat load, shock waves, and missiles. The chain continues through to the third unit (Figure 1c) In a real-life situation such a cascading effect would propagate as long as no more units are present within the danger zone created by the previous accidents.

Domino effect can be triggered by three types of primary accidents:

1) involving fire,
2) involving explosions leading to
   - blast wave effect;
   - missiles effect;
3) involving a combination of fire and explosion.

To forecast the occurrence and assess the consequences of domino effect, deterministic models in conjunction with probabilistic analysis have to be used (Latha *et al* .1992). Probabilistic models based on previous histories are

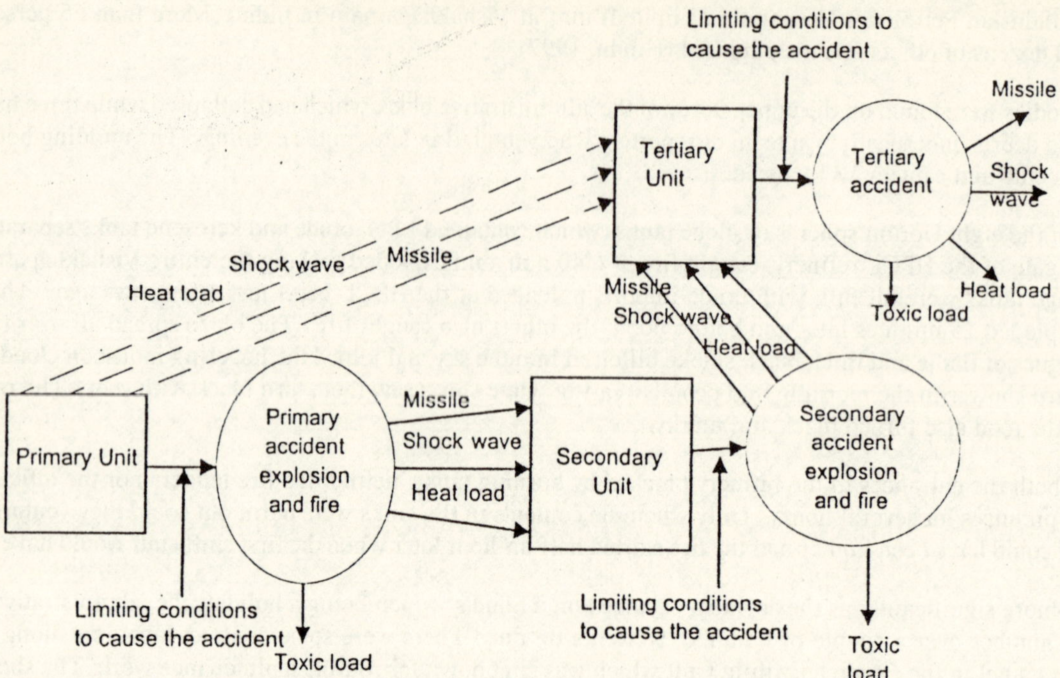

Figure 2. The mechanism of domino/cascading effect pertaining to modelling of chain of accidents in chemical process industries

useful in the assessment of event frequencies', equipment reliability, direction of projectiles' movement, etc. The physical and chemical processes, namely leak development, chemical discharge and dispersion, cloud formation, explosion, fire, vessel fracture, and related phenomena, can best be assessed by deterministic approaches.

Study of domino effect also requires an understanding of transient interchange of damage load (fire and explosion) between the initiator and receiver, and mechanics of vessel failure (Bagster and Pitblado, 1991). Figure 2 shows mechanism of domino effect modelling in chemical process industries.

Domino effect triggered by fire

Fire is caused when a chemical undergoes uncontrolled oxidation in the presence of air liberating heat. Important aspects of modelling domino/cascade effects due to fire (Figure 3) include prediction of flame heights, flame merging phenomena , and the effect of wind on flame tilt and length (Moorehouse, 1982; Considine, 1984; Latha *et al.* 1992).

The reception of thermal radiation by a target is most important for quantification of domino effects. It depends on the atmospheric transmitivity and the geometrical view factor. The latter depends not only on the shape of the flame, the distance, and position of the receiver but also on its orientation.

Many chemical plant installations are equipped with pressurised (liquefied) gas-filled tanks and storage vessels and study of their fire engulfment is important for the quantification of domino effects. The engulfment can be partial or total. The heat transfer and geometry analysis of engulfment of liquid-or vapour-filled vessels have been reported by Ramskill (1987), and Beynon *et al* . (1988).

To model the fire as an initiating event (Figure 3) following aspects, have to be taken into consideration:

I. transient nature of incident flame temperature, velocity, and emissivity:

II. various vessel shapes, e.g., cylindrical, spherical, cuboid, in vertical or horizontal disposition:

III. existence of several temperature zones in the fire-engulfed vessels:

IV. complex modes of heat transfer: fire to tank through radiation and convection; tank wall external to internal surfaces by conduction; tank inner wall to the vapour phase through radiation and convection; vapour to liquid phase by radiation and convection; and tank wall to the liquid phase by convection (natural and forced):

V. transfer of material from liquid to vapour phase during boiling (nucleate or film process) and from vapour to atmosphere during vent operation.

Domino effect triggered by explosion

Generally an explosion generates three damaging events (henceforth referred as characteristics of explosion) :

i) blast waves/overpressure,

ii) heat load, and

iii) missiles, which when encountered by the secondary unit can lead to failure of unit, either through rupture, uprooting or through strain failure (Figure 4).

The term 'blast wave' is used here to mean the shock wave caused by an explosion. The blast wave from all chemical explosions has a definite and measurable pattern. Upon detonation a sudden and violent release of energy causes the surrounding air pressure to rise rapidly creating a region of positive pressure known as "overpressure". As the blast wave moves away from its source at high velocity the overpressure increases sharply to a peak value, known as the peak overpressure, and then gradually reduces. The overpressure phase is followed by a region of negative pressure or underpressure.

Damage and injury as a result of blast wave is largely a consequence of diffraction loading . Diffraction loading is related to the peak overpressure of a blast wave as it passes over and around an object or structure. Peak overpressure refers to the pressure above ambient at a given location (often termed side-on overpressure). Diffraction loading refers to the force exerted on an object or structure during blast wave envelopment. The loading consists of two components

1. resulting from the pressure differential that exists between the front and the back of an object/structure prior to envelopment, and

2. static loading ('cruising' forces) due to the pressure differential between internal and external environments.

Blast wave damage is also a function of rate of pressure rise and wave duration. As a consequence of this, impulse is also used as a measure of blast damage. Impulse is a function of both overpressure and wave duration. The characteristics of blast wave as damaging event have been discussed by Maurer (1977), Baker*et al*. (1983), Martinsen *et al* .(1986), Medard (1989), Prugh (1991), Greenbook (1992) Venerate *et al*. (1993), Van den Berg and Lennoy (1993), Davies (1993), and Khan and Abbasi (1996).

The fragments which are generated as a result of explosion, can cause significant damage (Figure 4). Energy delivered to fragments from blast waves cause the former to become airborne and act as missiles. Such missiles could be either primary or secondary. Primary missiles consist of casing and/or container fragments from the exploded vessel. The secondary missiles consist of fragments from objects located close to the explosion source which have interacted with the blast wave. The characteristics of the missiles - primary or secondary -which are important in the study of domino effect are:

i) velocity ,

ii) shape,

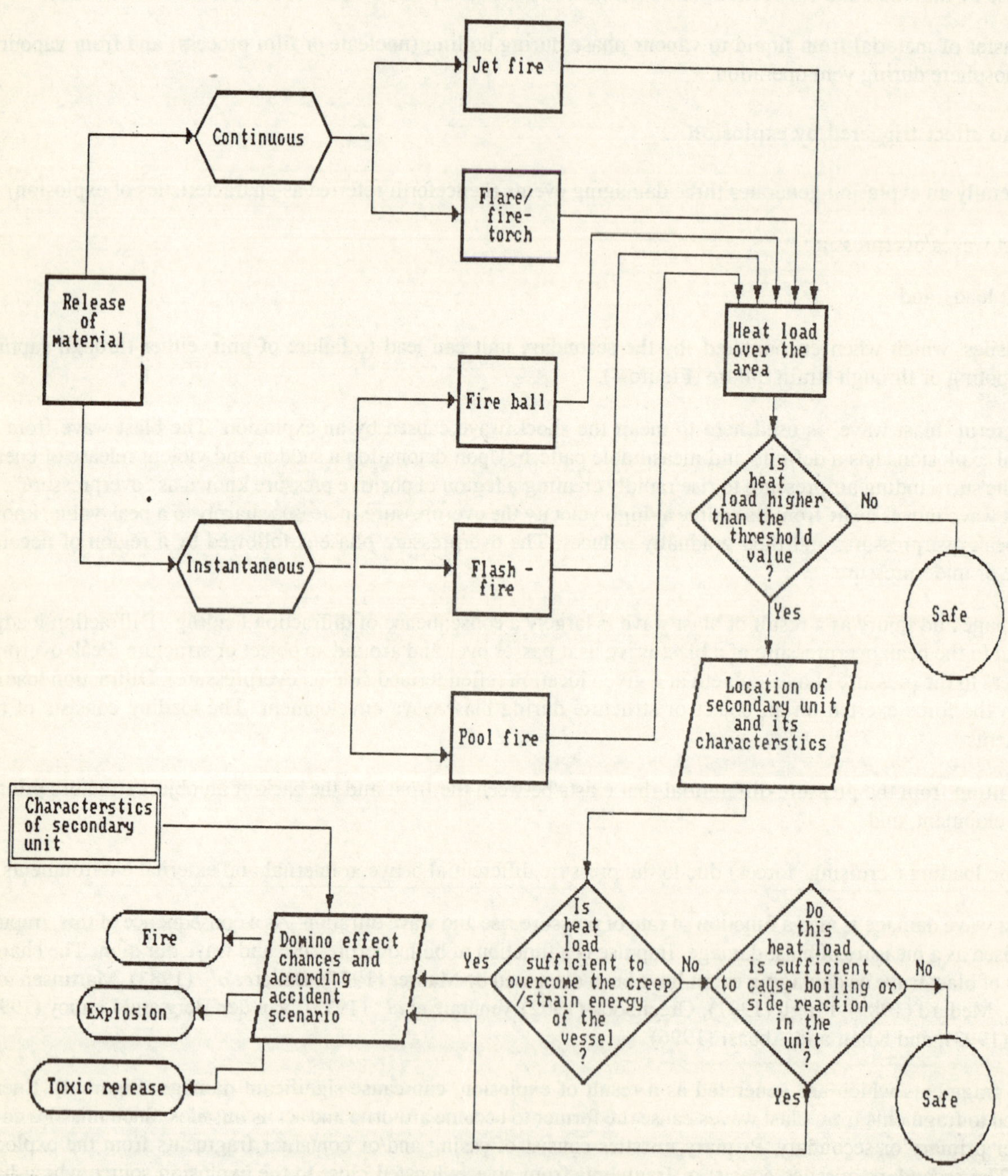

Figure 3. Procedure for domino effect analysis triggered by fire

iii) kinetic energy ,

iv) penetrative ability ,

v) direction.

The history of past accidents (Kletz, 1985; Marshal, 1987; Raghavan and Swaminathan,1996; Lees, 1996; Khan and Abbasi, 1996;1997a; Hindu, 1997) reveals that more often than not industrial accidents generate a combination of different impacts (explosion, fire and toxic release) rather than a single impact. Thus to study domino effect, the probability of occurrence of each type of primary impact (heat load, blast wave, and missiles) should be estimated and combined according to the anticipated sequence of events in order to forecast the nature and intensity of the secondary accident. (Khan and Abbasi, 1997a, 1997b).

THE DOMIFFECT SOFTWARE

We have developed DOMIFFECT (DOMIno eFFECT) as one of the tools for conducting risk assessment in chemical process industries, sequence of steps is shown in (Figure 5). DOMIFFECT is menu-driven and interactive, capable of the following:

- estimation of all possible hazards from toxic release to explosion;
- handling of interaction among different accidental events (generation of domino or cascading accident scenarios);
- estimation of domino effect probability;
- estimation of domino effect consequences.

The software incorporates state-of-the-art models for studying a) the hazards of fire, explosion, toxic release, or combination of these present in a chemical process industry; b) the damage potential of likely accidents, assessed on the basis of credible scenarios the tool develops; c) the likelihood of second accident being triggered by the first, d) the scenarios of the second accident, their damage potential, and the probability of their causing a third accident (steps similar to a-c above), and so on. A major feature of DOMIFFECT is the module automatic analysis. This module uses a knowledge-base built into DOMIFFECT, estimates the detailed consequences, and checks the probability of occurrence of secondary or higher order accidents at different locations.

DOMIFFECT is a PC-based software with object oriented architecture coded in C++. It consists of six main modules DATA, ACCIDENT SCENARIO, ANALYSIS, DOMINO, GRAPHICS and USER INTERFACE. The Architecture and message flow sequence of DOMIFFECT is shown in Figure 6. Each module consists of several submodules and functions.

Data, accident scenario, and analysis modules

The data module is similar to the one incorporated in our package MAXCRED-II (Khan and Abbasi, 1997c, 97e). Accident scenario module also has several features similar to the ones included in MAXCRED II, with the following additions:

i) automatic scenario generation sub-module of DOMIFFECT consists of more elaborate knowledge-base (implemented in terms of rule network; Figure 7) than the corresponding MAXCRED-II sub-module

ii) a different and faster inference engine (combination of forward and backward chaining; Figure 8) is used for retrieving the knowledge from knowledge-base;

iii) user-defined scenario generation sub-module consists of more advanced models for explosion and fire . It also treats gaseous dispersion in much more elaborate fashion incorporating density effects (heavier than air), atmospheric conditions, and terrain characteristics (Tables 1-3).

The analysis module has the features contained by the corresponding module of MAXCRED-II. In addition it contains newer models (Tables 1-3).

DOMINO MODULE

It analyse the damage potential of the primary event at the point of location of the secondary unit and checks for the likelihood of the occurrence of the secondary accident. If the probability of the secondary accident is sufficiently high then the appropriate accident scenarios are developed and analysed for consequences.

This module has an independent set of information which should be provided by the user. The information pertain to the operational details of the secondary unit, chemicals used, meteorological conditions, and topological characteristics. This module consists of various sets of mathematical models for estimating the damage consequences (Tables 1-3), and probability of occurrence of secondary accidents due to the effect of the primary ones (Table 4)

The main Domino module is classified into four sub-modules based on different type of accident initiating events: heat_load, blast_load, and missile_load. The probability of domino effect is estimated through F_prob function defined in main Domino module and inherited by all submodules. The models used, and the framework within which they are to be used, has been described by us in detail elsewhere (Khan and Abbasi, 1997h). Relevant probit equations are recapitulated below in brief.

Heat load

i) Failure of the second vessel due to high pressure build-up caused by the primary accident.

The probability of secondary accident due to heat absorbed by the chemical in the target vessel:

$$0.40*q*Ar = M* Cp *DT \quad (1)$$

where, Cp represents specific heat of chemical (kJ/m²/°C), DT is temperature difference, M is mass of chemical (kg), Ar is area of vessel (m²), and q is heat load incident over the vessel.

At temperature T_2 , the fraction of vapour generated is (Kayes, 1986; Greenbook, 1992):

$$f = 1\text{-}\exp(-Cp*(T_2 - T_1)/Hv) \quad (2)$$

and

$$Vvap = f * V \quad (3)$$

where, Hv is heat of evaporation (kJ/kg), V is total volume of chemical (m³), f is fraction of vapour and Vvap is volume of vapour generated (m³).

The pressure developed in the vessel:

$$P_2 = n*R*T_2/Vvap + P_1 \quad (4)$$

If P_2 is greater than the relief pressure, it may lead to release of the chemical contained in the vessel and if it is greater than the design pressure then the vessel may burst. The degree of excess pressure and the mechanical properties of the material of construction of the vessel would bear upon the severity of the secondary accident The probability of an accident due to rise is pressure is given by:

$$Prob_{heat2} = (P_2 - P_{relief}) / P_{relief} \quad (5)$$

ii) Vessel rupture due to material failure.

The second vessel may fail due to loss in the strength of the material of construction . The probability of this

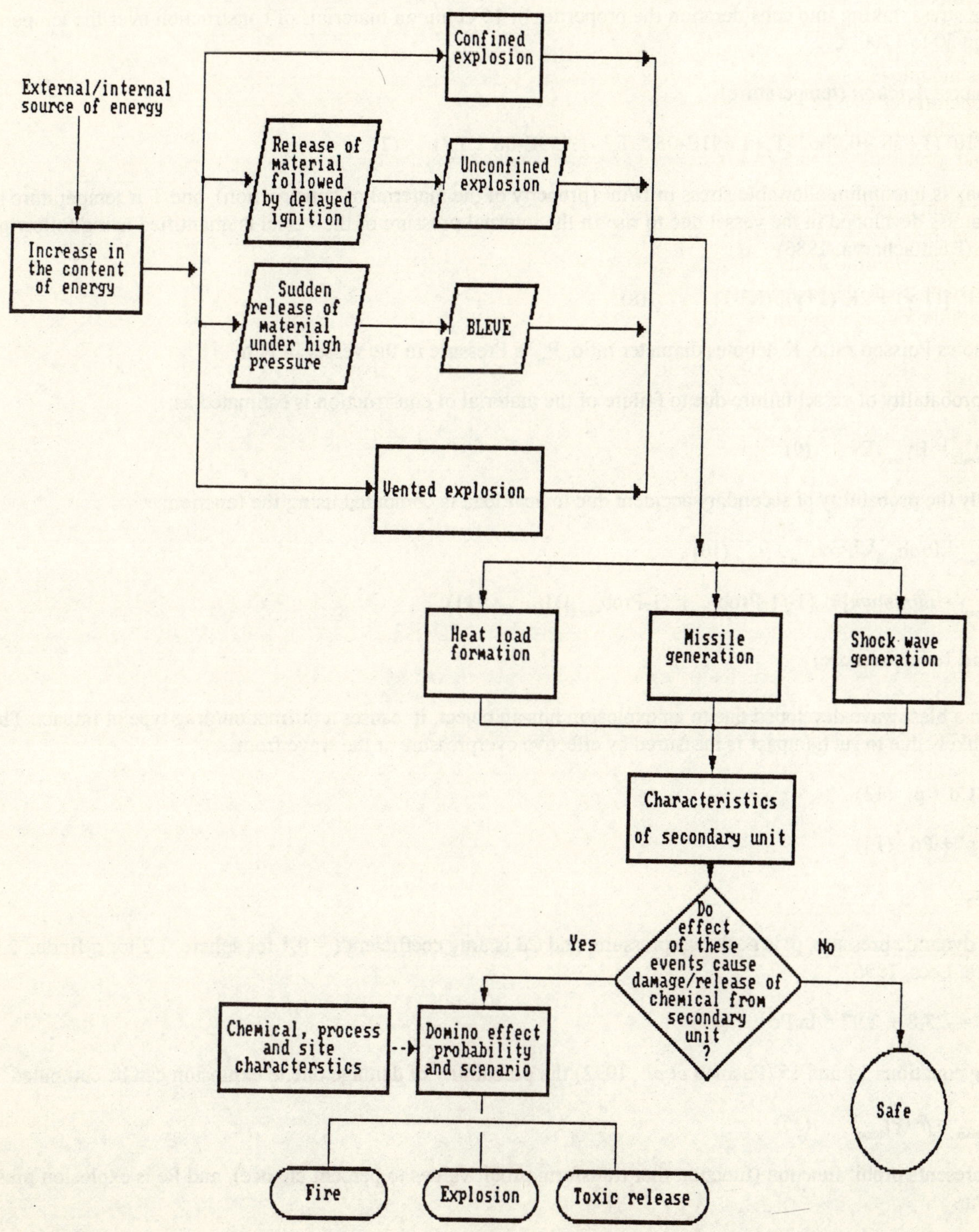

Figure 4. Procedure of domino effect analysis triggered by explosion

occurrence can be computed using maximum strain theory (Bhattacharya, 1986). Heat load developed due to fire would raise the temperature of the vessel wall (radiation is the dominant mode of the heat transfer). This rise in the temperature will reduce the maximum allowable stress of the vessel. This phenomena is quantified by:

$$T_2 = [(\varepsilon^*\sigma^*T_{fire}{}^4 - q)/(\varepsilon^*\sigma)]^{1/4} \quad (6)$$

These authors have developed an empirical equation to quantify the impact of temperature on the maximum allowable stress, taking into consideration the properties of 15 common materials of construction over the temperature range 50 to 1200 °C .

Eymax = *function* (temperature)

$$= 1*10^8 (1.858 - 0.0062*T_2+1.691E\text{-}05 * T_2^2 -1.959E\text{-}08 * T_2^3) \quad (7)$$

Eymax is maximum allowable stress in N/m^2 (property of the material of construction), and T is temperature in °C. The stress developed in the vessel due to rise in the internal pressure of the vessel is quantified using following equation (Bhattacharya, 1986)

$$Ey = P_2 [(1-\gamma) + 2K (1+\gamma)]/(K^2-1) \quad (8)$$

g denotes Poisson ratio, K denotes diameter ratio, P_2 is Pressure in the vessel in N/m^2.

The probability of vessel failure due to failure of the material of construction is estimated as:

$$Prob_{heat2} = Ey_{max}/Ey \quad (9)$$

Finally the probability of secondary accident due to heat load is computed using the function:

$$Prob_{heat} = Prob_{heat1} \cup Prob_{heat\,2} \quad (10)$$

$$Prob_{heat} = minimum[1, \{1-(1-Prob_{heat1})*(1-Prob_{heat2})\}] \quad (11)$$

Blast load (overpressure)

When a blast wave developed due to an explosion hits an object, it causes a diffraction/drag type of impact. The damage likely due to such impact is measured by effective overpressure at the wave front.

$$Pd = Cd * p^\circ \quad (12)$$

$$Pe = p^\circ + Pd \quad (13)$$

Where,

Pd is dynamic pressure, p° is peak overpressure, and Cd is drag coefficient (= 0.1 for sphere, 1.2 for cylinder, 2.0 for square; Lees, 1996).

$$Pr_{blast} = -23.8 + 2.92 * \ln Pe \quad (14)$$

Using equations 14 and 15 (Pasman *et al.* 1992) the probability of damage due to explosion can be computed:

$$Prob_{blast} = fr\,(Pr_{blast}) \quad (15)$$

fr represents probit function (function that transform probit values to percent chance), and Pe is explosion pressure in Pa.

Missile load

The impact of missiles on the secondary units is assessed using three parameters:

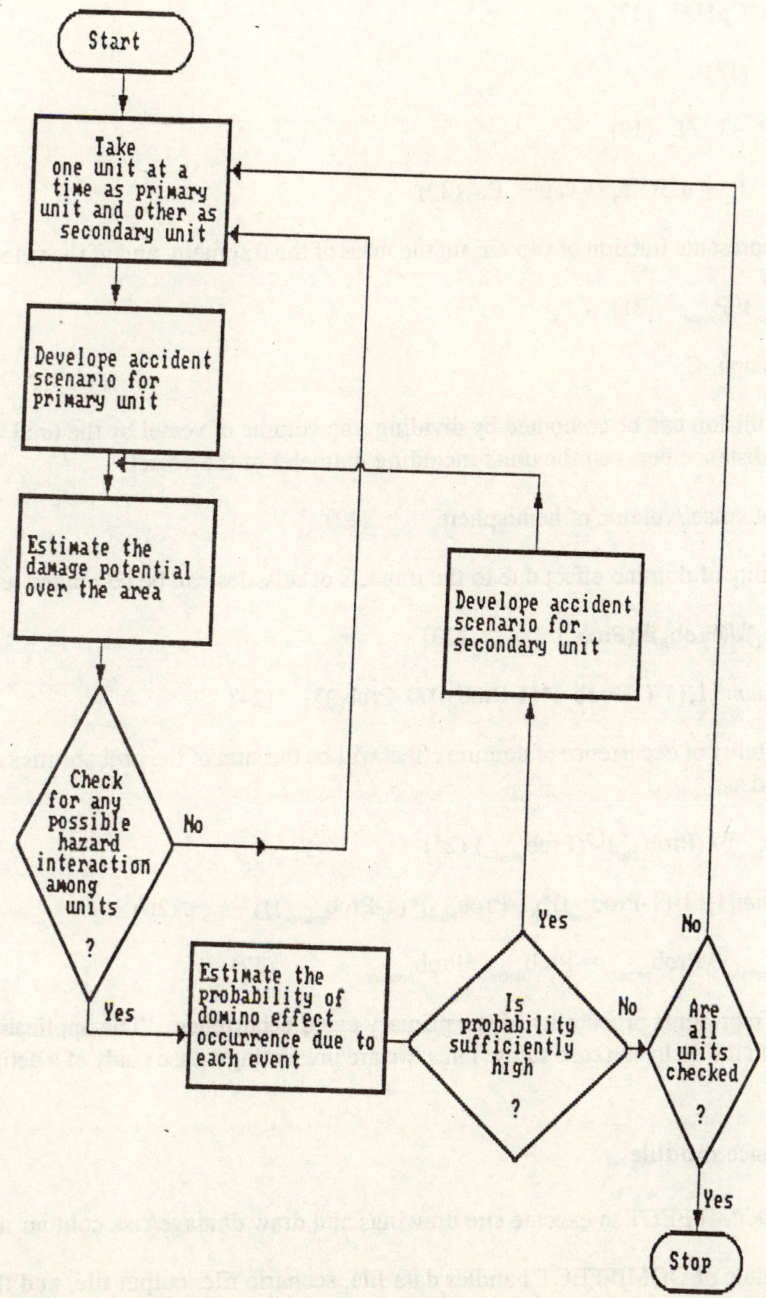

Figure 5. Algorithm of DOMIFFECT

i) **penetration strength, A:**

$Prob_A$=(penetration strength-thickness of vessel)/penetration strength (16)

ii) impact energy, B:

As reported by Davies (1993) and Lees (1996) about 40-50% of total impact energy is utilised in raising the temperature of the contents of the secondary unit. Hence

$1/4^* \; mf^*vf^2 = M^*Cp^*DT$ (17)

$T_2 = T_1 + DT$ (18)

for gases $P_2 / P_1 = T_1 / T_2$ (19)

for liquefied gas $P_2 = n^*R^*T_2 /Vvap + P_1$, (20)

Vvap = f*V; f represents fraction of vapour, mf the mass of the fragment, and vf the velocity of the fragment.

$Prob_B = (P_2 - P_{relief}) / P_{relief}$ (21)

iii) Probability of collision, C:

The probability of a collision can be computed by dividing the volume of vessel by the total volume of the hemisphere of radius equal to distance between the units including diameter of the vessel.

$Prob_C$= volume of vessel/volume of hemisphere (22)

Thus the probability of domino effect due to the impacts of missiles can be computed as:

$Prob_{missile} = (Prob_A) \cup (Prob_B) \cup (Prob_C)$ (23)

$Prob_{missile} = \textit{minimum}\ [1,\{1-(1-Prob_A)^*(1-Prob_B)^*(1-Prob_C)\}]$ (24)

Finally the probability of occurrence of domino effect will be the sum of the probabilities of each contributing event and can be estimated as;

$Prob_{domino} = (Prob_{heat}) \cup (Prob_{blast}) \cup (Prob_{missile})$ (25)

$Prob_{domino} = \textit{minimum}[1,\{1-(1-Prob_{heat})^*(1-Prob_{blast})^*(1-Prob_{missile})\}]$ (26)

$Prob_{domino} = Prob_{domino} \cap Prob_{primary} = Prob_{domino} {}^* Prob_{primary}$ (27)

Where $Prob_{primary}$ represents probability of the primary event occurrence. The applicability of the scheme can be well understood with the help of a case study. Thus, we are presenting a case study of a petrochemical complex in coming section.

Graphics and user interface module

This module enables DOMIFFECT to execute site drawings and draw damage/risk contour maps.

The user interface module of DOMIFFECT handles data file, scenario file, output file, and flow of information. This module works as 'information manager': it provides the necessary information to each module and sub-module for carrying out the desired operations, and stores the results in appropriate slots.

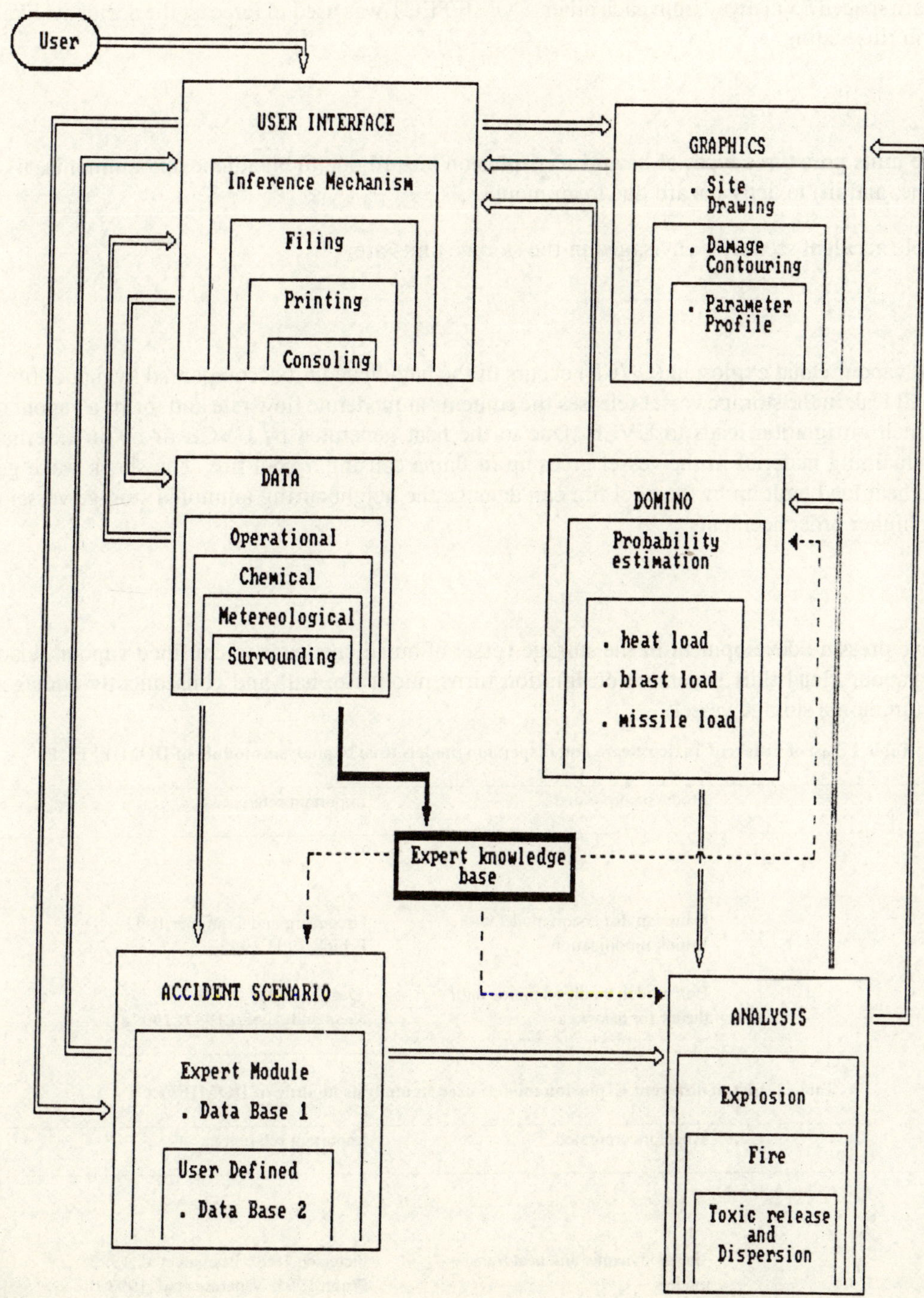

Figure 6. Architecture and message flow diagram of DOMIFFECT

APPLICATION OF DOMIFFECT - AN EXAMPLE

Preamble

In a chemical industry butadiene (C_4H_6) and ammonia (NH_3) are stored (in liquefied state) at -25 °C,-55 °C, and 3.5 atm, 6.5 atm, respectively. The storage capacities the two tanks are 10 metric ton, and of 5 metric ton respectively. The two units are spaced 75 m away from each other. DOMIFFECT was used to forecast the accidents likely and their consequences in this setting.

Results

The storage units pose three types of hazard: i) explosion hazard due to butadiene and ammonia, ii) fire hazard due to butadiene, and iii) toxicity hazard due to ammonia.

The plausible accident scenarios envisaged in the storage units are:

Scenario 1

Unconfined vapour cloud explosion (UVCE) occurs in the butadiene unit accompanied by a pool fire. This shall happen if a small leak in the storage vessel releases the contents at moderate flow rate and forms a vapour cloud in the atmosphere which on ignition leads to UVCE. Due to the heat generated by UVCE or by an external source of ignition, the remaining material in the vessel gives up in flame causing a pool fire. The shock wave generated by UVCE and the heat load built up by the pool fire can damage the neighbouring ammonia storage vessel and trigger secondary and higher order accidents.

Scenario 2

An excessive pressure development in the storage vessel of butadiene leads to confined vapour cloud explosion (CVCE). The vapour cloud thus generated on ignition turns into a fire ball and consequently damages the other storage vessel (ammonia storage vessel) .

Table 1 List of different Toxic release and dispersion models used in analysis module of DOMIFFECT

Event	Model incorporated	Important references
Toxic release		
Light gas	Gaussian dispersion model with Erbink modification	Greenberg and Crammer,1992 Erbink,1993,1995
Heavy gas	Box model, modified plume path theory for heavy gas	Deaves,1992; Khan and Abbasi,1997f,1997g

Table 2 List of different Explosion models used in analysis module of DOMIFFECT

Event	Model incorporated	Important references
Explosion		
BLEVE	thermodynamic and heat transfer models	Pietersen,1990, Pasman et al.,1992 Prugh,1991, Venerate et al.,1993
VCE	vapor cloud explosion Prugh,1992; Lees,1996	Ven den Berg and Lennoy,1993; Prugh,1987
CVCE	vapor cloud explosion in confinement (vessel or building)	Singh,1988; Pietersen,1990; Lees,1996, Pritchard,1989; CCPS,1994

Table 3 List of different Fire models used in analysis module of DOMIFFECT

Event	Model incorporated	Important reference
Fire		
Flash fire	flare model, fire torch and spontaneous combustion	Kayes,1986, Greenberg and Crammer,1992 CCPS,1994
Pool fire	combustion of liquid pool	Roberts,1983; Mourehouse,1982, Davies,1993; Greenbook,1992
Fire ball	spontaneous combustion of vapor cloud	Roberts, 1983; Davies,1993 Prugh, 1994

Scenario 3

An excessive by high pressure development in the storage vessel of butadiene leads to BLEVE. The unburned vapour cloud thus formed on ignition leads to a fire ball. As the damage potential of a BLEVE is expected to be less severe compared to CVCE or UVCE, the ammonia storage vessel would not be affected.

Scenario 4

An instantaneous release of ammonia.

Table 4 List of different models used in domino module of DOMIFFECT

Event	Model incorporated	Important references
Heat load	thermodynamic models, fluid expansion models, probit function, heat transfer models	Pietersen,1990; Bagster and Pitblado,1990; Prugh,1994 Latha et al. 1992; Khan and Abbasi, 1997h
Blast waveload	shock wave model, pressure-impulse model pressure loading, pressure-temperature interaction, empirical probit models.	Pritchard,1989; Pietersen,1990, Davies,1993;Khan and Abbasi,1997h, Lees,1996
Missile load	missile impact model, thermodynamic models, heat transfer models, and empirical models for probability estimation.	Bowen,1980; Davies,1993, Khan and Abbasi, 1997h

Analysis

A UVCE as per *scenario* 1 would give rise to heat radiation effects, shock waves, and missiles. In addition there would be secondary impact of burning of released material in the dike/vessel which would again lead to additional heat load. In *scenario* 1, missile effect is not significant (Table 5). However, shock waves of intensity high enough to damage all objects coming in their way would be occurring in an area of ~250 m radius. The combined impact of heat radiation, UVCE, and pool fire would be lethal over an area of ~500 m radius. The damage contour for more than 50% probability of damage/lethality would be extended over an area of ~500 m radius (Table 6). This scenario has 29% probability of causing secondary accident (release of ammonia), which may propel the gas in lethal concentrations over an area of ~500 m radius.

The CVCE in butadiene tank as per *scenario* 2 would generate shock waves and missile effects (Table 7). These would cause damage over a wider area than likely as per *scenario* 1 (Table 8). The butadiene released from the vessel

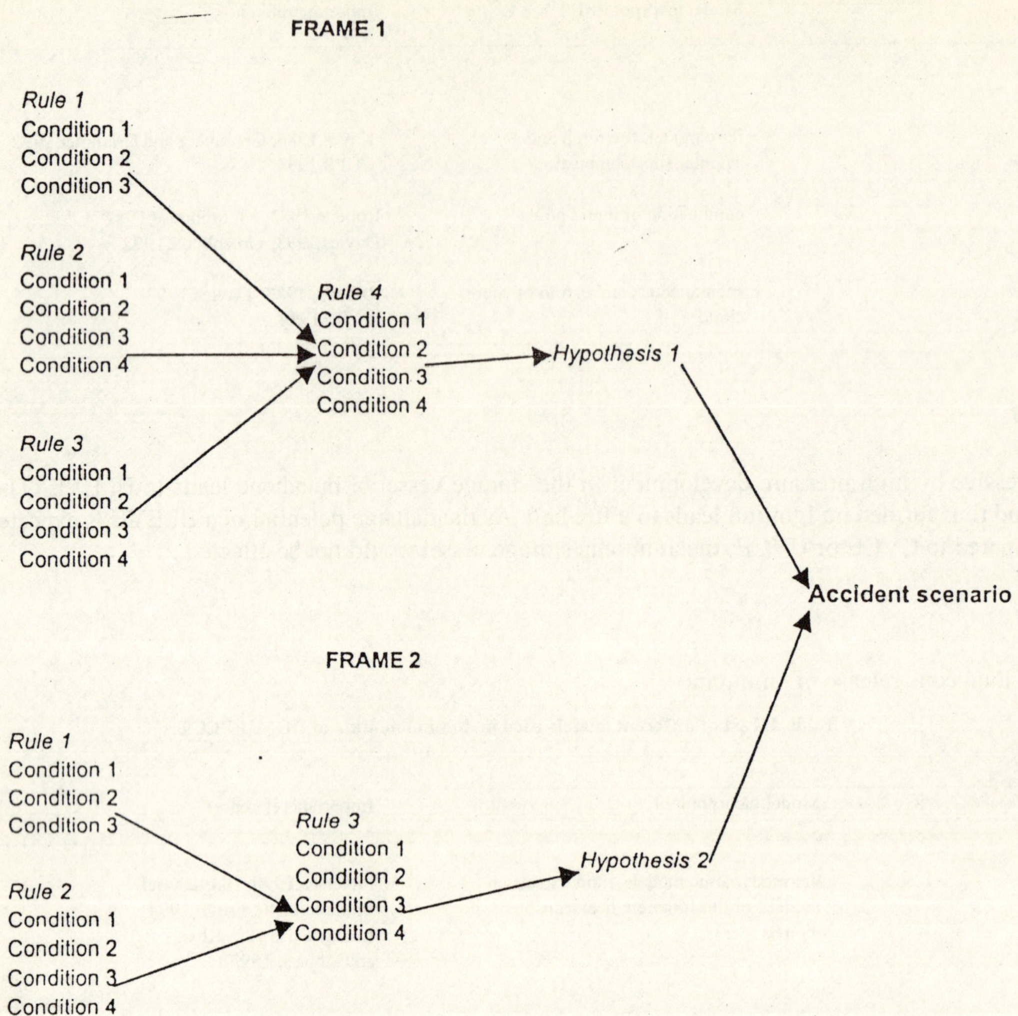

Figure 7. Typical rule network for automatic accident scenario generation module

would form a vapour-air mixture which on ignition would cause fire ball lethally effecting an area of ~500 m. The probability of a secondary accident (release of ammonia) due to this accident is about 47%. The secondary accident would cause build-up of ammonia over a wide area. All-in-all a region of ~700 m radius would be at great risk due to heat load, shock waves, and toxic load (Table 8) .

The DOMIFFECT outputs of *scenario*s 3 and 4 are presented in Tables 9 and 10 respectively. As per *scenario* 3 BLEVE would generate shock waves as well as missiles. In addition, there would be secondary impact of the released material getting ignited and forming fire ball thereby generating additional heat load. The output of DOMIFFECT for this scenario is presented in Table 9. The lethal impact of shock-waves, heat load, and missiles would go upto a radius of ~150 m (Table 11). As per *scenario* 4 (Tables 10 and 12), a lethal toxic load would be persistent over an area of ~500 m radius. The probability of secondary impacts (domino effect) is low in both the scenarios. The damage potential (50% probability of damage) of *scenario*s 3 and 4 as a function of distance from accident epicentre is presented in Tables 11 and 12 respectively.

Table 5. The result of DOMIFFECT for accident scenario 1

DOMIFFECT
F I Khan & S A Abbasi, Pondicherry-605 014, India
Result for scenario UVCE followed by Pool fire with domino analysis

Parameters		Values
PRIMARY EVENT		
Explosion : UVCE		
Total energy released by explosion	(kJ) :	4.9E+06
Peak over pressure	(kPa) :	224.6
Variation of over pressure in air	(kPa/s) :	84.3
Shock velocity of air	(m/s) :	450.9
Duration of shock wave	(ms) :	35
Missile characteristics:		
Kinetic energy associated with missile	(kJ) :	1.49E+05
Initial velocity of fragment	(m/s) :	156.3
Penetration ability at distance of 250 meter :		
Concrete structure	(m) :	0.0340
Brick structure	(m) :	0.0434
Steel structure	(m) :	0.0044
Fire : Pool fire		
Radius of the pool fire	(m) :	247.0
Burning area	(sq.m) :	191781.8
Burning rate	(kg/min) :	1574.8
Heat flux	(kJ/sq.m) :	932
SECONDARY EFFECT		
Domino Checking		
Distance of study for secondary unit	(m) :	75.0
Heat load	(kJ/sq m) :	215
Probability of domino effect due to heat load	(%) :	6
Domino effect due to over pressure :		
Peak over pressure	(kPa) :	72
Probability of domino effect due to explosion is	(%) :	23
Domino effect due to missile :		
Missile velocity	(m/s)	44.3
Probability of domino effect due to missile	(%)	2
Domino analysis : Toxic release and dispersion		
Box continues model : Elevated source		
Concentration at distance of 200 (m),	(kg/cu.m) :	6.65111E-05
Heavy gas plume Characteristics		
Ground level concentration of plume	(kg/cu.m):	6.61186E-05
Ground level concentration on plume axis	(kg/cu.m):	8.24479E-04
Width of plume	(m) :	2.50936E+02
Maximum ground level concentration	(kg/cu.m) :	3.49569E+01

DISCUSSION

Scenario 2 is the one most likely to cause domino effects as missiles, shock waves, and radiation loads would be generated simultaneously and units dealing with hazardous chemicals (flammable and toxic materials) are situated within the striking distance of the impact area of this scenario. *Scenario* 2 also represents the worst likely disaster within the realm of credibility as it has the largest area-of-lethal-impact (shock waves, lethal heat load, and lethal concentration of ammonia over an area of ~1000 m). *Scenario* 1 is also likely to cause secondary accidents but its adverse impacts would be lesser than of *scenario* 2.

In conclusion, DOMIFFECT reveals that, *scenario* 2 is the worst as far as the largeness of its impact area is concerned as well as in terms of its potentiality of causing secondary accidents. It follows that all strategies for minimising or eliminating risk should be based on the forecasts of *scenario* 2. Emergency preparedness plans should also be formulated keeping in view the worst possible impacts forecast by *Scenario* 2.

Table 6.
Probabilities of different extent of damages atdifferent distances from the epicentre of the accident for scenario 1

Damaging effect	at a distance of (meter)			
	200	500	700	1000
50% lethality by heat load	100%	55%	32%	11%
50% injury due to shock load	100%	65%	23%	5%
50% damage due to missile effect	34%	14%	1% --	
50% lethality due to toxic load	100%	65%	40%	16%

SUMMARY AND CONCLUSIONS

A new computer automated tool DOMIFFECT (DOMIno eFFECT) has been described which can be used in studying the probabilities of occurrence and the likely impacts of 'chain of accidents' or 'domino / cascading' effects in chemical process industries.

DOMIFFECT enables one to know a) whether domino effects are likely to occur in a given setting, b) if they do what would be the likely accident scenarios, and c) what would be the likely impacts of the different scenarios. Finally, the tool guides us towards strategies needed to prevent domino effects.

The package has been coded in C++ and attempts have been made to give it the following attributes:

a) Wide applicability and sophistication - to this end DOMIFFECT has been studded with state-of-the-art models capable of handling a wide variety of accident situations with precision and accuracy;

b) user-friendliness - this has been enhanced by consciously making the packages easy-to-use and by incorporating adequate facilities for generating graphics;

c) flexibility - the modular structure of DOMIFFECT makes it easy to link it with other a risk assessment tools; the package is also easy to 'add to' or 'revise'.

4. Bhattacharya, B C, (1986). Chemical equipment design, *CBC publication*, Delhi, 214.

5. Bowen, J H, (1980). Missile problems in the chemical and nuclear power industries, *Nuclear Engineering*, **19**, 149.

6. Centre for Chemical Process Safety-CCPS, (1994). Fire and explosion guidelines, *CCPS Publication*, AIChE, New York.

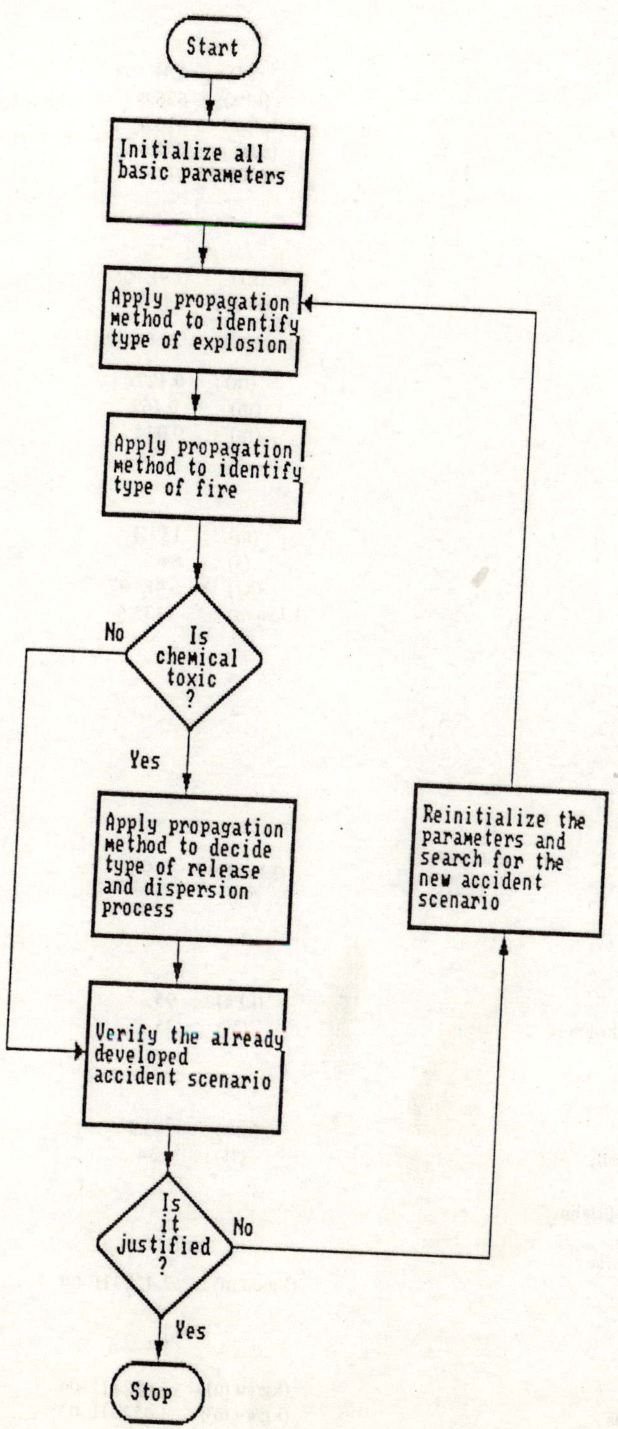

Figure 8. Inference engine of DOMIFFECT to decide the accident scenario

Table 7. The result of DOMIFFECT for accident scenario 2

DOMIFFECT F I Khan & S A Abbasi, Pondicherry-605 014, India Result for scenario CVCE followed by Fire ball with domino analysis

Parameters		Values
PRIMARY EVENT		
Explosion : CVCE		
Energy released during explosion	(kJ) :	2.4E+08
Peak over pressure	(kPa):	626.4
Variation of over pressure in air	(kPa/s):	420.4
Shock velocity of air	(m/s) :	763.6
Duration of shock wave	(ms) :	41
Missile result		
Kinetic energy associated with fragment	(kJ) :	3.9E+06
Initial velocity of fragment	(m/s) :	252.9
Penetration at distance of 250 meter :		
Concrete structure	(m) :	0.127
Brick structure	(m) :	0.162
Steel structure	(m) :	0.024
Fire : Fire ball		
Radius of the fire ball	(m) :	157.4
Duration of the fire ball	(s) :	64
Energy released by fire ball	(kJ) :	6.4E+07
Radiation heat flux	(kJ/sq.m) :	1435.6
SECONDARY EVENT		
Domino checking		
Distance of secondary event : 75.00		
Heat load :		
Heat load	(kJ/m2) :	545
Probability of domino event due fire	(%) :	14
Domino effect due to over pressure :		
Peak over pressure	(kPa) :	95
Probability of domino effect due to explosion is	(%) :	35
Domino effect due to missile :		
Missile velocity	(m/s) :	115.2
Probability of domino effect due to missile	(%) :	6.34
Domino analysis : Toxic release and dispersion		
Box instantaneous model : Elevated source		
Concentration at distance of 200 (m),	(kg/cu.m) :	3.45231E-04
Heavy gas puff Characteristics		
Ground level concentration of puff	(kg/cu.m):	3.45231E-04
Ground level concentration on puff axis	(kg/cu.m):	3.45231E-03
Cloud radius	(m) :	1.16753E+02
Maximum distance traveled by the cloud	(m) :	7.87457E+02
Maximum ground level concentration	(kg/cu.m):	4.3

Table 8. Probabilities of different types of damages at different distances from the epicentre of the accident for scenario 2

Damaging effect	at a distance of (meter)			
	200	500	700	1000
50% lethality by heat load	100%	71%	42%	22%
50% injury due to shock load	100%	76%	49%	25%
50% damage due to missile effect	50%	22%	3%	--
50% lethality due to toxic load	100%	100%	73%	51%

Table 9. The result of DOMIFFECT for accident scenario 3

DOMIFFECT
F I Khan & S A Abbasi, Pondicherry-605 014, India
Result for scenario BLEVE followed by fire ball with domino analysis

Parameters	Values	
PRIMARY EVENT		
Explosion : BLEVE		
Total energy released	(kJ) :	12890.0
Peak over pressure	(kPa) :	65.8
Variation of over pressure in air	(kPa/s) :	0.67
Shock velocity of air	(m/s) :	389.0
Duration of shock wave	(ms) :	300
No missile effect		
Fire : Fire ball		
Radius of the fire ball	(m) :	88.1
Duration of the fire ball	(s) :	36
Energy released by fire ball	(kJ) :	1.0E+06
Radiation heat flux	(kJ/sq.m) :	745.6
SECONDARY EVENT		
Domino Checking		
Distance of Study	:	75.0
Heat load :		
Heat load	(kJ/sq m):	156
Chances of domino event due fire	(%) :	2
Domino effect due to over pressure :		
Peak over pressure	(kPa) :	34
Chances of domino effect due to explosion is (%) : 2		
Domino effect due to missile :		
No chance of domino effect due to missile		
Domino analysis : toxic release and dispersion		
No analysis		

Table 10. The result of DOMIFFECT for accident scenario 4

DOMIFFECT
F I Khan & S A Abbasi, Pondicherry-605 014, India

Result for scenario toxic release and dispersion with domino analysis

Parameters		Values
PRIMARY EVENT		
Toxic dispersion		
Heavy Gas : Dispersion characteristics		
Box Instantaneous: Model		
Concentration at distance 200.00 (m),	(kg/cu.m):	2.374443E-4
Puff characteristics:		
Puff concentrationat centre of cloud	(kg/cu.m):	2.37443E-4
Concentration at cloud edges	(kg/cu.m):	2.37443E-3
Distance along down wind	(m):	259
Maximum distance traveled	(m) :	599
SECONDARY EVENT		
Domino checking		
No hazard interaction , Go ahead!		

Table 11. Probabilities of different types of damages at different distances from the epicentre of the accident for scenario 3

Damaging effect	at a distance of (meter)			
	200	500	700	1000
50% lethality by heat load	35%	11%	<1%	--
50% injury due to shock load	65%	23%	3%	--
50% damage due to missile effect	--	--	--	--
50% lethality due to toxic load	--	--	--	--

7. Considine, M, (1984). Thermal radiation hazards ranges from large hydrocarbon pool fires, *SRD report number R297*, U K atomic energy authority.

8. Davies, P A, (1993). A guide to the evaluation of condensed phase explosions, *J Hazardous Materials*, **33**, 1.

REFERENCES

1. Bagster, D F, and Pitblado, R M, (1991). The estimation of domino incident frequencies - an approach, *Process Safety Environ*, **69B**, 196.

2. Baker, W E, Cox, P A, Westin, P S, Kulesz, J J, Strehlow, R A, (1983). Explosion hazards and evaluations, *Elesevier Science Ltd.*, Amsterdam..

Table 12. Probabilities of different types of damages at different distances from the epicentre of the accident for scenario 4

Damaging effect	at a distance of (meter)			
	200	500	700	1000
50% lethality by heat load	--	--	--	--
50% injury due to shock load	--	--	--	--
50% damage due to missile effect	--	--	--	--
50% lethality due to toxic load	100%	100%	73%	51%

3. Beynon, G V, Cowley, L T, Small, L M, and Williams, I J, (1988). J *Hazardous Materials*, **20**, 239.

9. Deaves, D M, (1992). Dense gas dispersion modelling, *J. Loss Prevention in Process Industries.*, **5**(4), 219.

10. Erbink, J J, (1993). The advanced Gaussian model STACKS, *Proceeding of ERCOFTAC work shop on Inter comparison of Advanced Practical Short range Atmospheric Dispersion Modelling*, Manno, Switzerland.

11. Erbink, J J, (1995). Turbulent diffusion model from tall stacks, *Ph.D. thesis submitted to VRIJ University*, The Netherlands.

12. Greenbook , (1992). Methods for determining of possible damage to people and objects resulting from release of hazardous materials, *Rep CPR 16E*, Voorburg, Warrington.

13. Greenberg, H R and Crammer, J J, (1992). Risk Assessment and risk management in chemical process industries, *Van Norstand Reinhold*, New York.

14. Hindu , (1997). Major fire in Vizag refinery, *The Hindu publication*, September 15, 1.

15. Kayes,P J, (1986). Manual of industrial hazard assessment technique, *Technica Ltd.*, London.

16. Khan, F I, and Abbasi, S A, (1996).Simulation of accidents in a chemical process industry using software MAXCRED, *Indian J of Chemical Technology*, **3**, 338.

17. Khan, F I, and Abbasi, S A, (1997a). Risk analysis of epichlohydrin manufacturing industry using new computer automated tool MAXCRED, *J Loss Prevention In Process Industries*, **10**(2), 91.

18. Khan, F I, and Abbasi, S A, (1997b). Risk analysis of a cloralkali industry situated in densely populated area, *Process Safety Progress*, **16**(3), 172.

19. Khan, F I, and Abbasi, S A, (1997c). optHAZOP an optimal and effective procedure to conduct HAZOP study, *J Loss Prevention in Process Industries*, **10**(3), 191.

20. Khan, F I, and Abbasi, S A, (1997d). Inherently safer design based on Rapid risk analysis , *J Loss Prevention in Process Industries*, (accepted).

21. Khan, F I, and Abbasi, S A, (1997e). MAXCRED: a new software package rapid risk assessment, *Environmental Modelling and Software*, (accepted).

22. Khan, F I, and Abbasi, S A, (1997f). Modelling and Simulation of heavy gases based on the Modification in Plume Path Theory, *Atmospheric Environment* (under consideration).

23. Khan, F I, and Abbasi, S A, (1997g). Application of the recently modified plume path theory on the dispersion of some heavy gases, *Sym. of Air Quality Management at an urban, regional, and global scale*, 23-26 September, Istanbul.

24. Khan, F I, and Abbasi, S A, (1997h). Models of Domino effect analysis in chemical process industry, *Process Safety Progress*, November.

25. Kletz, T A, (1985). What went wrong, *Gulf Publication Company*, England.

26. Latha, P, Gautam, G, and Raghavan, K V, (1992). Strategies for quantification of thermally initiated cascade effects, *J Loss Prevention Process Industries*, **5**(1).

27. Lees, F P, (1996). Loss prevention in process industries, (2nd edition), *Butterworths*, **1-3**, London.

28. Mahoney, D G, (1990). Large property damage losses in the hydrocarbon-chemical industries: a thirty-year review, *M & M Protection Consultants*, New York.

29. Martinsen, W E, Johnson, D W, and Terrell, W F, (1986). BLEVEs:Their causes, effects and prevention, *Hydrocarbon Processing*, **65**, 11.

30. Marshall, V C, (1987). Major chemical hazards, *John Wiley & Sons*, New York.

31. Maurer, B, (1977). Modelling of vapour cloud dispersion and deflagration after bursting of tanks filled with liquefied gas, *2nd International Symposium on Loss Prevention in Process Industries*, Heidelberg , VI-305.

32. Medard, L A, (1989). Accidental explosions, *Ellis Horwood*, England.

33. Moorehouse, J, (1982). Scaling criteria for pool fires derived from large scale experiment, The Assessment of Major Hazards, *Institution of Chemical Engineers*, Rugby, 165.

34. Pasman, H J, Duxbury, H A, Bjordal, P, (1992). Major hazards in the process industries, : achievements and challenges in loss prevention, *J Hazardous Materials*, **33**, 1.

35. Pietersen, C M, (1986). Analysis of the LPG disaster in Mexico City, *Loss Prevention and Safety Promotion*, **5**, 21.

36. Pietersen, C M, (1990). Consequence of accidental release of hazardous materials, *J of Loss Prevention Process Industries*, **3**, 136.

37. Pritchard, D K, (1989). A review of methods for predicting blast damage from vapour cloud explosions, *J Loss Prevention Process Industries*, **2**(4), 193.

38. Prugh, R W, (1987). Evaluation of unconfined vapour cloud explosions, *Proceeding of International Conference of Vapour Cloud Modelling*, Boston.

39. Prugh, R W, (1991). Quantitative evaluation of BLEVE Hazards, *Chemical Engineering Progress*, **87**(2), 60.

40. Prugh, R W, (1992). Modelling and mitigation of the consequence of accidental release of hazardous materials, *Plant Operation Progress*, **11** (1), 19.

41. Prugh, R W, (1994). Quantitative evaluation of fire ball hazards, *Process Safety Progress*, **13**(2), 83.

42. Raghavan, K V, and Swaminathan, G, (1996). Hazard assessment and disaster mitigation in petrochemical industries, *Oxford Publishing Company*, Chennai.

43. Ramskill, P K A, (1987). Description of engulf in a Computer Code to Model the Thermal Response of Tank Totally Engulfed in Fire., *UKAEA Report no. SRD/HSE/R354 and SRD/HSE/070/WPL*, UK.

44. Roberts, A F, (1983). Thermal radiation hazards from pressurised storage, *Fire Safety*, **4**, 197.

45. Singh, J, (1988). Explosion propagation in non-spherical vessel: simplified equations and applications, *J Loss Prevention in Process Industries*, **1**(1), 39.

46. Van den berg, A C, and Lennoy, A, (1993). Methods for vapour cloud explosion blast modelling, *J Hazardous Materials*, **34**, 171.

47. Venerate, J E S, Rutledge, G A, Sumathipala, K, and Sollows, K, (1993). To BLEVE or not to BLEVE: Anatomy of Boiling Liquid Expanding Vapour Explosion, *Process Safety Progress*, **12**(2), 67.

¨ Reproduced from *Journal of Environmental Modelling and Software*, The Netherlands

Part VII

Methods of HAZARD Identification, Screening and Ranking

In the penultimate part of this thesis we present the system HIRA (Hazard identification and Ranking) developed by us to quickly identify and rank hazards present in a chemical process industry with the help of indices. In developing HIRA we have used the knowledge and experiences gained by us during the studies presented in the previous chapter. But, in practice, HIRA would form the first step in the total risk assessment system proposed by us (chapter 1).

17

ACCIDENT HAZARD INDEX : A Multi-attribute Method for Process Industry Hazard Rating*

Traditionally, the severity of accidents in chemical process industries has been gauged on the basis of the human lives lost (Lees, 1996; Wyler and Bohnenblust,1994; Khan and Abbasi, 1996;1997). However, factors such as loss of assets, contamination of the surroundings, and the resultant trauma also contribute to a very large extent towards the adverse impacts of such accidents.

We have developed accident Hazard Index (AHI) as a new system for a comprehensive yet rapid assessment of the damages caused by accidents in chemical process industries. The index can also be used to assess the impacts of accidents likely in a yet-to-be-commissioned industry on the basis of site characteristics and the industry's process and operational details; the index thus enables one to chose between possible sites for setting up a new industry.

Keywords: Hazard indices, hazard identification, hazard ranking.

INTRODUCTION

Right from the days of industrial revolution accidents have been occurring off-and-on in chemical process industries. But the frequency as well as severity of these accidents have significantly increased during the past few decades as thc pace of industrialization, as well as density of population near industrial complexes, have both incrcased rapidly with time. Table 1 presents examples of some of the bigger accidents of the last 25 years. It may be seen that the adverse impacts of the accidents depend not only on the type of the industry but also on the type of surroundings the effected industry had.

Most of the accidents in chemical process industries are caused either by material failure (such as crack in the storage vessels), operational mistakes (such as raising the pressure/ temperature/flow-rate beyond the critical limits), or external perturbation (such as damage caused by a projectile). Some accidents have catastrophic consequences. For example Bhopal Gas Tragedy of 1984 killed or maimed over 20,000 persons and the LPG terminal accident at Mexico city in the same year claimed 600 lives. There have been numerous other accidents in which the death toll would have been as high as in Bhopal and Mexico, if the areas where the accidents took place were not less densely populated.

Apart from causing damage to property and claiming human lives, many accidents also cause long-term contamination of the surroundings. For example, in the well-known Seveso Disaster (Abbasi et al 1997), which occurred near

* Reproduced from *Trans IChemE (UK), 75 B, 217-224, 1997.*

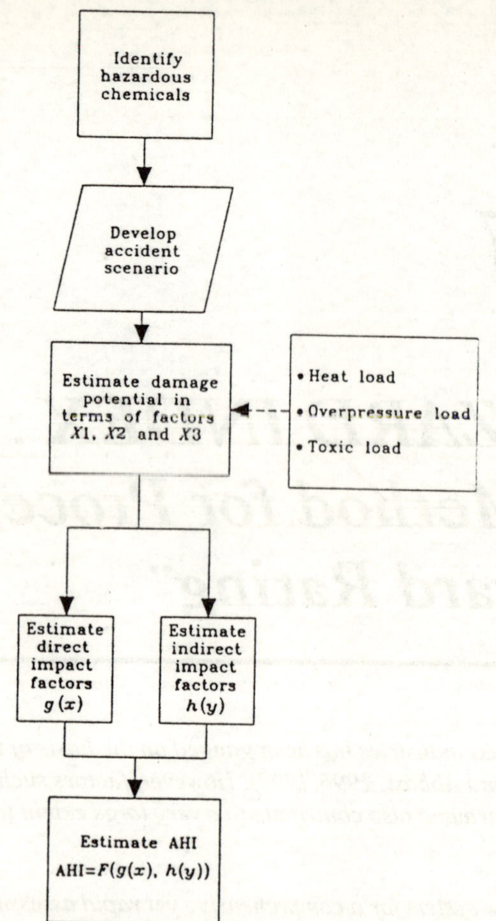

Figure 1. Systematic procedure of AHI computation.

Milan, Italy, in 1976, about 2 kg of TCDD (tetrachloro dibenzo dioxin) was released. TCDD is one of the most toxic and persistent chemicals known (Abbasi at al, 1997) and decontamination of effected area posed a very serious problem inspite of the low quantities of TCDD involved. Some authors believe that the area could never be decontaminated and the adverse effects of TCDD on humans are witnessed to this day.

Yet, traditionally, the severity of an accident is measured by the number of fatalities it causes. On March 12, 1995 a tanker carrying benzene dashed into a passenger bus and a tractor on a highway, about 50 km from the city of Chennai (Madras). The triple accident caused the tanker to explode. The resulting missiles, shock waves, and fire ball killed 150 persons (Frontline, 1995). Had the same event occurred after the tanker had entered the populous Chennai city, the number of fatalities would have run into thousands, and the accident would have assumed the dimensions of a notorious disaster.

Indeed, the number of fatalities is a very important parameter in assessing the damage potential of an accident. But there are many other parameters which have more or less the same importance and contribute in equal measures to the damage potential of an accident. These include long-term contamination of the environment, damage to property and other support systems which bring socio-economic depression in the areas surrounding the accident sites, trauma caused to injured - especially debilitated persons, and to the relatives of the deceased.

To characterize the hazard associated with any process industry, it is essential that all the probable accident scenarios are identified, their magnitudes quantified, their impacts assessed, and the knowledge used to work out net losses of lives, assets, and damage to ecosystems. But such an elaborate study of the likely causes, likely accidents, and likely consequences would require substantial inputs of experts personnel, time, and money. If one has to screen a large number of industries and industrial sites within a short span of time and limited budget, it is necessary to have an appropriate ranking technique which is quick to execute yet has adequate accuracy and precision. In the literature we find reports on the identification and ranking of hazards in process industries; the noteworthy among these include Dow Index (Dow, 1987; Scheffler, 1994), Mond Index (Mond, 1985) and Toxicity Index (Tyler, 1994). We, too, have developed an index HIRA (Hazard Identification and RAnkng) for this purpose. But all these indices take into account only the premises of the industries and do not consider the surrounding population, environment, and assets at all. But, as elaborated earlier, these factors can have a very strong influence on the damage caused by accidents. Indeed these factors determine the *real* magnitude of an accident's adverse impacts. Furthermore all these factors must be taken into consideration when deciding on the location of new industries from among the various potential sites.

Keller et al. (1985), Wyler and Bohnenblust (1991) and Christen et al. (1994) have proposed schemes to rank past accidents keeping some site characteristics in view but these schemes can only be used to rank the accidents that have already occurred and not in *forecasting the damage likely to occur* at different sites from the same type of accident. Among these the scheme proposed by Christen et al. (1994) is most modern and takes into account many parameters. It uses a scale of 0 to 1, to characterize the severity of an accident. However, it does not incorporate site specific attributes such as proximity to sensitive ecosystems, and nature of support facilities medicare, fire-fighting, transportation, etc.

To overcome the aforesaid limitations, the authors have proposed a scheme to rank probable or already occurred

Table 1. Comparison of index values for accidents

Accident	Even (s)	Financial Deaths	Christen's loss. million $	disaster index (DI)11	Significance as per DI	Accident hazard index (AHI) g (x)	h(y)	AHI	Significance as per AHI
Flixborough (1974)	Explosion+Fire	28	450	0.50	Sever accident	6.5	3.7	7.5	Severe accident
Beek (1975)	Explosion+Fire	14	10	0.33	Incident	3.5	2.7	4.4	Accident
Seveso (1976)	Toxic release	-	350	0.70	Catastrophe	6.5	5.5	8.5	Catastrophe
Dhurabar (1983)	Explosion+ Fire	47	25	0.44	Incident	5.8	3.1	6.5	Severe accident
Cubatao (1984)	Fire	100	50	0.43	Severe accident	4.3	3.5	5.5	Severe accident
Bhopal (1984)	Toxic release	2500	350	1.0	Catastrophe	10.0	5.4	10.0	Catastrophe
Basel (1986)	Fire + Toxic	-	245	0.51	Catastrophe	5.5	3.8	6.7	Severe accident
Arzamas (1988)	Explosion + Fire	23	55	0.57	Catastrophe	5.5	4.1	6.8	Severe accident
Ufa (1989)	Explosion + Toxic	7	570	0.75	Catastrophe	7.5	4.6	8.8	Catastrophe
Bangkok (1990)	Fire + Toxic	17	55	0.41	Severe accident	3.5	3.3	4.8	Accident
Bombay (1990)	Fire	10	145	0.46	Severe accident	4.4	3.1	5.4	Severe accident
Panipat (1993)	Explosion + Toxic	3	85	0.39	Incident	3.7	3.5	5.1	Severe accident
Dronka (1994)	Toxic release	4	25	0.33	Incident	3.4	2.7	4.3	Accident
Madras (1995)	Explosion+ Fire	150	45	0.57	Catastrophe	6.1	2.1	6.4	Severe accident
Bombay (1996)	Fire	2	150	0.27	Incident	3.5	1.8	3.9	Accident

g(x) represents value of damage potential as well as direct impact
h(y) represents value of indirect impact

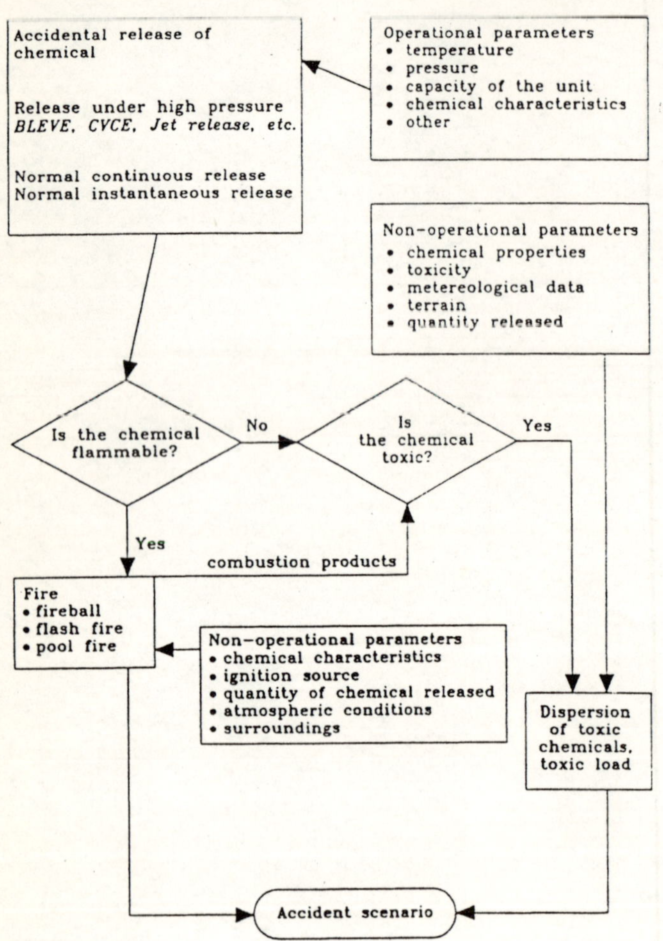

Figure 2. Logistics associated with the generation of scenarios.

accidents. This index can be used as a tool to rank an industry in terms of hazard to the plant as well as the surroundings. The technique incorporates the effect of various parameters such as chemicals in use, site characteristics, direct/indirect damage to surrounding population and the environment. A brief description of the importance of the various parameters and the methods employed by us to work out the index is presented below.

ACCIDENT HAZARD INDEX

AHI (accident hazard index) represents the consequences of an accidents on a scale of 1 to 10. The AHI algorithm is shown in Figure 1. The algorithm starts with the anticipation of the most credible accident scenario. The scenario is then processed for estimating its damage potential. Subsequently impacts of other factors on the severity of the accident are evaluated. These impact factors influence the severity of an accident through two different routes:

1) direct impacts,

2) indirect impacts.

Direct impacts are due to those parameters which have direct relation with accident consequences and have instant (with a maximum delay of a few hours) effects. Three most important direct impact parameters considered here are:

i) population,

ii) asset, and,

iii) ecosystem.

The indirect impacts are due parameters which have secondary relation with accident consequences. Three main indirect impacts considered in the present study are:

i) soil environment,

ii) water environment, and,

iii) ecosystem.

The indirect impacts are due to those parameters which have secondary relation with accident consequences. Three main indirect impacts considered in present study are:

i) soil environment

ii) water environment, and

iii) air environment

These impacts (direct and indirect) have a major contribution in characterizing an accident severity. The steps of

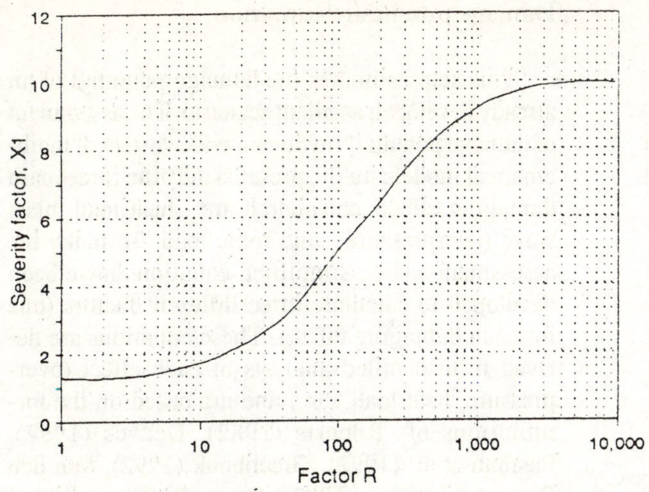

Figure 3. Profile of severity factor XI due to heat load.

AHI algorithm and method to quantify direct and indirect impacts are discussed in subsequent sections in detail.

Accident scenario

An accident scenario is a description of an expected situation. It basically depicts different likely events that may occur in an industry leading to an accident. The expectation of a scenario does not mean it *will* occur, but it means it has a *reasonable probability of occurrence*. The accident scenarios are generated based on the properties of chemicals handled by the industry, physical conditions under which reactions occur or reactants/products are stored, geometry and material strengths of the vessels and conduits involved, valves and safety arrangements etc. External factors such as site characteristics (topography, presence of trees, ponds, rivers in the vicinity, proximity to other industries or neighborhoods, etc.) and meteorological conditions are also considered.

Construction of a scenario aims to achieve the following objectives:

i) It is the basis of risk study; it tells us what may happen so that we can devise ways and mean of preventing or minimizing the possibility.

ii) A scenario forms a focal point of a heuristic process. It enables use of the wisdom of hindsight (experiences of past accidents) and state-of-the-art knowledge (to evaluate its impact) in forecasting accident situations. The forecast is fed back to the past and the present knowledge for generating new knowledge. A scenario is thus a reference point as well as a link between the past, present, and future.

In this step of AHI calculation accident scenario is generated for the industry under study. It is a very important input for the subsequent steps. The more realistic the accident scenario is, the more accurate is the forecasting of the type of accident, its consequences, and associated risks.

From the studies reported in literature (Chary, 1995; Contini et al., 1991; Raghvan and Mallikarjunan,1986) one gathers that generally the authors have considered only one or a few more obvious accidental scenarios, leaving out several other credible accidents from considerations. We have discussed this aspects in detail elsewhere (Khan and Abbasi, 1996;1997), bringing out how the entire complexion of the risk assessment and disaster prevention/management strategies can changes if the scenarios of all credible accidents are taken into consideration. For example, the scenario for an accident in ethylene storage vessel (storage under high pressure in liquefied state) is generally visualized as confined vapor cloud explosion (CVCE) followed by a fire ball. It is because a high pressure build-up in the storage vessel either due to external heat absorption, or due to some run-away reaction because of impurities present, would cause the vessel to fail with a CVCE and, as the released chemical is highly flammable, it would generate a fire ball. But a toxic release may also occur, leading to overpressure load along with toxic load due to the violence of the sudden release. Unless all such credible accidents are considered and their impacts carefully evaluated one can miss out on the various possibilities and the damage control exercises would accordingly be incomplete and inadequate.

Visualization of such accident scenarios can be achieved by analyzing the chemical characteristics and operating conditions in detail with the help of thermodynamic, heat transfer, and fluid dynamic models. The logistics associated with generation of scenarios are presented in Figure 2.

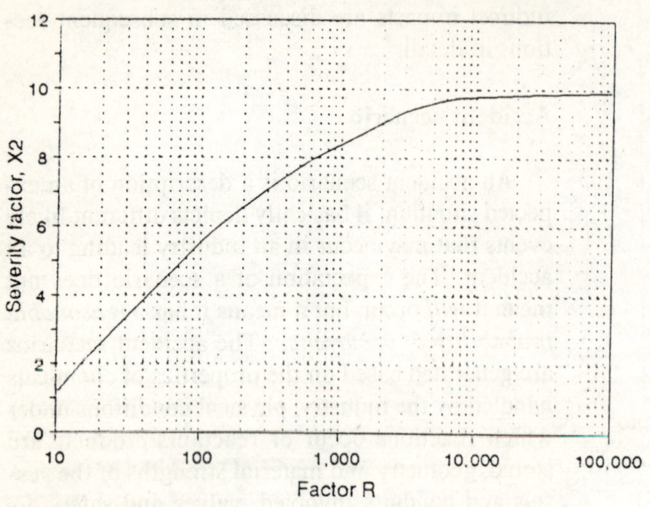

Figure 4. Profile of severity factor X2 due to toxic load.

Damage potential estimation

This step estimates the damage potential of an already developed accident scenario. The assessment of damage potential involves a wide variety of mathematical models. In the present study the three main damaging effects considered are - heat load, blast wave (overpressure), and toxic load. To make the assessment easier, simplified equations have been developed to calculate three different factors (one for each damaging effect). These equations are derived from detailed analysis of each effect (overpressure, heat load, etc.) and are based on the formulations of Roberts (1982), Deaves (1992), Pasman et al. (1992), Greenbook (1992), Van den Berg and Lannoy (1993), Davis (1993), and Lees (1996).

Heat load

The damage potential due to heat load can be estimated using;

$$R = K1*(Hc*m)^{1/2} \qquad ...1$$

$$X1 = f1(R) \qquad ...2$$

Where, K1 is a constant having a value 51, Hc is heat of combustion (kJ/kg) and m is quantity of chemical involved in the event (kg); all parameters are measured in SI units.

Later, the factor 'R' is used to predict severity factor *X1* using Figure 3. The Figure 3 has been drawn through a detailed study of heat load potential and its impact over the surroundings. A scale of 0 to 10 has been used to characterize this factor. This characterization has been done with the help of CCPS (1989), Roberts (1982), Lees (1996), Christen et al. (1994).

Overpressure load

The effect of overpressure can be quantified as;

$$R = K2*(Hc*m); \text{ where } K2=7.0*E\text{-}06 \qquad ...3$$

$$X2=f2(R) \qquad ...4$$

The severity factor '*X2*' is a measure of severity of damage potential due to overpressure on a scale of 0 to 10. *X2* can be estimated using Figure 4. This severity factor has been designed by using equations reported by Petersen (1990), Pasman et al. (1992), Davis (1993) and Van den berg and Lannoy (1993).

Toxic load

The consequences due to toxic effect can be quantified as:

$$R=(q/LC50)^{1/3} \qquad ...5$$

$$X3=f3(R) \qquad ...6$$

Where, q represents quantity released (in kg) in one hour (release rate * one hour) for continuous release and total

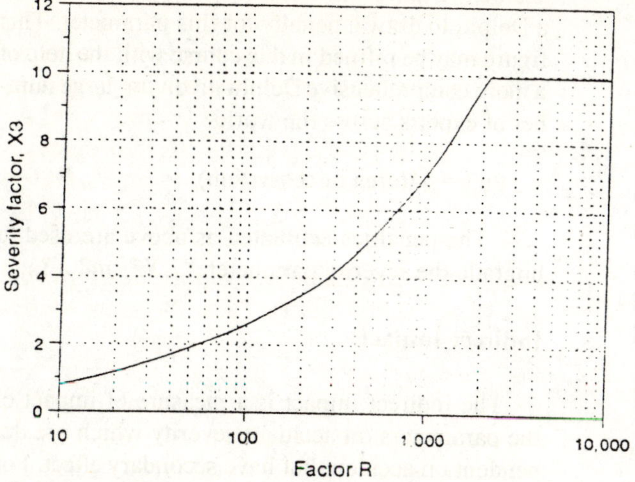

Figure 5. Profile of severity factor X3 due to over-pressure.

quantity release (in kg) for instantaneous release, LC50 (based on the exposure limit of 4 hours; Tyler, 1995) represents lethal concentration (50% probability of death) in kg/m^3. This severity factor X3 can be estimated by using Figure 5. This figure is drawn by considering dispersion under slightly unstable condition over a flat terrain and instantaneous exposure (short term exposure limit) through inhalation as the basis (Deaves, 1992).

Direct impact factors

The severity factors *X1,X2*, and *X3* estimated in the last steps represent severity of each damaging effect due to inherent characteristics of an industry or process. As discussed earlier the direct impact parameters are also major contributors to the severity. In this section, the effect of these parameters will be discussed in detail and accordingly the weightage (penalty) will be estimated for each parameter.

Population

As mentioned earlier, population density is one of the important factors which contribute to the severity of an accident. For example, an accident occurring in Connaught palace (a congested market place), New Delhi(population density 6139 person/sqkm) will have much more disastrous consequences compared to exactly similar accident occurring in Jaselmair, (a desert area) Rajasthan (population density 9 person/sqkm). The impact of population on severity of accident is assessed by the penalty pn1 which is a function of population density of the area. The penalty has a maximum value 1 corresponding to population density of Connaught Palace and least 0 corresponding to Jaselmair. The penalty of any intermediate population density can be estimated using Figure 6. Figure 6 has been drawn with the help of references Keller et al. (1985), Wyler and Bohnenblust (1991), Greenbook (1992) and recommendations of experts (Arya and Abbasi, 1995; 1997).

$$Pn1 = g1(\text{Population density}) \qquad ...7$$

Asset

Loss of assets is another very important factor contributing to the severity of an accident impact. This type of impact is assessed through penalty 'pn2'. It is a function of the asset density of the area. The maximum value of pn2 is 1 for market place (Connaught place) and a value of 0 for a remote area. Intermediate values of penalty can be drawn using Figure 7.

$$Pn2 = g2(\text{Asset density}) \qquad ...8$$

Ecosystem

Impacts of accidents on the surrounding ecosystems have been rarely considered because such impacts are much less visible than loss of lives and assets. But damages to ecosystems can have serious long-term consequences. For example the release of TCDD (tetrachloro dibenzo dioxin) at Seveso, Italy (Abbasi et al., 1997) and pesticides at Basel, Switzerland (Christen et al., 1994), caused long-term contamination of the environment with long-lasting adverse impacts.

The impact on ecosystem is assessed in terms of area of ecosystem getting affected by the accident. Further, high penalties are assigned if some sensitive or important ecosystem happens to be coming within the periphery of an

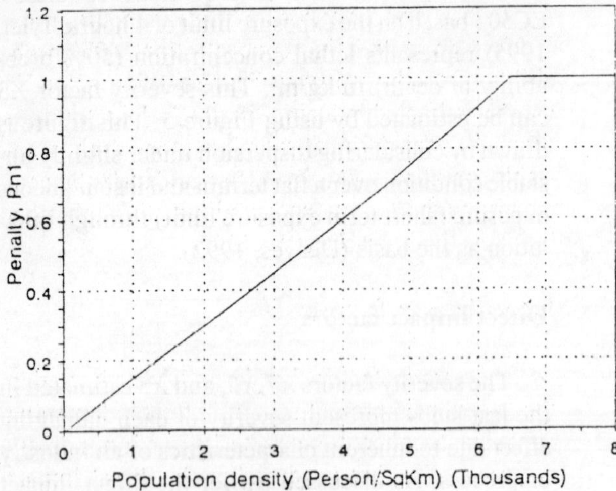

Figure 6.Cure for penalty estimation to assess damage to the population

accident. Figure 8 is tentatively suggested based on a Delphi to draw a penalty for this parameter. This figure may be refined in due course with the help of a more comprehensive Delphi involving large number of experts across the world.

$$Pn3 = g3(\text{area of ecosystem}) \qquad ...9$$

The penalties estimated as above are used to upgrade the severity parameter *X1,X2*, and *X3* .

Indirect Impact

The indirect impact is a measure of impact of the parameters on accident severity which are dependent on accident but have secondary effect. For example, release of hazardous liquid has chances to contaminate water, part of the liquid may evaporate and hence contaminate air and some liquid may be absorbed by soil and so contaminate the land. Thus, release of a hazardous chemical affects the air, water, and soil environment which later affect living organisms including humans.

The curves to assess the weightage of such impacts are presented in Figures 9-11. In order to develop these index components for the indirect impacts we have once again taken recourse to a Delphi as there in no other means to provide an 'importance' weightage for such impacts (Arya and Abbasi-1995,1997). In due course the components can be refined by a more comprehensive Delphi.

INDEX COMPUTATION

As discussed earlier AHI is a function of damage potential, direct impact and indirect impact, and hence can be expressed as;

$$AHI = F(g(x),h(y)) = \text{minimum of } (10, (g(x)^2 + h(y)^2)^{1/2}) \qquad ...10$$

where, g(x) is a function defining damage potential and direct impact while h(y) is a function specifying indirect impact.

The function g(x) can further be expanded as;

$$g(x) = \text{minimum of } [10, \{\{(g1(x1))^p+(g2(x2))^p+(g3(x3))^p\}*(1+z)\}^{1/p}] \qquad ...11$$

Where 1,2,3, specify the damaging effects due to heat load, peak overpressure and toxic release respectively, and P is a fuzzy expression parameter. Past studies suggest p value to be 3 (Zimmermann, 1987, Christen et al., 1994, Wyler and Bohnenblust , 1991).

The function gi(xi) can be as;

$$gi(xi) = \sum_{i=1-3}[Xi\{\prod_{j=1-3}(1+Pnj)\}] = \sum_{i=1-3}[Xi(1+Pn1)(1+Pn2)(1+Pn3)] \quad (12)$$

where, Xi represents the damaging potential of a particular effect, pnj represents the penalty of the direct impact of each parameter. The factor 'z' represents the hazardous characteristic of a chemical. NFPA (National Fire Protection Agency) rating has been used to calculate factor `z'. The rating has been scaled-down to a scale of 0 to 1 (instead of NFPA's 0 to 4) without disturbing its significance.

Similarly the function for indirect impact h(y) can be expanded as

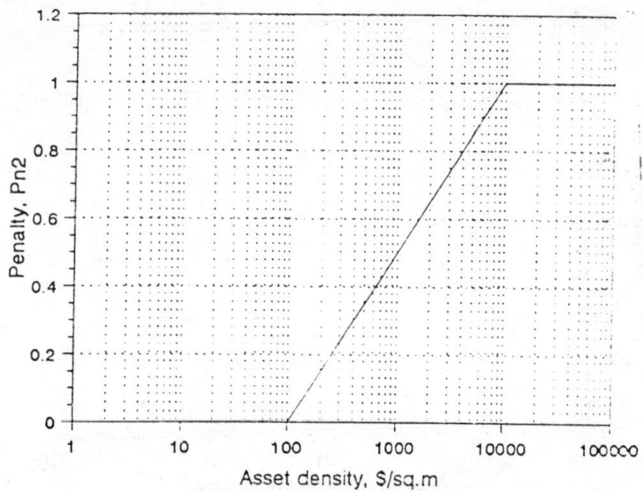

Figure 7. Cure for penalty estimation to assess loss of asset.

$$h(y) = \text{minimum of } [10, \{(l1(y1))^p+(l2(y2))^p+(l3(y3))^p\}^{1/p}] \quad ...13$$

where, li(yi)i=1,2,3 represents the indirect impact of an accident on the different environmental component and 1,2,3, represents the broder impacts on soil, water and air environment respectively. The function li(yi)i=1,2,3 can be further explained as;

li(yi=1-3) = *f*(hazardous properties, quantity release and condition of release) ..14

Curves to estimate the li(yi) values are presented in Figures 9-11.

As mentioned earlier, AHI is categorized on a scale of 0 to 10, where severity of damage is maximum at a value 10 and minimum at 0. The classification of accident and hazard potential according to AHI value has been done as;

0-1	—— Normal Operation	—— minor hazard
1-3	—— Incident	—— low hazard
3-5	—— Accident	—— significantly high hazard
5-8	—— Severe accident	—— severe hazard
8-10	—— Catastrophe	—— extremely severe hazard

The two classifications —accident type and hazard potential-— are interrelated. A minor hazard potential would always be there in any process operation (normal operating conditions), whereas an accident may have wide range of hazard potential from low to extremely severe. This is qualitative classification based on the values of AHI index which represent the severity of hazard. An industry or plant posing AHI value higher than 3 need to go for detailed evaluation of their safety system, whereas a value higher than 8 needs immediate attention and necessity to conduct detailed study to identify various vulnerable locations and development of strategies to control them.

CASE STUDY

AHI has been calculated for various past accidents. The list of accidents and their corresponding index values are presented in Table 1. The input data and the results of intermediate calculations for the Bhopal Gas Tragedy of 1984 are presented in Tables 2 and 3, respectively. The results presented in Table 1 are compared with the rating proposed by Christen et al. (1994). It is observed that the AHI has a wider range to enable more distinct characterization, whereas disaster index ranking (Christen et al. -1994). has a much narrower scale with lesser sensitivity and precision.

SUMMARY AND CONCLUSION

The indices reported thus far for ranking the severity of accidents in chemical process industries either do not take into account the surroundings (population density, assets, and sensitive ecosystems), or do not possess features to enable forecasting of impacts of likely accidents on the surroundings.

In this paper we have emphasized the necessity of considering the surroundings of an industry as crucial inputs in determining the severity of accidents occurring in the industry. An elaborate Accident Hazard Index (AHI) has been developed which incorporates direct and indirect impacts of accidents in chemical process industries on the population, assets, and ecosystems present within the striking distance of the accidents occurred, or likely to occur, in an industry. The special ability of AHI to not only rank past accidents in terms of severity but also to forecast the impacts of *likely* accidents makes it valuable as a management tool in choosing between potential sites when setting up a new industry.

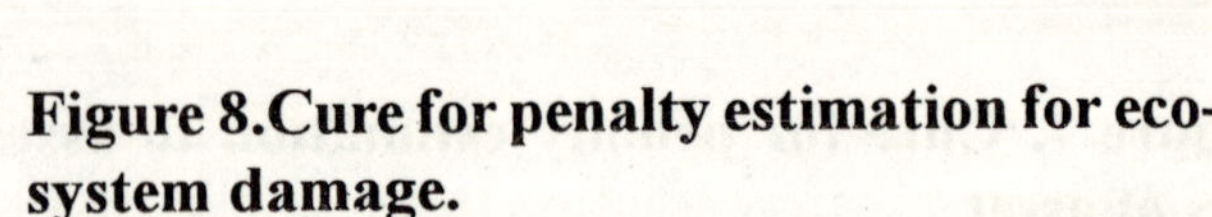

Figure 8.Cure for penalty estimation for ecosystem damage.

ACKNOWLEDGMENT

Authors thank All India Council for Technical Education, New Delhi for instituting the Computer-Aided Environmental Management (CAEM) Unit which enabled this study.

NOMENCLATURE

f1 = Function relating heat load to severity factor X1

f2 = Function relating overpressure load to severity factor X2

f3 = Function relating toxic load to severity factor X3

g1 = Function relating population impact to penalty pn1

g2 = Function relating asset impact to penalty pn2

g3 = Function relating ecosystem impact to penalty pn3

Hc = Heat of combustion (kJ kg-1)

LC50 = Lethal concentration kg/3

m = Mass of chemical (kg)

q = Chemical released (kg)

Pn1 = Penalty due to population

Pn2 = Penalty due to asset

Pn3 = Penalty due to ecosystem

g(x) = function representing direct impacts

h(y) = Function representing indirect impacts

X1 = Severity factor due to heat load

X2 = Severity factor due to overpressure load

z = Hazard characteristic of chemical

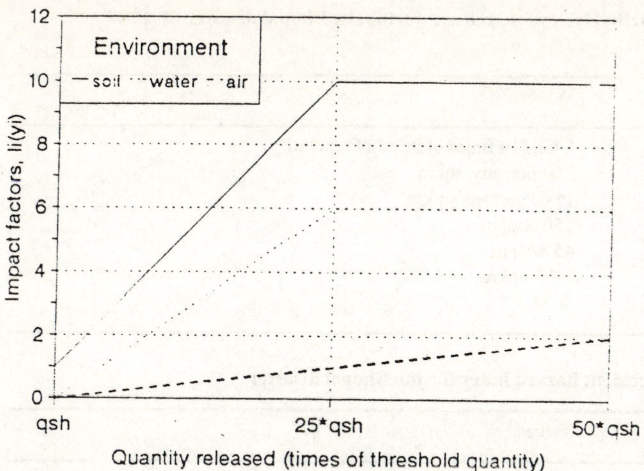

Figure 9.Indirect impact factors due to solids deposited; qsh represents threshold quantity in kg.

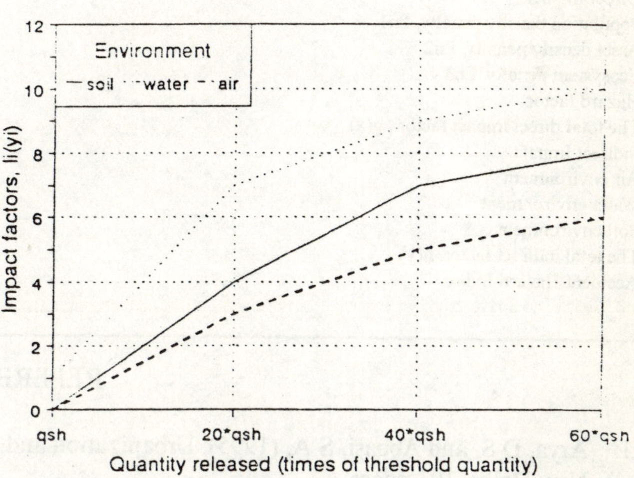

Figure 10. Indirect impact factors due to liquid releases; qsh represents threshold quantity in kg.

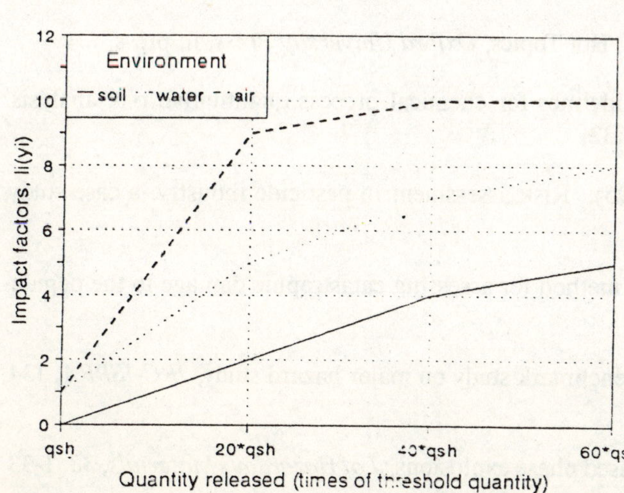

Figure 11.Indirect impact factors due to gaseous releases; qsh represents threshold quantitiy in kg.

Table 2. Input data to estimate accident hazard index for methyl iso cynate release during the Bhopal disaster of 1984.

Parameters	Values
Total quantity of MIC released	5 ton (10 times of threshold quantity)
Population density of with in plant	350 persons /sqkm
Population density of surrounding area	1540 persons/sq km
Asset density with in plant boundary	250 $/sq m
Asset density of surrounding area	45 $/sq m
Ecosystem got damage	2.25 sq km
Hazard potential of MIC (on scale of 0-1)	0.75

Table 3. Intermediate calculation step of accident hazard index for the Bhopal disaster

Parameters	Values
Bhopal Disaster, 1984	
Accident scenario : Toxic gas (MIC) release	
Factor, R	1651
Severity factor, X2	8.3
Direct Impact	
Population density penalty, Pn1	0.15
Asset density penalty, Pn2	0.10
Ecosystem penalty, Pn3	0.34
Hazard factor	0.75
The total direct impact factor , g(x)	10.0
Indirect Impact	
Air environment	5.2
Water environment	2.5
Soil environment	1.6
The total indirect factor, h(y)	5.43
Accident Hazard Index	10.0

REFERENCES

1. Arya, D S, and Abbasi, S A, (1995). Urbanization and its Environmental Impacts, *Discovery Publishing House*, New Delhi, 101 pages.

2. Arya, D S, and Abbasi, S A, (1997). Environmental Impact Assessment - existing Methodologies, Emerging Trends, *Venus Publications*, New Delhi, in press.

3. Abbasi, S A, Krishnakumari, P, and Khan, F I, (1997). Hot Topics, *Oxford University Press*, in press.

4. Centre for chemical process safety (CCPS-1989). Guidelines for chemical process quantitative risk analysis, *American Institute of Chemical Engineers*, New York, 32.

5. Chary, S V, Suryanarayana, G, and Rao, K C K, (1995). Risk assessment in pesticide industry: a case study, *Journal of IAEM*, **23**, 27-35.

6. Christen, P, Bohnenblust, H., and Seitz, S., (1994). A method for assessing catastrophic damage to the population and environment, *Process Safety Progress*, **13**(4).

7. Contini, C.A., Amendal, A., and Ziomas, I, (1991). Benchmark study on major hazard study, *JRC-ISPRA*, 134, Amsterdam.

8. Davis, P A, (1993). A guide to the evaluation of condensed phase explosions, *J of Hazardous Materials*, **33**, 1-33.

9. Deaves, D M, (1992). Dense gas dispersion, *J.of Loss Prevention Process Industries*, **5**(4), 219-227.

10. Dow fire & Explosion Index (1987). Hazard classification Guide, 6th edition, *Dow Chemical Company*, U.K.,

11. Frontline, 1995. Madras disaster, *The Hidu Publications*, April 15, 1995, pp 17.

12. Greenbook, (1992). Methods for the determination of possible damage to people and objects resulting from release of hazardous materials, *Report CPR 16E - TNO*, The Netherlands.

13. Keller, A Z, Wilson, H and Kara-Zaitri, C, (1985). The Bradford disaster scale -*Disaster Prevention and Limitation Unit*, University of Bradford, Bradford, U K.

14. Khan, F I, and Abbasi, S A, (1997). Hazard Identification & Ranking (HIRA): a multi-attribute indexing technique, *Research Report CPCE/RA 17/97*, Pondicherry University, India.

15. Khan , F I, and Abbasi, S A, (1996). Accident simulation in chemical process industry using MAXCRED, *Indian J. of Chemical Technology*, **3**, 338-344.

16. Khan, F.I., and Abbasi, S.A., (1997). Risk analysis of Epichlorohyding industry using computer automated tool MAXCRED, *J of Loss Prevention in Process Industries*, **10**, 234-256

17. Lees, F P, (1996). Loss prevention in chemical process industries-(4th edition), *Butterworths publication* , volume **1-3**, London.

18. Pasman, H J, Duxbury, H A, and Bjordal, E N, (1992). Major hazards in the process industries : achievements and challenges in loss prevention. *J of Hazardous Materials*, **30**, 1-38.

19. Petersen, C M, (1990). Consequence of accident release of hazardous material, *J. of Loss Prevention Process Industries*, **3**,136-141, .

20 Raghvan, K.V., and Mallikarjunan, M.M., (1986). An approach to Maximum Credible Accident Analysis of cluster of industries, Proc. Envirotech International conference, Bombay.

22. Roberts, A F, (1982). Thermal radiation hazards from release of LPG form pressurized storage, *Fire Safety J.*, **4**, 197-212.

22. Scheffler, N.E., (1994). Improved fire and explosion index hazard classification, *Process Safety Progress*, **13**,(4), 214-218.

23. The Mond Index, (1985). 2nd edition, *GDG associates*.

24. Tyler, B.J., (1995). A Toxicity Hazard Index, *I Chem Symposium Series No. 134*. 213-245.

25. Van den Berg, A C, and Lannoy, A, (1993). Method for vapor cloud explosion blast modeling, *J. of Hazardous Materials*, **34**, 151-171.

26. Wyler, E, and Bohnenblust, H, (1991). Disaster Sealing: a multi-attribute approach based on fuzzy set theory, *International conference on probabilistic safety assessment and management*, Los Angles, USA.

27. Zimmermann, H.J., (1987). Fuzzy sets, Decision making and Expert systems, *Kluwer publication* , Boston.

¨ Reproduced from *Trans IChemE*, UK

18

MULTIVARIATE HAZARD IDENTIFICATION AND RANKING SYSTEM[*]

Risk analysis in chemical process industries is an elaborate process involving several steps from preliminary hazard identification to development of credible accident scenarios, to preparation of strategies for prevention or control of damage.

All this requires substantial inputs of time and money. In order to get an approximate yet workable assessment of risk at much lesser costs, indices have been developed which link typical findings of elaborate risk analysis to 'scales of risk'. The 'scales', in turn, provide workable measures of hazards/risks/safety.

In the past, indices have been reported for swift risk assessment - the noteworthy among them include Dow fire and explosion index, Mond fire, explosion and toxicity index, IFAL index, and mortality index. A few rapid ranking techniques have also been proposed.

This paper presents a new system of methodologies for Hazard Identification and RAnking (HIRA). The system consists of two indices: one for fire and explosion hazards and another for the hazard due to likely release of toxic chemical. The magnitudes of these indices indicate the severity of the likely accident; in terms of the size of the area of impacted area.

HIRA has been applied to a typical chemical process industry - a sulfolane plant - and its performance has been compared with that of the Dow's and the Mond's indices. The study reveals that HIRA is more sensitive and accurate than the other indices.

Key words : Hazard identification, industrial hazards, hazard ranking, risk assessment

INTRODUCTION

The first step of any risk assessment procedure involves hazard identification, or answering the question : what can go wrong? This is also the most important step because hazards that are not identified will not be quantified, leading to overlooking or underestimation of risk. Therefore it is very important to devote adequate resources to this step so as to insure comprehensives.

But hazard identification is easier said than done. And it is becoming exceedingly more difficult as the depth of

* Reproduced from *Journal of Loss Prevention in* Process Industries, UK.

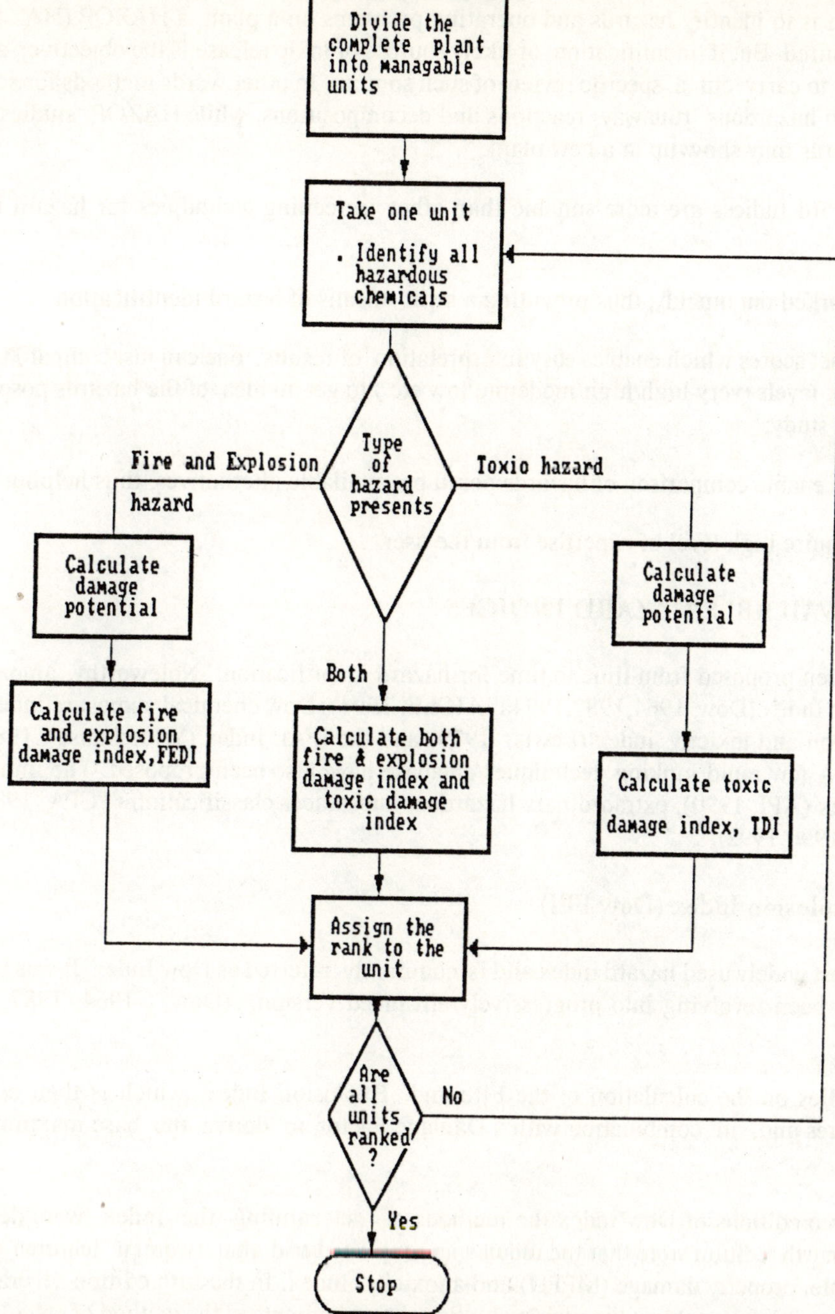

Figure 1. Algorithm of Hazard Identification and Ranking (HIRA) system

technology is continually increasing. The hazards, as well as the strategy for reducing them, are both traceable in the man-machine management system that runs any chemical plant. It is not always easy to discover the weaknesses in such a system. The hazards do not lie on the surface, accessible to simple visual inspection. With the gradual increase in the complexity of the man-machine system, it is becoming increasingly difficult to locate the soft spots. At the same time a whole lot of new tools are now available for hazard identification to facilitate risk analysis. Table 1 lists some of these stages and the corresponding hazard identification techniques. No single procedure is ideal or uniformly applicable (Anderson, 1990); different system suit different types of industries and processes. For example, a firm involved in the manufacture of a large number of organic chemicals is likely to be much more interested in techniques of screening chemicals for toxicity than a petroleum refinery of which the emphasis shall be on explosions and fires.

The choice of hazard identification technique also depends on the purpose for which the study is done. For example if the aim is to identify hazards and operating problems on a plant, a HAZOP (HAZard and OPerability) study would be required. But if identification of likely sources of toxic release is the objective, a hazard assessment would be necessary to carry out a specific review of such sources. In other words methods for screening and testing would be useful in hazardous runaway reactions and decompositions, while HAZOP studies would identify how often familiar hazards may show up in a new plant.

We believe hazard indices are more suitable than other screening techniques for hazard identification. Their virtues are:

a) they can be worked out quickly, thus providing a swift means of hazard identification;

b) they provide net scores which enables easy interpretation of results: one can just compare the net score with the designated risk levels (very high/high/moderate/low etc.) to get an idea of the hazards posed by the chemical or the unit under study;

c) net scores also enable comparison of hazards posed by available alternatives, thus helping in decision-making;

d) they do not require high level of expertise from the user.

PREVIOUSLY AVAILABLE HAZARD INDICES

Indices have been proposed from time to time for hazard identification. Noteworthy among them are the Dow fire and explosion index (Dow, 1964,1987,1994a; AIChE, 1994), Dow chemical exposure index (Dow, 1994b), the Mond fire, explosion and toxicity index (Lewis, 1979) and the IFAL index (Whitehouse, 1985), Mortality index (Marshall, 1977). A few rapid ranking techniques/database have also been proposed. The important ones are: substance hazard index (API, 1990); extraordinary hazardous substances classification (TCPA, 1987), and NFPA ranking (NFPA, 1989,1990,1992).

Dow Fire and Explosion Index (Dow FEI)

This is the most widely used hazard index and is commonly referred as Dow Index. It was first reported in 1964. Since then it has been evolving into progressively advanced version, (Dow , 1964, 1987,1994; AIChE, 1994, Scheffler, 1994).

The Index relies on the calculation of the Fire and Explosion Index which is then used to determine fire protection measures and, in combination with a Damage Factor, to derive the base maximum probable property damage (MPPD).

In the first three editions of Dow index the methods of determining the index were developed and refined. Changes in the fourth edition were that the index was simplified and that two new features were introduced: the maximum probable property damage (MPPD) and a toxicity index. In the fifth edition several new features were added: a new framework for making the risk evaluation, improvements in the method of calculating the index, Loss Control Credits, and Maximum Probable Days Outage. The toxicity index was taken out. In the sixth edition, a risk analysis package, including business interruption and a toxicity penalty to reflect emergency responses, was introduced (Dow, 1987). In the seventh edition some of the codes of good practice were updated but no major conceptual changes were made.

The Dow FEI is calculated as follows. First a material factor (MF) is obtained. It is a measure of the potential energy released from the material. It is determined by considering the flammability and reactivity of the material and falls in the range 1-40. Then two penalty factors (F1 and F2), one for general process hazards (GPHs) and one for special process hazards (SPHs), respectively, are determined. Next the process unit hazards factor (PUHF) (F3), which is the product of these, is calculated. The Dow FEI is obtained as the product of the MF and PUHF (Scheffler, 1994).

General Process Hazards (GPHs), are sum of the penalties due to the type of reaction/process, type of chemical handled in the process unit, (SPH), and drainage and spill control of chemical. SPHs account for the penalty due to operation under hazardous conditions, quantity of chemical handled in the unit, and characteristic of chemical. Using these three parameters (MF, SPH, GPH) MPPD is estimated, and utilising credits for hazard control strategies and safety system, the 'actual probable property damage' (APPD) is calculated. The damaging radius is derived empirically from FEI by using the following equation:

$$\text{damaging radii} = 0.84 * \text{Dow FEI} \quad (1)$$

Table 1. Hazard identification techniques applicable to different stages of project

Hazard identification techniques	Project stage
Management and safety system audits Checklists Feedback from workforce	All stages
Screening and testing for Chemicals *toxicity, instability, explosibility) Reactions *explosibility) Impurities Pilot plant	Research and development
Hazard indices Insurance assessments	Pre-design
Process design checks Unit processes Unit operations Plant equipments Pressure systems Instrument systems	Design
Hazard and operability studies Failure modes and effects analysis Fault trees and event trees Hazard analysis Reliability assessments Operator task analysis and operating instructions	Commissioning
Checks against design, inspection, examination, testing Non-destructive testing, condition monitoring Plant safety audits Emergency planning Inspection, testing	Commissioning
Inspection, testing Non-destructive testing, condition monitoring, corrosion monitoring, malfunction detection, plant degradation audits Plant safety audits	Operation

The Mond fire, explosion and toxicity index (Mond FETI)

This is an extension of the Dow Index. Mond FETI was developed at the Mond division of ICI and the original version has been described Lewis (1979). The alterations in Dow FEI which lead to the Mond FETI involve (Tyler, 1982; Lees, 1996):

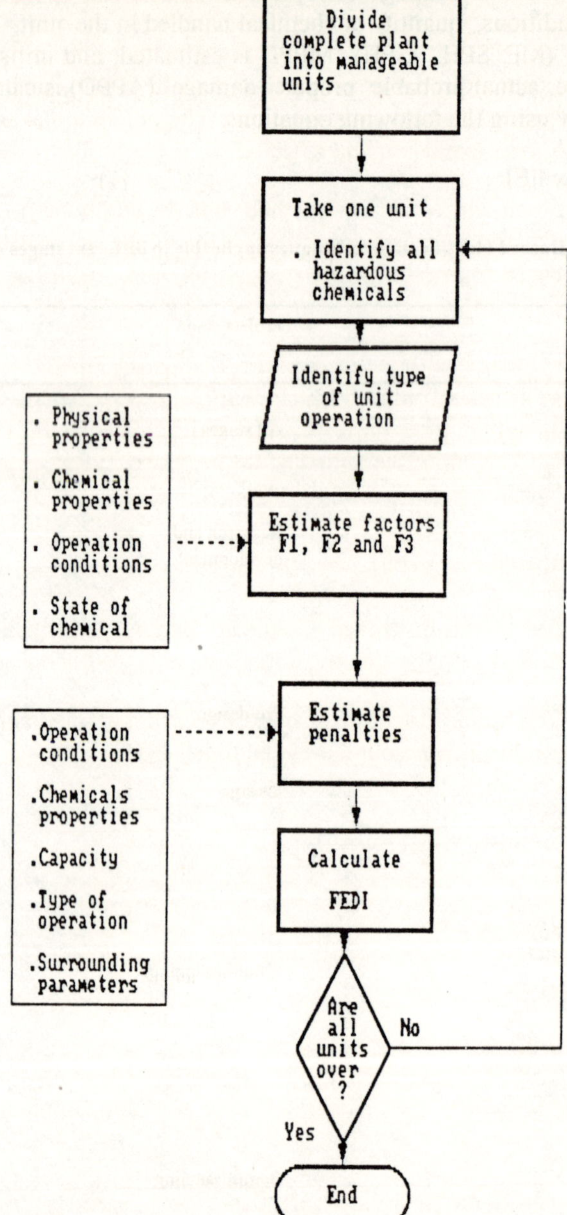

Figure 2. System procedure for Fire and Explosion Damage Index (FEDI) calculation

1. study of a wider range of processes and storage installations;
2. covering the processing of chemicals which are recognised as having explosive properties;
3. offsetting difficulties raised by high heat of combustion per unit mass of hydrogen and enabling distinctions to bc made between processes where a given fuel is reacted with different reactants;
4. inclusion of a number of additional special process types of hazard considerations that have been shown by a study of incidents to affect the level of hazard significantly;
5. enabling toxicity to be included in the assessment;
6. inclusion of a range of offsetting factors for good design of plant and control / safety instrumentation systems to enable realistic hazard levels to be assessed for plant units under varying levels of safety features;

7. indication of how the results of the method can be applied logically in the design of plants having a greater degree of 'inherent safety'.

The Mond FETI involves making an initial assessment of hazard in a manner similar to that used in the Dow FEI, but taking into account additional hazard considerations. The potential hazard is expressed in terms of the initial value of a set of indices for fire, explosion and toxicity.

The material factor is determined as in the Dow method, but in addition special material hazard factors are introduced. Again as in the Dow method, use is made of factors for GPHs and SPHs although the particular factors are different. A quantity factor, based on the inventory of material, and layout hazard factors are also introduced. There are also factors for toxicity hazard.

The toxicity index is calculated using health factor, quantity of chemical in use and the toxicological properties of chemical. Recently Tyler et al. (1994) has introduced some modifications in toxicity index calculation procedure. He has proposed a toxicity index calculation procedure which is similar to Mond FETI but includes consideration of the effect of acute concentration and layout of the area. He has proposed ranking of toxicity index on a seven point scale, from low to severe.

The instantaneous fractional annual loss (IFAL) index

The IFAL index was developed by the Insurance Technical Bureau, UK, primarily for insurance assessment purposes (Singh and Munday, 1979; Insurance Technical Bureau, 1981: Whitehouse 1985).

The method of calculation of IFAL index involves examining each major item of process equipment to assess its contribution to the index. The main hazards accounted by the index are

1. pool fires
2. vapour fires
3. unconfined vapour cloud explosions
4. confined vapour cloud explosions
5. internal explosions

In contrast to the Dow and Mond indices, the IFAL Index is too complex for manual calculation and is carried out using a computer program.

Dow chemical exposure index (Dow CEI)

The Dow CEI (Dow, 1994b, AIChE, 1994) is a measure of the relative acute toxicity risks. It may be used for initial process hazard analysis (PHA), calculation of a Distribution Ranking Index (DRI), and in emergency response planning.

The information needed for the calculation of the Dow CEI a) includes physical and chemical properties of the material; b) a simplified process flow sheet, c) showing vessels and major pipe work with inventories; and d) an accurate plan of the industry and its surroundings.

Mortality index

This index, proposed by Marshall (1977), is a measure of the lethality of the hazardous materials. It is computed on the basis of the number of deaths per tonne of material involved.

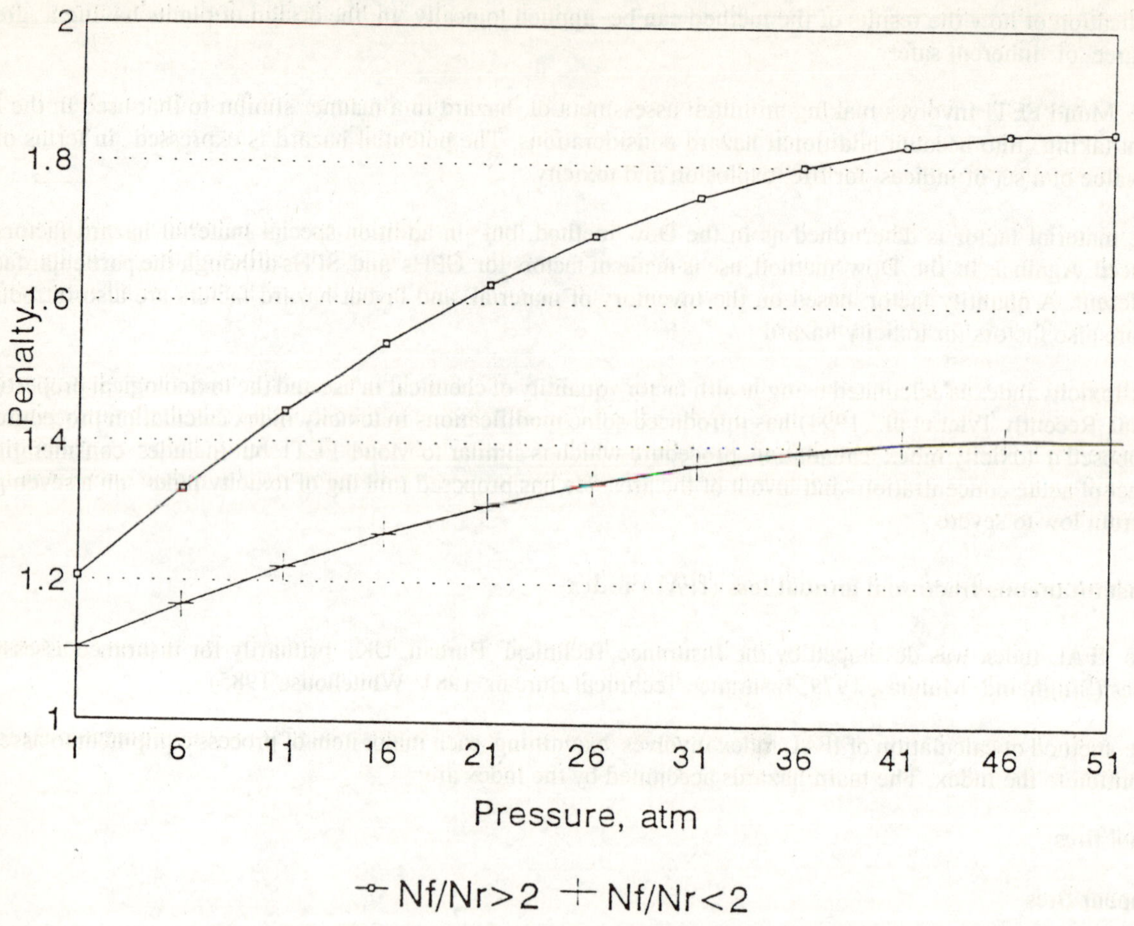

Figure 3. Penalty due to the severity of pressure

Rapid ranking techniques

Various agencies have proposed 'rapid ranking techniques'(RRT) and databases for hazard identification which are mainly based on the three main characteristics of chemicals: toxicity, reactivity and flammability. These techniques and database are used in different forms in different RRT procedures to identify the type of hazard present in the unit.

Substance Hazard Index (SHI)

A hazard system ranking proposed by American Petroleum Institute (API, 1990), is based on the vapour pressure and the toxicity of the chemical being assessed. It postulates that a high vapour pressure substance disperses more rapidly and an acutely toxic substance can pose damage even at low emission level. The substance hazard index, SHI is calculated as:

SHI=EVC/ATC

Where EVC denotes equilibrium vapour concentration (substance vapour pressure in mm Hg at 20 °C multiplied by 106 and divided by 760) and ATC denotes acute toxic concentration in *ppm*. An SHI value of greater than 5000 is considered to represent hazardous substance. This procedure can enable ranking of a chemical only at normal operating conditions. It does not incorporate any other effects such as effect of temperature/pressure on the operation, operating conditions, type of unit operation process, site characteristics, etc.

Extraordinary Hazardous Substances, (EHS)

In the 'toxic catastrophe prevention act' USA (TCPA, 1987), a list of such substances has been notified based on toxicity which, on human contact, may cause permanent adverse effect, including death. This list has been prepared on the basis of experimental evidence of toxicity as well as physico-chemical properties of the chemicals. In comparison to SHI, EHS is less common and effective.

National fire protection association (NFPA) ranking system

National Fire Protection Association (NFPA)-704M has developed a system of hazard identification and ranking (NFPA, 1989,1990,1991,1992). The chemicals are ranked using three different indices for toxicity, flammability and reactivity, 0 to 4 (least to most hazardous) scales.

It is presently the most recommended technique for ranking hazardous chemicals. However, its application has been restricted to specify hazard associated with chemicals; the effect of other relevant parameters such as (operating conditions and site characteristics) has to be accounted externally. Consequently the use of NFPA ranking system is restricted in assessing hazards under normal conditions.

THE PROPOSED SYSTEM

Hazard Identification and RAnking (HIRA) system

On the basis of the foregoing review we deduce:

i) good ranking procedures and databases are available to assess the hazards inherent in the chemicals used in process industries —flammability, toxicity, corrosivity and explosivity— under normal condition. However, when such chemicals are used under elevated temperature and/or pressure - which is quite often - their hazard potential is significantly increased. Further, the risk posed by a chemical (or a process using a chemical) is also a function of its surroundings (such as proximity to other sensitive units, populous neighbourhoods, fragile ecosystems) and such transient environmental factors as atmospheric stability and wind direction.

ii) The Dow and the Mond indices have been popular and have served useful purpose. We feel there is scope of improving them in terms of:

a) the main basis of the Dow and the Mond indices is the material factor (defined under 'introduction'). It is estimated empirically based on the reactivity of the chemical and its vapour pressure. We believe that reliance on a single parameter (material factor), which too, is empirically derived, may not give reliable measure of hazards. It accounts only for chemical energy (due to reactivity),major hazards are also present due to physical energy (pressure energy).

b) The 'material factor' as used in the indices is independent of the type of operation/process and process conditions. But each process may have hazards specific to it. For example in a unit involving a chemical reaction hazards would exist due to chemical energy (reactivity of chemicals), as well as physical energy (pressure and temperature). In other units, such as the ones associated with storage, the hazard is mainly due to physical energy (pressure, temperature and state of chemical). Moreover, these hazards can be easily quantified using common formulae of thermodynamics and fluid dynamics.

c) It follows that the system of assigning penalties in the two indices also suffers due to the lack of completeness in quantifying hazards. As the penalties are assigned on the basis of the risks posed, wherever the extent of risk is assessed inadequately the penalties assigned are also inadequate.

d) In Mond and Dow indices estimation of penalties for general process hazard and special process hazard steps are independent of process unit/operation. In this regard authors feel that penalties should be estimated depending upon process/operation type, which will reduce the working load by eliminating the unimportant penalties and giving due emphasis to important penalties.

Keeping these points in view we have proposed a systematic, comprehensive, but easy to implement system, called hazard identification and ranking(HIRA).

HIRA is essentially a combination of two indices

i) The fire and explosion damage index (FEDI),

ii) The toxicity damage index (TDI).

The procedure for development of each of these is discussed below (Figure 1)

THE FIRE AND EXPLOSION DAMAGE INDEX (FEDI)

For the purpose of developing FEDI, the various units of an industry are classified as follows:

i) storage units,

ii) units involving physical operations such as heat transfer, mass transfer, phase change, pumping and compression.

iii) units involving chemical reactions

iv) transportation units

v) other hazardous units such as furnace, boilers, direct-fired heat exchangers, etc.

Table 2. Hazard ranking according to the fire, explosion and toxic damage index

Fire and explosion damage index(FEDI)	Toxic damage index (TDI)	Hazard characterization
FEDI>500	TDI>700	extremely hazardous
500>FEDI>400	700>TDI>500	highly hazardous
400>FEDI>200	500>TDI>200	hazardous
200>FEDI>100	200>TDI>50	moderately hazardous
100>FEDI>20	50>TDI>05	less hazardous
else	else	no hazard

Estimation of FEDI involves the following steps (Figure 2):

i) classification of the various units in an industry into the five categories mentioned above;

ii) evaluation of energy factors;

iii) assignment of penalties;

iv) estimation of damage potential;

v) estimation of FEDI.

Each of these steps is described below.

Storage units

These units involves storage, and intermediate-process inventories of chemicals (chemical hold-up). To estimate the FEDI due to these units, three energy factor(F1,F2 and F3) are defined, which takes into account physical and chemical energy.

The factor F1 (which takes into account chemical energy) is calculated using the following equation.

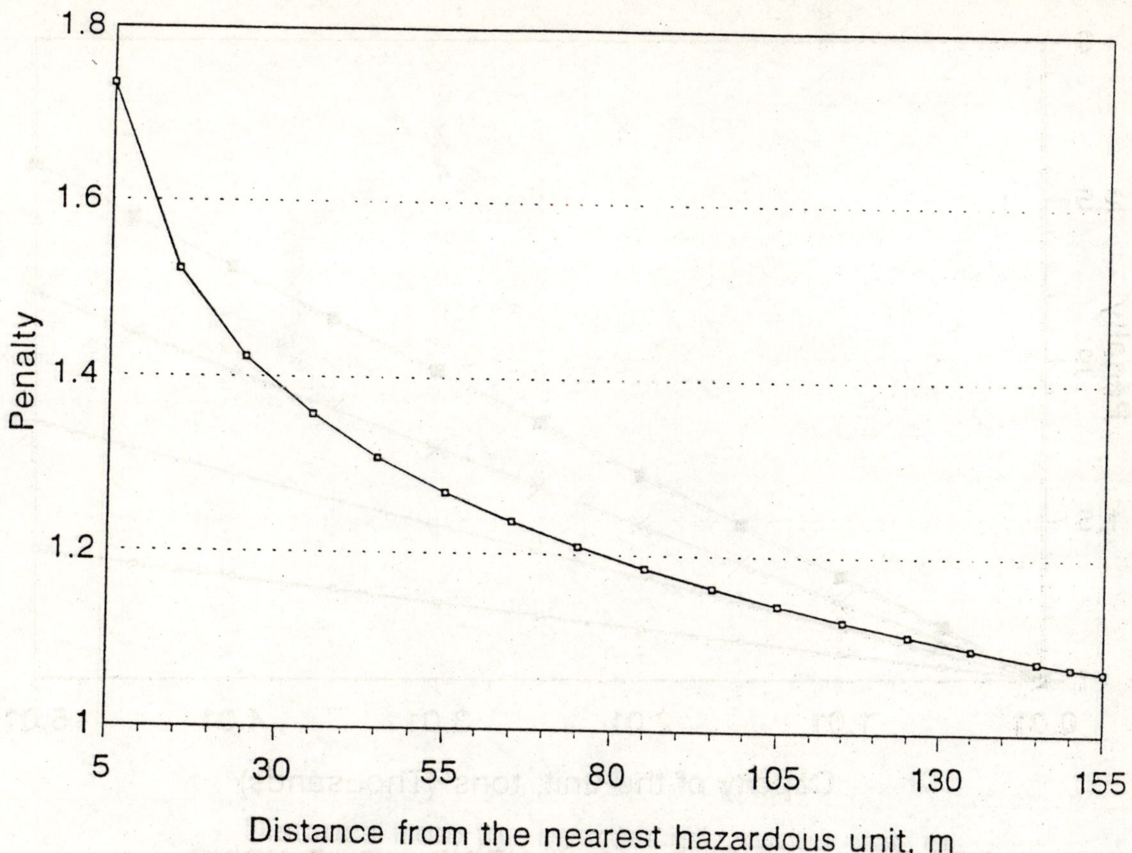

Figure 4. Penalty due to location of the storage unit close to other hazardous units

$$F1 = 0.1*M * (Hc)/K \qquad (2)$$

The other two factors F2 and F3 account for physical energy, and are computed as:

$$F2 = 6/K*PP*V = 1.304 * 10^{-3}*PP*V \qquad (3)$$

$$F3 = 1.0*10^{-3}*1/(T+273)*(PP-VP)^2*V \qquad (4)$$

These equations have been derived from the complex thermodynamic equations for isentrophic expansion of pressurised gases and liquids (Lewis, 1984; Lees, 1996).

Other than these three energy factors, penalties have been assigned to account for the impact of various parameters on the total damage potential which is subsequently transformed to the FEDI.

The impact of temperature is measured in terms of penalty (pn1) by considering the flash point and the fire point of the chemical, and operating temperature of the unit. This penalty is derived by comparing the operating temperature with the limiting condition proposed by API- RP750M (API, 1990), and NFPA (1990,1992). The impact of pressure is quantified in terms of two energy factors F2 and F3 and one penalty (pn2). The penalties for other parameters such as location of the nearest hazardous unit, quantity of chemical stored, and characteristic of chemical and space occupied by the units in a defined area (% of the area occupied by the units within an area of 30 meters radius around the unit) have been quantified with the help of process safety design code (CCPS, 1989; OSHA, 1990; Kavianian and Brown, 1992; Greenbook,1992) storage area classification guidelines (WHO,1984); Dow index (AIChE-1994) and NFPA ranking procedure (NFPA, 1989-92). The formulation for estimating these penalties are briefed below.

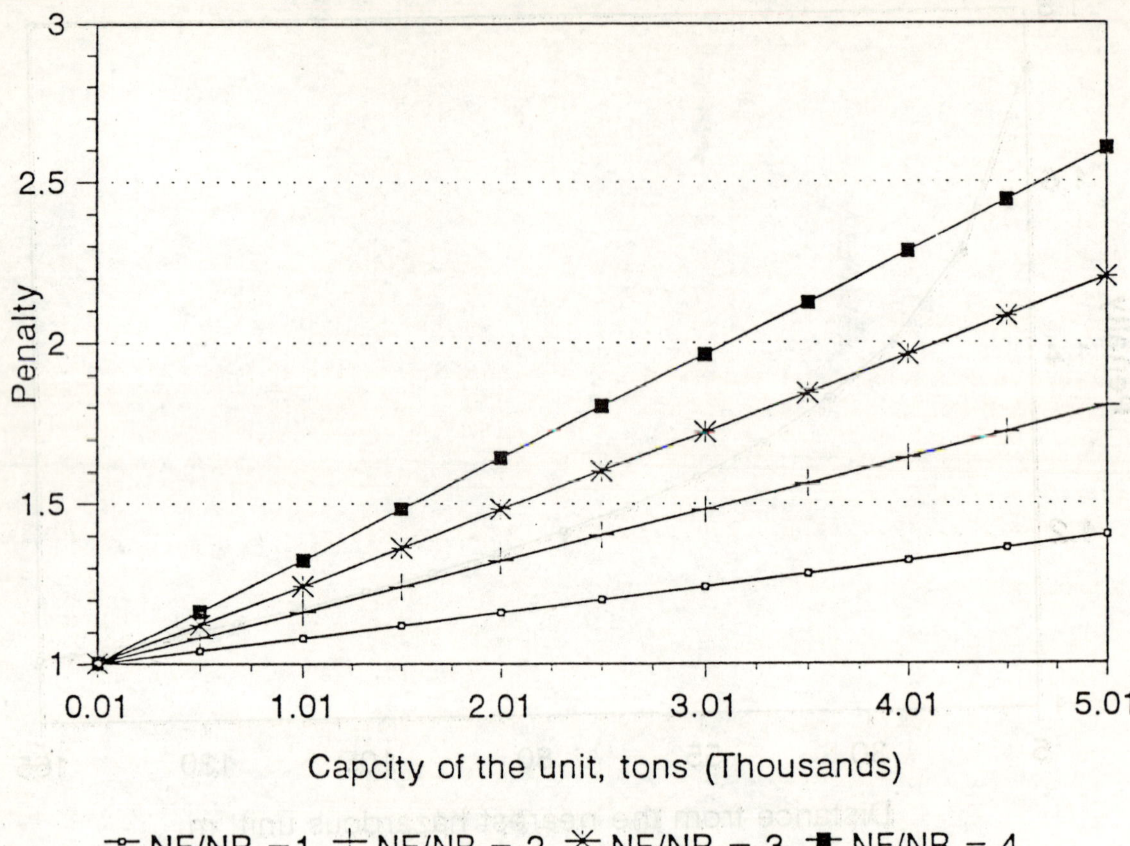

Figure 5. Penalty due to quantity of chemical handled in the storage units

Temperature

pen1 = ft1(flash fire,auto ignition,and working temperature) (5)

Where ft1 is a function representing the set of conditions for assigning the penalty. It is defined as:

ft1(flash, fire, auto ignition temperature)=

if(Temperature > Flash Point < Fire Point)

pn1=1.34 (6)

else if(Temperature>Fire point< auto ignition temperature)

pn1=1.55 (7)

else

pn1=1.1 (8)

Pressure

The impact of pressure is quantified as follows:

if(VP > AP)

if(PP > VP)

F = F2 + F3 (9)

pn2 = f(operating pressure) (10)

else

F = F2 (11)

pn2 = f(operating pressure) (12)

else

F = F3 (13)

pn2 = f(operating pressure) (14)

The function f(operating pressure) is plotted in Figure 3. This function is derived from the detailed analysis of pressure effect on fire and explosion described by Davies (1993) and Lees (1996).

Location of the nearest hazardous unit

The effect due to the presence of nearest hazardous unit(s) is quantified as:

pn3 = floc (distance) (15)

Where function floc(distance) is plotted in Figure 4. This figure is drawn with the help of Dow index guide (AICHE, 1994) and hazard assessment manual (WHO,1984; OSHA, 1990).

Table 3. Guidelines to assign the penalty due to the type of reaction and undesirable side reaction

Type of reaction	*Penalty*
Oxidation	1.60
Electrolysis	1.20
Nitration	1.95
Esterification	1.25
Reduction	1.10
Aminolysis	1.40
Hallogenation	1.45
Sulfonation	1.30
Hydrogenation	1.35
Alkylation	1.25
Polymerization	1.50
Pyrolysis	1.45
Undesirable side reaction	
Auto-catalytic reaction	1.65
Non-auto-catalytic side reaction probable to occur at above normal reaction conditions	1.45
Non-auto-catalytic side reaction probable to occur at below normal reaction conditions	1.20

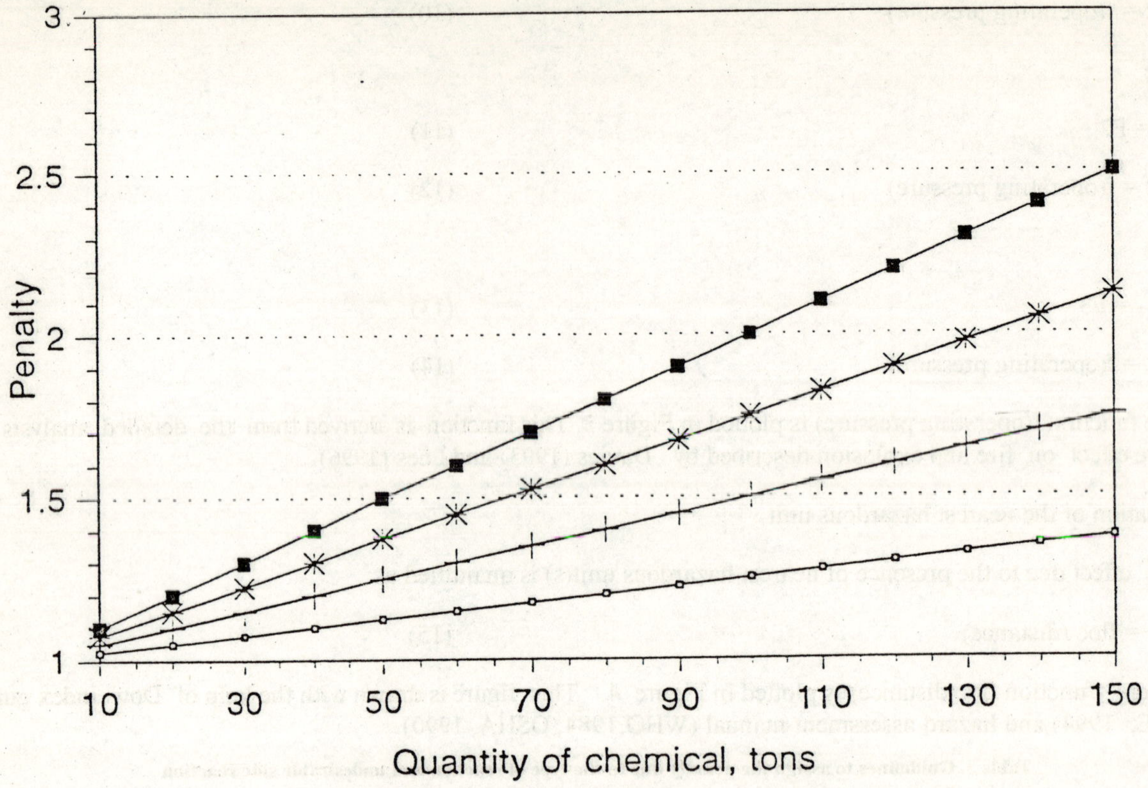

Figure 6. Penalty due to chemical handled in the unit involving physical changes.

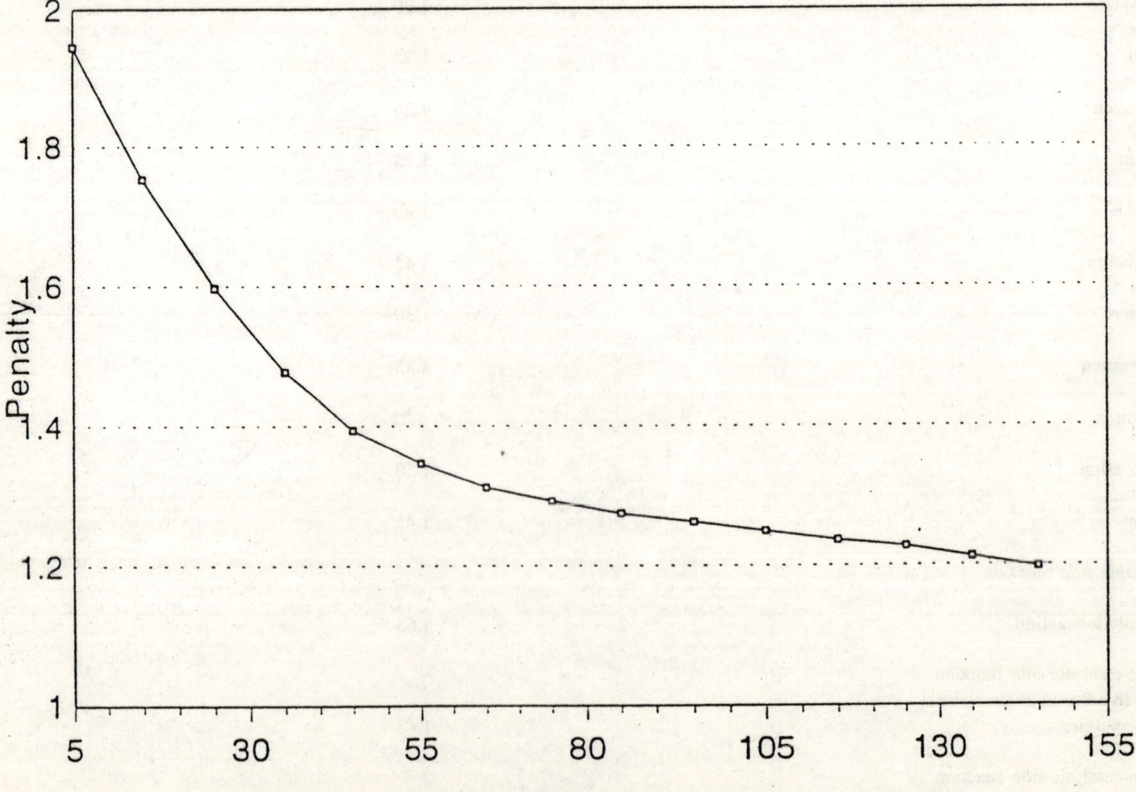

Figure 7. Penalty due to location of the unit involving physical changes close to other hazardous unit.

Capacity

The effect due to the quantity of the chemical handled in the unit (capacity of the unit) is quantified as:

pn4 = fqur (quantity in tons) (16)

The function fqur has been derived on the basis of past reports (WHO, 1984; CCPS, 1989; OSHA, 1990). The function has been plotted in Figure 5.

Table 4. Table to estimate factor A

NFPA rank	Liquid	Liquefied gas	Gas	Solid
4	4.00	8.0	13.40	0.1300
3	0.40	0.8	1.34	0.0130
2	0.20	0.4	0.67	0.0060
1	0.07	0.1	0.25	0.0025

Characteristics of chemical

The effect due to flammable and/or reactive characteristics of a chemical is quantified as

pn5 = 1 + 0.25*(NR + NF) (17)

Where NR and NF are NFPA ranks for reactivity and flammability of the chemical respectively (NFPA,1990).

Density of the units

The penalty due to the density of the units at the site (% of space occupied by the units), where the unit under study is located, is estimated with the following equation:

pn6 =(1+%space occupied by the unit in an area of 30m radius from the unit /100) (18)

The energy factors and the penalties as estimated above, are then combined to give damage potential which is further transformed to the FEDI. The damage potential and the FEDI are computed as follows:

damg.pot = (F*Pn2+F1*Pn1)*pn3*pn4*pn5*pn6 (19)

FEDI =4.76 $(\text{damg.pot})^{1/3}$ (20)

Where FEDI represents the damage radii in meters, and is a tool for ranking different units. Equation 20 has been derived with the help of the damage distance relation proposed by Jarret (1968) , Baker et al. (1983) and Lewis (1984). A ranking system based on FEDI as suggested by authors is presented in Table 2.

Units involving physical operations

Units involving operations such as heat transfer, mass transfer, heat transfer combined with mass transfer, compression, have been dealt under this classification. These units normally process chemical(s) in various phases and under conditions of very high or low temperature and pressure.

For these units, too, three type of energy factors and six type of penalties have been considered. The method of calculating energy factors for these units is same as for storage units but the formulation for calculating penalties are different. The effect of temperature(pn1)is assessed by comparing the operating temperature with flash fire and auto ignition temperature. The level of penalty here is higher because most of the operations are temperature - sensitive. The pn1 (penalty due to temperature) has been assigned a maximum value 1.95 when operating temperature is greater than fire point temperature of the chemical. This penalty is derived with the help of ranking procedures reported by API-RP750 (API, 1990), and NFPA-325M (NFPA, 1991). The intermediate value of penalty is quantified as:

pn2=ft2 (flash, fire, auto ignition, working temperature) (21)

where ft2 is a function defined as:

Table 5. Damage and Risk index values for different units of sulfolane plant

Units	HIRA's units specification	Chemical	Type of Hazard	Fire and explosion damage index	Toxic damage index
storage 1	Storage	Butadiene	Fire & Explosion	440.3	118.5
storage 2	Storage	Sulfur dioxide	Toxic release	75.4	477.5
Storage 3	Storage	Hydrogen	Fire & Explosion	277.1	88.0
line 11	Transportation	Butadiene	Fire & Explosion	83.2	46.5
Line 12	Transportation	Sulfur dioxide	Toxic release	45.3	337.5
Line 14	Transportation	Sulfolene	Fire and Toxic release	65.4	71.0
Line 19	Transportation	Hydrogen	Fire,Explosion & Toxic	105.4	57.0
Reactor 1	Reaction unit	Sulfur,Butadiene	Fire,Explosion & Toxic	271.6	128.5
Reactor 2	Reaction unit	Hydrogen,Sulfolen	Fire,Explosion & Toxic	205.4	97.0
Evaporator	Processing unit	Sulfurdioxide, Sulfolene	Fire and Toxic release	179.6	321.5
Pump 3	Processing unit	Sulfurdioxide	Toxic release	9.5	198.0
Pump 5	Processing unit	Butadiene	Fire & Explosion	34.5	77.0
Pump 7	Processing unit	Hydrogen	Fire,Explosion,&Toxic	41.7	106.5

if(Temperature > Flash Point < Fire Point)

ft2=1.45 (22)

else if(Temperature > Fire Point < 0.75 Auto ignition temperature)

ft2=1.75 (23)

else if(Temperature > 0.75 Auto ignition temperature)

ft2=1.95 (24)

else

ft2=1.1 (25)

The effect of pressure is assessed in two ways:

i) deciding combination of energy factors F2 and F3;

ii) estimating penalties by comparing the operating pressure with vapour pressure.

if(VP > AP and PP> VP)

pn2 = fp1(PP, AP,VP) (26)

F = F2 + F3 (27)

else

pn2 = fp2(PP, AP, VP) (28)

F = F2 (29)

if(AP>VP and PP> AP)

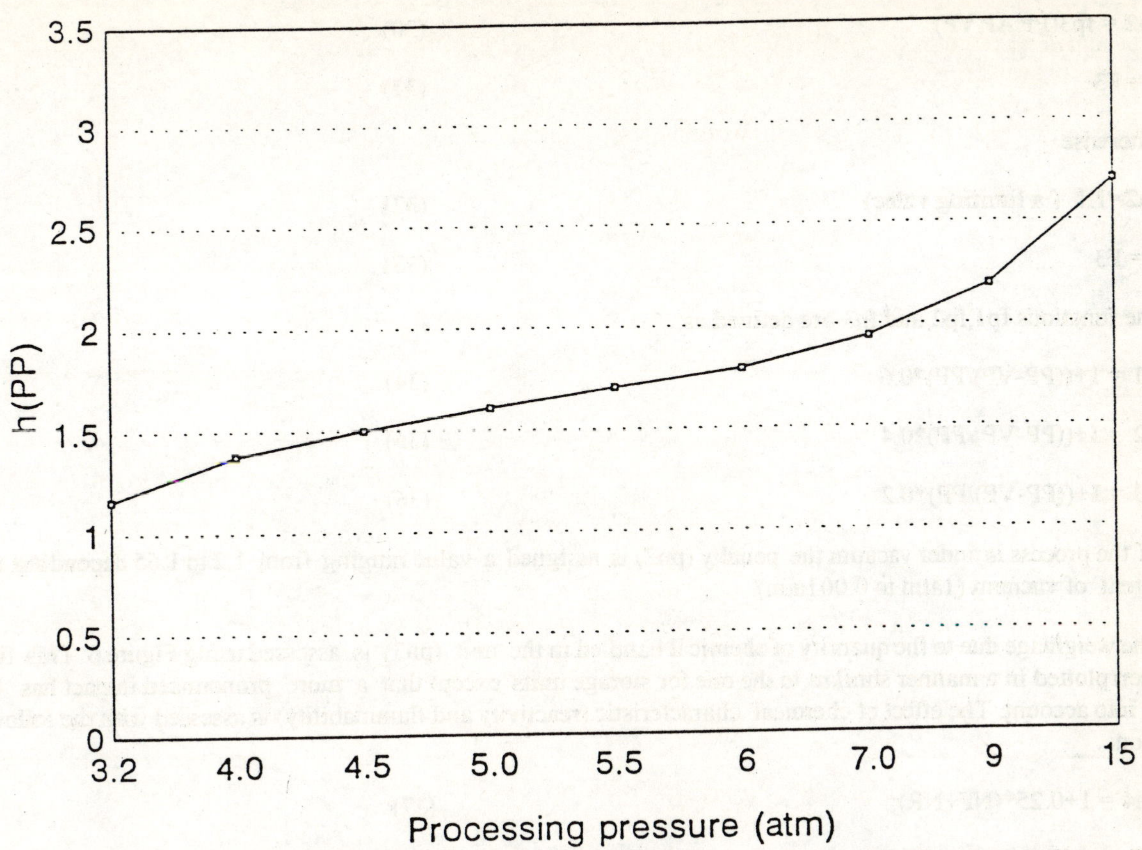

Figure 8. Penallty due to seveirty of pressure (above atmospheric pressure) for toxicity damage index estiamtion.

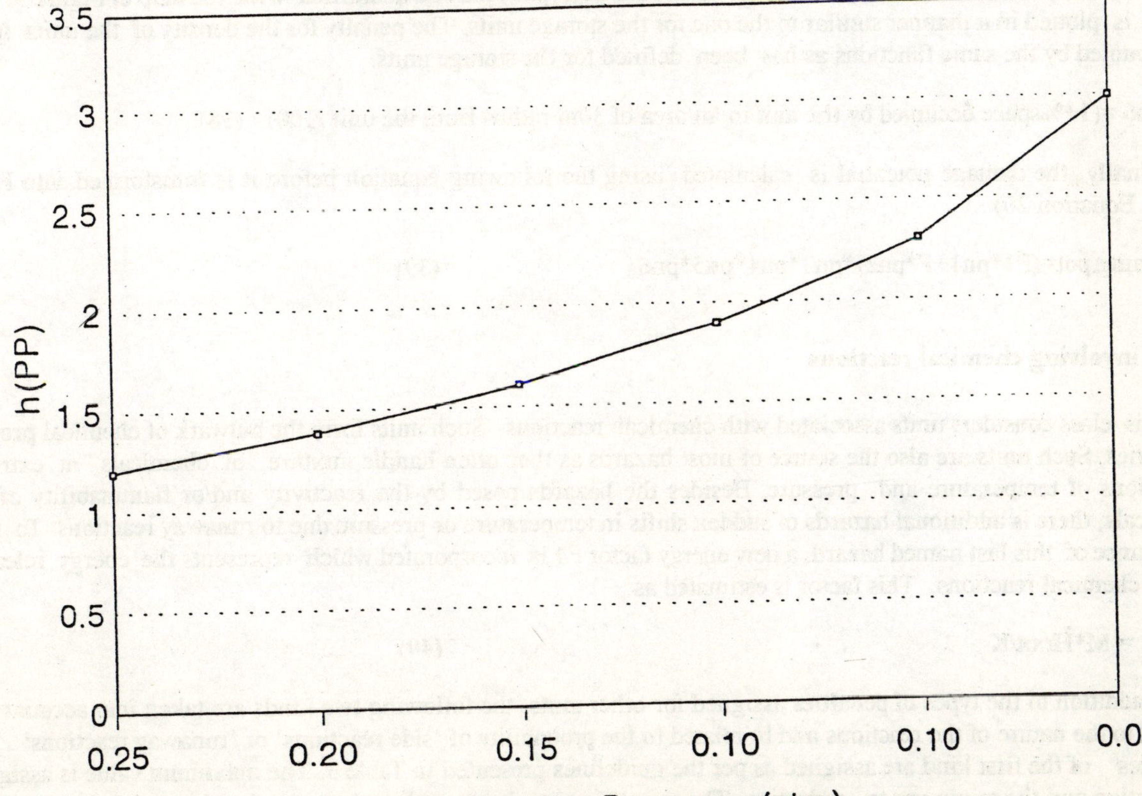

Figure 9. Penallty due to pressure seveirty (under vacuum) for toxicity damage index estiamtion.

pn2 = fp3(PP,AP,VP) (30)

F = F3 (31)

otherwise

pn2=1.1 (a limiting value) (32)

F = F3 (33)

The functions fp1,fp2 and fp3 are defined as:

fp1 = 1+((PP-VP)/PP)*0.6 (34)

fp2 = 1+((PP-VP)/PP)*0.4 (35)

fp3 = 1+((PP-VP)/PP)*0.2 (36)

If the process is under vacuum the penalty (pn2) is assigned a value ranging from 1.2 to 1.65 depending upon the extent of vacuum (1atm to 0.001atm).

The weightage due to the quantity of chemical handled in the unit (pn3) is assessed using Figure 6. This figure has been plotted in a manner similar to the one for storage units except that a more pronounced impact has been taken into account. The effect of chemical characteristic (reactivity and flammability) is assessed with the following equation:

pn4 = 1+0.25*(NF+NR); (37)

Where NF and NR are NFPA ranks for flammability and reactivity (NFPA,1990).

The effect of the location of the nearest hazardous unit (pn5) may be quantified with the help of Figure 7. This figure is plotted in a manner similar to the one for the storage units. The penalty for the density of the units (pn6) is accounted by the same functions as has been defined for the storage units.

pn6 =(1+%space occupied by the unit in an area of 30m radius from the unit /100) (38)

Finally the damage potential is calculated using the following equation before it is transformed into FEDI (using Equation 20)

damg.pot=(F1*pn1+F*pn2)*pn3*pn4*pn5*pn6 (39)

Units involving chemical reactions

This class considers units associated with chemical reactions. Such units form the bulwark of chemical process industries. Such units are also the source of most hazards as they often handle mixture of chemicals at extreme conditions of temperature and pressure. Besides the hazards posed by the reactivity and/or flammability of the chemicals, there is additional hazards of sudden shifts in temperature or pressure due to runaway reactions. To take cognisance of this last named hazard, a new energy factor F4 is incorporated which represents the energy released due to chemical reactions. This factor is estimated as:

F4 = M*Hrxn/K (40)

In addition to the types of penalties assigned for other units, the following two kinds are taken into account - a) related to the nature of the reactions and b) related to the probability of 'side reactions' or 'runaway reactions'. The penalties of the first kind are assigned as per the guidelines presented in Table 3. The maximum value is assigned to nitration and the minimum to reduction. The quantification has been based on reactive hazard index (Austin, 1993; Crousal and Lowver, 1990) and considerations of risks from hazardous reactions (Fowcett and Wood, 1993, Raghvan and Swaminathan 1996).

The possibility and the impact of side reaction is quantified in terms of penalty (Pn7), which depends upon the likelihood and the type of the side reaction. The penalty has been based on the studies of Austin (1993); Crousal and Lowver (1990), Dow (1987), and Kavianian and Brown (1992). Higher values have been assigned to the side reactions likely to occur at above normal operating conditions (Table 3). It is because the probability of occurrence and damage consequences of side reactions occurring above normal operating conditions are both higher (Kletz, 1984, 1985, 1991).

Finally, The damage potential and FEDI for these units are calculated:

damg.pot = (F1*pn1+F*pn2+F4*pn6*pn7)*pn3*pn4*pn5 (41)

The damage potential is later converted to FEDI (using Equation 20)

Table 6. Intermediate steps for fire explosion damage and toxic damage index calculation

Parameters	*values*	
Fire explosion damage index		
Unit	: Reaction	
Chemicals	: butadiene, butadiene-sulfone	
Energy factors		
Factor 'F1'	: 4.89E+04	
Factor 'F2'	: 5.90E+03	
Factor 'F3'	: 22.067	
Factor 'F4'	: 1213.91	
Severity factors (penalties)		
Reaction temperature	: 75 oC	Pn1=1.75
Reaction pressure	: 5 atm	Pn2=1.35
Capacity of unit	: 5 ton	Pn3=1.1
Location of the unit	: 95 m away	Pn4=1.25
Degree of congestion	: 25%	Pn5=1.25
Type of reaction	: sulfonation	Pn6=1.35
Side reaction	: above atm conditions	Pn7= 1.57
The damage potential	= 1.857E+05	
Fire and explosion *damage index*	= *271.6*	
Toxic damage index		
Chemical	: sulfur dioxide	
Release rate	= 3.98 kg/s	
G factor	= *3.191*	
Health hazard factor 'h'	= *3.0*	
Severity factors		
Temperature	: 70 oC	Pnr1 =1.65
Pressure	: 5 atm	Pnr2 =1.34
Vapor density	: 2.34 kg/cu m	Pnr3 =2.77
Toxicity of chemical	: Nh = 3.0	Pnr4 =1.60
Site characteristics	: 3214 (Persons/sqkm)	Pnr5 =1.45
Toxic damage index	= *128.5*	

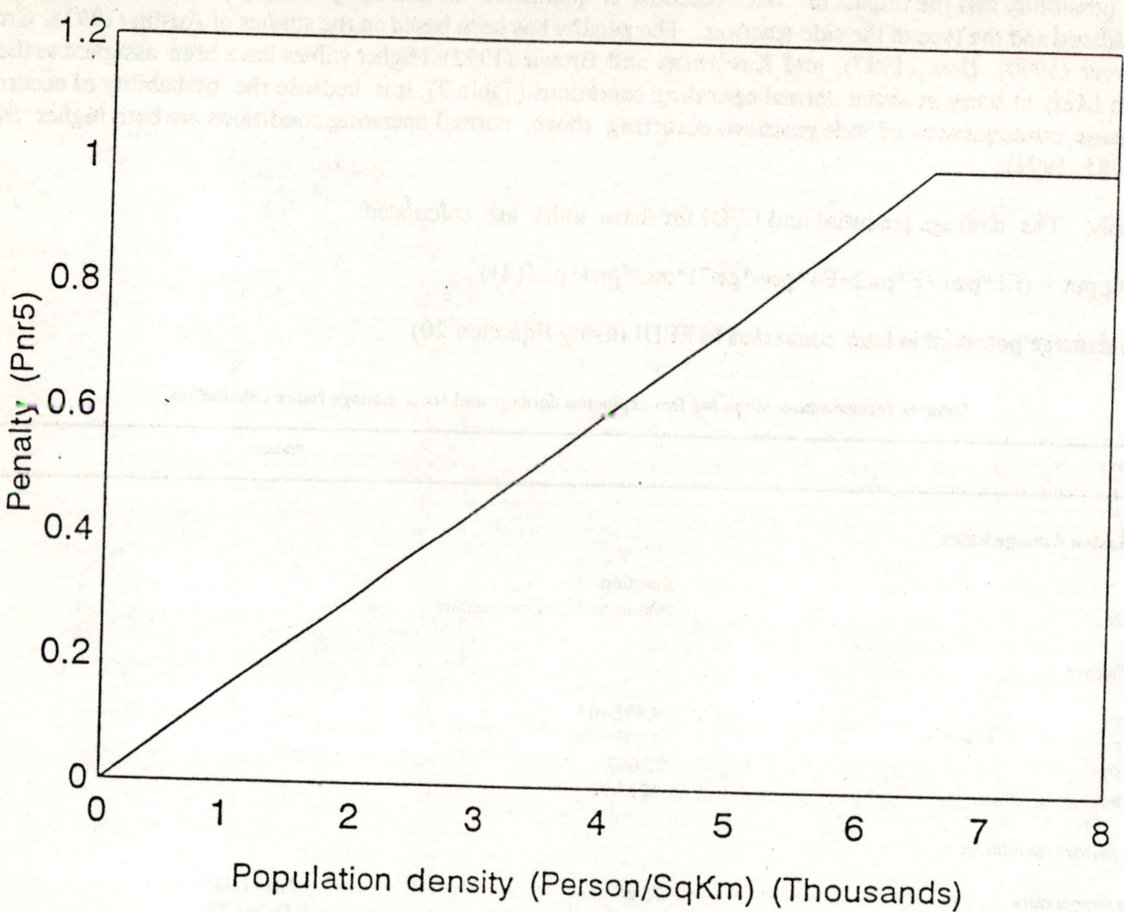

Figure 10. Penalty for population density.

Transportation units

The transportation of chemicals from one unit to another is associated with hazards of different types and magnitudes. When the transportation involves chemicals under such extreme conditions as highly pressurised or superheated state, the hazards are very great. Thus it is essential to provide adequate weightage to such conditions as temperature, pressure and flow rate. We have therefore assigned penalties relating to transportation temperature (pn1), transportation pressure (pn2), quantity transported (pn3), characteristic of the chemical such as flammability, reactivity (pn4), physical state of the transported chemical (pn5), location of the nearest hazardous unit(pn6) and density of the units in the area (pn7). The energy factors F!, F2, and F3 are similar to the ones used for other units.

The effect of temperature is estimated with:

pn1 = ft2(flash, fire, auto ignition temperature) (42)

The penalty due to severity of transportation pressure is estimated as follows:

TP>AP< 3*AP ;

pn2=1.2 (43)

TP>3*AP<5*AP;

pn2=1.4 (44)

TP> 5*AP;

pn2=1.6 (45)

For transportation under sub-atmospheric pressure the penalty (pn2) is quantified based on the extent of vacuum (pn2=1.2-1.8). The penalty for transportation by road is estimated using Figure 5, and by transportation through pipe line is estimated using the equation

$$pn3 = 1.0 + \frac{\text{quantity transported (Kg/min)}}{1000} \quad (46)$$

The effect of chemical characteristic is estimated as:

Pn4 = minimum (1, 0.20*(NF + NR)) (47)

and the penalty due to the physical state of the chemical is estimated as:

Pn5 = function(physical state) (48)

Gaseous pn5 = 1.45 (49)

Liquefied gas pn5 = 1.65 (50)

Liquid pn5 = 1.25 (51)

Solid particles pn5 = 1.30 (52)

The penalties due to the location of nearest hazardous unit(pn6) and density of the units(pn7) are estimated using functions similar to the ones described for storage units.

Pn6 = loca (distance); using Figure(4)

Pn7=(1 + %space occupied by the units in a radius of 30 m from the unit/100) (53)

The energy factors and penalties are combined to estimate damage potential:

damg.pot = (F1*pn1+F2pn2)*pn3*pn4*pn5*pn6*pn7 (54)

Finally, as before, damage potential is transformed into FEDI using Equation 20.

Other hazardous units

This class covers ancillary units such as boilers, direct-fired heat exchangers, flares, furnaces, etc. which do not fall under the other four classes. In such units physical energy (due to the internal pressure of the unit) is not important. Therefore factors F2 and F3 are not considered. Instead a few more penalties has been added to account for the effect of type of fuel(pn1), physical state of the fuel (pn2), and rate of the use of the fuel (pn3). Penalties have also been assigned for the location of nearest hazardous unit(pn4), density of the units (pn5) and temperature of the unit (pn6).

The penalty due to flammability is estimated with the equation

Pn1 = minimum (1, 0.25*(NF + NR)) (55)

The penalty due to physical state of the chemical is estimated with

Pn2 = f(physical state) (56)

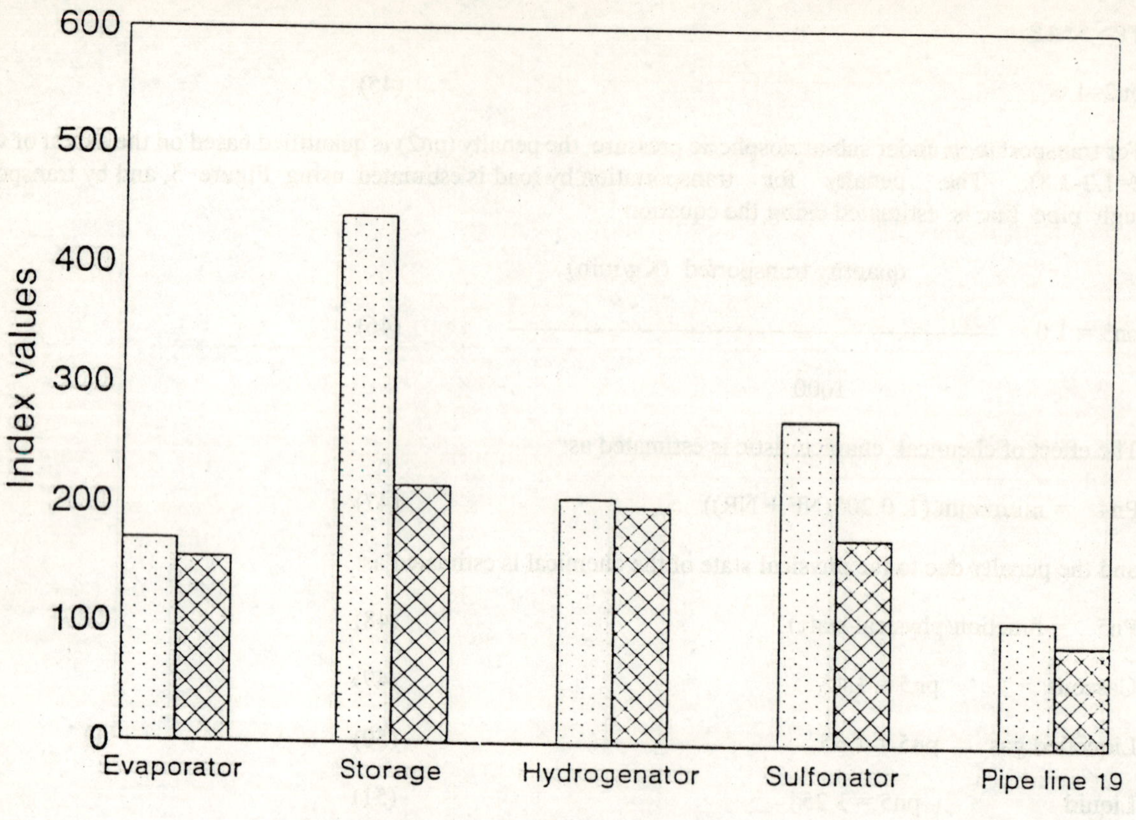

Figure 11. Typical plot showing comparision of FEDI with damage radius estimated by Dow F E Index.

where function f(physical state) is defined as:

Solid

solid dust particle size > 150 micro meter

pn = 1.25 (57)

solid particle size < 150 micro meter

pn = 1.40 (58)

Liquid

pn2 = 1.35 (59)

Gaseous

pn2 = 1.65 (60)

Liquefied gas

pn2 = 1.80 (61)

The penalty due to the quantity of the fuel used in the unit is estimated using the following expression:

$$Pn3 = 1.0 + \frac{NF}{1000} * \text{quantity in use per hour (tons/hr)} \qquad (62)$$

The quantification of other penalties pn4,pn5, and pn6 are done using same functions as proposed for units involving physical changes.

The damage potential for these units is computed by multiplying energy factor with all the penalties. This is subsequently transformed to FEDI using Equation 20.

$$damg.pot = F1*Pn1*Pn2*Pn3*Pn4*Pn5*pn6 \qquad (63)$$

TOXIC DAMAGE INDEX (TDI) METHODOLOGY

Toxic damage index (TDI) is a representation of lethal toxic load over an area. It is measured in terms of radius of the area (in meters) getting affected lethally by toxic load (50% probability of causing fatality). This index is derived using transport phenomena and empirical models based on the quantity of chemical(s) involved in the unit, the physical state of the chemical(s), the toxicity of the chemical(s), the operating conditions, and the site characteristics (Fowcett, 1993; Tyler et al., 1994). The dispersion is assumed to occur under slightly stable atmospheric conditions. We have opted for 'slightly stable atmospheric conditions' as these represent a median of high instability and high stability. Furthermore such conditions are often prevalent during accidents - as had happened at Bhopal, Basel, Panipat and other places (Cristen et al., 1994 ; Lees, 1996; Khan and Abbasi, 1997a).

The estimation of TDI is done with one core factor named as 'G factor' and several penalties. The G factor takes into account the following:

i) during the accidental release of super-heated liquid (liquid stored or processed above its normal boiling point) from the unit, a part of the liquid would flash to vapours and the remaining part would form a liquid pool which would subsequently evaporate;

ii) the release of gases would directly lead to dispersion in the atmosphere and would cause build-up of lethal toxic load;

iii) liquefied gases would have two-phase release, followed by dispersion and build-up of toxic load;

iv) pyrophilic solids would give toxic vapours which would generate toxic load in the air.

The G factor is quantified as:

$$G= A*m \qquad (64)$$

the value of A is dependent on the release conditions (Table 4), and m is anticipated release rate in kg/s.

The G factor forms the base or the 'core weight' which provides dimensions to the various types of penalties. The penalties take into account i) operating temperature, ii) operating pressure, iii) vapour density, iv) toxicity of chemical, and v) site characteristics.

The effects of temperature and pressure are estimated through penalty pnr1 and pnr2 respectively. These penalties are derived with the help of TCPA (1987), OSHA (1990), Tyler et al (1994), and API-750RPM ranking technique (API, 1990). The set of conditions used in estimating pnr1 and pnr2 are as follows;

Temperature

if (chemical is flammable)

if(Temperature> Flash Point < Fire Point)

pnr1 = 1.45 (65)

if(Temperature> Fire Point < 0.75 auto ignition temperature)

pnr1 = 1.75 (66)

if(Temperature > 0.75 auto ignition temperature)

pnr1 = 1.95 (67)

else if (chemical is toxic or corrosive)

if (Temperature > 4 * ambient temperature)

pnr1 = 1.55 (68)

else if(Temperature > 2 * ambient temperature)

pnr1 = 1.35 (69)

else

pnr1 = 1.1 (70)

Pressure

if(VP>AP)

if(PP>3.0*AP)

pnr2=h1(PP) (71)

else

pnr2 = 1.3 (72)

else if(PP<VP)

pnr2 = -h2(PP), (provided, PP<0.3*AP) (73)

else

pnr2 = 1.2 (74)

The functions h1(pp) and h2(pp) have been plotted in Figures 8 and 9 respectively; the values of penalties can be directly computed from these Figures.

Vapour density

Gases or vapours having density higher than air take more time to disperse and their plumes tend to be closer to the ground due to gravitational effect. Thus, such gases would cause build up of lethal toxic load closer to the ground and for longer duration than lighter gases. This effect has been quantified with the help of the model developed by us earlier (Khan and Abbasi, 1997b, 1997c, 1997d).

Pnr3 = 1.2 * Vapour density/air density (75)

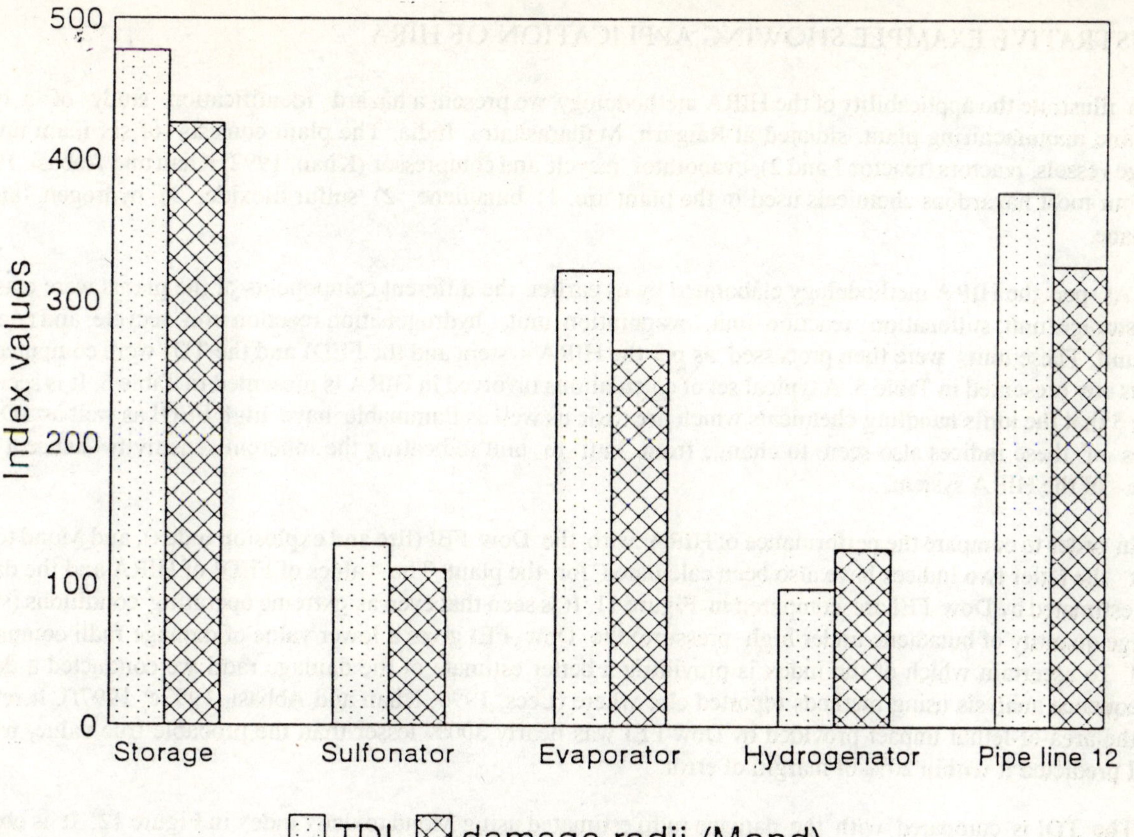

Figure 12. Typical plot showing comparision of TDI with damage radii estimated by Mond toxicity index.

Toxicity of chemical

The penalty due to the toxicity of the chemical is assessed using NFPA-49 (NFPA-1990) health factor (NH) as

pnr4 = minimum(1, 1+ 0.5* NH) (176)

Where, NH represents NFPA ranking for health hazard (NFPA, 1990).

Site characteristics

The effect of site characteristics has been accounted on the basis of population density at the site. The penalty is quantified with the help of criteria mentioned by Less (1996), Christen et al. (1994), and Khan and Abbasi(1997d), and is plotted in Figure 10.

pnr5 = fpop(population density) (77)

Finally the G factor and the penalties are combined to give TDI using the following equation.

$$TDI = b(G^* pnr1^* pnr2 * pnr3^* pnr4^* pnr5)^a \quad (78)$$

Where, a and b are constant and are estimated by studying release and dispersion of a range of chemicals (super heated liquids, liquefied gases, gases, etc.). The most appropriate values of a and b are estimated as:

a = 25.35, and b = 0.425.

ILLUSTRATIVE EXAMPLE SHOWING APPLICATION OF HIRA

To illustrate the applicability of the HIRA methodology, we present a hazard identification study of a typical sulfolane manufacturing plant, situated at Raigarh, Maharashatra, India. The plant consists of six main units — storage vessels, reactors (reactor 1 and 2), evaporator, recycle and compressor (Khan, 1992; Khan and Abbasi, 1997e). The four most hazardous chemicals used in the plant are: 1) butadiene, 2) sulfur dioxide, 3) hydrogen, and 4) sulfolane.

As per the HIRA methodology elaborated by us earlier, the different components of the plants were classified into: storage unit, sulfonation reaction unit, evaporation unit, hydrogenation reaction unit, recycle, and compression unit. These units were then processed as per the HIRA system and the FEDI and the TDI were computed. The results are presented in Table 5. A typical set of calculations involved in HIRA is presented in Table 6. It is seen from Table 5 that the units handling chemicals which are toxic as well as flammable have high FEDI as well as TDI. The values of these indices also seen to change from unit to unit indicating the inherent sensitivity -hence a major virtue - of the HIRA system.

In order to compare the performance of HIRA with the Dow FEI (fire and explosion index), and Mond toxicity index, the latter two indices have also been calculated for the plant. The values of FEDI of HIRA and the damage radii estimated by Dow FEI are compared in Figure 11. It is seen that even at extreme operating conditions (storage of large quantity of butadiene under high pressure) the Dow FEI gives a lower value of damage radii compared to FEDI. To ascertain which of the index is providing a better estimate of the damage radii we conducted a detailed consequence analysis using methods reported else where (Lees, 1996; Khan and Abbasi, 1997e; 1997f). It revealed that the area-of-lethal impact provided by Dow FEI was nearly 300% lesser than the probable true value, whereas FEDI predicted it within 20% of margin of error.

The TDI is compared with the damage radii estimated using Mond toxicity index in Figure 12. It is observed that unlike Dow FEI, Mond toxicity index is responsive to process unit type. This is due, probably to the fact that the latest version of Mond toxicity index (Tyler et al. 1994) has incorporated more factors such as health effect, conditions of release, plant layout, etc. which has made the index more comprehensive and sensitive to different setting of the process. Still, TDI is by and large more sensitive than the Mond toxicity index.

SUMMARY AND CONCLUSION

The indices for fire and explosion (FEDI) and toxicity (TDI) proposed here have some advantages over the conventional indexing techniques formulated by the Dow and the Mond chemical companies, and IFAL (instantaneous fractional annual loss). HIRA is more systematic, predicts results with more reliability as it takes into accounts larger number of parameters, and leads to quantification. HIRA methodology is simple in implementation, modular in structure, and can be easily automated to reduce expert time. The important features of HIRA are:

i) it take into consideration impact of various process operations, and the associated parameters for hazard identification:

ii) it provides quantitative results of good reliability;

iii) most of the penalties used in computing FEDI and TDI (on which HIRA is based) are derived from the well-tried and tested models of thermodynamics, transport phenomena, heat transfer, and fluid dynamics (CCPS, 1989; API, 1990; Greenbook, 1992). A few penalties are quantified with the help of empirical models and hazard ranking procedures such as NFPA (NFPA, 1989-1992) and EHS (EHS, 1987) ;

iv) it does not need case-to-case calibration as its magnitude directly signifies the level of hazard;

v) it may be used for very rapid reconnaissance of risk.

NOMENCLATURE

M = Mass of chemical, kg or mass release rate (kg/s)

Hc	= Heat of combustion, J/mol
lw	= Latent heat of vaporisation of water, kJ/mol
pf	= Explosion pressure, kPa
pn	= penalties for damage index estimation
pnr	= penalties for toxic damage index estimation
SP	= Specific heat ratio
Vow	= Volume of vessel, cu m
MW	= Molecular weight
PP	= Processing pressure, kPa
VP	= Vapour pressure, kPa
AP	= Atmospheric pressure, kPa
beta	= 1/(process temperature), K-1
Hrxn	= Heat of reaction, kJ/kg
K	= Constant (3.148)
C	= Constant (2152)
F1,F2, &F3	= Core energy factors used in damage index estimation
G	= Core toxic load factor used in toxic damage index estimation
damg.pot	= damage potential
NF	= NFPA ranking for flammability
NR	= NFPA ranking for reactivity
NH	= NFPA ranking for health hazard

REFERENCES

1. AIChE, (1994). Dow's Fire and Explosion Index classification guide, **AIChE Technical manual LC 80-29237**, *AIChE*, New York.

2. Anderson, P, (1990). Comparison of methods of hazards Identification at Plant Level, *J Loss Prevention in Process Industries*, **3**(4), 339-345.

3. API, (1990). Management of Process Hazards, *American Petroleum Institute Recommended Practice 750* (1st Ed.),Washington D C.

4. Austin, T G, (1993). Hazards of Commercial Chemical operation and Chemical Reaction, Safety and accident prevention in chemical operation, (ed. Fowcett and Wood), 2nd ed., *John wiley*, 61-86.

5. Baker, W.E., Cox, P.A., Westin, P.S., Kulesz, J.J., and Strelow, R.A., (1983). Explosion hazard and evaluation, *Elesvier*, Amsterdam.

6. CCPS, (1989). Guidelines for chemical process quantitative risk analysis, *AIChE*, **32**, New York.

7. Cristen, P, Bhnenblust, H, and Seitz, S, (1994). A method for assessing catastrophic damage to the population and environment, *Process Safety Progress*, **13**(4).

8. Crousal, D A and Lowver, J F, (1990). Chemical Process Safety: Fundamental with Application, *Pritence Hall*, USA.

9. Davies, P.A., (1993). A guide to the evaluation of condensed phase explosion, *Journal of Hazardous Materials*, **33**, 1.

10. Dow, (1964). Dow's process safety guide, *1st edition*, Midland.

11. Dow, (1987). Dow's fire and explosion index hazard classification guide. 6th edition, Midland,

12. Dow, (1994a). Dow's fire and explosion hazard classification, Midland,

13. Dow, (1994b). Dow's chemical exposure index, *AIChE*, New York

14. EHS, (1987). Extremely Hazardous Substances, *Environmental Protection Act-40CFR part 355*, Washignton D C.

15. Fowcett, H H, (1993). Toxicity versus Hazards, Safety and accident prevention in chemical operation. (ed. Fowcett and Wood), *John Wiley*, 245-260.

16. Fowcett, H.H., and Wood, W.S., (1993). Safety and accident prevention in chemical operation (Third ed.), *John wily*, New York.

17. Greenbook, (1992). Methods for determining of possible damage to people and objects resulting from release of hazardous materials , *Report CPR 16E*, Voorburg, Warrington.

18. Insurance Technical Bureau, (1981). *IFAL Factor Workbook* , London.

19. Jarret, D.E., (1968). Derivation of the British explosives safety distances, New York *Academy of Science*, 152(1),18.

20. Kavianian, H R, J K and Brown G V, (1992). Application of Hazard Evaluation Techniques to the Design of Potentially Hazardous Industrial Chemical Processes. Report. Div. of Training and Manpower Dev., *Nat. Inst. Occup. Safety and Health*, Cincinnati, Ohio.

21. Khan, F I, (1992). Manufacture of sulfolane: a technical report, *Department of Chemical Engineering*, Aligarh Muslim University, Aligarh, India, 1992.

22. Khan, F I, and Abbasi, S A, (1997a). Risk analysis of Epichlorohydrin industry using computer automated tool MAXCRED, *J. of Loss Prevention in Process Industries*, **10**(3), 213-234.

23. Khan, F.I. and Abbasi, S A, (1997b). Modelling of dispersion of heavy gas based on modification in Plume Path Theory, *Atmos Environ* (in press).

24. Khan, F.I., and Abbasi, S.A, (1997c), Application of the recently modified PPT on the dispersion of some heavy gases, *10th regional IUAPPA conference*, Istanbul, 23-26 September, Turkey.

25. Khan, F.I., and Abbasi, S.A. (1997d) Modelling and simulation of 'heavy gases' released by petrochemical industries, *2nd Speciality Conference on Environmental Progress in the Petroleum and Petrochemical Industries*, November, 17-19, Bahrain.

26. Khan, F I, and Abbasi, S A, (1997e). Rapid risk analysis of a typical chemical industry using MAXCRED-II, *Indian Jr. of Chemical Technology*, **4**, 167-179.

27. Khan, F I, and Abbasi, S A, (1997f). Accident hazard index: a multi-attribute method for process industry

hazard rating, *Transaction of IChE Part B*, (in press).

28. Kletz, T.A. (1984). The industrial approach to hazard identification and analysis and setting criteria for risk, In Major hazard installations: planning and assessment (ed. Petts, J I), *Dept. of Chemical Engg.*, Loughborough University.

29. Kletz, T.A. (1985). What went wrong? case histories. *Hydrocarbon Processing*, **64**(12), 81.

30. Kletz, T.A. (1991). Process safety - an engineering achievement. *Proc. Instn Mech. Engrs*, **205**, 11.

31. Less, F P, (1996). Loss Prevention in the Process Industries, *Butterworths*, London.

32. Lewis D J, (1979). The Mond fire, explosion and toxicity index - a development of the Dow Index. *AIChE on Loss Prevention*, New York.

33. Lewis D.J. (1984). Hazards of scaling up, *Haz. Cargo Bull*, **5**(4), 24.

34. Marshall, J.G., (1977). Hazardous clouds and flames arising from continuous release in to the atmosphere, *Chemical Process Hazards*, **VI**, 99-104

35. NFPA, (1989). Identification of the hazardous of material, *National Fire Protection Agency -Code 704*, Quincy, Massascusestests.

36. NFPA, (1990). Industrial fire hazards handbook, *National Fire Protection Association*, New Jercy.

37. NFPA (1991). Hazardous chemical data, *National Fire Protection Association code-325M*, New Jercy.

38. NFPA, (1992). Hazardous materials response handbook, National Fire Protection Association, USA

39. OSHA, (1990). Process Safety Management of highly hazardous chemicals, 29CFR1910.119, U S Occupational Safety and Health Adminstration, Washington, D.C.,

40. Raghavan, K V, and Swaminathan, G, (1996). Hazard assessment and disaster mitigation in petrochemical industries , *Oxford Publishing Company*, Chennai.

41. Scheffler, N E, (1994). Improved fire and explosion index hazard classification, *Process Safety Progress*, **13**(4), 214-218.

42. Singh J, and Munday G, (1979). IFAL: a model for the evaluation of chemical process losses. Design 79 , *Instn Chem. Engrs*, London.

43. TCPA, (1987). Toxic catastrophic Prevention Act, *New Jercy Environmental Protection Agency*, USA.

44. Tyler, B J, (1982). Using the Mond index to measure inherent hazards, *Plant/Operation Progress*, **4**, 172.

45. Tyler B J, Thomas A R, Doran P, and Grieg T R, (1994). A toxicity hazard index, *Hazards*, **XIII**, 351.

46. Whitehouse H B, (1985). IFAL - a new risk analysis tool. The assessment and control of Major hazards, *Instn Chem. Engrs*, Rugby, 309.

47. WHO, (1984). Major Hazard Control : A practical manual, *International Labour Office*, Geneva.

·· Reproduced from *Journal of Loss Prevention in Process Industries*, UK

Part VIII

Application of Risk Analysis in Process Design

In the concluding part of the thesis we have made a case for inherently safer design as the mother of all risk-reduction exercises. We have also presented a methodology developed by us, and a case study to illustrate its maner of use, to facilitate inherently safer design. The following chapter is a reproduction of the paper accepted for publication in Journal of Loss Prevention in Process Industries.

19

INHERENTLY SAFER DESIGN BASED ON RAPID RISK ANALYSIS*

The importance of inherently safer design (ISD) as a strategy to minimise risk of accidents in chemical process industries is being repeatedly stressed in recent years. The increasing frequency, and extents of damage caused by such accidents across the world have contributed to this thinking. However even as the need for ISD is being underscored, there are very few reports on the precise methods to implement this concept. Significant recent reports are by Berge (1993, 1995) who has suggested a scenariobased design procedure in which construction of accidents scenarios in a structured manner is made the basis of ISD.

We have been developing and applying the concept of rapid risk analysis (Khan and Abbasi, 1995;1996a; 1997a; 1997b). In this paper we present an approach to ISD utilising this concept. We believe, as detailed in this paper, that this approach is a significant improvement upon Berge's procedure in terms of ease, speed, and effectiveness.

Key Words: Risk analysis, inherent safety, Inherently safer design, hazard control

INTRODUCTION

Risks of accidents in chemical process industries, especially the ones handling hazardous substances and/or the ones involved with unit processes operating at extreme conditions of temperature and pressure, can be reduced in two essential ways:

a) providing safeguards such as early warning systems and damage control devices, once the plant is commissioned;

b) incorporating risk assessment as an essential input right at the design stage of a plant.

The second of the options, which confirms to the adage, 'prevention is better than cure' is finding increasingly larger number of supporters from among the industries as well as governmental regulatory agencics. This has resulted from the increasing awareness that the risks posed by chemical industries has increased over the year due to three factors:

i) an ever larger *numbers* and *types* of new chemicals and processes are being handled,

ii) the capacities of the plants are getting larger and larger,

* Reproduced from *Journal of Loss Prevention in* Process Industries, UK.

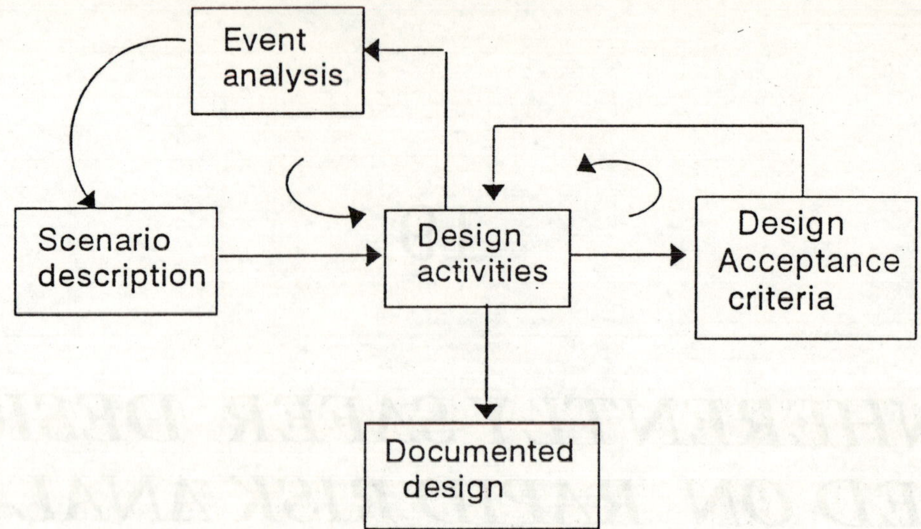

Figure 1. Scenariobased design method (Berge-1995)

iii) the general trend of increasing population and habitation around industrial cites has increased the risk to life and property from industrial accidents,

We can see that those of the industries where safety has been taken care of at the beginning of design are more inherently safe than others (Kletz, 1990a;1990b). For example, handling of large quantities of toxic and or flammable materials are inherently unsafe, while small quantities and/or non-toxic and non-flammable materials are inherently safe. Once a problem begins in an inherently unsafe plant, it may escalate catastrophically, while in an inherently safe plant such a problem should not arise but, if it does, it is self-correcting or may escalate but to easily controllable extent (Kletz, 1991a; Marshall, 1987; Lawrence *et al.* 1993). Therefore, it is almost self-evident that an inherently safe chemical plant is to be preferred over an inherently unsafe one, no matter how safe the latter is made by controlling the hazards. Furthermore, it is always preferable to achieve safety inherently rather than by modification, because then the probability of unforeseen events causing a problem is drastically reduced.

Safety and economy: Central to the concept of inherently safer design (ISD) is the criteria of safety-cost optimisation. These aspects of safety and economy are both equally important to the interest of society. In the course of designing any plant one often has to balance parameters which pull in opposing directions vis a vis benefit-cost considerations. While attempting ISD, the main challenge before the designer is to use the different design parameters such that the product satisfies both the safety and the economy aspect. As design is basically an interactive process, starting with an idea and ending with a final product through a number of modifications, short iterative loops linking modifications, costs, and safety benefits would increase the opportunity to find optimal solutions with lesser time and effort.

APPLICATIONS OF RISK ANALYSIS TECHNIQUES TO ISD

Risk analysis has been used in the chemical process industries to assess the risk posed by the operation of equipment and processes (AIChE, 1989; Khan and Abbasi, 1995). In other words, risk analysis has been a means to evaluate dynamic processes constituting a number of activities associated with chemical industries. Historically, the use of risk analysis has been as a means of verification of design and is performed subsequent to design. For this reason, risk analysis has had a rather passive role and has not been normally considered as a design tool. Admittedly, the safety aspects have been considered as a part of the design premises, but have not been handled as among the parameters which control the basic design strategy. Thus, safety aspects have been mainly serving as the verification criteria with a week feedback to the design process. This appears to be an illogical way of handling the safety aspects and has not been contributing to the cost-effectiveness of the design. Worst still, keeping risk analysis outside the purview of design engineering creates the impression that design engineers are free from the responsibility of considering risk as one of the design parameters.

We find two main reasons for introducing risk analysis as a tool for inherently safer design:

I. design premises should be extended to incorporate environmental and accidental aspects in addition to purely technical requirements;

II. the new elements of design premises include physical processes that are complex and difficult to predict with traditional analytical mathematical methods. An uncertainty in predicting the behaviours of such parameters may cause errors which subsequently may lead to total and catastrophic failures.

Inspite of being of great importance, and having high potential of solving hazard-related problems, application of risk assessment studies during design stage have not been given proper attention. In deciding any strategy, dealing with hazardous chemicals or severe operating conditions, risk assessment is ignored most of the time. This situation is particularly serious in developing countries which do not give as much importance as is warranted to the environment and social safety.

In general, industries consider capital investment, operational costs, maintenance costs and smooth operation as the only relevant factors for design and associated decision-making. However, when a mishap or accident occurs either due to a mistake of an operator or malfunctioning of an equipment, the consequences are often devastating. The accidents which have occurred at Flixborough in 1976, Bhopal in 1984, Besel in1984 and Mumbai in 1995 and hundreds of other places are examples, which illustrate this point. Even if the frequency of occurrence of such accidents is low, they need very serious consideration because once the accident does occur, its impact is often catastrophic.

The past attempts on the application of safety study during early stages of design have been made by Ramshaw (1985), Butcher (1990), Kletz (1990a,1991a,1991b), Rogers and Hallam (1991) and Mansfield and Cassidy (1994). Kletz has discussed inherent safety, need of inherent safety, and effectiveness of inherent safety. Rogers and Hallam (1991) have reiterated the need of inherent safety and have suggested an approach based on characteristics of chemicals. This approach highlights the implementation of inherent safety by evaluating the characteristics such as: intermediates produced, reagents used, material compatibility, catalysts used, and solvents used. Rushton *et al.* (1994) have discussed inherent safety in the context of computer-aided design. The authors gave an overview of inherent safety, computer aided design, and need of considering inherent safety in computer aided process plant design. Edwards and Lawrence (1993) have discussed inherent safety and the cost of its implementation. They have also proposed an index to assess the inherent safety of the plant either in operation stage or in design stage. The index considers 16 different parameters empirically. By and large past reports on inherent safety have emphasised the importance of this concept and some authors have suggested implementation of inherent safety by virtue of removing hazardous options, which is essentially a qualitative approach. Thus far, no systematic and structured scheme or procedure has been suggested to quantify and rank the hazardous options (particularly at design stage) in order to implement inherent safety.

Berge (1993) has proposed a 'scenariobased' method for design, considering safety at initial stage. Subsequently he has further modified this concept (Berge, 1995). The resultant procedure consists of four steps: establishment of proposed solution, identification of loads (hazards), prediction of hazards, and measuring consequences against acceptance criteria (Figure 1). The second of these steps- identification of hazards - is implemented by developing scenarios. In the third step, the developed scenarios are assessed in detail for the consequences. Finally these consequences are compared with the acceptance criteria.

This is a good scheme for considering safety as an input to design at the initial stage of the design process but has the following limitations.

i) It recommends the use of *event analysis* for the development of scenarios (Figure 1). *Event analysis* is a cumbersome process which needs extensive data inputs (reliability data of each component, operational data, etc.) and considerable time to develop an accident scenario (event tree development and evaluation). These inputs are not available during the early stages of design. Further any error in this type of data may lead to erroneous scenarios and may seriously effect the final design. Moreover, event tree development and evaluation for generating accident scenarios is an additionally tedious task.

The authors believe that their alternative of developing the most credible accident scenario (MCAS) on the basis of past experience, frequency of occurrence, operation details, and quantity of chemicals in the process is a better approach , as it gives sufficiently reliable scenarios with considerably lesser efforts (Khan and Abbasi, 1996a; 1997a; 1997b). Moreover, at this stage of the design process, the designer is more concerned about estimation of probable hazards rather than exactly determining sequence of events, so that the final design takes that into consideration. It has been observed by past case studies (Marshall, 1987; Pietersen, 1990; Lees, 1996; Khan and Abbasi, 1996a; 1997a; 1997c) that scenarios developed using maximum credible accident scenario (MCAS) concept give good estimation of scenario (around 90% the same scenario as been reported by sophisticated techniques i.e. event analysis with reasonably accurate reliability data).

ii) This scheme consists of two iterative loops, one for generation and verification of accident scenarios, and second for the verification of design as per acceptance criteria. These authors feel that the first of these iterative loops can be eliminated by using a simpler and easy-to-use technique such as MCAS. This would lead to faster implementation of procedure (saving of about 30% of the total time) without any change in the accuracy of the final results.

iii) Scenariobased method has suggested six different acceptance criteria and also described a link between a particular type of accident scenario (damaging events) with particular acceptance criteria. It makes the design process still more tedious, because for a plant there would be a number of accident scenarios of wide variety (at least one scenario for each unit) and hence designer has to check each time what criteria should be followed.

The authors feel that a common acceptance criteria (sufficiently incorporating the effect of each type of damaging effect) would solve this problem and would make the whole design process simpler and faster (saving ~15% of the time).

Keeping the above points in view, the authors have proposed a simplified and easy-to-implement design procedure termed as *rapid risk analysis based design*. A comparison of *rapid risk analysis based design (RRABD)* procedure with *scenariobased design* method is given in Table 1. A brief discussion on inherent safety and a description of the RRABD design procedure developed by us is presented below. A case study illustrating the use of our procedure is also presented.

Table 1. Comparison of scenariobased design method (Berge-1995) with these authors' rapid risk analysis based design procedure

Scenario based design method	Rapid risk analysis basaed design process
1. It requires two iterative loop	1. It requires one iterative loops
2. Scenarios are developed using	2. Scenarios are developed event analysis using MCAS concepts
3. The final design is based on the damage potential estimated using computational fluid dynamics models.	3. The final design is based on risk factors which represent cumulative effects of damage potential and probability of occurrence
4. It suggest use of different acceptance criteria according to the type of damaging events	4. It suggests use of a single acceptance criteria based on risk factor
	5. For a sample case study (discussed in detail in this paper) it has been observed that this procedure takes 45% less time compared to scenario -based procedure, with comparable accuracy

INHERENTLY SAFER DESIGN

The concept of inherently safer design was first expounded by Kletz (1976) while discussing the lessons of Flixborough. He has spoken about and published widely on the subject ever since. At first, interest in inherent safety was limited, but the appalling loss of life at Bhopal in 1984, which was associated with the convenient, but not essential, storage of a highly toxic reactive intermediate (Methyl-isocyanate), gave a strong impetus to discussions on inherent safety. A few important papers on this topic have appeared recently (Kletz, 1991a;1991b;1992; Rushton *et*

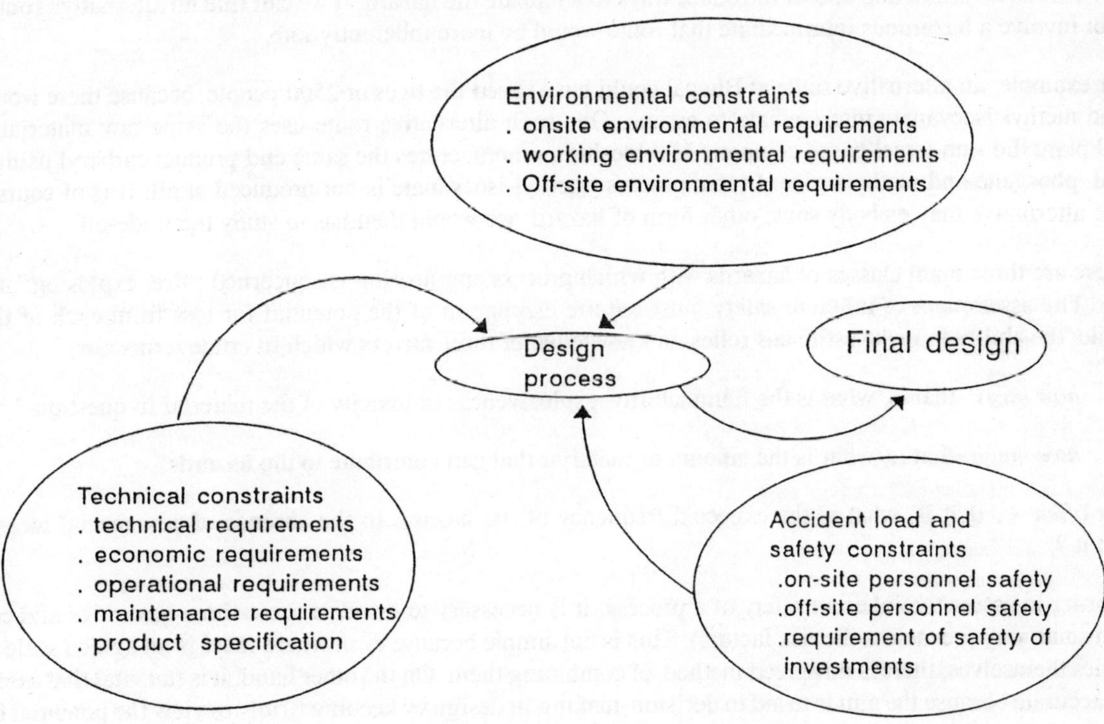

Figure 2. The main constraints involved in the design process.

al. 1994; Edwards and Lawrence, 1993; Roger and Hallam, 1991; and Lawrence *et al.* 1993). One possible reason that ISD has not caught on as much as it should have, is the perception that ISD is a costly and non-optimum approach. These authors have examined these. This is not true. If one analyses the total cost and financial loss due to any mishap with the probability of occurrence, then of course, the optimum solution will be the more safer design. For example, storage of a toxic chemical under a high pressure can be done in a number of storage vessels other than installing one big storage vessel. This, of course, (more number of vessels) will increase capital investment. However, on considering hazard potential and frequency of occurrence, it will be the optimum solution. A detailed description of optimisation and safety has been discussed by Kletz (1990b,1991b,1992), and Taylor (1982).

The essence of inherently safer design is to avoid or remove hazards rather than add protective equipment to control them (which would add to the costs) ISD is built on the edifice of five actions (Kletz, 1990a; Edwards and Lawrence, 1993):

intensification -using less of a hazardous material;

attenuation -using a hazardous materials in a less hazardous form;

substitution -using a safer material;

limitation -minimisation of the effect of an accident;

simplification -reducing the opportunities for error and malfunction.

It is imperative that inherent safety is considered right at the outset of the design process, when fundamental decisions which could have a large impact on inherent safety and cannot be altered later, are made. The choice of route (process and its step) is the key early design decision which influences the inherent safety of the plant. For example, if the route involves a hazardous intermediate, it would be unavoidably present in the final plant and we can only try to reduce its amount, and/or introduce ways to attenuate the hazard. If we can find an alternative route which may not involve a hazardous intermediate that route would be more inherently safe.

For example, an alternative route at Bhopal could have saved the lives of 2500 people, because there would have been no methyl isocyanate intermediate to escape. One such alternative route uses the same raw materials as the Bhopal plant did - an Israel-based company Makhteshim, manufactures the same end product carbaryl using alpha-napthal, phosgene and methylamine. In this process methyl-isocyanate is not produced at all. It is of course likely that the alternative may embody some other form of hazard; we would then has to study the trade-off.

There are three main classes of hazards with which process engineering is concerned : fire, explosion, and toxic release. The assessment of inherent safety must require estimation of the potential for loss from each of these. In principle, the ability to make estimates relies on knowledge of three factors which in crude terms are:

how nasty -that is, what is the flammability, explosiveness or toxicity of the material in question ?

how much -that is, what is the amount of material that can contribute to the hazards?

how often - that is, what is the expected frequency of the hazard, in the absence of any special measures to prevent it ?

In order to assess the inherent safety of a process, it is necessary to estimate these three quantities and combine them in some way (i.e. assess the risk factors). This is not simple because even where there is an agreed scale for the quantities themselves, there is no agreed method of combining them. On the other hand, it is not vital that assessment is very accurate because the aim is to aid to decision-making in design by keeping firmly in view the potential for loss. The quantification of inherent safety is not an end in itself. For this reason, indication of the direction and magnitude of change in inherent safety consequent on a given decision is valuable, even if the positions before and after the decision can not be quantified (Kletz, 1992; Rushton *et al.* 1994).

Not only the hazard but costs and energy consumption may also be reduced by employing smaller quantities of hazardous substances. However, this aspect is not entirely simple; it is difficult to say whether a smaller quantity of a more hazardous chemical is preferable to a larger quantity of a less hazardous chemical because there is no agreed scale of measurement of 'total hazard'(Rushton *et al.* 1994; Khan and Abbasi, 1995;1996a;1997b).

Rapid risk analysis based design (RRABD) is a tool to aid in such decision-making and in general implementing ISD. A brief description of RRABD in presented below.

RAPID RISK ANALYSIS BASED DESIGN (RRABD)

A rational application of inherently safer design concept calls for techniques which may evaluate each design option in terms of associated hazard and its impact on the plant and the surroundings. Rapid risk analysis based design is a new procedure we propose for such a study. By using RRABD approach it is easy to evaluate various design options and select the optimal one.

Design premises include a lot of requirements that need to be fulfilled (Figure 2). These are often in conflict with each other and the optimum solution is rarely straight-forward. Figure 3 illustrates the interactive and iterative nature of a design process.

If we apply the typical design process as shown in Figure 3 with safety consideration, we get a design cycle as illustrated in Figure 4. This design cycle (rapid risk analysis based design) describes the frame of reference for the inherently safer design. The main steps that constitute the RRABD procedure are as follows:

a) Define a set of accident scenarios, based on legislation, standards, codes and experiences. Use them as design premises.

b) Define acceptance criteria for the project. Consider the acceptance criteria also as part of the design premises.

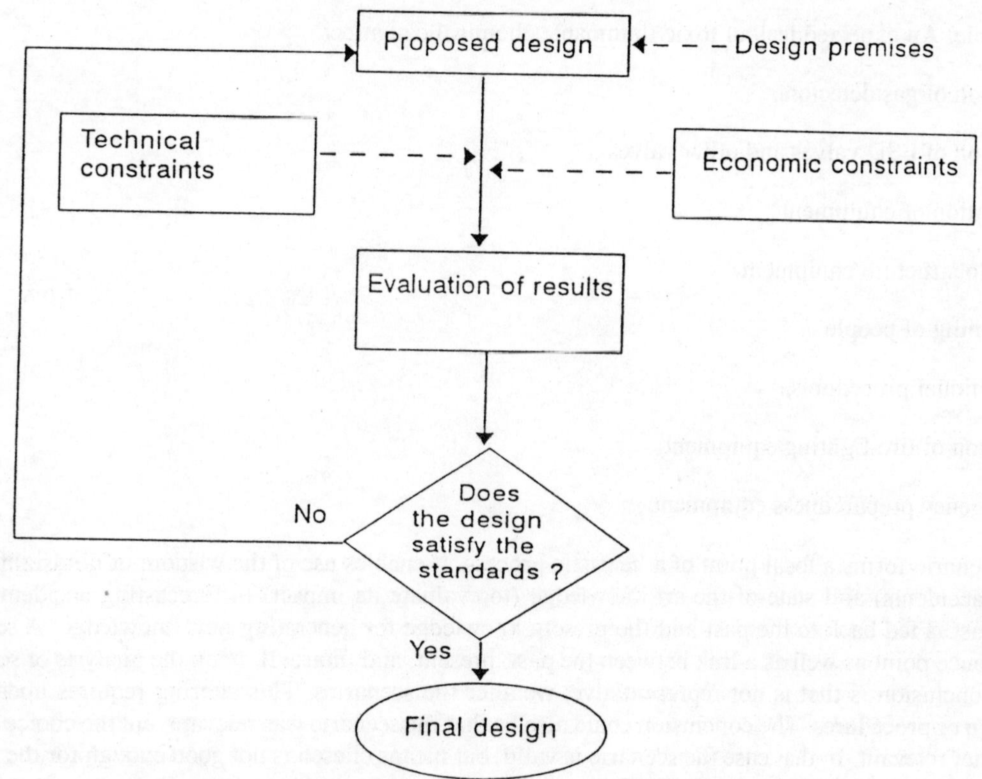

Figure 3. Conventional cycle of design process.

c) Propose a design solution (or modification to existing design).

d) Perform deterministic calculations on the basis of defined accident scenarios and the proposed geometry.

e) Evaluate the results (risk factors) against acceptance criteria.

f) Repeat step c) to e) until acceptable design is reached.

g) Evolve the acceptance criteria during the design process to cope with the specific elements in the proposed design.

A brief description of the key elements of RRABD is presented below.

Accident scenario generation

An accident scenario is a description of an expected situation. It contains single events or combinations of events. The objective of the design would be to avoid the scenario or drastically reduce the probability of its occurrence. We shall henceforth call accident scenario simply scenario.

The expectation of a scenario does not mean it will indeed occur, but that there is a reasonable probability that it would occur. A scenario is neither a specific situation nor a specific event, but a description of a typical situation that covers a set of possible events or situations (Berge, 1993; Mansfield and Cassidy , 1994; Lees, 1996).

The purpose of a scenario

Construction of a scenario achieves the following objectives:

i) It is the basis of risk study; it tells us what may happen so that we can devise ways and means of preventing or minimising the possibility. A scenario can influence several aspects of the design.

Example: An expected leak of toxic/flammable chemical can affect

- location of gas detectors,
- location of ESD valves and other valves ,
- insulation of equipment,
- load to structure/equipment,
- poisoning of people,
- operational procedures,
- location of fire fighting equipment,
- emergency preparedness equipment.

i) A scenario forms a focal point of a heuristic process. It enables use of the wisdom of hindsight (experiences of past accidents) and state-of-the-art knowledge (to evaluate its impact) in forecasting accident situations. The forecast is fed back to the past and the present knowledge for generating new knowledge. A scenario is thus a reference point as well as a link between the past, present, and future. If, upon the analysis of scenario we reach the conclusion is that is not representative, we alter the scenarios. This altering requires updating of existing design or procedures. The conclusion could also be that the scenario was relevant, but the choice of design means was not relevant. In that case the scenario is valid, but means chosen is not good enough for the purpose. That is also a useful input in RRABD and ISD.

A scenario description contains two sets of information: a description of the situation and the expected frequency of occurrence. The description of the situation must not reduce the freedom of finding solutions and must not restrict the means available for solution. A good accident scenario should describe the most prime cause of an event. As an example: define a leak rate instead of explosion pressure because here, one could go further and describe the cause of the leak as well. However, the purpose of a scenario is to be input to a deterministic calculation (consequence analysis).

Definition of scenarios must take place in the beginning of a project; the earlier the better. At this time little knowledge may be available about the proposed product; too little to perform an *event analysis*; event analysis being defined as a systematic analysis of the proposed design to identify accidental events and their frequency of occurrence (reliability assessment). The analysis concludes with a set of relevant scenarios that represents the events identified. The analysis may also consider operational procedures to decide scenarios which in reality may not be available at such an early design stage. It is therefore practical to define scenarios on the basis of maximum credible accidents; in other words accidental scenarios with a reasonable likelihood of occurrence.

Consequence analysis

Consequence analysis involves assessment of likely consequences if a scenario does materialise. The consequences are quantified in terms of damage radii (the radii of the area in which the damage would readily occur), damage to property (shattering of window pans, caving of buildings) and toxic effects (chronic/acute toxicity, mortality). The assessment of consequence involves a wide variety of mathematical models. For example source models are used to predict the rate of release of hazardous material, the degree of flashing, and the rate of evaporation. Models for explosions and fires are used to predict the characteristics of explosions and fires. The impact intensity models are used to predict the damage zones due to fires, explosion and toxic load. Lastly toxic gas release and dispersion models are used to predict human response to different levels of exposures to toxic chemicals. The dependence among various consequence models is shown in Figure 5.

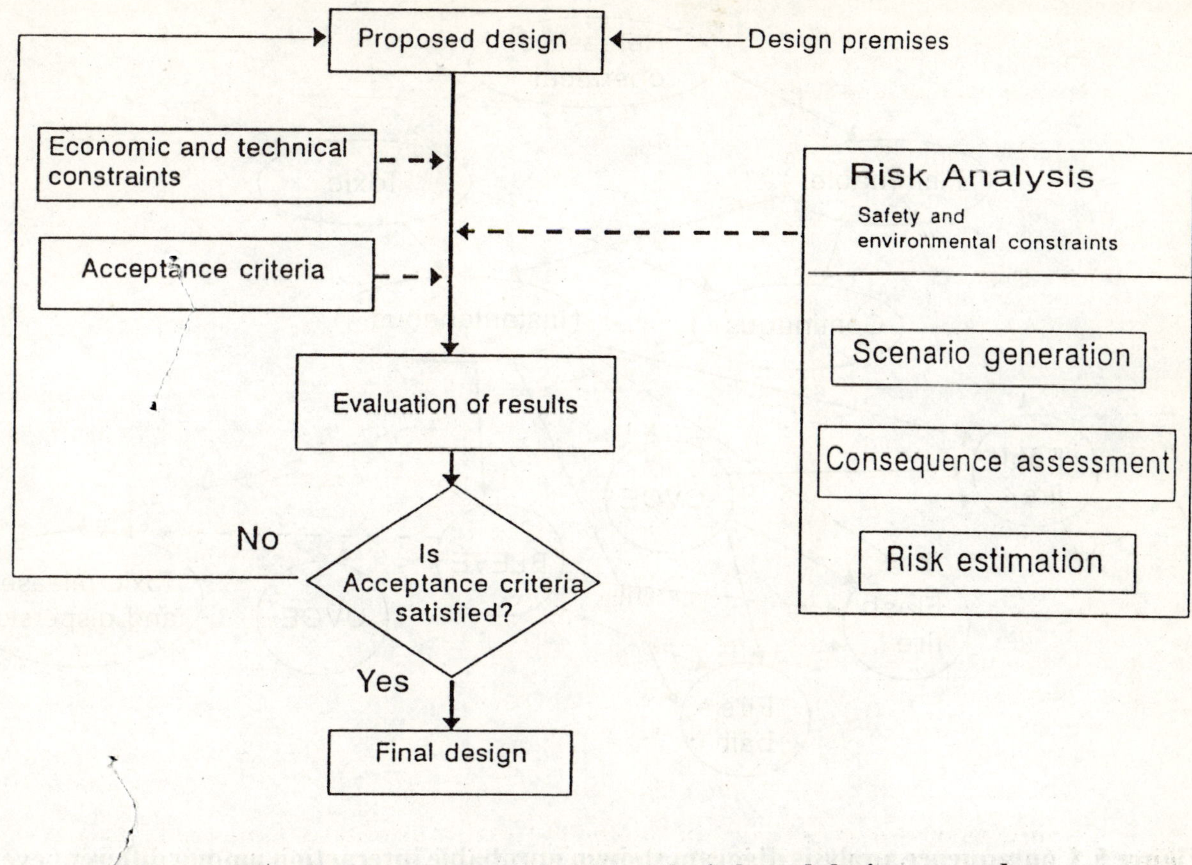

Figure 4. The algorithm of rapid risk analysis based design procedure.

As consequence analysis is a part of an iterative cycle (RRABD design cycle); the ability to perform the calculations quickly is vital for the ability to reach optimum solutions within acceptable time-span. Today cost means a lot and the difference between 'good' and 'not so good' solutions can be the difference between a profitable and a not profitable investment.

Acceptance criteria

Risk is commonly defined as likelihood of an undesirable happening; its severity being a combination of its propensity for damage and the frequency of the occurrence. Attempts have been made since long to find a general way to express risk so that one may be able to compare risk between different kinds of activities. But despite all the past efforts the closest we have reached to this goal is to divide risk into three classes: risk to personnel (individual), risk to economy and risk to environment.

There are three groups of design acceptance criteria:

1. system related criteria that sets the acceptance level for a system;
2. single component related criteria that set the acceptance level for single components;
3. dynamic related criteria that set limitations for an abnormal situation's dynamic development;

Example of a system related acceptance criterion is: The main structure shall maintain it's integrity for all type of loads with a frequency above 10^{-4} year. Example of component related acceptance criterion is: an instrument connections shall remain sealed under influence of loads with a frequency above 10^{-4} year. Example of a dynamic related design acceptance criteria is: an abnormal situation must not have the probability of more than 0.1% to escalate to a more critical abnormal situation.

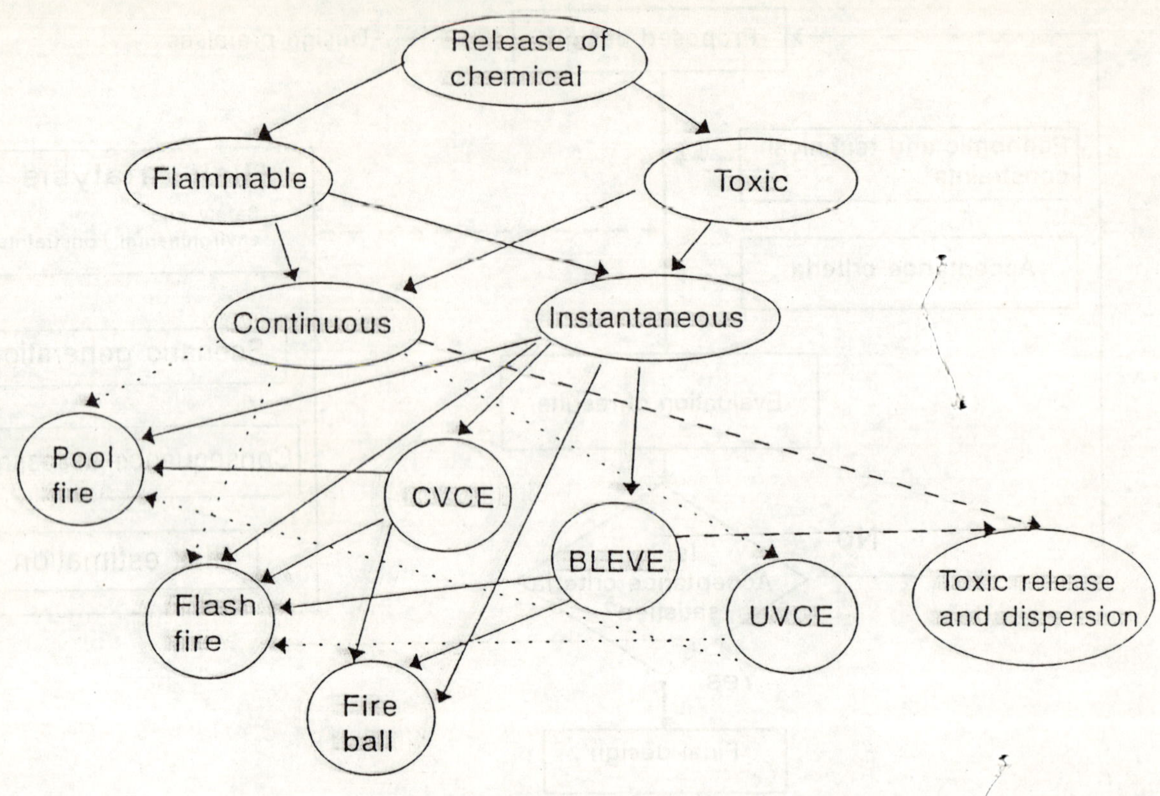

Figure 5. Consequence analysis diagram showin gprobable interaction among different events.

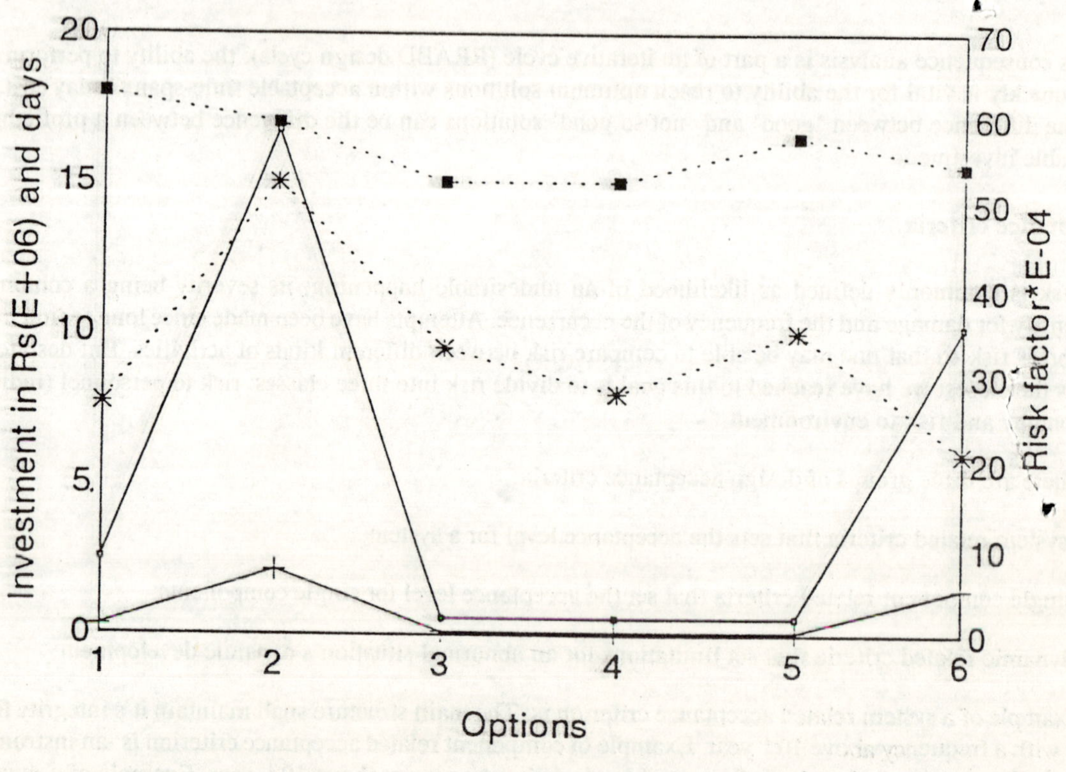

Figure 6. Various parameters plotted against different options for propylene storage.

I. There must be a logical connection among the three groups of design acceptance criteria. We may develop other criteria based on these criteria. Here are some examples of other types of acceptance criteria:

II. *FAR (fatal accident rate)* criteria. It is most commonly used as measure of risk.

III. *ALARP (as low as reasonable practicable)* principle. It has no defined risk level, but reduction of risk being a continous endeavour, it allows for as low risk as prevailing technology allows; in other words what is, economically defensible.

IV. *Prescriptive solutions*. It recommends standard prescriptions as solutions and methods for design of equipment and systems. This is a rigid criterion with little room for situation-adapted solutions.

V. *Prescriptive functionality*. It prescribes the functionality of a system or a component. This criterion provides the opportunity for situation-adapted solutions. At the same time, it requires documentation of the fulfilment of the functionality. The principle calls for competence, innovation and advanced engineering tools in order to have its potential realised to the full.

VI. *Accepted influence*. All kinds of activities influence their environment to a certain degree. The accepted influence criterion is based on the principle that restrictions on activities should relate to their influence on the surroundings. The acceptable level of influence is determined by the resilience of the surrounding to get back to its original start after the perturbations has caused and the surrounding's ability to maintain its function during the perturbations.

There are two conditions an acceptance criteria must meet to be a valuable in design:

i) The designers must understand the criteria; in other words engineers working in the different disciplines must understand the implication of the criteria.

ii) It must be possible to compare the results from consequence analysis with the criteria.

For RRABD these two conditions are crucial; as it is the designer's obligation to compare his proposed solutions with the acceptance criteria. In the opinion of these authors ALARP is the best criteria.

We now present a case study in which RRABD design procedure has been used in taking decisions pertaining to design.

CASE STUDY

Problem statement

The case study pertains to an industry engaged in manufacturing glycol and polyol, by using propylene and propylene oxide as main raw materials.

The industry procures the two raw materials from a nearby petroleum refinery. As there are frequent interruptions in the availability of raw materials, the production gets interrupted at least once every month. To circumvent this problem, the management of the industry has decided to enhance the storage capacity of the two key chemicals (propylene and propylene oxide) in order to meet the requirements of the plant for 15 days without interruption. After a detailed cost-analysis study, the industry has come out with six different options (design of various type and variant capacities of storage vessels) to meet the said requirements. These options are listed in Table 2. The management is most interested in option 6 as it is the most cost-effective.

A detailed study is carried out for each option using the RRABD design procedure detailed earlier before making any firm design decision in order to achieve inherent safety. The step-by-step results of the study are presented in the following sections.

Scenario generation

Propylene

The most credible accident scenario for propylene storage has been generated (taking the help of past case studies and considering the vulnerability of the unit) for each option as listed in Table 3. The accident scenario for options 1,3,4 and 5 has been envisaged as BLEVE (boiling liquid expanding vapour explosion) followed by a fire ball. The accident may be caused as follows: a leak in pressurised storage vessel of propylene may cause sudden release of chemical. The boiling liquid expanding vapour may meet an ignition source -even heat energy generated due to explosion could be sufficient to ignite propylene - turning into a fire ball.

The accident scenario for options 2 and 6 have been developed as CVCE (confined vapour cloud explosion) followed by a fire ball. It is because high pressure build-up in the vessel, either due to heat stratification, over-filling or shock absorption, may lead to an explosive release of the chemical as CVCE. The released chemical on meeting heat source may ignite instantly resulting in a fire ball. This scenario has been verified by the past case studies in which similar accidents have been reported to have occurred (Marshall, 1987; Prugh, 1991; Lees, 1996).

The accident scenario anticipated for options 2 and 6 is different from options 1,3,4 and 5 because options 2 and 6 involve storage of chemicals in large quantum (horton spheres with large capacity) under extreme conditions of pressure and temperature. This makes the system more vulnerable to failure as confined explosion because the high pressure build-up in a vessel is directly proportional to the capacity of the chemical, storing pressure and such physical properties of the chemical as vapour pressure and specific heat.

Propylene oxide

The accident scenario for propylene oxide has been developed as BLEVE (boiling liquid expanding vapour explosion) followed by fire ball (Table 4). This accident may occur in a manner similar to that explained for propylene vessel. A leak in the storage vessel may lead to sudden release of propylene oxide (stored under high pressure) forming BLEVE and as the chemical is highly flammable, it soon gets ignited to a fire ball. This scenario is common for all storage vessels (spheres as well bullet shaped ones). It is because, , the pressure and temperature at which propylene oxide is stored are not so high as to easily exceed explosion pressure limit and causes CVCE. Thus, the most credible accident scenario for these vessels is visualised as BLEVE followed by fire ball.

Table 2. List of options and their details

Option Number	Number of vessels *capacity (MT), shape	Operational Temperature oC	Conditions Pressure kPa	Capital Investment Rs(lakhs)	Inventory (days)
Propylene					
1	2*125 bullets	30	1500	77	18
2	1*400 spheres	30	1500	150	17
3	2*80 bullets	30	1500	95	15
4	2*80 bullets	30	1500	80	15
5	3*80 bullets	30	1500	100	16.5
6	1*250 sphere	30	1500	60	15.5
Propylene oxide					
1	1*300 sphere	10	250	75	18
2	2*150 bullets	10	250	106	17
3	2*134 bullets	10	250	100	15
4	2*100 bullets	10	250	85	15
5	3*134 bullets	10	250	150	16.5
6	1*250 sphere	10	250	65	15.5

Table 3. The damage potential of each option for propylene

Options	Accident scenario	Damge distance, meters, due to			Maximum damage distance, m
		overpressure	missile$	heat load	
1	BLEVE*+ fire Ball	975.7	1173.4	225.7	975.7
2	CVCE@ + fire ball	1822.1	2130.4	403.7	1822.1
3	BLEVE + fire ball	739.0	1094.3	180.5	739.0
4	BLEVE + fire ball	739.0	1094.3	180.5	739.0
5	BLEVE + fire ball	739.0	1094.3	180.5	739.0
6	CVCE + fire ball	1123.5	1937.2	319.2	1123.5

* Boiling liquid expanding vapor explosion
@ Confined vapor cloud explosion

Consequence analysis

The software MAXCRED (Khan and Abbasi, 1996b) has been used to estimate the damage potential (consequence assessment) of each option of storage of propylene and propylene oxide. The results of MAXCRED -based simulations are presented in Tables 3 and 4. It is clear from Table 3 that option 2 (sphere of 400 MT capacity) has maximum damage potential due to the simultaneous impact of various damaging effects (heat load, overpressure, missiles). Damage of 50% probability due to overpressure (shock wave) would be occur across an area of ~1822 meters radius. Similarly, Table 4 which presents the damage potential for propylene oxide storage reveals that options 1 and 6 have maximum damage potentials. The radii for 50% probability of damage would extend upto ~400 meters from the accident epicentre. It is evident from the Tables 3 and 4 that the damage potential for various options of propylene oxide storage are lower compared to that of propylene.

Further a detailed study has been conducted to analyse the likelihood of domino effect (chain of accidents). For this purpose a software package DOMIFFECT (Khan and Abbasi, 1996c) has been used. The results are presented in Tables 5 and 6. Table 5 reveals that option 2 has maximum probability (~65%) of causing an explosion in a near-by vessel (propylene oxide vessel if separated by a distance of 78 meters or lesser). The total damage in terms of assets and fatality would be maximum in accident scenario for option 2 followed by accident scenario for option 6.

The result of DOMIFFECT for propylene oxide has been presented in Table 6. It is clear from the table that probability of occurrence of secondary accident due to an accident in propylene oxide vessels are low compared to propylene. The total damage (in terms of loss of assets as well as fatality) has been observed maximum for accident scenario of option 1 and subsequently followed by accident scenario of option 6.

Table 4. The damage potential of each option for propylene oxide

Options	Accident scenario	Damge distance, meters, due to			Maximum damage distance, m
		overpressure	missile$	heat load	
1	BLEVE* + fire ball	499.9	954.4	285.7	499.9
2	BLEVE + fire ball	396.7	900.4	201.7	396.9
3	BLEVE + fire ball	382.2	875.2	190.9	382.2
4	BLEVE + fire ball	346.7	809.5	164.9	346.3
5	BLEVE + fire ball	382.3	875.2	190.9	382.3
6	BLEVE + fire ball	425.7	924.5	210.2	425.7

* Boiling liquid expanding vapor explosion
$ The probability of meeting target is not considered

Risk estimation and decision making

The risk factors have been computed for various available options of propylene storage (Table 5) as well as propylene oxide storage (Table 6). In order to enable easy understanding and swift decision -making, risk factors of different options are plotted along with other factors such as, cost of each option, inventory for the number of days (Figures 6 and 7). It is evident from Figure 6 that as far as installation cost and the number of days of inventory are concerned, option 6 is optimal. However, this option is highly vulnerable to accidents and entails severe risk both in terms of fatality and financial loss. On considering risk factor also as a design constraint, option 4 comes out the optimal in all respects (financial loss, fatality, cost of the project and number of days of inventory).

This problem can also be optimised by formulating the mathematical expressions for each variable and minimising for a set of boundary condition (days of inventory). When we did so, it also confirmed that the option 4 is an optimum solution. Similarly Figure 7, which represents the curves of different parameters for propylene oxide storage options reveals that option 1 and option 6 are optimal in terms of the cost and inventory for a limiting number of days. However, the risk potential is maximum for option 1, closely followed by option 6. On considering all the constraints (cost, inventory and risk factors), option 4 comes out as optimal.

All-in-all by simply observing the two Figures (Figures 6 and 7) it can be concluded that for propylene storage as well as for propylene oxide storage, option 4 represents the optimum. Thus, compared to all other options, option 4 is inherently safer and hence the plant can be designed in an inherently safe manner by selecting this option. We must mention that the plant would still need some more hazard reduction measures after it is commissioned; inherently safer design would minimise the need and the costs of such measures.

Table 5. Results of domino effect analysis for propylene

Options	Area under severethreat (meters)	Probability of domino effect (%)	Risk factor	
			asset	fatality
1	225.70	15	8.88e-04	1.05e-04
2	403.7	65	5.86e-03	7.54e-04
3	180.6	8	1.96e-04	3.74e-05
4	180.6	8	1.96e-04	3.74e-05
5	180.6	8	1.96e-04	3.74e-05
6	319.2	57	3.56e-03	5.36e-04

Table 6. Results of domino effect analysis for propylene oxide

Options	Area under severethreat (meters)	Probability of domino effect (%)	Risk factor	
			asset	fatality
1	285.7	15.4	1.43e-03	1.88e-04
2	201.2	11.2	5.07e-04	7.18e-05
3	190.5	9.3	8.41e-04	2.10e-05
4	164.4	7.2	6.90e-05	9.05e-06
5	190.5	9.3	8.41e-04	2.10e-05
6	210.5	15.7	0.35e-03	1.88e-04

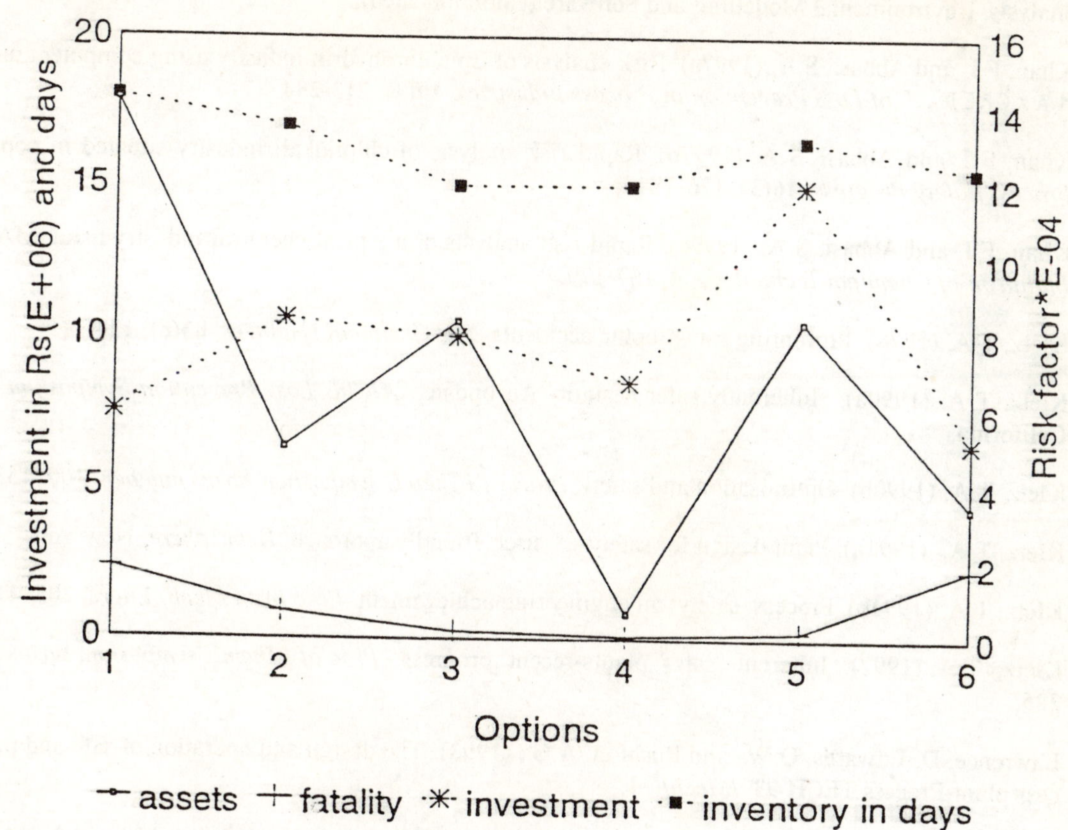

Figure 7. Various parameters plotted against different options for propylene oxide storage.

REFERENCES

1. AIChE (1989). Guidelines for chemical process quantitative risk analysis, *American Institute of Chemical Engineers*, New York.
2. Berge, G, (1993). Scenariobased design, a new approach to the safety issue in design, *3rd International Conference and Exhibition on Offshore Structural Design - Hazards, Safety and Engineering*, London.
3. Berge, G, (1995). Description of scenarios in Scenariobased design -proposal of methodology and relation to acceptance criteria, *14th International Conference on Offshore Mechanics and Arctic Engineering*, Copenhagen.
4. Butcher, C, (1990). *The Chemical Engineer*, **468**, 17.
5. Edwards, D W, and Lawrence, D, (1993). Assessing the inherent safety of chemical process routes: Is there a relation between plant cost and inherent safety, *Trans I ChemE*, **71 Part B**, 252.
6. Khan, F I, and Abbasi, S A, (1995). Risk analysis: a systematic method of hazard assessment and control, *Jr. of Industrial Pollution Control*, **11**(2), 89-88.
7. Khan, F I, and Abbasi, S A, (1996a). Accident simulation in chemical process industries using MAXCRED, *Indian Jr. of Chemical Technology*, **3**, 339-344.
8. Khan, F I, and Abbasi, S A, (1996b). MAXCRED : A tool for rapid quantitative risk analysis, *Environmental Modelling and Software*, (in press).
9. Khan, F I, and Abbasi, S A, (1997d). DOMIFFECT : A computer software for domino (series of accidents)

analysis, Environmental Modelling and Software (communicated).

10. Khan, F I, and Abbasi, S A, (1997a). Risk analysis of Epichlorohydrin industry using computer automated tool MAXCRED, *J. of Loss Prevention in Process Industries*, **10**(3), 213-234.

11. Khan, F I, and Abbasi, S A, (1997b). Rapid risk analysis of chloralkali industry situated in populated area, *Process Safety Progress*, **16**(3), 176-184.

12. Khan, F I, and Abbasi, S A, (1997c). Rapid risk analysis of a typical chemical industry using MAXCRED-II, *Indian Jr. of Chemical Technology*, **4**, 167-179.

13. Kletz, T A, (1976). Preventing catastrophic accidents, *The Chemical Engineer*, **83**(8), 124.

14. Kletz, T A, (1990a). Inherently safer design - An update, *AIChE Loss Prevention Symposium*, San Diego, California.

15. Kletz, T A, (1990b). Optimisation and safety, *Proc. of IChemE symposium series number 100*, 153.

16. Kletz, T A, (1991a). Plant design for safety- A user friendly approach, *Hemisphere*, New York.

17. Kletz, T A, (1991b). Process safety: an engineering achievement, *Proc Instn Mech. Engrs*, **205**, 11.

18. Kletz, T A, (1992). Inherent safer plants-recent progress, *Proc of IChemE symposium series number 124*, 225.

19. Lawrence, D, Edwards, D.W., and Rushton, A.G., (1993). The design and operation of safe and profitable process plant-Process TECH 93, *IMechE*, 1.

20. Lees, F P, (1996). Loss prevention in Process industries, *Butterworths*, 2nd edition, **Volume 1-3**, London

21. Mansfield, D, and Cassidy, K, (1994). Inherently safer approaches to plant design. The benefits of an inherently safer approach and how this can be built into the design process, *Institution of Chemical Engineers Symposium Series-134*, 285-299.

22. Marshall, V C, (1987). Major chemical hazards, *John-Wiley & Sons*, London.

23. Pietersen, C M, (1990). Consequences analysis of accidental release of hazardous materials, **3**, 136-141.

24. Prugh, R W, (1991). Quantitative evaluation of 'BLEVE' hazards, *J. of Fire Protection Engrs*, **3**(1), 9-24.

25. Ramshaw, C, (1985). *The Chemical Engineer*, **416**, 30.

26. Rogers, R L, and Hallam, S, (1991). A chemical approach to inherent safety, *Proc. of IChemE Symposium Series number 124*, 235.

27. Rushton, A G, Edwards, D W, and Lawrence, D, (1994). Inherent safety and computer aided process design, *Trans I ChemE*, **72 Part B**, 83.

28. Taylor, J R, (1982). Evaluation of costs completeness and benefits for risk analysis procedures, *Roskilde RisoNational Laboratory*, **N-14-82**.